HOT WIRED GUITAR: THE LIFE OF
JEFF BECK
MARTIN POWER

HOT WIRED GUITAR: THE LIFE OF
JEFF BECK
MARTIN POWER

OMNIBUS PRESS
London / New York / Paris / Sydney / Copenhagen / Berlin / Madrid / Tokyo

Exclusive Distributors
Music Sales Limited,
14/15 Berners Street,
London, W1T 3LJ.

Music Sales Corporation
180 Madison Avenue, 24th Floor,
New York,
NY 10016,
USA.

Macmillan Distribution Services
56 Parkwest Drive
Derrimut, Vic 3030,
Australia.

Every effort has been made to trace the copyright holders of the photographs in this
book but one or two were unreachable. We would be grateful if the photographers
concerned would contact us.

Printed in the EU

A catalogue record for this book is available from the British Library.

Visit Omnibus Press on the web at www.omnibuspress.com

Contents

Chapter 1

Detective Work

I thought we'd won."

It was a phrase you heard a lot in the United Kingdom during the post-World War II years. A phrase steeped in irony, pickled in humour but still carrying just the right amount of righteous indignation to ensure anyone hearing it nodded wearily in agreement. "I thought we'd won," said it all, really.

After near six years of bloody conflict, which saw the death of millions on various battlefields throughout Europe and Africa, the Allies formally accepted the unconditional surrender of Nazi Germany's armed forces on May 8, 1945. Adolf Hitler's dreams of a thousand year Reich were left smouldering with his ashes just outside a bunker in Berlin. As King George VI and Prime Minister Winston Churchill flicked victory salutes to the assembled throng from the balcony of Buckingham Palace, the mood was one of celebration – a just and fitting end to what one esteemed historian recently called "the last just war". Happy days, as they say, were here again. Or so you'd have thought.

The reality of life in post-war Britain was somewhat different. Having already been blitzed, bombed, rationed, made to shelter in tube stations or take refuge in hastily constructed sheds under the cover of 'blackout', the UK's civilian population were due a break. Like their military counterparts, those left at home had witnessed hard times, with over 60,000 dead after Nazi bombing missions decimated cities like Hull, Liverpool, Birmingham, Sheffield,

Nottingham, Glasgow, Swansea and many others. London saw the worst of it, the Luftwaffe turning the skies red for 76 consecutive nights over England's capital from September 1940 to May 1941, but most of the country had been affected one way or another. Yet, it would take nearly a decade or so before things eventually righted themselves, as industry, schools and homes were slowly rebuilt, and petrol, soap, clothing, fruit and milk again became available to the general public without need of government-stamped coupons. An austerity-ridden, black and white, gritty and grimy time for all concerned then, and one in which the phrase "I thought we'd won" made perfect, horrible sense.

Some 37 minutes' train ride from the bomb damage of London's Victoria Station was Wallington, then in the county of Surrey, now in the London borough of Sutton. Deriving its name from the Anglo-Saxon Waletone – which literally means 'Village of the Britons' – Wallington had actually gained a mention in William The Conqueror's Domesday Book of 1086, its eight acres of meadow, two mills and 11 hides worth the princely sum of £10 at the time of the census.

And that, more or less, was how Wallington remained until the mid 19th century: a moderate-sized community of largely agricultural means dependant on pig farming and the production of lavender to bolster the coffers of the local populace. But with the expansion of Britain's railway network in the mid 1800s and a growing need for housing outside of London, Wallington and its neighbouring parish, Beddington, were finally fused together to create a unified borough in 1915 – both villages now becoming towns under one, shared motto: 'Fess embattled'. Given the events of World War II and what it brought to Wallington and its surrounds, 'embattled' was an apt word to use.

When the United Kingdom went to war with Germany for the second time in 21 years, Wallington, Beddington, neighbouring Carshalton and their considerably larger first cousin Croydon – just two and a half miles up the road – all took their fair share of hits during the Battle of Britain and subsequent Blitz. Then London's major landing field, and a principal RAF fighter station, Croydon Airport was attacked in the first wave of German bombings, killing

2

six servicemen and 60 civilians in nearby factories in just one night. Like Croydon, Wallington did not escape lightly. The Dukes Head Hotel, then the busiest pub in the area, was badly damaged during an air raid while Wallington County Grammar School was struck by a V2 rocket in the late summer of 1944, its windows blown out, its roof collapsing under the impact. Thankfully, a nearby field where teachers grew vegetables in an effort to augment rationed supplies for their pupils was not affected by the blast.

Just 600 yards away from Wallington County Grammar School, opposite Beddington Park and but a stone's throw away from St. Mary The Virgin Church was Demesne Road. A straight-lined, if not exactly leafy street of mainly white, mostly pebble-dashed houses, Demesne Road was only 10 minutes walk from Wallington station, with numerous cul-de-sacs and warrens running the length and breadth of its near mile-long distance. An old lane that had been turned into something far more substantial in the thirties, Demesne Road's close proximity to Wallington Grammar must have meant when the V2 struck, its residents might well have heard it – perhaps even waking an infant Geoffrey Arnold Beck from his slumber in the back bedroom at No. 206.

The son of Arnold and Ethel Beck, Geoffrey – or 'Jeff' as he came to be known – was born on June 24, 1944, a war baby who would have to grow used to such nocturnal intrusions for some months to come. By no means affluent, Jeff's parents were still reasonably comfortable in terms of wealth and status for the time, his father working as an accountant while his mother secured a part-time job in a local chocolate factory after hostilities ceased. Jeff was not the first addition to the Beck family, his sister Annetta arriving four years before him and throwing down quite the challenge for her younger sibling to follow as she showed a natural flair for horse-riding, languages, art and music: "My sister," he later said, "is a genius."

As evidenced, the circumstances Jeff grew up in were secure enough, though surely still marked by events of 1939–45. While fish and chips constituted a weekly treat for most British families, rationing ensured children did not get their grubby hands on a full complement of sweets, biscuits and chocolate until early 1953. They would have to wait at least another year until restrictions governing meat were finally lifted. Perhaps more distressingly, remnants of conflict were littered throughout Wallington's streets and fields. In Beddington Park, the nearest open space for Jeff to play in, hundreds of metal shards continued to be dug up by locals, these dangerous chunks dropped by German planes in an effort to confuse radar outposts as they began their bombing runs on Croydon Airport. Holes in the road, iron spikes in the grass, nearby buildings on the verge of collapse and small portions on the plate – Wallington was part of a scarred, fractured nation, slowly emerging from post-war torpor. No great time to be young, even for one who had experienced nothing else.

Faced with such external uncertainties, Jeff's early world was understandably sheltered, somewhat insular and one he would later refer to as "net curtain land". Like those around them, the Beck family lived quietly in a 'three up, two down' semi-detached house, a wooden garage at the back used mainly for storage with a small, shared driveway marking the boundary of where their house stopped and their neighbours' began. Space was tight, if not restrictively so, and there was always plenty of room for Arnold Beck to park his car, a rare enough thing in the forties: "Yeah, there was a car outside," Jeff remembered, "but it was in danger of being swept away from the oil leaking from underneath." In the living room, taking pride of place was Ethel Beck's piano, a baby grand from which she stole back the odd classical melody learned in her youth: "My mum played beautifully," Jeff later told *Guitarist*. "She was busy bringing my sister and me up, so her playing suffered a bit. But I used to love to listen to her play."

With Annetta already showing real promise on the instrument, it was perhaps inevitable that he too would be forced into lessons at an early age. Despite the best efforts of his teacher, Jeff's response to the piano was lukewarm at best, a boy reluctantly skipping over the odd scale or teasing out a melody or two when prodded or pushed, yet more content to stick his head under its lid and pluck the strings when left to his own devices: "Actually, I'd skip lessons, buy model airplanes with the money and mark my own book in an effort to fool my mother." Having amassed enough cash to purchase all the Airfix toys he wanted, Jeff's solution to ending his weekly torture tutorials was novel to say the least: "I tore one of the black keys off. My mother then got the idea that I wasn't too keen on it."

In fact, the piano was not the first instrument that Jeff had turned his attention to, having already attempted to master violin following a chance encounter with a mysterious box at his eccentric uncle's house: "[When I was] eight years old, I found my uncle's violins," Beck confirmed. "I looked in a box he'd told me never to look in and there were six in there. And he caught me, and said 'If I ever catch you doing that again...' He gave me a bit of a slap, and then said 'Well, do you want to learn to play violin then?'" But like the piano, Beck showed no great affinity with the instrument, his uncle's patience snapping before Jeff could do the same thing to the strings: "Learning violin was murder. I was so poisonous on it and my uncle would snatch it away. I don't think he could bear me playing it. [The violin's] the most torturous instrument in the wrong hands." A brief attempt to redirect the young Beck towards the cello met with a similar fate: "I started plucking it because I couldn't get on with bowing and he just stopped me and said, 'Get out'. No patience at all." Evidently, having to sound notes with a bow rather than his fingers got in the way of all Jeff's fun: "When you're a kid, you want to get at the strings and pull at 'em. It's a childhood thing." He would get his chance soon enough.

If Jeff's uncle was despairing of his nephew's lack of talent on violin and cello, he did provide the boy with other compensations: "My uncle used to look after me at weekends and one of my biggest thrills was having him take me out in his open-top 1947 MG (TC). I used to think this was the coolest thing, and he used to open it up on some of the open roads, getting it up to 75 mph. Now my dad's car couldn't even get up to 45 mph, so this was just... I hadn't witnessed anything like it." With its distinctive radiators, sweeping arches and wire wheels, the TC Midget was Jeff's first real exposure to a classic sports car and he was hooked. When the family missed seeing Queen Elizabeth II's coronation on March 24, 1953, Jeff used his father's sense of guilt to canny advantage, begging him for a copy of *Hot Rod And Custom* to make up for losing out on the sight of all those gaudy carriages, bearskin hats and waving monarchs. The same night, Beck's bedroom wall was newly festooned with photos of souped-up Ford Model A, Bs and Ts. A lifelong love affair with chrome engines, sleek angles and burning rubber had begun.

In perhaps a final attempt to divert Jeff's attention back to more worthy pursuits than stealing money for car magazines and following his "pipe smoking, celibate, violin-playing mechanic" uncle around the garage at weekends, Ethel Beck enrolled her son in the local church choir. Strangely, she seemed to dislike the results of this latest experiment as much as he did, and Jeff's dalliance with morning praise ended almost as quickly as it had begun. Singing hymns about God was duly replaced with a snare drum and set of brushes, so that the 10 year old could rattle along to his father's collection of Art Tatum and Fats Waller records, a discipline in which he soon became reasonably proficient: "I [instinctively] knew what the drummer was doing and practised and practised until you couldn't really tell that I was playing along with it." Unlike Arnold Beck, however, Jeff's uncle had little truck with jazz music and hated blues even more, snapping off his car radio when its emotionally charged, evocatively driven sounds crossed the airwaves: "I heard [blues] for the first time and I was transfixed," Jeff later confirmed, "but he immediately turned it off." The next time the boy visited, the radio had been flung in the dustbin. No explanation was forthcoming.

As evidenced, the first decade of Jeff Beck's life in post-war Wallington had been fairly emblematic of the time, a childhood populated with rare treats here and there, with several curiosities allowed to develop into abiding interests. It was quiet but comfortable enough, built on stumbling music lessons, model aircraft, pictures of hot rods and endless games of chess, another hobby that Jeff showed genuine interest in and a level of proficiency well beyond his years. But all this was thrown into serious doubt on November 2, 1955 when Jeff was hit by a car while riding his racing bicycle near the family home: "I was run over and suffered a massive fracture to the back of my head." Pinned to a wall on impact, Beck's injuries were substantial enough to take him out of school for some weeks while he recovered.

The accident could not have come at a worse moment, with Jeff having recently transferred from a small, privately educated faculty to the much bigger and state-funded grounds of Sutton East County Secondary Modern School – where making the right friends quickly was as critical as exhibiting strong academic promise with teachers. Plagued by headaches as a result of his fractured skull, Beck became easily distracted and prone to mood swings – two maladies that would pursue him with some vigour into adult life. The injury also changed the nature of his engagement with formal education, making Jeff doubt the logic, value and worth of his new surroundings: "When I was in the classroom, I wanted to be outside," he later told *Mojo*. "I felt resentment... about being forced by the government into a room full of people I didn't like. But there was just no alternative. To be honest, I found it difficult to get back to normal after that, [though] I think I grew into a strong enough character to resist it." Feeling trapped inside his swollen head, and not much liking what he saw outside of it, it was perhaps unsurprising that Beck turned his attention towards the one thing that had always fascinated him more than models, cars, pianos or chess: the sound of guitars.

While Jeff had loved to listen to his mother tinkling the ivories, or bash along enthusiastically to his father's Art Tatum 78s, such feelings paled into insignificance when it came to the sense of wonder he felt when hearing six strings. It was all music of course, and as such one clear path to one tantalising goal, but something about "the wire and the wood" just did for young Jeff Beck. The signs and augurs had been there for years. As a six year old, he had become temporarily obsessed with a zither belonging to "a neighbour, next door but one", stroking it tentatively when he felt all adult eyes were looking in another direction. Then there was the failed experiment with the violin, the frustration of having to bow notes rather than sound them with his fingers apparent to both himself and his impatient uncle. The cello was still only a miserable compromise: the boy liked its low, mournful tones, but again preferred plucking the thing like an upright bass rather than drawing a French bow across its strings. Though much better and certainly more immediate, the drums provided only partial succour. Good to hit, yes, even better when used to establish a rhythm, or impress his father. But drums didn't really provide a tune, and as time would come to show, Jeff loved nothing better than a tune – even if he also loved to occasionally mangle it a bit.

Away from the piano that dominated the Beck household, there was another music generator in the same room that had a profound

7

effect on Jeff's decision to gravitate towards the guitar. "The radio," he confirmed, "was like a surrogate nanny to me." By all accounts as central a feature as Ethel Beck's baby grand, the radio was nearly always turned on when the family were home, a habit established during the war years when government announcements regarding allied progress were many and still diligently adhered to during peacetime. As Jeff was too young to wander the streets with friends, the radio acted as a cheap and cheerful conduit to other, more exotic worlds and, as crucially, it allowed him to hear what probably sounded like an alien invasion in the early fifties: "I couldn't believe it when I first heard Les Paul," he remembered. "He played so many notes. It was a sound that was new, unlike anything before it."

Part comedian, part genius, Les Paul was America's first true 'stunt guitarist', a fact driven home by the early fifties hits 'How High The Moon', 'Bye Bye Blues' and 'Tiger Rag' he shared with his wife, Mary Ford. A jazz and country player who pioneered the development of electric guitar in the forties, Paul had also been key to the progress of recording methods such as overdubbing, phasing, multi-tracking and other tape effects. Blessed with an inventive, good-humoured technique that included slurs, trills and 'chicken rolls' as well as an extensive chord vocabulary, Les would think nothing of speeding up the reels or piling 'sound on sound' to create his orchestra of mad guitars. By 1952, he also had his own signature model, having worked alongside Gibson to create one of the first production line electric instruments of its kind – a woman-shaped, carved-topped wonder called the Les Paul 'Goldtop'.

"He was the first guy who came out with the really fast, trebly guitar, that slap-back echo. Nobody did that before him," said Jeff. "He had some trouble with the press saying it was all tricks, and to some extent it was, but it was also spectacular." The 'trick bag' element of Les Paul's playing was a point not lost on Jeff's parents, who were keen to reinforce the fact that this was not proper music, but little more than audio manipulation. But Beck was smitten by Paul's spark-flying style and would not be deterred. "When your parents try and stop you," he said, "you end up doing it more." In an effort to replicate Les' sonic experiments, Jeff took to building his own demon machine: "It was basically a cigar box with a big, thick rubber band. But I never forgot the thrill of changing the pitch by stretching the band." From little acorns...

After repeatedly petitioning his mother and father for a guitar without success, circumstances finally conspired to provide Beck with the object of his desire. "I had a friend with a TV set and I used to go round to his place on a Friday afternoon to watch *Popeye*. There on the sofa was a black 'cowboy' guitar... but it didn't have all the strings on it," he later recalled. "And each time I visited him there were less strings on it, so I began to understand he didn't really care about it. When it got down to two strings, he said, 'Do you want to borrow it?' So I took it and he never got it back." Several decades later, Jeff's memory of liberating the instrument from its uncaring owner was still strong. "I remember carrying it home in the rain," he told *Guitarist*'s Jamie Crompton in 2009, "and taking off my coat to protect it. Right there and then, I had a protective thing to the guitar." According to Beck, it really was love at first strum. "When I first picked up that guitar, I thought this was the instrument that was made for me."

As the guitar was missing several strings, and Jeff's parents were unwilling to take the chance of buying a new set for what might turn out to be yet another whim, Beck was forced to improvise. His solution was to use control line wire from his model airplane collection to plug the missing gaps. This was hardly ideal, as unlike a properly gauged set of guitar strings, the control wire was all of one thickness. But given that Jeff didn't know any better at the time, it worked well enough. With everything in place, albeit oddly, he set about learning his first melody, Anton Karas' zithering 'Harry Lime Theme' from the 1949 film *The Third Man*.

In an effort to steer their son on the right path, Beck's mother and father began dropping heavy hints as to what they considered "suitable influences". An avid fan of classical music, Ethel Beck tried to focus her son's attentions towards Spanish guitar, pointing to the likes of Segovia as a fine potential role model. The jazz-loving Arnold Beck, on the other hand, was keen to push Django Reinhardt as someone Jeff might care to emulate, the gypsy guitarist's magnificent, quicksilver runs with 'The Hot Club' in the twenties and thirties often imitated but never bettered: "My dad would say

'This guy can really play guitar, forget all the others'," said Jeff, "so naturally I ignored him." What Beck wouldn't, simply couldn't ignore was the call of rock'n'roll. Sweeping across the Atlantic in an ever-building series of immaculately pompadoured waves, American rock'n'roll would eventually engulf the British Isles with a force and intensity that has been virtually unrivalled ever since. A mystical hybrid of blues, gospel, country, hillbilly and rockabilly styles aligned to an infectious 'boogie-woogie' backbeat, rock'n'roll was music you could dance, rebel and make love to, its impact on popular culture still resonating even now.

The first splashes of rock'n'roll made their way to the UK in January 1956 with Bill Haley & The Comets' 'Rock Around The Clock', a single that topped the charts and created an immediate dancehall craze. 'Rock Around The Clock' was certainly not the first rock'n'roll single (the other, decades-spanning candidates are simply too numerous to name here), and the cowlick-haired Haley was nearly 30 years old when he recorded it. But 'Rock Around The Clock''s 12-bar, jumped up blues construction, endlessly repetitive, yet infuriatingly catchy chorus and driving, insistent rhythm were enough to ignite the emotions of a nation's youth still used to twirling around ballroom floors to the sounds of crooners like Al Martino, Frankie Laine and Perry Como. As the authorities wept at the vulgarity of it all – pointing to the music's resolutely "black roots" and the fact that such "jungle beats" might incite riots and sex parties outside parliament – England's previously germ-free adolescents simply greased back their hair, donned draped or leather jackets and, in simpatico with their American counterparts, got on with inventing the 'Teenager'.

As ever, the UK soon put its own particular, artful spin on things. While gangs of 'Teddy Boys' manifested on every street corner, happily scaring grannies with their combination of Marlon Brando/ James Dean sneers, "Day-Glo socks and brothel creepers", Lonnie Donegan was busy introducing 'skiffle' to everyone else. The punk of its time, skiffle required only the most basic of musical tools to make its point: a wildly strummed acoustic guitar, well-scrubbed washboard and 'bass' constructed from bits of string and a tea chest. Skiffle's sparse melding of Appalachian mountain song and Leadbelly-style country/jug blues was easy to play and easier to hum along to. With Donegan's skittering 'Rock Island Line' dominating the radio throughout 1956, and scores of would-be teenage skiffle groups forming in every living room (much to the general delight of their bemused parents), it appeared that the advance of rock'n'roll might actually be derailed by the sound of a tea chest.

Then came Elvis Presley. Metaphorically swivelling his hips across the ocean from Memphis, Tennessee in a perfectly cut pink jacket and well-heeled pair of blue suede shoes, Elvis was young, electrically handsome and possessed of "a black man's voice in a white man's body". Though more strictly 'rockabilly' than 'rock'n'roll', Presley re-ignited the UK's love affair with "rebel hellcat music", he and his band's fusion of raw blues beats and country honk pushing them into the UK singles chart over a dozen times in 1957 alone. The door now truly blown off its hinges, a second wave of US performers that included Eddie Cochran, Carl Perkins and new black superstars such as Chuck Berry and Little Richard were free to flood British airwaves, their supercharged approach to rock'n'roll delighting the young and scaring the old. For a generation that had known only ration books, petrol sanctions and the anodyne pleasures of the Mantovani Orchestra, this was all something worth getting excited about – the first time in their young lives that the words 'I thought we'd won' might be forever discarded in favour of bold new frontiers.

Jeff Beck's personal call to arms came neither from Elvis Presley nor Bill Haley, but Gene Vincent & The Blue Caps. Without a television in their house, Jeff had heard and loved both Presley and Haley on the radio, but unlike most British kids hadn't actually witnessed the miracle of rock'n'roll for himself. "I used to hear what Elvis looked like from friends at school." All that changed with a trip to the cinema in the late spring of 1957, when Beck's mother took him to a screening of *The Girl Can't Help It*. "Imagine coming out of school at four o'clock, and by six o'clock there's your Technicolor dreams on screen. It was unbelievable." A slight comedy starring Tom Ewell and then 'It Girl' of the moment, the pulchritudinous Jayne Mansfield, one might have thought that the teenage Jeff's hormones had been inflamed by Mansfield's more outstanding talents in *The Girl Can't Help It*. In light of later escapades, they probably were. Yet it was the movie's musical cameos by Little Richard, Eddie

11

Cochran and, in particular, Gene Vincent and his Blue Caps that set fire to Jeff's head. "Gene Vincent's voice was so animal-like, he was screaming like the heavy metal kids today," he later confirmed. "It was street rock'n'roll... one electric guitar, an acoustic rhythm guitar, drums and an upright bass."

Once Beck had got past the primal roar of Vincent singing the immortal 'Be-Bop-A-Lula', his attention began to fixate on the sound of the guitar behind the voice. "The singing was so high... like manic breathing, like some sort of psychopath singing in the highest register he could get. Then the guitar took two screaming solos. I just thought 'This is where I belong...'" As Jeff was soon to discover, the "screaming" six strings backing Vincent belonged to Cliff Gallup. "Cliff Gallup. Oh God. Wild ridiculous runs. It was like listening to the future." In fact, by the time Jeff saw *The Girl Can't Help It*, Gallup was long gone. A 26-year-old married man with no real interest in touring, Cliff had ceded his position in the Blue Caps to lead guitarist Johnny Meeks soon after 'Be Bop...'s initial success; more happy to stay at home and work as a plumber than hit the road with the wild, bottle-swilling and totally unpredictable Vincent. But before making his decision to leave, Gallup had cut 35 tracks with the singer and Beck was determined to unearth each and every one. "I knew then that I wanted to play the lead guitar breaks... the fiery stuff, like Cliff Gallup. I knew I didn't just want to be a strummer."

His mission now clear, Jeff pursued guitar playing with a new vigour and determination, excitement falling away to obsession, fingers left bleeding as a result. In short, it was time to get serious. Like a prospector panning for gold, Beck raided his older sister's record collection for all the golden nuggets he could find, to analyse and emulate on his own wonky set of strings. Though Annetta expressively forbade such lightning raids on her room – always checking for Jeff's telltale thumbprints on singles – he still managed to unearth the goods wherever she hid them. A priceless copy of Elvis' 'Heartbreak Hotel' here, a rare 78 of Eddie Cochran's '20 Flight Rock' there, Beck found the lot. And when he couldn't find what he was looking for at home, there was always Croydon's Record Rendezvous, where the mock-respectful teenager would persuade the headmasterly owner to play copies of Little Richard's 'Lucille',

Roy Orbison's 'Go Go Go (Down The Line)' and Jerry Lee Lewis' 'Whole Lotta Shakin' Goin' On' while he stood transfixed at the listening post. At night, it was back to the radio, where Beck would attune his ears to the static-laden magic of Radio Luxembourg.

"Radio Luxembourg… was one of those stations that you could *just* tune into, as if it were coming from the far-flung regions of Africa or something, when in fact, it was just Luxembourg," he said. "It was all so muffled and indistinct…you had to strain your ears so much to hear the guitar." But when he was just about ready to give up, Jeff would be rewarded with little droplets from heaven. "Glorious cascades of guitar notes would come out and then just fade away again. Radio Luxembourg was like tuning into God or something."

During this bout of frenzied activity, Beck decided to dispense with the services of his friend's now ailing 'Black Cowboy' and build his own guitar. In preparation for the task, he had already been busy expanding his original cigar-box design: increasing the number of overall boxes, sticking an unsanded fence upright on top to act as a neck, painting the odd fret marker and putting nut and bolts where he felt the machine heads might sit. Jeff solved the string issue by simply double looping aircraft line wire for the heavier gauges. Perhaps unsurprisingly, it failed to render much of a tune. Next on the building block was an "absurdly out of proportion instrument" made from plywood that weighed a ton, had a neck the length of a football field and sported even more painted frets. Beck was prouder of this effort, and though it was still largely unplayable, he liked to place it on a chair and just look at it. Sadly, his father was less given to 'The Plywood Sports Model' and after an argument with his son, threw it in the garden. "The joints let go and the top of the body just went like two pancakes. That was the end of that."

For effort number three, Jeff enlisted help: "Next door to my bike-racing buddy's house, I heard the sound of a guy sawing in his workshop," he confirmed. "My friend said 'That's Jack, he can make anything'. So I went to see him and got him to make me a guitar." The design shape Beck provided his potential saviour with was that of a Fender Stratocaster, a "thing" Jeff had first seen being wielded by Buddy Holly as he sang 'That'll Be The Day', another slice of early rock'n'roll genius that dumbfounded the teenager when he heard it:

"When I saw Buddy Holly, I wanted a Strat." Alongside the Gibson Les Paul Goldtop and later 'Custom' models, the Fender Stratocaster was destined to become one of the most famous, genuinely beautiful and eminently playable guitars of all time. Designed by Leo Fender, Freddie Tavares and George Fullerton in 1954, its double-cutaway body, extended top horn, sleek contours and revolutionary tremolo arm made it appear like something out of a science fiction movie – an American guitar truly made for the dawn of the nuclear age.

Unfortunately there were no Fender Stratocasters in England at the time, and even if there were, neither Beck nor his parents could afford one. He was therefore only able to provide roughly drawn pictures, or at best photographs torn from a Fender guitar catalogue as a template for the mysterious Jack to work from. The end result proved predictably monstrous, but surprisingly pretty: "We knew they had to be solid. No guitar could be that thin and be hollow. So I rounded up [Jack] with a band saw... to cut this piece of wood. I can't tell you what a funny shape it came out. The neck was four times too long, but it was a good bedroom mirror guitar. I had it sprayed yellow." As Beck's co-designer had furnished the instrument with "about four hundred frets", Jeff finished the job himself during woodwork class. But being no luthier, 'pinpoint accuracy' and 'scientific measurement' eluded him. "We found out about fretting scales and stuff, [but I] had to scale up from photographs off albums, or just guess. The annoying part was you'd pick up a piece of crap guitar in a shop – like a five quid acoustic – and it still felt better than [the] home-made one." After several botched attempts to 'guesstimate' the correct fret dimensions, Jeff finally had something that resembled a working model, even if "the scale was so bad, it was only playable with a capo at the fifth fret". With true serendipity, Beck was forced to constantly bend strings to pitch – inadvertently creating one of the strangest, most beguiling and soon-to-be copied techniques in the history of rock.

The second but last piece of the puzzle was to animate Jeff's 'Frankenstein's Monster' by making it into a true 'electric' guitar. "You know, I didn't really know what an electric guitar was," he later laughed. "I thought 'electric' meant steam irons and cookers." To effectively emulate the sounds of his new heroes, Jeff had to dispense with any notions of running on just acoustic power and equip his instrument with a 'pick-up'. Essentially a transducer device that captured the vibration of a string and then converted it to an electrical signal that in turn could be amplified or recorded, the pick-up had first surfaced in the thirties. Then appearing as little more than horseshoe magnets that arched over the strings of guitars such as the Rickenbacker A-22 'Frying Pan', the pick-up's progress was shunted into a different and altogether more important place when the peerless Charlie Christian began using a Gibson ES-150 with the Benny Goodman Orchestra in 1939. Instead of the pick-up being located above the string, Gibson had moved it below "the resonating wires" and into the body of the guitar itself, an elegant and revolutionary solution that allowed an amplified Christian to make himself heard above all the woodwind, drums and brass. With just one flick of the proverbial switch, Charlie was now as much a lead instrument as the trumpet, saxophone or piano, a fact he took full and spectacular advantage of until his untimely death in 1942.

A precedent set, Gibson, Fender and, indeed, many other guitar manufacturers such as Gretsch were soon at the forefront of 'electrified' sound – with mass-production line Les Pauls, ES-335s, Strats, Telecasters and Duo-Jets (the last two will be returned to in due course) soon making their way into the hands of blues and rock'n'roll artists like Muddy Waters, Chuck Berry, Buddy Holly and Cliff Gallup. In such hands, and with the right amplification, the guitar could now be as caressing as a lover or as slippery as a snake, a six-stringed machine capable of seemingly endless tones and only limited by the capabilities of its user. Of course, the teenaged Beck wasn't quite cognisant of all this as yet. He simply wanted a pick-up. Sadly, as with most things in Jeff's life, his parents were unable (or, as likely, unwilling) to provide him with the money for it. Taking the view 'needs must when the Devil drives', he just walked into a music shop and stole one: "I really couldn't have cared if I got thrown in jail. I had to have my pick-up." Screwing it into place in the hole he had already burrowed into his makeshift guitar, there was now only one thing stopping him from realising his true vocation in life. "When you had the pick-up, you had to have the amplifier."

For Beck, that meant returning to school. Forsaking woodwork class this time for the science department, he set about building a veritable monolith to technology – a mammoth 15ft by 1ft cabinet crammed with an Axiom 300 speaker and driven by 10 watts of power: "It took over the entire house." One can only wonder how Jeff got it home. In honour of his heroes Paul and Gallup, Beck set the treble at maximum and dug in as hard as he could: "I think my mum started to realise there was *something* there, even if the noise was unbearable," he later said. "But it was still a guitar. When you want your son to play piano and impress all your neighbours with Rachmaninov and all you got was Chuck Berry, well..." Impressed by his drive, but driven mad by the noise, Jeff's parents consigned the amplifier to the garage and asked their son to plug into the back of the radio instead. Initially reluctant to compromise, Beck soon realised there was one redeeming feature to the new arrangement: "Well, I could hear myself on the radio." The next step was to hear himself in the concert hall.

Before that, however, Jeff got to see at close quarters what rock'n'roll looked, sounded and, in all probability, smelled like when he attended a Buddy Holly & The Crickets concert at Croydon's Davis Theatre on March 12, 1958. Already a huge fan of the bespectacled singer/guitarist, Beck reportedly didn't sleep the night before the gig, the excitement of actually seeing one of his idols in the flesh proving all too much for his young brain to cope with. The teenager's first concert was a then typical showbiz affair, with Holly supported by an all-round entertainment package that included the on-the-rise crooner Gary Miller alongside singing hoofers of "stage, radio and recording fame" The Tanner Sisters. Providing compere duties and "comedy with the modern style" was a young Des O'Connor, his effervescent smile, perma-tan and wobbly way with a ballad as yet unknown to the TV audiences he would duly terrorise in coming decades.

Given that his Davis Theatre appearance was the 12th night of a 25-date, 'two shows an evening' UK tour with no breaks in schedule, Buddy Holly was probably already tired when he hit the stage, but Jeff didn't notice: "He actually made the effort of coming over to England, to Croydon in the fifties, to play for us," he remembered. "When I saw him live, it was the best thing [I'd] ever seen." Wielding a pristine Sunburst Fender Stratocaster, Holly gave Beck his first opportunity to see what the guitar of his dreams could do in the right hands: "On 'That'll Be The Day', it was just 'Oh God'. I never heard another Strat tone like it. He must have been an electrician or something." Duly inspired by Buddy Holly & The Crickets, Jeff redoubled his efforts on guitar, now determined to learn every chord, slur, double stop and dragged rhythm rock'n'roll had to offer.

The Great British public didn't have long to wait before they could see Beck's progress, the 14-year old making his own performing debut at Carshalton Hall & Youth Centre in May 1958. Exhibiting early signs of the behaviour that would come to define his approach to such engagements, Jeff had resolutely refused to appear on a float as part of the town parade. Instead, he only agreed to appear in front of a captive, indoor audience. Armed with his home-made Strat and a small amp, Beck was accompanied on stage by a six feet, three inch duffel-coat wearing art student who had reluctantly consented to play bass – or more specifically, plucked upright cello: "It looked ridiculous. I kept saying 'Put it on a chair, put it on a chair!'" In the end, the mismatched duo managed to get through half a song (probably 'Be-Bop-A-Lula') before pleading "technical problems" and fleeing to the wings. Astoundingly, their short brush with fame got a positive review in the local paper, though 'Jack the woodcutter' turned up after the gig demanding the £5 he was still owed for building Jeff's guitar: "He made a complete twat out of me by telling everyone I hadn't paid him for it," said Beck. "I'd just been the belle of the ball, and he said 'Right, I'm going to tell you about your mate Jeff, you owe me £5, you cheapskate bastard!' I thought 'Right, for that, you won't get your money!'" As much as he fought hard against it in subsequent years, the tragicomic conclusion to Beck's first gig was indicative of things to come, with every step taken towards victory just as likely to end in defeat or downright farce. Then as now, it remains an essential part of his appeal.

Back in 1958, however, all was seriousness. Despite not yet acquiring a proper guitar with which to practise, Beck was intent on mastering the instrument, even consenting to his parent's wishes that he take lessons with a Spanish guitar tutor. It did not go well: "The teacher played acoustic. I wanted to play electric. He told me I was wasting my time. No meeting of minds there. I just said 'Bye...'"

Instead, Jeff continued to do his own detective work, a process he referred to as, "Drilling for oil. It became my life quest to find out who made those noises, who recorded them, and how they did it." For Beck, the more he investigated, the more he wanted to know. In Cliff Gallup's case, it might have begun with mimicking the sly twang of 'Be-Bop-A-Lula', but soon moved on to learning about Gretsch Duo Jets, Bigsby tremolo arms, flat wound strings, Fender Tweed and Standell amps and lashings of spring reverb. He also wanted to learn the source of Gallup's inspiration, where the jazz had come from, how he imitated pedal steels or skittered across the neck country-style on tracks like 'Blue Jean Bop' and 'Race With The Devil'.

While looking for such clues, Jeff found Chet Atkins, one of Nashville's most influential country/jazz pickers and a major influence on the likes of Gallup and Les Paul: "If you listen to Chet, and put a more abrasive edge on his playing, you've got rockabilly," Beck later said. "I used to sit there and wonder how the hell one guy did all that. It was a great blackboard when you start learning how to pick." Atkins' technique – which in itself was based on another country great, Merle Travis – involved using the thumb and up to three fingers of his right hand to play simultaneous bass lines, chords and solo melodies. Obsessed with getting it right, Beck started work on supposedly simpler picking patterns such as 'Windy And Warm' and 'Trambone', only to find they weren't simple at all: "The whole bass, rhythm, lead thing was daunting. [It's the] interaction of the fingers and the brain... everything's accurate, nothing's thrown away."

Having made a major breakthrough with the discovery of Atkins, Jeff now widened his net, taking in the work of sailor, boxer and pioneering rockabilly guitarist Paul Burlinson, who as a founding member of Johnny Burnette's Rock & Roll Trio had gifted the world with 'Train Kept A Rollin'' and 'Honey Hush'. An early advocate of the one-pick-up Fender Esquire (which Jeff would grow exceedingly familiar with in due course), Burlinson's fizzy tone had reportedly come about when he dropped his amp and a tube came loose – thus creating one of the first examples of 'distortion' on 1956's 'Tear It Up' and the following year's 'Rock Billy Boogie'. From there, it was a case of swimming backwards and forwards to find the likes of Johnny Carroll & The Hot Rocks' 'Hot Rocks', Jim Flaherty's Caravan-rocking 'Real Gone Daddy' and Art Adams' 'Dancing Doll': "If you listen to a million rockabilly records," he said, "they're not worth a toss lyrically or compositionally, but the sound [was] just fantastic." Ever the student, Beck's next lesson came from listening to James Burton's seminal 45s with teen idol Ricky Nelson. Using super-light strings, with the high B and E stolen from a banjo, Burton not only emulated steel guitar bends but skipped around the scales at lightning speed. As fascinated by the Telecaster-wielding Louisiana boy as he was with Cliff Gallup, Jeff's first properly learned solos were Burton's heart-stopping passes on 'Hey Babe' and 'It's Late'. "Burton," said Jeff with some understatement, "was incredible".

From Merle Travis-style claw hammer picking to false harmonics and faux-steel guitar bends, it was all grist for the mill to Jeff Beck, his ever-adapting style pulling in ideas from rockabilly, country, jazz and just about everything else. In fact, the only thing he seemed unconcerned about at the time was emulating the King of rock'n'roll himself: "I wasn't really interested in that Elvis, 'swivelling hips' kind of thing. All I wanted to hear was guitar." Still trying to save up the money for a real instrument, Beck had to content himself with peering through the windows of central London music stores to feed his addiction: "I saw the light by staring in the window through a quarter inch of glass of Jennings on Charing Cross Road, looking longingly at guitars I couldn't afford. Me, separated from them by only a quarter inch of glass. Then, I slowly summoned up the courage to ask to try out those guitars, and after a respectable amount of time, go back to those guitar shops, hoping that the staff had forgotten you so that you could try out those guitars again. They knew we didn't have the money, but they let us have a go anyway. Well, actually we got banned a couple of times, but it turned out all right."

For Jeff, the longing sometimes got so much, he literally lost his marbles: "When you're a kid of 14 and you see a piece of equipment that you dream about touching, never mind owning... well, I went into a trance [and] got the wrong bus home, it just blew my brains apart. It hasn't been any different since, really." Seeking consolation, Beck would often raid the likes of Jennings and Lew Davies' stores for the latest Fender and Gibson promotional booklets, salivating over images of the Strats, Teles and Les Pauls he simply could not own: "It was guitar porn, simple as that."

A confirmed 'teenage hot rod nut' who by now sported a quiff, white T-shirt and jeans, and rode around Wallington on a racing bike with his beloved yellow guitar strapped to his back so that everyone could see it, Beck must have been quite the prize for his parents: "Yeah, I remember my mum took me to the cinema when I was about 12 for a nice afternoon out. It was the worst thing she ever did. The 'B' feature was called *Hot Rod Gang*, and she tried to drag me out of the theatre when it came on. The opening sequence showed Deuce Roadsters racing down the pavement on both sidewalks, and she said, 'This is for hooligans, you can't have anything to do with it.' So I crept back and watched it on my own. [Another] film that changed my life."*

Though Jeff was doing reasonably well at school, his progressive mania concerning guitars and rods was still a worry for the Becks, with their son's class books and bedroom walls festooned with pictures of modified Ford Model Ts and white, red and sunburst Strats. At the age of 10, he had been a model student and keen chess player, whose worse excesses ran to breaking piano keys. Yet, by 15 he appeared for all intents and purposes like Wallington's answer to James Dean, but with six strings and a spanner in his back pocket. Slowly but surely, Jeff Beck had shed his childhood skin to become a professional rebel who harboured tantalising dreams of also becoming a professional rock'n'roll guitarist.

His world, then, must surely been knocked off its axis when, in Beck's own words, "The lights went out." After near five years of unrivalled domination, rock'n'roll and the change in culture it brought seemed to be falling into rapid, inexorable decline. In truth, it had been fighting a rearguard action for some while. In October 1957, for instance, Little Richard found God while on a flight over Australia, and renounced his previously evil ways to become a lay preacher. Worse, Jerry Lee Lewis had married his 13-year-old cousin, Myra Gale Brown, on December 12 of

---

* The movie's name was actually changed to *Fury Unleashed* in Croydon because of worries of violence.

the same year, an act apparently reasonable in Ferriday, Louisiana, but not one prying English journalists were likely to view with the same positive spin. Barraged with an unending stream of negative press while on tour in the UK, Lewis' musical career was all but shot to pieces as a result. Tragically, just 11 months after Jeff had shouted his approval at Buddy Holly from the foot of a stage in Croydon, the charismatic singer/guitarist was killed in a plane crash with fellow rockers The Big Bopper and Ritchie Valens, making February 3, 1959 one of the worst days in Beck's young life. Even Elvis had left the building, having been inducted into the army on March 24, 1958 with no way out until March 2, 1960. When Chuck Berry was arrested under the Mann Act for transporting a 14-year-old waitress across US state lines in December 1959, one could almost sense the buzzards descending. "I reckon on December 31, 1959, somebody pulled the big 'off' switch' for rock'n'roll," said Jeff. "A certain section of it died right there. 'The Twist' completely broke my heart. I hated it."

When Chubby Checker's catchy but puerile 'The Twist' introduced a new, parentally approved set of dance steps for the UK's youth to follow in the summer of 1960, rock'n'roll suddenly seemed as passé as Doris Day's 'Que Sera Sera' or Frank Sinatra's 'Three Coins In The Fountain', a fad whose days were not only numbered, but rubber stamped 'dead': "It just got extinguished," Beck confirmed to *Guitarist*. "Everything started to turn around, and for bands in [the UK], all that kind of 'Be-Bop-A-Lula' stuff just wasn't worth pursuing. Things were running at a million miles an hour and radical changes were being made."

In general, this was a terrible time for Jeff Beck. Now 16 years old, and committed to rock'n'roll, cars and guitars as if his life depended on them, the rug was in imminent danger of being pulled from beneath his feet, leaving him to face an uncertain future and, worse still, the prospect of a proper job.

It was time to get busy.

Chapter 2

Two Big Fish, One Small Pond

If rock'n'roll had been pronounced dead at the end of 1959, nobody was brave enough to tell the corpse, which continued to twitch away in semi-animated fashion throughout the spring and summer of 1960. In the UK, this amounted to a couple of fine singles, including the glacial thrills of Johnny Kidd & The Pirates' chart-topping 'Shakin' All Over' and the B-side of Vince Taylor's 'Pledging My Love', the marvellous 'Brand New Cadillac', which continued to pick up some airplay at the time. But in comparison with just two years before when Elvis' 'Jailhouse Rock' and Jerry Lee Lewis' 'Great Balls Of Fire' traded number one spots in consecutive weeks, it was small beer.

Even Cliff Richard, once touted as England's answer to Elvis Presley with his scorching debut 45 'Move It', had given up the ghost, now more content to sing about 'Livin' Doll''s over a somnambulant musical background than burn up the floor in his brothel creepers. The same was almost true of Richard's backing group, The Shadows. Led by the highly esteemed and hugely influential British guitarist Hank B. Marvin and his partner in rhythm Bruce Welch, The Shadows had once lit a real fire behind their singer, Marvin's precise, echoing and tremolo-heavy solos issuing forth from his trademark red Stratocaster, the very first of its kind in Britain. Yet by 1960 and the group's debut instrumental, 'Apache', it was all change. A beautiful, even haunting melody perhaps, but 'Apache' was light years away from the growling chug and bristling lead lines of 'Move It'.

For those like Jeff Beck, who still held out hope that rock'n'roll was simply suffering from a bout of flu rather than a fatal heart attack, news that Gene Vincent was to tour Great Britain in April 1960 must have been an absolute godsend. One of the 'original architects', Vincent's hell-for-leather image, bone-rattling voice and hell-raising Blue Caps had sent Beck into spasms of delight in 1957, and he was now gifted the opportunity of seeing them in his own backyard. Sadly, the group had recently disbanded, meaning that Jeff was not only denied his chance of communing with the long absent Cliff Gallup, but also his white Strat-wielding replacement, Johnny Meeks. He survived: "I was a naive, trusting kid and [Vincent] was playing with these guys who looked like they had just walked in from a bar," Beck remembered. "They were pretty good though, but when Gene appeared it was amazing. He was so menacing that you forgave him that he didn't have his own band. One always naively assumed that it was Vincent's choice not to have his band but he probably didn't have a say in it. Then, tragically, I watched [his] demise. He got overweight, lost his hair, and drank too much... typical rock'n'roll."

While Gene Vincent would soon enough descend into alcoholism, various legal battles and an ever-dwindling career that almost saw him desert his roots in favour of folk music, there was still enough life in the medallion-wearing, black-gloved holy terror in 1960 to give Jeff fresh hope. Having already chanced his arm in a number of local bands on the youth club circuit, Beck struck out for his first professional audition with The Bandits. An instrumental act from Hampshire who had won a contract backing various Presley and Vincent impersonators for a UK summer package tour, The Bandits had no knowledge that Jeff had changed his surname to 'Mason' for the audition. In the end, it didn't really matter. He got the job. Donning a grey suit, tie and freshly bleached pompadour, 'Mason' struck out on the road with the group – getting a real taste of driving up and down motorways in the back of a small van, and if reports are correct, witnessing a fight or two for his troubles: "We basically backed Gene-alikes."

To mark his passage from spirited amateur to semi-professional musician, Beck also got a halfway decent guitar, persuading his father to purchase a Guyatone LG-50 from Lew Davies' music shop on Charing Cross Road for the then not inconsiderable sum of £25, seven shillings and six pence: "It had purfling around the body and a maple veneer, so it wasn't such a bad old thing." Branded as an 'Antoria' in the UK, the Guyatone was a respectable enough Strat copy and regularly used by Hank Marvin in The Shadows until Cliff Richard gifted him the real thing: "The Guyatone felt great in comparison with the home-made one I'd had," said Jeff, "so it was good enough for me."

Despite earning his first real crust in a working band, Beck's tenure with The Bandits was brief. By Monday, September 19, 1960 he was once again back in full-time education, having left behind the unsatisfactory experiences of Sutton East Secondary Modern for a new life as a student at Wimbledon College of Art. Then among a growing wave of teenagers seeking a career outside the more conventional perimeters of a nine-to-five existence, Jeff had enrolled on a two-year fine art course that might provide him with the skills to enter advertising, graphic or even costume design, if he so wished. But like so many of his time and mind-set, Wimbledon College really represented little more for Beck than an opportunity to appease his parents while figuring out how he might find a permanent way into the music business. "If I took it seriously, I'd probably be designing cornflakes packaging now," he later confirmed. "So many English musicians came to their music by going to art school. It was an excuse not to work. You got a grant and you'd dress up in silly clothes. You didn't really have to answer to anybody, and you were part of this elite group. You could walk around with a Van Gogh under your arm and pretend you did it. A Van Gogh, some paint brushes and a Miles Davis album... those were your tools. But art school was a dead loss to me. It was just a rude awakening to all the art forms: painting, sculpture and so on. And you then realised that you didn't know anything about that, so my dedication to music took over."

What Jeff failed to make clear in his self-deprecating, though exceedingly accurate remarks about his time in the art school system was the degree of talent he brought to Wimbledon College. By his own admission not exactly a model student while at Sutton East Secondary Modern, Beck had nevertheless shown genuine flair with both brush and pen, being one of the more promising fine art pupils in his year. But a wilful streak had frequently seen him doodling Strats and Deuce Roadsters rather than following the more stringent assignments set by his teachers. Again, Jeff's head was not set on a traditional course: "I only used to go to [art school] because they had good meals." As Beck reluctantly dragged himself out of bed five days a week to travel the six miles to Merton Hall Road for oil painting classes, he was simultaneously planning his long-term escape into stardom. That plan depended on securing the lead guitar spot with an up-and-coming local covers band, The Deltones.

Jeff's first impressions of The Deltones were both aesthetically pleasing and musically sound. Having regularly seen the group's van – their proud name emblazoned on the side – parked outside various concert venues in Croydon and Wimbledon, Beck had ventured inside once or twice to actually check them out: "They had pink jackets, which I thought were great." A friend of the band's left-handed guitarist Ian (formerly Jim) Duncombe since his early teens, Jeff began to attend the odd band rehearsal at the Trojan car factory where they practised, their resultant noise neatly muffled by a nearby Tizer bottling plant and 'Power's Accounting Machines'. Aside from Duncombe, an (unknown) bassist and drummer, The Deltones also boasted a cherub-faced singer called Derek Burchell, whose name had been changed to the more pop-friendly 'Johnny Del' by the group's manager. All Tom Cruise teeth and greased black hair, Del's image was wholly indicative of the Cliff Richard, Marty Wilde and Billy Fury school of 'cheeky, but moody chappies' then drawing screams from schoolgirls across Britain, a fact mirrored by The Deltones' impressive pulling power in South and West London's dance halls.

Unlike Beck, The Deltones were also seasoned semi-professionals, all in their early twenties with their own self-pressed promo disc and a residency at the famed Hammersmith Palais already behind them. In Jeff's eyes, this was the big time: "Around our way, they were a hot item." His chance came when Duncombe announced to his colleagues he was moving to Germany to play nightly spots at Hamburg's Top Ten Club, leaving the position of lead guitarist potentially wide open. Though there were real doubts that the spotty 16 year old had either the skills or experience to fill Duncombe's place, a hastily arranged audition where Jeff unveiled his latest acquisition – a brand new red and gold Burns Vibra Artiste – and an astounding gift for mimicking Cliff Gallup put paid to all such concerns. "That Burns [had] about six pick-ups and about a hundred knobs on it," he later said. "I never knew what any of them did."*

In a perfect world, when The Deltones gave the thumbs-up of approval, Jeff should have simply taken the gig there and then. But he held back, only agreeing to join the group if John Owen accompanied him on rhythm guitar. The story behind Beck's stalling tactic was actually a touching one. Friends since childhood, John had often boosted Jeff's esteem during frequent periods of self-doubt, persuading him to reconsider packing in the guitar in favour of drums during a particularly low period when in his early teens: "Even then, [John] believed in me." Reluctant to cut their wages five ways, but mindful of securing Beck's skills, the band agreed to his request and Owen was in.

Now officially a Deltone, Beck was introduced to life on the road with a semi-pro act. As later published photographs confirm, he took to the sartorial side of his responsibilities with real enthusiasm, dressing in a natty blue suit, white shoes and splashed blond quiff, a pink handkerchief stuffed in his jacket pocket nicely setting off the whole ensemble. But Jeff was less enthused with the material the band had to play nightly in concert halls throughout the South East. "All the pre-'59 stuff had become a bit passé and taboo, you know. It was like 'Don't touch that, it's gone.'" Instead, The Deltones' set was peppered with tearjerkers of the day, Johnny Del more likely to break hearts when singing the likes of The Everly Brothers' 'Cathy's Clown' or Elvis' '... His Latest Flame' than scaring those in attendance with Gene Vincent's 'Double Talkin' Baby'. The closest

---

* Actually the guitar in question had three pick-ups, six knobs and a vibrato arm that looked like it could cut bread, but one shouldn't quibble too much.

thing Beck could really get to showing off his guitar skills was throwing down a few lead lines during their cover of The Shadows' 'Apache'. "Hank Marvin tended to pick the string near the fretboard end, and that gave him a very pure, round kind of sound – that and a very clean amp [setting]," Jeff later said. "He hardly ever clanged it and I admired him. You never heard him make a fluff." But away from the moderate treats of emulating Marvin's bell-like tones, the opportunities to rock out remained few for the guitarist. "It was easy stuff that any band with some proficiency could learn in a day."

There was the odd comedic moment or two to be had among the disappointments. Though Beck was enormously fond of John Owens, he wasn't above pointing out that his friend's white Fender Telecaster was a far better instrument than the Burns "Tri Sonic" he owned – and as lead guitarist, he should really be playing it. For a while Owens agreed to swap, though when confronted with the difficulties of controlling the Burns' seemingly endless knob configurations each night, soon asked for his Telecaster to be returned. Beck was again left with a model he was growing to despise until fate intervened. "I was standing at a bus stop and a gust of wind from the bus knocked the case over and smashed the (Burns') toggle switch, so that was the end of that." Jeff's choice of replacement, the Futurama, at least sounded promising from the advert he saw: "Go Modern, Go Hofner 'Futurama', the world's most advanced electric guitar… microscopic tuning, a cambered fingerboard with nickel silver frets, a vibrato arm that flattens and sharpens by half a tone, and seven tone changes from three matched pick-ups, instantly selected by three simple push button controls." Sadly, the Futurama, which was made in Czechoslovakia and imported into the UK by Selmer, hence its inclusion in a Hofner catalogue, didn't quite live up to its hype. "The switches were useless," said Beck. "The vibrato arm was a disgrace to technology… it was just rigid."

Rather than murder Owens to reclaim the Telecaster, Beck went cap in hand to his mother after seeing the guitar of his dreams in the window of a West End music store: "It turned out Fender Strats weren't £1,000, but actually £147. I thought maybe if I sold everything I had, I might be able to get the money together. In the end, I got it on HP." With Ethel Beck co-guaranteeing the agreement, Jeff finally had a sunburst Fender Stratocaster of his own. "A marriage," he later remarked, "made in heaven." With the purchase of the Strat came a whole new set of challenges, not least of which was finding the cash to make the monthly repayments. Now bored beyond measure by having to drag himself out of bed after a night's gigging to attend classes he hadn't the faintest interest in, Jeff made the decision to follow the money, go for the fame and pack in art school. "The standard was so outrageously high there, it just wasn't worth staying." There was a back-up plan of sorts. "Well, I thought 'If it all goes wrong in two years, I'll go back and learn how to paint properly.'" Though his parents probably wanted to throw a bucket of water over his head, Beck left Wimbledon College on May 22, 1961 to pursue his interest in 'the alternative arts'.

Over the coming two years, he probably wished he hadn't as his new career as a musician skittered, stopped, restarted, only to stop and then start again, leading to a bewildering number of associations with bands, artists, paint shops and golf courses along the way. For Beck, it was a true introduction into the joys and perils of a life less ordinary. Within months of throwing his lot in with the local promise offered by The Deltones, the group had splintered in two with Johnny Del taking his half of the name to another West London-based act, The Crescents. Unsure of what to do, Jeff followed Del into the line-up, again scratching a living by playing soppy ballads and Shadows covers to courting couples and singletons from Heathrow to Richmond. One good thing did come out of his decision, with Beck making his recorded debut on 'Wedding Bells', an old Deltones tune The Crescents demoed and then shopped to record companies in the autumn of 1961. Though no-one bit, 'Wedding Bells' had at least one, albeit dubious fan. When Jeff played an acetate copy to his mother, she thought the song so good, she refused to believe he had played on it.

After Beck drifted away from The Crescents (or, as plausibly, the band folded in late 1961), he seemed to enter his wilderness year, with rare sightings confined to pick-up bands and favours done for old friends. During 1962 Jeff was certainly seen loitering with Brian Howard & The Silhouettes – an act put together by Brian Somerville, whom Beck knew from art school days and was now trying to follow a similar path to Cliff Richard around Sutton and its surrounding areas. When this failed to work, Somerville formed the brilliantly named, but similarly doomed, 'Im & The Uvvers, who again used Beck's guitar skills on an occasional basis throughout the summer of '62. Other sources have Jeff playing with Kerry Rapid's Blue Stars around the same time, though tracking his movements during this period are akin to finding Jesus when he went on a 40-day stroll around the Sinai desert.

One thing that remains certain is that Jeff was by no means a full-time musician at the time, having to earn a crust by several other means, and sometimes by any means necessary. According to Beck, his first 'proper' job was driving a tractor around a golf course, which he enjoyed principally because it left him on his own for long periods. However, it was not without its drawbacks, with Jeff having to leave home at six in the morning for a long walk to the course. When he got there, he was also in some danger of serious injury: "The [golfers] were a right bunch of snooty bastards, I can tell you that," he told *Record Collector*. "They'd shout 'Fore!' after they hit the ball and then it'd go bouncing off my tractor. Having a ball coming in from 58,000 feet, it was murder." Reluctant to be used as target practice, Beck soon left for a spell as a painter/decorator before once again gravitating towards cars and bikes. At last finding regular work with a garage near his home, he settled into a variety of vehicle-related jobs, including panel-beater and paint sprayer. "The money wasn't that bad," he said. From now on, Jeff would become renowned for turning up to gigs covered in paint, grease or worse, another endearing if somewhat messy addition to his curious legend.

By the start of 1963, building slowly on the back of the trad jazz and Leadbelly-influenced skiffle boom of the previous decade, interest in urban American blues was about to reach fever pitch in Great Britain. Since the mid-fifties, jazz band leader and trombonist Chris Barber had been tireless in his promotion of American folk and blues forms, arranging the first UK tours of Big Bill Broonzy and Muddy Waters (even if audiences expecting to see the latter strumming a plain acoustic box top were shocked when he arrived wielding a thoroughly electrified Fender Telecaster). As the import record market continued to grow for such sounds – electric or otherwise – so did demand for home-grown alternatives. First to take up the challenge were former Barber employees Cyril Davies and Alexis Korner: the former, a pale, balding labourer's son from Buckinghamshire, who nevertheless sang and blew harp as if he had been born at the proverbial crossroads; the latter a Paris-born immigrant whose own spare gifts as a singer/guitarist did little to obscure a colossal and overwhelming love for black music. "All I ever wanted to do," Alexis once said, "was play the blues."

Together, Davies and Korner formed Blues Incorporated, "a revolving door" of a band whose various line-ups provided inspiration for a host of young disciples eager to hear the sounds of the Mississippi Delta performed on their own doorstep. Taking over a residency at London's sweaty, but seminal, Marquee Club in 1962, Blues Incorporated gigs became a training ground for the likes of rising stars Long John Baldry, Graham Bond, Danny Thompson and many others mentioned in due course throughout these pages. Always keen to nurture talent, Korner also implemented an 'open mike' policy for those souls brave enough to mount the boards backed by his ever-changing group. As a consequence, a promising slide guitarist named Brian Jones (then trading under the blues-friendly nom-de-plume 'Elmo Lewis') became friends with fellow stage crashers Mick Jagger and Keith Richards, the trio soon planning a band of their very own, The Rolling Stones.

Like any burgeoning cult, the blues boomers were destined only to grow. While Korner and Davies ruled the roost at the Marquee, other venues and halls sprang up or consolidated their appeal, catering for an ever-growing audience keen to escape the insipid pop then sugar-coating Britain's radio airwaves and make the blues their own. In Richmond, Surrey for instance, the Crawdaddy Club opened for business – giving the now fully formed Rolling Stones a chance to perform their occasionally irreverent, but always furious brand of up-tempo blues and R&B covers on Sundays to packed houses. By the time the Stones broke into the UK charts with a cover of Chuck Berry's 'Come On' in the summer of 1963, giving the 'Thames Delta' its first real hit, the Crawdaddy was simply too small to house their army of fans – the band now forever lost to the club, its manager and the locals who pushed them up the hill to stardom. But as time came to show, the Crawdaddy's loss would soon be Jeff Beck's gain.

Though he was first mesmerised by the low, insistent moan of the Mississippi Delta as a nine year old when his uncle's car radio began inadvertently spilling out some still unknown melody, Beck had fought shy of exploring the blues until lent an LP by a friend named Ian Stewart. A founding member of The Rolling Stones, Stewart had lost his spot as the group's pianist on the grounds of image, his "brickie jaw and wide shoulders" deemed unsuitable and six in a group considered one too many by their newly acquired manager, Andrew Oldham. However, 'Stu' remained within the Stones' inner circle, working onstage with the band as an unofficial sixth member and offstage as their road manager.

Liking Jeff's down-to-earth attitude and mightily impressed by his playing, Stewart lent the guitarist a slew of blues albums, providing proper introductions to old-school giants such as Big Bill Broonzy, Robert Johnson and a pre-electric Muddy Waters. Suffice to say, Beck devoured them all, using their example to extend his vocabulary of licks and further inform the slide-guitar technique that was to become a key component of his signature style. "It was *Folk Festival Of The Blues*," Jeff later confirmed. "I just wore out the album." A riveting live snapshot of all the Chicago blues scene had to offer, *Folk Festival...* featured cuts from the untouchable Muddy Waters, sly-sounding Sonny Boy Williamson and snake-charming Howlin' Wolf, as well as two tracks by Waters' 26-year-old protégé, Buddy Guy. As with Cliff Gallup, Beck was astounded by Guy's talent, his superb, imploring voice accompanied by some of the most experimental lead guitar work ever let loose on a 12-bar. "It was total, manic abandon that broke all the boundaries. Long, developing solos, just the opposite of all the pop stuff at the time."

Buddy's mastery of a Fender Stratocaster on songs such as 'Worried Blues' and 'Don't Know Which Way To Go' was a persuasive and compelling route into the blues for Beck. Crucially, it allowed him to connect the dots from fifties rock'n'roll right back to Rolling Fork, Clarksdale and Lettsworth, Louisiana, while also squaring a circle with the crisp, new soul and R&B sounds offered by Irma Thomas, Stevie Wonder, Otis Redding and Booker T & The MGs:

31

"Steve Cropper's playing on 'Green Onions' was just exquisite."

As ever with Jeff, initial contact with something he loved led to exhaustive exploration. Though not immediately drawn to the soul-sucking, pre-war acoustic country blues of legends such as Robert Johnson, Blind Lemon Jefferson, Tampa Red and Son House (too little electricity for Beck), he did become duly obsessed with many others; the likes of Otis Rush, John Lee Hooker and his cousin Earl Hooker all landing on Beck's turntable at some point or another. "My interest in blues," he later told journalist Tom Hibbert, "really started when the Chicago albums began to reach England. Muddy, Buddy Guy, Howlin' Wolf... there [was] a special way the guitars sounded, tinny and rough."

Another venue that did exceedingly well from its association with the British blues scene was Twickenham's Eel Pie Island. Set up by former junk-shop owner turned promoter Arthur Chisnall in 1956, Eel Pie Island was originally a down at the mouth hotel in the middle of the Thames that – under his guidance – became a home-from-home to the trad jazzers of the time. By 1963, Chisnall had turned his eccentric but captivating club into one of the biggest draws in the South East, catering for a thousand mad-eyed blues, soul and R&B fans each weekend. Dubbed by the media a "Beatnik-infested vice den" where young men "went on the pull" and "the girls didn't seem to mind", Eel Pie Island might have been a smelly, even pungent location with a rotting dance floor that bounced like a trampoline, but it was also great fun. While Chisnall was more than happy to accommodate the likes of Acker Bilk, Cy Laurie and George Melly & The Temperance Seven, he was also quite the bluesman, booking Jesse Fuller, Howlin' Wolf and Buddy Guy to appear on Eel Pie's swaying stage – all witnessed by an enthusiastic Jeff Beck.

For The Nightshift, a group Beck helped put together with vocalist/harmonica player Brian Wiles and drummer Dave Elvidge, both the rise of Brit-blues and the flowing hundreds that crossed over Eel Pie Island's rickety, narrow bridge on a Saturday night to see it for themselves was very good news indeed. Unlike any of the acts that Jeff had previously dabbled with, The Nightshift were, by all accounts, heavily influenced by the blues and R&B movement sweeping across London and the South East at the time. Though not destined to become a serious, long-term proposition, The Nightshift established enough of a following to gig regularly, not only at Eel Pie but also several notable London venues, even grabbing a much-coveted spot at the 100 Club on Oxford Street.

The Nightshift continued to perform on the South East concert circuit until 1965, and released two singles, 'Stormy Monday'/'That's My Story' and 'Corrina, Corrina' on Piccadilly Records*. While Beck reportedly returned to play on at least one 45 as a favour to the group, he had actually left their ranks during the autumn of 1964 (see below), with several key factors behind his move, most of which were driven by his newfound status as a married man. In something of a whirlwind romance, Jeff had married Crawley-born Patricia Brown in July 1963. A music-loving teenager like Beck, Pat was an attractive, doe-eyed girl with a mass of brown hair and a love of fashionable clothes, which she turned to her advantage by securing a job as a dressmaker. Again like Jeff, she shared a love of animals, in particular horses and dogs, the couple's first real acquisition being a huge Afghan hound, who would bring both joy and havoc to the newlyweds in times to come.

With marriage, of course, came increased financial responsibility and Beck's regular gig with The Nightshift – while satisfying enough – simply didn't pay enough to cover the couple's rent, let alone the price of dog food. Thankfully, his increased profile on the Thames Delta meant that other job offers were coming in. A spot with future Manfred Mann bassist Tom McGuinness' then promising group The Roosters was duly considered only to be turned down on grounds of cash. Elsewhere, a relatively new band led by John Mayall called Bluesbreakers were also seeking a lead guitarist, but again, Jeff was reluctant to commit. "John Mayall phoned me up [when] I was still living with my mum," he later told journalist Douglas J Noble. "My mother said, 'This John Mayall sounds a very nice chap!' I remember being pestered by a lot of phone calls though. In the end my mother

---

* 'That's My Story' was actually written by Tim Rice, who later found fame with Andrew Lloyd Webber as the lyricist behind the musicals *Joseph And The Amazing Technicolor Dreamcoat, Jesus Christ Superstar* and *Evita*.

would say, 'Answer the bloody phone, we all know who it is!' It would have been a great experience but you can't be two people. Those days were really crazy, every day something new would be happening." In the case of both The Roosters and John Mayall's Bluesbreakers, another Surrey-born guitarist would soon come to the rescue, his talent with six strings closely rivalling Beck's own.

After a period of hesitation, Jeff finally solved the dilemma of 'where next?' by throwing in his lot with The Tridents – a band The Nightshift had already supported once or twice at Eel Pie Island. The Tridents were led by two brothers, Paul and John Lucas, who covered lead vocals/bass and harmonica/backing vocals/rhythm guitar respectively, and completing the line-up were Ray Cook on drums and a fine lead guitarist named Mike Jopp. "John was a great rhythm and harp player who sang backing vocals and harmonies," says Jopp. "Paul played bass and sang the majority of our set. The Lucas brothers themselves came from a big family in Chiswick, though we actually rehearsed in a big house in Kilburn. That was through another of the Lucas family's connections." Already established as a strong live draw, The Tridents were wholly indicative of the type of blues/R&B act then making waves throughout London and the South East. "John and Paul were blues mad," says Mike, "so we were playing a lot of Howlin' Wolf, Muddy Waters, Bo Diddley and Little Walter covers, with two sets a night at venues like Eel Pie. It was a unique, great place to play... tons of people, very laid-back, just a bloody big hall with a beer counter in the middle and a tiny dressing room at the back."

Both the Lucas brothers and Jopp were aware of Jeff's reputation well before he actually joined the band. "When I first heard Beck, I just thought 'What the fuck was that?'" Jopp confirms. "There was this guy with a Telecaster and a Binson Echorec and the notes were just flying everywhere. Nobody at that point was doing anything like it. He was incredibly flash – I mean in terms of his technique – and doing things that we and the audience had just not heard before. Jeff was playing right at the top of the neck, off the fingerboard near the pick-up. He'd press the strings down at the top, detune them, just making these unbelievable noises."

Regrettably, when Beck made his interest in joining The Tridents clear, it was Jopp's position that was in jeopardy. "I was happy with

The Tridents but Jeff really wanted to get into a much better band, so he made it quite clear to them he'd like to join. And frankly, the guys called me up and said 'Look, Jeff wants to join'. Well, I just said 'OK, you've got to have him because he's incredible'. He was just so head and shoulders above everyone else. I was a little upset, of course, but also relaxed because Jeff was clearly in a league of his own. I actually saw them play the 100 Club after he joined, and he was incredibly nice to me, both before and after joining the band, actually." For Beck, taking on lead guitar duties with The Tridents not only allowed him access to bigger audiences and better wages, but also provided the opportunity to influence the sound and direction of the group in a way he had not enjoyed before. "I was screaming to be recognised," he said, "and I finally found this little R&B band which I thought was great. I [could help] build them up and play good, authentic blues."

In subsequent years, Beck's tenure with The Tridents has assumed almost mythic proportions, the tales surrounding him akin to turning water into wine, or at least six strings into "liquid gold". If such reports are to be believed – and there is no reason to doubt them – then Beck's playing has seldom been wilder, less restrained or experimental. Certainly, 'Nursery Rhyme', a live track recorded by The Tridents at Eel Pie Island in 1964 and later released on 1991's 3CD collection *Beckology*, goes some way to prove that he was not so much pushing the limits of technology and technique of the time as smashing them into little pieces. Armed with a white Fender Telecaster and Vox AC30 'Top Boost' (the sunburst Strat had fallen prey to a bad respray, faulty rewiring job and then been sold on to buy a Ford Zephyr), Beck's work on 'Nursery Rhyme' borders on genius – albeit of the maddest variety: trills, dissonance, double stops, overbends, hammer-ons, pull-offs and picking above the nut and around the pick-ups all present and correct over a resolutely dragged Bo Diddley beat. "You could do anything over a Bo Diddley beat," he later reasoned. In 1964, this must have sounded not unlike the arrival of the four horsemen of the Apocalypse: "Jeff was just uniquely talented," said an admiring Mike Jopp. "He had this stunning technique and an incredible touch. He was the most gifted guitarist I'd ever heard or seen."

Of course, a key component to this audio madness was Beck's use (and ritual abuse) of the Binson Echorec, a device he began experimenting with during 1962 when it first arrived on the UK market. Originally designed with drums in mind, the Binson was an expensive proposition, its £140 price tag making it then more costly than a Vox AC30 amp. But for Jeff, the Binson's ability to provide up to 12 echo settings, plate/room reverbs and valve compression meant he had personal access to the same sonic palette his hero Les Paul drew from during the forties and fifties. "The crowds didn't always want straight blues," he later said. "They wanted sci-fi noises as well and that was all right with me." In addition to his use of the Binson, Beck was also a dab hand with a Klemt Echolette, which allowed him to programme alternate delays of an eighth, quarter and half second's duration, and even create rudimentary loops. Unfortunately the device was prone to temperature changes, meaning that "the tape would snap halfway through the first number and all my tricks were gone". Stung by criticisms that he was wholly dependent on such effects to create his sound, Jeff reportedly played part of one gig with a Spanish acoustic fed through a vocal mike to prove his doubters wrong.

Beck's penchant for "abstract harmonic manipulation", or as one critic more simply put it, "sonic mangling", did The Tridents no harm at all, with the band regularly drawing upwards of 800 people at Eel Pie Island, while also playing to 'House Full' signs at London's 100 Club, Studio 51 and Windsor's Ricky Tick. The group even shared Eel Pie's highest ever attendance record when they supported Leroy Fuller to an audience of 1,500 in mid-1964. "Eel Pie was an elite club," Beck later told journalist Gene Santoro. "People wanted you to emulate their idols. That's when I really started to kick some butt. I remember detuning the low E and A strings and just whining the hell out of them, making ridiculous noises and everyone went berserk. There wasn't an ounce of musical sense to it, but they loved it because it was different." Beck was not exaggerating either the elite nature of Eel Pie's core attendance or their desire for new sensations. Peopled by rollnecked beatniks, moustachioed jazzers, pill-popping R&B heads and, later, a sharp-suited mod contingent that included future Who guitarist Pete Townshend and singer Roger Daltrey, who remembered being "stupefied" by Jeff's antics with The Tridents, Eel Pie was a cult all its own. "I didn't know what impact I was having on the music scene," Arthur Chisnall later admitted. "You've got to remember that my job was to create a world for people and I created that world. The people who were originally there were 300 art-school people and they remade themselves until, bang, you had The Who and so many others."

One element of Beck's fearsome bag of tricks that has led to much subsequent debate among music critics was his use of 'controlled feedback' – and more specifically, whether he was the first British guitarist to exploit it on a concert stage. In simple terms, feedback is a 'loop' created when an electric guitar's pick-ups capture sound from the amplifier's speaker and then regenerate the signal through said amp, providing an eerie, high-frequency whistle that can be further manipulated into drones or, in the right hands, even tunes. There is some evidence to suggest that blues players such as Johnny 'Guitar' Watson, Guitar Slim and the wonderful Albert Collins were toying with the effect as early as the fifties. But it remains unlikely that their experiments were as bold or musical as Beck's, who according to some witnesses was setting up a feedback-delay loop via his Binson echo unit with one guitar while playing along with the results using another. "It's like a cycle of sound that builds up in the pick-ups that you can even play tunes with and I've been experimenting with [it] since 1960," he later confirmed. However, attributing the discovery of controlled feedback to Beck alone remains something of a sticky wicket, with Pete Townshend and The Kinks' Dave Davies also staking a claim to its screechy throne. "To tell the truth, Dave Davies, Jeff and me have got a tacit agreement that we'll all squabble until the day we die that we invented it," said Townshend. "I think possibly the truth is that it was happening in a lot of places at once. As the [volume] level went up, as people started to use bigger amps, and [some of us] were still using semi-acoustic instruments, it started to happen quite naturally."

One of the few people able to enter into such a debate with any real authority was Jimmy Page, though his loyalties – then as now – would probably have been with Beck. After all, the two were practically relatives from the moment they met. "Jeff came round my house with a guitar and played James Burton's solo from Ricky Nelson's 'My Babe'," Jimmy told *Guitar Player*. "We were immediately blood brothers." The only child of a personnel manager and doctor's secretary who lived in Epsom, Surrey – just six miles up the road from Wallington – Page was the same age as Jeff and from a similar social background. But they also shared another, far more important interest. "We were both guitar freaks," laughed Beck. Tying down the exact date, or even year, when they became friends is no easy task. Despite the fact Jeff and Jimmy both recall their first meeting taking place during their early teens, this seems unlikely. Instead, all reasonable evidence points to the fact that their paths probably didn't cross until they were at least 16 or even 17 years old.

However, the exact circumstances of their introduction remain in little doubt. "Well, my sister Annetta was at the same college as Jimmy," said Beck. "And though we had a fight at the time, she just couldn't resist telling me there was another nerd with a guitar at college. I had to travel miles on a bus to see him, but the fact that he was as insane as me about guitars, well, it was worth it. Suffice to say, a strong friendship developed." The faculty in question was Sutton Art College, which Page began attending in 1962 as a fine arts student. "I lived in Epsom, Jeff in Wallington, two towns not far apart," Jimmy later recalled. "Anyway, people sort of knew I was playing guitar... and I was friendly with a record collector [Barry Matthews], who knew Jeff's sister. She was a little older than Jeff, who in turn was just a little [younger] than me. But the thought was 'Maybe we should get these two guys together'. So we met up. We had home-made guitars and regular guitars at that point and just played." To ensure all went well, Annetta accompanied her younger brother to Page's parents' house. "She knew where he lived and we both went over on the bus to Epsom," Jeff said. "Jim was there and he sang us a Buddy Holly song. His mum made us a cup of tea."

As the two traded guitar licks – Page precisely tracing Scotty Moore's jumpy solo from Presley's 'Baby, Let's Play House', Beck responding with a blast or two from Vincent's 'Race With The Devil' before they both settled into James Burton's break on Ricky Nelson's 'It's Late' – Jeff became aware Jimmy was no neophyte when it came to six strings. "Christ, he was much more advanced than me, he knew all Buddy Holly's stuff. He was an only child you see, and his mum bought him all the goodies!" In fact, Page was already something of a star before meeting Beck. An early convert to Lonnie Donegan's skiffle movement, Page had appeared on BBC 1's *Huw Wheldon Show* in 1957, performing 'Mama Don't Want To Skiffle Anymore' and 'Cottonfield' with a bunch of like-minded amateur enthusiasts. When 13-year-old James was asked by the host whether he played any other guitar styles, he confirmed, "Yes, Spanish and dance," before adding that he wanted to pursue "biological research" after leaving school. Given later evidence, he certainly achieved his ambition on a practical, if not scientific level...

By age 16, Page had quit education in favour of a full-time career in music, soon taking up the post of lead guitarist with local rockers Neil Christian & The Crusaders, whom Beck saw in person while on a visit to nearby Richmond. "Jimmy was playing with Neil Christian," he confirmed. "I went to see them in 1961 or 1962... a lunchtime gig at The Boathouse in Kew Bridge. I saw this human beanpole with a Gretsch [Country Gentleman] four times bigger than he was." In the end, Page's time with Christian was relatively brief, the teenager falling prey to repeated bouts of glandular fever which eventually forced him to hand in his cards with the band and return to academia. "[I was] travelling around all the time in a bus. I did that for two years after I left school, to the point where I was starting to get really good [money], but I was getting ill," Page said in 1975. "So I went back to art college. And that was a total change in direction. As dedicated as I was to playing the guitar, I knew doing it that way was doing me in forever. Every two months I had glandular fever. So for the next 18 months I was... getting my strength up. But I was still playing."

Thanks to Annetta Beck's timely introduction Jeff and Jimmy were soon visiting each other's homes on a regular basis, endlessly exchanging guitar riffs and ideas while their parents provided tea and biscuits. As ever, Beck championed the more extreme advocates of the art, turning Page onto the new pleasures of pedal steel player Alvino Rey, jazz great Barney Kessel and his beloved Cliff Gallup. That said, Jimmy's taste was no less eclectic, the young guitarist already familiar with the wild overbends of Buddy Guy, the economical beauty of Howlin' Wolf's Hubert Sumlin and even the lush Indian sitar stylings of Ravi Shankar, of whom Page was an extremely early and vocal supporter. All such ideas and influences, from Elmore James' shivering slide on 'Dust My Broom' to Les Paul's near unplayable intro to 'How High The Moon', were pored over, assimilated and catalogued for possible future use. For the most part, however, the duo fixated on their shared love of rock'n'roll. "In our area, there weren't many guitarists... we were really the only two," Jimmy later confirmed. "I mean, we just used to go mad. We were over-keen on guitars and records and used to get little pictures of all the old rock'n'roll stars. You know, just being kids really."

By 1964, Beck and Page were still proverbial peas in a pod, but now inhabiting extremely different worlds. While Jeff was the undoubted attraction within The Tridents' ranks, his guitar prowess justly celebrated each week in venues across the South East, Page's career had taken a new and interesting turn, leading him into the heart of London's session scene. While still at art college, Jimmy had begun jamming with Cyril Davies and Alexis Korner, joining The All Stars and Blues Incorporated on stage at the Marquee whenever he could. Inevitably he was spotted, with John Gibb of Brian Howard & The Silhouettes asking him to play on several singles for Columbia Records. As was often the case with such things, Jimmy was offered further sessions, leading to regular work with Decca Records where he contributed guitar to (former) Shadows Jet Harris and Tony Meehan's No.1 single 'Diamonds'. As Page was still fragile from his brush with glandular fever, landing a role as a well-paid studio musician where he could continue to play – but in the luxury of a controlled environment – seemed to offer the best of both worlds. Crucially, it also gave Jeff Beck a potentially lucrative contact at the heart of the British record industry.

In his own generous way, Page had already tried to help jumpstart Beck's professional career as far back as the autumn of 1962, when he suggested Jeff replace him as lead guitarist in Neil Christian & The Crusaders. Unfortunately, Beck's audition did not go well, with Christian reportedly listening to the teenager for only a few moments before offering him the bus fare home. However, two years later and things were markedly different, with Page's championing of his friend's talents carrying more weight within the musical community. Hence, Jeff began to pick up the odd session here and there when Jimmy was unavailable for work. Though details and dates of these studio appointments remain sketchy, Jeff possibly contributed spirited guitar breaks to Mancunian harmony act Fitz & Startz's single 'I'm Not Running Away'/'So Sweet', Johnny Howard's irritating 'Rinky Dink'/'Java', the former of which became Radio Caroline's theme tune for a time, and Phil Ryan & The Crescents' 'Mary, Don't You Weep'/'Yes I Will'.

Jeff's most memorable session during 1964 was surely alongside Screaming Lord Sutch on the oddball but entertaining 'Dracula's Daughter'/'Come Back Baby'. A genuine English eccentric who later formed the Official Monster Raving Loony Party and stood for election as an MP on several occasions, David 'Lord' Sutch's horror-themed stage show and wild theatrics had certainly served him well enough as a concert attraction. Indeed, his ever-evolving backing band, The Savages, offered a veritable finishing school for several notable musicians, including Deep Purple's Ritchie Blackmore, and Jimmy Page appeared briefly alongside 'The Good Lord', helping out occasionally on guitar from January to May 1964. But thus far, Sutch had no luck in translating his live successes to the singles chart. Alas, Beck's presence on 'Dracula's Daughter' did not change that, though the mock screams and slides he provided on the guitar track were a genuine hoot, perfectly adding to the cod-humour of the overall song. "Lips are blue, eyes are red, a laugh like gurgling water," sang Sutch, "but I can't resist that passionate kiss, I'm in love with Dracula's daughter…"

A man who knew Beck and Page as they both began making their mark on the stage and in the studio was Roger Mayer. Then working as an acoustic engineer for the Admiralty department on various research projects, Mayer was also obsessed with the sound of rock'n'roll and spent much of his spare time trying to work out how those noises were made. "Well, The Ventures had just done a record called '2,000lb Bee' and it had this 'fuzz' sound," he says. "Soon, one or two of the music stores in London's Charing Cross Road had the new Maestro Fuzz Box, and that's when I first became aware of the possibilities of heavy, transistorised distortion. Obviously, there had been American records before that had [got that sound] by turning the amplifier up, but this was genuinely new."

By then of course, Mayer had made the acquaintance of two guitarists who were conducting their own rudimentary investigations into distortion. "I grew up near Epsom and Jimmy and Jeff were always playing in local bands at youth clubs and elsewhere. This was 1962, 1963. Back then, Jeff was really good, very rock'n'roll in his playing. In fact, he was the most American sounding rock'n'roll guitar player around at that point. Pagey had a slightly more blues-influenced thing going on. He had that technique down already. Anyway, we'd all be around at Jimmy's house listening to various records by Freddie King and other blues guys, and there'd always be a focus on these guitar players from the American scene. For Pagey, he'd be listening to James Burton from Ricky Nelson's band while Jeff was more into rockabilly. He was always a little more rockabilly sounding."

According to Mayer, another later Beck trademark was also fully in evidence. "Jeff would show up at gigs or around my house with his hands covered in paint and grease because he'd been working on cars. I used to say he was the best guitar-playing car mechanic I'd ever heard. It was always difficult to know with Beck which he loved better: cars or guitars. At that time I also knew a lot of people from the Cooper car company, who produced Formula One racers, so there was always a lot to talk about."

As discussions deepened, Page approached Mayer about the possibility of turning his knowledge of acoustics to the business of guitar effects. "Jimmy came to me when he got hold of the Maestro fuzz and said, 'It's good, but it doesn't have enough sustain... it's a bit staccato.' I said, 'Well, I'm sure we can improve on that...' That conversation spurred me on to design my first fuzz box." Borrowing some of his configurations from the Maestro unit, Mayer concocted one of his very own for Page. "There had to be similarities, of course, because there were only three terminals to work from, but I managed to build one that had much more sustain." The 'Mayer Mk1' was probably first used on PJ Proby's 1964 singles, 'Hold Me' and 'Together'. "Well, there's some dispute about whether it's on 'Hold Me'," said Roger, "but Pagey told me it was my device. Anyway it was definitely there when PJ recorded 'Together'. *"

After Mayer's initial success with building a fuzz box, both Beck and Page were near-constant visitors to his house: "Jeff and Jimmy were always after new sounds. I'd have a go at making some treble boosters, and they were after those. They'd come by the house on Sunday morning just to try them out." For Mayer, the guitarists' devotion to their cause was total. "Absolutely. If I remember right, Jeff even played at his own wedding! But he was one of the very finest out there. No question. Jeff was innovative as a teenager and that was just going to grow. We were young, we were all having fun and pursuing something that had its roots in the blues and rockabilly. But I think we also knew even then that we were creating something very British and something very new. Everyone had a slightly different agenda, but yes, I think we all knew we were on to something. And we were right." As time came to show, Roger Mayer's contribution to "something very new" was in its own way as important as any solo Jeff or Jimmy ever cut to disc.

Given such circumstances, it seems unusual that Beck and Page did not work together more frequently during 1963/4. Yet, as history shows, despite a number of home recordings made in the Page family's front room – which are unlikely ever to see the light of day – the pair were captured only once on tape at the time, albeit with pleasing results. The jam in question took place soon after Christmas 1964 with Jimmy in the producer's chair and two former members of the Cyril Davies All Stars, Cliff Barton and Carlo Little, providing support on bass and drums respectively (Cyril Davies had sadly died in January 1964). Augmenting the line-up was a fine pianist named Nicky Hopkins, then recovering from a lengthy spell in hospital, but already making his own way towards becoming a brief, though important player in Jeff's overall story.

---

* Page subsequently used the Mayer fuzz on several other singles, including releases by Carter-Lewis And The Southerners and the Who B-side 'Bald Headed Woman', while Beck's earliest, frankly astounding experiments with such a device can be heard propping up Screaming Lord Sutch's 'Come Back Baby'.

By all accounts, five tracks were recorded on the day, though only two strongly featured Jeff on lead guitar. In the case of 'Chuckles', it was all about "the boogie", as Beck shot straight out of the traps with a fierce, blues-inflected solo over a shuffling backbeat. 'Steelin'', on the other hand, was a much more sedate affair, again allowing Jeff to show off his increasing mastery of slide, the trebly tone employed deeply redolent of Earl Hooker and Fred Roulette's work on 'Anna Lee' and 'New Sweet Black Angel'. Even allowing for the fact that Beck and Page were keen to carve out their own separate identities, this tantalising glimpse of what might be achieved by pooling their resources surely planted the seed for future, if sometimes stormy, collaborations.

It was an impromptu affair and the tracks were never meant to be released. But when Page signed an in-house production deal with Immediate Records in 1965 the company claimed the tapes as its own, eventually putting them out as part of an 'All-Stars' compilation LP, *Blues Anytime*, in 1968. (The songs continue to find their way onto various collections even now, though all parties have repeatedly disowned them.)

For Jeff, this slow but sure move into a brave new world of talented friends, sporadic session work and guest appearances must have given him some confidence. Still only 20 years old, he had already disengaged himself from family expectations, the confines of art school and a potential career "designing cornflakes packets" in exchange for a life of spitting guitars, fledgling distortion boxes and the occasional standing ovation. Yet, there were also problems that refused to go away. While The Tridents could sometimes command a salary of £8 each per night – very good money for 1964 – their gigging schedule remained sporadic and such sums proved the exception rather than the rule: "More like up and down the motorway for three quid," Beck later recalled. And unlike Page, whose growing appointment book would soon generate enough money for him to buy a plush boathouse, the lack of steady concert engagements meant Beck was still reliant on spray-painting cars for a regular income. This often meant a full day's work at the garage before embarking on a mad sprint across London to make it on time for 'curtain up'. A thrilling enough ride, perhaps, but surely less than ideal for either Beck's health or marriage.

Away from continuing money problems and potential exhaustion, there were other concerns. The Tridents were a good, sometimes great band, a fact evidenced by the sheer numbers that turned out to see them. There was also no doubting that Jeff had become something of a local hero, his ability to torment a musical scale or twist it into bold, new shapes marking him as one of the most innovative and gifted guitarists on the circuit. But unlike The Rolling Stones, who had left the clubs for a far broader stage, The Tridents were still trapped on the South East circuit, their ambition stymied by the lack of a record deal or strongly connected management. In short, getting the boat out of the Thames Delta and into international waters just wasn't happening quickly enough for Beck's liking. "They were lightning times," he said, "everything was changing hour by hour, minute by minute and if you didn't watch out, you'd get stuck." Having watched the Stones go through their paces regularly in Twickenham, jamming with their bassist Bill Wyman in May 1964 and even persuading Ian Stewart to sit in with The Tridents onstage, Jeff must have felt as if he was waving goodbye from the dock as the proverbial ship set sail.

And then there were The Beatles. From the moment they had arrived on the music scene in October 1962 with their first single, 'Love Me Do', The Beatles had simply changed everything. Mop-topped, loveable and utter rascals to a man, the Liverpool quartet not only boasted quirky charm and winning smiles, but also killer melodies in abundance – their songs and image heralding a new golden age of pop. More, they seemed to have timed their entrance into popular culture with almost preternatural clarity, the group's natural optimism and boundless energy reflecting Great Britain's rise from post-war indolence to reinvigorated world power. If America had exported rock'n'roll and 'The Teenager' to UK shores at a time when they were desperately needed, then The Beatles, their deliciously evil alter egos The Rolling Stones and a dozen other home-grown bands were now ready to return the favour. The 'Swinging Sixties' were just around the corner and it was going to be a global affair.

During his early adolescence, Beck's aspirations had been simple enough: "I just wanted to be at the front of the stage, watching Jerry

Lee Lewis, or seeing my reflection in Little Richard's boot." But things had grown more complex by the end of 1964. Now that he was a gigging musician and occasional sessioneer, there was little doubting either the depth of his talent or sweep of his ambition. In fact, though he didn't know it – or more probably, wouldn't even entertain the idea – Beck was possibly the most gifted guitarist on British soil, "a six-string freak of nature" whose technique and passion for the instrument made him potentially extraordinary. Yet, the world was getting bigger and the opportunities endless as a result. If he didn't act quickly, he might find himself left behind.

The next 20 months would be an extraordinarily creative spell for Beck, his sneakered feet dragging themselves across a battlefield of shattered instruments, smashed amplifiers and crumpled bed sheets, with each step taken bringing him ever closer to his final destination as a legitimate 'guitar god'. For precisely these reasons, it's worth investigating The Yardbirds' story in some detail.

Chapter 3

Escape Velocity

When The Rolling Stones climbed to the top of the British singles chart with a surprisingly faithful cover of Willie Dixon's 'Little Red Rooster' on November 21, 1964, it was a clear signal to all concerned that the Thames Delta blues scene had hit ramming speed. Just the week before, a South-West London based R&B band called The Yardbirds also scored moderate chart success with their sprightly rendition of Sonny Boy Williamson I's 'Good Morning Little Schoolgirl', the song peaking at number 44. Though this version bore little resemblance to the wheezy, harmonica-driven country blues of Williamson's original, being more Tin Pan Alley than Tennessee, it did feature a stinging electric guitar solo that both emptied the lungs and pricked the ears. Eric Clapton – or 'God' as he would come to be known – had announced his arrival.

The Yardbirds officially formed in May 1963, when singer Keith Relf and bassist Paul Samwell-Smith broke up their previous band, The Metropolis Blues Quartet, to join forces with lead guitarist Anthony 'Top' Topham, rhythm guitarist Chris Dreja and drummer Jim McCarty. Taking their name from a passage written by the American Beat author Jack Kerouac in which 'Yardbirds' were described as railroad drifters moving from station to station in search of work, the group were an eclectic bunch from the very start. In 21-year-old Relf they had a genuine beatnik, who divided his time reading cult US literature, drinking copious amounts of beer and, despite a severe case of asthma, blowing a very fine harmonica.

Samwell-Smith also leaned towards the rebellious, his keen intellect and City gent demeanour undermined by a complete inability to conform either at school or work. McCarty, on the other hand, was down to earth and downright funny, qualities mirrored by his good friend Dreja – a witty, urbane type who shared Samwell-Smith's gift for the seditious. The baby of the band was 15-year-old Topham, a gifted guitarist who often butted heads with his parents in order to attend late-night rehearsals.

Driven by a "mutual and psychotic" love of blues and inspired by The Rolling Stones' growing dominance of the Thames Valley scene, The Yardbirds quickly picked up gigs at Eel Pie Island and Studio 51 on central London's Great Newport Street. "At that point, our set was wholly covers, mainly drawn from the Chicago scene," said Dreja. "I suppose we were blues 'impostors' really, but we genuinely worshipped the music. Blind Lemon Jefferson, Muddy Waters, Bo Diddley, Jimmy Reed, Jelly Roll Morton, Lightnin' Slim. To us, it all seemed so otherworldly. And these guys had such extraordinary names. Take Howlin' Wolf. I mean, what's a 'Howlin' Wolf' when you've been brought up in Surbiton?" As their reputation grew on the South London live circuit, the band secured a residency at Richmond's Crawdaddy, ably replacing the Stones, who had by then grown too popular for such an intimate venue.

At the Crawdaddy, The Yardbirds also gained a manager named Giorgio Gomelsky. Exotic, "pan-European" and distinctly forward thinking, the Georgia-born Gomelsky had crammed much into his early years, including a spell in the Swiss Air Force and time spent documenting the UK's nascent traditional jazz scene on film. As much a blues fanatic as The Yardbirds themselves, Giorgio had set up the Crawdaddy as a "Mecca for English R&B acts", hoping to relocate the Marquee's sweaty central London atmosphere to suburban Surrey. It had worked too, with the Stones proving such a successful draw that the club had to move from its original venue opposite Richmond Station to the larger athletic ground clubhouse. Yet, while Giorgio had acted as 'unofficial manager' and close confidant to the fledgling group, his financial rewards proved minimal. When Gomelsky flew to Switzerland to attend his father's funeral, Mick Jagger and co. chose to mark his absence by taking on ex-Beatles publicist Andrew Loog Oldham as their manager. Burned by such ingratitude, Giorgio was not about to make the same mistake again when The Yardbirds came his way, grabbing their signatures without delay before another manager swooped in for the kill.

"Giorgio wasn't that much older than us and soon became like our sixth member," said McCarty. "But he spoke several languages, drove a sports car... just a real character from the off. And he had so many ideas, mad ones, bad ones and brilliant ones." One idea that Gomelsky was committed to shone above all others. "I didn't want a copycat Stones," he said. "The element that was missing from them was instrumental improvisation. I needed a band and guitarist that could play solos, brilliant solos."

Sadly, 'Top' Topham wasn't to be that guitarist. Struggling to find his identity on the instrument at the time and increasingly pressured by his parents to drop out of music in favour of a university education, Topham left The Yardbirds in September 1963. His replacement was an old school acquaintance of Dreja's whom Relf had also come across while attending Kingston Art College. Something of a clothes horse, who spent his weekends scouring tailors' shops on Shaftesbury Avenue looking for 'Ivy League'-style threads, Ripley-born Eric Clapton was a hideously devoted blues player who worshipped at the twin altars of Freddie King and Big Bill Broonzy. "When I heard Freddie King's 'Love That Woman' as a teenager it sent me into a complete ecstasy," Clapton said. "It also scared the shit out of me. I'd never heard anything like it and I'd never thought I'd get anywhere near it on guitar."

Clapton had already made a reasonable name for himself with local part-time R&B covers outfits The Roosters and Casey Jones & The Engineers, but was still working on a building site alongside his grandfather when he joined The Yardbirds. Quiet and reserved on first meeting, Eric's initial awkwardness was mistaken for arrogance by some of his new bandmates. "He seemed very cocksure of himself, very confident," said McCarty. "Eric was very... strong when he first played with us. To be honest, I took an immediate dislike to him."

Dreja, who shared a room with Clapton for six months on his arrival in the group, was somewhat more forgiving of the guitarist's eccentricities: "A very shy guy, especially at the start, was Eric. But he was incredibly devoted to his instrument. He would spend a weekend rehearsing a phrase or even just holding the guitar. In fact, Eric borrowed my guitar once just to work out his stance."

For Clapton, such personality traits were inextricably linked to his own self-image. The illegitimate child of a Canadian soldier posted to England during World War II, Eric had been raised by his grandparents as their own, only learning during his teenage years that his older sister was actually his real birth mother. "Throughout my youth, my back was against the wall," he later said. "The only way to survive that was with dignity, pride and courage, and I heard that in the blues. It seemed to me it was always one man with a guitar, with no options but to sing, play and ease his pain. That echoed what I felt."

Again following the Stones' example, The Yardbirds were soon venturing to central London clubs such as the Marquee to expand their fanbase. In addition to a growing command of blues and R&B covers, they had also evolved the "rave up", a formidable technique where the group would double the pace of a song during its mid-section, creating a sheet of sound over which Clapton's guitar and Relf's harmonica would solo furiously. When the mood took them, rave ups could last for a good 10 minutes or so before returning to a more traditional structure. "The audience would go mental," said McCarty, "and frankly, so would we..."

By March 1964, Giorgio Gomelsky had secured The Yardbirds a deal with EMI Records and the band began the process of transferring their wares to a national level, touring the regions, Scotland and Wales. At this point, the endless hours Clapton spent poring over the neck of his guitar had borne rich fruit, transforming him from a musician happy enough to play tentative lead lines behind an amp to a formidable onstage presence. He had even gained a nickname, 'Slowhand', in honour of the lingering handclaps of his devotees while he changed broken strings. "In the beginning," said Jim McCarty, "we were a typical band in that all the attention went to our singer, Keith. Then, after a while, we noticed a crowd building on Eric's side of the stage. Girls and boys. So, he must have been doing something right, though I'm really not quite sure exactly what." Such devotion to their lead guitarists was something The Yardbirds would have to get used to in coming years.

Having backed one of their idols, Sonny Boy Williamson II, for a series of gigs at the Marquee (a recording of which would finally see light of day as the Fontana album *Sonny Boy Williamson & The Yardbirds* in 1966), the band released their first single, 'I Wish You Would/A Certain Girl' in May 1964. Soaked in reverb, throaty harp fills and galloping bass courtesy of Samwell-Smith, 'I Wish...' might have been bereft of any crisp lead lines from Clapton, but it still acted as an able calling card, securing them their first TV spots in the UK. Following an enforced lay-off to allow Keith Relf to recover from a collapsed lung, the group returned with 'Good Morning Schoolgirl' and their debut LP, the Marquee set *Five Live Yardbirds* in December. Though both releases placed Clapton squarely at the forefront of The Yardbirds' assault, with his Freddie King-inspired solo bursts now marking him as one of the UK's pre-eminent blues guitarists, he appeared increasingly dissatisfied with his lot in the band.

As The Yardbirds moved ever further from their hardcore, blues-loving audience, joining pop package tours headlined by the likes of Billy J Kramer and providing support to The Beatles for their Christmas shows at Hammersmith Odeon, Clapton's overall mood seemed to blacken. He started to turn up late for gigs and even missed one Odeon performance altogether, leaving Dreja to fill in on lead guitar. Worse still, while Eric's face beamed from the pages of the music press alongside new madcap friends such as The Who's Keith Moon and The Pretty Things' Viv Prince, he had become a virtual stranger to his own group. "We were pretty fed up with Eric, really... he always seemed unhappy," said McCarty. "We'd be travelling from show to show in a cramped van, and he'd just sit there looking glum. Don't get me wrong, it wasn't always like that. Clapton did have a good sense of humour, often pulling 'gurns' and funny faces to break us all up. But we knew something was amiss."

Matters came to a proverbial head with the recording of the group's next single, 'For Your Love', in January 1965. A melancholy, yet strangely memorable tune that flicked between major and minor chords to make its emotional point, 'For Your Love' was the hit The Yardbirds had been seeking. "Ronnie Beck, the music publisher, brought us the song," remembered Dreja. "It had been written by Graham Gouldman – then of The Mockingbirds, later of 10cc – and there was just something about it. I think we all knew 'For Your Love' was special."

The demo version that Gomelsky played the group was by all accounts minimal, featuring just vocals, guitar and bongos. But Samwell-Smith, who with his manager's blessing had now assumed a semi-official role as 'musical director' within the ranks, loved the sparseness of the sound, cannily suggesting the bongos be augmented with only a harpsichord and bowed upright bass. Any guitars were to be limited to a brief rave-up section during the middle eight. Evidently, this was not the sound of Chicago and Clapton was feeling distinctly mutinous. "I saw there was a way forward for us without it becoming totally commercial," he later confirmed. "Giorgio almost gave us an exam... he told us we were [going to do a single], and we each had to come up with an idea. The closest I could come without compromising our ideals was an Otis Redding song. But what we ended up doing was 'For Your Love', which was a great song for any band. But I really didn't want our first record of any stature to harness that kind of image that quickly."

Clapton's protestations fell on deaf ears and the recording session went ahead. With harpsichord provided by Brian Auger (soon to form Steam Packet alongside Long John Baldry) and bongo beats courtesy of DJ Denny Piercey, Relf was left to add an uncharacteristically keening vocal while McCarty tapped rather than thumped his drums in the background. Clapton and Dreja's contributions arrived a minute into the song – a pair of angry, prodding guitars that disappeared some 18 seconds later – submerged by the trills of Auger's neo-classical keyboard. Samwell-Smith did not even play on the track, a session bassist whose name now escapes all providing the bottom end. "My God, there was real static in the studio when we recorded it," recalled Dreja. "It just felt absolutely right. Ah, but Eric..."

Ah, but Eric indeed. For a devout blues purist such as Clapton, 'For Your Love''s gothic pop qualities were all too much. "We'd had two singles which were covers of blues and R&B songs by then, and they just didn't happen," he later remembered. "Then, this joint decision to use someone else's song written for the charts... written specifically to be a hit. I started to feel uneasy, because I could see a motivation going on that I didn't have any sympathy with whatsoever. That's really what 'For Your Love' was all about. I didn't actually walk out on the session, though they could see I was on the verge of walking out. [And] they gave me the middle eight to play a riff on, to keep me placated for a time, because there was a great deal of real friendship in the band. But for me, it was the end."

After handing in his cards, Clapton took to the hills, literally. Escaping London in favour of the Oxford countryside, Eric joined his former Roosters bandmate Ben Palmer who, disenchanted with the music scene, had abandoned piano playing in favour of a wood carving/antique restoration business. "We sat up every night talking about the way things should be," Clapton later told *Guitar Classics*, "and how pointless it was [in aiming] to be a serious, struggling musician when in England, all you really had to be was a pretty face. For two, three weeks, I actually thought I was going to do something else."

The errant guitarist also had time to reflect on the possibility of darker hues influencing his decision to 'leave' The Yardbirds: "You know, I think there might have been another agenda going on. I wasn't a very likeable guy... and I really wasn't. I was a very nasty piece of work: unreliable, dogmatic, antisocial. And I think the guys saw me as the fly in the ointment. Perhaps they thought 'Once we've got rid of Eric, we can get on with this...'"

Even now, such notions are rejected by the group, though no-one is disputing Clapton's departure ever hurt them commercially. "It was more a case of right time, right moment," said Dreja. "At that point, we were a blues band, but *Thames* Delta rather than Mississippi Delta. We weren't the real thing, and we really needed to start making our own music, creating our own identity. Well, Eric was steeped in the blues, no bad thing, but when he left, he actually did us a favour because it enabled us to follow our own instincts. It freed us up to do all the things we wanted."

For Relf, who later conceded that some of The Yardbirds' essential charm was forever lost with Clapton's exit, it was more a case of the guitarist finally surrendering to the inevitable. "Eric just loved the blues so much," he said, "and I suppose he didn't like it being played badly by a white shower like us."

Within weeks of leaving The Yardbirds, Clapton had abandoned any notions of wood whittling in favour of a new home with John Mayall's Bluesbreakers, where he would soon play 'Guitar Jesus' to Mayall's 'John The Baptist'. "Like me," Eric said, "John was happy to make money... and be successful making records just as long as he didn't have to bend too much [from the blues]. That was integral to me."

Of course, Clapton's gradual ascent to the status of deity was of little consequence to The Yardbirds in February 1965. In 'For Your Love', they had a tasty new single – one that might give them real chart success – but no lead guitarist with which to promote it: "Yes, I knew Eric before he officially became 'God'," laughs Dreja, "but it didn't really matter then. We just needed another bloody guitarist..."

For both band and manager, there was one candidate that rose above all others: a model professional regarded as London's pre-eminent session dandy. Jimmy Page might have been but 21 years old but he was also a veritable "king of the strings" and The Yardbirds wanted him. "Well, Jimmy seemed ideal," said McCarty. "He was an established session guitarist, Giorgio knew him well and he seemed the obvious choice."

By January 1965, Page had long secured his place as *the* 'go to' guitar player with a list of session credits as long as his very long arms. Since committing to full-time studio work only a year before, he had provided support for the likes of Marianne Faithfull, The Nashville Teens and Them's cover of 'Baby, Please Don't Go'. Through his association with producer Shel Talmy, Jimmy had also bolstered recordings by harder-edged acts such as The Kinks' debut album and The Who's first single, 'I Can't Explain', though he only played on the B-side, 'Bald Headed Woman'. From Petula Clark's life-affirming 'Downtown' to Dave Berry's sad-eyed 'The Crying Game', Page had played on a lot. He was also friends with Eric Clapton. "Well yes," Page confirmed, "I knew Eric. I mean, we all did, really."

Exact details of Page and Clapton's first meeting have sadly been lost in time. But their paths had certainly crossed at the Marquee by mid-1964, where Jimmy was playing alongside pianist Andy Wren in a casual pick-up band, stealing interval spots at Alexis Korner's regular

'Thursday Blues' jam. According to Page, Clapton approached him after the set, genuinely complimenting his "Matt Murphy-style" lead lines on the standards 'I Got My Mojo Working' and 'Sweet Home Chicago'. "As I'd been listening to Matt Murphy a lot at that point, I was impressed by Clapton spotting that." A respectful friendship ensued, not one that could be classified as enormously close, but close enough for the two to share the occasional dinner.

"We got on pretty well," Jimmy later remembered. "We'd go out, eat, and just talk about everything. Once, he took me around this guy's place who had tapes of obscure musicians like Poppa Hop. Eric was getting into that and was becoming really interested in getting something across on his guitar." Admiring Clapton's fervour, and finding him genuinely likeable to boot, when Giorgio Gomelsky approached Page about joining The Yardbirds, he was hesitant. "After my earlier experiences with Neil Christian, I was still nervous about getting ill. Also, I was doing quite well money wise with the sessions – three a day, five days a week – and honestly, I wasn't quite sure about the politics with Eric because we were friendly." Stuck in an unfortunate position, but still eager to help, Jimmy made a fateful suggestion: "I recommended the guy I'd been friends with for years. I told them about Jeff."

In a perfect world, the very mention of Jeff Beck's name should have brought sighs of recognition from Giorgio and the band. After all, Beck had steadily built a small but select list of session credits for himself, a tasteful contrast to the sheer bloody pandemonium he was creating weekly at Eel Pie Island with The Tridents. Yet, both The Yardbirds and their manager drew a unanimous blank. "Being 100% honest," said Dreja, "we'd never heard of Jeff or The Tridents." McCarty was equally mystified. "It really was a case of 'Jeff who'?"

Still, Page persisted that Beck was the man for the job. "Well, it took about two months to get it going, though finally, they agreed to go and see him." But not before the former incumbent of The Yardbirds' guitar chair had snuck a look. "I'd heard that the band were considering Jeff, so I popped along to see him with The Tridents," Eric Clapton later revealed. "There was this guy with long hair, tearing into the guitar, echo bouncing off the walls. I thought, 'I wonder if they know what they're letting themselves in for'. To be honest, my mind-set was, 'I'll leave and the whole thing will collapse without me'. In fact, they were just about to get better."

If The Yardbirds were completely uninformed regarding Beck's talents, he at least was broadly familiar with their work. When 'Good Morning Little Schoolgirl' tickled the UK charts in November 1964, Beck had picked along to the song on the radio. "It wasn't bad," he later said, "but I wasn't overly impressed either." He was also well informed as to Clapton's particular gifts. "Oh yeah," said Mike Jopp. "Back then, all the guitar players were like gunslingers, each aware of the other guys in town. I remember having a meal with Jeff when he was in The Tridents and asking him, 'What do you think of Eric?' He replied 'Well, Eric's great, but he can't play slide and I can.' Of course, Eric rectified that later."

Beck's opinion of Clapton's overall talents changed when Page played him a copy of *Five Live Yardbirds*, which included a slow-burning treatment of Eddie Boyd's 'Five Long Years'. All snarling harmonica and gritty outbursts from Clapton, the version allowed Beck to view the band and their now former guitarist in a more favourable light. When Page asked the question, "Would you be interested in joining them?" Jeff nodded slowly in the affirmative. But it was to be another month before Gomelsky and his right-hand man, Hamish Grimes, finally joined the audience at Oxford Street's 100 Club for a sweaty night with The Tridents. "By then, the clock was ticking," confirmed Dreja. "'For Your Love' was about to start its climb up the charts."

According to Beck, The Tridents' 100 Club date had been "an absolute stormer, we'd taken the doors off the place". So he was caught by surprise when the hefty forearm of Grimes wrapped itself around him after the gig. "Hamish said, 'You're going to be in a great fucking band this week.' To be honest, I was a bit pissed off because I already thought I was in a great band." Resisting the urge to shout, "Go away, you nasty little man," Beck just smiled when Grimes said, "Be at the Marquee on Tuesday at four." No mention of The Yardbirds was made, nor indeed anything else, leaving the guitarist a tad confused. "I didn't link it [to them]," Jeff remembered. "I actually thought I might have been auditioning for The Beatles."

Though never fully confirmed (because no one can actually

remember), Beck's first and only audition with The Yardbirds probably took place at the Marquee on Tuesday, February 23, 1965. Beck himself has said there were several other guitar players in attendance but Jim McCarty will have none of it. "There have been stories that we were auditioning loads of people that day. Completely untrue. There was just the band and Jeff." Whatever the case, Beck's appearance initially caused a sharp intake of breath from all concerned: "It was a bit of a shock," McCarty continues. "This guy with really long hair and greasy hands walks in. He looked like he'd come straight from working on a car." By Jeff's own admission, he probably had. "God, hair down to my shoulders, terrible spots. God." After the shock had struck, it was Keith Relf who recovered first, bounding off the Marquee stage to greet Beck with a firm handshake "and an inhaler. He said 'What sort of music do you like to play?' I said 'The blues'. That was the right answer."

Within minutes, Jeff was sparring some choice Buddy Guy licks with the band. "Not only could he play all the Eric stuff, but also a lot more," said McCarty. "There was the Les Paul thing, the rockabilly thing, the whole bloody lot. His style was also kind of futuristic. We were impressed." Dreja echoed these sentiments, seeing Beck's love of experimentation as a welcome antidote to Clapton's strict adherence to the blues: "When Jeff came into The Yardbirds, we recognised a talent, a man who could work with new ideas without getting all uptight about it." According to Beck, one minor irritation came when he was told to disconnect his beloved echoplex. "They said 'Get rid of the echo... no one uses echo in Chicago blues'. They actually said that." Despite this gaping hole in the band's understanding of Buddy Guy's recording techniques, Beck took the job.

By March 2, Beck had formally handed his notice in to The Tridents' John Lucas, confirming his position as a full-time Yardbird. "In a way, it was a tragedy because The Tridents had built up a great following," he later said. "They were a real band, but there was no way I could exist, because they just weren't paying me anything. I didn't even have the price of guitar strings." With a vacancy in their ranks, The Tridents again turned to lead guitarist Mike Jopp, who helped the band soldier on following Beck's departure. "Well, The

Yardbirds gig was paying much better money so it was obvious Jeff should take it," said Jopp. "Anyway, John and Paul Lucas got straight on the phone to me and said, 'Help, we need you back'. By that time, they'd recorded a single called 'That Sound' or 'That Noise' I think, which had this Bo Diddley-type riff. Jeff certainly did a demo version of it. Of course, when I rejoined the band, they wanted me to play all this crazy stuff like Beck. And really, I shouldn't have tried to do what he did, mainly because I didn't have his technique and also because it just wasn't me. I should have stuck to what I'd done before which was more blues guitar."

Like so many potentially promising bands, the lure of regularly paid employment became too difficult to ignore and The Tridents called it a day in the summer of 1966. "We probably lasted for about another year," Mike recalled. "The trouble was that both John and Paul had day jobs and didn't want to give them up. They were very traditional guys that came from a family with a good, strong work ethic. I guess they didn't feel strongly or confident enough that they could make a go of it. So they decided they'd be better off getting on with their lives in other ways. Big mistake really, because it was a bloody good band." Jopp, on the other hand, persisted on the music scene, first securing a sales job at Ivor Mairants' esteemed guitar shop in central London before joining a promising progressive jazz outfit named Affinity. Signed to Vertigo in 1970, the band's self-titled debut album has since attained something approaching cult status, its clever mix of jazz, rock and Latin themes a step ahead of other acts of the time. "Yes, I suppose Affinity has become something of a cult group. Weird, that," laughs Jopp.

For Gomelsky, acquiring the services of Jeff Beck was a huge step forward for The Yardbirds. "I was very happy with Jeff because he had this emotional thing that Eric just didn't. Of course, the emotion was there in Eric, but with Jeff it wasn't bubbling under the surface. It was there in your face." That said, if Clapton's steely British reserve had held him back in overt displays of onstage emotion, he more than made up for it in terms of sartorial elegance – a quality wholly missing in Beck: "I was bad. I mean, bad. A mess." Fellow guitarist Chris Dreja was given the job of easing Jeff into the band, which began with an emergency trip to one of central London's swankier boutiques. "I brought him down to Carnaby Street and got some clothes for him, got him a haircut, which kind of brought him in line with our image at the time." McCarty agrees: "Well, he just didn't look like one of us. So Chris took him into London and got him cleaned up, which Jeff quite liked. He came back looking a bit more like a pop star."

Chris Dreja: "Not long before, we'd done The Beatles' Christmas show in Hammersmith, and for some reason – probably Giorgio's idea – we thought we'd wear suits. In fact, Eric designed them. They had two collars, and one suit was in black, the other in white. Anyway, I suspect Jeff might have ended up wearing one, paired with sneakers, of course."

As the new boy, Beck may have found wearing his predecessor's clothing an onerous task, but he was reticent to sound any protests as yet: "Yep, I got a free suit when I joined The Yardbirds. Luckily, it fitted." Reportedly, Eric's red Fender Telecaster and Vox AC30 amp were also passed to Jeff as part of the new deal, though McCarty remains sure that while Beck might have suffered the suit and speaker, forcing Clapton's old guitar on him was a step too far: "Nice story, sounds good. But no, I doubt it. I sincerely doubt Jeff would have played Eric's guitar." Beck, however, was not about to turn down the money that came with the gig. "They wanted a guitar player," he later told *Q*, "and I fitted the bill for £20 a week. It stayed that way for all the time I was with them. Bastards."

Within a week, Jeff Beck had left his former band behind, joined a group with a potential hit single, had his hair shorn while simultaneously gaining a second-hand suit. One would surely forgive him if he had been caught a little off balance. Yet, there was an even more difficult task ahead: negotiating the subtle politics of a band who had known each other for years – one fully aware of their various strengths and weaknesses and whose drive to succeed remained overwhelming. "We were all very close, really," said Dreja. "Various reasons. We went to the same schools, had history together and I guess it was quite difficult for Jeff at first. He was very shy, and a bit of a rough diamond...pretty scruffy, working with cars at the time – some things never change – and he really just communicated through his guitar to begin with. He always had a guitar with him, and used to play these wonderful passages that were like speech. That's how Jeff talked to us at the start."

If Beck was quiet at the beginning of his tenure with The Yardbirds, he nevertheless understood what the band offered. Despite their original blues leanings, and Clapton's sincere wish to bring Freddie King to the masses, 'For Your Love' represented something genuinely new, genuinely modern, in fact. Simultaneously sad and uplifting with a spirited mid section that Beck could let fly on during live performances, the song marked a major turning point for the group of which he was now a part. The possibilities – both musical and financial – were endless. "Giorgio and the guys wanted to see something new come out of the blues," Beck remembered, "a different take on things. And you know, that's what people really wanted. They didn't want to hear me play definitive blues, they wanted this nutter with this guitar doing these weird noises. And that was all right with me."

Chapter 4

Fuzzbox Voodoo

Jeff Beck's honeymoon period with The Yardbirds lasted a matter of hours – sleep, at least for the time being, becoming a fond childhood memory. "From the minute I got the gig, we were off and running." Of vital importance was the quick absorption of the band's live set. For training purposes, Beck was handed a copy of their first LP. "I was given four days to learn the songs, including the odd rehearsal." And so it was on March 5, 1965, that The Yardbirds took to the stage of Croydon's Fairfield Hall to introduce their new guitarist to the demands of the rave up. Though the quintet were only second on the bill to The Moody Blues, with BBC disc jockey Simon Dee on compere duties, Beck's nerves were probably jangling on the night. After all, he was replacing the mighty Eric Clapton, a crowd favourite then as now, whose departure was still being mourned by those assembled. In his favour, Fairfield Hall was the closest thing Beck might get to a home audience, with Wallington but a short bus ride away. Perhaps it was a soothing thought to hold onto when the curtains unfolded.

Reportedly, Beck was quiet but calm backstage, puzzling his new bandmates with one of his more eccentric practices: the fine art of not tuning up. "In all my time with the band," Relf remembered, "Jeff just didn't tune his guitar. He'd get it about halfway there, then leave it. If you asked, 'What's going on?' he just say, 'Don't worry, I'll sort it out'. Then, we were on, and was he bending the strings to pitch – bending the strings into tune. It was bloody amazing." When Beck was later asked about stepping onstage with The Yardbirds by the BBC, the answer was brisk but telling: "One person shouted out 'Where's Eric?' I said, 'Haven't you heard? Read the papers. He's gone'."

What Beck undoubtedly meant was that Clapton had been exorcised in a blast of feedback, wild string bending, unbridled distortion and mad stunt guitar. "It was," Chris Dreja asserted, "quite the debut." Jeff filled in the gaps in a 1997 interview with *Guitar World*: "I did my first job with them and blew the place apart. I thought 'Well, this is interesting, I'll stick around'."

Things took a comedic turn at encore time when a pretty young woman began yelling her approval from the side of the stage, causing Beck his first real case of the jitters that night. "Normally," said Dreja, "there was a throng of girls screaming. Very nice too. But here, there was one girl in particular shouting 'Jeff! Jeff!', and I remember him saying 'C'mon, hurry up, that's my wife.' Wife? We didn't even know he was bloody married! I thought 'He's kept that one quiet...'" As part of his continued diplomatic mission of easing the guitarist into the band, Dreja invited the Becks to dinner with him and his then girlfriend Patricia at their small Wandsworth flat. "We had a place in Fernside Road. We had to use an outside phone box... it was the only reach to the world we had. Anyway, Jeff and his wife Pat came over. As ever, Beck was quiet. I mean, he didn't even tell anyone he'd been to art school. That would have been instant kinsmanship. We had a few drinks and it turned into quite a funny evening, but it was hardly a meeting of the Algonquin Round Table Club."

Behind the scenes, Jeff and Pat were already experiencing matrimonial difficulties, the two cooped up in a microscopic apartment in nearby Balham with living areas partitioned off by pieces of hardboard. Things were only made worse when the couple's impressively sized Afghan hound began wreaking havoc in their makeshift surroundings. As a result of such pressures and Jeff's new life on the road, their marriage began to falter over the coming months.

With momentum continuing to gather around The Yardbirds' new single, the group played a string of London dates at their old 'home from home', the Marquee. It was at this juncture that a young physics student and keen amateur guitarist called Brian May saw Beck for the first time. "Jeff became a huge influence on me," he remembers.

"[When] he succeeded Clapton in The Yardbirds, I couldn't believe what he could do. I remember seeing him put the guitar down, make it feed back, and play a whole tune without even touching the fingerboard. I was at the Marquee very soon after Beck joined... pretty amazing stuff, I'll never forget that."

Perhaps even more so than at Croydon's Fairfield Hall, Beck's explosive performance at the Soho club had proved there was a future beyond Clapton for both The Yardbirds and himself: "Of course, it was a tough act to follow, going on at the Marquee where they're all waiting for Eric. But I just went for it, pulled out every trick I had in my book, got lucky, and got a standing ovation."

Having acquitted himself admirably upon the concert stage, Beck now had to learn the fine art of the promotional appearance on programmes such as *Top Of The Pops* and *Ready Steady Go!*. Both shows – transmitted on Thursday and Friday nights respectively – announced the beginning of 48 or so hours of casual mayhem for teenagers across Britain. Transmitted from modest studios in Manchester and Kingsway, London, in pearly black and white, the likes of *TOTP* and *RSG!* were all cardboard sets, faux spiral staircases, nail-chewing girls and hosts who appeared to be learning their jobs live on set. But appearing on such rickety stages was also a sure-fire way of launching a single, giving new bands two or three minutes of quality time with a television audience of millions, a fact not lost on The Beatles, The Rolling Stones and countless others who benefited from such exposure.

Though The Yardbirds had done TV spots before to promote 'I Wish You Would' and 'Good Morning Little Schoolgirl', this was different. The band knew that with 'For Your Love', they had the goods to hand. It was just a matter of selling things correctly. Cool as a proverbial cucumber, Relf locked eyes with the camera, a gnarly Brian Jones look-alike offering the "moon, sun and the stars above for your love" while Messrs Dreja, McCarty and Samwell-Smith kept admirably straight faces behind him. Meanwhile, to the left of the stage, a sullen, heavy-fringed pipe cleaner of a guitarist stared moodily into the distance, occasionally summoning up enough courage to look directly into the lens. Whether Beck's apparent dissatisfaction with the rigours of promotion was the result of shyness, tiredness, boredom, or, more probably, having to play Clapton's lines instead of his own mattered not. The image of Jeff Beck as "moody guitar icon" had been cast and it would help, hinder, define and distract from his capabilities in equal measure over the next five decades: "We did [our first] TV show," Beck told journalist Gene Santoro, "and I raced home to tell my mum. The people next door cutting their hedges said, 'We saw you on TV, very good'. They were the same people who, up to that point, were yelling at me to turn it down all the time. All of a sudden, I was somebody..."

The Yardbirds' short but important spots on *TOTP* and *Ready Steady Go!* proved successful, adding enough extra heat around 'For Your Love' to propel the song to number three in the UK charts on March 20, 1965. "And so it was," laughed Dreja, "that we became pop stars." In fact, Samwell-Smith was so happy with this turn of events he immediately began dating one of the girls on *RSG!*'s production team, an act of apparent serendipity that nonetheless ensured the band became regulars on the show. As The Yardbirds embarked on a near month-long British tour supporting The Kinks on April 30, group nerves were beginning to finally settle. Yet, as was the case with such things in the mid-sixties, there was little time for celebration. To capitalise on the success of 'For Your Love' and maintain their momentum, another killer single was required in weeks rather than months. Again, The Yardbirds were on a timer.

The band's follow up was 'Heart Full Of Soul', another melancholy gem penned by Graham Gouldman – who as a member of *Top Of The Pops* warm-up act, The Mockingbirds had watched Beck perform 'For Your Love' on the TV show. "Everyone clamoured around," he later told the BBC, "and there I was just part of an anonymous group. I felt strange that night, hearing The Yardbirds play my song." Recorded at a block session at London's Advision Studios the group undertook with Beck soon after he joined in April 1965, 'Heart Full Of Soul' was to be potentially even more outlandish than its predecessor. Seizing on the fact that Brian Auger's novel use of harpsichord on 'For Your Love' had set the song apart from The Yardbirds' beat-orientated contemporaries, Gomelsky was determined 'Heart...' repeat the trick in even more impressive fashion. His solution was to bring in an Indian sitarist and tabla player to augment the song's undulating riff. However, while the tablas added a certain something to proceedings, the sitar sounded distinctly queasy in the mix. "Oh, it was another one of Giorgio's mad ideas," said Jim McCarty. "It was fine in principle, but while the tablas sounded OK, the sitar just wasn't up front enough. It just didn't cut through."

As the studio clock ticked on, it was also becoming obvious to all concerned that the sitar player was having real trouble with the song's distinctly Western time signature. "I remember the session well," Beck confirmed. "[He] couldn't play it in straight 4/4. Instead, [he was] playing it in some weird time signature, like 18/4." Jeff's solution was reductionist, but inspired. "Beck said, 'Well, hold on, I could do that sound on the guitar,'" McCarty confirmed, "and then he disappeared for a while." Knowing that Jimmy Page was working on a session in an adjacent studio, Jeff asked to borrow his friend's Roger Mayer-made fuzz box "for experimental purposes". Though Mayer's device was still being perfected by the designer at that time, its impressive ability to simultaneously distort and sustain notes allowed Beck to replicate the wide sweep of the sitar's 20-odd strings with just two of his own: "It sounded outrageous. I could [create] the D-drone and the octave above, so from my point of view, job done." Happy with his work, Jeff presented the results to the band. "This great-sounding riff emerged," said Dreja. "I mean Beck just nailed it." Jeff later returned to Advision with his own pedal, probably a Sola Sound Tone Bender MK1 – "It came free with a packet of cornflakes," he once joked – and cut the guitar track. When later asked where the idea to fuzz up 'Heart...'s signature riff came from, Beck pointed towards Southern Asia: "Well, the sitar player Ravi Shankar was certainly an influence. Jimmy and I would be listening to some records that he had, pondering away on how to get that sound."

Aligned to another moody vocal turn from Relf, whose rumbling tones suited Gouldman's compositions beautifully, 'Heart Full Of Soul' provided The Yardbirds with their biggest chart hit yet. Backed by 'Steeled Blues', a slow "Chicago style" number that marked Jeff's recording debut with the band and featured some impressive Hawaiian-sounding slide guitar, 'Heart...' bolted into the UK Top 10, peaking at number two on July 17. "We suddenly took a ninety degree detour from the blues with our A-sides," said McCarty.

"Really, we just couldn't get a hit doing straight blues, then 'Heart Full Of Soul' took off and so did we." With the benefit of hindsight, Beck's use of the Tone Bender on 'Heart Full Of Soul' and, indeed, the tune's distinctly subcontinental vibe were genuinely ground-breaking. While the manufactured fuzz box had already appeared on The Ventures' 1962 single '2000lb Bee' and PJ Proby's 1964 hit 'Together', and been used to rousing effect by Keith Richards on The Rolling Stones' seminal '(I Can't Get No) Satisfaction' only weeks before 'Heart...'s release, no one had approached the device with such exotic abandon.

Equally, through embracing the music of India, The Yardbirds were at least six months ahead of their competition, outrunning The Beatles' sitar-inflected 'Norwegian Wood', which appeared on their *Rubber Soul* album in December 1965. By comparison, the Stones' own attempt at Eastern whimsy, 'Paint It, Black', sounded positively old fashioned when it finally hit the charts in May 1966. Though he was often prone to rubbishing many of his subsequent efforts, groaning loudly when anyone complimented him on a solo, song or album, Beck has never actually derided his work on 'Heart Full Of Soul'. Perhaps even he has to admit there is a certain genius to it.[*]

With two genuine hit singles under their belts, The Yardbirds found themselves with an open invitation to the sights, sounds and sensations of Swinging London during the summer of 1965. "Well," Dreja quipped, "there was lots of talk about 'Swinging London', but it didn't start really swinging for us until 'Heart Full Of Soul'." Legitimate pop stars, the band had access to the finest boutiques on Carnaby Street, a free pass to the best clubs and an opportunity to test drive one of the new, Union Jack-festooned Mini Coopers then making their debut on the capital's streets. Sadly, the realities of pop-star life were somewhat different. Knowing their time had come,

---

[*] For those wishing to hear 'Heart...' with the original sitar part in place, it can be found on *Shape Of Things*, a retrospective seven-LP box set released in 1984. Three other tracks recorded at the first Advision sessions with Beck – 'I'm Not Talking', 'My Girl Sloopy' and Keith Relf's lively 'I Ain't Done Wrong'– charted as *Five Yardbirds*, an EP which reached number two in the UK 'specialist' chart in August, 1965.

Gomelsky was busy shuffling the group between press conferences, television studios, concert halls and other increasingly bizarre PR opportunities. One such moment had them dressing up in medieval armour while prancing around in a Windsor cow field for an early promotional film to accompany 'For Your Love'. With the pressure of success now snapping at their heels, each Yardbird reacted to the demands of fame in his own novel way. "Giorgio had us running around like mad men," confirmed McCarty. "He'd never turn down a request, no matter how bizarre. So, when we got a break, it was every man for himself."

For Relf, this translated to either falling dog-tired into the arms of his wife, April, or holing up in a hotel room with as much drink as possible. Samwell-Smith was also fond of the notion of retreat, though for him it was more often than not a trip to his girlfriend's Hampstead flat, where he largely replaced booze with a novel. The jokers in the pack, McCarty and Dreja were always in pursuit of their next escapade: checking out other groups, finding new bars, avoiding arrest, things of that nature. But when it came to Beck, tracking his movements was an altogether more subtle proposition. With his two-year marriage now in its death throes, Beck reportedly disappeared into the night in pursuit of more earthly pleasures. "Well, Jeff was always a bit of a magnet for women," confirmed Dreja. "It wasn't just the guitar playing that made him attractive. I think they liked his 'Neanderthal' thing. I mean, look at his bloody hands. This is a guy who can produce the most sublime sounds in the world. Then, you see his hands and you think 'Fuck. I thought you were meant to have long, elegant fingers.'"

Evidently, while Beck might have had engine grease under his nails, it certainly didn't detract from the attention he received from a growing female fanbase. "Look," Jeff later pointed out, "we'd come back to the tour van and it'd be covered in phone numbers written in lipstick..."

Despite his growing reputation within The Yardbirds as a ladies man, the guitarist was also giving thought to the band's advance into battle upon the bloody fields of the UK music scene. Obviously, there was no catching The Beatles who – like Elvis Presley in America – had escaped the traps first and were to a large extent making the rules up for everyone else as they went along. The Stones too were essentially immune to competition, their combustible mixture of blues, R&B and pop – coupled with an anti-authoritarian, bohemian image – allowing them the role of 'House Devils' to The Beatles' 'Street Angels'. Still, when pitted against the likes of The Animals, Them, The Kinks and The Who, there was all to play for. After all, The Yardbirds had an edge to them unlike all others, aligning a gift for the unconventional in the studio with an aggressive, unconstituted spirit on the stage. "I felt we started the punk movement in a lot of ways," Jeff later said. "It was just 'Go get 'em, kill 'em,' experimental soloing and banging it and crashing it and aggression." In Relf, the group also had the makings of a truly unique front man – part angel, part demon, all angles. "I didn't know what to make of him at first," Beck later confirmed. "Keith didn't have the greatest singing voice by any means, but he meant it. He made up for lacking that strutting, macho thing and some vocal shortcomings with sheer belief. Yeah, he had trouble with the pop stuff, but he could really do the wild blues thing."

Having staked his own claim in The Yardbirds with the fuzz-box voodoo of 'Heart Full Of Soul' and played a major part in a string of scorching summer performances – which included coming dangerously close to upstaging The Beatles at Paris' Olympia Theatre on June 20 and inciting a full-on stage invasion at Richmond's fifth annual Jazz & Blues Festival on August 6 – Beck was settling in quite nicely. "As a band, we were going up," said Dreja, "and Jeff was the perfect person to join a guitar band because of his wonderful creative streak. He was malleable, wanted to work with us and we were coming into our golden age. The timing, location and people just knitted together perfectly. Honestly, if Jimmy Page had come into the band at that point, I don't think it would have been the same." A fair point. But Jeff still felt a strong degree of gratitude towards his friend. "Jimmy set it all up," Beck later said. "He was always in London on sessions and I hated London. So, without him, it probably wouldn't have happened." How exactly Beck might repay Page for his favour would have to wait a while yet.

Enthralled by the sound of its roaring engines as a child, brought to puberty among the throaty screams and howling machinery of its native music, 21-year-old Jeff Beck was finally about to fall into the arms of America.

Chapter 5

Oh Say Can You See...

Since hooking up with Giorgio Gomelsky in the autumn of 1963, The Yardbirds had travelled far and wide, their manager booking the band into Swiss chalets, French hamlets and a bewildering array of UK venues from Southampton to Dumfries. And as their success increased, so did the number of gigs. "Anywhere there was a crowd, Giorgio got us there," recalled Chris Dreja. "It didn't matter how far." The upshot of Gomelsky's approach was that the group became a formidable concert attraction. Mutating their early blues mimicry through the passion of the rave up into even more peculiar climes, The Yardbirds' original gift for live performance had now reached a new level. By acquiring the services of Jeff Beck, they had also added goodly measures of volume, sex appeal, sweat and moody theatrics – his ability to play the guitar behind his head or simply place it atop his amplifier, allowing the thing to feed back and create a tune all its own – leaving most audiences open-mouthed in wonder. "I just went out to kill them," said Jeff, by way of explanation. When one conjoined the hit singles, the group's increasingly high profile and the thrilling allure of their one-man sonic circus, it was little wonder Gomelsky made the decision to take The Yardbirds to the USA.

As ever, The Beatles had led the charge when it came to exporting a sparkling new British pop scene to America. Leaving behind some 4,000 screaming fans at Heathrow Airport on February 7, 1964, the Liverpool quartet were singing in front of a TV audience of 74 million just two days later, their appearance on *The Ed Sullivan*

Show sparking what was soon to be called 'The British Invasion'. By April of that year, The Beatles occupied the top five positions on the *Billboard Hot 100* singles chart and the race was on for other UK acts to follow, the likes of Dusty Springfield, The Animals, Manfred Mann and The Rolling Stones all achieving US chart success in their wake. With 'For Your Love' having already reached number nine in the American charts on June 3, 1965 and its cobbled together, parent album of the same name securing the number 96 spot (Eric Clapton, not Beck, featured on this release, even though Jeff was pictured on the sleeve), The Yardbirds' trip across the Atlantic was a foregone conclusion.

Though Giorgio hadn't secured an exact date for their departure, the band more or less ceased to play gigs as their manager negotiated a difficult path between the UK Musicians' Union and United States Embassy to allow his charges access to the States. "We played the Marquee, I think," said McCarty, "but there was no touring. And very little in the way of royalties either." The main sticking point was the UK's bizarre 'exchange agreement' with the USA, meaning that until a suitable American act agreed to travel to Britain, The Yardbirds remained grounded on English soil. For Jeff, who had eagerly secured his first passport for the trip, such delays were simply infuriating. "Oh, it was ridiculous," he told the BBC. "Waiting for a man in a bloody suit to OK whether you can play or not." Eventually, a traditional jazz band fulfilled the criteria of suitable "musical exchange students", and The Yardbirds left from Heathrow on September 2, bound for New York City.

Accompanying Beck on the trip to America was a relatively new recruit to his guitar arsenal. "When I first joined the group," he said, "[I'm sure] I was using Eric's old red Tele, which I think actually belonged to them and they leased back to him... oh, they were bastards! Obviously I wanted my own. Fender had just started making Teles with rosewood necks, but I wanted one with an original maple neck. Thankfully, we'd gone on tour with The Walker Brothers, and John Maus [their singer/guitarist] had a maple-neck Tele. He wanted about £75 for it, which was only £10 cheaper than the new ones in the shops, but he wouldn't budge. So I dug out the money, bought the guitar from him and I never regretted it." In Jeff's words a "battered specimen", the Telecaster in question (carrying the serial number 1056 on its neck plate) was actually a 1954 Fender Esquire, the absence of a front pick-up marking it as such. Maus had already cut contours into the Esquire's swamp-ash body to make it comfortable to wear, in line with its more expensive brother, the Stratocaster. Beck's only modifications were to change the guitar's scratch plate from white to black and replace its steel bridge saddles with brass ones. Light-bodied, with a fast neck and surprisingly deep voice for a Telecaster-style instrument, the Esquire remained at the heart of The Yardbirds' sound during his tenure with the band.

After a brief stopover in Ireland, an Aer Lingus jet finally deposited its charges on New York soil, or more specifically, tarmac. On clearing customs, the band were immediately whisked up by Premier Talent, their American booking agency, into the back of a black stretch limousine, en route to a fine midtown restaurant. "Being used to Morris Minor vans, this 50ft 'thing' did impress," laughed Dreja. Having bonded well in previous months, McCarty was sharing a room with Jeff for the tour. "We were on something like the 40th floor in this huge New York hotel," he remembered. "Beck was looking out the window saying 'Look at those cars, all those American... cars'. He was absolutely transfixed. Well, we both were really." Dreja was equally overwhelmed by the prospect of bringing the blues home to Uncle Sam. "To be young, to travel, to blow the establishment out of your brain... it was just bloody marvellous."

And a tad confusing. After they left New York for their first concert at a funfair in the middle of rural Oklahoma, continuing administrative problems around both the terms of the exchange programme and their work visas brought The Yardbirds' tour to a shuddering halt. In essence, the band were simply not allowed to perform. "We had terrible problems with visas and the Musicians' Union... bloody 'artist exchanges' and such like," said Chris, "so it became increasingly difficult to actually get any gigs." Another unanticipated problem was the group's appearance. While shoulder-length hair and sharp suits cut quite the dash on Carnaby Street, they took on a wholly different connotation in the American Midwest. "Oh yeah, we got some grief at times with the long hair," McCarty confirmed. "I think they thought we were trying to avoid the Vietnam War, that we were draft dodgers, you know. Well, that or just a bunch of dropouts."

Despite such reservations, their plight also offered some relative compensation for Beck. "We arrived in the days of checked shirts... all the guys hating every minute [of us] because their girlfriends were freaking out at [our] long hair," he told *Guitar For The Practising Musician*. "I was thinking 'Where's the rock'n'roll, the greased sideburns, Elvis and Chuck Berry?' All of a sudden, we realised – us spotty oiks from England were actually happening, that we carried more weight than those guys." As Willie Dixon once said, "The men don't know, but the little girls understand..."

Unable to play any gigs, but with visits already confirmed to several American cities, Gomelsky was forced to improvise. Hence, the band were carted to and from a plethora of radio stations, with Giorgio forcing his charges onto the air to promote their wares while DJs struggled to ask appropriate questions of musicians they had met only moments before. "It wasn't exactly ideal," said McCarty with some understatement. Nonetheless, another brainstorm from Gomelsky actually proved a stroke of genius. "Sam Phillips was on a fishing weekend," recalled Dreja, "and somehow, Giorgio got hold of him on the phone and told him we were coming to Memphis to make a record. Unbelievably, he went for it."

Even in 1965, before rock'n'roll was handed to the historians to ensure its early gods were appropriately honoured, Sam Phillips was a sizeable deity. A no-nonsense Alabama boy, who moved to Memphis in his late twenties to open a recording studio, Phillips' subsequent decision to launch his own label in 1952 changed the face of American music. Within the space of just four years, Sun Records had activated the careers of Howlin' Wolf, Elvis Presley, Jerry Lee Lewis and Johnny Cash, Phillips producing early rock'n'roll and rockabilly classics such as 'That's All Right', 'Blue Suede Shoes', 'Folsom Prison Blues' and 'I Walk The Line' in his studio at 706 Union Avenue. Though Sam had wound down much of his recorded output in favour of other business opportunities by the time The Yardbirds came calling, it was still a considerable coup to have him produce their session.

Arriving on a Sunday evening in mid-September, the band was shocked to find that the hallowed halls of the 'Memphis Recording Service' were in fact nearer the size of their hotel rooms. "Sun Studios was like a little shop, almost the size of a kitchen," remembered Dreja. "A tatty old amp over there, a drum kit fixed to the floor. You couldn't touch anything because Sam had everything worked out. The distance of the microphone, the correct volume, everything was in place. But God, it worked. Phillips really understood sound." McCarty was even more shocked when he approached the drum kit he would be playing: "There was this little, beaten up old kit in the corner with this sandbag thing in the bass drum. I took one look and thought 'Christ, what's this going to sound like?' Anyway, I sat down, started playing and it was just fantastic. Sam had the sound down to perfection... it was a sound we just couldn't get in England. It literally breathed."

Just as he had been days before when confronted by traffic passing below his New York window, Beck was utterly transfixed by his surroundings. "I mean, Sun. Elvis, Jerry Lee, Carl Perkins. We were listening to playback from the same speakers that Presley first heard his songs. It was like, 'Come on...'"

Of the tracks cut at Sun that night, the most memorable was surely 'Train Kept A-Rollin'', an old Beck teenage favourite that he personally suggested for the session. From the moment Jeff's guitar volume swells emulated the sound of a train's departure whistle to Jim's ungodly cymbal crash some three minutes later, The Yardbirds beat the living daylights out of Tiny Bradshaw's jump-blues classic. Regrettably, while Phillips was complimentary of the band's anarchic take on 'Train...' he was less enamoured with their lead vocalist, making it clear to all they should ditch him. "Sam didn't really take to Keith, mainly because Keith was drunk," said McCarty. "Unfortunate really, because he thought everyone else was OK, but Keith... well, Keith liked a drink." Dreja put Phillips' negativity towards Relf more down to cultural differences: "I think you have to understand that Sam had worked with the likes of Elvis, Carl Perkins, Howlin' Wolf and a sensitive British popster like Keith would not have ticked his box. Of course, he could recognise a great guitar player like Jeff, but Keith was different. He was an English white kid with his own sense of delivery and his own sense of dynamics."

Though Beck kept his counsel during the face-off, he was privately seething at Phillips' attitude. "I felt quite protective of Keith that night," he later said. "I didn't really understand the animosity then. But looking back, what we sounded like must have been frightening [to Phillips], like The Sex Pistols arriving. He hadn't quite adjusted to 'Rolling Stones-itis'."*

Days later, The Yardbirds made their second visit to hallowed ground, this time convening at Chicago's rightfully lauded Chess Studios, then located at 2120 South Michigan Avenue. For some, Chess Studios was *the* home of American music. Set up by brothers Leonard and Phil Chess in 1950, the recording facility and its titular record label had captured and released some of the finest blues, R&B and early rock'n'roll singles, giving the world its first proper taste of Muddy Waters, Memphis Slim, Buddy Guy, Bo Diddley, Chuck Berry and so many more. Having weaned themselves on such acts, The Yardbirds felt Chess was akin to a spiritual home where, like Sun Studios, they might capture their onstage essence: "We were a high-energy live band – a lot of power, a lot of audience interaction – but we just couldn't get that sound on tape, at least not in England," reasoned Dreja. "But the Americans were geared up for recording, and when Giorgio got us into places like Chess and Sun, we knew we were in proper studios."

The band took full advantage of their brief time at Chess, cutting an incendiary version of Bo Diddley's 1955 hit 'I'm A Man', a mid-tempo blues they had previously recorded live with Eric Clapton. Sticking reasonably close to Diddley's version for the intro, right down to Relf's eerie Billy Boy Arnold harmonica impersonation, things changed radically at one minute, 28 seconds into the song when Beck's foot smashed into his Tone Bender. Though the jarring increase in guitar volume was initially a shock to the ear, what happened next was a genuine revelation. As The Yardbirds doubled the tempo behind them, Beck and Relf chased after each other in a manic harmonica/guitar interface, notes swooping in and out of

---

* Relf's vocals on 'Train Kept A Rollin'' were subsequently re-recorded in New York, while Beck retains misgivings about the band's performance even now.

the mix before Beck's Esquire scratched and howled its way to a shattering close. "When we heard the playback," Jeff later told *Guitar Player,* "we went berserk. The bass drum was shaking the foundation of the building... there was just so much excitement there." Alongside their work at Sun Studios it was the closest the group had yet come to capturing the sound of the 'rave up' on tape.

Following the Chess sessions, Gomelsky returned to his continuing war with officialdom, resulting in The Yardbirds picking up the odd gig in Chicago and Arizona – each concert drawing them inexorably nearer to their dream destination of California. But the band was given a sharp lesson in the realities of what "being black" actually meant in the States when they entered Los Angeles via the district of Watts, where only weeks earlier some of the worst civil rights protests in US history had flared. Poor housing, bad schools and an astronomical unemployment rate had brought on a six-day riot by angry African Americans, leading to 34 deaths, over 1,000 injuries and nearly 4,000 arrests. A sharp contrast to their experiences at Chess Studios only days before, history of the most disturbing kind was being made right outside the band's tour-bus window as they drove past broken shop fronts, still smouldering cars and street graffiti promoting 'Black Power'. While The Yardbirds had long been supporters of black American music, they quickly came to realise the actuality of being "a person of colour in the States" was an altogether more complex thing. "England after the war was pretty dirty, pretty grimy, with very little for young people to do," said Dreja. "Everything was very establishment-minded, so America was unreal to us. But it was also home to our idols, black musicians, though we didn't really know there was segregation or bad treatment. Our understanding of that only came when we saw things for ourselves."

For Gomelsky, this clear partition between cultures and the violence that arose from it was as inherently stupid as the attitudes he encountered when speaking about home-grown blues artists with US record industry types. "The worst thing about America is that white people have no idea about the fantastic talent of black musicians," he said at the time. "When we said we wanted to go to Chicago and see Muddy Waters, they just said 'Who?' They'd never heard of him. There are three or four black radio stations in every region, but white people just don't listen to them. It's not prejudice, it's simply ignorance."

What The Yardbirds encountered when they arrived in Beverly Hills was an altogether different America, one that Beck instantly recognised from the movies of his youth. "London might have been swinging, but California was sunny," he said. "[There were] 17, 18-year-old girls driving around in convertible cars... God. It truly was the land of milk and honey. And smog." To celebrate, Beck hired a sparkling new Corvette Stingray, driving backwards and forwards along Sunset Strip in a state of automated bliss. "Endless sunshine, Beach Boys songs on the radio, Hollywood women walking up and down the streets," said Chris Dreja. "It was another world, but in Technicolor – like something from a movie we'd watched at home... but now we were in it. Jeff even got a colour television for his hotel room."

And a visit from the police. Within a day or so of setting foot in LA, Beck's beloved new Esquire was stolen, threatening to put an enormous dampener on the guitarist's Hollywood experience. Mercifully, the LAPD soon found and returned it (covered in fingerprint dust), thus allowing Jeff to get back to the delights of road-testing his hired car. The band also marked their visit to the city by filming a spot on the TV show *Shindig*, Beck moodily stroking a 12-string Gibson acoustic on 'For Your Love', before unleashing his now safe Esquire and a rare smile for an excellent live rendition of 'Heart Full Of Soul'. The presence of Hollywood starlet Raquel Welch performing 'Dancing In The Street' while dressed in turtle-neck sweater and white boots no doubt underlined the fact Jeff was no longer on Wallingford's Manor Road.

In fact, Beck was soon to find a Hollywood princess of his very own, albeit through the increasingly surreal – and entirely accidental – business machinations of his manager. Ever the creative type, Gomelsky had circumvented The Yardbirds' on-again, off-again concert schedule by booking them on the party circuit or, more specifically, one very big party. While in LA, Giorgio had been introduced to a young socialite named Bob Markley, who was in the process of putting together his own group, soon-to-be cult favourites The West Coast Pop Art Experimental Band. Said introduction had been made by yet another of Gomelsky's friends, the inimitable Kim Fowley, then "a major face" on Sunset Strip, who would go on to manage Seventies all-female quintet The Runaways, among other things. In conversation, Giorgio learned that Markley's oil tycoon father owned a plush mansion in the Hollywood Hills, currently occupied by various artistic types. Within minutes, a plan was hatched: the mansion's doors would be opened, a party would be held and The Yardbirds would be house band for the night.

After some 45 or so years, memories of the actual event have become a little clouded. Suffice to say, Markley's party was the zenith of The Yardbirds' first (non-tour) of the USA. "Everyone turned up," recalled Dreja, "or so we were told. Filmmakers, artists, even Marlon Brando, Bob Dylan and The Byrds' Roger McGuinn were meant to be attending. And I'm sure they did, though sadly we never saw them as we were playing in the living room behind a sofa..." Even comedic legend Lenny Bruce made an appearance, throwing a boot at McCarty as he packed his drum kit into a van. While Bruce was practising his shoe-flinging skills from a window above, Beck was busily trying to acquire the telephone number of a girl one floor below.

The object of his affections was Mary Hughes, a stunningly attractive 21-year-old, then best known for uttering a line or two in such B-movies as *Muscle Beach Party* and *Beach Blanket Bingo*, innocent 'sun, sea and fun' romps where key plot developments occur only when an actress changes her swimwear. Hughes' soaring height, combustible figure and way with an on-screen quip had made her "Queen of the beach bunnies". She was also Markley's girlfriend at the time. "Well, you can't blame Jeff for that," reasoned Dreja. "Like the rest of us, Jeff had come from black and white and California was in full-on Technicolor. Mary Hughes, well, she was all the colours of the rainbow. A lovely, vivacious, blonde woman, a mini Bridget Bardot. I think she blew his mind. She'd blow most people's minds, actually." Though Beck and Hughes' blossoming relationship was placed on temporary hold as The Yardbirds returned home, their romance would have far-reaching implications for the guitarist, both in terms of song and career plans.

If the band's first visit to the US had been a jarring experience, full of stops and shunts along the way, there were relative compensations. Following their appearance on *Shindig* and another pop show, *Hullaballoo* – which fellow guest, King of Comedy Jerry Lewis, jokingly nicknamed 'Fuckaballoo' – 'Heart Full Of Soul' had risen to number nine in the American charts, giving The Yardbirds transatlantic pop-star status. Additionally, the group's thinking had been profoundly influenced by their trip, the likes of Fowley introducing them to a vital LA music scene that would eventually produce The Doors, Love and Frank Zappa & The Mothers Of Invention. The band also became aware of San Francisco's growing psychedelic movement only 350 miles away, where acts such as The Charlatans, Jefferson Airplane and The Warlocks (who would soon change their name to The Grateful Dead) were also intent on "pushing back musical boundaries and blowing minds" with the aid of a hallucinogenic drug called LSD. While Beck personally had little truck with hippies or acid trips, preferring the odd beer and cigarette for his sins, he was aware that pop was growing up quickly and his brand of guitar playing might greatly influence its ascent to adulthood.

This realisation was curiously prescient on The Yardbirds' next double A-side single, 'Evil Hearted You'/'Still I'm Sad'. Again written by Graham Gouldman (though it would be his last contribution to the band), 'Evil Hearted You' had a hint of the Spaghetti Western scores of Italian composer Ennio Morricone, with Beck's contribution taking it to a whole new level of excitement, his clattering, heavily reverbed guitar and shimmering, two-octave slide solo sounding almost ghostly. He was equally impressive on 'Still I'm Sad', The Yardbirds' first self-penned hit, written by McCarty and Samwell-Smith during a lazy night at the piano in Hampstead. Driven by a mock-Gregorian chant, Beck added volume swells and splash chords to enhance the tune, occasionally pecking at Relf's sonorous vocal with a lead line here and there. Funereally paced and very European sounding, 'Still I'm Sad' had almost nothing in common with the blues band The Yardbirds sought to be only two years before. "We were just trying to do something different," explained Dreja. "The 12-bar blues was very predictable, and now we wanted to make things more exciting, for us and the audience. We had the rave up and it was now time for something new. And of course, Jeff had all these sounds, this... orchestra of sounds, and we really wanted to use them."

How Beck was "used" by The Yardbirds was rather like "dropping a bomb on the song from above". In essence, the band would work on tracks as a quartet, with Samwell-Smith overseeing the process while his colleagues cut their parts. "The drum sounds always took the longest," he said, "with four or five mikes dotted around the kit. I'd then equalise it, [bounce] the drums and bass onto one track, and then you could do whatever you liked with the guitars." As Samwell-Smith revealed, once the backing track was captured on tape, Beck would be given free rein to light the fireworks. "It was easier all round," said McCarty. "The way four-track recording worked at the time, we could lay down the backing, then Keith's vocals and then let Jeff come in and do his thing. In hindsight, we put him under an awful lot of pressure without realising it. We'd expect Jeff to sound like a chicken and a tank at the same time, but the thing was he always managed to do it." Beck's own memories of this time echo McCarty's remarks, even invoking similar military imagery. "I'd be skulking in the corner, shuffling my feet, twiddling my thumbs, just waiting to go off like a fucking cannon."

As 'Evil Hearted You'/'Still I'm Sad' climbed to number three in the UK on November 6, 1965 (a chart position no doubt helped by Gomelsky joining the band dressed as a monk for their *Top Of The Pops* appearance), The Yardbirds prepared for yet another British tour. This time, there were some 16 dates to negotiate, with two nightly performances alongside Manfred Mann, Paul & Barry Ryan and Inez & Charlie Foxx beginning at the ABC Cinema, Stockton. As ever, Beck remained a quiet presence on the road, though friendships with his bandmates were now starting to coalesce. "By then," said McCarty, "I'd got to know Jeff a bit better. He was still 'of himself', if you see what I mean, but a nice guy all the same. Like Eric, he'd be in the back of the bus, staring into the distance. Then all of a sudden, he'd start pulling these mad faces. Believe me, having a sense of humour when you're on the road driving bloody miles to the middle of nowhere can only help."

Beck's gift for gurning must have faced a mighty test on November 22, when en route to a show at Bradford's Gaumont the band's tour bus sustained a puncture, stranding them on the M1 during the worst blizzard England had seen in a decade.

To escape the terrible cold of a British winter, The Yardbirds headed back to the States on December 16 for their first problem-free tour and, in Jeff's case, another opportunity to rendezvous with Mary Hughes. Since leaving the country only two or so months before, the band's clattering version of 'I'm A Man' had given them another US hit, reaching a respectable 17. More, their second US album, *Having A Rave Up With The Yardbirds*, had climbed to number 53 in the *Billboard* charts, the LP destined to flit around the Top 100 for a further 30 weeks. A strong collection made up of tracks from *Five Live Yardbirds* (with Clapton), previously released singles such as 'Heart Full Of Soul' and the Sun/Chess wallop of 'Train Kept A Rollin'' and 'I'm A Man', ...*Rave Up* also featured another nascent classic in the making: 'Mr. You're A Better Man Than I'. Part philosophical ode to the rights of the individual, part attack on the stupidity of war and racism, 'Mr...''s championing sentiments were in fact co-written by Manfred Mann's Mike Hugg and his brother, Brian. Lyrically robust for its time, the song was indicative of the future themes The Yardbirds would explore, diluting the optimism of the burgeoning hippie era with altogether blacker philosophical hues. It also featured a very nasty free-form solo from Beck, all screams, sighs and stinging vibrato. "On the tracks [present on] *Having A Rave Up...*," *Guitar Player* later confirmed, "Jeff Beck emerged a fully-fledged guitar hero: menacing, flamboyant, ungodly energetic... he laid down the shape of things to come."

Indeed he did, as The Yardbirds temporarily broke away from their US concert schedule to record their next single – the stunning 'Shapes Of Things' – at Chicago's Chess Studios on December 21. A landmark for the band written by Samwell-Smith, McCarty and Relf, there is some dispute as to whether work on 'Shapes...' had actually begun at Chess the previous September, though there is no doubt it was finished at LA's RCA Studios in early January 1966. Quibbling over recording dates aside, the song remains arguably The Yardbirds' finest moment, where 'beat' fused with the burgeoning psychedelic movement to create something wholly new – even if the melody was actually based on an old Dave Brubeck riff.

It would also be impossible to downplay Beck's part in establishing the song as a future classic, his combination of Indian raga-influenced lead lines, nascent feedback and chiming chords opening up possibilities for a generation of guitarists to follow. Admittedly, his efforts came at some cost: frustrated by the limitations of how far he could bend notes, Beck changed guitars several times throughout recording, choosing in the end to play his solo just on the G-string: "I wanted the bends to sound like Buddy Guy, but it was hellish work." The final version incorporates all of Beck's lead breaks, though the main solo – at least until the note starts to feed back – is from a single pass. "It was all too good to be true, really," he later confessed. "Walking into the same place Bo Diddley and Muddy Waters had cut 'I'm A Man'. You know, 'Shapes Of Things' was the pinnacle of The Yardbirds, our best single." It certainly was. Full of shy hope, harmonic innovation and containing a strong pro-environment message years before it became fashionable to even talk of such things, 'Shapes Of Things' thoroughly deserved its respective numbers three and 11 placing in the UK and US charts when released as a single in March and May of 1966.

Back in December 1965, The Yardbirds were enjoying some of the finest notices of their career, even if their travel arrangements between American gigs remained less than ideal. "God, the touring was mad," said Dreja. "Strange, strange situations. Sometimes you'd get on a plane and find yourself seated next to a dead deer." The benefits, however, largely outweighed the disadvantages, especially for fans seeing the band for the first time. One such admirer was a very young – and soon to be very good – guitarist called Neil Giraldo. "The Yardbirds played this little club in Cleveland called The Cob, and because I wasn't old enough to get in, I had to sneak in," he told *Guitar World*. "Jeff Beck just blew me away. I will never forget that night. [From then] apart from Beck, I really didn't listen to that many other guitar players." Giraldo learned from Beck extremely well, going on to work with (and, indeed, marry) rock vocalist Pat Benatar, with whom he recorded one of the late Seventies more memorable guitar solos on the US Top 10 single 'Hit Me With Your Best Shot'.

Having been grasped to the bosom of Seattle at a memorable New Year's Eve concert, The Yardbirds left behind icy rain in favour of the warmer climes of LA, performing a four-night residency at the Hullaballoo Club on Sunset Strip. By now, their live set bore little or no relation to their days at the Crawdaddy, the old Jimmy Reed and Chuck Berry covers making way for warped treatments of 'Still I'm Sad', 'Heart Full Of Soul' and virtually unrecognisable renditions of 'I Wish You Would' and 'I'm A Man'. "Nothing was 'named' back then, it wasn't 'psychedelic' or 'rock', it was just music," said Dreja. "Like touring for us, there were no road maps... just fewer boundaries. Things happened. We were inventing every night to keep ourselves interested. God, I mean you would, being on the road endlessly. We were doing it for ourselves, for the audience. We were young and there were people who wanted to explode with us. So we went for it."

For Beck, recently christened "the boy who is Mick Jagger's double" by *Disc* music paper, this was truly the band's golden age. As The Yardbirds departed from the West Coast for more dates in New York, where the open arms of pop artist Andy Warhol and his merry band of Factory 'Superstars' led to a whirlwind tour of the city's more outlandish nightclubs, Jeff must have felt like visiting royalty. "At that time, I came into my own as a guitarist," he later said. "I was allowed to go wild onstage and I did. It was all experimentation, anarchy, and we were at the forefront of the psychedelic thing... some would say we even invented it. The underground was coming up and things were really moving. We had a passport to the world. I mean, what could I complain about?"

Things change.

Chapter 6

Pressure Drop

By January 1966, The Yardbirds had entered the imperial phase of their career. Loved at home and abroad, their recent successes had seen them embraced by both the pop market and the growing underground scene, placing them at the epicentre of Swinging London with an 'access all areas' pass to the West Coast and edgy, arty New York. From an outsider's perspective, the stars had aligned and manna was slowly descending from heaven. Unfortunately for the band, while milk and honey might have been flowing in abundance, the cash certainly wasn't. "All these hit singles, these American tours and we were coming back with nothing," confirmed Chris Dreja. "We just weren't making any money."

The man behind The Yardbirds' financial predicament was Giorgio Gomelsky. Though possessing a quite brilliant mind, full of genuinely innovative ideas about promoting the group's artistic direction, Gomelsky was simply not watching the purse strings as well as he might. "The thing about Giorgio was that, above all else, he was a creative man," said Dreja. "He was the sixth member – the sixth artist – in the band, and he had some wonderful ideas that took us in interesting directions. But it's not such a good thing to have an artist in a strict management role. We weren't benefiting financially from him." As the record sales went up and the gate receipts doubled, The Yardbirds' collective feathers began to rustle. "The only time you get resentful," Beck said, "is when you come to the realisation that money was there and you've missed it. Quite understandably, you start to get pissed off."

For Beck, the situation worsened considerably at the end of January when Gomelsky's artistic gifts also appeared to desert him. To appease The Yardbirds' Italian record label, he had entered the group in the decidedly upmarket San Remo Song Festival where they recorded and performed two songs especially for the occasion: the sub-Eurocheese ballad 'Questo Volta' and the unfortunately named 'Paff... Bum'. When Jeff heard the tunes, and learned they would be playing for an audience of "jewellery tinklers and penguin suits", he point blank refused to be involved. After some subtle negotiation by Gomelsky, Beck partially relented, agreeing to appear live with the band and play a solo on 'Paff... Bum', though he "still wouldn't touch 'Questo Volta' with a sodding bargepole".

On the night, The Yardbirds actually took matters into their own hands, giving the assembled throng of diplomats and fashionistas quite the spectacle. "This was a black tie, bejewelled, moneyed event – almost operatic, actually," said Dreja. "But hey, why not have a punk band go down there and mix it up? After all, we were the first. Anyway, we just went for it. Jeff nearly took their heads off." Predictably, the band didn't receive a standing ovation. "They even hissed and booed at us when we walked onstage, but hell, we did it. At the time of course, it seemed like a disaster. But with hindsight, it was another thing that helped create the atmosphere and myth of the group."

In the aftermath of the San Remo Song Festival, Giorgio's role as manager began to become untenable. During sessions for the band's next album, curiously christened *A Yardbirds' Eye View Of Beat* by Gomelsky himself, Paul Samwell-Smith played the part of Fletcher Christian to Giorgio's Captain Bligh, sacking him on behalf of the others. "I helped Paul Samwell-Smith develop his career and made him musical director of The Yardbirds," Gomelsky later told writer Chris Welch. "That was one reason why Eric left, because of Samwell-Smith calling the shots. And then Paul's girlfriend complained about my management. She said she had a friend who could do a better job. Paul talked the others into firing me... it was a heartbreaker." Heartbreaking perhaps, but Giorgio was smart enough to take some insurance with him. "I had a contract with them," he said, "and I wanted the rights to all the songs I produced."

Assuming that their entire back catalogue would be unlikely to generate much income in the coming years, the band agreed to hand it to Gomelsky. "Bad mistake," said Dreja. As The Yardbirds' and Jeff Beck's reputations as musical innovators grew over the next two decades, so did demand for their product – a fact not lost on Gomelsky, who found new and ever more lucrative ways of repackaging their earliest hits and recording sessions. Yet, there now seems to be no bad blood between the two parties, who have since mended all fences broken in 1966. "There was no one moment with Giorgio," confirmed Jim McCarty. "It had just built up over time. He had so many ideas – sometimes they were brilliant, sometimes not. We'd been on the road for ages and were tired of living in transit vans rather than travelling in huge Greyhound buses or in planes, as you might today. Also, we were a Top 10 band, but we hadn't really seen any money. It was just time for a change."

As work ceased on the band's next album – and Gomelsky walked away with the tapes – The Yardbirds appointed Simon Napier-Bell as their new manager. A London scenester, who had recently co-written the lyrics to Dusty Springfield's first UK number one, 'You Don't Have To Say You Love Me', Napier-Bell had precious little managerial experience, his only charges thus far being boy/girl duo Diane Ferraz & Nicky Scott. Yet, what he lacked in experience, he more than made up for in attitude. Living in a plush bachelor pad near Buckingham Palace, the 31-year-old smoked cigars, was on first name terms with every club owner in London and drove a brand new Ford Thunderbird. Jeff Beck could only look on with envy. Or perhaps not. "Yeah, it was a very impressive car," confirmed Napier-Bell. "The electric hood went up, then disappeared into the boot. The first time I went to see The Yardbirds at the Marquee, I took the Thunderbird with me. After the show all the kids are coming out, walking past this beautiful car, so I pressed the button – you know – so the hood would rise and it'd look great. Anyway, halfway up, it jammed. I had to call the AA. God, there I was, scuttling away trying to fix things as these decidedly unimpressed teenagers walked past laughing..."

Thankfully, things went a little better when actually meeting the group. "Paul Samwell-Smith's sister was actually my secretary and Vicki Wickham, who I co-wrote 'You Don't Have To Say You Love Me' with, persuaded her that I might be the right choice for manager. I didn't know that much about management at that time, but I saw it as a test of my bravery," Simon laughed. "Anyway, I met the guys in a plush Soho restaurant, it went well, and we took it from there. What surprised me was how nice they all were. I was expecting them to be bloody monsters like The Rolling Stones, and I got these gentle souls with good manners. From that moment on, I was trying to keep ahead of them really, because I was relatively new to the pop business and they'd been around the block. That said, I did have a natural instinct for pulling off scams."

According to Dreja, Napier-Bell's more orthodox approach to management was a real change of tact from Gomelsky's 'sixth member' status. "We were a top-down, on-the-road band... a little cynical by then," he said, "and I don't think Simon could really relate to us at all personally. He was very 'hands off' in style compared to Giorgio. But he also was a lovely man who did several good things for us, starting with the renegotiation of our publishing contract and the securing of our rights."

Some £25,000 better off thanks to an advance against royalties from EMI negotiated by Napier-Bell on his arrival ("I felt my job depended on it"), The Yardbirds set off again on the concert circuit, this time to France for a tour beginning at La Locomotive club in the Moulin Rouge, Paris. But events took a rapid downturn when a year on the road finally caught up with their lead guitarist, who passed out backstage in Marseilles, falling down a set of concrete steps in the process. After an emergency run to the local hospital, doctors at first thought Beck was suffering from meningitis, though a more thorough check-up reduced the risk rating to a severe case of food poisoning, coupled with suspected tonsillitis. "Inflamed tonsils, inflamed brain, inflamed cock," being Beck's expert medical assessment of his condition.

There was no real time for rest. After only a few days' recuperation in France, the still weak guitarist rejoined his colleagues at London's Advision Studios during April to record the follow-up single to 'Shapes Of Things', then beginning its descent from the UK Top 10. The tune chosen as successor to 'Shapes...' actually began life as a loose jam based around Bill Haley's immortal 'Rock Around The Clock'. "We cut the song with Jeff playing bass," said McCarty. "Then, as usual, he disappeared only to come back a few hours later with this fuzz guitar riff. My first thought was 'Eh? How does that riff go with that boogie?'To be honest, it sounded mad. But then, when you heard it again, it started to make sense. I ended up loving it."

Almost impossible to replicate because of its unique bends, Beck's hypnotic, snake-charming riff took listeners off on a wild middle-Eastern jaunt before shuttling back via the Mississippi Delta by the end of the song.When Napier-Bell suggested chanting 'Over Under Sideways Down' over the chorus, The Yardbirds had their title and another hit single. "'Over Under...'s a good example of Jeff at work," reasoned Dreja. "He's a wonderful enhancer, with a pure artistic streak, though he's not as spontaneous as people might think. He likes to go and work with a song – feel it out – before producing something extraordinary. Which by the way, he did." A personal favourite of Beck's ("Great song, a bit mad, you know..."), 'Over Under Sideways Down' reached number 10 in the UK charts on June 4, and number 13 in the US a month later.

Having abandoned work on their album when sacking Giorgio Gomelsky,The Yardbirds once again took up the baton in early June, returning to Advision for another try. "Advision was a big white room," said Beck, "lots of air with space to record." Unlike Gomelsky, Napier-Bell saw himself as no great producer."I listened to five of their singles, and it taught me nothing. Every one was different – chanting with monks to raw blues, then out and out pop – they didn't have a homogenous sound. Here they were, in my opinion the third biggest band in the world after The Beatles and the Stones, and I couldn't really fathom it.Then when you saw them live, they were completely different again, all jams and long rave ups, with Jeff just screaming away. Though I didn't know a thing about record production at the time, luckily Paul had that covered. He was always a sharp thinker, very focused with a gift more for pop than blues, perhaps. For me, it was more about marketing and opportunity, pulling it together." Deadlines around the project, however, were watertight."We had five days to record the LP," said Samwell-Smith, "writing all the numbers ourselves. If only we had the studio for a month, it would have been fantastic. [But] we had to rush it out all over the world."

Assisting the band in beating the rush was recording engineer Roger Cameron, who inadvertently gave the album its nickname, *Roger The Engineer*. "Roger was a lovely guy, very BBC, but he really didn't want to be BBC, if you know what I mean. He wanted to escape that," said Dreja. "In those days, people like Roger did wear suits, white coats, suede shoes and were quite proper. For us, Roger was a little like The Beatles' producer, George Martin, in fulfilling a role. Not as musical as George, but very helpful. He never said 'You can't do this, or you can't do that'. There was no 'Turn down, shut up, go away', he just really allowed us to try everything. Really, it was stroke of genius from Simon. He thought Paul and Roger would get on very well and it worked out brilliantly." Looking for something to do during downtime Chris casually took to drawing sketches, his caricature of Roger Cameron sadly making his way across the studio floor, one hand burdened with tape, the other with headphones, becoming the cover of the LP. "Yes, it turned out quite well," quipped Dreja.

Roger The Engineer – or to give it its official title, *Yardbirds* – was a quantum leap forward for the band, its 12 songs still justly celebrated as a mad confection of psychedelic blues, exotic instrumentation and nascent hard rock. Though a little ragged around the edges at times (a fault, no doubt, of limited studio time), the LP nevertheless had several real highlights, including 'Hot House Of Omagarashid', a bizarre experiment in world music (replete with Rolf Harris-style wobble board), the ungodly drones of 'Ever Since The World Began' and 'Turn Into Earth' and the Chicago-influenced, tub-thumping crunch of 'Rack My Mind'. "Yes, it was a pivotal album for us," said Dreja. "Lots of creativity, following lateral thoughts, just a wonderful time. And though Jeff wasn't there for some of the process, when he did come in, the stuff he did was just wonderful."

Still recovering from his recent illness, Beck's contributions to *Roger The Engineer* were recorded in a concentrated blast toward the end of the sessions. They were also quite breathtaking in their intensity. "Jeff was nailing each song," said Dreja, "quick takes and all fire. Beck wasn't a writer *per se*, but he was a virtuoso... a genius, I'd say. You can just hear he was born to play guitar on that album." Coiled in a corner while the others pulled together strands of songs, Jeff was almost at breaking point when his bandmates finally called him in. "I was twiddling my fingers, waiting for my chance to get in and rip it in half," he later told *Guitar World*. "They [were watching] the flame build." This anger is nowhere more evident than on 'Rack My Mind', where after peppering the track with a series of ringing harmonics, Beck's guitar break veers off into a succession of wild octave jumps and descending arpeggios. 'He's Always There' also greatly benefited from Jeff's annoyance, his squished fuzz solo building from quiet indignation to full on 'killing face' in just 50 seconds.

Of even greater significance was Beck's performance on 'The Nazz Are Blue'. Based on Elmore James' masterful 1951 interpretation of the old Delta standard 'Dust My Broom', and originally cut as 'Jeff's Blues' almost one year before for the *Having A Rave Up* sessions, 'The Nazz Are Blue' has become something of a defining moment in the annals of rock guitar. Sung by Beck himself, the song adheres to a traditional 'slide blues' structure until its middle section, when Beck confounds all expectations by sounding a single note, which then whistles into feedback across the entire solo section. Yet, when he first recorded the take in Advision, band, engineer and manager all thought it was a mistake. "They really weren't getting on, Jeff and the group at that point. But then we all knew he was the best musician in the line-up," said Napier-Bell. "I think Jeff was tired and genuinely angry with the way he thought he was being treated. Anyway, he walked into the recording booth to cut the solo for 'The Nazz Are Blue' and just held this one note until it started to feed back, played nothing else and then just stopped. Everyone was saying, 'What the hell was that? You've fucked it up!' Then we heard the tape. God. Of course, it's since become this amazing moment in rock, Jeff holding back the storm with one note, wavering there with so much tonality and feel. But to this day, I don't know whether it was deliberate or whether he did it just to piss off the band."

Beck's startling, quite deliberate conceit on 'The Nazz Are Blue' (and to a lesser extent on 'Lost Woman') remains a watershed moment in the use of controlled feedback, providing inspiration for a wave of forthcoming psychedelic/heavy metal musicians. It also predates the work of another extraordinarily gifted guitarist who would soon seriously challenge Jeff's supremacy in all matters of sound manipulation.

Beck's other contribution of real note to *Roger The Engineer* was a blistering display of guitar pyrotechnics entitled 'Jeff's Boogie'.

Originally released as the B-side to 'Over Under Sideways Down', 'Jeff's Boogie' had been around in one form or another since his Tridents days, a showcase for the guitarist that amalgamated all his formative influences with cheeky snatches from well-known classical and jazz melodies into one delightful trick bag. Based in part on 'Guitar Boogie' by Chuck Berry, Beck later dismissed the instrumental as "a loony thing I came up with because we needed some filler material". Possibly true, but like 'The Nazz Are Blue', its impact was far-reaching at the time, guitarists on both sides of the Atlantic grappling with Beck's intricate runs in order to join the elite club that had actually mastered the tune. Full of staccato picking, false 'clock chime' harmonics, hammer-ons, pull offs and overbends, Beck paid homage to Les Paul, Buddy Guy, and in particular Cliff 'Cruisin' Gallup throughout 'Jeff's Boogie', quoting phrases and passages from their work but making the overall tune uniquely his own. "There was always that little bit of swing in there with The Yardbirds," said McCarty. "Back in school, I'd played in different jazz-type bands and Jeff liked that swing feel. If you listen to him on '... Boogie', he's got that wild jazz feel to his playing."

A fine album, *Roger The Engineer* reached number 20 in the UK charts when released in July 1966. The American version, named *Over Under Sideways Down* in order to monopolise on that single's US success, inexplicably dropped 'The Nazz Are Blue' and 'Rack My Mind' from its running order, though the US LP admittedly benefited from some novel remixes of certain tracks, with Beck providing a markedly different solo on 'Hot House Of Omagarashid'*. "We'd been playing some of the songs live before laying them down, such as 'What Do You Want', 'Jeff's Boogie' and a few others, so we knew they worked with an audience," said McCarty. "But on other tracks, we threw our ideas into the pot and went from there. I don't think anyone knew what we'd achieved then, but it seems to have stood the test of time. All in all, *Roger The Engineer* was a very democratic album."

Though Jeff Beck had secured his place as *the* pre-eminent English guitarist with *Roger The Engineer*, the strain of continuing illness and the

---

* Both mono and stereo versions of the LP are now available on a single CD.

role of "musical stuntman" within The Yardbirds was now taking a serious toll. Worse, the band were due back on the road for several UK dates before again heading to the US in the summer for another elongated tour. "Before that tour even started, Jeff had been really ill," McCarty said. "He was a nervous guy by nature, and now he was nearing exhaustion. And remember, they thought at one point he'd got meningitis. But Jeff, well, he didn't always express himself. He'd bottle it all up."

For Dreja, the combination of Beck's late entry into the group and the demands for increasingly novel ways in which to desecrate a guitar signal was gradually wearing him down. "Maybe Jeff considered himself something of an outsider, I don't know. We'd all known each other in the band for so long when he joined, he might have felt that. But you know, he always got on well with us. We were fond of each other. That said, I think we put him under some real pressure. We expected him to come up with these wonderful things and he always did. But even though we all knew he was a genius, to expect him to come up with miracles every time, it just wasn't fair."

According to Napier-Bell, Beck had to actually be coaxed back into the group around the time of *Roger The Engineer*, the manager tracking him down to his parents' South London home one afternoon for a genuine heart-to-heart. "I remember being shown up these stairs to this room at the back," he said. "I open the door, and Jeff's sitting there cross-legged, guitar in hand in the middle of this single unmade bed. Classic guitar hero pose, you might say. We spoke and he just wasn't happy, really grumpy, really moody. I think he felt a bit stranded, as if we were taking advantage of this great talent he had. But he did agree to come back."

For Beck, his rapid ascent into the rarefied atmosphere of pop stardom and the attendant pressures that came with it were starting to wear thin. "I had to keep delving into the bottom of my bag to see what I could come up with," he later said. "I was trying to impress the band with my playing all the time and I felt pretty unbalanced. I was 20 when I went from rags to riches... and it had started to mess me up."

Psychically and physically frail, feeling distant from his bandmates, isolated by his talent and worn down with the effort it took to harness it, Jeff was in a proverbial dark corner. It was time to phone a friend.

Chapter 7

The Devil Rides Out

Rumour has it that Jeff Beck actually drove himself to The Yardbirds' appearance at the Oxford May Ball on June 18, 1966. A prestige event held for students at the University that marked the end of their academic year, the May Ball was all black ties, formal dresses and heavy drinking. It was also quite the coup for The Yardbirds – a well-paid, highly respectable diversion from the more familiar sweat pits they had made their own in previous years. "The student committee had spent a lot of money on the May Ball," said Chris Dreja, "and there were some wonderful backstage amenities. Lots of food, lots of drink, and lots of time in between sets to indulge. It was going to be fun."

In the passenger seat of Jeff's ageing maroon Ford Zephyr Six sat Jimmy Page. Still the closest of friends, the two had even recorded together only a month before, a subject to be returned to in some detail in later pages. Though the conversation during their journey to Oxford went unrecorded, Beck was perhaps extolling the virtues of his latest purchase, a 1959 sunburst Gibson Les Paul, bought from Selmer's in London's Charing Cross Road for £170. Having already heard the searing yet thick "woman tone" Eric Clapton had unearthed from the same instrument and a Marshall combo on John Mayall's soon to be released *Bluesbreakers...* album, Jeff was eager to capture some of the Gibson's creamy sustain for himself. Jimmy Page may have made a mental note to buy a Les Paul of his own, though finding one might prove difficult as the guitar had been discontinued due to poor sales in 1960, a situation that would change drastically due to Clapton, Beck and Page's championing of the model in future years. On the other hand, Page was as likely to have been voicing his dissatisfaction with the increasing claustrophobia he felt doing endless sessions in darkened studios, while Beck bathed in the lights of the concert stage. Maybe they were just content to talk about the weather. Whatever the case or conversation, the night ahead was to prove eventful.

As soon as Keith Relf arrived at the May Ball with his fellow Yardbirds, he had but one mission in mind: to get uproariously drunk. "Yep," said Jim McCarty, "Keith was on one. The Hollies were also on the bill with us, and their singer Allan Clarke soon had this karate thing going on with Keith... daring him to have a go at these bits of chair and metal trays." Dreja saw first-hand the result of Relf's new-found interest in the martial arts. "He broke three fingers trying to smash up six trays and didn't even feel it until two days later." Though Relf made it through the band's first set more or less intact, his continued backstage drinking rendered him next to useless for The Yardbirds' second appearance of the night. "By the time he got on stage, we almost had to tie him to the mike. He was absolutely wrecked," said McCarty. "He forgot the lyrics, didn't really seem to know where he was and then started taking the piss out of all these Hoorah Henrys, blowing raspberries, that sort of stuff." With their singer well and truly "off with the fairies", The Yardbirds' set became one extended guitar solo, an amused Jeff Beck filling in the spaces where Relf should have been singing. For Jimmy Page, this was all marvellous stuff. "Keith was rolling around, grappling with the mike, blowing harmonica in all the wrong places, singing nonsense words," Page later told *Mojo*. "But it was great, just fantastically suitable for the occasion."

Unfortunately, Paul Samwell-Smith didn't see it that way. Incandescent with rage at Relf's behaviour, the bassist started shouting at him from the moment The Yardbirds left the stage: "It didn't sit well with Paul," said Dreja. "A lovely man, but a square peg in a round hole in the world of rock'n'roll, a world he didn't think was particularly civilised. Paul felt it was important to act stiff in front of all these academic types, so in his mind Keith let him down." For Jim McCarty, Samwell-Smith's reaction to Keith's antics was more connected to his upbringing: "Paul was such a snob, he liked all these people. I mean they'd changed their family name to 'Samwell-Smith' because his mother didn't want to be called (plain) Mrs. Smith!"

As the students slowly left the hall "to go dancing into the village doing the bloody conga", things reached boiling point backstage with Samwell-Smith handing in his resignation. "Paul was absolutely furious," said Dreja, "and just left the band on the spot." Embarrassed on behalf of Page, who was watching the drama unfold from the wings, Beck started to apologise to his friend. Yet Jimmy was having none of it. "I went backstage and there was a huge argument going on with Paul leaving the group. But I thought it was brilliant... this marvellous, anarchistic night. I just said 'I'll play bass if you like'." Though the band had potentially just lost their friend, musical director and producer, Chris Dreja couldn't help but see the funny side of it all: "What a wonderful gig for Jimmy to come to. And it was wonderful. Like Johnny Rotten meeting the Queen. Pure theatre, pure punk. It didn't surprise me at all when Jimmy put his hand up and said 'I want a piece of this'."

In reality, the events of the May Ball were more final straw than singular disaster for Paul Samwell-Smith. "To be honest, that night was the tip of the iceberg for Paul," said McCarty. "He was tired, fed up with the touring, and just didn't want to keep going." Simon Napier-Bell also confirmed Paul's growing dissatisfaction with his role in the band: "Paul was getting drunk at gigs, actually more than Keith if truth be told. I remember walking with him in Paris and he said to me, 'I really can't tell you how much I hate touring. I genuinely hate it.' So the writing was on the wall. When I heard about his decision to leave the next morning, I said, 'OK'. But looking back, I really fucked up because Paul was at the heart of it. He was a really good overseer – he made The Yardbirds a team."

As the smoke cleared, Beck spoke with Page to see if his offer to join the band on bass guitar still stood. The song remained the same. "I was just so brassed off at the studios at that point," said Jimmy, "and going along to [gigs at] The Marquee and Eel Pie, I could see it was all happening. I wanted in." It was a decision that didn't thrill the band's manager. "I knew Jimmy from my days organising sessions," said Simon. "He was a really good guitarist, but even though I didn't know him character wise, my instinct said, 'No'. I just couldn't see it from an 'ego' point of view. It meant Jeff would have an equal in the group with him. But they all kept saying, 'No, no, no, he's just going to play bass.' Well, that wasn't really going to happen, was it?"

For Jeff Beck, Jimmy Page joining The Yardbirds was in his own words "a dream come true". Feeling sometimes lost among 'the old boys' network', having Page in the ranks potentially consolidated his position and crucially gave him an ally both in the studio and on the road. Additionally, with Jimmy seemingly happy to play bass guitar, any potential rivalries between the two would be circumvented. "Well, when Paul Samwell-Smith wanted to play at producers and didn't want to go on the road any more, calling on Jimmy made real sense," he later said. Just three days after the May Ball debacle, Page made his first official appearance with The Yardbirds at The Marquee. "Actually, he was very good," Beck recalled, "with this real, thrashing sound." To celebrate Jimmy joining the group, Jeff soon presented him with his own 1959 Fender Telecaster, the words 'Jeffman' sprayed on the back. A valuable piece of kit, Page made it his own, painting it in psychedelic colours and equipping it with a sliver scratch plate so it might catch the light onstage. The Telecaster would soon become Jimmy's main workhorse, a guitar that carried him through The Yardbirds and far beyond. Given future events, Beck might have been better served buying him a Fender Precision bass.

In reality, Jimmy Page had come to The Yardbirds at a curious point in their career. Sensing various niggles within the ranks, Simon Napier-Bell had reactivated one of Giorgio Gomelsky's ideas, and planned for the group to cut a raft of solo singles. As mentioned, Beck had already taken to the idea admirably well, drafting Page and several other well-known musicians into Olympic Studios a month before the May Ball to record a promising instrumental for potential release. But the only song to actually see the light of day at the time was Keith Relf's 'Mr. Zero', a fine Jacques Brel/Scott Walker pastiche that deserved much better than its disappointing placing at number 50 in the UK charts. For Beck, Relf might have benefited more from visiting an alcohol treatment centre than making a play for solo stardom. "It'd be 12 noon, and we'd be on the tour bus," Jeff told *Uncut*. "[Then] you'd hear a fizz as Keith opened a can of beer. And then, five minutes later, another one. And another. I think he needed hands-on help at the time, but no one gave it to him." Worse still, drinking seemed to bring out a maudlin streak in Relf that unsettled Beck: "I think he was a manic depressive. He wanted to kill everybody. He used to read *Guns And Ammo* to work out how to commit the perfect murder. No, really, he was just cynical about everything."

According to Simon Napier-Bell, Relf's behaviour may have been the result of family ties linked to the group: "Keith was always an enigma. His dad was tour-managing the band, and to be honest, you really don't want relatives around. Tour managers are extremely influential and I think his dad subdued Keith in many ways. A lot of Keith's sullen drinking might have been down to suppression. We all wanted him to come out of himself, because I think there was much more to him that we ever saw. He could have been much bigger, much better, but then again, I might be wrong. It's back to that enigma thing."

Or perhaps Relf realised that during the majority of his tenure as front man of The Yardbirds, he had in fact been sidelined by a number of superb lead guitarists. "Well, there might be truth in that," Jeff once said. "After a while, it became apparent to me that there were more people on my side of the stage than in front of Keith." Though he was a newcomer to proceedings at the time, Page echoed Beck's sentiments: "I think Keith did have a thing about being overshadowed by Jeff, which really was nonsense." Chris Dreja, however, had his doubts, pointing to Relf's pragmatic approach to any such imbalances within the quintet. "I think Relf was always aware we were a band with the spotlight firmly placed on the lead guitar," he said. "And he was pretty much OK with that. He knew what his strengths were and exactly how to use them. Keith was an extremely sensitive man who wrote great lyrics, but like many alcoholics, he had a schizophrenic aspect to him. But please don't forget, Keith's role in The Yardbirds was huge."

An element of genuine disquiet hung heavily over The Yardbirds' next single, 'Happenings Ten Years Time Ago', a song that began life at Keith Relf's flat during an impromptu writing session between the singer and Jim McCarty, before developing into something altogether more quixotic in the studio: "Keith and I got the idea together around at his place, then it was recorded in two distinct sessions." Though Jimmy Page was covering bass live, he probably played guitar on the track with a promising young session man/arranger named John Paul Jones taking on four-string duties. "Jonesy played bass on it," continued McCarty, "though I can't actually remember Jimmy cutting his part. Jeff came in later to add his bit, which was the icing on the cake."

A strange, mesmeric tune with Beck, Page and Jones' guitars sounding as if they were rapidly falling down a set of stairs as mock explosions and car crashes sounded around them, the sense of uneasiness in 'Happenings Ten Years Time Ago' was compounded by Relf's déjà vu-like lyric: "It seems to me I've been here before, the sounds I heard, and the sights I saw, was it real, was it in my dreams, I need to know what it all means…" If The Yardbirds had invented or at least heavily contributed to the birth of psychedelic music in their past, they had come to define it with 'Happenings…'

In addition to providing some vicious solo flights, Beck also contributed a spoken word interlude during the song's middle eight, his mocking tones aping several sleazy questions asked by a doctor of sexually transmitted diseases when a Yardbird or two reportedly visited his West London clinic in the mid-sixties: 'Pop group, are you?', 'Why you all got long hair?' 'Bet you're pulling the crumpet, aren't you?'

"I think 'Happenings…' reflected the confusion of the sixties," Beck later said, "It's quite a chaotic record." And one far too chaotic for their fans, who unlike previous efforts largely avoided buying it, the single stalling at a dismal number 43 in the UK and 30 in the US when released in October, 1966. "'Happenings Ten Years Time Ago' was so ahead of its time," said Chris Dreja. "Perhaps not appreciated then, but much loved now. Funny, isn't it? There we were forging ahead, and sometimes the audience, our own fans, didn't even get it." For their manager, Simon Napier-Bell, who also produced the session, its chart failure was entirely expected. "It was all a bit off," he said. "I think it was the first single recorded with a click track. Clem Cattini played the original drums, which I believe Jim replaced. But Jeff arrived at the session without his bloody guitar. I said to him, 'Where is it?' and he replied, 'Oh I've forgotten it. Sorry about that.' I mean, how can the lead guitarist turn up without his bloody guitar? Anyway, we found him one. I know 'Happenings...' is now seen as a real ground-breaker, but to be honest, I've always thought it was a bit stiff sounding."

To both placate Beck's continued gruffness around the band and also take advantage of his ever-growing popularity with audiences, the guitarist was asked to provide lead vocals on the B-side to 'Happenings...', a sly re-reading of Chuck Berry's 'No Particular Place To Go' named 'Psycho Daisies'. Essentially a Yardbirds-eye view of the charms of America, there was no mistaking from the lyrics where Jeff Beck most liked to visit while in The States: "New Orleans is the home of the blues," he howled, "But California's my home with Mary Hughes..." For Dreja, 'Psycho Daisies' remains one of the group's lesser-known gems: "There's a great sense of humour on that one, though I think people sometimes missed that funny, satirical side we had." As with 'Happenings...', Jimmy Page also reportedly contributed some guitar lines to 'Psycho Daisies', though the squealing solo flights that punctuate the track are surely all Jeff's work.

Beck's next chance to fall into the tanned arms of Mary Hughes was unavoidably delayed at the end of July, 1966 when he fell victim to another bout of tonsillitis, putting off The Yardbirds' third trip to the US by a week. When the band finally arrived in Minneapolis on August 4, the still ragged guitarist was committed to a punishing tour schedule due to end exactly one month later in Honolulu. "I was shattered before I even got on the plane," he later confirmed. As ever, The Yardbirds' physical appearance set them apart from the crowd, causing Beck some justifiable paranoia at the band found itself booked to perform at a number of state fairs throughout the Bible belt. "We always used to wear our stage gear in the street and there was an incident every day," he later told *Uncut*. "We were threatened with knives, guns, you name it. Serious nutters in the backwoods that wanted us dead. I had an armed guard outside my room. I'd tell Jim 'Give me two knocks if they give you any trouble'. There was a guy out in the woods with a gun pointed at our room. All kinds of weird stories..."

As Chris Dreja confirmed, Beck's increasing vigilance was not the result of recurrent illness or hallucination. For the group, the threat of potential violence in the US was ever present on their collective radar: "America was deep in the shit of the Vietnam War then. We were touring the US during a period when aluminium coffins were coming out of the back of the plane at the same time as our luggage, and servicemen were everywhere. Of course, they didn't really get us. While it might have appeared everyone was hip, 90% of the country was very... American. Bible belt, military, crew-cut types or hard-edged businessmen. Don't imagine the whole country was about 'loving the music'. So yes, they gave us a bit of a hard time. In fact, I was always surprised we got back in one piece. Let's be clear, though. It wasn't just America. You were as likely to be beaten up by the local boys in Dumfries or John O'Groats as in Texas. So we developed this marvellous ability to befriend local people, who almost ended up becoming our bodyguards. Know your enemy!"*

Afraid of standing too long in front of a hotel room window, and probably too tired to even fight his corner if trouble came knocking, something had to give – which in Jeff Beck's case, proved to be his guitar amplifiers. "By then, we were pioneers of 'the gruelling schedule'," said Jim McCarty. "Endless nights, endless touring, we were knackered all the time, and it took its toll on your nerves, including Jeff's, who was a very wound up and sick guy at that point. So, if he didn't get his sound right, he'd just kick the amps offstage." For Beck, amp smashing was somehow akin to blessed relief. "I only really got angry on stage if the amp had blown up, my guitar was out of tune or Keith was coughing and spluttering," he told journalist Steven Rosen. "He used to have this respirator [for his asthma],

---

* This philosophy didn't always work. When Page and Beck later wore identical coats festooned with German Iron Crosses at a gig in Scotland, they were spat upon by the audience.

and you'd sometimes hear this 'Ssshhist, ssshhist, ssshhist' with this respiratory thing in the middle of a blues solo! Oh Christ, I mean there's nothing more frustrating than going onstage with so many things to say, and so many things on your mind... and there's only one way out, break that guitar. But it's almost impossible to break it, unless you swing them around full blast. So I used to give it angry little jabs at the speaker, and if it completely went up in a cloud of smoke I was happy. If it just stayed there stubbornly, or it wouldn't move, or made crackling noises, then I'd give it some more stick."

Beck's new-found love for the wilful destruction of his back line drove his manager to distraction. "Because all the airlines were on strike we had to do the tour on a charter plane," said Napier-Bell. "So when Jeff smashed up his amp, he was left with nothing. I was phoning all over the place trying to find the right one. And it was very difficult, with suppliers refusing to provide Voxs or new Marshalls, which he'd gotten into by then. But there were only about 20 Marshalls in the States at that time. The band were saying, 'Well, we could use something else', but Jimmy Page was really testing me. He said, 'No it absolutely has to be the right amp. Simon's our manager, it's up to him to sort it out.' Well, I finally found the right amp, but the only way to get it to the next gig was to charter a plane. I mean, this was ridiculous. Chartering a plane was going to cost five times as much as buying a new amp. But I did it. Then, of course, Jeff broke it again. And again."

And again. Becoming progressively more irritated by the limits of technology, Beck was now taking amp punishment to a whole new level as he crossed the US. "The electronic equipment just wasn't up to the sounds I had in my head," he said. "When we got to America, everything I'd hoped for got washed down the drain in technological shortcomings. You'd get to a gig and find the PA was nonexistent, and I felt we'd be better off in the small clubs in London. So, I'd just fly into rages and tantrums, purposely play the wrong notes and bend strings in complete contempt of the situation. But that [ended up] aiding and abetting my whole guitar style."

The whole thing threatened to get seriously out of hand during a performance at a Phoenix nightclub, remembered in three markedly different ways by those both on and offstage. "It was an incredibly hot gig and we were on the first floor, with a window just by the stage," said Jim McCarty. "Anyway, we'd got hold of these... Jordan amps I think, but remember, I'm just the drummer. Simon might have got a deal on renting them and I gather they were pretty crap. Of course, Jeff didn't take to them and the next thing you know, the amp's gone out the bloody window. Thank God there was nobody below."

According to Napier-Bell, the amp in question was probably a Marshall and Jeff didn't care for it at all. "Actually, I think we were on the second floor when he slung it out the window. There were people and cars below. It was lucky he didn't kill someone."

Beck's side of the story is again somewhat different, though death from above was never a real consideration for the population of Phoenix. "I just went crazy... smashed the amp, pushed it over and the top went through the window. It was dangling outside, swinging about. The thing that saved someone's life down below was that it had a locking cannon plug."

Unfortunately, even the threat of being hung for murder in the Southern States didn't stop Beck. "Of course it didn't stop him," his manager said. "The next night he just did it again. Every bloody night, he was smashing amps and I was in the hotel room afterwards phoning around, trying to find him another one. Obviously, the tour didn't make much of a profit because all I was doing was buying amps and chartering planes to put them on."

But for Jeff, his bad moods had now taken on the aspect of performance art. "I'd worked the whole act so that we were bringing in bits of destruction to illustrate a point. It was like an action painting... we all sort of threw our guitars at it." Chris Dreja, standing stage right and no doubt trying to avoid the carnage several feet away, was less convinced by Beck's explanation. "Jeff is prone to mood swings, and full of testosterone on stage. He didn't smash anything up as part of 'an act'. He just smashed up amps because they were pissing him off."

As Napier-Bell manned the phones in a frantic effort to replace Jeff's back line, the tour progressed to the Eel Pie-like setting of Catalina Island, where The Yardbirds played to a packed house at the Casino Ballroom on August 23. "They played a fantastic gig that night," he remembered. "It was one of the true highlights of my life watching Jeff play this blues solo. Really, it was just one of the greatest things I ever saw. He played for a long time, maybe five minutes, but it was right up there with BB King. Perhaps it was his anger or angst in the playing that night... perhaps it was the fact he was ill. I really don't know. But such emotions often bring out the very best in musicians. What I know for sure is that I'll never forget it."

Two nights later, Beck again collapsed, his throat now completely shot with infection, his body just about ready to give up. As Jeff sought treatment, The Yardbirds took to the stage of San Francisco's Carousel Ballroom with Jimmy Page on lead guitar. "The show has to go on," reasoned Chris Dreja. "Jimmy was wonderfully professional at that point. He'd come from a background where if you were five minutes late, you were fined. He understood the finer points of contracts, music publishing and the mechanics of the music industry were already under his belt. He was also very fresh, whereas we had been touring for years and he just stepped up to the plate."

For Dreja, his own switch to bass guitar – though bittersweet – was wholly pragmatic. "Switching things around was the obvious thing to do at that point. As I said, the show had to go on. And for me, it was a case of 'They've given me the bass guitar. I can play these huge deep notes. Bloody wonderful'."

Justly nervous, Page nevertheless rose to the occasion. "[Jeff] simply couldn't make it so I took over lead that night," [he] confirmed. "Yes, it was really nerve-racking, because this [was the] height of The Yardbirds' concert reputation and I was [not quite] ready to roar off on lead guitar. But it went all right, and after that night, we stayed that way. When Jeff recovered, it was two lead guitars from then on."

Following his release from hospital, Beck stayed with Mary Hughes for a few days before returning to the UK and the prospect of a modified Yardbirds line-up. Having provided some righteous-sounding noises on 'Happenings Ten Years Time Ago'/'Psycho Daisies' and carried the burden of the band's remaining US dates, it was obvious to all concerned that Jimmy Page should retain his lead guitar status. Equally, he, Beck and the group had already discussed the possibility of a dual six-string attack in the recent past, though the circumstances of the Carousel Ballroom "had accelerated things a bit". For Jeff, Page's move had its advantages.

He would retain his role and, as evidenced, have a good friend working alongside him – someone perhaps who could take some of the burden from his weary shoulders: "I guess I always knew it'd work out that Jimmy would take that role," Beck said later. "I mean, at the time, my worry was that people weren't ready for one lead guitarist, let alone two. But then, it might be easy to blend the guitars together because The Yardbirds had a strict musical policy and Jimmy and I got off on the same things." It was time to make the partnership work.

To that end, Beck and Page convened at the latter's Thames-moored Victorian boathouse in an effort to blend their distinctive styles together. The two started by practising Freddie King solos in unison and then progressed to exploring dual harmony lines. When this was accomplished to their satisfaction, they turned their attentions to The Yardbirds' own material, picking their way through the likes of 'I'm A Man', 'Rack My Mind', 'Shapes Of Things' and '... Better Man Than I'. Despite their different approaches – Page sticking more closely to the demands of the material while Beck fluttered around the melody – a mutual understanding was found. "Yeah," Jimmy said, "it was good. It worked well. We could harness the collective energy. Well, at least for a time..."

The first test of The Yardbirds' new guitar team came on September 23, 1966 at the Royal Albert Hall where the band began supporting The Rolling Stones on a 12-date tour of the UK. Also on the bill that night were the crazy/beautiful R&B duo of Ike & Tina Turner, whose life-affirming 'River Deep, Mountain High' had recently soared to number three in the British charts. As Ike could rightly claim some ownership to birthing rock'n'roll with his piano/guitar arrangement for 'Rocket 88' – a distorted jump blues recorded by Jackie Brenston & His Delta Cats at Sun Studios in 1951 that actually predated the sound of Chuck Berry and Elvis Presley by some four years – he might have proved a difficult audience to impress. But on hearing Jeff Beck warming up backstage, Ike told his wife, Tina, "Man, these guys can play over here." Tina herself also made a mental note of Beck's keen guitar skills, putting him to fine use on two of her own songs some 18 years later.

In Jeff's mind, The Yardbirds' set at the Royal Albert Hall was an unqualified success, the Stones beaten into submission by a combination of canny showmanship, dual guitar sorcery and sheer bloody volume, an opinion seconded by Simon Napier-Bell. "Beck and Page played all Jeff's original solos in unison and the crowd just loved it. It was amazing to watch, given that there were no proper mixing desks in those days." Unfortunately, *New Musical Express* begged to differ, dismissing the band as distinctly average and Jeff as little more than a guitar gymnast. Though he would soon be voted 'Best Lead Guitarist of 1966' in *Beat Instrumental*, the review sat badly with Beck. As a consequence, Jeff's attitude soured towards the music press in general for several years, his already measured approach to journalistic enquiry descending into a series of clipped responses, quips, scowls, vacant stares and downright obfuscation.

As the tour progressed so did Beck's difficulties, his onstage pairing with Jimmy Page providing audiences with either agony or ecstasy depending on the night. "It was incredibly hairy when we became a two-guitar line-up," reasoned McCarty. "They just started competing with each other. Jeff had his style – he'd never play the same thing twice – while Jimmy was an experienced session musician who was used to playing what people wanted, playing the right part. For me, it was nerve-racking. Sometimes, it was marvellous, these two guitars playing in perfect unison. Other times, it could be all over the place. I'd always be thinking 'God, how's it going to be tonight?'"

Chris Dreja, who was now trying desperately to anchor the chaos in front of him alongside McCarty, felt the same about Jeff and Jimmy's two-guitar onslaught: "Oh, we'd definitely entered the age of the gunslinger. More missed gigs, more smashed amps and pure dynamite onstage – good and bad. Things were always on edge. And I think if we're honest, people like bands who are on the edge. Jeff might have been quiet behind the scenes, but under the lights, he was king. Nobody had ever got in his space. I tried to enhance everything he did as best as I could, because that was my role. But when Jimmy came along, well... Jeff knew how good Jimmy was. It was like someone had stepped into his underpants."

Of course, Page knew his joining the band might have an impact, though even he was unprepared for Beck's endless deviations from their agreed approach. "Well, I was doing what I was supposed to while something totally different would be coming from Jeff," he later told *Guitar Player*. "That was all right for improvisation, but there were other parts where it just didn't work. Jeff had discipline occasionally, in that when he's on, he's probably the best there is. But at the time, he had no respect for audiences. When I joined, he supposedly wasn't going to walk off any more. Well..."

Accentuating the positive, on those nights that Beck and Page's styles coalesced and egos were set aside, there were moments of genuine beauty to be had: guitar notes dovetailing together into space, solo flights of breathtaking complexity and the sheer exhilaration of hearing two of the world's best players mutate 12-bar blues into something never heard before. But, by his own admission, these moments were often at the mercy of Jeff's moods. "To be honest, I was frustrated with the business and not wanting to play in front of people, but having to do it," Beck later told *Guitar Classics*. "That led to an unpredictable vibe onstage. I was acting like a naughty boy, really."

For manager Simon Napier-Bell, by bringing Jimmy Page into The Yardbirds Jeff had actually destabilised his own role within the group, the end result a volatile and impassable conclusion. "They were great friends, but struggling," he said. "Jeff couldn't help but be very resentful of Jimmy's new role in the band. These were Jeff's solos, but Jimmy was getting the applause on them. And of course, Jimmy had no particular feeling of triumph, because he was playing Jeff's stuff. Most creativity comes from conflict, not resolution, and the best music often comes from war. But this was a no-win situation." Though such a realisation must have hurt at the time, Beck admitted his folly years later in an interview with the BBC. "I didn't like my territory being encroached upon," he said. "I wanted to *be it*. Of course, [by bringing in Jimmy] little did I know I was doing myself out of half of a job..."

Jeff last real hurrah with The Yardbirds came at the conclusion of the band's support slot to The Rolling Stones, when film director Michelangelo Antonioni inadvertently committed the only real footage of the Beck/Page guitar line-up to celluloid. Following the European successes of *L'eclisse* and *Il Deserto Rosso,* Antonioni had flown to the UK during the summer of 1966 to begin production on his English-language movie debut, a "metaphysical murder mystery" set in 'Swinging London' entitled *Blow-Up*. The plot, such as it was, required a trendy photographer (played by David Hemmings) to look simultaneously cool and befuddled, sleep with supermodels and then struggle hopelessly in trying to establish a relationship between subjectivism and consensus reality. There was also a murder in there somewhere. As part of his ludicrous quest, Hemmings' character, Thomas, had to visit a typical London nightclub where a suitably rocking band happily destroyed their instruments before an oddly detached audience. Given that The Who's Pete Townshend was a leading proponent of such activities at the time, Antonioni approached the band's irascible manager, Kit Lambert, with a view to them starring in his film.

Thanks to the machinations of Simon Napier-Bell, however, things went badly between Lambert and Antonioni. "Kit told me over dinner that Antonioni was coming into town to make this great art film called *Blow-Up* with David Hemmings. Well, I knew this already because of my connections in the film business. Anyway, Antonioni wanted The Who to star in it because they had a reputation as great amp smashers and he loved all that destruction. I was incredibly jealous, of course. So, when Kit asked me what sort of money he should ask for, I said 'A minimum of £10,000 and don't forget to get absolute control of the film's final edit'. I knew he wouldn't get it. Also, Kit was very pompous when it came to requesting things. He'd never give way. So he did exactly what I told him, went in guns blazing. He came down slightly on the money, I seem to remember, but wouldn't budge on the edit – banging the table, demanding complete control. So Antonioni just threw him out, which I was hoping might happen." After his stand-off with Lambert, Antonioni considered several other groups, including The Velvet Underground and The In Crowd. But visa problems and scheduling conflicts scuppered the chances of both acts, allowing Napier-Bell to step into the fray and finally put Jeff's destructive impulses to sound financial use: "I called Antonioni and said 'The Yardbirds are much better at smashing equipment than The Who ever was'. And like that, though he hadn't heard of the band, we were in."

The Yardbirds' fleeting brush with cinematic fame was, by all accounts, as barking mad as the plot of *Blow-Up* itself. "Well, it was frankly odd," said Jim McCarty. "For three minutes of screen time, we had to turn up for at least five days. We were staying in a hotel in Knightsbridge and the band was picked up every morning by a driver who then took us to Elstree Studios, near Borehamwood." The film set, too, was a surprise for all. "It had been made to look exactly like our old haunting ground, the Ricky Tick in Windsor," continued Jim, "which again was frankly baffling." For Jimmy Page, who had never visited the Ricky Tick, creating a club from the ground up for the purposes of a film only added to his overall air of bewilderment: "I'd never been there but the other lads said it was just identical to the Ricky, brick for brick, cobweb for cobweb." Things became even more perplexing when they enquired what *Blow-Up* was actually about. "Nobody in the crew seemed to know what it was all about when we asked them," Page told author John Tobler. "It sounds ridiculous, but [that's] absolutely true."

Antonioni's appearance on set was brief. Greeting the band, he explained in broken English that the scene required them to perform in front of a cast of extras standing emotionless before them. During the performance, one of their number – namely Jeff Beck – should become progressively more irritated with his malfunctioning amplifier before flying into a rage and smashing his guitar. "Typecasting then," laughed Chris Dreja. But when the director suggested that Beck actually destroy his own Les Paul, he was given short shrift: "No fucking way," being Jeff's alleged response. To placate matters, Antonioni arranged for a huge box of £25 Hofner guitars to be delivered to Elstree, which Beck could then mutilate to his heart's content. "Those guitars were just destined to be smashed," Jeff later said. The group hardly saw the filmmaker again.

The Yardbirds were originally set to play 'Smokestack Lightning' for *Blow-Up*, but the number was considered too slow for Antonioni's purposes. Instead, the band's version of 'Train Kept A Rollin' – re-christened 'Stroll On' for copyright purposes – was used. During the course of filming, Beck got through the box of Hofners, the company's representative gleefully handing over guitar after guitar for Jeff to turn into matchwood. "After four days of being on set, told where to stand, do this, do that, and then some... girl sponging my nose with make-up, I'd have broken the guitar even if it wasn't in the script." Of equal irritation was performing his auto-destruct sequence to a cast of automatons: "The extras just stood there, gazing at us," McCarty recalled. "I guess Antonioni wanted them to look mesmerised. Or just drugged out of their heads. Anyway, Jeff hated the whole bloody thing, apart from smashing the guitars, obviously."

The Yardbirds' appearance in *Blow-Up* remains to this day a mouth-watering taste of what might have been if Jeff Beck had been able to resolve his issues with the band and Jimmy Page. Though the recording of 'Stroll On' itself is something of a mess, with Jeff's lunatic solos flying everywhere in the mix while Jimmy's guitar remains curiously inaudible, the sight of the two onstage together still has the power to shake those of a certain age even now. And if Beck's almost quaint attempts to dismantle his guitar and Vox AC30 amp in a display of bad-tempered pith has lost something in the face of latter day stage-wreckers such as Jesus And The Mary Chain and Rammstein, it matters little. One only has to look at those tight trousers to thoroughly confirm he was enjoying his moment in the sun: "I had a fucking hard on, man!" he laughed. "I took my mother to the film and there you were... this horrible, sinister thing hanging down the side of the screen."

A delightful screen curio in the midst of an otherwise baffling movie, the band's cameo in *Blow-Up* netted them some £3,000 for just five days' work. "That was probably the best thing Simon pulled off for us," said Chris Dreja.

As the others sensibly banked the money, Beck spent his share on a 1963 Stingray Corvette, the very same model he had fallen in love with as a teenager and hired to drive Mary Hughes through the Hollywood Hills. "I used to have a picture of it on my wall," he later said. "It was the most beautiful thing I'd ever seen." A 1932 black Ford T-bucket with a V8 engine would follow in 1968, Jeff literally restoring the car from a shell to its former glory. It wouldn't be the last time he'd dabble in such restoration.

With *Blow-Up* behind them, The Yardbirds' next move was a return to the States on October 29, 1966, where they joined *American Bandstand* host Dick Clark's 'Caravan of Stars' tour, a supposedly glitzy affair bringing young musical talent to the very doorsteps of US teenagers. In reality, 'The Caravan of Stars' was a 33-date jaunt across America lasting 27 days and crossing 16 states. SAS operatives had cracked under less pressure. "Yeah, 33 dates, I think, and of those, 25 were doubles [two shows in one night]," said Jimmy Page. "You'd think a double would be played in the same town, but it wasn't – it was two different towns. The show was in two halves. When the first half finished, and there was an interval... the [performers] would get on the coach driving to the next venue, while the second half carried on. Then, they in turn carried on to the next place, where the others had [by then] finished."

Worse still, travelling conditions for the bands on board were appalling. "'Caravan of Stars'? More like the 'Caravan of Hell'," said Dreja. "I think Simon thought he was doing us a favour by keeping us working. But there were no luxury, cocktails-in-the-side-pocket super-liner buses then, I'm afraid. These were more like second-hand Greyhound buses with all the seats still installed. And we'd be sitting there, these supposed 'stars', who were then wheeled out to do two or three shows a fucking night, before getting back on the bus and off again a few hundred miles away for the next one. We were human beings stuck in a rat hole. It was so undignified, it was a joke. Actually, it was a bit like being sectioned. You don't know why you're there – because you're actually sane – and yet there you are. Clever man though, Dick Clark. You'd have to give him that."

Even their fellow prisoners could provide little relief. "It was absolutely dreadful," confirmed McCarty. "The other acts had little or nothing in common with us. Sam The Sham & His Pharaohs. Brian Hyland. I mean, they were just so different, though Sam had his moments. Anyway, when they let us off the bus, we'd go onstage and they'd shout 'Turn the guitars down!' Jimmy was getting through it because he was a professional. Chris and I stood up to it because we were creating humour from all sorts. Keith was drinking his way along. But Jeff..."

Jeff Beck's 20-month tenure with The Yardbirds came to an impenetrable impasse a few dates into the 'Caravan of Stars' tour, when after a cruelly hot night in Texas playing to a room of teeny-boppers, he exploded backstage: "We finished the gig, came offstage and Jeff completely lost it," said McCarty. "He just smashed up his guitar – this Les Paul, just a beautiful guitar – into bits. Then, according to Jimmy, Jeff walked up to him a bit later and said 'Well, you could have stopped me doing that.' There was just no way we could have done anything – he'd gone fucking crazy." Burnt up, bummed out, racked by illness and crushed by exhaustion, Beck had finally hit the wall. "Stuffed... like an animal in a bus with 50 other people driving 600 miles [to] play two numbers," he later told *Mojo*. "It was like 'Come out, here's a few biscuits, go and play'. That throws an incredible magnifying glass on your life. So I had a freak out and left the band." For those witnessing Jeff's behaviour at the time, it might have appeared that the guitarist had a complete breakdown. Yet, according to Chris Dreja, additional factors may well have been at play: "I suppose he had a quasi-mental breakdown although there was Mary to factor in. In short, he got hooked on her and, as a result, got a bit pissed off having to do the actual job."

Realistically, Jeff Beck's decision to quit The Yardbirds was a combination of several factors, with stress, money (or the lack of it), illness, ego, internecine politics, creative torpor and love all playing a part. "I think I did have a breakdown," he said. "I just couldn't handle it. I saw the end of the line, but [also] couldn't see any creativity going on in The Yardbirds. I was putting everything I had into it and the songs weren't coming. I didn't write, all I did was wait for them to come up with this threadbare stuff and try and make something of it – for which I hardly saw any money. Also, Keith was drinking a lot. It was just difficult to cope with the success. In a way, I loved it, but Keith just hated human beings sometimes, so he wasn't easy to have around. I was tired of touring and on my last legs, really. Twenty two years old and quite fucked up." Beck was also smitten with Mary Hughes. "My logic was simple. Why go through shit when I could have a wonderful time with her?"

As Beck departed Corpus Christi Airport on October 31 for California, where he might find some peace with Hughes, The Yardbirds' manager was already picking up the pieces back in Texas – albeit with comedic results. "Jeff just walked out the door and disappeared into the night. That was the end of it. I had to go on television the next day to announce why the gig was cancelled. Rather kindly, the band gave me an exploding cigar – unbeknownst to me, of course. Keith and Jim had gone out earlier to get it and there I am on TV, sucking on this cigar, explaining away what's wrong when the fucking thing blew up in my face." With some 30 dates left on their collective contract with Dick Clark the decision was made to press on, the ever reliable Jimmy Page now covering all guitar parts for the remainder of the tour. "Jimmy was always a real pro, whereas Jeff was a man of emotion," Chris Dreja told *Guitar World*. "I think Jeff always found it harder than Jimmy because he was prone to playing according to... how he felt, whereas Jimmy's idea was always, 'We're professional entertainers'." Again, the show had to go on.

Eventually, The Yardbirds caught up with Jeff Beck in Los Angeles, where conversations reportedly took place as to whether he might return to the band. Other sources claim that Beck was officially sacked at this time. Simon Napier-Bell remains adamant that the latter course of action did not take place. "Listen, he wasn't pushed out by me. Jeff Beck was the best thing about The Yardbirds. I never thought of Jimmy as equal to Jeff, in terms of feeling. Jimmy was a technician. Clapton, too. But I never heard either of them play blues like I heard Jeff play blues. I know he eventually moved on in his playing, but he was always the one with that essential blues feeling, that pure expressiveness."

Despite a complete lack of credible evidence, rumours have also occasionally surfaced that the band themselves – and Jimmy Page in particular – might have engineered Beck's departure, the guitarist's penchant for emotional histrionics finally getting the better of them. Again, any such unpleasantness was firmly denied. "Jimmy had an eye on the future for sure," reasoned Dreja, "and there was friction there even though they were great friends. But it was more like a ménage à trois that went wrong. Jeff, Jimmy, but only one guitar. It just wasn't going to work." Napier-Bell echoed Dreja's sentiments, acknowledging that while Page may have had designs concerning the band's future direction, he was unlikely to have ever betrayed his friend to gain complete control. "Jimmy and Chris got on very well on an intellectual level. They were like great planners. Jeff, on the other hand, wasn't that interested in talking. He just wanted to play or be by himself. If there were ever any [rumours] in that area, it was probably about Jimmy and what happened next. I think he had it in mind by then that he was going to take over The Yardbirds. But beyond the odd squabble... Jeff didn't fight with Jimmy, ask to go, or even talk about going. He just went."

Following Beck's exit, The Yardbirds shifted yet again, with a dual announcement to the press on November 30 confirming Beck's departure on the grounds of ill health and Page's promotion to sole lead guitarist. Behind the scenes, it was also all change on the managerial front. "The band were looking at the possibility of exploring a much more commercial direction," explained Napier-Bell. "So I took them to the pop producer Mickie Most and said, 'Do you want to take them on?' Mickie said, 'OK,' but his 'associate' Peter Grant then said, 'I'll manage them'. I said, 'Fine. I'll have Jeff and you have The Yardbirds'. I thought at the time I made the right choice, certainly at that time. I found Jimmy very narky and difficult. He was just so awkward to deal with." For Page, the feeling was mutual: "Bloody right. We did four weeks with The Rolling Stones and then an American tour and all we got was £112 each!"

With Mickie Most and Peter Grant now acting as producer and manager respectively (again, we shall return to both parties in some detail in due course), The Yardbirds soldiered on for another 19 months, sadly with ever diminishing returns. Despite the odd inspired single ('Little Games'), a lost classic ('Think About It') and an increasingly theatrical live show that saw Page taking a violin bow to his guitar in an effort to expand The Yardbirds' gift for experimental textures ('Dazed And Confused'), they eventually called it a day on July 7, 1968 after an underwhelming gig at Luton College. "If we had taken time off, regrouped, things might have been different," said Chris Dreja. "It was a shame, really. If we'd made it to the seventies intact, where things were a little more relaxed – where albums were more important, who knows? But then, it was all about singles, and nobody cared about LPs."

According to Jim McCarty, Jimmy Page was eager to soldier on, but time and tide had changed within the band. "We could have gone on, yes. I know Jimmy didn't want to stop, but Keith and I, we'd had enough. It was time for something new."

As Dreja moved into a parallel and mightily impressive career as a professional photographer, Samwell-Smith found just acclaim as a record producer with Cat Stevens, and Relf and McCarty joined forces to form the progressive folk-rock outfit Renaissance, Page was left to stoke the ashes of the band into new life – resulting in a phoenix-like resurrection that exceeded even his loftiest ambitions.

Looking back, all parties happily concede that Jeff Beck's time with the band bore the sweetest fruit. "His overall capacity for the instrument, the sheer variety in his playing, it was all there," said Jim McCarty. "He didn't just stick with the blues like Eric and he took it a little further than Jimmy, who worked within certain limits. In short, for me The Yardbirds with Jeff was the best line-up, no question." Dreja was also incredibly giving to Beck's particular gifts. "What Jeff is, his gift if you like, is just sheer genius with a guitar. He's always so thoughtful and artistic in his approach, like a painter. And if you hear him for just a second, you know it's him – it's just unmistakeably 'Beckola'. A divine, mad genius."

For Jimmy Page, it was only ever about lost horizons. "Jeff leaving was such a shame," he reasoned. "We'd only just got things going..." Yet it was perhaps Keith Relf, who had lost out most to Beck's mercurial onstage personality, that best summed up the nature of his talent. "He had this unbridled spontaneity," Relf confirmed in 1974. "When Jeff really got in on, you know, when he forgot himself and just blew... when he forgot his problems, now that was really something to behold."

Within the space of a decade, The Yardbirds passed from also-rans to legends, their importance confirmed, their legacy assured. Starting life as "blues impostors", they progressed to being psychedelic pioneers of a new musical age, while also unleashing three of the finest guitar players Great Britain would ever produce. "Yes, but no one had a clue at the time," said Chris Dreja. "We were just all kids together really. Eric was brilliant, tentative and a bit screwed up, Jeff was moody and weird, but could play exquisitely and Jimmy was great and on a mission. To be honest, when the band broke up, there was no talk about making history. It was more a case of 'How much do I have in the bank? Ah, I'd better get on with things.' Personally, I loved them all one way or another. You know, it was all great fun, we produced a fantastic back catalogue and sealed our place with a wonderful history and legacy to boot. What more could you ask for, really?"

For Jeff Beck, the memory of his time with the band was more bittersweet – a mad ride that introduced him to the masses, defined his public image and provided the cornerstone upon which he would build his own musical empire, albeit at some emotional cost. "When Jimmy joined, I lost focus as to where The Yardbirds could – or should – have been going," he confirmed. "We were overqualified in the guitar department and underqualified in the writing department. We really should have taken stock there and then, waived the final tour and said, 'We're not ready for that'. But we took it on and it just burned itself out." Despite such attendant pitfalls, Beck later came to enjoy his place among "The Yardbirds' holy triumvirate", acknowledging that in their short lifespan, the group had launched a trio of guitarists that went on to cast an almighty shadow over the development of blues, rock and jazz-fusion. "It's peculiar when you talk about The Yardbirds and me, Jimmy and Eric," he told *Guitar World*'s Alan Di Perna in 1995. "We're all from the same country and all [grew up] within about a 12 mile distance. That's extraordinary. I really don't know what it was. Maybe that part of the planet has some kind of energetic vibe about it. Or maybe it was something to do with the education system that drove us to leave school and listen to rock'n'roll. The Yardbirds were the focal point of it. Without that band...things might have been very different for me."

Indeed.

Chapter 8

Every Cloud...

During his 20-month tenure with The Yardbirds, Jeff Beck's application for the position of 'Guitar Hero' had been processed, stamped, approved and then advertised throughout the world. More, Beck's brooding reputation and the fearful tales of havoc he had wrought only enhanced the almost sulphurous air of mystery surrounding him. "Jeff Beck is like James Dean," observed one critic, "but with longer hair and better weapons." Given Jeff's rebellious streak and teenage love of Americana, he was probably secretly pleased with such a comparison. But building his public image solely on burning angst and psychic implosion actually did him a grave disservice.

When one swept away all the rubble of missed appearances, lingering illnesses and quasi-nervous breakdowns, Jeff Beck's contribution to The Yardbirds had been little short of majestic. From his spiralling, one-note solution to the solo on 'The Nazz Are Blue' and manic interjections on 'Someone To Love (Part Two)' to the shimmering chords supporting 'Still I'm Sad' and distorted, eerie drone of 'Heart Full Of Soul', Beck's work with the band would emanate a radioactive glow for years to come. Chicken scratches, controlled feedback, wild octave jumps, peerless slide work and lyrical, voice-like soloing. In short, he was so far ahead of the game when it came to stunt guitar theatrics, it was almost funny.

But Beck was also out of a job. "Basically, three of The Yardbirds were friends before I joined and that's fatal," he complained to journalist

Val Wilmer shortly after his departure from the group. "They went to school together, virtually lived together... so no matter how much friction there was they'll swallow it and get back together. But the person who joins as an outsider, no matter how good he is, will get into these arguments and be left out all the time. Anyway, I couldn't wait to get out." Jeff Beck's exit from The Yardbirds might have left a sour taste in his mouth, yet for nearly two years the group had kept him in fashionable clothes, airline tickets to dream destinations, top-of-the-line guitars and more than a few amps. Those ties had now been severed and, worse still, his position as *Beat Instrumental*'s "Best Guitarist of 1966" was about to take some severe bombardment.

Only a month or so before Jeff's tenure with The Yardbirds came to a colourful end, 23-year-old James Marshall Hendrix arrived in London with $40 in his pocket, a small suitcase and a Fender Stratocaster. A native of Seattle, Washington, Hendrix had acquired his first guitar during his teens, learning to play by listening to R&B, Elvis Presley and Chuck Berry songs on the radio. At 19, he had enlisted in the US 101st Airborne Division, serving an undistinguished year before being discharged by his unimpressed superiors. The US Army's loss proved to the Chitlin Circuit's gain, with Hendrix eking out a reasonable living as a backing guitarist to singers such as Sam Cooke and Jackie Wilson on the demanding black music scene of the American south. Frustrated by the constraints placed upon him by bandleaders, Hendrix soon left New Orleans for New York where he again secured employment backing The Isley Brothers and his teenage hero, Little Richard.

After a spell fronting his own group, Jimmy James & The Blue Flame, he was discovered at The Cheetah Club in January 1966 by Keith Richards' then girlfriend, Linda Keith. She in turn recommended him to Animals bass player, Chas Chandler, who was about to leave the band in favour of a managerial career. Suitably impressed by Hendrix's fiery cover of the traditional American murder ballad 'Hey Joe' and his novel treatment of Bob Dylan's recent hit 'Like A Rolling Stone', Chandler signed him to a production deal alongside ex-Animals manager Mike Jeffrey. He then booked Hendrix a flight to London with the intention of the guitarist forming a band and securing a record deal. Feeling that 'James' or 'Jimmy' didn't quite cut the mustard as a pop star name, Chas rechristened his charge 'Jimi' Hendrix. Within hours of arriving at Heathrow Airport on September 23, Jimi was onstage jamming with the house band at Soho's Scotch of St. James Club, and by October 5 had pieced together his own group – 'The Experience' – featuring Mitch Mitchell on drums and Noel Redding on bass guitar. Three days later, Hendrix met with rapidly ascending amp designer Jim Marshall and bought a 100-watt Marshall stack, which he used to record his first single, 'Hey Joe', for Track Records. By January 6, 1967, the single was number six in the UK charts. It really was as simple as that.

What Chas Chandler had known when he bundled his new charge on a plane bound for stardom was that in addition to a warm, distinctive singing voice, Jimi Hendrix was a truly terrifying guitarist. With his rhythmic skills honed to perfection by the demanding schedules of the Chitlin' Circuit, and in possession of an extensive blues and R&B lead guitar vocabulary, Hendrix also had a frightening command of harmonic trickery, a gift for uninhibited stagecraft and an uncanny ear for melody. Wildly experimental and beautifully musical, Jimi Hendrix was very probably the best rock guitar player in the world – a fact Jeff Beck was about to find out. "Some girl rang me up and said, 'You've got to hear Jimi Hendrix. I saw him last night...and he was unbelievable'," Beck remembered, "I said, 'Right, thanks.' Just what you want to hear first thing in the morning. Anyway, I went along to see him in a club, Blazes I think, and he was just... it was like a bomb blowing up in the right place. He came out with Dylan's 'Like A Rolling Stone', and I thought 'Oh Christ, all right, I'll become a postman'."

For Beck, Hendrix's complete lack of onstage inhibition was as thrilling a sight as his complete mastery of a Fender Strat and newly acquired Marshall stack. "The thing I noticed when I first saw him was not only his amazing blues but his sheer physical assault on the guitar," he later told *The Telegraph*. "His actions were all of one accord, an explosive package. In a way, me, Eric and Jimmy, we were cursed because we were from Surrey. We all looked like we'd walked out of a Burton's shop window. Then there was Jimi with his military jacket, his hair about 14 feet in the air, playing with his teeth.

He looked like an animal, played like an animal, and everyone went crazy. We would have loved to have done that."

Roger Mayer, who would soon become Hendrix's right-hand man in his quest for new sounds, creating – among other startling guitar effects – the 'Octavia' pedal used on 'Purple Haze', 'Little Wing' and 'Machine Gun', believed it was Jimi's quest to escape his background that led to such overt displays of showmanship. "A lot of English musicians didn't have that freedom of approach or simply have the experience of playing in R&B bands that Jimi had," said Mayer. "It was an incredibly competitive environment, and God, you had to really try hard to survive it. For a lot of black players at that time, being successful in those bands was the only way out of a difficult life. And, of course, there were a lot of guitar players who'd gladly take their place. Sadly, things haven't moved on that much now, if you look at black athletes, football players, boxers and the like. So, if like Jimi, you'd been given a talent by the grace of God, you are going to pursue it all the way. It's your escape. In comparison, English players had no frame of reference to that. Imagine if Jeff had grown up in similar circumstances to Jimi in America. I mean, think what he might have sounded like!"

By his own admission, Beck was severely shaken by his first encounter with Hendrix. "I was sick when I saw him, I'll tell you that," he laughed. "It was like 'What the hell am I going to do tomorrow?' It was hopeless, actually. Everyone I talked to said, 'Have you heard Jimi Hendrix?' and I was like, 'Yep, thank you...'" But an inner compulsion to understand more about his new rival (and a burning need to figure out how he was actually achieving his sound) drove Jeff back to revisit the guitarist several days later. "Well, I followed him around for a bit, and then eventually got to meet him." To Beck's astonishment, Hendrix not only knew who he was, but had seen him perform with The Yardbirds when they had appeared in New York. More, Jimi was also highly complimentary of Jeff's work. "I couldn't believe it. He even said, 'You know that lick you did on 'Happenings Ten Years Time Ago'?' I swiped that. That meant we could actually *talk music*. He was an inspiration. So wild, so unchained." Bonding over a mutual love of Buddy Guy, Hendrix made a recommendation that Beck later took to heart.

"I was looking at his fingers, which were at least an inch longer than mine, when he asked what type of strings I used," said Jeff. "I was using super-light strings at that point, 0.08s, which made bending notes easier. He just said, 'Man, you got to get rid of those rubber bands!'" *

Though Beck and Hendrix were to become close in the coming months, their paths crossing occasionally while both were on the road, Jeff remained in shock at the American's talent and what it personally meant for him. "Jimi hit me like an earthquake when he arrived in 1966," he later said. "I had to think long and hard about what I did next. The wounds were quite deep actually, and I had to lick them on my own. I was constantly looking for other things to do on the guitar, new places to take it. I had to feel that 'this is mine' [because] if it didn't feel special, I just didn't do it."

Jimi Hendrix's arrival both coincided with and contributed to a whole new era in music – one which placed firm distinctions between pure pop and a growing underground scene that demanded instrumental virtuosity, strong improvisatory skills and probing lyricism. The Yardbirds and Beck himself had been partially responsible for such forward movement, the likes of 'Shapes Of Things' and 'Happenings...' pushing boundaries toward psychedelic music and beyond. But by late 1966, things had transformed yet again, with Hendrix's "wild guitar God archetype" nestling alongside another new category of performers: the supergroup. And once again, Eric Clapton had warmed the seat before Jeff Beck had a chance to sit on it.

Having ascended to the level of virtual deity himself with John Mayall's Bluesbreakers after the release of the 'Beano' album – where recording his Gibson Les Paul through a Marshall 2X12 combo amp at onstage volume had given birth to the 'Woman' tone – Eric Clapton had now become the thinking man's guitar hero. All across London (or at least outside Islington Underground Station) walls were daubed with white paint proclaiming 'Clapton Is God',

---

* To access greater tonal possibilities and more sustain, Jeff later made the change to heavier gauge strings, moving up to 0.09s before eventually equipping his guitars with wires so thick one could tug a boat with them.

a mark of how one man's unswerving obsession with the blues – if marketed correctly – can lead to others eventually claiming his omnipotence. With typical obstinacy, Eric had reacted badly to all the fuss by turning his back on the rigours of saving the 12-bar, leaving John Mayall in the lurch and heading off to help invent the first supergroup.

Joining forces with ex-Graham Bond Organisation drummer Ginger Baker and bassist/singer Jack Bruce, two strongly gifted (and exceedingly headstrong) jazz musicians who could turn their hand to almost any kind of music, Clapton formed Cream in July, 1966, their very name implying they were 'the cream of the crop'.

Predictably, the band were an immediate success from their unofficial debut at Manchester's Twisted Wheel club on July 29, 1966 – their thumping, free-form blues–rock jams and extended, improvisatory soloing opening a doorway of possibilities to what could be achieved by three exceedingly good instrumentalists, spirited vocals and a hell of a lot of volume. Already a fan of Clapton via his work with John Mayall, one of the first things Jimi Hendrix did on arriving in London was seek Cream out at Central London Polytechnic, leading to a jam on the old Howlin' Wolf standard, 'Killin' Floor'. Following Hendrix's display of string–chewing, fleet-fingered guitar acrobatics, Eric was stunned, reportedly asking Jimi's manager Chas Chandler, "Is he always that fucking good?" at the show's conclusion. Again as with Beck, Hendrix and Clapton were to become friends, the latter stating in his autobiography: "Jimi was a force to be reckoned with. He scared me because he was clearly going to be a huge star... the real thing."

As Hendrix marked his coming with 'Hey Joe' and Cream's debut album, *Fresh Cream*, headed for number six on the UK charts, it was perhaps understandable that Jeff Beck's initial reaction was to pull the bed sheets above his head and pretend it simply wasn't happening. Without a band, he was forced to watch from the sidelines as Jimi and Eric staked their individual claims to the title of ultimate guitar hero, with each song and solo dictating what rock music might eventually become. "Jimi made it possible for people to see what could be done with a guitar," said Beck. "I had been doing similar things, but not in such an ostentatious way. I was messing around with tape echo, feedback, wang bars a bit, but he came along with big amps, big sounds. The change had come."

For precisely such reasons and a few more besides, the first few weeks after leaving The Yardbirds were a thoroughly depressing time for Jeff. Without an established source of income and his girlfriend Mary Hughes some 3,000 miles away, he slipped into something of a funk, going to ground in a "shitty flat" while trying to work out precisely what to do next. Still contracted to Simon Napier-Bell, Beck did pick up the odd session, working on a track called 'I See Love In You' with singer John Maus (aka Walker) of The Walker Brothers, the very man who had sold him his beloved Esquire. He also contributed a few lead lines to the single 'But She's Mine' by John's Children, another of Napier-Bell's pop acts of the time, who are now best remembered for providing young Marc Bolan with a temporary home before he left to form Tyrannosaurus Rex (later T-Rex) in August, 1967. Yet, phoning in the odd solo on (an admittedly good) 45 did not a career make. It was time for positive action.

In January 1967, Jeff Beck returned to the studio to record his first single as a solo artist with Columbia records, having signed a convoluted management contract some weeks before that saw his affairs overseen by both Simon Napier-Bell and Peter Grant while Mickie Most handled all production duties. The words 'out of the frying pan into the fire' didn't even begin to cover it. "I signed a fabulous contract," Jeff later said, "that guaranteed I wouldn't get anything, no matter what." While Napier-Bell was reasonably new to the manager's game, both Grant and Most were seasoned hands and soon to become as legendary as some of their charges.

In the case of Peter Grant, his reputation as one of the entertainment industry's "genuine hard men" often threatened to disguise a superb business brain and at times almost-smothering loyalty to the acts he represented: six feet three and skirting 270 lbs (he would become considerably heavier), Grant was brought up by his mother in the then distinctly working class London neighbourhoods of Norwood and Battersea during the worst of the Blitz. Abandoning formal education at 13, he worked as a stagehand, soldier, rent collector, bit-part actor and bouncer before a brief stint as 'Count Bruno

Alassio of Milan', the stage name Grant gave himself while treading the boards as a professional wrestler. Having grown tired of sitting on his opponents, Peter settled into behind-the-scenes entertainment, first chauffeuring then tour-managing the likes of Gene Vincent, Bo Diddley and The Everly Brothers whenever they toured the UK. It was during this period that he acquired a reputation for being able to get just about any job done, no matter how difficult.

When, for instance, Gene Vincent injured his one good leg before a performance, it was Grant who reportedly stuck a microphone stand through the back of the rocker's leather jacket and propped him up onstage. Even more ingeniously, a hissy-fit-throwing Little Richard was bundled up in his hotel room rug, slung in the boot of a car and delivered screaming to the doors of London's Lyceum Ballroom, where he was scheduled to appear. And appear he did. The protégé of the original hard man/manager Don Arden, who had even found work for a thirties-styled novelty act – The New Vaudeville Band – during the height of the pop boom, Peter Grant was now not only managing Jeff's old group The Yardbirds, but Beck too. "All I saw in the office was this vast chair with a huge jacket draped over it," Jeff said when recalling his first meeting with Grant. "Then later on, this big gentleman walks in and there was a twinkle in his eye..." The two would bond in due course.

Occupying the same Oxford Street office space as Peter Grant was Mickie Most. The Simon Cowell of his time, Aldershot-born Most (formerly Hayes) was the son of an army sergeant major who left school at 15 to work as a singing waiter in Soho's then pre-eminent music biz haunt, the 2i's coffee bar on Old Compton Street, where Grant was the doorman/bouncer. Failing to find immediate stardom among the espressos, he cut his losses and formed a number of singing duos/groups, the most successful of which were Mickie Most & The Playboys who scored 11 consecutive number ones in South Africa when Most and his wife emigrated there in 1959. Three years later, Mickie was back in England and in a new job: record production. It proved to be an inspired career move. Within 12 months, he had overseen The Animals' 'House Of The Rising Sun' and Herman's Hermits' 'I'm Into Something Good', both monster hits that won him a 'Producer Of The Year' Grammy award in 1964. Setting up shop with Grant, who he had first met while waiting tables at the 2i's, Most's forte was the creation of pop stars, as Jeff Beck was about to find out in the bluntest possible terms. "It seemed the gateway to the whole world was right there in Mickie Most's office," Beck remembered. "I went to see him and he said, 'Right. Do you want to be a star? Then do what I say. I get all the writing credits, you don't get anything, but you get to be on TV. You're going to sing this song, it's going to be a smash. Good luck, all right?' Or at least that was the way it seemed..."

The result of Jeff Beck's first collaboration with Most, 'Hi Ho Silver Lining' and its B-side, 'Beck's Bolero', remain compelling evidence of the quandary the guitarist found himself facing as he moved beyond the shadow of The Yardbirds and into the light of new possibilities. Even now, Beck describes '... Silver Lining' as "having a pink toilet seat hanging round my neck for the rest of my fucking life", while summing up '...Bolero' as "one of my favourite songs. A defining moment that showed me there was promise there. Ah, why can't there be more of those?" Given such strident opinions and the strong emotional response both tunes provoke in Jeff, they are surely worthy of some examination.

In defence of 'Hi Ho Silver Lining', the song is probably nowhere near as bad as Beck would have it, though it was a disastrous choice for establishing his credentials as a major player in a new 'serious rock' market. Essentially three minutes of perfect pop fluff, punctuated by a hastily recorded double-tracked guitar solo (the very mention of which can irritate Jeff even now), '... Silver Lining' did have some redeeming features: the lyric, for instance, was a surprisingly astute attack on the blind optimism of the blossoming flower power movement with lines such as "Going down the bumpy hillside in your hippie hat" and "Saying everything is groovy, when your tires are flat" pointing to the potential folly of 'turning on, tuning in and dropping out'. Additionally, its ominous, droning backwards piano intro was of some interest, creating a real sense of unease before John Paul Jones' string arrangement arrived like a dawn chorus to scare any potential menace away. And love it or hate it, one cannot deny '... Silver Lining''s chorus was incredibly catchy, albeit in that Archies 'Sugar Sugar'-type way: "Well, Mickie did say to me 'You'll be hearing this for a long time'," Beck later said, "... but I just hated singing on it."

For Jeff, the experience of singing on 'Hi Ho Silver Lining' was akin to having his wisdom teeth removed without benefit of anaesthetic. "It was," he told *Making Music*, "a humiliating experience. My voice sounded like a fucking boy scout and I absolutely hated every minute of it." Never possessing the greatest of voices, Beck reportedly went to some lengths to avoid his turn at the microphone, but as we will learn, Mickie Most was intent on ignoring other – perhaps more suitable – candidates at the time so that '... Silver Lining' remained a Jeff Beck solo single. "Jeff said he wanted to be a pop star," Most remembered. "I asked him if he·could sing and he said, 'Not very well', but then none of the rest of the [backing] group could sing very well either, so we recorded it as a bit of fun. Jeff's singing wasn't very good and it was a bit of a struggle. In fact, I was singing most of the chorus and I'm not much of a singer myself. Between us, we almost ruined the record but we got away with it."

Written by Scott English and Larry Weiss (who co-authored The American Breed's similarly poppy 'Bend Me, Shape Me'), and featuring Clem Cattini on drums and Dave Ambrose on bass, '... Silver Lining' gave Jeff Beck the hit Mickie Most was hoping for. Released in March 1967, it reached number 14 on the UK charts, sticking around the Top 50 for a further 14 weeks. At the time, Beck was reasonably content to toe the party line as to the song's success, though one could almost hear his teeth grinding between the lines of newsprint. "'Hi Ho Silver Lining' was aimed at people who don't really know me, and yes it's different from what I've done before, but it's just a commercial record," he told *Record Mirror* in 1967. "Of course, people who knew me before were surprised by it, but it did the trick. I just hope it goes even higher."

As stated, Jeff would enjoy a love-hate-total enmity relationship with '... Silver Lining' in later years, his response to its subsequent cult status as "an end-of-office party classic" and theme song for Wolverhampton Wanderers FC alternating between real embarrassment, shy pride and sly humour. "As I came out of recording the song," he told *The Telegraph* in 2010, "even the receptionist was singing it. I knew I was in trouble then. But if you've got to have one, it's not that bad, I suppose. And if it makes people happy at Essex weddings, then so be it." According to Beck, not everyone was as grateful as the residents of Essex: "'Hi Ho Silver Lining"'s played at the end of every police ball and I still get speeding tickets. After all the pleasure I've given them..."

If 'Hi Ho Silver Lining' managed the job of making Jeff Beck hugely irritated and a pop star all at once, then 'Beck's Bolero' brought about equal feelings of huge pride and lost opportunity. The instrumental would also spark a long-running and still-unresolved debate about who wrote and produced it, though no one is in any doubt as to the musicians who recorded it. '... Bolero' was actually cut on May 16–17, 1966 at London's IBC Studios (nearly eight months before '... Silver Lining') by a one-time only cast of players that might have caused the combined might of The Jimi Hendrix Experience and Cream to nervously study their ranks before running for the hills. On drums was The Who's resident madman, Keith Moon, whose talent for lunacy was almost as impressive as his skills with the sticks. Filling in for Moon's bandmate, John Entwistle, who originally agreed to play bass on the session but pulled out at the last minute, was recurring session ace John Paul Jones. Adding some classically-influenced sparkle to proceedings was keyboard player Nicky Hopkins, a child prodigy/Royal Academy of Music graduate who had carved a fine career as a studio musician, working with The Beatles, the Stones and The Who. And completing the line-up were Jeff Beck and Jimmy Page, then only a month away from attending the Oxford May Ball where events would change the terms of their relationship from the best of friends to duelling gunslingers.

The '... Bolero' session was conceived as part of Simon Napier-Bell's plan for The Yardbirds to engage with various side projects in an effort to ease mounting tensions within the group, and part of the same nest of recordings that produced Keith Relf's 'Mr. Zero'. In advance of the booking at IBC, Beck had visited Page to work up some suitable material for potential solo release. "Well, The Yardbirds were dying and Simon suggested I do something to keep me quiet," Beck told *Elsewhere.com*, "so I went around Jimmy's place and he came out with this rhythm on a 12-string guitar (actually a Fender Electric XII). We wanted Keith, who was one of my favourite drummers, to play on it." The rhythm in question was inspired by *Bolero*, a classical piece written in 1928 by the composer Maurice Ravel as an accompaniment to Russian choreographer Ida Rubenstein's short ballet of the same name. Built on a persistent, repeating motif supported by a snare drum, the piece displayed Ravel's genius in re-creating the Spanish 'bolero' dance pattern for full orchestra, using flutes, horns and oboes to add melody to the steady yet insistent tempo – thus matching the steps of said dancers as they built toward a slow-burning crescendo upon the stage.

In his treatment of Ravel's original idea, Jimmy Page opened up Ravel's original two-chord progression and transposed it from the key of 'C' to 'A', thus using the 12-string guitar's rich chiming quality to emulate the distinct, orchestral 'bolero' sound. That said, who actually wrote the haunting melody that sits on top of the chords remains a sticky point for both Beck and Page. According to Jeff, he is solely responsible: "Jimmy was playing the bolero rhythm and I played the melody on top of it. I don't care what he says, I invented that melody." Not so, according to Page: "I wrote it, played on it, produced it," he later told *Guitar Player*, "and I don't give a damn what [Jeff] says. That's the truth." Page certainly took the sole writing credit for 'Beck's Bolero' when it appeared on the B-side to 'Hi Ho Silver Lining', though Beck has become more philosophical than angry over time regarding his part in writing the instrumental – even if he does still claim the melody as his own. "No, I didn't get a song-writing credit," he said, "but you win some and lose some down the years."

Beyond such disputes over authorship, 'Beck's Bolero' has also taken on an important status in the annals of rock history because of the musicians involved in its recording, their unique collaboration on the track pointing the way towards what might have been rock's first true supergroup. Then unhappy that The Who's guitarist and principal songwriter, Pete Townshend, was receiving the lion's share of cash in the band, both Keith Moon and John Entwistle had let it be known that they might be interested taking their talents elsewhere. Picking up on the rumour, Page and Beck contacted the duo and asked whether they would consider working on some material, with a possible view to even forming a band. Fearing possible reprisals from Townshend and Who manager Kit Lambert if discovered playing away from home, but still interested in what might come out of the session, Moon asked that the recording be conducted in total secrecy. "Keith told us he could only give us about three hours before his roadies would start looking for him," said Jeff.

Evidently, such clandestine activity proved too much in the end for John Entwistle who ending up ducking out, though Keith Moon's nerve did hold – even if he went to extraordinary lengths to disguise his involvement. "Moon got out of the cab that morning wearing dark glasses and a bloody Cossack hat," laughed Beck. Keith Moon's contribution to 'Beck's Bolero' was well worth the daftness, his unique, propulsive drumming style adding much to the track's mid-section rave up. "It was my idea to cut off in the middle, Yardbirds-style," said Jeff. "Keith upped the tempo and gave it an extra kick. It's like a bit of The Who, a bit of The Yardbirds and a bit of me." In fact, such was Moon's enthusiasm for Beck's idea, he managed to smash a $250 microphone with his drumstick as the band doubled the pace, thus rendering the sound of his kit inaudible but for the cymbals. "You can actually hear him screaming as he does it," Beck confirmed to *Guitarist*.

A wonderfully judged tune, 'Beck's Bolero' featured Jeff at his very best, the guitarist weaving his way across an alternating major/minor melody before launching a barrage of sighing slide effects that soaked the track in slow waves of echo and reverse phasing. When '... Bolero''s tempo picked up, Beck was again equal to the task at hand, providing a thick-toned, descending riff that eerily presaged the coming era of hard rock and heavy metal. "The riff in the middle of 'Bolero' is the first heavy metal riff ever written and I wrote it," he later said with some pride. What makes 'Beck's Bolero' potentially even more scintillating is the knowledge that it wasn't the only track recorded that morning. "I think there were two or three tracks in all," Jeff confirmed. "They're lurking about somewhere. But those were the days that when you left the studio, you left the tapes. No cassettes, just reel-to-reels."*

Yet another hotly contested issue concerning '... Bolero' is who

---

* Legend has it that future Deep Purple guitarist Ritchie Blackmore was also involved in some capacity at the sessions, though this has never been confirmed.

actually produced the track, with three candidates eager to claim it as their own. "Well, the track was done and then the producer, Simon Napier-Bell, just disappeared," Jimmy Page told *Guitar Player*. "He was never seen again. He simply didn't come back. [Simon] just sort of left me and Jeff to it. Jeff was playing and I was [at the recording console]." According to Napier-Bell, his input was far more considerable. "I produced it," he said. "But I was naive about 'Bolero'. When Mickie Most took Jeff, he asked if there were any productions knocking around and I said 'Yes, we've got '... Bolero'. So it eventually came out as a Mickie Most production, which has always pissed me off because it was such a great record. My fault, no one else's." Whether Most refined, enhanced or, in all probability, did absolutely nothing to the tapes he received is ultimately irrelevant. '... Bolero' bears his name alone as 'Producer'.

Arguments aside, 'Beck's Bolero' remains a delightful curio of the band that could have been but never was, their efforts hermetically sealed within the walls of an instrumental lasting just shy of three minutes. Upon its completion, Keith Moon immediately returned to his full-time position as The Who's lunatic-in-residence, though his act of infidelity soon came to the attention of Pete Townshend, who took to calling Beck and Page "flashy little guitarists of very little brain" whenever the mood took him. Elsewhere, Nicky Hopkins was now firmly back on Jeff's radar, his impressive orchestral swells at the end of the track alerting Beck to the possibilities of adding keyboards to any future endeavour. But it was Jimmy Page and John Paul Jones who probably gleaned most long-term benefit from '... Bolero', the session planting seeds in both their minds of potentially good times ahead. "'Beck's Bolero' was Jimmy, Jeff, Me, Nicky Hopkins and Keith Moon," Jones told *Uncut*. "Moon was just brilliant, [the] life and soul of the party at all times... plenty dangerous to go and party with, but never dull. We all thought, for about half an hour, that it would be brilliant to take this line-up on the road, though Moon said it would go down like a lead Zeppelin..."

Jimmy Page didn't capture Moon's joke on tape. But he did remember it.

Chapter 9

God Bless *The New York Times*

In May 1966, Jeff Beck had been part of a three-hour experiment that – if things have gone differently – may well have produced one of the sixties most important bands. Sadly, when Page and Beck tried to find a possible vocalist for the fledging project, their entreaties were met with some resistance. "Well, it was going to be either Steve Marriott from The Small Faces or Stevie Winwood [from The Spencer Davis Group]," Jimmy told *Guitar World*'s Steve Rosen. "In the end, the reply came back from his office [saying] 'How would you like to have a group with no fingers, boys?' Or words to that effect." Evidently, Marriott's manager Don Arden was in no mood to entertain the guitarists' creative impulses.

Yet, some six months on from '… Bolero' Beck had actually solved the problem of finding a world-class singer – but as ever with Jeff, things were seldom straightforward. As Beck was now signed to Columbia Records in his own right, his new producer Mickie Most simply didn't want to know about anyone else singing lead vocals when it came to the matter of single releases. "I said 'All right, we'll get Rod on 'Hi Ho Silver Lining'," Beck told *Guitarist*. "But Mickie said, 'No, I don't want that silly poof singing on this record, you're the star'. That's what he said." The 'silly poof' in question was Rod Stewart, the first recruit to support Beck's real aim for the future: forming a band that would seriously challenge the likes of Jimi Hendrix, Cream and a whole raft of emerging progressively themed acts at the time.

Rod Stewart had already done his time in various bands before hooking up with Jeff Beck. The son of a Scottish master builder and English housewife, Stewart was raised in the North London district of Highgate, a German V2 missile striking the local police station only minutes before his birth in January, 1945. Following a stalled apprenticeship as a silk-screen printer, Rod joined Brentford FC as an apprentice striker at 16, but a slight build, severe dislike of journeying 10 miles west to the ground each morning and an intense hatred of cleaning the first team's boots brought his football dreams to a swift end. Spells as a grave digger, fence erector and sign writer followed before Stewart finally gravitated towards a singing career, first busking his way around Leicester Square before taking on occasional vocal/harmonica duties with Ray Davies' pre-Kinks band, The Ray Davies Quartet, and Jimmy Powell & The Dimensions.

Rod's first real break came after attending a Cyril Davies & The All Stars gig at Eel Pie Island, where he was spotted by blues singer Long John Baldry drunkenly howling his way through 'Smokestack Lightning' while waiting for a train at Twickenham station. "John heard me singing and playing the harmonica," said Stewart. "You know, I'd had a few drinks... and he said 'Why don't you join our band? You know, I need someone to sing. I need someone to warm the audience up'. I was absolutely petrified but I gave it a go, you know. That's how I got started [in] 1964." By 1965, Baldry's Hoochie Coochie Men had morphed into Steampacket, a jazz, soul and R&B revue-type act managed by Giorgio Gomelsky, which heavily featured Rod on vocals. But contractual issues around various band members saw the group stall and Stewart head off in the direction of Shotgun Express, another bluesy affair that paired him alongside future Fleetwood Mac guitarist Peter Green and Mick Fleetwood on drums. But like all Rod's previous enterprises thus far, Shotgun Express were soon floundering, leaving the singer potentially without a band by the end of 1966. As fate would have it, Rod Stewart again had a glass in his hand when fame came calling for him a second time.

Still smarting after his exit from The Yardbirds, Jeff Beck had been persuaded by a road manager friend just back from the States to put his woes behind him and head out for a beer at The Cromwellian – a well-known music haunt opposite Exhibition Road in South Kensington. Once inside the venue Beck spotted Stewart, who had impressed him during a Steampacket performance a year before. "This particular evening... Rod was somewhat worse for wear through drink and I just thought there's the guy – the one guy – I would like to sing in my band," Jeff told journalist Douglas J Noble. "I was pretty down as well – totally out of The Yardbirds, nothing going, no money. I hadn't got anything to lose so I asked him if he would be interested and he said, 'Yep'. Amazing." Though pleasantly soused at the time, Stewart was still sober enough to ask Beck to call him at noon the next day to prove he was serious. When Jeff did, the two agreed to meet – somewhat oddly – at a war museum. They were soon full of talk about forming a group, and headed back to Jeff's Putney flat where they listened to records by The Four Tops, The Temptations and Dionne Warwick's sublime single 'Walk On By'. "When Rod arrived," Beck later said, "it was like a huge, big table with jelly and cakes in front of me. You [had] a guy who could sing great blues, but was prepared to step outside the 12-bar thing."

Rooster-haired, rogue handsome and probably one of the better all-round singers of the sixties, Rod 'The Mod' Stewart was an extraordinary find for Jeff Beck. But, as evidenced, Mickie Most was having none of it. In his mind Beck was a pop star, pure and simple, and Most knew a lot about pop stars. By diluting Jeff's already established appeal as an ex-Yardbird within a new group fronted by a little-known and still unproven singer, there was much to lose and little to gain. "Mickie just wasn't interested in Rod at all," Beck said. Peter Grant, however, had more expansive ideas. Having seen the potentially rich pickings offered by the nascent US college circuit as current manager of The Yardbirds, and fully aware this new and vital trend was being mirrored throughout cult London clubs like UFO, The Art Lab and Middle Earth, Grant knew there might well be a place for a 'Jeff Beck Group'. Far too astute to fall out over the piddling aesthetics of the guitarist's career, a deal was quietly agreed between Most and Grant. Mickie would go on creating the pop star while Peter handled the rock bit. Sadly, Beck would have to handle both, leading to a truly schizophrenic existence before the whole collapsed on him some two years later.

With Stewart now on board as the sole member of Jeff's new group, the race was on to find suitable candidates for the vacant positions of bass guitar and drums. The first to be auditioned at a Goodge Street studio in January, 1967 was the unlikely pairing of ex-Shadow Jet Harris and former Pretty Thing Viv Prince. But despite their sturdy backgrounds – and some excellent sounding rock'n'roll names – Harris proved unreliable, Prince proved unsuitable, both loved the bottle too much and neither made it past initial rehearsals. That said, Ronnie Wood did stick, joining the fledgling band on rhythm guitar. An acquaintance of Jeff's since The Tridents had shared the stage of the 100 Club with Ronnie's band The Birds in 1964, Wood had even jammed once before with The Yardbirds, taking on harp duties when singer Keith Relf's asthma temporarily got the better of him. A known face about town, Hillingdon-born Ronnie was a multi-instrumentalist, a 'Water Gypsy' by birthright, an art school graduate and, crucially, able to find the funny side in just about anything – a skill that would soon be tested to its absolute limit by Beck in months to come.

In the meantime, Jeff was being sorely tested by his management team. Keen to start seeing a return on their investment, Peter Grant, Mickie Most and nominally Simon Napier-Bell (who still had an interest in Jeff's affairs at this point) had arranged for the new group to join a 32-date UK tour package supporting Roy Orbison, The Small Faces and Paul & Barry Ryan in early March. When Beck received news of said tour while holidaying in Brussels, it was the third week of February, giving him days rather than months to pull together a band. In a desperate attempt to meet the deadline, Jeff recruited his former Tridents cohort Ray Cook on drums while Ronnie Wood was gently but firmly asked whether he might cover bass. Not owning a four-string at the time, Wood strolled up from the group's Chinatown rehearsal space to Selmers on nearby Shaftesbury Avenue where he "obtained" a Fender Jazz. "I had no money," he later told *Guitar Player*. "I couldn't pay for it so I just borrowed it and never took it back. About five years later I paid for it, after they tracked me down." *

The Jeff Beck Group made their debut on March 3, 1967 at the Finsbury Park Astoria, later to become The Rainbow. To mark the occasion, the band all wore white jackets, apart from Jeff who, as leader, dressed in black. Spirits were allegedly high backstage. Given what happened next, that's where the band should have stayed. "Oh God, the first night was unbelievably bad," remembered Napier-Bell. "They hadn't rehearsed properly, the curtain fell down on Ronnie, The Small Faces pulled the plug on the electricity. In short, it was a complete disaster."

Within the space of two minutes, all that could go wrong for The Jeff Beck Group did. According to some accounts at least, the band made it through their first number more or less intact, but then the lights were mysteriously cut – leaving Beck and his cohorts completely in the dark and Ray Cook reportedly silent behind his drum kit. As Jeff walked offstage in disgust, a hastily descending curtain struck Ronnie Wood on the head as he and Stewart tried to waddle into the wings. It was at about that time that Rod realised the zipper on his trousers had been undone for the duration of the show. He really needn't have worried. He could do it up in time for the second set.

The show was a complete disaster from start to mercifully quick finish, and Beck was absolutely furious afterwards, seeking retribution – and possibly blood – from The Small Faces' Ian McLagan who may well have sabotaged the band's lights and equipment. "We thought he'd done it because we might steal their limelight," Stewart later reasoned. Unfortunately, the Finsbury Park debacle marked Ray Cook's last appearance with The Jeff Beck Group. "In the end," Rod told *Zig Zag*, "we made (Ray) take the blame. It was a real shame because his father had bought him a new drum kit for the tour and he was sacked on the first day. Very sad."

---

* In an alternative version of the tale, Wood admitted to walking into the music shop, spotting the bass positioned closest to the door, grabbing it and then running like hell.

It also marked the end of Simon Napier-Bell's professional association with Beck. "To be honest, I'd chosen Jeff over The Yardbirds, though I utterly fucked up what came next," he said. "They'd done about five rehearsals, and at each one, Beck had used different musicians. The only constants were Rod and Ronnie. I sort of gave up. I didn't call because I couldn't stand the arguments and because I was still reasonably new to management, I really didn't know how to deal with difficult people. After the Astoria, I didn't have a group to manage. I wasn't talked to and I didn't talk. To my mind, I just hadn't been competent and, in their mind, I'm sure it was the same feeling. So I just ran away from it and left Jeff to his own devices."

Following the events that played out at Finsbury Park, Jeff Beck was probably thinking about running away himself. Though he immediately pulled the band from all remaining dates to mitigate any further damage, it was still too late to stop the *Melody Maker* printing a sour review of the gig. "The group were seriously under rehearsed," wrote journalist Chris Welch, while adding, "Jeff seemed to have difficulty even playing a good solo." The last comment must have really stung. "Yeah, we were lousy," Jeff later admitted. "Absolutely rotten. But you know, it drew attention to us..."

Ray Cook's enforced departure signalled the installation of a new revolving door marked 'Drummers This Way' outside The Jeff Beck Group's rehearsal room. First to enter was Micky Waller, who came to Beck's aid for a BBC *Saturday Club* radio session taped just four days after the events of Finsbury Park. Bookish and bespectacled, the university-educated Waller listed his favourite pastimes as "reading, motorcycles and being alone", marking him as an unlikely candidate for the heavy duty blues rock Jeff was planning. Yet, as the quality of the BBC broadcast illustrated, Micky was very probably the man for the job. A funk specialist with a great appreciation for the Detroit Stax/Motown sound so beloved by Beck in his adolescence, Waller's resumé was also impressive, including stints with Little Richard, Cyril Davies' R&B All Stars, John Mayall's Bluesbreakers and Rod Stewart's old band, Steampacket. But Micky was also committed to a series of concert dates with The Quotations, thus ruling him out of a forthcoming appearance for Jeff's newly relaunched band at the Marquee on 11 April and a short tour thereafter.

Forced back to the drawing board, Beck again made several switches to his line-up. With Waller unavailable, future Stealers Wheel and Strawbs drummer Rod Coombes was drafted in to warm the back seat. Meanwhile, Ronnie Wood again found himself promoted to rhythm guitar while Dave Ambrose, another of Stewart's former cohorts from Shotgun Express, took over on bass. While chaos reigned behind the scenes, Beck was beginning to enjoy a real measure of solo chart success with 'Hi Ho Silver Lining', its poptastic chorus being sung along to by the housewives of Great Britain as the guitarist's hardcore fanbase simply scratched their heads in confusion. For Rod Stewart, who had been relegated to backing vocals on the single when Mickie Most decided "Jeff was the star", this was all priceless stuff: "Well, we felt sorry for him [singing] really, and thought we'd better help out. For a guitar player like that to do 'Hi Ho Silver Lining', well, it's a crime."

Jeff Beck's situation started to right itself at The Marquee, where an audience of over seven hundred (and still close friend and current Yardbird Jimmy Page) witnessed a fine performance by his band. "The Marquee was where we put matters right," Jeff later said. But there were still some tinkering to be done before Beck was satisfied. Dave Ambrose was the first to be let go, though he soon found alternative employment with Brian Auger, whose harpsichord lines on 'For Your Love' had originally helped push The Yardbirds to fame. With a vacancy now on bass guitar, Jeff again turned to Ronnie Wood, though this time his move from six to four strings proved permanent. "Some people thought, 'Oh, you can't go to bass, it's an inferior instrument if you're a guitarist,' but it [was] the other way around," he told *Guitar Player* in 1975. "Jeff and I had a nice feel between us, so there was never any competition. I didn't know too much about it, [so] I just played what I felt."

A fan of Paul Samwell-Smith, Wood used the Yardbirds bassist's galloping runs as a stylistic guide to the instrument, while Jeff lent him old Chicago blues records in a further effort to help. By mid-April, The Jeff Beck Group had also acquired a new drummer in the form of Aynsley Dunbar, who had run a very close second to Mitch Mitchell when Jimi Hendrix was putting together The Experience in October, 1966. A fine, innovative player who had again worked briefly with John Mayall's Bluesbreakers, Dunbar's fearsome command of his kit seemed to genuinely inspire Beck at the time. "Our direction in music is strange," he said. "Aynsley lays something down and I follow it, then someone else follows me. He's fantastic, and has [this] strange technique... it's like the rhythm of the chain gang workers in the deep southern states of America."

Keen to avoid the package-tour format that did for them at Finsbury Park, The Jeff Beck Group struck out on the club circuit throughout April, 1967, playing dates at St. Albans' Market Hall, Nottingham's Beachcombers and Malvern's Winter Gardens. With each gig they got better, disregarding calls for old Yardbirds material in favour of high-energy Chicago blues covers and newer Motown songs. Hence, fans were treated to Buddy Guy's 'Stone Crazy', Howlin' Wolf's 'I Ain't Superstitious', The Four Tops' 'Loving You Is Sweeter Than Ever' and The Temptations '(I Know) I'm Losing You', a particular favourite of Rod Stewart's. Keen to keep his vocalist happy (and take advantage of the recognition factor his Steampacket associations brought in certain areas of England), Beck occasionally allowed the band to be billed as 'Jeff Beck and The Rod Stewart Show'. Yet, Rod's status as a simple 'de facto' band member was not subject to any change. In fact, like the rest of the group, he was not even signed to Grant and Most's RAK Management organisation, a contractual loophole that Stewart would exploit in due course.

Following their jaunt across the provinces, The Jeff Beck Group next appeared in the pleasant environs of London's Saville Theatre on July 2. Keen to bring together the very best of the UK's current music scene under one very well-made roof, Beatles manager Brian Epstein had booked the Saville Theatre for a series of shows throughout July, creating a must-have ticket during 'The Summer Of Love'. The band was scheduled to appear alongside John Mayall's Bluesbreakers and Cream, who had just returned from recording their second album, *Disraeli Gears*, in New York. Though Beck hadn't even managed to get his first LP in the shops, there was no real jealousy between him and Clapton, the two having put any potential differences aside when they met towards the end of Jeff's tenure with The Yardbirds. "I walked into a club and there he was," Jeff later said. "I really didn't know what to expect, but it all turned out all right... we gave each other a hug and that was that." Jeff had checked out Cream's first show at The Marquee.

Like Cream, The Jeff Beck Group had diligently tried to avoid any overt associations with the flower power movement, more eager to establish their own identity than be seen as pandering to trends. All that changed the minute the band stepped onstage at The Saville Theatre. Arriving in an explosion of kaftans, wild flowers and patchouli oil, their previously hippy-baiting guitarist had even donned a fur coat and floppy hat for the occasion. For blues purist Aynsley Dunbar, it was all too much, the drummer making a mental note to escape sooner rather than later.

Dunbar was still behind the drums when Jeff Beck released his next single, the pleasing but slight 'Tallyman'. Written by Graham Gouldman, the pen behind 'For Your Love', 'Heart Full Of Soul' and 'Evil Hearted You', 'Tallyman' was another example of the Mickie Most hit factory in action, its recording taking place in hours rather than days. Still, Jeff's guitar work was at least worthy of some admiration, his Gibson Les Paul issuing forth a series of fine unison bends, well-judged slide interjections and some tasty, staccato chord work reminiscent of The Who's Pete Townshend at his very best. As before, Rod Stewart was not allowed behind the mike for 'Tallyman', with Beck again forced to hand in a queasy vocal supported by the milky harmonies of session veterans (and Most stalwarts) Ken Lewis and John Carter: "Oh God," Stewart said. "It was Jeff this and Jeff that. I couldn't get a look in."

Of far more interest was 'Tallyman''s B-side, 'Rock My Plimsoul', a hot-wired retelling of BB King's 'Rock Me Baby' which the band had been performing live on and off since their fearful debut. Chockful of spiteful blues fills from Beck, 'Rock My Plimsoul' would soon become a cornerstone of their concert set and the centrepiece of their debut album, Stewart's salty reading of the song making a mockery of his then current position of 'silent lead vocalist'.

Aynsley Dunbar finally handed in his cards after a well-received set at Windsor's Seventh Annual Jazz & Blues Festival on August 12, just two weeks before 'Tallyman' reached number 30 in the UK charts (somewhat ironically, Dunbar's new band, Retaliation, also had a supporting slot at Windsor). What he was leaving behind was actually starting to sound rather good as a well-thumbed bootleg of the show still confirms. Blasting off with a spirited version of The Drifters' 'Some Kind Of Wonderful', all parties were in excellent form, the loose ends and rough edges of their earliest incarnation now sewed up and sanded down by several months on the road. From bold makeovers of Elmore James' 'Talk To Me Baby' and Marvin Gaye's 'Can I Get A Witness' to a comedic, but rousing version of 'Hi Ho Silver Lining', Jeff and his merry band were "really getting the hang of it".

As Beck had confirmed to *Melody Maker* in April 1967, Dunbar had laid down beats he was willing to "follow", and replacing his authoritative thump was not going to be easy. Jeff solved the dilemma by once again turning to Micky Waller, who was now free to join the band, full time. The immediate change in the group's sound was on display when Waller made his live debut with Beck at The Marquee on September 26. Moving away from a strong, sinewy rhythm section where Ronnie held down the chords while Jeff cartwheeled around him, the quartet were now an altogether crisper proposition, where the space between notes was as important as the notes themselves. Wood took full advantage of Waller's lighter touch by pursuing a more improvisational style, skipping in and out of the beat with Jack Bruce-like abandon. In short, by adding Waller, The Jeff Beck Group might have lost the thump, but they had found the funk.

Unfortunately, there was little to hop, skip and jump about when it came to 'Love Is Blue', or to give it its proper title, 'L'Amour Est Bleu'. Originally written by French composer André Popp for Greek chanteuse Vicky Leandros to sing as Luxembourg's entry for 1967's Eurovision Song Contest, 'Love Is Blue' was a sugar-coated, anaemic and astoundingly good example of the type of material Jeff should have rightly run a mile from. Instead, it was to be his next single. Of course, there were no prizes for guessing who came up with the idea. "One of the stipulations of the contract with Mickie Most was that I had to play the songs he provided or approved of," Beck later told *NME*. "I couldn't come up with anything he liked, so he suggested a cover of 'Love Is Blue'." When Jeff rightly pointed out to Most that there were a number of covers of the tune already in circulation, Mickie replied: "Ah, a guitar instrumental version, then. Basically, we cut it for the European market."

There is little to be said of Jeff Beck's version of 'Love Is Blue' other than it does him absolutely no favours. All twinkly keyboard trills, dampened drumbeats and somnambulant female choirs, it's no wonder Beck sounds bored beyond all comprehension, his dead-eyed Hank Marvin impersonation coming to life only at the end of the song when he stops copying the vocal melody and lets rip with some angry slide fills. The grand finale was too little, too late. When released as a single in February 1968, 'Love Is Blue' could only make it to number 23 in the UK charts – pipped at the post by Paul Mauriat's superior orchestral version of the tune (which went on to sell over a million copies in the States alone). Even for Jeff's most enduring supporters, this syrupy turn of events had to be a step too far. "Actually, I was disgusted by the reaction the tune got," he reasoned after the fact. "People who knew my playing were so blind they couldn't see the humour in it. They deserved to be offended." Or perhaps they simply deserved better.

In his defence, the winter/spring months of 1967–68 were a particularly low point for Jeff Beck and his band. Though they had gained a creditable following on the club circuit, house attendance rarely numbered above 1,000 people and money remained tight. Moreover, Beck's constant ping-ponging between blues-rock credibility and pop puppetry proved a destabilising influence within the ranks, a fact underlined in a press announcement of the time stating he might even record a 'guitar concerto' album. Rock, pop, now classical – it was all getting very confusing. Privately, such uncertainty had led to a band member or two looking (or being forced) elsewhere for possible avenues of escape. Constantly stymied by Mickie Most's refusal to record a Jeff Beck A-side with him on vocals, Rod Stewart had his first solo single 'Little Miss Understood' released by Immediate Records in March 1968 – a cautious toe dipped in the waters to see if there might be a market for "solo Stewart". It didn't trouble the charts.

Ronnie Wood too was exploring other possibilities, having temporarily broken with – or possibly been fired by – Beck for reasons unknown. To keep the cash flowing, Wood briefly joined his old friend Kim Gardner's pop-art quartet, The Creation, who had scored a minor UK hit in 1966 with 'Painter Man' (the irony here was that Gardner in turn had been turned down as bassist with The Jeff Beck Group only a year or so before). Recording three singles in rapid succession with The Creation, Wood shortly returned to Jeff's good graces after his replacement, Tomorrow's John Woods, proved unsuitable following a short European tour with Beck in April, 1968. God only knows what Micky Waller made of it all.

Locked into a low-paying contract that forced him to release below-par singles wholly unrepresentative of his undoubted talent or preferred musical direction, and with a band now on the verge of desertion, Beck continued to prop up his income with the odd session. The most notable of these was an inspired contribution to the B-side of ex-Manfred Mann singer Paul Jones' single 'And The Sun Will Shine', cut in the early spring of 1968. Written by the Gibb Brothers – aka The Bee Gees – 'And The Sun...' was a fairly innocuous example of late-sixties pop balladry. But its flip side, 'The Dog Presides', was much more rewarding to the ear. Cut at Abbey Road's famous Studio II, 'The Dog Presides', featured an all-star cast of musicians and fashionable London faces. Making his debut as a producer was Pete Asher of Peter & Gordon, a singing duo that had already achieved considerable notoriety with four million-selling singles, the best known of which was 'A World Without Love'. The brother of Jane Asher – then dating Beatle Paul McCartney – Pete had asked McCartney to attend the session at which he ended up playing drums. Also along for the ride was Jeff's former bandmate and now producer in his own right, Paul Samwell-Smith, who added bass guitar. To give things an extra helping of top-end sheen, Nicky Hopkins brought along his keyboard, leaving Beck to provide some typical fiery runs from the neck of his Gibson Les Paul. The result of all this superstar jamming was a cracking little tune, sung beautifully by Jones, whose panicky harmonica fills were a perfect complement to Jeff's growling lead lines. For Beck, who reportedly earned a week's rent from 'The Dog Presides', there was only one regret: "Well, all I remember [about it] was hoping Paul McCartney would sing."

That Jeff remained a musician in high demand was also evidenced in December 1967, when a promising new underground act reportedly approached him with a view to taking over from their ailing 'unofficial leader' on lead guitar. At the time, Pink Floyd were experiencing the first flush of real success with two Top 20 singles, 'Arnold Layne' and 'See Emily Play', and well-received debut album, *The Piper At The Gates Of Dawn*. But a growing love affair with LSD had led their talisman and principal songwriter, Roger 'Syd' Barrett, to mentally unravel at the seams – his behaviour becoming more unpredictable, his place in the band untenable as a result. A shortlist of players to replace Barrett was drawn up by Floyd's bassist, Roger Waters, drummer, Nick Mason and keyboardist, Rick Wright, with Beck at the top. However, word of the band's interest failed to reach him. "I may have seen Pink Floyd at The Speakeasy," Jeff revealed in 2010, "but with all the psychedelic lights, they could have changed personnel and I wouldn't have noticed. I only heard recently they were thinking of asking me to join. I wouldn't have thought they'd have given me light of day." Floyd's Rick Wright told *Record Collector* in 1996 that an approach was made to Beck at the time: "He was definitely approached. I can't remember exactly what his answer was, but it obviously wasn't yes!" The man found to first work alongside – before permanently replacing – Syd Barrett was another gifted guitarist, Dave Gilmour. A huge fan of Beck's before joining the group, and destined to become a close friend and extremely vocal supporter of the guitarist in years to come, Gilmour once speculated on what might have become of Pink Floyd had they been more insistent in their entreaties: "I think the only other person the band had in mind was Jeff Beck, which, heh... well, it really would have been slightly different..."

In this hazy light of financial uncertainty, occasional sessions, arcane approaches from desperate bands, ill-conceived musical flings and a quite awful solo single, The Jeff Beck Group managed to finally snatch victory from the jaws of defeat by becoming enormous in America. As already evidenced, having closely managed The Yardbirds since Simon Napier-Bell had cut ties with the band in January 1967, Peter Grant had become progressively more aware of the cash rewards bands could glean from traversing the US college circuit and the inexorable rise of album sales to that market. Now in danger of becoming the 'overground' rather than 'underground', Stateside university students had slowly turned their affections towards LPs rather than singles, with 1968 becoming the first year that albums sold more than 45s. The reasons for such changing behaviours were numerous. When The Beach Boys' *Pet Sounds* and The Beatles' *Sgt. Pepper's Lonely Hearts Club Band* had opened up the possibilities of what might be achieved with sound by treating the recording studio as another instrument, the album was destined to become big business. Instead of just listening to an LP, one actually pondered it: the sleeve, the songs, the lyrics, the hidden messages – all were analysed, dissected and pored over in microscopic detail, the experience made even more satisfying when combined with the odd joint or tab of acid so beloved by the new hippie generation.

Equally, with the advent of heavy touring by the likes of Iron Butterfly, The Doors, The Grateful Dead and Jefferson Airplane, rock music was now on the very doorsteps of the campuses and local halls that housed their core audience, with such bands growing up at the same rate as the people who bought their records. When the steady growth of college radio stations was also factored in – allowing listeners direct access to experimentally driven sounds they would never hear on Top 40 AM networks – the album's rout over the single was all but complete. Sensing that The Jeff Beck Group could exploit this sea change in tastes, Peter Grant made the decision to bring them to America. "Peter was fantastic," Beck later told *Uncut*. "What he realised, long before the others, was there was a sizeable audience for an underground scene away from the Top 40. We'd been playing shitholes in England and then he took us to America..."

From their debut at New York's Fillmore East on June 14, 1968 supporting The Grateful Dead, The Jeff Beck Group were an instant – if wholly unexpected – success in the US, thanks in large part to a gushing review of their performance by *The New York Times'* Robert Shelton. "Jeff Beck and his band deal in blues mainly, but with an urgency and sweep that's hard to resist," wrote Shelton. "[They're] wild and visionary... lean and laconic... the climaxes [are] primal, bringing the 'Big Beat' of the English rock school forward." In reality, the evening could have been a total disaster. Used to playing in front of crowds numbering 1,000 at best, the band found The Fillmore packed to the rafters that night, The Grateful Dead's headlining status guaranteeing an audience of 3,000 or so. To confirm this fact, opening act The Seventh Sons were little more than a tasty aperitif for the 'Deadheads' in attendance, being barracked offstage only moments after summoning up the bravery to set foot upon it.

Still finding his own feet as a front man at this point, Rod Stewart was genuinely horrified by the surly reception accorded The Sons. According to Beck folklore, he became even more fearful upon hearing rising star Janis Joplin singing 'Summertime' to a group of musicians and roadies backstage. So astounding was Joplin's rendition of Gerswhin's classic jazz standard that both Rod's nerve and voice deserted him – the singer spending the first five minutes of his American debut croaking furiously behind Jeff's amplifier: "I remember the first time we played the Fillmore East," Stewart later told *CNN*'s Larry King. "I was so scared, I sung the first two or three numbers from behind the amps. I just wouldn't come out. I was actually hiding. Basically, there was no singer on the stage because I was so terrified."

Thankfully, the hoarse-voiced Stewart remembered that he and Ronnie Wood kept a small bottle of brandy in a bag near Waller's drum kit. One large hit later, Rod's courage kicked in, Jeff stopped playing solos to cover his vocalist's stage fright and Robert Shelton started writing his review: "Bang," said Ronnie Wood, "once the *New York Times* published that, the rest of the country was intrigued." Seizing the moment and a copy of *The New York Times* with his two very large hands, Peter Grant telegraphed a copy of Robert Shelton's kind words to the head of Epic Records, who in turn offered The Jeff Beck Group an immediate album deal. "That one gig," continued Wood, "just built the band's reputation."

Further dates consolidated Shelton's viewpoint, with the newly confident quartet handing in an assured appearance at Staten Island's Daytop Music Festival before beginning a week's residency at New York's Scene Club on June 18, during which Jimi Hendrix frequently joined them onstage. "I'd already jammed with Jimi [at Daytop]," Beck confirmed, "and The Scene was just six nights of bliss. He used to come on at the end of our set. With Jimi, you felt like you were part of something massive, history being made."

In town to work on his third album, the career-defining *Electric Ladyland*, Hendrix had already conquered America the previous year at 1967's Monterey International Pop Festival, setting fire to his Stratocaster with lighter fuel and a smile during the finale of The Experience's legendary performance.

Though now regarded as "part-shaman, part alien guitar god", Hendrix had thankfully lost none of his enthusiasm for jamming with anyone that might have the courage to share a stage with him. This fact was confirmed by Roger Mayer, who had continued to work with Jimi in his ever-evolving quest for new guitar sounds and effects. "Hendrix just really loved to play, but the problem from his point of view was that other guitarists were sometimes intimidated. Everyone's got an ego, and they'd get frightened by the prospect of jamming with him. I'm sure Jeff, Pete Townshend or Eric Clapton would agree. You see, when he landed in England, not only was he a great guitar player, he was also an extraordinary showman and singer. Maybe that combination was a bit strong for some. But Jimi was also a courteous guy, very giving to other players... he didn't want 'Being Jimi Hendrix' to get in the way. Really, he wanted to have fun." Confirming Mayer's theory, Hendrix's appearances alongside Beck in New York weren't just confined to fiery guitar duels.

Instead, he would take whatever instrument came to hand while onstage, including wearing Jeff's guitar upside down or simply using Ronnie Wood's bass guitar. "Jimi liked Ronnie Wood so much," said Jeff, "he actually gave him a basset hound as a present." Another visitor to The Scene Club was Eric Clapton, who jammed alongside both Beck and Hendrix one memorable night. "Sadly," said Jeff, "no one has a bootleg tape of it."*

After the events of New York, The JBG (as they had come to be known) spread their wings throughout the US, sharing stages with the likes of Moby Grape, The Grateful Dead and Sly & The Family Stone, whose unique mixture of rock, funk and soul Beck genuinely worshipped. Like the band's ever-growing profile, the

---

* Though no recordings were made of these jams, Beck later received a photograph from a fan of him and Jimi Hendrix playing at The Scene Club. The photo has yet to be made available to the public.

venues they played also became considerably bigger, ranging from Detroit's respectably sized Grande Ballroom to Philadelphia's Kinetic Playground, where audiences topped the 5,000 mark. It was at one such gathering in Boston that future Aerosmith guitarist Joe Perry first saw his hero. "The first time I ever saw Beck live was when I was 17, 18," he later confirmed. "The Jeff Beck Group played at the Boston Tea Party and I remember the band walked through the crowd carrying their instruments to the stage. Jeff plugged into these huge amps and I was just blown away. He was playing blues but his take on it was totally different to what I'd heard before. Plus, he was really flash and knew all the tricks. Jeff had a sense of humour about his playing… it was like he'd thumb his nose at you by playing certain notes. I remember waiting around afterwards and Jeff came down walking on his own with his Les Paul case in his hand. I stopped him and said, 'I just got to shake your hand, you're the best.' He just nodded, said 'Thanks' and walked on. The next day I decided I was going to buy a Les Paul. It was the first time I had seen anybody play one." As with so many of Beck's admirers, Perry would eventually trade licks with the guitarist, seeking to both acknowledge and repay a debt of inspiration while also fulfilling a long-held teenage dream in the process.

Following a six-date stopoff at promoter Bill Graham's Pacific-facing Fillmore West in San Francisco during July, The JBG finally concluded their first US tour at Los Angeles' cavernous Shrine Auditorium on August 3, 1968, offering able support to both Sly Stone and veteran blues master Albert King. The last time Beck was faced with such a schedule in the States, it almost killed him, the guitarist running headlong into the Texas night before various inflammations put him in a wooden box. Yet, under the ample guardianship of his manager Peter Grant, he had seen his latest venture flourish, America embracing the band's potent brew of blues and rock in their thousands. For Beck, this was justice. "America really was a last-ditch thing for us from Peter's point of view," he said. "Then within months, [we were] selling out…arenas without even having a record in the charts."

But not for long.

Chapter 10

The Grit In The Oyster

As The Jeff Beck Group were gathering up their belongings in LA for a long trip home to London, their debut album, *Truth*, was beginning its ascent on the US charts. The result of a "four day blitzkrieg session" at Abbey Road studios on May 14, 15, 16 and 25, 1968, the LP had been rush-released Stateside to capitalize on the band's recent concert success – its contents produced, mixed, mastered, pressed and thrown into the shops within two months of recording. Essentially a collection of road songs honed into shape while "playing glorified toilets and real small clubs" throughout the UK, *Truth* was mostly cut live with minimal overdubs and precious little in the way of embellishments. As time has come to show, it was also one of the best albums of the sixties.

It is difficult to imagine in an age when bands are given months – or in the case of Guns N' Roses, decades – to capture their best performances on tape the amount of pressure The Jeff Beck Group were under while making *Truth*. Yet, the circumstances of the day demanded product quickly, with singles often cut in hours, and an acetate copy of the results sometimes circulating at radio stations within days. As evidenced, The Beach Boys and The Beatles were bucking that trend by 1966/67, their 'power of sale' allowing them more time to get things right before any product escaped the studio. But The Jeff Beck Group had no such power at the time, being piddling minnows in a very large sea of basking sharks. Also, *Truth*'s producer, Mickie Most, was a man known to have little truck with indulging his acts' penchant for excessive experimentation. A product of old-school production values, Most's style was 'wheel 'em in, stick to the brief, press record, listen back, enhance the chorus and hope for the best'. But the very fact that Beck and his band were working within such tight perimeters still gives *Truth* a freshness, sparkle and spontaneity that most performers would gladly lose a digit or two for some four decades on.

From track one, *Truth* was keen to exhibit its class, the album beginning with a substantially reworked and damn sight more aggressive version of The Yardbirds' 1966 hit 'Shapes Of Things'. A pivotal moment in Beck's back catalogue, 'Shapes...' had been slowed down to a virtual crawl, with Jeff now dragging the song's chords behind him rather than launching them ahead of the beat. Full of gravelly-sounding slide fills (courtesy of a Sho-Bud steel guitar Beck had recently purchased), the highlight of 'Shapes...' was its 'pistols at dawn' mid-section, which found Jeff and Micky Waller chasing each other through a maze of drum rolls, crashing cymbals, slashing power chords and creamy arpeggios. Quite the start, then. Next up was 'Let Me Love You', which began life as a live cover of Buddy Guy's tune of (nearly) the same name, but was now credited to 'J.Rod'. Despite the undoubted cheek of Beck and Stewart claiming Guy's work as their own, there was actually little resemblance between their version and Buddy's own – the band upping the level of menace and soaking it in funk textures. Featuring a wonderfully salty performance from Rod, 'Let Me.' was also a showcase for Jeff's fearsome blues power, his guitar carefully tracking Stewart's melody line before breaking free in a bold display of flattened fifths and grumbling 16th notes. He was at it again on a newly recorded version of 'Rock My Plimsoul', letting Rod walk through the track with an almost conversational vocal before unleashing an inspired solo full of unison bends, slow string releases and much neck shaking (again, though 'Rock My Plimsoul' was a modified update of BB King's 'Rock Me Baby', the song was credited to 'J.Rod).

Peppered among *Truth*'s blues-rock attack were a couple of genuine surprises. Aside from the presence of 'Beck's Bolero' ("It was just too good to just throw away on the back of a single"), 'Morning Dew', 'Old Man River' and 'Greensleeves' were all examples of The

Jeff Beck Group stretching themselves admirably beyond the limits of the 12-bar. In the case of 'Morning Dew', Beck and Stewart had first heard the song at Brian Epstein's Saville Theatre extravaganza the previous July, where it was performed by American singer-songwriter Tim Rose, the man responsible for bringing 'Hey Joe' to Jimi Hendrix's attention. Entranced by the melody, and knowing full well original material was thin on the ground, Jeff suggested covering the tune for *Truth*. To strengthen the chances of Rod singing it, he readily agreed when the vocalist suggested adding bagpipes to the mix. "He said 'I want bagpipes', because he loves bagpipes," Jeff said in the album's sleeve notes, "so we got this bagpipe player in who was just dreadful, which you can hear."

Despite Beck's reservations about the "slightly sharp" pipe blasts and "misty, bloody naff Scottish Highlands at dawn thing", 'Morning Dew' allowed the world to hear what a superb singer Rod Stewart really was, his imploring vocal drawing out the inherent melancholy present in the lyrics: "What they've been saying all these years has come true, you know, and only you know, that there's no more morning dew..." The band's cover of Jerome Kern and Oscar Hammerstein's 'Ol' Man River' was even more left-field, with Rod singing along to a timpani drum (played by an 'incognito' Keith Moon) while Beck covered both slide and bass duties in the background. And for those wanting to know what a Beck 'classical album' might have sounded like, Jeff kindly provided a curiously faithful rendition of 'Greensleeves', delicately picking out the tune of the old English traditional folk song on a Martin D-18 acoustic guitar borrowed from Mickie Most.

But *Truth* was really at its best when The Jeff Beck Group abandoned the bagpipes, odd percussion and wooden box tops in favour of their original blues/rock template, a fact underlined by the album's three remaining tracks. On 'Blues Deluxe', the JBG were in 'slow burn mode' with Stewart first teasing, then screaming and finally hollering his way through the song before a visiting Nicky Hopkins elbows him out of the way to provide some spirited piano tinkling to a 'fake' live audience. "It really does sound live, too, doesn't it?" Hopkins later said. "Mickie Most did an excellent job of putting fake applause on the track. [It's like] an audience, you know, a crowd." Yet, the listener is never left in doubt as to whose show this actually was. Having waited impatiently in the wings for the best part of five minutes, Jeff Beck stepped into 'Blues Deluxe' like a visiting cyclone, bringing with him a rapid succession of growls, wild overbends and double stops, notes shooting this way and that before he again dropped out of sight 60 seconds later.

Beck also stamped his authority on an explosive cover of Muddy Waters' 'You Shook Me' (originally written by Willie Dixon), where in his own words, "The last note of the song is my guitar being sick... well, so would you be if I smashed your guts." Again accompanied by Nicky Hopkins' organ and piano flourishes, Jeff's solo at the end of 'You Shook Me' indeed lived up to his claim, vomiting all over Rod's shoes at the tune's conclusion. But Beck – and indeed his band – saved the best for last by transferring their spirited live rendition of Howlin' Wolf's 'I Ain't Superstitious' to Abbey Road studios mercifully intact. A showcase in rhythmic dynamics, with Wood and Waller using economy and occasional silence to mark the passing of phrases and chords, '... Superstitious' was still wholly owned by Beck – his inspired use of a Cry Baby wah-wah pedal issuing forth a guitar orchestra simulating angry dogs, horny cats, beached whales, dying swans and revving hot rods. "Actually, I wanted it to sound like a war club," he laughed.

Jeff's thick, commanding and endlessly adaptable tone throughout *Truth* was undoubtedly the result of leaving behind the Vox AC30 that defined his sound while in The Yardbirds for the newer Marshall amplifiers he now favoured both live and in the studio. As revealed, Beck first made the switch to Marshalls in mid-1966, having heard what Eric Clapton had achieved with the amp on the 'Beano' album. But the demands of now being heard in large halls across the US had seen him 'go one louder', settling on "a 200-watt Marshall amp with four cabinets", which he further distorted with either a MK II Colorsound Tonebender or (unknown brand) treble booster. Beck's famed '54 Esquire and back-up Fender Telecaster were also spending more time in their cases as the creamier sounds gleaned from his '59 Les Paul sunburst took greater precedence. "Well, Peter Green from Fleetwood Mac was using one, as was Eric," he later said, "so the Les Paul just seemed to be the way to go. Playing it through a combo or bigger amp [led to] thicker chords... it just sounded so rich."

Another innovation used to enhance Beck's tone while at Abbey Road came from engineer Ken Scott. Charged with overseeing recording during Mickie Most's frequent absences as he dashed to Olympic Studios in Barnes to produce Donovan's new LP, *The Hurdy Gurdy Man* (to which we will later return), Scott came up with a novel idea:"I said to Ken,'I'm just off to Olympic and I won't be long'," said Most,"so I want you to get a nice heavy guitar sound for Jeff'. [We got it] by putting Beck's amplifier in a cupboard in the studio, closing the door of the cupboard and putting the microphone outside.That was a good band," Mickie concluded,"they were quite creative."Though the Marshall 200 amp/Les Paul/locked cupboard combination may have been at the heart of *Truth*, Beck did not stop there. As the album was cut at relatively low volume, Jeff reportedly also used a Marshall 1987X 50-watt head through a 4 × 12 cabinet ("They sounded like you were blasting away at a million watts"), and might even have toyed with the odd Fender amp or Sunn amp head and Univox cabinet – a combination he put to use at head-crushing volume in later years.

A landmark album, both for guitarists and music historians who regularly cite its powerhouse approach, sore-throated vocals and riff-heavy content as being "the prototype of heavy metal", *Truth* is perhaps best enjoyed without the weight of history. Instead, it should simply represent Beck's then stated desire "to just blow minds" or, as probably, stake a legitimate, compelling claim for himself and his band alongside the likes of Cream and Hendrix in the increasingly competitive field of blues rock: "When you listen back to *Truth*," he said in 1986, "[it] doesn't sound like heavy metal to me. But I suppose when you hear Rod screaming, the varicose veins standing out on his neck and the loud guitars, yeah... I suppose they pointed towards that road, but not the heavy metal you recognise today." In this, he is surely right. When compared with the likes of Black Sabbath, Judas Priest, Iron Maiden, Metallica or latterly Pantera and Avenged Sevenfold, *Truth* has a swing to its step and an occasional lightness of touch wholly absent from that genre. It seems while such bands were happy to take the overloaded grunt and groan of Beck's guitar tone, they were also willing to leave behind the overt blues and funk influences that framed it: "You know, I don't like over-the-top heavy metal," Jeff once said. "I can't stand it. Too many amps, too much volume, it's just flat-out ear assault. I'm sure there's a lot of deaf people out there."

Regardless of the genres, sub genres or hearing loss it might have inadvertently inspired, *Truth* sat well with US audiences of the time, the LP banking at number 15 in the States during August, 1968. It also received a glowing review from the then all-important *Rolling Stone*: "*Truth* is a classic, much the way the Clapton-Mayall album is.... The singing is gorgeous and... first-rate throughout [and] as a band, they swing like mad..." Sadly, *Truth* didn't fare as well in the UK, where The Jeff Beck Group were still to make as substantive an impact as they had in America. While the album garnered a cult following among musicians, British journalists and *Radio One*'s John Peel, who played it relentlessly, such praise didn't translate into firm sales with *Truth* failing to chart when released on home soil in early October. More troubling still was the fact that the JBG had performed at a number of festivals during the late summer to audiences alert to their continued presence, including a prestigious spot at the eighth National Jazz & Blues Festival on August 10. Perhaps if Columbia Records had released the LP during that time, instead of reluctantly dragging it into the stores in mid-autumn, things might have been different.

After a brace of appearances in Denmark and Sweden, The Jeff Beck Group headed back to America on October 11 to drum up further sales of *Truth* and again take advantage of the lucrative earnings available on the ever-expanding rock circuit. There to witness their opening show at Chicago's Kinetic Playground on North Clark St. was Mickie Most, who had finally acceded to Peter Grant's endless requests and come to America to see what all the fuss was about. According to Beck, there were few things more pleasurable than watching his producer's jaw fall open as the band walked onstage to a full house of howling fans. "That was the end of any more fucking pop music," he wryly observed. For Most, this must have been a true 'Road to Damascus' moment. A firm believer in the pop ethos, he was now confronted with a new and exciting rock scene where performer and audience were separated in age by months rather than years, with both equally committed to crushing what had come before.

By the time Jeff and the band ventured to New York for a return visit to Fillmore East, they also had a new member in their ranks. After several years as London's most in-demand "studio rat", Nicky Hopkins had finally tired of the world of sessions and thrown in his lot – and Wurlitzer piano – with Beck. "*Truth* went over so well [in the US]," Hopkins later said, "and when Jeff got back [from the first American tour], he wanted me to do the second tour with him. At that point I said, 'Okay, well several bands have asked me to join them and do tours of the States before'. I was so locked into the session thing, which I really enjoyed... but then it just began to be really too much. So I said, 'The next person who asks me to join, I'm going to join'. I chose Beck."

The acquisition of Nicky Hopkins was a major boon. Probably the best keyboard player on the London circuit, Hopkins was renowned for being able to learn a tune in seconds, his classical background and strong improvisational skills sought by every major band of the time. Yet, he had also been dogged with persistent health problems since his youth when Crohn's disease was diagnosed. As a result, Nicky had never strayed far from the studio, preferring to work in a controlled environment rather than submit his stick-thin body to the potential abuses of the road. Obviously, following endless nights of recording with The Rolling Stones, he had come to the conclusion it was more beneficial to at least see the world from the back of a tour bus than through the endless haze of Keith Richards' cigarette smoke.

As the band rolled across the East Coast for a return visit to The Boston Tea Party, tragedy struck when Beck's beloved Les Paul sunburst was dropped by one of the road crew, splitting its neck. Though on a whim Jeff had recently stripped the guitar of its original finish, it remained his favourite instrument and would not be easily replaced. Hence, a variety of stand-in Strats and Teles were either purchased or pulled back into action before Beck found an able successor: a 'Tiger Stripe' Les Paul sunburst with Zebra pick-ups sold to him by future Cheap Trick guitarist Rick Nielsen. Sadly, when his favoured Gibson was returned by the repair shop, its replacement neck was half the size of the original, causing Jeff much disgust. To add insult to injury, the enterprising repair man had also torn out its highly prized PAF pick-ups and inserted standard replacements, causing it to squeal at high volume. Evidently cursed, the same guitar would suffer further humiliations in years to come, with more accidents, botched paint jobs and unrequested customisations eventually forcing its retirement, before a kind-hearted repair man took pity on Beck and provided a fine replacement.

After more dates in Philadelphia and Michigan alongside the likes of Alvin Lee's 100-miles-an-hour blues howlers Ten Years After, the JBG once again returned to the West Coast, appearing at LA's Shrine auditorium before making a final four-night stand at the Fillmore West on December 5–8. By now, Nicky Hopkins had become thoroughly versed in the pleasures of road life. "My God, there was some guy backstage at Fillmore West," he said. "I don't know whether it was [The Grateful Dead's] Jerry Garcia or whether it was somebody who just looked like him... [but he] kept passing me these enormous joints. I said, '*No*', [but it was] 'Go on, have some more!' By the time we got onstage, by about halfway through it, Beck was doing a solo and I just put my head down on the piano and went to sleep. One of the road managers came over and said, 'Nicky, wake up!' Well, I woke up and carried on with the set. I'd smoked so much grass, it was incredible..."

Another set of visitors to greet Hopkins backstage at The Fillmore were much more likely to wake him up than send him to sleep. Known to many a band visiting LA in the late Sixties, Girls Together Outrageously (or GTOs, for short) were "groupies to the stars", their apparent mission the bedding of whichever rock musician took their particular fancy. Graced with names such as Miss Pamela, Miss Sparky, Miss Lucy and Miss Cynderella, the GTOs enjoyed a reputation as fun-loving, occasionally whip-cracking doyennes of the Sunset Strip. Their erstwhile benefactor, Frank Zappa – who was steadily building a reputation as one of America's more creative, if downright weird composers – had recently suggested they make an album and the GTOs were determined to recruit Jeff Beck on guitar. Ever the musical philanthropist, Beck readily agreed to help, dragging along a none-too-protesting Rod Stewart and Nicky Hopkins with him to a recording session overseen by Zappa. The results of their endeavours surfaced on the 1969 LP *The GTOs: Permanent Damage*, an inessential, often unlistenable collection of out-of-tune vocals, show-tune pastiches and other listless experiments that Frank couldn't persuade his band The Mothers Of Invention to take seriously, but the likes of Miss Pamela were more than happy to howl over. For the record, Beck's guitar can be heard sounding like a wounded elephant at the end of 'The Eureka Springs Garbage Lady', while he adds a slide lick or two to 'The Ghost Chained To The Past, Present And Future (Shock Treatment)' and 'The Captain's Fat Theresa Shoes'. Given the fact that Jeff had earned something of a reputation on the groupie scene during his Yardbirds years, it was probably his turn to share the joy.

What happened next, however, brought Beck no joy at all.

At precisely the time the JBG were enjoying their first wave of US success, his old band The Yardbirds were imploding. As stated, after nearly two years of wobbly singles such as 'Ha Ha Said The Clown' and 'Goodnight Sweet Josephine' and a fair to middling album, *Little Games* (all produced by Mickie Most), The Yardbirds had finally downed tools at Luton College of Technology on July 7, 1968. Yet, while Chris Dreja, Jim McCarty and Keith Relf collapsed in an exhausted heap – their minds and bodies shot by five years on the road – Jimmy Page was in no mood to give up the ghost. Still contracted to fulfil a Scandinavian tour beginning in September, Page set about rebuilding the band with a new line-up, provisionally christened 'The New Yardbirds' – even resuscitating an exhausted Dreja to cover bass duties. At around this time, various drummers from the guitarist's past life as a session musician flitted in and out of view, including Clem Cattini and Paul Francis, but Page really wanted to find the right vocalist first. To that end he approached another Mickie Most protégé, Terry Reid, who had enjoyed a modicum of radio success with the single 'Better By Far'. A fine singer and guitarist, Reid was already committed to a US tour in support of Cream, but suggested Jimmy consider a young unknown from Stourbridge named Robert Plant, then covering vocals with the little-known Band Of Joy.

With Robert Plant came another piece of the puzzle, as Page's new recruit in turn recommended his friend, Redditch-born

John Bonham, for the position of drummer. The group apparently complete, a temporary spanner was thrown in the works when Chris Dreja graciously backed out to return to his original love, photography. "It was suggested to me while at art school, 'Dreja, you're doing fine art, perhaps you'd be better off doing photography'. So I gravitated back towards the camera, which eventually became as kind to me as music had been." Hearing of Dreja's decision, Jimmy's old friend from session days, bassist/arranger and multi-instrumentalist John Paul Jones, stepped into the breach. Following one swiftly arranged, though very promising rehearsal under a record shop in Gerrard Street, where the assembled quartet covered Johnny Burnette's 'Train Kept A Rollin'', Jimmy Page reported back to manager Peter Grant that he had found 'the right stuff'. On completion of their Scandinavian dates as The New Yardbirds, a new name for the band was required. Remembering Keith Moon's joke at the 'Beck's Bolero' session that their line-up would go down like "a lead Zeppelin", Page had his moniker, though the 'lead' was modified to 'Led' after Peter Grant raised concerns that the word might be mispronounced in America. One lost character later, Led Zeppelin were born.

By November 1968, Peter Grant had secured Led Zeppelin a $200,000 advance from Atlantic Records, a monstrous sum at the time, and all the more staggering when one considered the terms of the contract between band and record label. In addition to the money, Grant had brokered the right as to when Zeppelin would release albums and tour, and further, how such releases were packaged and promoted. They also retained final say when it came to singles, the group rather than Atlantic deciding not when but *if* said singles were appropriate for release. In a final thumbing of the nose, Zeppelin had even formed their own company, Superhype Music Inc., to deal with publishing rights to all group-related material. Even by Grant's own inimitable standards, this was impressive stuff. The cause of Atlantic's capitulation was the sheer quality of material Grant had presented to them. Instead of securing cash from a record label to finance their first disc, Led Zeppelin had simply done it on their own, entering Olympic Studios with Jimmy Page in the producer's chair upon their return from Scandinavia. Some 30 hours later and at a cost of £1,782 – including money set aside for a cover – the band had nine complete songs which Grant could hawk to the highest bidder. In this way, both band and manager were able to fully control their product, image and the terms under which they entered into a business agreement. Of course, the whole thing would fall down under the weight of its ambition if the songs were of dubious quality, but as Jeff Beck soon found out, Jimmy Page hadn't produced a dud.

Beck first engaged with Led Zeppelin's debut album at New York's Americana Hotel, where Peter Grant played him an acetate copy. At first, he was impressed by what he heard, until the LP got to track three, a fine version of Muddy Waters' 'You Shook Me', which Jeff had recorded only months before with his own group. Despite a slightly altered arrangement, which slowed the song down to a low rumble and emphasised Page's way with a slide, Zeppelin's take on 'You Shook Me' bore more than a passing resemblance to Beck's own. "I was mortified when Peter Grant played me the acetate," he told *The Guitar Magazine's* Vic Garbarini. "[At first] I thought 'Oh great, this is a great tribute to us'. So I asked 'Okay, where's the album?' And he said 'This is the fucking album, you're listening to it!' I said 'You're joking, we did that... months ago.' And Peter said, 'Yeah, but Jimmy loves this version and Robert sings it differently'. Well, I was both upset and flattered."

In an alternative take on the story, Page himself was present at the unveiling and Beck was more upset than flattered: "[Jim] said 'Listen to this, listen to Bonzo, this guy called John Bonham that I've got'. And my heart just sank when I heard 'You Shook Me'," Beck revealed to author John Tobler. "I looked at him and said 'Jim, what?' and the tears were coming out in anger. I thought 'This is a piss-take, it's got to be.' I mean, there's *Truth*, still spinning on everybody's turntable, and this turkey's come out with another version. Then I realised it was serious and he did have this heavyweight drummer. I thought 'Here we go, pipped at the post again...'"

If Beck made it to the LP's closing tune, 'How Many More Times', at precisely three minutes, nine seconds in he would have also heard Jimmy re-creating the melody line of 'Beck's Bolero'. One suspects

Jeff was long gone by then – as both the acetate and Page might well have gone out of the closest window.

Establishing the rights and wrongs of 'You Shook Me'''s appearance on Led Zeppelin's debut album, and indeed, whether the JBG were a major influence on Led Zeppelin, is a path fraught with difficulties. According to Page, a long-shared similarity in musical tastes was what led to the song being covered by both bands. "You've got to understand that Beck and I came from the same sort of roots," he told *Guitar Player*. "If you've got things you enjoy, then you want to do them... to the horrifying point where we'd done our first LP with 'You Shook Me', and I heard Jeff had [also done it]. I was terrified that they'd be the same. But I hadn't known he'd done it, and he hadn't known we had." Fair enough. But there is no doubting the fact that Page had accompanied Peter Grant to several Jeff Beck Group gigs when they first played America, and was therefore a clear witness to the dynamic interplay between Jeff's guitar and Rod's voice. He would also have seen the fluidity and strength of the band's rhythm section – two more vital elements of Led Zeppelin's future sound. During a 1976 interview with *NME*'s Billy Altman, Beck attested to this fact, stating that "[Jimmy] was going with us from city to city, taking things in". Rod Stewart made a similar claim about Page on a US radio show during the eighties. The situation takes on a murkier hue when one contrasts Jimmy's claim that he wasn't aware of Beck's version of 'You Shook Me' while recording *Led Zeppelin* against the fact that his future bandmate John Paul Jones was present at the sessions for *Truth*, even contributing Hammond organ to 'Ol' Man River'. '[But] Jonesy didn't say 'Oh, I've just done this with Jeff',' Jimmy said, "because the two [versions] were so different."

In Page's defence, the observation that he and Beck shared the same roots does hold water. Close for years, and long in the habit of raiding each other's record collections, swapping guitar licks and even sharing a stage with The Yardbirds, it isn't beyond the realms of possibility that the two drew – albeit unknowingly – from the same well for inspiration, or even the same Muddy Waters EP. Similarly, John Paul Jones' appearance on 'Ol' Man River' does not imply that he was present throughout the whole recording process. His remit as a hired session musician would simply not allow it. But

Page's presence on the JBG's first US tour, at a time when they were already performing 'You Shook Me', is less easy to explain away. An avid student and collector of the blues, Jimmy would surely have recognised Beck's source material and his novel treatment of it.

Perhaps what most annoyed Jeff Beck about Page's "freak accident" and, indeed, Led Zeppelin as a whole, was his friend's success in assembling a band that exactly met the requirements of the new age. Louder and more aggressive than Cream, more 'catholic' in their approach than Hendrix and less prone to internal strife than Beck's own group, Zeppelin emerged as a completely formed unit – one made up of a world-class singer, drummer and multi-instrumentalist – while their leader was one of the most business-savvy, talented guitarists on the world stage. As Chris Dreja said, "Jimmy was a man on a mission," and with Robert Plant, John 'Bonzo' Bonham and John-Paul Jones, he had found the troops to help him achieve it. "[Zep] had a better looking lead singer [with] golden, curly hair... a bare chest and the girls fell in love with him," Beck later confirmed. "They also had Bonzo... creating all sorts of pandemonium. It was a much better package than I had."

For some, this might have been precisely the time to 'rise to the challenge', 'fight them on the beaches', 'get back on the horse' – things of that general nature. But once again, Jeff was embroiled in a war in his own backyard that distracted, deterred and ultimately undid any chance of mounting such a challenge.

Chapter 11

All The King's Horses

The coming of Led Zeppelin in late 1968 and more specifically Jimmy Page's shock treatment of 'You Shook Me' seemed to unnerve Jeff Beck, who in his own words was "stunned, annoyed, flattered... and just a bit miffed by the whole thing". Caught unawares by his friend, and no doubt staggered by the terms of Zeppelin's new deal with Atlantic Records – a deal brokered by his own manager, Peter Grant – Beck once again began to seriously doubt the merits of his own band. With John Bonham, Page had found a sticksman of outstanding quality, the sheer thump of his bass drum enough to put the fear of God in those gathered at the back of a concert hall, let alone the front rows. In comparison, Micky Waller's lighter, funkified touch now sounded anaemic, or at least incapable of competing with the likes of Bonham. It was again time for a change.

Beck's solution was to fire Waller on February 11, only three days before his group were due to return to the States for a third tour. His replacement was Tony Newman, who began his musical career backing the likes of Gene Vincent, Sam Cooke and Jerry Lee Lewis on several UK concert packages, before joining Sounds Incorporated – an instrumental group who supported The Beatles at their now legendary Shea Stadium appearance in 1964. Though a louder, more aggressive proposition than Micky Waller, Newman's love of jazz drummers such as Louie Bellson and Buddy Rich meant that the JBG would retain its sense of swing, a quality Jeff was keen not to lose by shuffling the line-up. He was, however, perfectly happy to lose Ronnie Wood, who was sacked by Peter Grant in a terse phone call the same day Waller received his marching orders. An understandably shocked Wood was celebrating his girlfriend's 21st birthday at the time.

The umpteenth version of The Jeff Beck Group arrived at Worcester, Massachusetts on February 28 to begin the first date of their heavily rescheduled tour. On bass this time was Douglas Blake, a former member of Junior Walker & The All Stars, who had been hastily absorbed into the band only a day before. He lasted two gigs. "Beck had sacked Ronnie and Micky and got Tony Newman on drums and an incredibly bad Australian bass player who rehearsed with us once, the night before we went onstage," said Rod Stewart. "We died an all-time death. So the bass player [got] sent back to Australia and Jeff calls back Ronnie again... who by this time, is incredibly pissed off."* The fact that Ronnie Wood returned at all beggars belief, though a lack of employment at the time and subsequent offer of a wage rise may have helped calm his sense of outrage.

That said, the endless reshuffles, pointless sackings and general air of uncertainty were now starting to drive a wedge between Beck and his own band. Stewart and Wood had become firm friends in recent months, the two not only sharing hotel rooms while on the road, but also the same impish sense of humour. "With Rod and Ronnie, it was water fights, endless moonings, drinks on tap, midnight charges down hotel corridors, heads popping out of doors – not always theirs, I hasten to add – just rank insanity of the highest order," confirmed assistant US tour manager Don Murfet in 1998. Outside the group, they also inhabited similar circles, with Stewart dating Sarah Troupe, the best friend of Wood's partner, Krissy Findlay (whom Ronnie would marry in 1971). Things were further undermined when Rod was occasionally mistaken backstage by visiting record company employees as 'Jeff Beck'. "Nobody at Epic Records even knew Jeff," he told *Rolling Stone*. "They'd actually come up to me and say 'Hey Jeff, you sang great, fucking good guitar player you got in the group too...'" Even the normally placid Nicky Hopkins privately doubted

---

* Douglas Blake was actually from New Zealand.

how long it was before it all went pear-shaped: "Really, I was losing interest as far as all the bullshit was concerned."

In a troubling re-creation of his Yardbird days Beck once again grew ill, collapsing at a gig in Minneapolis on March 23, just three weeks into the tour. More troubling still was his band were no longer moving tickets in the same numbers they had only months before – the sales of *Truth* being easily usurped by Led Zeppelin's debut album, which had just entered both the UK and US Top 10. With more product required to reactivate interest in the JBG, all remaining US dates were cancelled and Beck and his cohorts flew home to begin work on a new LP in early April, 1968.

In the light of such growing unrest, The Jeff Beck Group's second album, *Beck-Ola*, was actually a surprisingly strong effort, if not quite as beguiling a prospect as the mighty *Truth*. Cut at De Lane Lea Studios in London's Soho district, *Beck-Ola* diligently followed the same red-eyed schedule as its predecessor, though the band were given the luxury of six rather than four days this time around to re-create the power evident in their concert appearances. Recording took place on April 3, 6, 8, 10, 11 and 19, 1969, with a further five days allowed for overdubs and mixing. Again overseeing production was Mickie Most who, thanks to his brief spell on the road with Beck in the US, was now marginally more sympathetic as to what he was trying to achieve. Sadly, Most was still in a position to do little or nothing about it, his pop ears simply incapable of steering the group towards true 'rock glory'. But when one pushed past the deficiencies in sound, there was much to admire about the LP, even if it consisted of only seven songs – and two of them Elvis Presley covers.

Of the material present, the instrumental 'Rice Pudding' was particularly pleasing, its opening riff still a mainstay of Beck's concert set some four decades later. First premiered at a BBC radio session in September, 1967 when it bore the title 'Old Mother's Rice Pudding', the track was all subtle twists and turns, Nicky Hopkins' nimble fingers matching Jeff's own as the band slowed, then quickened the tempo behind them. Unfortunately, 'Rice Pudding' also suffered from one of the worst endings in recorded history, the tape inexplicably cut stone dead instead of fading out into a pleasant abyss of white noise. "Without doubt," Beck once told *Guitar World*, "the dumbest thing I ever did was sign with Mickie Most." Perhaps he was thinking of the end to 'Rice Pudding' at the time. Most did get it right on the marvellous 'Spanish Boots' where The Jeff Beck Group managed to swing like James Brown while simultaneously out-pummelling Led Zeppelin, Ronnie Wood's outro solo also forever defining the term 'lead bass guitar'. 'Plynth (Water Down The Drain)' was equally impressive, its tight but loose, funk-rock structure providing a template for the likes of Deep Purple and Aerosmith to follow in subsequent years, as well as being a fine example of what new recruit Tony Newman brought to the quintet.

For those seeking proof of Beck's continued ability to dazzle on six strings, his madcap solo on 'The Hangman's Knee' provided compelling evidence, the track awash with throaty slide fills and a distinct lack of respect for anything approaching a musical scale. 'Hangman's Knee' also marked the 'official' debut of Jeff's love affair with the Fender Stratocaster, whose tremolo arm he tortured with Jimi Hendrix-style abandon throughout. "When we did *Beck-Ola*," he later said, "I'd just got fed up with the sound of the Gibson. In the studio, it didn't sound all that different from [Clapton and Green] in John Mayall's Bluesbreakers. It's a lovely sound, but every track ends up sounding similar." The Strat taking Beck's punishment was a 1954 model which he had stripped of its original finish and paired with a Marshall 100-watt stack. Coupled alongside a Dunlop Cry Baby, (unknown) delay unit and ever-present Colorsound Tonebender, the guitar's single coil pick-ups provided a lighter, but still stinging tone that can be heard throughout *Beck-Ola*. Like most of his instruments, Beck fell in and out of love with the '54 Strat over subsequent years, finally decommissioning it from live performance in the late seventies.

A much more gentle side of the JBG could be found on 'Girl From Mill Valley', "a pretty understated piece" written by Nicky Hopkins honouring a love affair he had begun with a young woman living among the Redwood trees, big skies and plunging canyons of Mill Valley itself. "It's just outside of San Francisco," Hopkins explained. "I totally fell in love with it [when] she took me out there. Just a magical place." Unfortunately, the band's covers of Elvis Presley's 'All Shook Up' and 'Jailhouse Rock' couldn't be deemed exactly magical, though they were certainly sprightly enough. Bearing little resemblance to Presley's fifties cuts, both tunes had been substantially rearranged to showcase Rod Stewart's exquisitely sore tonsils while also affording Beck an opportunity to abuse his favourite new toy, the 'whammy bar'.

A good, if not truly great, album, *Beck-Ola* perfectly illustrated the strengths and weaknesses of Jeff's current band. Accentuating the positives, Tony Newman was a strong find, working well with Beck on the arrangement to 'Plynth...' and providing a steely but swinging backbeat that allowed Ronnie freedom to take his bass excursions to ambitious new levels. Wood, Stewart and Hopkins also aided Jeff in the writing department, contributing melodies and chord ideas on the likes of 'The Hangman's Knee' and 'Spanish Boots' that could be developed by the group to full execution. But with only five new songs written in the last year to call their own, doubts had to be raised as to whether the JBG were a self-sustaining proposition or, more likely, a band that would always struggle in finding material strong enough to bring them to the next level. A possible clue as to that dilemma came from a dedication to fans in the album's sleeve notes: "Today, with all the hard competition in the music business, it's almost impossible to come up with anything totally original. So we haven't. However, at the time this album was made, the accent was on heavy music. So sit back, listen, and try and decide if you can find a small place in your heads for it." Honest as hell perhaps, but this was hardly fighting talk.

"*Beck-Ola* was an emergency album, really," Jeff later admitted. "At that point, the band was starting to act a bit childish. Especially Rod, who was really acting like a schoolgirl. I said, 'Look, we either start acting like adults on the road or head off to make a record'. *Beck-Ola* was the result. Sometimes, we might not have had the songs, but the LP had a nice cover." It certainly did. A reproduction of the Belgian surrealist René Magritte's 1952 painting *The Listening Room*, *Beck-Ola* bore a huge green apple on its front sleeve, while on the back – beside the album title – ran the words 'Cosa Nostra', the famous phrase used by the Italian Mafia to imply one shared aim, or literally 'Our Cause'. Beck had actually been handed the phrase by Mickie Most: "He said, 'Why don't you call [the LP] 'Cosa Nostra'," Jeff told John Tobler, "'because there's an evil overtone to it and it's kind of underhanded. It suits you, it suits the band's music... and it's a great title for an album'." But one the record company wanted to run a mile from. Fearing possible links being made to the real Mafia, or even reprisals from disgruntled Sicilian crime families, Epic strongly suggested Beck choose something a little less controversial. Given that Peter Grant's nickname for the guitarist was 'Beckola', a phrase he in turn adapted from the old 'Rockola' jukeboxes once found in the 2i's coffee bar: "I thought 'Why not use that for the title?" Beck said. It stuck.

In a perfect world, *Beck-Ola* would have been released to coincide with a well-organised globe-trotting tour, its sales bolstered by concert appearances, its success helping to heal the wounds of all recent discord within the band. Of course, this didn't happen. Instead, The Jeff Beck Group found themselves quickly back in the States to make things good with concert promoters and the Musicians' Union following the hasty cancellations of the previous March. Worse, there were arguments back in London with their record company and Peter Grant over both image rights issues around the album cover and the use of the word 'Cosa Nostra' on its sleeve. It was precisely against this backdrop that the quintet arrived at Fillmore East for a two-night stand on May 2, 1969: a strong new LP in the can, several new songs to air, but no album in the stores for fans to purchase. One could almost see the vultures circling.

To their credit, the band pressed on throughout May, performing at The Boston Tea Party, The Kinetic Playground and to placate a rightly irked Bill Graham – who had lost thousands of dollars in promotion costs when Jeff brought his naughty schoolboys back to London – a storming set at Fillmore West. Yet, backstage the atmosphere was becoming poisonous. By now, Beck and Stewart had all but given up even trying to resolve their differences, the two simply avoiding each other wherever they could. "It was getting too ridiculous for words," Rod said. "We were trying to hide from each other all the time." The situation was exacerbated by the group's post-concert arrangements, with Jeff reportedly staying at the finest hotels while his group were forced to share rooms and fight over food in lesser accommodation. Further, previous grumbling behind closed doors about unpaid wages was now slowly making its way to Beck's own ears, as old session hands Nicky Hopkins and Tony Newman began to ask what had happened to all the money. "Well, besides Stewart and Beck not getting along, there was a nice amount of hate between Nicky and Jeff, though I suppose a lot of that went into the music," Ronnie Wood told *Guitar World's* Gene Santoro. "Nicky would always come with the briefcase and the Mac. [Then] there was... Tony Newman, a real businessman. [He'd say] 'You mean you're being paid what?' Mickie Most is doing what? You need somebody to get organised'. And on and on." According to Newman, he simply did not realise how big a proposition the JBG were in the USA until he saw the audiences they commanded: "I had no idea until we got to the States of the magnitude of the group. And remember, I'd been around the block a few times when this came up..."

Already experiencing difficulties fulfilling his role as band leader, Jeff Beck was probably in no mood to act as an accountant or auditor. But even he could see something was very wrong with the group's finances. In comparison with the dip of previous months, gate receipts for the JBG had actually gone up on their latest tour, with houses of 2–3,000 generating $8,000 profit for a night's work not uncommon. Yet, neither he nor his bandmates were seeing anything close to those sums. "They wanted to know where the money was going to, and of course, I was getting the rap for it," he later told *Crawdaddy*. "We were getting ripped off." Regrettably, Beck's only recourse to action at the time was swift words with Peter Grant, who had built his reputation on ensuring the acts in his care were fully compensated for services rendered. But Grant was occupied elsewhere, helping Led Zeppelin take over America on very different terms. Not for the first time, Beck felt as if he was on his own.

The fractures began to resemble mighty cracks in June 1969, when pianist Nicky Hopkins either jumped from a sinking ship or walked the plank straight into a new job with established West Coast psychedelic rockers Quicksilver Messenger Service, led by the silvery fingers of guitarist John Cipollina. "Every opportunity was there but we blew it constantly, cancelling tours," said an aggrieved Hopkins. "We'd wake up one morning in the States only to find out Jeff had left the night before and was back in England." Hopkins himself would be gone within a month. As the JBG came off the road to lick its wounds, Stewart finally decided to take advantage of the loophole in his de facto band membership by signing a solo deal with Mercury Records. He and Ronnie Wood also began to establish close ties with Ian McLagan, Kenney Jones and Ronnie Lane, once three quarters of the wonderful Small Faces, but now without portfolio following the departure of their leader, guitarist/vocalist Stevie Marriott. Bored by constant in-fighting with Beck and sensing his future lay elsewhere, Wood agreed to taking over on guitar from Marriott, while a more cautious Stewart secretly tested the waters as a potential singer by playing two under-the-radar dates with the quartet in Surrey and Cambridge, billed as 'Quiet Melon'.

While all this skulduggery and potential double-dealing went on behind the scenes, to the outside world at least, The Jeff Beck Group were actually doing rather well: released at the end of June, the band's second album bounced into the US Top 30 at number 15, equalling *Truth's* chart placing a year before. Additionally, a lightning session the group had cut with 'Sunshine Superman' Donovan while recording *Beck-Ola* was also starting to bear sweet fruit. Though Donovan had originally been launched as the UK's answer to Bob Dylan in 1964, enjoying a string of hits with the whimsical, psychedelic folk-pop of 'Catch The Wind', 'Mellow Yellow' and 'Jenifer Juniper', changing times left him at an uncertain crossroads by the end of the sixties. With typical alacrity, producer Mickie Most decided to halt any further decline in sales by toughening up his sound, first with the single and album *The Hurdy Gurdy Man* (to which Jimmy Page contributed some robust guitar lines) and then by teaming him up with The Jeff Beck Group for the single 'Barabajagal (Love Is Hot)'. "Donovan was... on a sticky wicket at the time and needed some beefing up," said Jeff. "He wasn't making it very big on the airy-fairy butterfly stuff he was singing and Mickie thought it would be bizarre to have a wild heavy rock band behind him."

According to Donovan, 'Barabajagal...' began life as a simple two-chord vamp he played on acoustic guitar to Most. "Mickie said, 'Let's do it as a single'. Then he raised the question of which musicians to use." As Most was working on *Beck-Ola* at the time, he suggested dragging Jeff's band into the mix. "Well, I knew Jeff to be a hot-rod enthusiast and a mean mother on Fender guitar," said Donovan, "so we went for it." By all accounts, the recording of 'Barabajagal' was a chaotic pleasure, with Beck turning up late to the session covered in grease and without an instrument to play. "He said, 'Where's my fuckin' guitar?' and the group said, 'Oh no! It's locked in the van!'" Donovan told journalist Paolo Vittes. "So they phoned up and rented the best Fender Stratocaster they could find in London." While roadies began a frantic search to provide Beck with six usable strings, Nicky Hopkins reportedly sat at his piano reading Silver Surfer comics, idly watching Donovan teach the rest of the group his song. "Nicky could pick up a melody in seconds flat," Ronnie once said. "Never seen anything like it, before or since." The eventual result of the two-hour session produced a thoroughly unexpected pleasure for both Jeff Beck and Donovan fans, with 'Barabajagal...' still sounding as fresh as a daisy some 40 years on. Full of Latin-influenced beats, quasi-mystical, spoken-word interludes and a snapping guitar part from Jeff, the tune also featured some rousing backing vocals from Rod Stewart, Madeline Bell and Lesley Duncan. "In the end, it turned into a 'head' session, really," said Donovan. "Just like voodoo. Ronnie Wood, Rod, Jeff, it was rocking." A fine single even the similarly themed Happy Mondays would be proud to call their own, 'Barabajagal (Love Is Hot)' charted at number 12 in the UK during July 1969, its success leading to further collaboration between Donovan and Beck in subsequent years.

As 'Barabajagal...' warmed things up at home, an ailing but still active Jeff Beck Group made their fourth visit to the States, playing various dates on the East Coast, including a well-received appearance in New York's Central Park on July 7. Nearly a week later, they were again in New York, this time supporting Vanilla Fudge at Queens' Singer Bowl. For Beck, this was an opportunity to experience at close quarters a band he had long admired. Comprising of singer/keyboardist Mark Stein, Vince Martell on guitar, Carmine Appice on drums and Tim Bogert on bass, Vanilla

Fudge had provided American audiences with a home-grown link between the psychedelic movement and a new era in rock – their grinding 1967 version of The Supremes' 'You Keep Me Hangin' On' pointing towards a promised land of stabbing organs, sludge-laden guitars and windswept vocal harmonies. Jeff was especially taken with the Fudge's technically superb rhythm section of Appice and Bogert, watching in silent admiration as the duo demolished both the walls and audience of London's Speakeasy club when Vanilla Fudge made their UK debut there in mid-1967. Bottom-heavy, but with the ability to soar when the occasion demanded it, Fudge's self-titled debut LP had been regularly spun on Jeff Beck's turntable and also proved a minor influence on the sound of *Beck-Ola*.

"Their version of 'Shotgun' was [also] really near to me in style, and I thought 'Christ, these guys can really play'," Beck later told *Sounds*. "I wouldn't have associated my style with [Carmine's] grand, showy stick–twirling stuff and those harmonies... but when I heard 'Near The Beginning', that changed. I remember... being really flabbergasted by the drums."

Inevitably, the JBG's appearance at the Singer Bowl turned into something of a shambles, though it really wasn't their fault as events of the day overtook all concerned. Already scheduled to appear alongside Alvin Lee's Ten Years After, Beck was pleasantly surprised when several stray members of Led Zeppelin – some of them very drunk – also turned up at the show. Things went rapidly downhill from there, as the 'British contingent' began to wreak havoc both onstage and off. "Three English groups in one place has to add up to trouble," Jeff later quipped. Aside from covering Alvin Lee and his guitar with orange juice during Ten Years After's set, Beck's band were joined by Jimmy Page, Robert Plant and an extremely sauced John Bonham at encore time for a now historic – but in all probability bloody awful – rendition of 'Jailhouse Rock'. As Page struggled with a borrowed Telecaster and Plant tried to avoid being impaled by Jeff's 'mock' spearing of his genital region with the headstock of a Les Paul, Bonham began pounding out the beat to 'The Stripper' behind them, disrobing steadily as he went. Keen to get in on the act somehow, Rod Stewart then tried to insert a mike stand into the drummer's now bare posterior before the police made their move. "He got arrested, the cops pulled him off and I ran away," Stewart later told *Trouser Press*.

In the light of such insanity, Vanilla Fudge would have been well within their rights to fine their support act. "Well, as John Bonham stripped off and was running around nude... my parents were there," said Carmine Appice. "My mother was going, 'Who's the guy taking his clothes off?'" Yet, when Appice and Tim Bogert learned the next day from a now sober Bonham that Jeff loved their playing and might be interested in forming a band, they immediately sprang into action. "We said, 'Great, let's get word to him,'" Carmine told *The VF Journal*. "He'd already left... but we had his number. We called him and he wanted to do it." It was certainly during this period that Jeff first jammed with Vanilla Fudge on a commercial for Coca Cola, stepping up to the plate when the group's guitarist, Vince Martell, fell sick at a recording session. "Our guitarist Vinnie Martell got so sick that he had to physically leave the session," Tim Bogert told ainian.com. "There we were with the commercial producer ready to go and no guitarist. [Our roadie] Bruce said that he knew that Jeff Beck was in town staying at a hotel and offered to try to get him. We had been listening to *Truth* and *Beck-Ola*, and needless to say were excited at the prospect of having Jeff do the session with us. A short time later he just showed up, ready to play." Beck cut four different versions of the 'Things go better with Coke' advertisement in all, saying: "It was a funky thing and I got $300 for half an hour's work, which was great."

For Jeff, the very prospect of forming a band with Appice and Bogert was enough for him to call time on his own group. Burnt by Led Zeppelin's swift ascent to superstardom, and shackled to a bunch of musicians he had effectively lost control of, joining forces with Vanilla Fudge's drummer and bassist represented both an easy escape from his current woes and a fine opportunity to create an act technically capable of beating Jimmy Page at his own game. After a near onstage fight with Rod Stewart in Boston on July 24 and a blistering 'make-up' performance in Detroit two days later, Beck cancelled the band's remaining dates and headed back to London. If he had hung on just three weeks more, his band would have played to an estimated audience of over 400,000 people at the Woodstock

Festival in upstate New York, a four-day gathering that cemented Jimi Hendrix and The Who's statuses as rock giants, while also making stars of Carlos Santana, The Band and Joe Cocker. In fact, Beck's name was already on the posters for the event, though it gave him little cause for cheer. "No, I was never more pleased that I wasn't involved in that shit," he later told journalist Steven Rosen. "I never really felt at home with that – the headbands, the roses, the feet, the peace signs, all that bollocks. That wasn't me at all."

In other, even more candid moments, Beck has conceded that though his group were playing well enough to have benefited enormously from appearing at Woodstock, there were also genuine fears that it might all end in disaster. "No control of the PA... strange running orders, it wasn't going to happen. I just couldn't have stood the failure." The knowledge that the Woodstock festival was to be filmed for a possible movie release gave him an additional case of the jitters. "We weren't ready for 'the big screen'. I couldn't bear to be preserved on film playing out of my depth and having Rod hating the sight of me on screen."

Oddly, though Beck and Stewart were often at each other's throats during the final days of the group's last American tour, the guitarist was in no hurry to lose his singer. In fact, when Tim Bogert and Carmine Appice flew to the UK to meet with Jeff in September to discuss business issues around the formation of a new band, Beck was still trying to persuade Stewart there was a place for him in any proposed line-up. But Rod, with a new solo recording deal in his pocket and the formation of The Faces now only a whisper away, declined all Jeff's advances. "I'd [signed] with Mercury Records... just got a manager and they both said I [could] join The Faces and... make solo albums. That was it." Despite the fact that *Beck-Ola* had just broken into the UK Top 40 (albeit at number 39, and then only for a week), Stewart was having none of it. "I said, 'If that's what you want to do, then see ya'," Beck later offered. "I'm off to Heavy Street." The planned release of 'Plynth...'/Jailhouse Rock' as a single was subsequently shelved.

As Stewart sidled up to Ronnie Wood and his other new bandmates to begin rehearsals on The Faces' debut LP, *First Step*, and his first album as a solo artist, *An Old Raincoat...*, Beck finalised his own plans for a new group with Appice and Bogert. But on November 2, 1969, "it all went to rat shit." While out for a drive around Maidstone, Kent in a heavily customised 1923 Ford T-bucket, Jeff blew a tire and skidded into the path of an oncoming Morris. Though the other driver only broke a knee in the collision, Beck was not so lucky. Thrown from his vehicle on impact, he sustained multiple injuries, including a fractured skull, damaged back, deep facial cuts, smashed teeth and a broken nose – which still bears the scars of hitting the roadside some four decades later. He had been due to fly to America the following day to meet with Appice and Bogert. At first, Beck's injuries were thought to be relatively minor – or minor enough to warrant discharging him from hospital within two days. Yet, after begging doctors to re-examine his back, it was revealed that he had suffered severe trauma to the spinal region, resulting in a three-week stay on the wards sitting atop a wooden slate. Though Mickie Most and Peter Grant were quick to visit their ailing charge, Rod Stewart remained curiously absent. "When I had the car crash, well, that was it. Rod didn't even come to see me in the hospital," said Jeff. "When I came out of the coma, I picked up *Melody Maker* only to see he'd joined The Faces."

Beck's enforced hospital stay probably gave him an unwanted opportunity to review the recent past in horribly close detail. Just two years before, his band was on the cusp of creating something magical, and indeed with *Truth*, they had made good on that promise. An album soaked in delicious blues, funk and rock influences, with a wonderfully heavy soul, *Truth* might not have single-handedly birthed the thing we now call 'heavy metal'. But it was surely responsible for generating a slew of hard-rock bands that would strictly adhere to its richly drawn template of salty vocals, slashing guitars and tight-but-loose rhythms. And if *Beck-Ola* hadn't quite trumped the JBG's first LP, then it had at least come close to re-creating some of the magic, the likes of 'Spanish Boots', 'Plynth...' and 'Rice Pudding' closely skirting the majesty of 'I Ain't Superstitious' and the self-defining 'You Shook Me'.

Yet, while the albums were a fine snapshot of a game well-played, few had really come out of their time with The Jeff Beck Group covered in glory. A fine pop Svengali, Mickie Most's shortcomings as a producer had left glaring holes in the band's sound that Jimmy Page was able to plug with ease when recording his own group's debut disc. Equally, Most's blinding desire to see Beck only as a pop performer had threatened to destabilise the guitarist's career, confusing his fan base with several singles that continue to embarrass all concerned. Additionally, Peter Grant – perhaps still the finest manager of the modern age – had grown so tired of the JBG's endless squabbling that he threw his considerable weight behind Zeppelin at precisely the time Beck needed him most. Given the circumstances, some might not blame Grant for this. But Grant's strong hand might have given Jeff's band the extra push they needed to put aside their differences and attain their rightful place at rock's top table. Sadly, we shall never know.

As for the JBG itself, each member had their own take on why it failed. According to Nicky Hopkins, who was the only one among them to play Woodstock, as a stand-in keyboardist for Jefferson Airplane and The Jerry Garcia Band, the answers to their problems lay solely at Beck's own doorstep: "What can I say? Jeff was a brilliant guitarist who unfortunately lost one of the best bands we've ever had through foolishness."

For Rod Stewart, whose alleged "childish behaviour" alongside partner-in-crime Ronnie Wood drove Beck to thoughts of murder, it was more a case of fear in the ranks rubbing shoulders with poor leadership skills: "It was a great band to sit with, [but] I couldn't take all the aggravation and unfriendliness that developed," he said. "Do you know, in the two and a half years I was with Beck, I never once looked him in the eye. I always looked at his shirt, or something like that." In Jeff's mind, Stewart's claims were more a case of 'kettle and pot'. "Before the friendship between Rod and Ronnie cemented, everything was great and we were over the moon," he told John Tobler. "Then they starting acting like a couple of girls and I couldn't handle their girl-guide humour. We were self-destructing then, and I didn't want to go on with those silly vibes."

But as was the case with The Yardbirds, time proved to be a great healer for almost all concerned. With advancing years, the insults lessened – to be overtaken by a sense of pride in what the group had achieved. "You know," Rod told *Q* in 2002, "it was a wonderful learning experience, because the musicianship was just so high. Jeff, Ronnie, Micky, Nicky – a fabulous band to be in. And the way the vocals were used, I was a real instrument in that band. I didn't know how important *Truth* would become, creating a little bit of rock'n'roll history, influencing musicians and singers. It was truly great stuff." Wood too, became markedly more giving to his former employer: "Jeff was only after one thing – to blow minds. And he blew mine often enough. But I always loved the way he played."

As with the others, Beck knew it was all a case of lost opportunity. "Those were magic days," he told *Musician's* Scott Isler: "Rod had a freak voice. He is a freak. No one can sing like that. Everyone else, they're just copies. Rod Stewart was, is, the prototype." He also conceded that his own inflated sense of self-importance at the time was a factor in helping start the auto-destruct sequence that eventually did for the band: "I bought into that stuff about how great I was and how great my guitar playing was. Everyone," Jeff concluded, "goes through an ego trip."

Away from the mudslinging, self-laceration, petty squabbling about who-did-what-to-whom and "other pointless stupidity", the Rod Stewart-era Jeff Beck Group were – and always will be – a great rock'n'roll band. Pioneers to a man, they brought a brand new approach to bear on sixties music: gloriously heavy, inherently soulful and with lashings of world-class guitar, the JBG thoroughly deserve their place in history, a fact further underlined by recently unearthed live tapes of their final live performances at Bill Graham's Fillmore East, where the likes of 'Shapes Of Things' and 'You Shook Me' still sound vital, energetic and just a wee bit evil.

But as Beck once told *Melody Maker* in 1972, no matter how potent the brew, it was still governed by its sell-by date: "I read criticisms of groups for breaking up. But if they want to break up, it's up to them. It's not their duty to stay together if they've reached the end of their creativity. There's just no point..."

Chapter 12

Power Over Loudness

When casting an eye over Jeff Beck's long and varied career, it would be hard to find a more uncertain period for the guitarist than November, 1969. Following the injuries he sustained when thrown from his Ford T-bucket in Maidstone, Beck was informed by doctors it might take years, not months, until he was completely healed. In addition to the harm done to his back, Jeff's fractured skull was also of enduring worry – the latest impact wound only a matter of centimetres away from the area he damaged when hit by a car at the age of 11. In a true moment from *The Twilight Zone*, Beck realised that both accidents had taken place on exactly the same day some 14 years apart. As a consequence, he swore never again to venture beyond his own doorstep on November 2. Furthermore, when released from hospital Jeff began to realise the full extent of what had befallen him, with waves of nausea, blinding headaches and severe lapses in concentration all rocking his already unsteady frame. The worst malady, however, was an aversion to loud noises, not the easiest of symptoms to overcome for a man who made his living driving amplifiers to the point of overload. "My head," he said with some understatement, "was in pretty bad shape."

Having been told to rest for at least at least six months Beck was obviously in no position to work, a fact that forced Carmine Appice and Tim Bogert to finally abandon plans of starting a new group with him and move on to other pastures. Their solution was to form Cactus with ex-Detroit Wheel guitarist Jim McCarty and former Amboy

174

Dukes singer Rusty Day, a fulsome blues-rock quartet that would keep them busy for at least another 18 months. "[When] Jeff got in a car accident and he couldn't work... me and Tim didn't want to sit around and wait," Appice said. "In those days, when you broke up with a band, you usually didn't break up on good terms. So it wasn't like, 'Let's go back to Vanilla Fudge.' We had to keep moving ahead, so that's why we put Cactus together." Beck, on the other hand, was in no great position to do much of anything but stare into space, even avoiding the chore of listening to his old records when he could: "I couldn't relate to anything I'd done before... I had a kind of musical amnesia. My playing wasn't affected, but I had no sense of proportion on what I was doing."

Nonetheless, he could take some comfort from the circumstances around him, namely a recently acquired 1932 Ford Coupe and a two-seater Roadster that needed considerable restoration, a beautiful new home in the countryside and the continuing sympathy of his partner of nearly two years, the model Celia Hammond. In the case of the cars, Beck's interest required no real explanation. But the purchase of property was of perhaps more interest. Having grown tired of flitting between rented flats in places like Putney and Surrey, Jeff had made the decision to escape the rat race and buy a wooden-beamed, 16th-century cottage with 10 acres of grounds in a small village in East Sussex. Boasting a population of just over 1,000, with local amenities confined to The George pub, a small string of local shops and a football/cricket pitch, Beck's choice of locale was as telling as it was impressive. He had always hated the steady roar of London and now he had completely removed himself from it.

Accompanying him on the move was Hammond, whom Jeff had met after his relationship with the actress Mary Hughes ended. Like Hughes, Hammond was tall, blonde and quick with a quip, but the similarities really ended there. Perhaps second only to Jean Shrimpton as the UK's most recognisable model of the time, Celia's striking profile regularly graced the cover of *Vogue* during the mid-to-late sixties, her image captured by the likes of elite photographers Terence Donovan, David Bailey and Norman Parkinson. In fact, it is Hammond's face that was featured on the cover of The Jeff Beck Group's first album, *Truth*, in an arresting photo taken by Stephen Goldblatt. Yet it appeared that Celia had little truck with the modelling industry beyond the cash it provided: "[It was] a good way to earn money... and all good fun. [But] we'd fly to Greece to take a single picture." Matters came to something of a head as a snowballing interest in animal welfare and growing disgust at the practice of seal culling led her to refuse to wear fur during shoots. This stance was later celebrated by Beck's old friend Donovan, who wrote the song 'Celia Of The Seals' in her honour: "A cruel and heartless deed, Celia of the seals, she knows just how they feel...". The song can be found on 1971's *HMS Donovan*, an album on which Jeff contributes a brief guitar solo to the song 'Togetherness', actually recorded two years earlier.

By the time of their relocation, Hammond had largely abandoned modelling in favour of rescuing unwanted cats, their new cottage and its grounds now home to at least a dozen felines as well as Beck's ageing Afghan hound. The number of strays and abandoned animals would grow to much higher levels in subsequent years, with Hammond even earning the nickname 'St. Celia of the Cats' from visitors to their house. Jeff rarely objected to sharing his home with the growing brood. Instead, he took to the life with some pleasure, even becoming vegetarian in deference to his partner's beliefs: "I gave it a try and never looked back. Not very rock'n'roll, but there you are..." According to Beck, there were other benefits to be gained from such an essentially moral decision. "Being a vegetarian slows you, stops the animal aggression a bit," he told *Musician*. "But it also opens another door, of self-control. You can accept a lot more criticism without losing your temper. When I ate meat, I was much more aggressive. After eight months of not eating meat, I went for the throat of the guitar instead of other people's throats." Thankfully, Rod Stewart did not often call at Jeff's cottage to test the theory.

As one new decade rolled into another, Beck had sufficiently recovered from his injuries to attend Led Zeppelin's appearance at the Royal Albert Hall on January 9, 1970, a show which was filmed and later released on their DVD package of 2003 (Jeff can be briefly seen strolling around backstage, joking with Jimmy Page). During the period of his recuperation, Zeppelin had ascended from attendant superstars to virtual deities among rock audiences with the release of their second LP, *II*, which topped the charts on both sides of the

Atlantic – a fact Jeff was sorely aware of. "When Zep started doing huge concerts and I was just sitting in the garage with the cars listening to the radio I [thought] 'What's going on? I started this shit, now look at me!'" Seeing his friend's group decimate a London crowd with the likes of 'Communication Breakdown' and 'I Can't Quit You', while adding future classics 'Heartbreaker' and 'Bring It On Home' to the set, Beck's attention was again drawn to John Bonham: part drummer, part mythical beast, Bonham's terrifying intensity, unrivalled technical aptitude and sheer bloody loudness thrilled him beyond measure. It was time to find one of his own.

Beck's cautious return to public duty began with the recruitment of Colin Flooks or, as he was better known, Cozy Powell. A native of Cirencester, Gloucestershire, 23-year-old Cozy – who adopted his nickname in honour of jazz sticksman 'Cozy' Cole – was in many ways the original journeyman drummer, having already played with a slew of minor bands before joining forces with Beck. From his teenage years as a member of The Corals and The Sorcerers to later work with The Move's Ace Kefford, Tony Joe White and Big Bertha, Powell was no stranger to swapping drum stools when the mood took him. It was a habit he would never really lose. But like John Bonham (who was a close friend of Powell's), Cozy was an immensely gifted musician, capable of enhancing any group he joined. To a confirmed "drum freak" like Jeff, he was also a gift from the gods. The two met when Beck began auditioning an endless cast of would-be percussionists in a Hampstead rehearsal studio in February, 1970.

Powell was invited to attend by Peter Grant, who despite his ever-growing commitment to Led Zeppelin, continued to manage Jeff's affairs and this latest attempt at pulling together a group that might not kill each other if they ever got as far as the road. Knowing Cozy's reputation, Grant had asked him to step into a back office on his arrival in Hampstead, sending his own secretary to inform Beck he was wasting his time with auditions when the best candidate was sitting but yards away having a coffee. Powell took up the story in 1984 with *Modern Drummer* magazine: "He had a lot of guys that were tapping away at this little Hayman drum kit that was there. I brought my Ludwig kit down [with] the old red double bass drum kit and set it up right in front of him. I thought 'I'm just going to go for it, and if I don't get the job, at least I'll have left my mark. I've got nothing to lose.' Jeff was the sort of guy who would just be standing there saying 'next'. A drummer has got to be in charge of the band, so I just started one of the tunes and he put the guitar down halfway through it and said, 'You've got the job'."

For the best part of a year, Cozy was left to ponder exactly what "the job" was as Beck slowly, methodically, and no doubt infuriatingly for Powell, auditioned prospective band members while simultaneously dabbling in just about any project that piqued his interest as long as it bore no resemblance to sixties 'blues rock'. Still volume-sensitive after his accident, Jeff had spent little of his recuperation time listening to the 'strum and drang' that surrounded him while on the road with the JBG. In fact, he seemed keen to wash most of that period out of his hair completely. "I hated the sixties, he later said. "It was full of lost souls, ludicrous trousers and women in floppy hats. I had my music stolen and my fashion decided for me. All I was really interested in were the prettiest girls. Unfortunately, you had to go back to their place with a bunch of lunatics. I used to watch all their degeneracy for hours. People just coming apart."

Still an acolyte of fifties rock'n'roll at heart, the guitarist had approached the era of flower children with some disdain, its fashions, foibles and all-pervading drug culture an anathema to the sleek lines, slap-back echo and sharp suits of a decade before. "Flared trousers... long hair... headbands. I just couldn't really handle that," he told Steven Rosen. "I didn't really want to. I wanted the rockabilly stuff, Gene Vincent. That's what I wanted to see and I was robbed of that. I never saw any of that. I kept asking everybody, 'Where's Chuck Berry? Where's Gene Vincent? Where's Elvis?' And they'd say, 'Huh? Do you guys know The Beatles?' And we'd say, 'Fuck off.' Yeah, it was like that."

Yet, one part of the sixties that continued to make complete sense to Beck was Motown. Crisp, tuneful, immaculately produced and driven by a beat one could not only dance to but, in Jeff's own words, "Live to", Motown Records' "Hitsville" sound was a far cry from the frying valves and torn drum skins of his previous incarnation. And indeed, when one stacked the records of The Jackson 5, Marvin Gaye, Jimmy Ruffin and Diana Ross & The Supremes alongside the heavy thud of established rock acts like Led Zeppelin, Deep Purple and even more progressively themed, classically influenced newcomers such as King Crimson, Genesis and ELP, Jeff really was swimming against the tide. Still, funk rhythms had been at the heart of the early Jeff Beck Group, with Micky Waller and Ronnie Wood swinging to their hearts' content when the mood took them. There was also no doubt that Beck and Rod Stewart's earliest conversations when forming the band had centred on a mutual love of the Detroit scene, the two bonding over a pile of Four Tops and Temptations singles. But Jeff was not going to make it easy on himself by simply producing a carbon copy of the Motown groove. Instead, he wanted to toughen things up by superimposing the raw, overdriven tone of his guitar on a bed of sharp, melodic bass playing and incisive, groove-laden beats. In short, Jeff Beck wanted a 'deranged' Motown of his very own.

In the early summer of 1970, Beck got his wish, when he, Cozy Powell and the still ever-present Mickie Most flew to Motown studios, then located at 2648 West Grand Blvd. in downtown Detroit. The brief they gave record company executives was simple enough. Over the course of 10 days, Beck wanted to cut some instrumental tunes with Most producing. Powell would take care of the drums while Motown legend James Jamerson would sit in on bass. Several other session musicians would enhance the results, which in turn would form the backbone of Jeff's new album. Then it all went a bit wrong. First, Powell decided that Motown's drum kit simply wasn't going to work for him and took to dismantling it in favour of his own double-bass drum version. "I'd used two bass drums for about two years," he later explained. "It's not a gimmick. When you play these huge places... you need loud drums." A bemused Jamerson simply watched from a corner, while casually observing, "There goes the Motown sound."

The general mood slipped further into the abyss when Jamerson and his fellow backing musicians requested to see transcriptions of what they would be working on. Used to jamming rough outlines into usable shape with his former band, Jeff and Mickie hadn't thought about bringing any sheet music with them, which left the immensely talented but hardened sessioneers staring in disbelief, their irritation palpable. "I took some of my own tunes over. I didn't think I'd need the music for them because they were so simple, but things got pretty ugly because the musicians didn't want to think," Beck later said. "They usually have the music [written out] in front of them, but I went straight in laying down these chords on them and they didn't want to know. Well, actually they did for a while, because they found out they were being paid the same – only they had to work harder, which they didn't like."

The results of Beck's endeavours in Detroit – or "The Motown Sessions" as they have come to be known – have never been released. According to Jeff, the majority of his guitar parts were recorded directly into the studio console without benefit of amplifiers – thereby stripping the crucial 'rough house' element from his sound. Few, if any, solos were cut. Additionally, the famed billowing reverb that earmarked all Motown's classic releases seemed to be absent from the final tapes. Unusually, Mickie Most was not blamed for the oversight. "Without the trademark reverb," Beck later remarked, "The results were really bland." The tracks he managed to record at Hitsville included cover versions of The Temptations' 'I'm Losing You' and The Four Tops' immortal 'Reach Out (I'll Be There)', as well as rough mixes of lesser-known material such as 'Don't Give A Hoot' and 'I Can't Give Back The Love I Feel For You' – the latter of which Jeff would subsequently rework. Bitterly disappointed by the outcome, Beck, Most and Powell returned to London, the tapes forever filed away in a bomb-proof vault. "It was," Cozy later concluded, "the most obscure thing I've ever done."

There was a further, unwelcome diversion with the release of *Screaming Lord Sutch And Heavy Friends* during the summer of 1970, an album of drunken, late-night jams cobbled together by Beck's former bandleader from the previous year, which included contributions not only from Jeff but also Jimmy Page, John Bonham and Nicky Hopkins. While Beck was willing to laugh at Lord Sutch's cheek, dismissing his own solo on 'Gutty Guitar' with the words, "I must have known what I was doing [because] I vaguely remember recording it," Page was not feeling so humorous. Irritated by a photo and supporting caption of himself and Sutch printed in *Melody Maker* which seemed to imply his official involvement in the project, Jimmy wrote an angry, distancing letter to the music paper. "I just went down to have a laugh," he said, "playing some old rock'n'roll, a bit of a send-up. Then, the whole joke sort of reversed itself and became ugly." With the image of Led

Zeppelin now coalescing into an untouchable, four-headed beast, Page did not want any mistakes – no matter how insignificant – troubling his band.

Jeff, on the other hand, seemed to be willing to try just about anything to keep busy or divert him from the business of forming a group, including playing side man to Elton John on a possible American tour. Though not a household name as yet, John had already established his credentials as a promising singer-songwriter, his self-titled debut album of April 1970 causing a stir among the critics and producing a minor hit in the US with the single 'Border Song'. As its follow-up, 'Your Song' was likely to break Elton wide open in the States, the pianist had begun conducting rehearsals for a series of dates there in August. Having heard John's LP and its obvious country influences, Beck was initially sceptical. But a visit to see the pianist perform at London's Speakeasy club – where Elton provided a surprisingly rocking set – eased his concern. As with Beck's Motown experiment, things went badly with Elton. With the guitarist arriving an hour late for their first meeting at Hampstead Town Hall due to a malfunctioning car, John proceeded to bite Jeff's ear off for his tardiness. Once matters settled, they actually got on well enough, with the bespectacled one complimenting Beck on his highly melodic tone. But when the guitarist suggested replacing John's regular drummer, Nigel Olsson, with Cozy Powell, the two swiftly parted company.

Beck's next brief dalliance was with his former band The Yardbirds, who were threatening to reform for a short UK tour at the end of the year. Sensibly, Keith Relf abandoned the idea, but not before he had roped Jeff into laying down an impressive solo on 'If You've Got A Little Love To Give', the lone single release by The Holy Smoke – a temporary alliance comprised of Relf, his sister Jane and Jim McCarty, who had originally written the song and it's B-side, the impressive 'It's All In The Camera', for fading beat group stars The Dave Clarke Five.

Among all these false starts, odd liaisons and general acts of whimsy, Beck was also confronted with genuine tragedy when on September 18, 1970 Jimi Hendrix died at the London flat of his girlfriend, Monika Dannemann, after a mixture of sleeping pills and red wine caused him to asphyxiate on his own vomit. Only 27 years old, Hendrix had blazed an astounding trail since coming to prominence in early

1967, pushing the boundaries of guitar into hitherto unexplored territories. Yet, a never-ending schedule of tours, recording dates and the demands of publicity that surrounded them had exacted a heavy toll on the guitarist, pushing him ever further to the point of exhaustion and spiralling drug dependency. For Beck, this cocktail of insurmountable business pressures, questionable management practices and chronic lack of care for his well-being were as much responsible for Jimi's death as the mixture of drugs and drink that actually killed him: "People expecting miracles from him every night was too much for him, really," Jeff said. "I could see him going down as a result of it, his playing suffering as a result of it and then, unfortunately, the worst happened. It's a bloody shame there was nobody around to make sure it didn't."

Given Jeff Beck's longstanding admiration of Hendrix, it should have come as no great surprise that he toyed with offering the vacancy of bass player in his own fledgling group to Jimi's original Experience bandmate, Noel Redding, the pair jamming regularly throughout 1970. But when Jeff finally emerged after months of chasing his own tail with a brand new line-up for the JBG (Mark II) in the spring of 1971, it was a teenager named Clive Chaman who had secured the spot. "It took us about a year to find the right bass player... because Jeff wanted someone who could play in a sort of Motown style, but he couldn't quite put his finger on what he wanted," said Cozy Powell, with some understatement. "Then when Clive came along, he was really the ideal man." A native of Trinidad, Clive Chaman had been working with folk troubadour Cat Stevens when Powell extended an invitation to come and meet Jeff. Jamming in the improbable setting of a disused hair salon, the trio clicked almost immediately, with Beck greatly given to Chaman's "James Jamerson-style lines". "Playing with Jeff," said Chaman, "I felt I could just be myself."

The next to join up was Alex Ligertwood, a no-nonsense Glaswegian who reportedly arrived unannounced at a Beck rehearsal one afternoon to offer his possible services on vocals, bass, rhythm guitar or even drums. When Jeff learned Ligertwood had sung in a number of minor Scottish acts, including The Primitives and a 'White Soul' covers band called The Senate, he put him in front of the microphone. On hearing Alex's sinewy style – part Rod Stewart, part Robert Plant, with a little bit of Sam Cooke thrown in for good measure – Beck offered him the job. Last in, but certainly not in terms of talent, was a 25-year-old former dock worker called Max Middleton. Owning only one or two Horace Silver records at the time, the classically trained Middleton had only been playing professionally for a matter of months when Clive Chaman – whom he knew from the band Flare – alerted him that Beck was seeking a keyboard player. "When I came to rehearsals, Jeff was sitting up against the wall playing his guitar," Middleton confirmed. "He didn't actually look up when I walked in. No reason why he should, I suppose! Anyway, Cozy came over and shook my hand, and I thought, 'Oh, he must be the leader of the band'. I really didn't know at that point Jeff played guitar. But when I started to listen to him play, I just heard this strength. I could feel something there. I just loved his playing. After a while, Jeff just said, 'We're in Island Studios next week, do you want to make a record?' And that was the start of it."

Though Max Middleton was the least experienced musician to join Beck's band, he was also to prove the most important of this latest batch of recruits, his easygoing manner disguising a formidable mastery of Fender Rhodes piano and Hohner clavinet, as well as some keen songwriting skills. More, Middleton was also crucial in opening up Jeff's ears to the possibilities of jazz, a style which Jeff would gravitate towards in due course. "Max Middleton was the first musician I had played with who didn't make me feel embarrassed that I didn't know the names of the chords he was playing," Beck confirmed. "He would just go just through the notes in the chords and I would learn them." After an excruciating 12 months of "failed experiments and general fuck ups", it at last appeared that Jeff had found a group of musicians who could take his ideas forward to album stage. "Yes, it took about a year to find the rest of the group," he confirmed to *Sounds*. "I had Cozy and he was getting bored stiff. He just wanted to play [and] I just wanted to sit back and think."

Following a short period of rehearsals, the group entered West London's Island Studios at the end of April 1971 to begin work on a new LP, Beck's first in nearly two years. Replacing Mickie Most as producer this time around was the redoubtable New Yorker Jimmy Miller, who had not only overseen The Spencer Davis Group's finest single, 'Gimme Some Lovin'', but two great Rolling Stones albums, *Beggars Banquet* and *Let It Bleed*. Being a drummer himself, Miller was almost obsessive in his devotion towards finding the perfect percussion sound – this pursuit gloriously evidenced on the Stones' 'Honky Tonk Women' and a fact not lost on either Beck or Powell. But the sessions were mired in personnel, record company and management difficulties right from the off. Within days, representatives from CBS had rounded on Alex Ligertwood, apparently disliking his rough-hewn vocal style. "Alex was a great musician, nothing wrong with him at all," said Middleton, "But for some reason, the record company just weren't hearing it. Then, Jeff got a bit panicked..." As a consequence, Ligertwood was let go. "I felt terrible about it," Beck later said, "but I had to kick him out."*

As worrying was a behind-the-scenes feud brewing between Beck and Mickie Most. Unhappy with the general terms of a new contract being offered by RAK Management, and Most's hasty plans to put his band on the road by summer, Beck had walked away from any further negotiations. Most, on the other hand, was unimpressed by Jeff's growing penchant for 'Motown Rock' and the fact he was paying Jimmy Miller to record it. With Peter Grant now fully engaged in all matters Led Zeppelin, there was no mediator to calm the situation down. The stalemate was broken by Ernest Chapman, a former Lincolns Inn solicitor and in Max Middleton's words "a very straight shooter". Stepping in to resolve the dispute, Chapman soon learned that all Beck's royalties had been going directly to Most for distribution instead of to the guitarist himself. This was soon stopped.

The next step was to renegotiate the terms of Jeff's US record deal, which resulted in Ernest and Jeff flying to America for private talks with Columbia (Jeff would also sign a new UK agreement with CBS subsidiary label Epic). These actions did not sit well with Most, who arranged a 'cease and desist' order on Beck's new LP and duly confiscated all studio tapes. The matter was finally resolved to everyone's satisfaction by June, when Beck terminated his association with RAK and Most walked away with (and subsequently buried) the Island sessions, while also retaining a proportion of the profits

* Alex Ligertwood later resurfaced in the ranks of Santana and Dixie Dregs.

from Jeff's next LP. "There was nothing right about it," Beck later said of his time working with Mickie Most. "It was expensive both emotionally and financially." What Jeff had gained in addition to control over his future was a new and decidedly impressive manager in Ernest Chapman. Unswervingly loyal, incredibly patient and "a true gentleman" to boot, Chapman's clipped tones and astute business mind would serve Beck with distinction for the next 20 or so years.

Now a free man, Beck still had several pressing matters to attend to before he could finally get an LP in the stores. Having lost the services of Jimmy Miller in the management merry-go-round, he was now without a producer and, due to record company pressures, also had a glaring vacancy at the mike stand. Jeff resolved the first issue by taking on production duties himself and the second by installing one of bassist Clive Chaman's close friends, Bobby Tench, on lead vocals. As with Chaman, Tench was born in Trinidad, but had moved to London in the early sixties, where he formed Gass, a progressive rock/Latin/blues band with whom Jimi Hendrix and The Animals' Eric Burdon jammed several times. A multi-instrumentalist, who numbered piano and guitar among his talents, Bobby was also a first-class singer, his gritty voice redolent of singers such as Wilson Pickett and The Temptations' David Ruffin, and therefore very much up Beck's increasingly soulful alley.

Recording of the new LP began in July, though as Max Middleton confirmed, some of Beck's new band were still getting used to life working alongside a rock star. "Well, I turned up at nine in the morning and start practising away," said the keyboardist. "After a while I'm wondering 'When everyone's going to turn up?' Then, about seven that evening, they start rolling in. Jeff sends one of the roadies off for some food. That gets eaten, and Jeff says, 'Well, I'm a bit tired now. Shall we go down The Speakeasy?' And this happened for three days. I just sat there, thinking, 'Hmm. So this is what it's like being a professional musician.' Of course, we did get down to work eventually." Things were similarly confusing for Bobby Tench – who having recently had the good fortune to secure his position as singer – learned the early, relaxed atmosphere actually meant he was only given a week to write new lyrics and record vocals for the album. "Talk about being thrown in at the deep end," he laughed.

Jeff Beck and his new band (again christened 'Jeff Beck Group') emerged into the light and onto US record racks in October 1971 with *Rough And Ready*. It was an apt title if ever there was one. The album bolted both funk and soul grooves onto R&B and jazz melodies, with a generous portion of rock guitar poured right down the middle to remind listeners of Beck's hard-edged past. Truthfully, the LP was also something of a disappointment, its myriad styles and rhythmic swerves never really threatening to gel into one, cohesive whole. But, on occasion, this preponderance of influences did throw up the unexpected gem, leading one to wonder how good a disc it might have been if recorded in a more disciplined atmosphere.

On the plus side, opening track (and subsequent single) 'Got The Feeling' was a greasy, all-out affair, with Jeff's furious wah-wah pedal excursions predating Isaac Hayes' gorgeous 'Theme From Shaft' – if only by a matter of weeks. 'New Ways Train Train' also jostled the senses, as a series of undulating riffs, several bizarre key changes and a rhythmic pattern Sly Stone would have been proud of muscled things towards a satisfying, if jarring conclusion.

'Situation' too was pleasing enough, the song's spiteful opening and sour descending chromatic solo shunting the previous menace of Beck's old group nicely into the new decade, while 'Max's Tune' (originally called 'Raines Park Blues') also delivered a welcome change of pace – its poignant, jazzy piano, novel use of tubular bells and probing lead lines opening up another musical avenue for the band to explore. "I just liked the tune," said Middleton. "I didn't think about it too deeply, I just played it. And Jeff, who always liked working over a melody, wanted to play over the top." Yet, elsewhere there were misfires: 'I've Been Used' and 'Short Business' both struggled to find decent melodies amid an abundance of clever chords and odd tempo changes, leaving the well-meaning 'Jody' to close proceedings in dramatic, if slightly overstretched style.

Rough And Ready has sometimes been referred to as "the runt in Jeff Beck's litter", the LP's heady confection of adopted musical styles making it difficult to penetrate, with some critics and fans content to turn away altogether: "*Rough And Ready*," *Mojo* once reasoned, "is the *Plan Nine From Outer Space* of the rock world." Indeed, Jeff Beck did little to enhance its reputation, virtually disowning the album on

"The finest British guitarist of his generation." Jeff Beck stares directly into the camera and into his future circa 1966.
MICHAEL OCHS ARCHIVES/GETTY IMAGES

"Blues, pop, psychedelic and all points in between." The classic 1965 Yardbirds line-up (L-R): Paul Samwell, Chris Dreja, Jeff, Jim McCarty and Keith Relf. HARRY GOODWIN/REX FEATURES

Jeff in 1965, soon after his Carnaby Street clean up. HARRY GOODWIN/REX FEATURES

The Yardbirds record a TV spot at the *Ready, Steady Go!* studio in Wembley, London (L-R): Paul Samwell-Smith, Chris Dreja (partially obscured), Keith Relf, Jim McCarty and a Les Paul-wielding Jeff. IVAN KEEMAN/REDFERNS

A dandified Jimmy Page joins the ranks of The Yardbirds in 1966 (L-R): Jim McCarty, Keith Relf, Chris Dreja, Jimmy and Jeff.

Blood brothers. Though Jimmy and Jeff have remained friends for over five decades, their time together in The Yardbirds proved a brief, explosive affair.

Train Kept 'a Rollin. Yardbirds singer Keith Relf takes to the high ground in this rare publicity shot captured at an (unidentified) railroad station. PICTORIAL PRESS

"Rockabilly Rebel". A teenage Jeff Beck eats a pie and cracks a smile alongside Patricia Brown. The two married in 1963.

Jeff contemplates his new solo career while walking the dog near his South London home in May, 1967. TONY GALE/PICTORIAL PRESS

Posing at home with a cup of tea for *Beat Instrumental*. TONY GALE/PICTORIAL PRESS

Jeff backstage at London's Saville Theatre in 1967 soon after the formation of The Jeff Beck Group. PICTORIAL PRESS

"Wild and visionary... lean and laconic." The Jeff Beck Group captured at LA's Shrine Auditorium soon after beginning their mutual love affair with American audiences. Rod Stewart, Jeff and Ronnie Wood (back of shot). ROBERT KNIGHT ARCHIVE/REDFERNS

The Jeff Beck Group performing at London's Roundhouse (L-R): Rod Stewart, Jeff, Tony Newman and Ronnie Wood. RAY STEVENSON/REX FEATURES

Not a smile in sight. The Jeff Beck Group in moody repose (L-R): Rod, Aynsley Dunbar, Ronnie and Jeff. Like many drummers who worked with Beck at the time, Dunbar's tenure with the group could be counted in months rather than years.
DEZO HOFFMANN/REX FEATURES

its release: "I liked *Rough And Ready* after we first recorded it. I don't now," he told *Melody Maker* with typical frankness in 1971. "The second one we make might be more... listenable. The material will be less fiddly. I know, I'm never happy. But you've got to be conditioned not to be too satisfied."

In its defence, *Rough And Ready* did allow Beck to cut crucial ties with the limitations of his blues-rock past, while simultaneously pointing the guitarist's career in a new, albeit confusing direction. There was also no doubting the quality of his band, with Middleton's sophisticated, Erroll Garner-like keyboard lines, Chaman's economic but twisting bass fills and Tench's soaring, soulful vocals all enhancing the sound of Jeff's chipped 1954 Stratocaster and trebly Marshall stack.

Additionally, Cozy Powell was probably Beck's best drummer yet, even if he caused his employer a near heart attack at the conclusion of recording. "Cozy's timing was impeccable," said Max Middleton. "At the end of *Rough And Ready*, he said 'I've just got a brand new drum kit and I want to put it on the record'. But because we were using eight-track at the time, there was no room left. Cozy just said, 'Don't worry, I'll just re-record it over my drum tracks'. We said, 'But what if you get it wrong?' He just smiled and said, 'I won't'. Jeff said to him, 'If you muck this up, I'll actually kill you', but Cozy was confident, you know. So, he played the whole album from start to finish, and on 'New Ways Train Train' where it's literally just him and Jeff playing free-form, he still just did it. Unbelievable."

Best labelled as "flawed, if occasionally very fine", *Rough And Ready* did the trick of reconnecting Jeff Beck with his American audience, where the album stumbled into the charts at number 46 – not such a bad position when one factored in there had been a dearth of new product from the guitarist in over two years (Beck supported the US release of the LP with a series of dates throughout October and November, mainly concentrating on the East and West coasts). Yet, his comments to the UK music press regarding *Rough And Ready*'s shortcomings meant that British audiences took him largely at his word and avoided buying it when it was released at home in January 1972. "I am what I am and I can't change," reasoned Jeff. "This is an indisputably good band but that doesn't mean it's the best in the world.

We don't want to fizzle out, [but] I don't know if it'll last. That's up to the rest of the group."

Thankfully, a short English tour allowed old fans to see that Beck's latest group were actually a lot better than he had sold them to journalists, a fact proved by well-received gigs at Bristol Poly on January 31, Kent University, Lancaster Polytechnic, Coventry College and a concluding date at the Camden Roundhouse 'Implosion' on February 20. Treating crowds to vastly extended jams of *Rough And Ready* material, this Jeff Beck Group were both harder and heavier than on record, their workmanlike appearance masking an advanced command of jazz time signatures, funk rhythms and a guitarist who – despite his best efforts to rubbish his own work – was still head, shoulders and sideburns above most of his competition. "I've moved on a bit," he said at the time. "I'm now after power over loudness."

Beck was also still in pursuit of fusing that 'power' to the black music he so loved as a teenager. Having become obsessed with hot-wiring Motown for his own ends, Jeff now wanted to extend the perimeters of the model even further by adding the snap, crackle and pop of Memphis' Stax Records to his own group's sound. As previously stated, Beck had been driven to near ecstasy on hearing Booker T & The MGs' 'Green Onions' in 1962, the economy of Booker Jones' organ playing, Steve Cropper's clipped, precise guitar work and Lewie Steinberg and Al Jackson Junior's ultra-tight bass and drum patterns bewitching his youthful ears. Further exploration of Stax – and its sister label Volt – in later years unearthed even more treasures, with releases by Sam & Dave, The Astors, Otis Redding and Wilson Pickett all being swiftly added to Beck's record collection. But it was the power of Stax's own house band, The MGs and their accompanying horn section, The Memphis Horns, that most beguiled Jeff – a mixture of black and white musicians capable of stopping on a dime or prising a beat between atoms. Beck needed to re-create such precision if he was to truly realise the mad ideas kicking around his own head. Failing to harness that dream as a producer with *Rough And Ready*, the guitarist now decided to approach the very source of his adolescent fascination to solve the problem: Steve Cropper himself.

Beck's idea to ask his youthful hero to produce the next JBG album was as inspired as it was canny. In addition to leading The MGs, Steve

Cropper was also an accomplished soundman and tunesmith, having overseen production on several Otis Redding singles as well as co-writing '(Sitting On) The Dock Of The Bay', Eddie Floyd's 'Knock On Wood' and 'In The Midnight Hour' by Wilson Pickett. If Jeff could capture a set of tunes only half as good as these classic releases, his work on Earth would be done. But there was a problem or two to contend with. While Cropper readily agreed to helm the project, he had already left Stax Records to go it alone in 1970. That meant Beck and his band would not have access to 926 East McLemore Avenue, the former cinema which Stax had converted into a small, sloping studio to obtain their raw, deep sound. Instead, they would be cutting tracks at Steve's newly opened TMI recording complex around the corner in downtown Memphis.

"It came at a time when it seemed I could get anything I wanted," Jeff later confirmed. "I rang Steve Cropper and said we wanted to record with him. Sure enough, days later, we were on the plane and I was really looking forward to recording in Stax Studios, the old movie house. But when we arrived, we found ourselves in a brand new studio. I was really disappointed."

Beck was also initially wary of Cropper's methodical approach to production, with the former MG putting both Jeff and his group through the wringer in search of the perfect take. "The difference between the first and second albums was Steve Cropper," said Max Middleton. "With him, it was take after take as Steve wanted it to be perfect. But he idolised Jeff. He thought he was a wonderful guitarist." Though Beck was equally giving to Cropper's guitar style, he remained privately concerned that his new producer's background might preclude him from allowing the band to indulge their more experimental inclinations. "It was one of Steve Cropper's first efforts [outside Stax], and I think he couldn't handle it at times. We had a completely different approach to recording from his." In essence, Beck wanted Stax with added bite, power and requisite wildness. Cropper, on the other hand, wanted precision, discipline and a modicum of control.

In the end, The Jeff Beck Group's second, self-titled disc offered a bit of both. Christened 'The Orange Album' by fans due to the orange on its cover sleeve, Beck's latest effort was a much more refined proposition than *Rough And Ready*, its performances reasonably compact, its overall sound tighter and better balanced. But Jeff and his band had also sneaked a little insanity onto the record's grooves, with bass drums regularly flapping against the speakers, intrusive keyboard fills stabbing in and out of songs, and in several cases, guitar solos so beautifully unhinged, they were in need of psychiatric evaluation. As a result, 'The Orange Album' had a certain schizoid aspect to its nature, fluttering between delight and delirium often within the same tune.

On opening track 'Ice Cream Cakes' (a holdover from the first LP), the emphasis was wholly on greasy funk-rock, with Jeff's antics on his battered Stratocaster encompassing distressed chicken scratches, country rolls and flagrant whammy bar abuse. This approach was consolidated on a heavily fortified version of the old Carl Perkins tune 'Glad All Over', where Beck's free-form interjections reigned supreme – odd scales, snappily bent single notes and blunt double stops squeezing every drop of drama from Cozy Powell's stop-start rhythm. An almost Gospel rendition of Bob Dylan's 'Tonight I'll Be Staying With You' came next, allowing Bobby Tench to exercise his throat muscles before Max Middleton's strident piano announced the arrival of 'Sugar Cane', another attempt by Jeff to fuse wah-wah pedal lunacy to a jaunty jazz-soul-blues workout.

An impressive instrumental rendition of Ashford, Simpson and Holland's 'I Can't Give Back The Love I Feel For You' provided a teasing glimpse of what Beck's earlier, unsatisfying liaison with Motown might well have sounded like. First recorded by Jeff and Cozy at Motown's Detroit studios in June 1970, 'I Can't Give...' had been resurrected as a showcase for Beck's slide guitar skills, his lyrical, almost kazoo-like tones sitting atop a nest of fake sitars and sympathetic keyboard flourishes. In stark contrast, the JBG's treatment of Don Nix's lively blues 'Going Down' proved rather a muted affair, the inherent power of a song they had recently made their own in live performance somehow lost at the recording desk of TMI studios. That said, Jeff did his best to rescue 'Going Down' from the perils of mediocrity with a quite mad series of solos pulled from the neck of his tortured Strat. "He never bothered tuning up, you know," offered Max Middleton. "He'd just pull the notes into tune. Never the same solo ever. Just different takes, one after the other. Brilliant when you think about it."

After another potential stall with the pleasing but inconsequential 'Highways', things again righted themselves with 'The Orange Album''s concluding track, 'Definitely Maybe'. A beautifully judged tune, again benefiting from Beck's frightening control over both a steel slide and wah pedal, 'Definitely Maybe' was almost lost forever when Jeff decided it was too intricate for its own good. "Well, I wrote that for Jeff," said Middleton. "I wanted it to be quite long and it was also quite complex, with two or three parts and a counter melody. It was very difficult to sort through. Jeff actually wanted to give up on it, but Steve Cropper said, 'No, this is good, let's keep going'. And Beck's solo on that is lovely, it's just one note, but it's beautiful." Aside from giving Noel Gallagher and Oasis the title of their debut album, 'Definitely Maybe' has also become something of a cult favourite among Beck fans, with the guitarist still dusting down its haunting melody line at the occasional concert or two.

Like *Rough And Ready* before it, 'The Orange Album' was by no means a perfect distillation of Jeff Beck's abiding wish to master the complexities of the Stax or Motown sound. Yet, taken as a whole, the album was a much more satisfying experience than its predecessor – its melodies more robust, Beck's guitar playing more substantial. "Good memories, overall," said Jeff. "But in the end, we didn't really have the material. The good thing was we sounded like a really heavy Motown, Staxy band. Cozy bashing away... call it flawed but fun." As ever, UK audiences failed to connect with 'The Orange Album''s charms upon its release in May, 1972, the LP failing to chart. But across the Atlantic, it was accorded a much better reception, putting Beck back in the US Top 20 after an absence of three years: "Number 19 isn't bad," he joked. The disc's American success was no doubt helped by a two-month tour during April and May, where another of Jeff's youthful favourites, Stevie Wonder, appeared alongside him at Detroit's Cobo Hall.

As was the case with Steve Cropper, Beck had admired Wonder's formidable dominance of R&B, soul and pop for years, first coming on board with 1963's 'Fingertips (Part Two)', and staying close throughout the small miracles of 'Uptight', 'For Once In My Life' and Stevie's latest hit, 1970's 'Signed, Sealed, Delivered, I'm Yours'. Wonder was only 13 when he scored chart success with 'Fingertips...', marking his procession from "child prodigy to teen sensation" in some style. Able to get a tune from almost any instrument he touched, Stevie had already mastered bass guitar, drums, harmonica and keyboards by his recording debut. Yet, his advance into adulthood proved a tad more difficult to negotiate. Recurring squabbles over poor royalty rates and retaining complete control of his creative output had soured relations with his record company, Motown, by early 1972, with Wonder forced to withhold two albums of material from label boss Berry Gordy Jnr. until the situation was adequately resolved. After a protracted stand-off between the two parties, Motown acceded to Stevie's requests, with a new 120-page contract giving him a much higher royalty rate and free reign to compose, produce and issue his own material as he saw fit. Given the strength of the blind singer-songwriter's talent, Gordy would still make more than enough money to see him into luxurious dotage.

By the time Beck and Wonder met at Detroit Cobo Hall, the wheels were greased for collaboration. Jeff had ably covered Stevie's 'I Have A Song For You' on 'The Orange Album', while A&R types at Epic records were 'having conversations' with Motown about the guitarist taking a guest spot on Wonder's next LP. With Stevie's record company keen to reposition their prime asset in the adult market ("After the suit and bow tie episode of 'Fingertips'," Beck joked), having a "long-haired, moody six-stringer" offer some crossover rock appeal didn't seem a bad idea. From Jeff's point of view, the opportunity of adding a solo or two to a Stevie Wonder disc was reward enough in itself, though he also hoped that he might get a song out of it. "When I heard Stevie might write something for me, I was just speechless."

In May 1972, Beck joined Wonder at Electric Lady Studios in New York to record his contributions to the latter's new LP, provisionally titled *Talking Book*. The results of the session were two fine, jazzy solos from Jeff on the tracks 'Lookin' For Another Pure Love' and 'Tuesday Heartbreak', the latter sadly not released on the finished LP. Impressed by Beck's ability, Stevie invited him and his band back to the studio with a view to writing a tune. When the JBG returned days later for the first of several visits, they were all in shock at the sheer musicality of their host. "Stevie was just incredible, a wonderful piano player, a wonderful singer and a wonderful man," said Max Middleton. "You could say to him, 'Play this tune' or 'Play that tune', any tune really, and he'd just do it. He'd be sitting at his Fender Rhodes and be working on three songs at once. He'd cut ideas to tape on the piano, then ask for playback. He'd then sing the instructions to the engineers: 'OK, I'll play some bass on track two', or 'I'll add drums to track three', and the songs would be coming together there and then, with him singing along in that beautiful voice. The next day, you'd come back and the whole lot was finished. I've never seen anything like that in my entire life. It affected me profoundly just watching him work. Everything was so musical, and his output was simply colossal."

Beck's own appraisal of Wonder's musical skills was perhaps more succinct, but no less revealing: "I just sat there staring at him. Music comes out of his arse."

Over the course of the visit, Beck once again raised the subject of Stevie writing a tune for his band, even drilling out a possible drum pattern himself that might inspire Wonder into action. "I hoped he would write me one song to get me going, you know, in that new direction." Max Middleton takes up the story as to what happened next: "Jeff said, 'Give us a song'. Well, Stevie had a lot of songs, about 250 already recorded, there were tapes just hanging from the walls. So we went through them for hours, but there was nothing that caught Jeff's ear. So Beck said, 'Play me something funky.' Stevie said, 'OK, why don't you guys go and get a drink and I'll come up with something'. Jeff and the others left for a while, but I stayed there sitting next to him as he played clavinet. The next thing, he started this riff... it was magical. He built up the track, played the drums, started putting words together on each take. When we all came back the next day, Stevie had the whole thing finished."

The song Wonder had written was 'Superstition'.

When Beck first heard the result of Stevie Wonder's endeavours, his response was entirely predictable: "I thought, 'He's just given me the riff of the century." But Wonder was also aware that he had captured something truly spectacular. In fact, when Jeff and his band asked to record the song with him, Stevie made his feelings plain. "He said, 'Hold the session,'" Beck remembered, "I'm paying for it from right now'." The subsequent demo was quickly passed to Wonder's record label for a verdict. "When they heard it, Motown said 'No, you can't give that to anyone'," said Middleton. "which was very wise, when you think about it..." Within hours, Jeff Beck had one of the best funk riffs of the 20th century placed squarely in his palm, only to have it removed again before he could close his fist. "'Superstition' was this ideal, monstrous heavy metal funk thing," he later said, "and when [Motown] said, 'Beck doesn't get this', it hurt like hell. But you know, I thought, 'What better guy to get a hit with his own song than Stevie?'"

Back in the hands of its creator, 'Superstition' became the centrepiece of *Talking Book* and a huge worldwide hit when issued as a single in January 1973 – reaching number one in the US, where it sold over a million copies alone. It was the first Stevie Wonder single to do so since 'Fingertips (Part Two)' in 1963.

Though Jeff Beck was philosophical (if "gutted") to have lost 'Superstition', the fun didn't end there for him during the Electric Lady Studio sessions of May/early June 1972. As Wonder worked on elsewhere, a fight broke out between several band members in the control room, with Clive Chaman allegedly shouting at a startled Beck in plain view of the heads of Motown. For Jeff, who was still in pain from the results of his accident some two and a half years earlier, and once again doubting the worth of his latest musical pursuits, this was one headache he could do something about. Within days of returning from New York, his group were told that on fulfilment of forthcoming tour obligations, their services were no longer required. As with the 'Motown' sessions, the tapes cut with Stevie Wonder – including the band's version of 'Superstition' – were swiftly collected, placed in a box and never seen again. As a functioning unit, the second incarnation of the JBG had released two albums, one single and lasted just over a year.

When looking at the band's fate with the aid of a rear-view mirror, it seems obvious things were again destined to fail. As the serious rock scene had grown progressively more ambitious in its aspirations, veering into complex, neo-classical territories, Beck had steered his band in the completely opposite direction, using the economical precision of Motown and Stax to inform their sound. Further, the group had sometimes lacked for true quality material, with Jeff's overwhelming desire to innovate at any cost pushing aside a desperate need to consolidate their position with a few killer tunes. "Yeah, Jeff gets a lot of good ideas," Cozy Powell told *Sounds* in 1972, "only a lot of people seem to pick up his ideas before he does and put them out. That's a bit difficult to comment on, really." (Powell was no doubt taking a not-so-veiled pot shot at Jimmy Page and Led Zeppelin with this remark.)

Worse still, at the precise moment Beck finally found a song so perfectly right for his band that its success was virtually guaranteed, it was snatched away before the tape had even finished rewinding. When pitted against such odds, the argument that broke out at Motown – though no doubt irritating to Jeff and equally baffling to record company spectators – was not so much a sign of internal discord as a doomsday bell ringing the need for definite change: "I was caught up in a horrible carnival of clashing musics at the time, and really confused," he later told *Rolling Stone*. "It was a terrible feeling of insecurity."

As ever, almost every clue required to decipher Jeff Beck's contrary nature can be found in the music he recorded. Therefore, a quick spin of 'The Orange Album''s 'Going Down' reveals much about the man's mind-set of the time. As his band stomp along behind him, sticking more or less to the bones of Don Nix's bluesy Stax-approved tune, Beck once again takes a different road. "Persistently behaving like a kid in a dodgem car," wrote journalist David Sinclair, "[Jeff] bumps and bashes into 'Going Down' from all angles and with mischievous glee. Bewildering barrages of tremolo-swooped notes followed by Hank Marvin-type doodles completely counter to the rhythm... then flurries of country-style picking. Anything, in fact, except a blues sequence which is what 99 out of 100 other players would have done."

Good or bad, Beck never did obvious. Or so it appeared until June 1972.

Chapter 13

And Then There Were Three

Thus far, the early seventies had offered a cornucopia of choice when it came to music, with old and new acts alike elbowing each other out of the way to get their share of the spotlight. Having led the charge for so very long, The Beatles had finally fallen to pieces at the turn of the new decade, the band collapsing under the weight of sustained infighting, dubious outside influences, increased drug use and botched business decisions. In their absence, pop and rock had splintered, then split apart, only to reconstitute itself in bold new ways. With the advent of 'Glam Rock', the likes of David Bowie, Marc Bolan, Roxy Music, Slade and Sweet had cleverly aligned a love for retrograde rock'n'roll to new, experimental textures and some very impressive clothing – their startling visual appearance confusing parents and delighting teenagers in equal measure.

For more serious types, the psychedelic and blues-rock boom of the sixties had paved the way for a correspondingly serious music, with bands once content to delight in the pleasures of the 12-bar now turning their attentions to odd scales and even odder time signatures. Progression was the name of the game, as bands like Wishbone Ash, Yes, Focus, ELP and King Crimson (if they could stay together long enough to record an LP) all blurred the boundaries between classical, jazz, rock and folk. To prove their seriousness, performers in such groups actually sat down to play their instruments, donned large capes, stabbed their keyboards with knives or even yodelled. Songs were no longer even songs in the traditional sense, but 'movements', with individual solos sometimes lasting as long as the side of an album. And even the hardest of rock had become the heaviest of metal, as Black Sabbath and Deep Purple piled on the decibels, dabbled with flattened fifths and became 'War Pigs' or 'Speed Kings'.

In the US, things were equally diverse: Frank Zappa, once a delightful musical eccentric, was now a full-blown musical lunatic, pulling 20 band members onstage with him to play some of the weirdest, wildest tonalities known to man and goat. Country and folk music too had also evolved beyond its earliest three-chord roots in America to birth a new genre of 'soft rock', the likes of Bread, The Eagles and singer-songwriters such as James Taylor advising us to 'Take It Easy' because 'You've Got A Friend'. Whether it was old stagers The Rolling Stones offering *Exile On Main Street* or Pink Floyd silently gathering in the corners of Abbey Road studios to plan their journey to *The Dark Side Of The Moon,* rock and pop music had seldom been so diverse, pleasurable or plain bizarre.

Given Jeff Beck's gift for courting the unpredictable and his seeming inability to commit to one musical style for longer than one LP, this heady, ever-changing landscape of sights and sounds must have seemed an inviting prospect. Though his quest for a mutant hybrid of "Stax drums, fat bass and really cooking guitar" had proved ultimately untenable, there was now a clear opportunity to gather his thoughts, return to the drawing board and come up with something both artistically satisfying and commercially successful. It came as a genuine surprise then, when it was announced in July, 1972 that Beck's latest project would team him alongside the former Vanilla Fudge rhythm section of drummer Carmine Appice and bassist Tim Bogert. From the outside looking in, this appeared a case of 'one step forward, two steps back', with Jeff returning to previous plans to revitalise future efforts. Having gained a reputation for laying new foundations rather than ploughing old furrows, one might be forgiven for believing the guitarist had simply run out of ideas, or worse, was content to tread water while thinking up which direction in which next to swim.

But Beck's decision to re-establish ties with Appice and Bogert was based on two strong guiding principles: money and shared responsibility. In the first instance, Jeff may have been at times a contrary soul, but he could never be taken for a fool. By mid-1972, Beck had seen his friend Jimmy Page reap astounding rewards from bringing "light, shade, blood and thunder" to the masses, with Led Zeppelin now inarguably one of the world's biggest bands. Their fourth, strangely untitled, album had not only topped the UK charts in November, 1971 but also been a million seller in the US, Zeppelin's third disc in succession to achieve such an honour (LZ IV would eventually sell over 23 million copies in the States alone). And while Jimmy may have further broadened his group's remit to include Celtic, folk, blues and country influences, the high-energy, hard-rock stomp of songs such as 'Immigrant Song', 'Whole Lotta' Love', 'Heartbreaker' and latterly 'Black Dog' and 'Rock'n'roll' remained at the heart of their live appeal. If Jeff could build a machine with Carmine and Tim that equalled, or even surpassed, Led Zeppelin's gift for bombast, then he too would enjoy all the commercial benefits to be had from the US market. "We've never played what the people wanted to hear in America," he told *NME* in July, 1972. "They expect vicious, violent rock'n'roll. That's what I'm known for, but I was avoiding all that in the previous band. I was trying to play subtle rock'n'roll. That stuff was more suitable for clubs, not big stages. This new group will play much heavier music."

Of equal importance was the value of democracy. As was now becoming clear, Jeff Beck's particular gifts were more those of a guitarist, arranger and interpreter than principal songwriter, his skills often untouchable on six strings yet not often directed towards the rigours of composition. If this distribution of talent had been different, Beck might already have rivalled Jimi Hendrix, the Stones' Keith Richards or Jimmy Page as a composer capable of channelling the blues into new, exotic and exceedingly profitable shapes. But the mood for writing songs only seemed to strike him occasionally, leading to swift changes in musical direction, and his position as band leader sometimes undermined as a result. By Jeff's own admission, this odd but telling absence in his musical make-up had plagued him at regular intervals – making the guitarist often dependant on others for material – with the quality of his output suffering as a result. By aligning his skills to Appice and Bogert, the pressure of driving a band on his own would be lessened while the three could either co-author or seek out material ideally suited to their shared vision of "heavy music". Or that, at least, was the theory.

At first, Beck, Bogert and Appice were unwilling to entertain the notion of reinventing the wheel, or indeed, severing any potentially lucrative ties with their past. Though Carmine and Tim had officially served notice to their present group, Cactus, there were still a handful of US dates to fulfil before they were free to pursue other avenues. "Well, [Cactus] were just going in different directions and didn't see eye to eye any more," Bogert later concluded. "We had never really developed a formula, but were just four people working in a way that they knew. For a while, that was very compatible."

Jeff was also locked into several British shows before the JBG were again due to return to America for a tour beginning on August 1. Of course, there was the potential niggle that his backing band were actually 'out of contract' after their appearance at London's Roundhouse on July 23, leaving him light of a drummer, bassist, keyboard player and vocalist for the next round of gigs in the States. To avert a potential crisis (and some very sharp promoters' fines), Appice and Bogert flew to London a day after the Roundhouse date to join Beck for an intense period of rehearsals at The Rolling Stones' studios in Bermondsey. Along for the ride was pianist Max Middleton, who had agreed to at least stay on with Jeff for the American tour and a new singer named Kim Milford. New Jersey born, Illinois-raised and very blond-haired, the 22-year-old Milford's only experience of the concert stage thus far had been confined to supporting roles in musicals such as *Hair*, where he played the dual roles of Woof and Claude. That he could sing was never in doubt, but the stringent demands of a full-on rock audience were somewhat different to those of a polite theatre crowd, as Kim was to find out soon enough.

Still trading under the name 'The Jeff Beck Group', the new five piece's opening show at Pittsburgh's Stanley Theater on August 1 went over well enough, with their set comprising various bits and bobs from the recent 'Orange Album', *Rough And Ready* and a lengthy take on 'Jeff's Boogie'. To appease Appice and Bogert's stateside fanbase, extended versions of Vanilla Fudge's cover of Junior Walker's 'Shotgun' (always a particular favourite of Beck's) and Cactus' 'Oleo' (featuring a trademark, growling solo from Tim) were also bolted onto the set. But a string of ever more unpredictable performances – including a badly received show at New York's Gaelic Park – marked the end of Kim Milford's time with the band. "A good-looking lad and a nice bloke," Beck later said, "but the crowd just didn't want to know." Max Middleton concurred: "Kim just didn't have the image Jeff was looking for, perhaps. He might have been a little too straight, you know, long blond hair... just too good looking." Milford did not leave the group completely empty handed. The singer's strident turn on the old JBG outtake 'Justice' appeared on the soundtrack of Andy Warhol's 1972 movie *Ciao! Manhattan*, and was later released by CMP records in Denmark. With Kim Milford gone within six gigs, Beck once again turned to his previous vocalist, Bobby Tench, to plug the gap. Being a reliable sort, Tench flew out to the US where he joined the band onstage at Chicago's Arie Theater on August 9, before seeing out the tour at Washington's Paramount West Theater some two weeks later.

On the conclusion of these American dates, it was all change again. Based on their road experiences, Jeff, Tim and Carmine had come to the inescapable conclusion that they were best served as a trio rather than quintet, a fact that went down surprisingly well with Max Middleton. "Well, Jeff had always wanted a three piece like Jimi Hendrix," he said. "Now, I'd never seen Hendrix but I'd loved Cream, so I actually loved Beck's idea." Well used to his boss' ways, Bobby Tench was also fairly sanguine regarding Jeff's idea, first returning to session work with Linda Lewis, Junior Marvin and blues great Freddie King, before fronting his own groups, Streetwalkers and the much underrated jazz-funk outfit, Hummingbird (whom we will return in due course).

The reduction of the JBG from five to three members was as inevitable as Beck changing the oil of one of his ever-growing fleet of hot rods. "I thought Carmine was a real street thug, you know, with that double-sized drum kit of his," Jeff later said. "It was like having a tank behind you. And Tim, who was impossible, a total nutter, was also a fabulous player. It was like being in the first real street heavy metal band." Beck's observations were essentially correct. What Appice and Bogert offered the guitarist was the chance to venture into 'the music of extremity' – creating a three-headed black dog of a band that combined virtuoso musicianship with crushing volume, relentless thump and showy theatrics.

Additionally, the trio shared a strong camaraderie away from the stage, with Appice's fondness for practical jokes and easygoing nature acting as a soothing balm for Beck and Bogert's more unpredictable personalities. The fact they were all car and motorbike freaks certainly didn't hurt either, their shared fantasies of driving rods on stage, playing on speedway tracks or just racing "each other into oblivion" much more likely to inform backstage banter than anything else. A "high-decibel, high-energy street party band" that America could potentially take to its heart, it was all a far cry from Jeff's more measured experiments of only a year before. "You know," he said, "I was recovering from a bad accident, a bad blow to the head and any loud noise was just terrible." By all accounts, Jeff Beck's avoidance of loud noises was now at an end.

The strengths and weaknesses of the new group were there for all to see when they returned to live performance in the early autumn of 1972, opening their European account with dates in Holland, Germany and the UK, where they appeared third on the bill to Frank Zappa and Hawkwind at *Rock At The Oval* on September 16. Buoyed by the presence of high-powered Sunn amps and a veritable mountain of Univox speakers, Beck's tone was simply huge, no doubt aided by the recent purchase of a thick-blooded '71 white Fender Stratocaster. As bootlegs show, Tim Bogert was also immense in both volume and pitch, his combination of low-end fuzz rumble and top-of-the-neck excursions providing just evidence of exactly why his fellow bassists regarded him in such high esteem. "Tim wasn't a regular bass player," said Carmine. "He played lead bass." With a gong behind him and a mountain of hair on his face, Appice was also the band's real showman, a percussionist capable of swirling his sticks and geeing on the audience while simultaneously producing mad, intricate patterns from the two bass drums at his feet. "John Bonham learned a hell of a lot from watching Carmine," Jeff later said, "that whole double bass drum thing for a start..."

The band had several songs of real note: set opener 'Livin' Alone' was a boogie-friendly romp with Beck scuttling around its three-chord structure as Bogert and Appice gave frantic chase, while 'Lady''s multi-tempo, deep-blues rock could not fail to engage with audiences brought up on a staple diet of Cream and Hendrix. A surprisingly faithful version of Curtis Mayfield's gospel-tinged 1965 hit 'People Get Ready' also didn't fail to impress, though it was the trio's ultra-low frequency treatment of Stevie Wonder's 'Superstition' that was perhaps the highlight of their set. Replacing Wonder's jabbing clavinet and springboard rhythm with a highly overdriven Strat, well-deep bass and pounding tom-toms, the trio ably illustrated what 'Superstition' might have sounded like in the JBG's hands: "Super-charged, super-heated, super evil and covered in blood," being *Melody Maker's* verdict.

But away from the positives of the group's performance, there were other, creeping doubts. Beck, Appice and Bogert's musical approach often lacked a crucial element of light and shade, the band coming forward relentlessly without pause or measure. This was no doubt the intention, but it also meant that songs sometimes bled into each other, one indiscernible from the next. Of equal concern were the vocals, now mostly led by Carmine with Tim offering supporting harmonies. While the drummer and bassist could undoubtedly carry a tune, their voices only really shone when combined together. In a world where Zeppelin's Robert Plant, Deep Purple's Ian Gillan and The Who's Roger Daltrey could navigate their way from a scream to a sigh in microseconds, the lack of a single, charismatic and huge-lunged front man at the centre of the stage might ultimately halt the group's progress towards the superstardom they craved.

If there were any such concerns among the band's ranks, they must have been quelled by the impressive turnout for the remaining dates of their first UK tour, with positive word of mouth from the Oval appearance causing houses to fill up from London to Scotland. By September 23, Jeff was even confident enough to stop touring under the old 'JBG' tag in favour of a new moniker – 'Beck, Bogert, Appice' or 'BBA' – thus giving each member star billing, even if his name remained firmly at the front. A subsequent raft of gigs in Europe also went well, though the trio ran into trouble during a concert in Hanover, Germany, when a combined Stars & Stripes/ Union Jack backdrop inflamed a politically sensitive audience who vented their frustration by bottling the stage. The reception accorded Beck, Bogert, Appice in the States when they returned for a second 22-date tour later that month was mercifully trouble-free, with packed crowds of beer-swilling, dope-smoking, Quaalude-dropping teenagers immediately connecting with the "techno-boogie" coming in loud waves from speaker stacks. "Tim and Carmine were just amazing," Jeff later offered. "Two maniacs with the power to sound like eight people and me just trying to ride on top of it." This general satisfaction with each other's talents also translated to onstage practical jokes, as the front rows at several venues had to avoid flying custard pies thrown by various band members at the conclusion of the show. Ever the ham, Beck would fall to the boards in a mock-dead heap if Bogert or Appice occasionally hit their target.

Soon after their last US date at the 4,000 seater Warehouse in New Orleans on November 11, 1972, BBA began the process of trying to translate their big-boned sound onto tape. "I wanted a band that could outdo all the metal stuff around at the time," Jeff later reasoned. "[And] the energy levels were ridiculous. There was static electricity before we even went on stage." The man responsible for ensuring the group's debut album ably harnessed such power was Don 'Going Down' Nix, whose recent production credits included John Mayall & The Bluesbreakers and former Beatle George Harrison's *Concert For Bangladesh* in 1971. When preliminary recording in the UK went badly, the trio and their producer relocated to Chicago's Chess Studios in December, but frequent power outages, flooding and recurrent bouts of ill health saw them up sticks again in January, 1973 to LA's Village complex – a former Masonic temple with huge stone walls and a reputation for stoic professionalism in the face of even the maddest of rock star demands. Having blazed a trail across the Atlantic, then several Western states in little less than three months, Don Nix sounded exhausted by the end of studio sessions. "I don't know how I got the job," he told *Zig Zag* at the time, "but I'd sure like to get out of it…"

BBA's self-titled debut disc was eventually shipped to US stores on March 26, 1973 with UK fans having to wait a further two weeks before they could get their hands on a copy. Listening to the results, they might have got the better deal.

While *Beck Bogert Appice* was a reasonable enough calling card, showcasing the individual and collective musical talents of its makers, it nevertheless failed on three major fronts: distinctive songs, a strong individual vocal presence and, crucially, capturing the overwhelming testosterone of the band's live set in its grooves. In fact, for the first time in his career, Beck's searing guitar tone sounded almost muddy, fighting to be heard above Bogert and Appice's pounding bass and crunching back beat. When the tunes were tough enough to cope, as with BBA's rousing cover of 'Superstition', the aforementioned 'Lady' and the crispy-fried funk rock of 'Lose Myself With You', such quibbles could be ignored. But on material such as the weak, boogie-thud of 'Why Should I Care', one's ear grew tired of working through all that sludge. To their credit, the trio had tried to lighten the load with the inclusion of several gentler moments: 'Sweet Sweet Surrender', featuring Three Dog Night's Jim Greenspoon and Danny Hutton on keyboards and backing vocals respectively, was almost a love letter to the soft country rock of The Eagles, with a gorgeous wah solo from Jeff pushed nicely up in the mix. 'Oh To Love You' was also a tender attempt at soothing the brow of listeners, its Beach Boys-like harmonies and soulful piano interludes (courtesy of Cactus' Duane Hitchings) acting as a mellow alternative to the grunt and groan of previous tracks. And with a surprisingly sincere version of Curtis Mayfield's 'I'm So Proud', the band sounded almost romantic, floating down a river of dreamy mellotrons, luscious slide guitars and more stacked harmonies.

But when one withdrew all the grunge and thump in favour of these sparer, more contemplative arrangements, BBA's vocal shortcomings were thrust into full view. As a combined unit, Tim Bogert and Carmine Appice's voices could rival those of a barber shop choir. But when either sang solo it was an entirely different matter and one quickly picked up by the critics: "Appice is [often] the designated singer," said *Rolling Stone* in its review of the album, "and while he can at least carry a tune (even if at times he sounds like he's carrying it in a satchel), his tenor possesses little flair and scant individuality." For his sins, Jeff also contributed a rare lead vocal to *Beck Bogert Appice* on the Don Nix-penned 'Black Cat Moan'. Best described as 'mud rock', 'Black Cat Moan' was pushed slowly along on the back of Beck's best Duane Allman impression, his frequent slide guitar interjections mimicking a feline in heat. However, his singing was as ever limited, recalling why he seldom if ever took a turn in front of the microphone.

An album to divide kingdoms, *Beck Bogert Appice* also divided journalists, with some actually championing and deriding it within the space of one review: "Thankfully, BBA have managed to stay clear of all the foibles that blighted Beck's last band, and this album combines inventiveness, vitality and some all round knockout instrumental work from all three musicians," wrote the *Sounds* reviewer, before sounding a strong note of caution: "Yet in many ways BBA's first album is also a disappointment, for Beck has yet to come up with a record to match his and this band's stage brilliance. Nevertheless, there's enough here to keep you believing." As evidenced, *Rolling Stone* took an even sterner view: "The band's debut LP is surprisingly docile, when compared to their live show that summons recollections of the Fudge's savage version of 'Shotgun' united with Beck's swooping leads," wrote James Issacs. "Always a master of unrestraint, Jeff is often subdued here, depending far less on the sound effects and whooshing runs that dominated the two albums with Rod Stewart." Three decades on, Jeff himself offered an extremely erudite view of the album's failure to capitalize on the band's undoubted live power: "The songs were a bit naff, you know... just skinny blueprints to get some heavy guitar going. But maybe if we'd thought about the material a bit more... I don't know, we just couldn't harness all that energy."

If *Beck Bogert Appice* was at best an uneven effort, it certainly didn't stop people actually buying it, with the album reaching number 12 in the USA and 28 in the UK – the highest chart position Beck had achieved yet in terms of domestic album sales. To support the LP's release, BBA struck out on a comprehensive world tour in February 1973, beginning with a warm-up gig at London's Imperial College before further UK dates. At around this juncture, Jeff unveiled two new pieces of hardware to appreciative audiences – one destined to become iconic in its own right, the other praised either as a "bold addition to his sound", or dismissed as an outright gimmick. In the case of the former, the latest recruit to Beck's army of guitars was a striking, refinished 1954 Gibson Les Paul Goldtop, its original golden hues now a deep, black/brown colour Jeff called 'Ox-Blood'. The instrument was brought to his attention by fellow musician Buddy Davis, who originally traded the guitar into Memphis store Strings & Things, only to commandeer it again after a potential sale fell through. When Jeff offered Davis $500 for the Ox-Blood he dutifully accepted, later paying Strings … back for their trouble. "When I mixing it up in the sixties, most of the guys playing guitars were playing Les Pauls," he later said. "In a small band, they had a big, rich sound that with a Marshall, cut right through. And I was also aware of Les Paul himself, the giant, the man who had created 'How High The Moon'."

As stated, Beck had largely swung back to Fender Stratocasters after the death of his first group, but the high-volume, three-piece approach of BBA now demanded an even louder, thicker tone to compete with the onstage antics of Bogert and Appice. Purchased for $500, the Oxblood fulfilled such criteria in spades: mighty in weight, with precisely the type of thick neck Beck loved, the guitar was also equipped with a pair of meaty PAF humbuckers that had replaced its original standard P90 pick-ups. Capable of deafening the back of a hall or offering the sweetest, jazz-like tones when the volume control was rolled back, the Oxblood provided Jeff with a new signature sound for the mid-seventies.

Of more debatable worth was Beck's acquisition of 'the talk box', 'voice bag', or just 'the bag'. A devilishly complicated effects device that made the guitar sound as if it was talking, 'The Bag' was essentially a horn driver wrapped up in a "Mexican drinking bag", which was further encased in foam rubber. A piece of plastic tube was then inserted where the horn was usually placed, which kept any sound enclosed within the gadget itself, unless it was drawn up through said tube. "The extension leading from the amp," Beck told *Guitar Player,* "used this as an amplifier, [so when] you put the tube in your mouth and formed a voice box… you [could] mould the sound by the shape of your oral cavity." In other words, when Jeff placed the tube in his mouth and moved his orifice around a bit, his amplified guitar signal emulated speech or even singing. "You don't have to sing at all," he continued, "It comes over the microphone to be re-amplified."

Variations on the 'talk box' had been around for decades before Jeff had implemented its use on BBA's 1973 tour. As a childhood fan of

Alvino Rey, he would have heard the steel guitarist use a hot-wired carbon throat microphone to mimic similar "singing guitar" effects, while Nashville steel-pickers such as Bill West also toyed with the talk box to produce like-minded sounds. But Beck had first seen the device in action at Iron Butterfly's second gig on Sunset Strip in late 1966, when the band's guitarist Mike Pinera used a form of the bag to impress LA crowds. "They played one song for over half an hour," Jeff remembered. "I liked how they were willing to take that chance. Mike Pinera used [a bag] to do just bass-riff noise and guitar lines with it."

In reality, what Jeff originally wanted his version of 'the bag' to do was emulate the vowel-like sound of Stevie Wonder's clavinet for BBA's live version of 'Superstition', thus providing a funk-approved lift to the trio's resolute "wall of pound". But after hearing audiences howl with approval each time the bag was produced, he soon incorporated into other tunes, most notably on 'Beck's Boogie', where he got the thing to drone like a set of bagpipes or scream like a scalded cat. Yet, as other guitarists such as Joe 'Rocky Mountain Way' Walsh, Rufus' Tony Maiden and most notably Peter Frampton also began using the effect to produce similar reactions and several hit singles, Jeff consigned it to the dustbin. "Peter Frampton ripped off my entire act with that bloody bag," he once growled. "Then, when I saw heavy metal acts… standing up there… buzzing away with their teeth dropping out, I thought it was time to get rid of it."[*]

On completion of the UK leg of their tour at Cardiff's Top Rank Suite on February 18, BBA set out for Paris to make a rare TV appearance on music show *Pop Deux*, before again crossing the Atlantic for another 18 US shows, beginning with a gig at Boston's Music Hall on March 28. In front of their core audience of bell-bottomed teens, the 'BBA Monster Boogie Show' came into full effect as dry ice, an impressive lighting rig and wall-to-wall amplification tickled throats, illuminated the front rows and deafened everyone else in attendance.

Running this spectacle every night was Beck's new road manager, Ralph Baker, who had taken over the post when its previous

---

[*] According to some reports, Peter Frampton may have first used the talk box in concert with Humble Pie as early as 1969.

incumbent, Clive Coulson, decided to return to his former employer, Peter Grant, and help keep Led Zeppelin out of trouble while on tour. A wise and well-organised soul, Baker would soon become Jeff's right-hand man, second only to Ernest Chapman in matters of business and friendship.

While Ralph Baker could control the logistics of BBA's road life, he had little influence on growing dissatisfactions between band members while onstage. As the trio soldiered on across the US in April, 1973 it was becoming apparent that tensions were brewing between Tim Bogert and Jeff Beck over their respective playing styles. A technically superb bassist who had never been afraid to make himself heard, Bogert's habit of running up and down the neck rather than providing a solid bedrock of supporting notes and chords was now causing real problems each time Beck took a solo. "We were an all-out jam band," said Carmine Appice, "So when [Jeff's] solo would come, Tim would jam along with the solo, but [like] another soloist. Then, the bottom end would drop out. Jeff loved it at first, but it got old quick."

When the 'duelling banjos' approach worked – as on 'Lose Myself With You' and 'Livin' Alone' – Beck and Bogert sounded almost interconnected, a symbiotic organism feeding off Appice's monstrous energy behind them. But at other times, it could all sound like one giant, unending solo. "We could be uncreative and self-indulgent... thriving on excess and overplaying," Beck later confessed. "If you could zero in on the energy, you got the goods. Otherwise, it was a cacophonous, horrible racket. I was doing a bottle of Smirnoff a day just to survive it."

Little of this growing conflict or indiscipline can be heard on *Beck Bogert Appice Live In Japan*, an album recorded at Osaka's Koseinenkin Hall on May 19, 1973, during the trio's first (and only) visit to the Far East. As in the States, BBA had amassed quite the following in Japan, with Beck's moody persona and the band's technical wizardry appealing to a market obsessed with strong Westernised images and vivid displays of instrumental virtuosity. In fact, despite never visiting the territory before, BBA were selling out cavernous venues such as Tokyo's Budokan theatre with ease. "I don't really know why," Beck later confirmed, "but the Japanese love me and I love them." Cut especially for the Eastern region (though it would become a high-selling import throughout Europe and the US in both single and double-album formats), *BBA Live In Japan* remains probably the only document confirming that, when the occasion warranted it, Beck, Bogert & Appice were a peerless concert act. Riding the volume and piling on the theatrics, the trio's renditions of 'Superstition', 'Black Cat Moan' and 'Lady' frankly laid waste to their studio equivalents, while a heavily reworked medley of 'Plynth.../Shotgun' proved they could also twist older material into stunning new shapes. "It's not such a crime to be better live than on record," Beck said at the time, "because that way, people aren't disappointed when they see you. Any live album has to capture the magic the band puts over at a gig, and to be honest, some live albums I've heard have been terrible. Still, I always get the horrors when I record because I realise I need more practice. I like to put over moods when I play – humour, violence or whatever."

After the triumphs of Japan, BBA returned to their respective continents for a brief break before returning to the road for another elongated European tour. Privately, neither Bogert nor Appice greatly cared for leaving their American homes any longer than was strictly necessary ("Carmine and Timmy didn't like touring England, they just didn't like the touring life over here," Jeff later said), while Beck was in no hurry to up sticks from the rural quiet of East Sussex for the headier pleasures of the USA. "I've no aim to move permanently to America," he told *Rolling Stone* at the time. "Luckily we're in a position where we can afford to lead separate lives when we're not working."

This apparent love of England's green, pleasant and then strike-ridden land inadvertently allowed Jeff to be in precisely the right place and time to take part in one of the stranger episodes of his musical career. By mid-1973, David Bowie had managed to navigate a path from little-known, one-hit wonder best remembered for 1969's 'Space Oddity' to full-blown stardom with his wondrous alter ego, Ziggy Stardust. Spearheading the UK's growing obsession with glam rock, Bowie had reinvented himself as a flame-haired, stick-thin, ambi-sexual alien from the stars, his post-apocalyptic lyrical musings and strange yet beautiful songs offering just the right amount of weirdness for British youth to revel in. With his band, The Spiders From Mars, *Ziggy Stardust...* concept album and three legitimate hit singles, Bowie had become within the space of just one year the UK's most controversial and startling performer, as the rest of the world, including America, was starting to notice as he took his show on the road throughout 1972/3.

Jeff Beck had known of David Bowie long before he became an extraterrestrial or even a lad insane, checking out some of the singer's earliest shows at London's Marquee club. But he had been either in recording studios or touring with BBA during glam rock's peak, so was not fully aware of 'Bowie Fever' when invited with his partner, Celia, to attend a Ziggy show in Croydon during the summer of 1973. At a backstage party following the gig, David approached Beck directly, telling him that he had been a huge fan of The Yardbirds and that his recent hit 'Jean Genie' was based on the chords of 'I'm A Man'. Furthermore, Bowie informed Jeff that his own lead guitarist/arranger Mick Ronson worshipped him and would love an opportunity to play together. Having enjoyed his night, the music and Ronson's brisk, melodic guitar work – "He's potentially good, but... sounds a bit like me!" – Beck provisionally agreed to join David and Mick onstage for the final night of the 'Ziggy' tour on July 3 at London's Hammersmith Odeon. The evening ended on a surreal note when Jeff was then presented with a stuffed puppet which Bowie believed resembled him. "'Strange', I thought," he later joked.*

Ultimately, the night of July 3 proved memorable for a number of reasons. First, Bowie had chosen Hammersmith Odeon as the appropriate venue at which to retire Ziggy Stardust & The Spiders From Mars from public life – a fact neither his audience nor his band was privy to until he announced it from the stage. Secondly, it was Mick Ronson's birthday and Beck's agreement to join The Spiders at encore time was the guitarist's present. "Yep, didn't know about that," he later said. Finally, the gig was being filmed for potential cinema and TV release by film director D. A. Pennebaker, another

---

* Though Beck said yes to the Hammersmith appearance, he did not leave a contact number for David's management, resulting in a mad last-minute scramble to find him in time for the gig.

item of interest that Jeff hadn't been informed of until he arrived at the venue. To his credit he went along with all the chaos, providing slide guitar/talk-box theatrics on 'Love Me Do'/'Jean Genie' and Chuck Berry's 'Around And Around' alongside an ecstatic Mick Ronson, before Bowie brought matters to a close with the shock announcement he was breaking up the band. "Not only is it the last show of the tour," he said, "but it's the last show that we'll ever do. Thank you." Happy Birthday, indeed.

While Beck had been a good sport by showing up at Ziggy Stardust's final stand, and genuinely liked both Bowie and Ronson, he was less fond of his performance at Hammersmith Odeon and asked for it to be removed from the final cut of Pennebaker's film: "I thought because they sounded very upset, very abrupt and pissed off and they just weren't going to use it." Realistically, Jeff was right to ask for such an excision. Looking like a car mechanic who had accidentally stumbled into a kabuki-themed dress-up party, Beck was neither dressed for the part nor playing at his best, being content to trade casual, hammy licks with Mick Ronson rather than take things too seriously. It was with a degree of surprise then, that he learned some months later that his unrehearsed jam with Bowie had already been broadcast as part of an *In Concert* series throughout the USA. Not one to take such matters lying down, Jeff threatened to sue unless the three songs on which he appeared were promptly cut. However, despite some initial awkwardness around the situation, it did not sour relations between him and Bowie, who was apparently unaware of D.A. Pennebaker's mistake at the time. In fact, David continued to wax lyrical over Beck's talents for decades to come. "Jeff and I have talked about doing a very special project at some point," he said in 1997. "And I'd very much like to work with Jeff. I still think he's one of the most undervalued guitar players. I think he's absolutely extraordinary and I'd like very much to work with him."*

---

* Though the two have never made good on their conversations, Bowie did perform a striking cover of The Yardbirds' 'Shapes Of Things' on his *Pin Ups* album of October 1973, which co-incidentally featured Beck's former bandmate Aynsley Dunbar on drums.

Only five days after his Hammersmith Odeon appearance, Jeff rejoined his BBA colleagues for a brief swoop across Europe, taking advantage of the lucrative summer festival circuit in Holland, West Germany and France. From there, the trio returned to America to commune with their most devoted fanbase, planning a comprehensive raid on the East and Southern states. But on July 17, only six dates into the tour in Florida, Bogert and Appice awoke to the news that Beck had returned to England to deal with an urgent, unspecified crisis. In reality, the crisis in question turned out to be a simple case of road fever, with Jeff just too tired to continue being pummelled by 100 plus decibels of 'super boogie' each time he strapped on a guitar. If Tim and Carmine had known their colleague's previous history of sudden disappearances – and what they eventually led to – they might have been more worried. But Beck assured both that once rested, he would begin work on the band's second album which they were due to produce themselves.

Keeping to his word, Jeff rejoined Tim and Carmine for initial rehearsals for the aptly named *BBA Two* in Devon during September, 1973, before transferring to Abbey Road to begin recording. But these sessions proved disastrous, resulting in another move to Beck's former stomping ground of De Lane Lea Studios in London's Soho. Once again things went wrong, when Bogert took a spill from his motorcycle and broke his foot. Perhaps in sympathy, Carmine then contracted a heavy dose of flu, which he in turn passed on to the already ailing Tim. Surprisingly, BBA managed to deliver a strong performance at the Crystal Palace Music Festival during all these upheavals.

As Bogert and Appice pulled themselves back together and the band again considered switching studios in search of a better sound, a now robust Beck passed his time by visiting old friends or working with other artists. During this period, he attended initial rehearsals of the funky new Hummingbird, whose line-up included former JBG cohorts Max Middleton, Bobby Tench and Clive Chaman, and who would soon sign to A&M Records. Unfortunately, Jeff chose not to play on their self-titled debut album, perhaps feeling that their resident guitarist, Bernie Holland, had all bases covered. But he did lay down a fine solo on 'Watch Yerself', a track from former Crabby

Appleton front man Michael Fennelly's first solo LP, *Lane Changer*, which was then being recorded at CBS Studios with ex-Zombies/ Argent bassist Chris White in the producer's chair. "I knew I wanted a guest lead guitarist for 'Watch Yerself'," said Fennelly. "I asked Chris who he thought might be a good choice, and he said 'Why don't I give Jeff Beck a call?' I was pleased, to say the least, when Jeff agreed to do it."

When Beck arrived, Michael observed at close quarters the nature of his gift with six strings, and indeed, Jeff's sharp ear for fine equipment. "I remember, quite distinctly, sitting in the control room by Jeff as he learned the song, listening to the basic track and 'work' vocal," Fennelly confirmed. "I watched him noodle around, trying this and that. His technique was just incredible. So fluid, [like] liquid. He was playing through a little old blond Fender Princeton I'd brought along. Jeff wanted to buy the amp but I told him it wasn't for sale. It was quite a lovely classic, from the late fifties or early sixties." Working quickly, Beck aligned his lead guitar part – probably cut with a Tele and Marshall – to [ex-Crabby Appleton keyboard player] Casey Foutz's undulating synthesiser lines, resulting in some fine, swooping interplay between the two instruments. "I was very pleased with Jeff's playing on 'Watch Yerself'," said Fennelly. "I felt it added a flavour to the song that hadn't been there... a rich fluid twang over a track that was rather brittle, and a little harsh, by design."

'Watch Yerself' remains a little lost gem in Jeff Beck's back catalogue of session work, the song he contributed to redolent of a new, leaner hard-rock sound then gestating among bands such as Montrose and UFO that would soon enough overtake the likes of BBA. "I'd love to wax poetic about vision and fusion," Michael said, when asked about crafting 'Watch Yerself' and *Lane Changer*'s overall futuristic approach, "but honestly songs just happen and they cry out for specific approaches. So, I give them what they ask for."

Strangely, Beck seemed less than enthralled by his efforts on 'Watch Yerself' and asked to be withdrawn from the album's acknowledgements – an occasional practice in subsequent years. "I was disappointed to later learn that Jeff was less satisfied with his part. He asked us to leave his name off the credits, [so] we complied." It is worth noting that Jeff's only contribution to *Lane Changer* is on 'Watch Yerself', with all other guitars on the album played by Fennelly himself: "Flattering mistake, though," he joked.

Recording sessions recommenced for BBA's second album in October, 1973 at Kent's Escape Studios, only a hot rod's journey away from Beck's home. But despite considering several producers – including ex-Bowie guitarist Mick Ronson – and tinkering with the recording controls themselves, lightning again failed to strike. By this time, BBA had amassed some 14 partially completed demos, with the likes of '...Your Lovemaker's Coming Home', 'Solid Lifter' and 'Prayin'' already debuted in live performance. Additionally, there were other tracks such as 'Laughalong/Song For The Lovely Ladies', 'The Chant Song' and the fearsome instrumental 'Jizz Whizz' also in various stages of completion, as well as several covers under consideration by the likes of The Staples Singers and Freddy Scott. Yet Jeff remained unsatisfied with both the direction of the group and the quality of the tunes recorded. "We suffered," he concluded, "from an abysmal lack of material."

In a last-ditch effort to save the day, BBA enlisted the help of Jimmy 'JBG2' Miller and Led Zeppelin engineer Andy Johns, and moved to London's CBS studios where things went slightly better. But when miners' industrial action caused the Conservative government to again implement an energy-saving three-day working week in the winter of 1973/4, several studios were forced to close, leaving Beck and his colleagues wandering around London with no place to mix and master their latest efforts. As a result, all further work was abandoned, with Jeff taking the tapes home and throwing them in a dark corner, never to be seen again. "It all got a bit dead-ended," he later said. "You couldn't really dream up anything special for each song. They all demanded a certain style. There's a second BBA album somewhere in my house [with] mould growing off the tape. A nice crop of grass."

Despite various signs from God, pit workers and the government of the day, Beck, Bogert and Appice struggled inexorably on, though Jeff was not above dropping the odd hint or two about their probable future when meeting the press in January 1974: "The main fault of the group is the fact we don't work enough," he told *Sounds* at the time. "That's because I don't like being in America, and Tim and Carmine aren't quite at home here. I'd like to see the bond strengthened between us. I don't think the three of us know what should and shouldn't be played. They'll be playing by ear behind me, but half the time, I'm just playing along with them. There isn't really one member of the band that's more dominant than the others. We're all about equal. And that's good, because if I'm feeling rotten, they can carry things a bit." But the interview concluded on an ominous note: "This group could go on for a very long time or die out very quickly. I really don't know."

The answer to that question came in a series of fits and starts, with a previously contracted and long-delayed UK tour throughout January almost being cancelled again when Carmine Appice caught a fever and the band had to pull out of their opening Scottish dates. As before, Tim Bogert was the next to be struck down by the extremities of the British winter, hauling his exhausted, flu-ridden body up and down the M1 before BBA's flagship appearance at Finsbury Park's Rainbow Theatre on January 26. Given that Beck had already experienced one of the worst shows of his life at that venue, during which mysterious power failures and falling curtains all but destroyed the JBG's debut performance in March 1967, he was probably not that surprised when a backstage fight broke out between him and Bogert during sets. Though Jeff was reportedly flattened by Tim as the argument raged, bootlegs suggest the band's onstage antics remained wholly professional, with new material such as '…Your Lovemaker's Coming Home' and 'Prayin'' not sounding 'punchy' in the least.

One would have thought that the events of The Rainbow, and a couple of hastily rescheduled, but underwhelming appearances in Scotland would have brought a natural end to proceedings, with all parties content to give up the ghost and move on elsewhere. But after a short break to clear the air, Appice was again on the phone to Beck from the US with the news that Sly Stone was willing to produce their next album. A huge fan of Stone from the days of 1968's 'Dance To The Music' and 'Everyday People', Jeff duly took the bait and flew to Sausalito in the spring of 1974 with high hopes and several guitars. Sadly, Sly had reacted badly to the pressures of fame and was in the middle of a failing love affair with cocaine, PCP and America's Black

Panther movement. The resulting sessions were undistinguished at best, with Stone's frequent absences eventually leading Beck to hop back on a plane to London and finally call time on the group.

A fine, if ultimately stymied experiment, BBA were really a band out of time. If everything had gone to the original plan and Jeff not had his car accident in November, 1969, the group might have been potential world-beaters – their gift for elongated, technically dazzling jams and brute musical force a fine replacement for an absent Cream or even a rival to Led Zeppelin. But by delaying their arrival, and electing to retain a three-piece structure without benefit of a charismatic front man, they had a whiff of 'yesterday's men' to both their image and music.

"We were missing the boat a bit in the end," Jeff later admitted. "Cream had already done the extended solo thing. It just wasn't strong enough." Equally, BBA suffered from lack of a definite leader, with Beck's original wish for a "democratic unit" ultimately leading to uncertainty, indecision and excessive behaviour instead of truly fine songs. "I know that Carmen and Tim were frustrated guys, and they wanted me to lead them to new pastures. But, [again] we were existing in the wake of bands like Cream and Jimi Hendrix, which made it difficult to find those pastures," he said. "We overextended ourselves – we were the answer to the question 'What kind of music would these crazed guys make without any chastisement?'"

Of all the groups that Jeff Beck has joined, formed or walked out of over the years, he seems to retain the most affection for BBA, often citing them as an example of how extraordinary potential, excellent musicianship and unswerving drive can be undone by bad decision-making and a criminal lack of restraint. "Without blaming anyone, BBA needed more discipline," he said. "We were just three maniacs. Three utter, complete maniacs. It went on all day, onstage and offstage. If we'd sat down and thought about it... said to each other 'Look lads, we're going to sell 10 million albums if we do the right things', maybe we could have actually done it. But that was never going to happen, never to be, no way."

But it was precisely because of BBA's failure in these areas that Beck was once again forced to lick his wounds, readjust his thinking cap and ultimately embark on the most commercially successful period of his career.

Chapter 14

A Change Is As
Good As A Rest

Jeff Beck turned 30 years of age on June 24, 1974. A professional
musician for nearly half his life, he had been at various points
a Deltone, a Trident, a Yardbird, a band leader with two distinctly
different groups bearing his name, and latterly, a major part of a
well-meaning if botched experiment in "democratic unity". Widely
regarded as one of the world's pre-eminent lead guitarists, Beck had
led the way in matters of feedback and distortion, drone techniques
and legato, soloed his way across continents and been a major
influence on the birth of psychedelic, blues and hard rock. All in all,
it was quite an impressive resumé to have at hand. Yet, when asked
to assess his personal contribution to a music scene he in part helped
build, Jeff's response was not so much humble as self-flagellating.
"Mine is just 18–22-year-old yob music, really," he said. "It is."

Though Beck had often expressed misgivings about the worth
of his musical output before, and been quick to point out errors in
how he handled his career – resulting in missed opportunities, stolen
ideas and more than a little acrimony here and there – there was no
doubting his artistry. Never one to follow trends, Jeff simply made
up his own, whether that be his ground-breaking work with The
Yardbirds, or providing a sonic template for countless others to follow
with *Truth* and *Beck-Ola*. But recent years had seen diminishing
returns in pointing that undoubted creativity at the right target.

217

JBG2, while ambitious in its quest to fuse Motown and Stax grooves with overdriven guitars, had not been keenly received by the public. BBA, on the other hand, were greeted far more enthusiastically, yet failed to surmount the twin perils of instrumental overindulgence and middling tunes. "To be honest, we had no songs and no singer," Jeff said. "Well, we tried a singer but that was a disaster."

More worrying was that despite their undoubted gifts and live popularity, the band's free-wheeling, three-piece format was almost a dead art form at the time. With The Jimi Hendrix Experience and Cream already consigned to history, a new wave of sharper, more concise hard rock/metal acts such as Aerosmith, Thin Lizzy, Stray Dog, Montrose, UFO and Kiss were now ready to take their place and Beck was more than willing to let them get on with it. "Heavy metal, a term used to describe these awful bands that came after *Truth* and *Beck-Ola*," he later growled to *NME*. "That just turned me off rock n' roll for a while. It was like a complete desecration of rock's essential spirit as far as I was concerned."

As ever, Jeff Beck had profound reservations about the validity of his latest enterprise long before BBA officially shut its doors for business. Battered by long nights of shattering volume and endless solos, he had spent much of his downtime while recording the trio's ultimately aborted second album listening to a mysterious tape in the front seat of Carmine Appice's brand new Pantera sports car. "I thought it was Badfinger, because [Carmine] was always playing Badfinger. It wasn't. It was *Spectrum*." For Beck, every light in his head went on simultaneously. "*Spectrum* changed my whole musical outlook. I thought 'This is the shit we need.'" "The shit" Beck was referring to was a ground-breaking 'jazz-rock' LP released in October, 1973 by drummer Billy Cobham, a former employee of legendary jazz trumpeter Miles Davis, and then current member of John McLaughlin's Mahavishnu Orchestra.

The odd delights of jazz rock – or as it later became known, 'fusion' – were not unknown to Beck at the time. An essentially American phenomenon that mixed the improvisational qualities of jazz with the rhythm, tonalities and volume of rock (and occasionally funk), the genre's exact origins were hard to pin down, though most critics will point to the mid-sixties as a probable starting point.

218

Following pioneering work by The Free Spirits, featuring sublime guitarist Larry Coryell, and The Charles Lloyd Quartet – a line-up that included pianist Chick Corea and drummer Jack DeJohnette – things truly moved into a new age with Miles Davis' 1969 LP *In A Silent Way*. Comprised of two side-long improvisatory jams, ... *Silent Way's* loping beats, quiet but forceful grace and stunning instrumental passages acted as a finishing school for the jazz rock/ fusion stars of the future. Within just three years of the album's release, drummer Tony Williams, saxophonist Wayne Shorter, keyboardists Herbie Hancock and Joe Zawinul, and Corea had formed the likes of Lifetime, Weather Report, Headhunters and Return To Forever.

Providing guitar on *In A Silent Way* and Miles Davis' follow-up fusion discs, the magnificent *Bitches Brew*, *A Tribute To Jack Johnson* and *On The Corner*, was Doncaster-born John McLaughlin, who in 1971, had left his mentor to form the Mahavishnu Orchestra. A frightening technician, capable of sewing jazz, classical, rock, flamenco, Eastern and Indian styles into just one solo, McLaughlin's work with Mahavishnu again expanded the boundaries of what could be achieved with fusion, a fact conclusively proved on 1973's *Birds Of Fire*. For Beck, who had first encountered John's spectacular flights on Davis' ... *Jack Johnson* LP, *Birds Of Fire* was seminal, enviable and just a little humbling. "I try to incorporate dazzling playing into something that at the same time can be commercial," he told journalist Jas Obrecht while still with BBA. "But I can understand Mahavishnu because they've already done what I wanted to do, really. McLaughlin is far more technically knowledgeable than me. I mean, I don't know half of what he knows. I just never had to worry about those kinds of chords... because they weren't usable in what I was playing. McLaughlin wouldn't come and watch me with the group I have now, let me tell you that!" In fact, the more Jeff explored tracks such as 'Sister Andrea' from the album *Between Nothingness And Eternity* or listened to Mahavishnu's 1972 performance at Mar Y Sol (which featured on a live disc of the same name), he came to one, irrevocable conclusion: "McLaughlin's the best there is. Supreme, on another plane entirely."

But as much as he admired John McLaughlin's gifts, Beck still held slight reservations about the overall complexity of the Mahavishnu Orchestra, admiring from a distance rather than being wholly engulfed by the band's more exotic tendencies, which included quite bewildering changes in tempo and odd, chamber-music stylings. He had no such doubts about Billy Cobham's *Spectrum*, however. Though Cobham may have been a fully paid-up member of McLaughlin's band, the explosive power, volatile energy, funk grooves and fire-starting performances on *Spectrum* were something Jeff could not only understand, but actively wished to replicate. "Billy Cobham's *Spectrum* gave life to me at the time, on top of the Mahavishnu records," he said. "It represented a whole area that was as exciting to me as when I first heard 'Hound Dog' by Elvis Presley. They were so inspirational to me to the point that I started to adopt that type of music."

Another aspect of Spectrum that intrigued and delighted Beck was the synthesiser/guitar interplay between Mahavishnu graduate Jan Hammer and The James Gang's Tommy Bolin: "Tommy's guitar playing on *Spectrum* is fantastic, while Jan can flatten you with the first few notes." In fact, Hammer's Mini Moog synth lines were so creamy-sounding, dextrous and fleet fingered, it was often hard to distinguish them from Bolin's six-string attack – a fact Jeff gave great thought to while sitting in Carmine Appice's car. "Jan's sound," he later admitted, "just went straight into me..." When still a member of BBA, Jeff Beck could only listen to albums like *Spectrum* and *Birds Of Fire* without any real hope of emulating them, knowing full well there was little chance of persuading Tim and Carmine to embrace such a bold new direction for their own band. But by May of 1974, he was again a free man and able to pursue that fixation in stronger terms, subject of course, to the blessings of his record company. Thankfully for Jeff, Epic had seen the sales numbers on *Birds Of Fire* and the crowds Mahavishnu Orchestra, Weather Report and Return To Forever could draw to shows, and were therefore willing to indulge his latest whim.

In fact, Beck already had some form behind him when it came to the vagaries of jazz. As far back as 1971, his solo pass on Stevie Wonder's 'Looking For Another Pure Love' – with its rapidly descending chromatic scales and warm tone – certainly doffed a cap in the direction of Barney Kessel. Additionally, parts of 'Jeff's Boogie' had always contained a tribute phrase or two to his childhood hero Les Paul, Beck's skittering runs up and down the fretboard redolent of classic tracks such as 'Bye Bye Blues' and 'Tiger Rag'. But after hearing John McLaughlin and Billy Cobham, he had ramped up his interest in jazz and funk to new levels.

Aside from watching and occasionally jamming with Latin/jazz/reggae-themed pick-up band Gonzalez – whose core membership would go on to form Hummingbird – Beck also guested on several sessions of a distinctly experimental nature during mid-1974. Having been introduced through Gonzalez to a new jazz-funk-progressive act called Zzebra, which housed the likes of guitarist Terry Smith, saxophonist Dave Quincy and bassist John McCoy (who later found fame with Ian Gillan), Jeff cut a brief, but fulsome solo on 'Put A Light On Me' – a song released on the band's debut album, *Panic*, in 1975. He also made a small, but telling contribution to 'White Lady', the title track of Badger's first LP, a group led by ex-Yes keyboardist Tony Kaye that also featured the talents of bass player Kim Gardner, who in turn had auditioned without success for the original JBG in 1967. Keen to stay busy, Beck next joined ex-Cream writing partners Pete Brown and Jack Bruce in the studio, where he provided a lick or two on the witty 'Spend My Knights In Armour'. Though the session went well, with Max Middleton adding a suitably funky Fender Rhodes part to Bruce's noodling bass, 'Spend My Knights...' was not released until 1987, when it appeared on Brown's long-delayed solo album *Before Singing Lessons: 1969–1977.**

But by far the most jazz/funk/rock-approved acts that Jeff involved himself with at around this time were Eddie Harris and Upp, both associations providing clear pointers and real clues as to his future musical direction. In Harris' case, Beck's interest stemmed from the exhilarating freedom with which the tenor saxophonist approached both his chosen instrument and compositional theory as a whole. Best known for the daring, 'love it or hate it' approach of 'Freedom Jazz Dance', Harris revelled in taking chances – whether they be introducing amplified sax solos to the predominantly conservative jazz audience of the late sixties or debuting the 'reed trumpet' to the general disgust of critics at 1970's Newport Festival. Therefore, when Jeff learned that Harris was ensconced in London's Morgan

---

*	For completists, Pete Brown also wrote the lyrics to 'Livin' Life Backwards', a track scheduled to appear on BBA's second disc.

Studios at work on his latest album during August 1974, he was quick to offer his services. The result of their collaboration was the peculiar, but pleasing 'He's Island, Man', on which Beck's almost calypso-like run and novel use of octave divider (or an early ring modulation device) contrasted wonderfully with Eddie's dissonant sax blasts, offered a thrilling taste of Jeff's new approach to the art of soloing. Beck's efforts can be found on Eddie Harris' *E.H In The UK*, a disc that also features Deep Purple's Ian Paice on drums and the stunning country guitarist Albert Lee. To this day, Jeff remains uncharacteristically happy with his work on the LP.

Of equal importance was Beck's continued championing of Upp, a band he had first encountered in the summer of 1973 and who subsequently backed him for a prestigious appearance on the BBC documentary *The Five Faces Of Guitar*. Hosted by the legendary Julian Bream, the programme pulled together a dream cast of guitarists from almost all genres of music, including flamenco (Paco Peña), folk (John Renbourn), classical (John Williams) and jazz (Jeff's teen hero, Barney Kessell). Presumably, Beck was invited along to represent 'rock', but threw a spanner in the works immediately by providing viewers with a distinctly reggae-tinged treatment of The Beatles' 'She's A Woman' before letting fly an inspired, jazz/ blues solo on Upp's own funk-leaning 'Down In The Dirt'. As with his support of Eddie Harris, Jeff's interest in Upp's melding of "Cobham-type funk... and very spacey Moog" spoke volumes as to where he wanted to point his guns next. After Upp supported BBA on their final UK dates, Beck served as producer of their first, self-titled album, recorded in the summer of 1974 at London's CBS Studios and released a year later (it also remains the only occasion he has chosen to produce a group). Alongside drummer Jimmy Copley*, keyboardist Andy Clark, guitar player Dave Bunce and the aptly named Stephen Amazing on bass, Jeff provided solos on the tracks 'Don't Want Nothing To Change' and 'Dance Your Troubles Away', as well as appearing on the group's next disc, 1976's *This Way*.

---

* An excellent drummer and rare proponent of the 'open hand technique', Copley would remain firm friends with Jeff, their paths often crossing over the years, both socially and in the studio environment.

Having tested the waters with various sessions, brief experiments and more elongated pursuits in the areas of jazz, fusion and funk, Jeff was finally ready to make his next move. But after years of battling Mickie Most about guitar levels, watching helplessly as Steve Cropper reined in his band's finer excesses and even turning a hand to production himself, Beck wanted to ensure he had the perfect producer in place for potentially the most difficult album of his career. The man chosen for that job was George Martin, whose seminal work with The Beatles had seen them evolve from loveable, mop-topped popstrels into one of the most quietly subversive and genuinely experimental bands of the 20th century. Since The Beatles' break up Martin had been far from idle, first leaving the scene of his greatest triumphs, Abbey Road, to set up central London's AIR recording studios in 1969, before revitalising the success of US soft rockers America with 1974's million-selling album *Holiday*.

But it was Martin's recent alliance with John McLaughlin on Mahavishnu's latest album, *Apocalypse*, that had truly piqued Jeff's interest, with the producer perfectly aligning the group's own dense and complex sound to the myriad strings and railing brass of the London Symphony Orchestra. A superb arranger, strong composer and in The Beatles' own words "the man who showed us how to use the studio as a tool or another instrument", George Martin's agreement to produce your LP was a considerable honour and Beck knew it. "George was the father figure of The Beatles. I was so in awe of what he did with them... four guys who were basically rockers. The fact that he was even slightly interested in me gave me a tremendous boost."

Unbeknownst to Jeff, George Martin was also a longtime fan of his work and had been somewhat shocked when asked to consider the project. "[I was] immediately surprised that he would approach me because I'd always admired his playing enormously," Martin told Gibson. com. "I knew his work well, and Jeff was always very much a sort of heavy rock, heavy metal guy, but a hip guy... he wasn't just a basher. But I was quite surprised he approached me because I'd been tending to be doing much more soft work than the kind of things he was used to. And for that reason, I thought it was a surprising choice on his behalf. When he did approach me, I was very excited about it. I thought it was a great idea and I looked forward to working with him."

Work began on Jeff Beck's new album in October 1974 at George Martin's AIR studios with a small but important core of musicians – one a logical, inspired choice, the other a genuine surprise. Returning to the keyboard was Max Middleton, whom Beck had previously credited with adding sophistication to his sound and helping him learn some of the trickier chord voicings present in the work of JBG2: "Jeff called me up out of the blue, and said 'I've got an album to do. Want to join up?'" However, the presence of Carmine Appice behind the drum kit was slightly more perplexing, his crushing style seemingly at odds with the type of music Beck now wished to explore. "Carmine was just really, devastatingly good," Jeff later reasoned to *Guitar World*. "He was probably the last of the forties-style, big-band, fuck-off drummers. But he still had that forward-thinking Billy-Cobham-type feel." Rounding out the band was bassist Phil Chen, a fine musician who had often jammed with Middleton in Gonzalez. "Good grooves with Phil," said Max.

Initial sessions went well, with at least four tracks taking definite shape within the space of a few days. But confusion soon set in between Appice and Beck as to whether the album bore the drummer's name on its front cover. Apparently, when the duo first discussed the project, Carmine was under the impression that it was to be an equal collaboration, a fact later corrected by Beck's manager, Ernest Chapman. Given that Carmine's name was 'in lights' with BBA, his own management team took badly to the news, stating their charge was no side man. The situation became further complicated when Appice learned that to complete the terms of his own solo deal with Epic Records, he would have to be legally billed as a 'featured artist'. "Jeff, Carmine and I did a couple of days recording at AIR studios with George Martin," said Middleton. "Then, out of nowhere, Carmine said, 'I want this to be called 'The Carmine Appice and Jeff Beck Project'. Jeff said, 'Well, you can bugger off'. For him, it was just a solo album, no big deal, you know? He just wanted to make the best album he could, but..." Suffice to say, Appice left AIR studios, never to return.

Beck was now faced with a dilemma. "Jeff came to me and said, 'What are we going to do? We've been waiting months for George and the studio, now we've got no drummer'," confirmed Middleton. "So, I said, 'Don't worry, I know someone.'" Max's solution was to call Richard Bailey, a formidable, 18-year-old talent that he and Phil Chenn had worked with in Gonzalez. "There was no real worry about either Phil or Richard coming in and fitting with Jeff's style," said Middleton. "They were just really good musicians who instinctively knew what they were doing." With a band now in place, the tracks begun with Appice were further developed – including 'Scatterbrain' and 'Constipated Duck' – while several new songs (including 'Air Blower' and 'You Know What I Mean') were composed during breaks in rehearsal. As before, Max Middleton worked with Jeff on shaping chords and substitutions for guitar, while also finalising the structure of Beck's own material. "One of the good things about [Beck and my] relationship was meeting up with Max Middleton," said George Martin. "Max wrote a lot of the tunes with Jeff and a lot of the tunes by himself. It was kind of a three-way partnership really, because Max had the patience to spend a long time with Jeff, which I couldn't do. He was able to translate my thoughts into Jeff's medium. He was a good go-between [for] the two of us, between Jeff and myself."

As work began in earnest, Middleton was again reminded of Beck's eccentric practices about keeping to agreed studio hours. "Well, George Martin was like your favourite uncle. He said, 'Let's work from 10 in the morning until six at night. If it goes any longer, you can get tired. Or if you start at six, you'll still be here until two, three in the morning, so let's keep it respectable'. We agreed. But then, it'd be 10 in the morning and there'd be no Jeff. And at noon. And so on. Then, Jeff would come bounding in about six, when we were just about finishing. After two or three days of this George said, 'Why are you coming in so late?' So Jeff said 'It costs £2 to park out there and if you miss the meter, you'll get a ticket'. George just looked at him and said, 'But Jeff, you're wasting £1,000 in the studio...'. You see, the record company was paying for the studio but the meter was being paid for by Jeff. And he wasn't having it. After a few more days of this, I said, 'George, we may as well start recording something, we're here anyway.'" By all accounts, the decision to begin cutting tracks to tape in his absence sufficiently roused Beck to get in at an earlier hour. But despite such herculean efforts, his producer still remained a hard, if loveable taskmaster: "I would be trying to do these really difficult bits and George would say, 'Jeff, you played like an angel this morning but now you suck. Just take a break!' I loved that about him because I hate to be patronised about my playing."

Once principal recording at AIR Studios was nearly complete, Beck's hitherto concrete decision to abandon groups in favour of working as a solo artist was thrown into serious doubt when word came from The Rolling Stones camp that they were seeking a new lead guitarist, and he was their target. In December 1974, some five years after replacing the talented but unstable Brian Jones, Mick Taylor had quietly but firmly handed in his resignation with the Stones, citing both exhaustion and a need to explore new musical pathways as his reasons for leaving the band. Behind the scenes, it was a somewhat murkier story, with Taylor privately irked that two songs he had written for the group's latest LP, *It's Only Rock'n'roll*, were credited solely to Mick Jagger and Keith Richards: "I was a bit peeved about not getting credit for a couple of songs," Taylor later told journalist Gary James, "but that wasn't the whole reason [I left]. I guess I just felt like I had enough."

Replacing Mick Taylor was no easy task. As stated in *The New York Times* following his departure, "Taylor [was] the most accomplished technician who ever served as a Stone, [being] a blues guitarist with a jazzman's flair for melodic invention." If one simply changed the sentence to read "blues and rock guitarist..." then Jeff Beck instantly topped the list of likely candidates as Taylor's successor.

Flattered by the attention, aware of the copious income opportunities, but also wary of abandoning a potentially fine album and nascent solo career, a conflicted Beck flew to Rotterdam in late January 1975 to attend rehearsals with the Stones. "Well, who wouldn't want a private jet with a fireplace?" he later joked. Once there, however, it became apparent that the very fact that Jeff had boarded a plane was signal enough that he was willing to join the band. "When I got there, I spied 400 guitars all with different tags on. I said, 'Are these all Keith's guitars?' They said 'No, these are the guys coming to audition.' I said, 'What? I'm not auditioning!' They said, 'No, you've got the gig, they're going to tell the others not to come.'" Of further concern was his introduction to a novel concept known as 'Rolling Stones Time', where group members appeared or disappeared from the studio altogether as and when they saw fit, with songs starting up only to halt moments later when Keith Richards left the room. "The Stones never showed up at the same time to play," Beck said. "They just kept turning up at different times."

If bootleg dates are correct, Jeff Beck contributed to two sets of rough demos with the Stones on February 1 and 9 in Rotterdam, these sessions producing approximately 30 minutes of various riffs, snippets and potential ideas. The most complete song on these tapes is an early version of 'Slave', a sluggish three-chord vamp that later appeared (without Jeff) on the band's 1981 album, *Tattoo You*, with Pete Townshend replacing Beck on rhythm guitar and backing vocals. Elsewhere, Jeff can be (just about) heard contributing some tasteful slide flourishes to the cod-soul of 'Sexy Nite (Lovely Lady)', a bit of casual tremolo wobbling at the end of 'Blues Jam' and some pinched harmonics and chugging chords to 'Travellin' Man'. Of the other tracks present, such as the James Brown-like 'Come On Sugar (Let's Do It Right)', the Bo Diddley shunt of 'Shame, Shame, Shame' and the reggae-inflected 'Man Eating Woman', it is nigh impossible to confirm Beck is actually playing on them at all. Whatever the case, Jeff seemed to find the whole experience unsatisfactory: "Part of me would love to have been a Rolling Stone, but I was used to conceiving a notion, putting it down on tape and finishing it by the end of the evening. They just had trouble turning up."

Having made his mind up to "get the fuck out of Dodge", Beck turned to his old friend and current Stones road manager Ian Stewart to deliver the bad news: "I was being sucked into it you see, so that was the crossroads... what path was I going to take? But one rehearsal was really enough. When I played with the Stones it was so quaint. After the real violent riffs and wild Billy Cobham rhythms I was getting into, it would never have worked. So I slipped a note under Ian Stewart's hotel door [that] said, 'There's been a mistake,' and I was gone." As the years passed, Jeff was often questioned as to why he turned down one of the most prized jobs in rock'n'roll, but his answer seldom strayed far from one simple thread of logic: "In three hours, I only had to play three chords and I need a little bit more energy than that,"

After expressing interest in or even auditioning the likes of Irish blues maestro Rory Gallagher, two-handed fret tapper Harvey

Mandel and Southern session ace Wayne Perkins, the Stones finally settled on a guitarist well known to Beck: Ronnie Wood. Then a star in his own right, Wood had long since dispensed with the four strings that propped up JBG1's rhythm section for six all of his own, stroking his trademark Tony Zemaitis-made 'metal front' guitar every night onstage with The Faces. An accomplished slide-player, with a deceptively gentle touch and sure gift for teasing out the slightest of melodies, Ronnie's easygoing nature was also perfect for counterbalancing the complex personal and musical relationship between Jagger and Richards. Therefore, when The Faces split in the autumn of 1975 amid a clattering soundtrack of smashed bourbon bottles, inflamed sinuses and sour grapes about the continuing success of Rod Stewart's solo career outside the band, the Glimmer Twins had their man. "Good job I recommended Woody then, because he was the perfect fit," Beck later said. "Besides, I'd never have got on with Keith. But he's still the Guv'nor, isn't he? Keith defies all the laws of gravity and still manages to play with one string missing. He's got the slouchy thing going, and plays almost painfully behind, which I love to hear." But obviously not enough.

With his decision made, Beck returned to London to view the final artwork on his first official 'solo album', a cleverly painted image of the guitarist by artist John Collier, who had adapted it in turn from an existing photo of Jeff onstage circa 1973. A striking pose, showing Beck at work high on the neck of his beloved 1954 Oxblood Les Paul, its woody, almost classical hues certainly drew the eye, but questions remained whether the disc inside could actually deliver the goods. By dumping the old-school, but still profitable sound of BBA and moving towards the 'terra incognito' of jazz-fusion and funk styles, Jeff was taking the chance of his life. He could only hope that he took his audience with him.

"I had all this good, funky stuff wanting to come out of me," he said, "[And] I thought, you know I've got to have a go at this.'" When asked by journalists what the title of his new LP was, Beck responded with the words 'Blow By Blow'. "I think George might have come up with it," he said. "I didn't like it at first, but the more I heard it, the more it made sense."

He was right.

Chapter 15

Revenge Is Sweet

Blow By Blow was released by Epic Records to no great ceremony in March 1975. Based on Jeff Beck's already established profile, sales numbers generated by like-minded acts such as the Mahavishnu Orchestra and a strong tour to promote the disc, Epic could be hopeful of a Top 20 placing in the States, though as ever, all bets were off as to UK chart performance. Yet, there was also a mood of quiet confidence among the record company's A&R department that Beck's new all-instrumental album might be "a grower", a fact that both surprised and flattered the guitarist: "I didn't really think much of *Blow By Blow* when we were doing it. I thought it was probably a middle of the road mistake. But when [Epic] heard it, they rolled out a red carpet that stretched from my house to New York. I just went with it."

In fact, *Blow By Blow* proved to be more an overnight success than steady climber, with the LP sprinting up to number four in the US charts within weeks, its sales no doubt helped by the support of FM radio, which played it relentlessly on release. That *Blow By Blow* caught the mood of an ageing audience now content to leave behind their teenage fixations with high volume and stage theatrics to explore more 'serious music' was also surely a factor. But in the end, the album's positive reception and impressive retail figures were probably down to one, solid gold reason. *Blow By Blow* was really rather good.

In the run-up to the LP's release, Jeff Beck had talked much about his admiration of John McLaughlin and Billy Cobham, waxing lyrical about their striking modernity and the bold new sounds and unexpected textures they produced. But *Blow By Blow* mimicked neither *Birds Of Fire* nor *Spectrum*. Instead, it simplified their approach, making complex time signatures and clever chord changes accessible to ears that previously might have had trouble distinguishing them from white noise. Additionally, Beck had played to his strengths, using his gift for melody and lyrical phrasing to great advantage, providing listeners with tunes they could actually hum or even dance to. It was more akin to Miles Davis' *Kind Of Blue* than John Coltrane's *A Love Supreme*; Jeff, his band and George Martin had produced fusion's first bestseller, offering both jazz and rock neophytes an easily digestible but striking introduction to a genre that potentially offered much, but still scared the majority of horses.

Blow By Blow's opening track, 'You Know What I Mean', quickly mapped out where the album's focus lay, with Richard Bailey and Phil Chen's funky rhythmic patterns providing a sprightly, loose beat over which Max and Jeff could do their stuff. Immediately sounding in his element, Beck bounced off Middleton's lively keyboard, twisting and turning his solo in unexpected, but wholly melodic directions. The band's reggae-like cover of The Beatles' 'She's A Woman' was even better, with Jeff's guitar more or less tracking Paul McCartney's original vocal line during the verses before adding flashes of syncopation, falling blues scales and the occasional use of the voice bag to further enliven the tune. Though Beck had performed '...Woman' live several months before with Upp on the BBC's *Five Faces Of Guitar* documentary, he had first come across the song through Max Middleton. "Max was playing in a backing band [Gonzalez] for Linda Lewis," Jeff told *Guitar World*. "She was Jim Cregan's wife, who was Rod Stewart's guitar player, and she'd started making waves at Ronnie Scott's jazz club. Anyway, Max said, 'Linda does this song... and people go crazy'." Middleton took up the story: "I said 'Let's do 'She's A Woman'. I'd worked on it at home, and come up with a funny way of playing it, like a calypso. Well, George hated it, but Jeff loved it, so we did it."

There was more fun (and funk) to be had from 'Constipated Duck' and 'Theolonius', the latter of which Stevie Wonder had gifted Beck in return for his efforts on *Talking Book*'s 'Looking For

Another Pure Love', and which BBA tried to knock into shape for their second, unreleased album. On both cuts, Jeff again turned on the charm, using Middleton's clavinet as a springboard for some clever rhythm guitar work – and in the case of the aptly named '...Duck', a vividly drawn Wes Montgomery meets Chuck Berry solo flight. 'Freeway Jam' was probably *Blow By Blow's* most 'rock friendly' moment, taking its musical orders from Richard Bailey's marching, military snare and Phil Chen's walking bass before Jeff dug out the '71 Strat and pulled out all the stops. "I used the Strat to frighten people at that point, really," he later joked. Living up to its title, 'Freeway Jam' had come out of an impromptu air Middleton began fiddling about with during breaks in recording, though its exact origin stemmed back to JBG2's 'Orange Album'. "If you listen closely," Max confirmed, "the bridge in 'Definitely Maybe' has the same melody as 'Freeway Jam'." Despite the fact that 'Freeway Jam' has long established itself as a concert favourite for Beck fans, the guitarist himself never actually warmed to it. "I hate it!" said Jeff. "It felt like a slowed-down Irish reel to me."

An impressive album thus far, *Blow By Blow's* bid for enduring greatness was defined by two tunes: the first, a spare, soulful ballad, the other "a mad thing" that remains one of Beck and Middleton's more intricate and compelling compositions. In the first instance, Jeff once again returned to Stevie Wonder for inspiration. "I'd always closely followed [Stevie's] music," Beck later told *ABC Music*. "Well, he produced an album for his wife, Syreeta Wright, who was also a Motown act and I got hold of the LP. Then I heard this beautiful intro line that she sang, and I thought, 'Thank you very much, that'll do for me." The song Jeff was referring to was 'Cause We've Ended As Lovers', from Syreeta Wright's second solo album of 1974. "Actually, when I heard it," he continued, "I wasn't hearing Syreeta singing. I was hearing me playing. I picked up the guitar and there was this perfect song."

A masterclass in improvisation, Jeff's treatment of 'Cause We've Ended...' had him swooping, stabbing and stroking at the melody line, using different pick-ups and tonalities to tease out the bittersweet nature of Wonder's song. But it wasn't only Stevie Wonder who had inspired Jeff's lyrical approach to 'Cause We've Ended...', a point underlined by recurring use of volume swells, artificial harmonics and three-note overbends throughout Beck's mournful solo. Though Jeff had been using them a while, these particular techniques were also strongly associated with Roy Buchanan, then as now something of a secret among guitar players, and to whom Jeff dedicated the track. "I played that song with the same vibe [Roy] had," he told *Guitar Player*. "He...just blazed. I had the style already pretty much in my head, that sort of stroking strings... arpeggiated sort of chords and bending notes... but he actually made it more comfortable for me to play in that [way]. [Roy] was pure kick-up-the-bum stuff." Within a year, Buchanan returned the favour, writing the song 'My Friend Jeff' for his 1976 album, *A Street Called Straight*.

Later billed as "the world's best unknown guitarist", Buchanan's main instrument of choice was a battered but beautiful 1953 blond Fender Telecaster he nicknamed 'Nancy'. Oddly, Beck had also acquired a modified Telecaster of his own with which he used to cut 'Cause We've Ended...', a 'present' bestowed upon him by Seymour Duncan, and with a story all its own. Reportedly, Duncan was working as a part-time repair man at London's Fender Soundhouse in the early seventies when Jeff visited the store on a break from recording with BBA to get his beloved '59 sunburst Les Paul fixed once again. "[I'd heard] when Jeff got the guitar back, the pick-ups had covers on them... and the original Patent Applied For [PAFs] had been replaced with new Gibson humbuckers," Seymour told *The Guitar Magazine*. "I felt real bad, so I wanted to get Jeff a guitar with the tone of a Les Paul. I couldn't afford a [Gibson], so I came up with the 'Tele Gib'." Driven by guilt, Duncan brought Beck a heavy, ash-bodied 1958 Fender Tele with a specially modified humbucker to try. "The first humbucker I actually made was for Jeff Beck, who used it on the *Blow By Blow* album," he said. "I'd taken two PAF humbuckers out of Lonnie Mack's damaged old Flying V I found in Cincinnati [and modified] one of them, putting it in the guitar I gave to Jeff, which he used to record 'Cause We've Ended As Lovers'.

Over the moon with Seymour's work, Beck probably wasn't thinking too clearly when Duncan enquired whether he still owned his famous Yardbirds Esquire, and might want to swap. "I thought 'Has he lost his nut?', he's given me a guitar which is clearly better and he wants to swap it for this [bashed up] old guitar. Great. It was like 'Bye Bye, there goes my old workhorse'. Mind you, he got a lot of pleasure and enjoyment out of it, maybe more than me." Seymour recalls the tale slightly differently. According to him, once he had presented Beck with the Tele-Gib, a grateful Jeff sent Ralph Baker around the next morning to the Soundhouse with three guitars in a cloth bag from which Duncan could make his own choice. They included a '51 Tele, a mid-fifties Strat and the Yardbirds Esquire. Suffice to say, Seymour chose wisely. Ultimately, the end result remains the same: Jeff Beck got a wonderful guitar which still takes pride of place among his collection and Seymour Duncan not only received a thrilling substitute (later donated to the Rock & Roll Hall Of Fame), but also a long and profitable career as America's foremost designer of pick-ups – his original humbucker design for the Tele-Gib rechristened 'The JB1' and still in production today.

Of perhaps even greater value than desirable hybrid Telecasters and the wondrous solo that sat atop 'Cause We've Ended As Lovers' was *Blow By Blow*'s centrepiece, the bold, bizarre and quite beautiful 'Scatterbrain'. Marking its arrival upon 'Air Blower''s muted, yet soothing conclusion, 'Scatterbrain' started quietly but warmed up quickly, soon becoming a thrill ride of ever-changing tempos, dizzying solo interplay between Beck and Middleton and an almost miraculous string arrangement from George Martin that lifted the track to another level. A work of real genius, 'Scatterbrain''s manic riff actually began life as a warming-up exercise Jeff used to unlock his fingers before a gig. "I had 'Scatterbrain' in the can for about two years before *Blow By Blow*, but only the melody," he said. "I used to do it as an exercise, but we shifted the same figure [up the keys] and put different chords on it."

It was Max Middleton who took the guitarist's original idea and added some sprightly chords of his own. "Yep, Jeff had the riff so I wrote the chords and changes," he confirmed. "In a way, the process was simplicity itself, almost childlike. Then George stuck the strings on afterwards. Like 'Cause We've Ended As Lovers', Beck's solo was done in one take, by the way. He was banging them out that week." Driven along by Richard Bailey's brisk, inventive drum pattern (for which he surely deserves a medal), 'Scatterbrain' also ended on a supreme high: as the compound rhythms and band drop away, Beck is left alone to go barking mad with his Oxblood Les Paul, 200-watt Marshall stack and Colorsound Tonebender, discharging a barrage of malevolent-sounding, henpecked notes before his colleagues return in an attempt to rescue him from himself. "I was just trying to get out of there without any trouble," he later joked.

As Bernie Holland's mournful 'Diamond Dust' brought *Blow By Blow* to a slow but classy finale with luscious, James Bond–like strings again courtesy of George Martin, one was left with few doubts that this was Jeff Beck's finest album in years – perhaps even rivalling the mighty *Truth* as one of his strongest releases. "I enjoyed making *Blow By Blow* with George because there was an air of importance about the project," Jeff said. "But it wasn't like, 'C'mon, you bastard, we've been waiting two years for that.' I think it [was] the best guitar playing I've done since *Truth*." He also gave credit to Martin for instilling in him not only the courage to attempt an instrumental release, but also allowing the guitarist to forge a new identity in an already overcrowded marketplace. "George gave me the confidence to play on an instrumental album, and at that point I was absolutely cleared from any kind of 'direct' challenge to what Eric Clapton was doing, or anyone else for that matter, in terms of clashing styles."

Shifting more copies in a matter of weeks than Beck's combined back catalogue had done in years, *Blow By Blow* could only be seen as an unqualified success, and one Jeff was keen to emphasise, mercifully free of promotional gimmicks. "There wasn't much hype, everyone just sort of liked it," he told *Sounds* in 1975. "And that's the sort of music I want to play... music that makes the charts because everyone likes it, not just because six million people just decided to buy something because they're bored. So, they bought it because they liked it, not because it's 'new'. That's a big difference."

But though the LP might have leapt out of US stores, it was accorded a frostier reception on Jeff's home soil where, like *Truth* before it, *Blow By Blow* actually failed to chart. "Frankly, it's not very good," said *Melody Maker*. "But then, it's not amazingly bad either. It's just lame, about as lame as all the other guitar instrumentals he's ever done. The Stevie Wonder tunes crop up, only to be dealt with summarily, somehow emphasising the purposelessness of the whole project. *Blow By Blow*," the reviewer concluded, "is remarkable only for its vacuity."

Harsh words, and hardly conducive in persuading potential UK buyers to part with their cash for the album. Yet, *Melody Maker*'s somewhat tart review did identify one criticism of *Blow By Blow* that refused to go away at the time, and still holds water some three decades on. By chipping away at the hard corners of fusion and producing "an easily assimilated version" of the genre for broader public consumption, Jeff risked the ire of hard-core jazz critics who might look upon his latest offering as more pandering to the masses than creating true, experimental music. For the strongly principled Beck, who built his name on doing precisely the opposite of what might be deemed good for him, this was an uncomfortable dilemma and one he remained wary of for years to come: "Yeah, *Blow By Blow* went right up the [US] charts, but it dabbled dangerously with easy listening," he told *The Independent* in 2010. "I was actually getting these couples coming up to me that had conceived a child or made up some terrible rift while listening to that stuff. I thought, 'Oh dear, I smell big trouble. I smell patent-leather shoes.' See ya... not interested. It was a horrible realisation that Epic loved what I was doing. Whoops. We really had to think about that one. The record company liking the product was not what I envisaged."

Evidently for the rebelliously inclined guitarist, achieving mainstream popularity was a notion to be wrestled with, not revelled in. But the poor sales and critical sniffs accorded *Blow By Blow* in his homeland did have another less pleasing effect on Beck. Having pushed a boulder – Malthus style – up a hill with UK audiences for the best part of a decade, only to have it roll down on his head every time he thought progress had been made, Jeff took this latest slight to heart. Tired of trying to persuade British critics and crowds of his worth, he now concentrated his professional efforts elsewhere, refusing to tour the UK again for almost six years.

Back in April, 1975 and across the Atlantic, it was an entirely different matter as Jeff readied himself for three months on the road with the Mahavishnu Orchestra, a tour put together by John McLaughlin's manager, Nat Weiss, and the ever-reliable Ernest Chapman. "They said, 'Would you fancy a double-bill tour?' and I just leapt at it because I was on the verge of getting into that stuff," Beck told *International Musician*. "There's no way that the two musics are compatible, but that wasn't the idea of the tour. [It was more] to try and break away from all those white cop-out rock'n'roll licks." With the exception of Max Middleton, Beck chose not to bring the band that recorded *Blow By Blow* to the States, opting instead for the redoubtable Wilbur Bascomb on bass and Bernard 'Pretty' Purdie on drums. Session veterans who had worked with James Brown, Aretha Franklin and, in Purdie's case, just about anyone who entered a recording studio for more than five minutes, Beck's new rhythm section looked on paper like a formidable team, but even he took some getting used to their funky, no-nonsense style. "Jeff thought Richard Bailey was a little too young at that point and might be a little light for the tour," said Middleton. "though he wasn't sure about Purdie at first either because he was hoping to get someone like Billy Cobham. But Purdie had played with everyone. James Brown, Sinatra, who I absolutely loved. He wasn't one for mad time signatures, but Bernard could really adapt. He was a real groover."

Another concern for Beck was that the wild exoticism of Mahavishnu's sound might jar with his own, more "reasonable, gap-bridging" style, their two contrasting approaches likely to confuse audiences, or worse, alienate them altogether. "We're going to put a fence up in the middle of the audience to keep John's more intense followers away from my yobbo crowd," he joked. But given Jeff's love of McLaughlin's violin-toting, dimension-spanning Orchestra, and in particular, his admiration of John's sublime guitar excursions, it was a chance he was willing to take. "Jeff idolised McLaughlin," said Max. "He always said there was no one better. And look at the quality of his original band... Jan [Hammer], Billy Cobham, just astounding musicians."

Ultimately, Beck's enduring respect for John McLaughlin's mission helped immeasurably when, several dates into the tour, it was becoming apparent the majority of the crowd were there to see him. "John was doing very well and the plan was to tour as his support act," Middleton confirmed. "But by the time we got to the States, Jeff was number four in the charts and being played everywhere. So, Jeff was approached about actually headlining the tour. But because he had such respect for McLaughlin, he said, 'No, no, no, I can't do that'. So from what I remember, it turned out with Jeff saying to John, 'Look, tonight. Do you want to go first or do you want me to open up?' So they just swapped around. It was a very respectful show between friends."

Unlike previous visits to America, where Beck's band was fronted either by Rod Stewart or Bobby Tench, he was now offering a vocal-free night's entertainment, something that prompted the odd question from visiting journalists, but which Jeff had a witty riposte for: "Stevie Wonder can write a tune. He's got a great sense of melody. If a singer like Stevie came along, I'd be game to work with a vocalist. Otherwise, no." Equally, when quizzed about the validity of his new direction, and whether it was truly 'jazz rock', Beck had his answers ready: "I hadn't made what I considered to be a decent record in ages, so I threw all my ideas into it and tried to freeze that feeling," he said. "All I'm really playing is elaborated blues with progressive rock overtones." But thanks to Bernard Purdie, it was a 'progressive blues' people could dance to: "Purdie's swing was so infectious people would just start dancing," said Middleton. "Even though the stuff we were playing was instrumental, he made it sound like a hit. He just knew how to play to the people. 12,000 people just dancing. To be honest, because we had such a great band and such a great sound I'd stop playing and listen, thinking to myself, 'This sounds nice, I'll just play one chord'. I loved that about him, Wilbur and Jeff." Beck was also warming to Purdie's rootsy, simplified approach: "Plenty of power, Bernard, and his wrist is thicker than my leg."

It wasn't all sweetness and light. When Jeff sidelined his Oxblood Les Paul at the beginning of the tour and returned to using the panel-beaten '71 Strat of JBG2, a curse seemed to fall on the guitar, with pick-ups constantly fizzing and volume pots failing at the most inopportune times. The solution was to hire a new Stratocaster in every town or city the band visited – not so bad in Los Angeles, perhaps, but a real problem in the rural midwest. "Sometimes they'd turn up with a Strat and the strings were a foot off the neck," said Max. "Jeff would look at me and say, 'I can't play this!', but there he was onstage an hour later doing what he always did, making it sound sweet."

A near two-month, coast-to-coast trek that stretched from New York to California, and included time for a TV broadcast where Stones keyboard player Billy Preston sat in with Beck's band for four songs, the tour's end was marked by a typically kind gesture from John McLaughlin: "At the end, because Jeff was having so many problems with various guitars and was renting them from town to town, McLaughlin bought him a lovely white Strat which he took home with him," remembered Middleton. "Of course, Jeff being Jeff, he put the guitar in the back of his pick-up when he went to Ronnie Scotts one night. Then he's surprised when it's gone missing by the time he's come out..."

While back in England, Beck no doubt had the opportunity to assess his US triumph, casting his mind over an arena tour that had seen crowd attendance regularly top the 12,000 mark and *Blow By Blow* achieve gold status (500,000 copies sold) in a matter of three months. "I was absolutely flabbergasted," he said, with no sense of false modesty. Yet, as evidenced, while his American profile continued to soar, Jeff was still smarting from the muted reaction to *Blow By Blow* in the UK. "They still ask me about 'Hi Ho Silver Lining'," he told *NME* at the time. "I mean, that's a failure. It just doesn't seem that they're interested in what I'm doing now. It's all about The Bay City Rollers. I mean, c'mon, go and join the circus."

He was probably right to be irked. A key player in the creation of blues rock and, according to some, the architect of a sound stolen by others who had profited greatly from his original designs, Beck was – despite his Stateside success – best known at home for a single he hated with a vengeance. Perhaps some of this righteous indignation seeped into his witness statement of Led Zeppelin's five-night stand within the mammoth walls of Earls Court in May, 1975. "I'm sorry, I can't help you," he told journalist Steven Rosen when asked about his friend Jimmy Page's recent work. "I wouldn't be fair to myself if I made any excuse for him. I saw the show and I thought they were filth. It sounded like someone paralysed his arms or something." Even for a newly energised, newly reinvented Beck, old sins still cast long shadows.

By the autumn of 1975, Jeff was again back on the road in the US for a series of dates that saw him squeezed uncomfortably between a dying Rod Stewart & The Faces and a very much alive Aerosmith. Out for one last hurrah before calling last orders, The Faces had watched helplessly as Ronnie Wood joined The Rolling Stones for their own recent American tour, his contributions to their forthcoming album, *Black And Blue*, already in the can. For Beck, this must have been something approaching real comedy. Having turned down the Stones gig, he was now confronted by the sight of his old bass player mugging into the camera alongside Keith and Mick while simultaneously banging out 'Stay With Me' with his former singer who, for the record, he still carried some reservations about: "No, not interested," said Jeff. "[Rod's] gone right round the bend, silk trousers and silly hats."

Somewhat ironically, the last time Beck had seen action in the UK singles chart was when Mickie Most re-released 'I've Been Drinking' in May 1973. Originally the B-side of 1968's 'Love Is Blue', the song had been rebranded as collaboration between 'Rod Stewart and Jeff Beck' and reached number 27. A beer-sodden soul ballad, featuring a squealing solo from Jeff, 'I've Been Drinking' served to remind listeners of two essential facts: what a truly wonderful prospect the JBG had been, and why in God's name Mickie Most had relegated Stewart to B-sides when his voice was that good.

There were no such issues to negotiate with Aerosmith, who clearly worshipped Jeff and didn't care who knew it. Formed during the spring of 1970, the Boston quintet had recently broken the States wide open with their third album, *Toys In The Attic*, and hit single 'Walk This Way', which featured lead guitarist Joe Perry distorting his voice and Les Paul through the same type of talk box Beck regularly used in BBA. The connections didn't end there, either. Aerosmith's lead vocalist, Steven Tyler, had been a regular stalker of Jeff since his Yardbirds days while Perry had watched the JBG in slack-jawed wonder at the Boston Tea Party of 1967, becoming a fervent disciple ever since. "There isn't a guitar player around who doesn't look at Jeff and wonder how he does what he does," Joe once rightly said. "I used to idolise him when I was 18, now I come to believe he's from another planet." A gut-bucket, hard-rock act whose sound was indebted not only to Beck's previous incarnations, but also fellow Brits the Stones and Led Zeppelin, Aerosmith proved perfect touring partners for Beck, with the band watching from the wings while their audience "whooped him on" every night. "Good group, Aerosmith," said Max Middleton, "though I seem to remember Joe Perry still owes me a set of tyres..."

As the dust settled on his latest US jaunt, Beck returned to England for some rest before embarking on the next album. He did so in a new home, tucked nicely away in "my own little piece of Sussex", and some 30 minutes away from Wallingford where he had grown up. Benefiting from the spoils of two profitable American tours and a bestselling album, Jeff's latest purchase officially sealed his new financial status – a rambling, Tudor manor built in the late 1500s, and surrounded by 80 acres of woodland where his partner, Celia Hammond's, growing army of stray cats could roam uninterrupted. A perfect rock star setting then, to contemplate his next move while building a huge garage to store all the hot rods.

"There was no element of showbiz about Jeff, though," said Beck's former manager, Simon Napier-Bell, who would become reacquainted with his former charge in subsequent months. "I mean, he was happy to get the applause, but he really just wanted to play the guitar. Usually, the people who want to be stars have an overwhelming necessity to be applauded. Jeff never had that. Even Clapton found out after years of playing shyly, turning his back to the audience, he wanted to be a star. Maybe it's down to difficult childhoods, I really don't know. Obviously, Jeff was different in that area. Instead, he became that rare thing, a superstar musician."

Napier-Bell was undoubtedly correct about Beck's career trajectory. Though the path he had chosen was often difficult to navigate and occasionally horrendous to watch, Jeff had somehow managed to crack the US market without the aid of a singing Viking, eye-popping laser show or a 20-feet inflatable penis. Instead, he had placed his guitar playing front and centre and just hoped for the best. "*Blow By Blow* was really well recorded, the players were great and the material was great," he later said. "George knew what he was doing. He had the know-how to score the strings underneath the stuff I wrote with Max and we had a nice, commercial set of tunes appropriate for the time. It went well."

Now all he had to do was follow it up.

Chapter 16

Hammer Time

In a career already defined by several high-stakes ventures, Jeff Beck's decision to reposition his talents in the jazz-rock/fusion market was his most audacious gamble yet. By his own admission, Beck was no "jazzer", having come to that musical form via a solid, albeit extremely experimental blues, pop and rock background. More, aside from several piano lessons as a child – most of which ended in boredom and frustration for both student and teacher – he could claim no great credits in advanced compositional theory or major knowledge of harmonic intervals and stacked fourths. But as *Blow By Blow* made clear, Jeff could probably find a tune in a dustbin, his instinctive gift for lyrical phrasing and proven ability to adapt to almost any genre more important than recognising a diatonic scale when he heard it. "The audience doesn't clap because you've hit every little dot," Beck said. "They clap because they like what they hear."

With its Top Five US chart placing, *Blow By Blow* had proved him spectacularly right on this point, the album achieving gold status within months and eventually selling over two million copies worldwide. Its success also gave Beck critical distance from past associations, placing him a healthy acre or two from the likes of old rivals such as Jimmy Page and Eric Clapton, while also establishing a new stall from which to sell his more refined, but still user-friendly goods. "I want to do stuff that's not too far from the audience because that's not productive," he told *Creem* in 1975. "You can be great, but you can still miss the boat by a mile. Then when you die, everyone

241

picks up what you've done, and that's just totally frustrating. To me, the best formula is when what you're playing isn't beneath you, but at the same time keeps both you and the audience on its toes. Most performers turn things out to be consumed and digested. Then, the audience comes back for more and more until they get indigestion. That's overindulgence and I don't want that." When it came to following up *Blow By Blow*, Beck's solution to such 'indigestion' was to stick to his guns but ramp up the firepower, providing an album still heavy on funk and jazz grooves but with a harder-edged, more overdriven sound.

Recording of Jeff's second solo disc began in October 1975 at London's AIR and Trident studios. George Martin returned as producer, but the group of musicians assembled to aid Beck's latest vision had widened considerably since last time around. With session bassist Phil Chen having departed for a spot in Rod Stewart's new backing band, Wilbur Bascomb was free to take his place, still piping hot from several months on the road with Jeff. Like Bascomb, Max Middleton picked up where he had left off, providing keyboard textures and the odd tune when required. As for percussion, *Blow By Blow*'s Richard Bailey was invited to attend several sessions (as was newcomer Ed Green) though their place in the starting line-up was largely overtaken by former Mahavishnu drummer Narada Michael Walden. "Oh yeah, I always thought Walden was suitably insane enough to play with me," said Beck. "I saw him with John McLaughlin and he just blew me away. There are few drummers who have that ability to become such a central part of the music... maybe Keith Moon. He just made The Who jump. Unlike some drummers, Mooney would play the melody, just slamming away, and Narada's got some of that quality." A multi-instrumentalist, who played a mean honky-tonk piano when the mood took him, Walden was also a gifted composer who would eventually contribute four songs towards Jeff's new opus. "I loved working with Jeff and George on the record," he said in 2010. "They were so very calm and George was very easygoing."

However, unlike *Blow By Blow* – where the only real hindrance to progress was Beck's aversion to feeding the parking meter for his car – recording sessions on this occasion proved a more stilted affair, with George and Jeff not quite seeing eye to eye on the direction the album should take. "*Blow By Blow* was such a big success that in a way it made life difficult for Jeff because he's not the most secure of people," Martin said later. "And he thought, 'Well, having done that one, how can I follow it up?' So [it] became a much more difficult LP. [Jeff] was much more introspective, concerned about it and worried all the time." In turn, Beck was concerned that George Martin didn't understand his wish to 'supercharge' *Blow By Blow's* original conceit, pushing the sound in a direction that more ably reflected the guitarist's formative obsessions with jazz rock. "Halfway through it, I realised I was having trouble communicating with George," he said. "I wanted an ultra-heavy groove like Billy Cobham's *Spectrum* and I don't think George really got that."

In an effort to reconcile their differences, and no doubt take a break from the intense studio atmosphere at AIR and Trident, the two flew to Los Angeles' Cherokee Studios where they could concentrate on recording Beck's guitars in isolation. While at Cherokee, a then very young engineer named John Arrias witnessed the specifics of how Jeff and George went about their work. "As I recall, we set up Jeff's twin Marshall amps in the studio," John remembered. "Jeff then played in the control room instead of 'on headphones' so we were able to turn up the big monitors. He had several effects, including a volume pedal that he used to increase distortion when he wanted. But Jeff's a master at using the volume control on his guitar so the combination of effects, volume and distortion helped shape his sound. I'd like to take credit for it, but it really was just Jeff's playing."

As Beck fought various battles with his guitars and effects, Martin kept an ever watchful eye, but always from a respectful distance. "George Martin's production [style] allows the artist to just create rather than make the final decision as to what works and what doesn't," Arrias confirmed. "And his final choices on the album show that way of working with Jeff was correct."

Regrettably, neither Martin nor Beck was watching too closely when Arrias wandered out of sight to fix a sound problem during the recording process. "I needed to change the position of a mike so I went into the studio to do it," he said. "Well, Jeff was still in the control room at this point and didn't realise I was in there. He started playing and the volume was so loud it nearly blew my head off! I couldn't hear anything out of that ear for quite a while, but Jeff was so apologetic. He really felt bad about the mistake." Beyond the temporary hearing loss, John Arrias' livelihood was thankfully unaffected as his later production and engineering credits with the likes of Barbra Streisand, David Bowie and Chaka Khan confirm. "Being in the presence of Jeff Beck and George Martin in the studio is by far one of the highlights of my blessed career," he confirmed. "I've worked with Bob Seger, Barbra Streisand, Hall & Oates and many others, [but] that is a stand out."

Despite their best efforts, the Cherokee sessions marked a natural break point for Jeff Beck and George Martin, with the two parting on amicable, if mutually confused terms. "George was a very objective person to have around," Beck later said. "I wouldn't say he completely comprehended what I was doing, but I didn't either!" As the producer returned to London in February 1976 to involve himself in other projects, Jeff enlisted the help of a new collaborator who could help him pin down that elusive *Spectrum* sound.

The man chosen for the job was Jan Hammer. Born in Czechoslovakia, Hammer had come to music early when his mother, Vlasta Pru°chová, a well-known singer on the Czech jazz scene, encouraged him to play piano as an infant. Unlike Beck, Jan took to the keys instantly, starting his own jazz-classical trio at high school before earning a place at Prague's Academy of Musical Arts. When the Soviet Union invaded Czechoslovakia in 1968, he moved to the States, continuing his education at Berklee's prestigious College of Music. Within three years, Hammer had become a founding member of Mahavishnu Orchestra alongside John McLaughlin and Billy Cobham, creating a new form of jazz soon dubbed 'fusion'. Or not. "Well, 'jazz-rock' was a better name for it," he later told *Synthtopia*. "We didn't call it fusion....fusion sort of describes the leftovers, the music that came later. When Mahavishnu was happening, *it was like a stroke of lightning*. People weren't sure what to call it because it was basically an instrumental rock group with a heavy improvisational element."

After recording the ground-breaking albums *The Inner Mounting Flame*, *Birds Of Fire* and *Between Nothingness And Eternity,* the original

Mahavishnu Orchestra broke up in 1973, allowing Hammer to pursue other interests. Reuniting with Billy Cobham for *Spectrum*, Jan's Mini Moog synth textures and Spitfire like duels with guitarist Tommy Bolin were rightly lauded as some of the most dynamic and innovative playing of the time. "I think that [guitarists] hear something in my playing that they can bounce off," he confirmed. "It's sort of an inverted guitar approach... it complements their playing. You would overlap too much if you had two guitarists. The way the notes come together on a keyboard is just different than on a guitar." This was a point not lost on Jeff Beck, who as previously mentioned, "lost his mind" on hearing Hammer's approach to the synthesiser. "When I heard Jan's Mini Moog, I wanted to know all about it because it was so pure."

For Jeff, Hammer's combination of fluid, dextrous runs and seamless command of jazz, classical and rock idioms made him the perfect partner in crime for the type of instrumental pandemonium he was seeking to unleash: "Jan was the best guitarist ever to have played a keyboard..." Having been persuaded to join Beck's cause, Hammer lost little time in exerting a strong influence on the long-gestating album. Within two weeks, the keyboardist had completely remixed four tracks as well as contributed a new composition of his own entitled 'Blue Wind'. "Jeff came over to my studio [Red Gate in NewYork]," Jan confirmed. "He brought the tapes over from England and we did the soloing and overdubs." As the two bonded over tapes, spools and faders, it became abundantly clear that this was never going to be a purely short-term alliance: "Jeff completely got what I [did] and built on it. We would come together and pieces just came into place naturally. Many people don't realise this, but I was pushing more to rock and he was pushing more towards improvisation."

The results of Jeff Beck's latest endeavours, *Wired*, was finally released in June 1976. A praiseworthy disc with a strong collaborative centre, *Wired* had taken the themes on *Blow By Blow* and amplified them considerably, with the emphasis now firmly placed on 'rock' as much as 'jazz'. Taking his cues from Billy Cobham's *Spectrum*, Beck had also pursued a freer, less formal approach to the compositions at hand – allowing both him and the musicians to break quickly from principal melodies and get straight to the soloing. Hence, the album was awash with high-wire guitar and keyboard gymnastics, strange melodic twists and spirited leaps into the rhythmic abyss. Of the tunes Narada Michael Walden had written, 'Come Dancing' and 'Play With Me' were both lithe, funky affairs – the former strongly reminiscent of Allyn Ferguson's immortal 'Theme From Barney Miller', the latter benefiting enormously from Max Middleton's squelching clavinet lines and Wilbur Bascomb's burping bass fills. Walden's two remaining contributions were also distinguished, with 'Sophie'''s 7/8 time signature and ever-shifting chord pattern nicely challenging to the ear while 'Love Is Green'''s ballad-based structure allowed Jeff a rare chance to mix and match acoustic and electric guitars to soothing effect. "I don't often play acoustic guitar," Beck later laughed. "They're a pain in the ass and make you sound like a folk singer. John McLaughlin plays one better than anyone else, so I just leave it to him."

In 'Head For Backstage Pass', Wilbur Bascomb and co-writer Andi Clark had gifted Beck a peach of a riff, the bassist slapping and popping its opening lines before Jeff's solo soon ducked and dived through the holes left by Walden's snare and cymbal crashes. 'Led Boots' too, was enormously entertaining, its continued presence in Beck's concert set after 40 odd years ample proof of its enduring appeal. All bangs, crashes and whiplash guitar parts, 'Led Boots' was actually written by Max Middleton on his way to work. "Yes, I wrote it in my head on the way to the studio," he said. "Again, it's a simple song and very easy to learn. It was cut live but George hated it, so we forgot about it. Then, at the end of the album, we realised we were a bit short on running time, so I said, 'What about that one we cut at the start?' When we listened to it again with fresh ears it sounded good, so we put it on."

Though Beck has never confirmed or denied it, 'Led Boots' has often been viewed as a public swipe at Led Zeppelin – its title either an addendum to his remarks concerning the quality of their 1975 Earls Court concerts or the result of several years' festering resentment about the inclusion of 'You Shook Me' on the band's debut LP. Certainly, Jeff was no longer in touch with Jimmy Page at the time *Wired* was recorded – "I don't call Jimmy and he doesn't call me," he tellingly said in 1976 – but again, there is no 'definitive' proof to support such a hypothesis.*

As with *Blow By Blow*, *Wired* was essentially defined by two tracks – one pointing the way to possible futures, the other marking a personal milestone in the relationship between Beck and his Fender Stratocaster. With Jan Hammer's 'Blue Wind', all instruments were cut by Jan and Jeff alone, the two furiously trading riffs and solos in call and response style over a shifting background of tempo-flaunting stops and starts. Obviously born to play together, it was sometimes difficult to distinguish Beck and Hammer apart as one swooping guitar line coalesced into an ever-ascending synth part. "[We] really made the most of it," Jan later said. "Jeff really listened with the right attitude, [and we] really made it work… within that improvisational jazzy sort of rock beat." This simpatico of approach was all over *Wired* like a rash, the likes of 'Led Boots', 'Play With Me' and 'Come Dancing' resonating with dovetailing runs or mad-fingered sprints to the finishing line, though it was often impossible to pick a winner. "I mean, I don't sound like Jan, but obviously his phrases influenced me immensely," Beck later said of their similarities in style. Given this clarity of shared purpose and the sheer level of enjoyment they displayed in each other's work, it was only a fool who would bet against Beck and Hammer ending their association after just one LP.

Strangely, however, Jan Hammer was entirely absent from *Wired's* standout moment, 'Goodbye Pork Pie Hat'. A tribute to the fine tenor saxophonist Lester Young written by his friend, the equally irreplaceable jazz bassist Charlie Mingus, 'Goodbye…' had first come to Jeff via John McLaughlin, who had recorded a striking acoustic version of the tune on his own 1970 release, *My Goal's Beyond*: "John's version was so tasty, so original," Beck later told *Guitar For The Practising Musician*. "I wanted to make mine more commercial,

---

* Whatever the case, a superb reworking of Middleton's tune, 'Got My Led Boots On', appeared on Hummingbird's 1977 LP *Diamond Nights*. Sung by Bobby Tench, with bass from Clive Chaman, drums by Bernard Purdie, keys by Max and a fine solo from guitarist Robert Ahwai, 'Got My…' resembles a reunion of various JBG line-ups, but without their fearless leader at the helm.

a little more rock'n'roll. It was the perfect tune for me. The melody is simple, but the chords are all over the place... dynamically angular and aggressive, nasty and great. I play a simple line and it's supported by all this nonsensical chord work." Cut in just one take, Jeff's rendition of 'Goodbye Pork Pie Hat' proved a revelation as guitarist and melody simply melted into each other – his singing lead lines, frequent changes of pick-up to provide tonal variation and delicate, yet daring use of the tremolo arm to tease out additional notes and nuances all combining to provide that rarest of experiences: pure listening pleasure. But by all accounts, Jeff almost 'car-crashed' the solo midway through the take. "Well, on the take – which was going well – there was a note that started feeding back and I thought, 'Oh no, we're going to have to do it again'," remembered Max Middleton, who was providing a wonderfully sympathetic Fender Rhodes part at the time. "And just as I'm thinking this, Jeff started to control the note, then bend it, and if you really listen, he plays a phrase from 'Singing In The Rain'. Amazing, really. He did that solo start to finish in one take." For Middleton, Beck's performance on 'Goodbye...' surely remains one of his finest achievements. "Jeff's unique; his spontaneity, his intuition, his phrasing, his approach to melody. It's all there on that track." On hearing Beck's take on his song, Charlie Mingus sent Jeff a note saying how much he loved the new version. The note remains one of Beck's most treasured possessions.

A fine, if occasionally frenetic disc, *Wired* underlined Jeff Beck's continuing commitment to fusion while also reintroducing hints of the free-booting, high-volume theatrics of his days with JBG. Unusually for Beck, *Wired* also received a modicum of real praise from UK critics, who seemed eager to sound the record's chimes in one way or another. "Beck has taken to the demands of his new setting with a combination of skill and audacity that [originally] made him such a uniquely daring rock soloist," said *Sounds'* Dave Fudger. "And he's still prepared to interrupt a particularly plaintive, melodious run with a scuffing chord slide, a prancing idiot descending run or wavering tremolo bar manoeuvre." *NME* were also in a reasonably celebratory mood, with longtime Beck supporter Charles Shaar Murray again emphasising that, despite the odd power chord or two, the guitarist was unlikely to return to first principles anytime soon: "*Wired* is basically 'Son of *Blow By Blow*' in that it's Phase II of JB's divorce from all that nasty, horrible immature white rock'n'roll that he dug and played when he was young and stupid and didn't know any better. The end result of years of listening to Mahavishnu, Stevie Wonder and Herbie Hancock on car eight-tracks and feeling childish and inferior because he was still playing that greasy kid stuff."

The general public's appreciation of Beck's efforts was equally robust, with *Wired* initially reaching number 16 in the US charts (and soon achieving gold status), while strong reviews at home helped secure a reasonable number 38 placing in the UK. As with *Blow By Blow*, the LP eventually went on to shift more than two million copies, marking *Wired* and its predecessor among the highest-selling instrumental releases ever.

An undoubted factor in driving up *Wired*'s sales was the continent-spanning tour Beck undertook in support of the album, which kept him on the road for the best part of a year, and therefore well away from British tax officials keen to get their hands on a share of the profits generated by his recent success. To solve the problem of appropriate backing musicians for these dates, Jeff again turned to Jan Hammer, whose own band were then close to releasing their first LP, *Oh Yeah?*. Comprising Jan on keyboards, occasional Mahavishnu Orchestra violinist Steve Kindler, Detroit-born bassist Fernando Saunders and former Malo/Santana drummer Tony 'Thunder' Smith, The Jan Hammer Group turned out to be precisely what Beck was looking for. "Well, we were playing in a club in Ithaca, New York and Jeff came along," remembered Smith. "He was thinking of doing a big tour at that point and wanted Jan to open the show... maybe even sit in and do some songs with him. Then when he saw us play, he said 'Wow, maybe we should just be one band...'" A deal was subsequently struck that profited both sides of the equation. Hammer's group would open the shows, and then provide back-up for Beck during his set. "We'd do three or four tunes, not a complete set," said Tony, "then Jeff came on and we'd go off for nearly two hours."

Beginning their run with a hush-hush debut in support of Alvin Lee's Ten Years After at Camden Town's Roundhouse on May 23,

1976 (frustratingly, their only UK date), Jeff and The Jan Hammer Group journeyed across the Atlantic to begin a near seven-month sonic bombardment of the States. During this period, they either opened for or shared top billing with a plethora of American talent, including The Doobie Brothers, Jefferson Starship, Journey and old friends Aerosmith. "Jeff [was] with Jan Hammer's band in Boston and since [my then] wife Elyssa knew him, we took him to Paul's Mall to see Muddy Waters play," guitarist Joe Perry later confirmed. "[On tour], it was like me and Brad Whitford were watching a guitar lesson every night. We'd watch this insanity go on and then have to follow it. To me, it wasn't headlining, it was following. Jeff knew it. A lot of people of his stature wouldn't have opened for us but he did it that summer, 26 shows worth, mostly outdoors."

Perry's reward came on September 10 at Anaheim's Angels Stadium, when Beck joined him and the other members of Aerosmith onstage for an impromptu rendition of 'Train Kept A Rollin', the old Johnny Burnette/Yardbirds stalwart that the Bostonians had since made their own signature tune. "History was made!" said an excited Elyssa Perry, no doubt referring to the fact it was the first occasion Jeff had played live with a US act. That it was also Joe Perry's 26th birthday no doubt added to both his and her sense of elation.

To describe Jeff Beck's sets with The Jan Hammer Group as "intense" would be doing both parties a grave disservice. In fact, a better choice of words might be "sheer bloody lunacy". Night after night, Beck and Hammer seemed intent on soloing themselves into oblivion: Jeff armed with a new sunburst Strat, a set of Marshall amps and a wall of Univox speakers, Jan with his beloved Mini-Moog slung over the shoulder, its in-built 'pitch wheel' allowing him to bend notes as wildly as any guitar player. As a result, their duels on tracks such as 'Freeway Jam', 'Scatterbrain' and 'Blue Wind' can still freeze the blood four decades on: "Playing with Jan almost knocked all the soloing out of me," said Beck. "Taking exchange solos with someone like him can take you to the limits of your soloing. I mean, I've got tapes of us on the road playing 'Freeway Jam' and not once did he ever play the same solo or even in the same strain." Hammer concurred: "Jeff's sound is him, it's in his hands. It's how he handles – or manhandles – a guitar. I'm not a guitar player, I'm a very amateur picker, but I can tell you one thing: he gets away with things that are totally illegal on guitar. Beck is so astounding... sometimes you think he's playing two parts."

One would have thought that these nightly battles, which also included space for Steve Kindler's seering, inventive violin runs, might have taken their toll on the musicians involved. Not so, according to drummer Tony Smith: "If you can have the most fun ever, you don't care about money so much. It's more about going onstage every night and just 'slammin'". That's what we'd live for. To go around the world and show that to as many people as you possibly can and it's growing every night. You're so full of fun and energy, there's no tiredness – you can go on and on forever. And don't forget, there'll never be another Jan Hammer. I've heard keyboard players that are really great, and they'll get halfway there – some can even emulate it, but no, nobody can play like him. I mean, my God..."

Inevitably, there were always going to be problems to surmount, not least of which were connected to playing extremely complex musical passages in venues more suited to the landing of medium-sized aircraft. "[The soloing] was all right for clubs maybe, where you can hear every single note," Beck later remembered, "but in an arena, it must have sounded like a jet engine." There were also occasional tensions behind the scenes to contend with, including audience reaction to Hammer's opening spot. "Jan was doing a half-hour set before I went on, and people were... throwing tin cans. I thought 'If people throw tin cans at a talent like Jan, I want out of this game.'"

However, as road life began to take its toll, Jeff's concerns became more focused around balancing Hammer's 'ambitions' to use the tour as an opportunity to cross into the rock market against his own established profile as a 'featured performer': "He had strong ideas of carrying on as Jan Hammer... as a 'star', you might say. Whereas from the beginning, it was meant to be a two-way relationship. I was drawing the big crowds, and in return, he let me use his band." Things got worse before they got better. "At the time, we were arguing like mad," said Jeff. "He wanted to be 'Jan the big rock star' [but] he didn't want to give me anything in terms of credibility. He just felt I was huge enough not to worry about that. But I was trying to lay out a blueprint for a long-term thing." For Beck, Hammer was simply spending too much time "waddling around with his electronic stick..."

In Jan's defence, the keyboardist had made no bones about such desires to expand his fanbase. In fact, he was fully aware that Jeff's profile and previous history offered both he and his group a real chance to commune with crowds previously denied them. "His commercial appeal was so much wider," Hammer said, "because he had established a huge base from The Jeff Beck Group and The Yardbirds. You know, he was one of the holy trinity!"

Drummer Tony Smith also saw first-hand the value of Beck's crossover appeal when the group played San Francisco's 'Day On The Green' to an assembled crowd of thousands in 1976: "It was an amazing moment for all of us, looking out from the stage and seeing this sea of people. We'd actually got to the masses. You could see every type of face." After one particularly vigorous debate where Jeff's onstage frustrations carried themselves backstage (reportedly, at some volume), issues between he and Hammer eased considerably, allowing the tour to progress without further incident to Canada, Australia and New Zealand throughout early 1977.

To commemorate Beck and Hammer's year-long jaunt – and no doubt maximise profits while they were at it – Epic Records released *Jeff Beck With The Jan Hammer Group Live*, which popped into the US charts at number 23 in March 1977 (given Beck's still spectral UK profile, the album failed to chart at home). A seven-song disc recorded over four nights at various venues the previous October, ...*Live* captured both the strengths and weaknesses of Jeff's latest collaboration for all to hear. "We never thought 'This is being recorded'," said Tony Smith. "All you think about is when the first beat is played, hit that downbeat, and we're off and running." And off and running they sometimes were. On 'Full Moon Boogie' (featuring a fine vocal from Smith) and 'Scatterbrain' for instance, the group's performances was simply peerless, with Jeff's 'over the pick-ups' slide work on 'Freeway Jam' probably worth the price of the LP alone. Other highlights included squeezing a delightfully unexpected blast from 'Train Kept A Rollin'' into the middle of 'Blue Wind' as well as a nicely irreverent take on The Beatles' 'She's A Woman'. But elsewhere, things often resembled one long, interminable solo: a perfectly fine thing if one wanted to marvel at Jeff's anarchic use of his new ring modulator unit during 'Earth (Still Our Only Home)' or Jan's novel Oberheim bass setting on 'Scatterbrain', yet still somewhat difficult for non-musicians to fully appreciate or truly engage with. It was a point not lost on Beck. "I never wanted to put that album out," he later said. "[It was] just skinny exercises to do fantastic solos. I hated it."

Though there was the possibility of further dates throughout the summer of 1977, Jeff chose to call time on The Jan Hammer Group just before the release of ...*Live*, even if he remained willing to leave the door open for the possibility of future collaborations. "In the end," said Jan, "Jeff's unique and driven, the music just flows out of him and I knew we'd work together again." On the road for much of 1976 – and due to his tax exile status, based largely in Los Angeles while not on tour – the guitarist was probably eager to just return home to Celia Hammond, their various cats and dogs and, no doubt, a week's worth of sleep. That said, Beck left a lasting impression on those he worked with, including Tony Smith, who alongside bassist Fernando Saunders, would soon forge a lasting musical alliance with Lou Reed. "Jeff's one of the legends, one of a kind," said Smith. "There's a love coming from what he plays. He's the model, you know. He doesn't play for the dough, he just plays for the love of it and that stretches out to the people on the stage with him. It's like we were all in the same car and we're all loving where we were going."

As was so often the case with Beck, he had simply chosen to exit the vehicle before the ride began to get boring.

Chapter 17

The Invention of
Space Metal

Thanks to the back-to-back success of *Blow By Blow* and *Wired*,
Jeff Beck found himself in an enviable position during the
mid-to-late seventies. Financially secure for life, with a strongly
established American fanbase he could turn to whenever the coffers
needed topping up, the guitarist had also received the blessing of his
contemporaries as a slew of recent awards attested to. In addition
to a Grammy nomination for 'Best Pop Instrumental Performance
of 1976', Beck had won 'Best Guitar Album' and 'Best Rock
Guitarist' for the second year running from *Guitar Player*, as well as
receiving its vote as 'Best Overall Guitarist' for his work on *Wired*.
Even *Downbeat*, a magazine whose reputation for championing only
the most worthy and serious of jazz acts preceded it, had richly
honoured Jeff's efforts, naming him 'Rock/Blues Musician of the
Year'. Beck's response to such accolades remained predictably self-
effacing: "There were thousands of guitarists playing with their Les
Pauls cranked up bloody blaring loud at the time," he said. "I just
needed to try something new."

However, away from the platinum discs, various accolades and
endless nights on the road with The Jan Hammer Group, there was
also some sadness to negotiate. Both Beck's parents had recently passed
away, with Jeff taking his mother's baby grand piano into his own home
as a way of remembering who originally set him upon his musical path.

On a professional level, there was more bad news. Tommy Bolin, whose scorching guitar duels with Jan Hammer on Billy Cobham's *Spectrum* proved a major factor in Beck's decision to abandon 'foot to the floor rock' in favour of fusion, had died on December 4, 1976 from a heroin overdose in Miami, Florida. The tragedy was made worse by the fact that the former James Gang and Deep Purple guitarist was supporting Jeff on tour at the time. Jan Hammer, who played with Bolin not only on *Spectrum* but also his first solo album, 1975's wonderful *Teaser*, remembered Beck being genuinely bowled over by the strength of Tommy's abilities. "Jeff would stand in the wings offstage, listen and go 'Wow!'" he later told *The Tommy Bolin Archives*. "He just really appreciated what Bolin was doing."

An equally unexpected loss occurred on May 14, 1976, when former Yardbirds singer Keith Relf was electrocuted while playing an unearthed electric guitar at his home studio. Just 33 years old, Relf had been busy rehearsing new material for the regrouping of his band Renaissance under their new name, Illusion. "With Keith," Beck later said, "the certain type of approach that was needed for a pop song was something he couldn't really embrace. Yet he could do wild blues like 'Smokestack Lightning', where it didn't matter about the intonation, but was more about the energy and pure screaming attack." Relf's death came at a time when such qualities were wholly in the ascendant throughout the British music scene as punk threatened to undo a near decade of increasingly ludicrous and self-important progressive/rock dominance. Once an exciting medium, full of virtuoso performances, genuine experimentation and the odd, fabulous conceit, both 'prog' and rock were now in danger of collapsing under the weight of their own egos – with previously creditable musicians pretending to be wizards or writing frankly mad concept albums about long-dead British kings. As rock'n'roll had once electrified British teenagers bored with twirling around the dance floor to Eddie Calvert's 'Oh Mein Papa', punk's minimalist 'here's a chord, here's another, now go form a group' approach seemed intent on sweeping away such stupidity by returning music to a proverbial 'year zero'.

In fact, punk had been gestating in the bowels of downtown Manhattan since the early seventies when bands such as The Patti Smith Group, The New York Dolls and The Neon Boys began gigging regularly at venues like Max's Kansas City and CBGBs. By 1975, a second wave of acts that included The Ramones, Blondie and Talking Heads had attached themselves to the scene. Taking its cues from garage rock, old rock'n'roll/R&B standards, vestiges of glam and the occasional Stones/Velvet Underground/MC5 riff, punk was all about short, sharp tunes performed in a stripped-down, no-nonsense style. Though punk remained an essentially New York phenomenon in the States (at least for the time being), its spirit soon crossed over the Atlantic where it was taken on by the likes of Sex Pistols and The Clash. In the UK punk mutated even further, gaining a hard political edge that mirrored the dissatisfactions of British youth already ostracised by high levels of unemployment, race riots and the glaring prospect of 'no future' circa 1976.

To some old stagers, punk's rapid ascent represented the end of days, a new wave of no-talent wastrels hell-bent on returning music to its feral rock'n'roll origins. Of course, Jeff Beck professed to love it all, even if his tongue was thumping wildly against the inside of his cheek when singing its praises. "Every time I see a punk group pogo-ing up and down and thumping their guitars... I just think of The Yardbirds," he said in 1977. "It makes me think 'Wow, is this how The Yardbirds must sound to them? Is that how come they sound so bad, because they listen to The Yardbirds?'" A former, card-carrying rockabilly rebel himself, Beck at least seemed to understand the necessity behind a bit of good, old-fashioned youthful revolt every now and then. "The new wave that I've heard had really brought the spirit back into [rock'n'roll]," he told *NME*. "There's been a renaissance of getting back to basics. I love punk rock... [it's a] smack in the eye for the world."

Realistically, Jeff could at least admire some of the talent emerging from punk and the new wave scene that quickly followed: the low, humming "Panzer division" guitars of Sex Pistols' Steve Jones; the glass-cutting, atonal experimentation of Magazine's John McGeoch and Gang Of Four's Andy Gill; the curious, searching leads of Television's Tom Verlaine and Richard Lloyd. Even the eerie, bagpipe like wails of The Skids' Stuart Adamson must have held some fascination for him. On the flip side, however, Beck was precisely the type of target punks were keen to catch in the cross hairs of their vitriol-spitting rifles. A manor-dwelling former rock aristocrat, who had made his fortune overseas from parading the type of self-indulgent virtuosity they wished to put to the guillotine, Jeff's rebellious history with the likes of The Yardbirds or sterling background as a sonic innovator now stood for little. Punk showed no respect for the past, and at 34 years old, Beck represented an easy archetype, one the rock weeklies had recently taken to calling a dinosaur. Like the wisest of his peers, he chose to publicly ignore the insults while biding his time behind castle walls until the revolution blew over.

That said, Jeff Beck was not entirely idle while the Sex Pistols and their ilk threatened anarchy, stirred up Parliament and greatly enlivened Queen Elizabeth II's Silver Jubilee celebrations. Having appeared with Billy Preston several years before on the US pop show *Midnight Special*, Jeff contributed a fine, high-necked solo to 'Bad Case Of Ego', a salsa-influenced track from the Stones pianist's self-titled 1976 debut album. He also added a tasteful flourish or two to 'The Saint And The Rascal', one of the better tunes from Narada Michael Walden's 1977 LP, *Garden Of Love Light*. "The year after making *Wired*, I made my first solo album," Walden confirmed. "Jeff was very gracious to fly over [to the US] and play on it. I was very happy about that!" One of Beck's more unusual appearances during this time was on 'Inside Looking Out', a song from Dorian Passante's privately pressed debut disc. Described by one critic as a "gay-themed glam-psych marvel with heavy fuzz and a hard edge," Passante's music was a weird amalgam of *Rocky Horror Picture Show* theatrics and Jobriath-like glam rock'n'roll – his lyrics strongly referencing the experiences of an "out of the closet" performer in an age when such things still had some power to shock. Reportedly, Jeff had met Dorian while working with Eddie Harris in 1974 and agreed to cut a lead or two for his then in progress record. The result was a growling, bluesy solo that recalled some of Beck's best work during the sixties.

On a more comedic note, Jeff's old Yardbirds manager Simon Napier-Bell also approached him in 1976/77 with the novel idea of combining the guitarist's skills alongside those of the Regimental Band of the Coldstream Guards. "Yes," Napier-Bell laughed, "I remember something about that! Brass and rock. Don't think it happened, though it would have been good, wouldn't it?" In all probability, it would be far better than the next project Beck became involved with, which proved the nadir of The Bee Gees, Peter Frampton and Aerosmith's otherwise distinguished careers. Produced by Bee Gees manager Robert Stigwood and directed by Hollywood journeyman Michael Schultz, *Sgt. Pepper's Lonely Heart's Club Band* promised to be a lavish 'rock opera/movie', drawing on Beatles songs from not only the *Sgt. Pepper's...* album, but also *Abbey Road* to inform its storyline.

With the Gibb brothers and Frampton playing the heroes to Aerosmith's villains of the piece, ... *Lonely Heart's Club Band* was all set to give the likes of *Saturday Night Fever* and *Grease* a run for their money, or so the theory went. In reality, the film turned out to be a farcical mess which *The New York Times* described as "strung together so mindlessly... [it] has the feel of an interminable variety show". Thankfully Jeff kept his contributions to a bare minimum, dialling in a muted solo on the opening bars of 'You Only Give Me Your Money' as a favour to George Martin, who had been lumbered with producing the movie's soundtrack LP. However, the chance to work with Martin once again seemed to make Beck misty-eyed regarding his recent past. "With benefit of hindsight, I was too stupid to understand what George Martin was offering at the time of *Wired*," he later said. "George had been the core of a great album [*Blow By Blow*]. But with *Wired*, I was just after... wildness."

By the time *Sgt. Pepper's...* crashed and burned at the US box office in July 1978, Jeff was once again planning his next move. With punk now floundering after the death of the Sex Pistols in a San Francisco ballroom and The Clash starting to sound suspiciously like the proper rock'n'roll band they probably always were, it was as safe a time as any for the rich old dinosaurs to let down their drawbridges and take a peak outside. Truthfully, not much had really changed. America still remained in thrall to the soft-rocking, AOR-driven sounds that had defined its airwaves since the early seventies while the UK was now watching with interest as an abundance of new wave bands began to emerge in the wake of John Lydon's era-defining primal scream. Having already dodged the advances of former Deep Purple singer David Coverdale, who wanted him to join his new blues-rocking outfit Whitesnake, Beck now rolled up his sleeves and set to work forming yet another group for a proposed tour of the Far East and Europe.

The first recruit for this enterprise was Stanley Clarke. Born and raised in Philadelphia, Clarke was undoubtedly one of the finer bassists walking God's green earth. Introduced to four strings while still a schoolboy – he had arrived late for music class one day only to find that the acoustic bass was one of the few remaining instruments up for grabs – Stanley had nonetheless taken to it like a proverbial duck to water. Quickly assimilating various influences such as Motown, The Beatles, R&B, classical, rock and jazz, the breakthrough for Clarke came when he began exploring the work of Jimi Hendrix and jazz saxophonist John Coltrane. "When I heard Jimi Hendrix and then John Coltrane, it brought a lot of things together for me," he said. "It wasn't so much the music itself but the cry behind it, the passion that was driving it along. That's what I liked and that's what I responded to. With Coltrane, it was almost like rock'n'roll in that it was strong, new and carried the same amount of energy. The music was brave: it conveyed a lot of courage and stepped out of a box. That was my connection."

By 1971, he had left behind the Philadelphia Academy of Music for a new career at the centre of the New York jazz scene, working with established bandleaders such as Art Blakey, Dexter Gordon, Joe Henderson, Gil Evans, Stan Getz and others. During this time, Clarke met Chick Corea, who had recently made a name for himself with Miles Davis' electric band. The two musicians subsequently formed the ground-breaking Return To Forever, one of the first groups to be labelled with the fusion tag.

Establishing a parallel path as a solo artist, Clarke's debut album, 1973's *Children Of Forever*, gained him strong critical praise, but it was a track on his second, self-titled LP of 1974 that caught Jeff Beck's ear. Featuring guests Jan Hammer on keyboards, Bill Connors on guitar and the marvellous Tony Williams on drums, 'Power' was the type of tune that Jeff could really get his teeth into. "It was just good, chuggy rock'n'roll," he later remembered. Suitably enamoured, Beck took to playing 'Power' live with his own group on their 1975 US tour: "To my amazement, Stanley heard [I was playing it], and summoned me for tea at his house." Clarke takes up the story: "I didn't know much about it until I heard that some guy called Jeff Beck was playing my song, 'Power'. Now I sort of knew The Yardbirds, but not that much.

So I did a little research, and eventually there's a phone call from his management asking if we could meet. Anyway, I was at my house in Long Island, and I will never forget this – a long limousine pulls up and this guy gets out, knocks at my door and introduces himself. I loved that. Only Jeff would do that. Think about it. To turn up out of nowhere and say, 'Hey, I'm playing your tune, I'd like to talk about working together'. Well, I fell in love with him there and then."

A mutual admiration society duly established, Beck contributed a fine solo to 'Journey To Love', the title track of Clarke's next solo LP as well as throwing his weight behind 'Hello Jeff', a suitably funky workout Stanley had written in the guitarist's honour. "It was me, Jeff and Lenny White that cut the track," said Clarke. "It was a simple thing, almost naive, you might say. It was my way of saying 'Hello' to this guy, who had such a great energy and an almost child-like sense of freedom in his approach to music." Further collaborations followed, with Jeff adding a lick or two to Stanley's 1976 promotional single 'Life Is Just A Game' and a thumping power-chord progression and flighty solo on 'Rock 'N' Roll Jelly' – a track from Clarke's 1978 disc, *Modern Man*, that also featured Beck's old sparring partner Carmine Appice on drums. "Cutting that track, I was so worn out," Stanley said. "I'd been touring and was feeling a little burnt out, a little frazzled. Then, when I got to London, I also had jet lag. So I went to get some sleep. I get back the next morning and Jeff and the engineer were still there, two real warriors. When I heard the results, well, Jeff had played his ass off. He'd recorded it just as I wanted."

Having worked with each other on and off for the last three years, it made perfect sense to Clarke when Beck approached him about finally getting a group together. "Well, I suppose [at first], we came from fundamentally different musical backgrounds. Mine was connected to gospel and classical, and my mother was an opera singer," he said. "Then I had explored real progressive, maybe even extreme jazz, but still with a love of Hendrix. That all helped when I entered the genre of jazz-rock or fusion. Then there was Jeff, from a different part of the world, who'd taken a different musical journey. But as Mayo Angelou's poem 'Human Family' said: 'We are more alike, my friends, than we are unalike' and that's the way it was for us. There were no barriers. It wasn't like 'He's a rock musician' or 'I'm a jazz musician'. All that melted away because we had the right chemistry, connecting personalities and similar musical passions."

Beck and Clarke's original intention was to form a band in time for 1978's annual Knebworth Festival, where they would appear alongside an eclectic cast including Tom Petty & The Heartbreakers, Devo and Jefferson Starship in supporting headliners Genesis before a crowd of over 50,000. But Stanley's choice of drummer, Gerry Brown, was unable to make the gig due to scheduling conflicts and the trio were forced to pull out.

Still keen to do something ("Anything!" laughed Clarke), the duo set about finding the right line-up for their upcoming tour. At first, it appeared that Max Middleton would resume his role as keyboard player. As a possible alternative, Stanley floated the idea of David Bowie's former pianist Mike Garson for the job. "We didn't want it to sound directly like his thing or mine," Beck later said. "But the setback was the keyboard player he insisted on using didn't fit in. I had to say – in despair – to Stanley that he wasn't the right man."

Ultimately, neither Middleton nor Garson secured the position. One man that did, however, was drummer Simon Phillips. Barely 21 years old at the time, Phillips was already something of a veteran of the music wars, having regularly gigged with his father Sid's Dixieland-themed group from the age of 12 before taking up the drum stool in the West End production of *Jesus Christ Superstar*. From there, Simon quickly established himself as one of the London session scene's finest talents, his contribution to ex-Roxy Music members Brian Eno and Phil Manzanera's experimental art-rock act 801 only consolidating his growing reputation on the circuit. A drummer of outstanding technical ability, great emotional flair and an able composer to boot, Phillips was more than merely familiar with Beck's work when he received the call-up. "It was Max Middleton who first arranged for me to come down to Jeff's house and jam with him," he recalled. "At the time, Jeff was preparing for another record and was looking for 'new blood'."

Though these initial jams (which also included sessioneer John Giblin on bass) failed to produce a cohesive line-up, Beck was impressed enough with Simon's obvious skills to offer him a spot with him and Clarke. "Simon," reasoned Jeff "was just astounding."

The problem of finding a suitable keyboardist for the project was resolved when Phillips suggested using an old acquaintance of his named Tony Hymas, with whom he had worked on a brief project led by former Cream bassist Jack Bruce. "We were rehearsing at the Rainbow in Finsbury Park and I went up to the dressing room where I found Jeff and his manager, Ernest Chapman, discussing what to do about a keyboard player," remembered Simon. "I recommended Tony Hymas. They asked me to call him. I told Tony that I was going to Japan with Jeff Beck and Stanley Clarke and asked him whether he'd like to join us. He said he'd look in his diary and then told me he had a concert with Cleo Laine on one of the days we'd be out there. I just said, 'Tony, are you serious?' He started laughing and said 'No problem, I'd love to do it'."

Like Clarke and Phillips, Hymas came from a strong classical/jazz background, allowing him to flit easily between the worlds of sessions, live performance and orchestral arrangement – the latter proved by a spell conducting accompanying music for Dame Marie Rambert's prestigious Dance Company. Yet, the most unlikely addition to Tony's CV was a composing credit on the jaunty theme tune to the BBC's cult animated series *The Mr Men*, which gave Beck many an opportunity for some good-natured ribbing: "I'm going to do a heavy metal version of that..." Away from the bad jokes, however, the guitarist knew exactly what Hymas was capable of. "Tony's one of the greatest keyboard players I've ever heard in my life," Jeff said at the time. "He's a true original."

With things now in place, the quartet set off for a two-week tour of the Far East in late November, 1978. Neither Stanley Clarke nor Simon Phillips was prepared for exactly how 'Big in Japan' Jeff really was. "The Japanese fans just adored Jeff. He was a real superstar in their country," said Clarke. "Everywhere we went, people loved us. A great sound, a great crew, and we were just killing it onstage." For Phillips, the experience of playing to a packed house at Tokyo's legendary Budokan theatre was the closest he ever came to 'Beatlemania'. "Well, of course for me it was amazing to be finally playing in that arena. I'd wanted to play with Jeff and Stanley for a while, but never thought it would be with them both at the same time. Also, it was mind-blowing to go to Japan that early on in my career. Our promoter, Mr Udo, travelled with us everywhere and he took me under his wing. I was already very interested in Japanese culture and food so this was a fantastic first visit. I'd say it's the closest I've ever felt to being a 'pop idol'. The kids were actually reaching out and pulling our hair when we left the venue after a show."

Drawing on a diverse set list that included a powered-up version of Stevie Wonder's 'Superstition', an elegant reading of 'Goodbye Pork Pie Hat', as well as Jan Hammer's 'Blue Wind' and Clarke's own crowd-pleasing anthems 'Rock 'N' Roll Jelly' and 'School Days', Beck and the band were in their element. "My favourite thing was just getting on stage with Jeff," said Stanley. "That was even better than recording. You didn't need a singer, the music and energy were just all there. You see, Jeff is in his music. All the other shit around him is what it is. Just listen to the music, you'll hear it all there. Also, for me, Simon was this young, powerful drummer, while Tony seemed like a veteran. Simon was so young, he weighed about 100 pounds and you could hardly see him behind this mountain of drums. But he could play. Simon and Tony were truly great musicians."

In no mood to call it quits just yet, the group pressed on into Europe during the spring and early summer of 1979, where more concerts took place throughout Scandinavia, Austria, France, Holland and Spain. But due to continued tax issues around Beck's earnings, they never made it to either America or Great Britain. "Yeah, I know," said Clarke. "The only thing I regret about that tour is we didn't play live in the US and UK."

At the conclusion of festivities in July 1979, Stanley Clarke and Jeff Beck went their separate ways, though further collaborations would take place in due course. Clarke's next move was to consolidate his ever-growing association with the rock world by joining The Rolling Stones' Keith Richards and Ronnie Wood in their new, ad hoc jam band The New Barbarians, who supported Led Zeppelin for two memorable nights at Knebworth in August 1979. Beck, on the other hand, stayed busy with Simon Phillips, beginning the process of recording his first studio album in over three years. As before, Jan Hammer was heavily involved, having sent Jeff a cassette of six tunes for his consideration before arriving at London's Ramport Studios with several more ideas. "We recorded some songs with Jan at The Who's old studio, Ramport, with John Punter acting as the engineer," said Phillips, "but Jeff wasn't totally happy with the outcome."

Though three of Hammer's compositions would still make the final cut, Beck's dissatisfaction with the Ramport sessions saw him move the group to Abbey Road Studios in the spring of 1980 and take on a new co-producer, Ken Scott. Since engineering *Truth* in 1968, Scott's career had shot into the heavens as he scored joint production credits with David Bowie on the illustrious *Hunky Dory*, *Ziggy Stardust…* and *Aladdin Sane*, as well as part-overseeing Supertramp's platinum-selling *Crime Of The Century*. A patient type with an indisputable ear for melody, Ken was a perfect candidate for moving things onto 'Stage Two'. "There were all sorts of attempts to record until Ken Scott was finally brought in," said Simon. "Then we could actually get the job done."

Repeating a pattern long established throughout his career, Jeff again found himself searching for quality material with which to work. This time, the issue was resolved by the new writing team of Simon Phillips and a now returning Tony Hymas. "As I worked with him more, I realised that Jeff's not a 'composer' as such and he needed some material," said Simon. "The other thing is that many musicians make the mistake of thinking of Jeff as a 'fusion' guitarist. He's not. He's a rock/ blues guitarist through and through but with amazing versatility and technique. Therefore, he needs instrumental 'rock' music… [and] a vision of what that music should be. So I got together with Tony and the first song we wrote was 'The Golden Road'. We went down to Jeff's house and played him this tune and he just loved it. So we carried on writing and came up with the others." A languid, slow-burning composition with plenty of room for Beck to build up a head of steam before its emotive climax, 'The Golden Road' was indicative of the democratic approach Phillips and Hymas took when writing for Jeff. "I had this concept for a guitar ballad with a [real] groove," remembered Simon. "The first three notes of the melody were Tony's, followed by the next seven notes, which were mine. It just went from there."

With recording now well under way at Abbey Road, finding precisely the right bass player to augment their line-up became a pressing concern. Given the complexity of some of the songs already on tape, and a need to tie down the trio's flightier excesses with "a bit of solid bedrock", this was no simple task. Again, Simon Phillips offered Beck a possible solution. "I suggested Mo, who Jeff liked immediately. And that was the birth of the 'There & Back' band." The 'Mo' in question was Mo Foster, a former maths/physics student who, by 1980, had become one of the UK's pre-eminent session musicians. "Actually, I'd met Simon in 1976 where we'd done two weeks at the Paris Olympia with a French singer called Véronique Sanson," said Foster. "He was only a teenager at the time, but already brilliant. We'd also worked on a jazz-rock album, *Ready Or Not*, with the guitarist Ray Russell."

An immensely likeable soul, Foster began his musical career after abandoning a promising job as a laboratory research assistant in 1968 to join prog/jazz-rockers Affinity alongside former Trident Mike Jopp. When that group folded in late 1970, Foster found himself slowly but surely absorbed into London's session world, playing with the likes of drummer Clem Cattini, keyboardist Mike Moran and percussionist Ray Cooper on hundreds – if not thousands – of studio dates. From the Royal Philharmonic Orchestra, Judie Tzuke and Cliff Richard & The Shadows to Gerry Rafferty, Phil Collins and The Walker Brothers, Mo's bass guitar was in there somewhere: "Well, it was the beginning of a word of mouth situation which gradually mushroomed..."

Yet, Foster was genuinely shocked when he found out who else Beck had been considering for his group: "As far as I remember, Jeff had a shortlist. To my amazement, it included ex-Mahavishnu bassist Rick Laird and Led Zeppelin's John Paul Jones. Distinguished competition, you might say. Anyway, we went to a big cinema in Kilburn and just played. I knew Jeff's stuff by ear – I'd loved *Blow By Blow* – and it went well. The atmosphere was friendly, relaxed and the banter was good so I was in." For Foster, this was the dream gig to end all dream gigs: "We became a little team, an evolving friendship...getting used to each other slowly. And we really enjoyed playing together. Having grown up with Mahavishnu, for me, it was a pinnacle of playing the music I'd always wanted to."

Of course, there was a 'bedding-in' period to get through, which meant being on the end of the odd practical joke or two: "I was playing on 'Space Boogie' which is an incredibly complicated track.

It had to be done by a series of drop-ins. As I finished the final note, Simon and Tony were looking very glum behind the studio window. All of a sudden, they raised these pieces of paper with scores written on them. I felt like a bloody ice skater getting his marks!" As with most musicians who have worked with Beck, however, Foster spent a goodly proportion of his time in awe of the guitarist's ability: "Jeff doesn't really lead a band. He just expects you to come up with the stuff. Come up with ideas. There's no sense of pressure there. It's just the single-mindedness of it... his search. Miles Davis is probably a good comparison. Like Jeff, he had trouble articulating exactly what he was searching for, but then he'd do it... pointing to his musicians, driving them on, encouraging them. In that respect, they share the same thing... this continuous, ever-evolving pursuit of excellence. And Jeff, well, he doesn't read... actually he doesn't know what the chords are half the time. But you know, when you can play like that, you doesn't really need to know."

By July 1980, Jeff's latest album, *There & Back*, was in the shops, debuting at numbers 21 and 38 in the US and UK charts respectively. Sometimes overlooked in the Beck 'canon' because of its relative proximity to *Blow By Blow* and *Wired*, *There & Back* was nonetheless a fine disc, full of genuine surprises and often scary musicianship. If there was a fault to pick at, it was the record's somewhat schizophrenic nature, with Jan Hammer's approach to songwriting occasionally jarring against the material provided by Tony Hymas and Simon Phillips. But this 'Janus'-like element also kept things fresh, making *There And Back* an odd, but still captivating listen.

Of Hammer's three tunes, 'Star Cycle' was head and shoulders above the competition. Premiered live on Beck's Japanese tour of 1978, 'Star Cycle' was a wonderful, "undulating thing" that bubbled along atop Phillips' brisk stick work. As ever, Jeff and Jan remained keen to push each other to the limit, their guitar and synth face-offs often so spirited one found it difficult to mark where Beck's solos ended and Hammer's began: "What a compliment!" laughed Jeff. "When you're handed 'Star Cycle' by Jan Hammer, it's actually intimidating to aspire to that level of brilliance." An assured opener, 'Star Cycle' subsequently became the theme tune for UK Channel

4's flagship music programme *The Tube*, which ran from 1982–87.[*] Hammer's 'Too Much To Lose' – later released as a single in the US – and 'You Never Know' were also of reasonable calibre, both taking their cue from the hard funk edges found on *Wired*, with tight, musical structures one couldn't help but tap a foot to.

Of the Hymas/Phillips compositions (all of which featured Mo Foster on bass), 'The Pump'''s stately rhythm and dream-like atmosphere allowed Beck to set sail on an elongated guitar break, with his fingers circling, attacking or caressing the central melody. "Believe it or not," Phillips recalled, "my influence for 'The Pump' was the Beatles' 'I Am A Walrus'!" For Mo Foster, 'The Pump' was notable for another reason: "It was like driving without speeding up. That's very tricky to do." Destined to become a regular feature of Jeff's concert set, 'The Pump' also gained some notoriety when used as the musical backdrop for Tom Cruise's 'Porsche ride' in the 1983 movie *Risky Business*.

In comparison with 'The Pump''s drowsy elegance, 'Space Boogie' was in Beck's own words: "An absolute bloody killer." A frantic, crunchy and dislocated tune that stretched all the musicians involved to their absolute limits, 'Space Boogie' was born of two drum kits at Jeff's house one memorable evening in mid-1979. "We were jamming with Jeff in his music room and I'd brought a small Ludwig kit along with me," said Simon. "He had an old Premier kit set up and during the day I dragged over his kit and put them both together so I had two bass drums. We were playing a fast, boogie shuffle and I started playing seven over the 4/4 groove we had going. Jeff just loved it and that's when I made a mental note to write something with that groove. On the next writing session with Tony, I played him that groove... and he came up with the bass line. The rest, as they say, is history..."

Mad as a proverbial badger, 'Space Boogie' is probably one of the first real examples of 'Math' or 'Space Metal', it's complex structure requiring those playing it to constantly count bars lest things fall into total chaos. "Yeah," Jeff told *Guitar Player,* "it called for listening and

* When 'Star Cycle' was retired by the show in 1985, Beck provided another, untitled theme tune. Reportedly written with producer Trevor Horn, this stonking little instrumental still remains unreleased.

counting. You really need to be in the mood for that high-speed stuff. You have to be angry... to get that kind of naughtiness going and then let it out." Apparently, Beck had little trouble building said anger up, as at least 30 attempts were made before 'Space Boogie''s killer (and very agitated sounding) solo proved to his liking.

'El Becko' didn't let anyone – least of all Jeff – rest on their laurels, either. An intricately rendered tune full of flamenco-like flourishes, 'El Becko''s rattling tempo and "irritated feel" gave Jeff another chance to display his gift both for slide-guitar heroics and off-kilter, string-skipping runs. "Tony had already written the intro to 'El Becko' and then I added the riff," Simon recalled. "There's more of a Stanley Clarke influence on that from my point of view." However, *There & Back*'s strongest moment was saved for last. "I had asked Tony if he could write a 'featured' guitar piece," said Beck. "And then having asked that stupid question, I felt embarrassed because that's really something I should be able to do. Anyway, I just said I wanted some spaced-out chords that I could work between and that's exactly what we did. I was just making the guitar up on that... it really wasn't planned at all. He wrote the melody and I just cried a few times on guitar. It was just a locked-in mental thing between us."

The instrumental in question, entitled 'The Final Peace', was written by Hymas several weeks before it was recorded at Abbey Road. Nonetheless, while Tony did play Jeff its chord structure in advance, he was reticent to allow him any time to prepare a solo, preferring instead to capture his response live on tape. "'The Final Peace' was perfect for Jeff and I think [it] was Tony figuring out the best way to write for him," said Phillips. "Jeff is such a melodic player... you just have to give him enough melody, but also with enough room to manoeuvre, so he can extemporize and make it his own." The resulting take proved Hymas' theory correct, with Beck weaving a quite beautiful improvised melody over his shimmering chords – the tune awash with saxophone-like octave leaps, squealing harmonics and lingering grace notes. Though 'The Final Peace' was right up there with the best of Jeff's work, he was initially reluctant to include it on the album until a studio visit from his old drummer, Cozy Powell, persuaded him otherwise. "Well, Cozy heard it and went away glazed and glassy-eyed," Beck said. "So I had second thoughts."

The presence of 'The Final Peace' on *There & Back* also enabled listeners to hear Jeff's latest guitar, a 1954 sunburst Fender Stratocaster, in all its cobbled-together glory. A gift from The Small Faces' Steve Marriott presented to Beck after a drunken night out in 1976, the Strat was "heavy as hell" with an almost 'concrete' ash body. Bearing the serial number '0062', its original neck had been replaced by Marriott with one taken from an old Telecaster, which Beck in turn replaced with a '58 Strat neck of his own. Ever the tinkerer, Jeff had also removed its stock pick-ups in favour of "a set of Alnicos", making the '54 a beautiful mutant. Reportedly "a bitch to play", with an infuriating habit of going out of tune at the most inopportune times, the '54 still had a magical hold over its new owner. "The Strat is often an instrument of torture," he said, "so unless you get a hold of it by the scruff of the neck, you're not going to get much out of it." For the record, Beck's backline and effects for the recording of *There & Back* included the original Marshall head/amp combination he used on *Truth* coupled with an Ibanez booster – "a little yellow thing" – that allowed him to raise the volume "without overtly distorting it". Jeff also employed an exceedingly rare Tycobrahe Paraflanger on certain tracks, this wah-like device capable of sounding like the sea hitting the shore or a bath draining with just one sweep of its expression control.

Despite its undoubted merits *There & Back* received few positive reviews, with critics seeing it either as a lazy consolidation of Beck's previous work or, worse, out of step and out of time with a music scene now basking in the pleasures of new wave. "In the end," said *Sounds*' Steve Gett, "*There & Back* is strictly for devotees. [But] 'The Final Peace' is a must for everyone whoever wanted to hear guitar playing with feeling." *NME*'s Nick Kent was less impressed: "*There & Back* is an album that grates profoundly. It's too jittery to even act as decent background music. And Beck's obsolescence is made all the more glaring by the manoeuvres of other guitarists: Robert Fripp's experiments merit far more attention. Tom Verlaine has achieved a maverick shaping... of guitar that although more academic completely trashes Beck's blinkered conceits. [Even] Neil Young's playing on *Live Rust* steals the fire that Beck could once kindle." Though Kent's words were harsh, they did ably point to the still-wavering nature of Jeff's position circa 1980. As evidenced, punk had drawn clear markers between 'then and now', with respect only accorded those willing to embrace new frontiers rather than profit from old glories. That Beck had supposedly chosen to press on with electric rock and fusion flavours while roundly ignoring most developments post-1976 only underlined his old-school status. Given such a hostile atmosphere, it would have been a brave man indeed that pointed out Jeff had spent his entire career trying to avoid any form of repetition – rock, fusion or otherwise. The critics were getting younger, their memories ever shorter, the knives were getting sharper and Jeff – like many of his peers – was easy meat.

Of course, away from sniffs and slights of the rock weeklies Beck still had a healthy audience to attend to, as a six-month, sold-out world tour proved. Taking Simon Phillips, Tony Hymas and Mo Foster along with him for the ride, Jeff and the 'There & Back' band rolled across the US and Japan throughout the autumn/winter of 1980, playing "two lots of three-week runs" at a time. "On a good night, it was like a jazz gig," Foster recalled. "I'd shut my eyes without realising it and just float off. There was something... almost spiritual about it, if that's the right word. I'd then have to quickly realise I was supposed to be in the band and better join in. I was on auto-pilot, just elsewhere." Simon Phillips too, felt a similar type of exhilaration: "I was 22 years old, had endless amounts of energy, so there was no problem playing those songs. They were never fast enough for me!"

However, the subtle intricacies involved in performing 'Space Boogie' at various cattle sheds throughout America's midwest still remained a problem for all concerned. "When we starting touring in America, we were playing big halls and these places really echoed," Foster confirmed. "So I'd be looking at Simon trying to catch the first beat, because sometimes he'd be playing 14 beats, and we'd catch up on the 15th. Anyway, I'd do a movement with my neck [to indicate the first beat], and then we knew we were synchronised. That went OK for a few days, but then he'd start doing a similar thing which I took as his signal, except of course it wasn't. It was Simon just stretching his neck. So with the echo, and the lack of signals, we ended up just hoping for the best. That song was hard to play."

After a round of well-received Japanese dates ("At the end of each gig they'd just go crazy," said Mo), the group returned home to prepare for Beck's first UK shows in nearly seven years. Having either avoided, or been ignored by, the British market for so long, one might have thought it was high time for Jeff to finally bite the bullet and drum up some interest in his forthcoming concerts. But getting the guitarist in front of a TV camera was no easy task. "Jeff hated promotion. Hated it," said Mo Foster. "In his eyes, what you did on record or in the concert hall said it all. Anyway, when we were doing Hammersmith Odeon, the record company wanted him to go on *The Old Grey Whistle Test* and be interviewed by Annie Nightingale. But he just didn't want to do it, so a plan was hatched. A PR chap called Judd Lander was dispatched to Jeff's house very early one morning. So Jeff awakes to the sound of bagpipes in his driveway. There's Judd naked, playing away on these bloody bagpipes. Of course, Jeff loved this and invited him in for a coffee. Anyway, he finally agreed to do the interview, but only if Judd would re-create the naked bagpipe scene on TV. And to his credit, Judd did. Jeff's sitting there doing this serious interview with Annie, and suddenly this naked bagpiper walks on in the background. Now, that's PR at its best." Actually, Beck was equally funny with or without bagpipes. When asked by host Annie Nightingale why he was now appearing in the UK after a seven-year gap, the guitarist was a deadpan delight: "Basically, it's to let everybody know I'm not dead."

If Beck had been unfairly overlooked by the Great British public for a near-decade (and reacted accordingly), one wouldn't have known it from the rapturous applause he received at London's Hammersmith Odeon on March 9 and 10, 1981. "By the time we got to Japan and the UK we were on fire as a band," confirmed Simon Phillips, "and those shows at Hammersmith were some of our best." Appearing genuinely shaken by the crowd's reaction as he walked onstage, Jeff managed to stumble through a word or two of introduction before the opening bars to 'Star Cycle' quickly reminded him of where he was and what he was meant to be doing. "I was very nervous beforehand," he later admitted, "but it thrilled me the way the audience really listened." The second night at Hammersmith took on even deeper significance as Beck was joined onstage at encore time by his old friend Jimmy Page.

Only six months before, Led Zeppelin's unrivalled domination of the international rock scene had ended tragically when drummer John

Bonham died at Page's Windsor Mill House following a prolonged drinking bout. Faced with the prospect of recruiting a replacement or simply ending the band, Zeppelin issued a carefully worded press statement that neither confirmed nor denied either option: "We wish it to be known that the loss of our dear friend, and the deep sense of undivided harmony felt by ourselves and our manager, have led us to decide that we could not continue as we were." While this missive left some room for ambiguity regarding the group's prospects, the reality was somewhat different. Since Bonham's death on September 25, 1980 Page had withdrawn from public view, with rumours of poor health and possible drug problems leading to his retreat. It was therefore a relief to all concerned when a decidedly frail, but still Les Paul-wielding Page emerged from the wings to accompany Beck on a spirited, if shambolic rendition of 'Going Down'. Though Jimmy's progress would remain slow for some time to come, if there ever had been a feud between the two, it surely ended that night.

Back onstage in England after a seven-year break – indeed, back on stage with Jimmy Page for the first time in over 14 years – if Jeff had been looking for a suitable ending to his world tour, then the Hammersmith Odeon appearance was as good a way as any to do it. "*There & Back* was really about getting together a collection of really good melodies and seeing if they were suitable for my guitar style," he said at the time. And it had worked. By no means Jeff's finest album, *There & Back* was still a creditable enough step forward – "A possible bridge," as journalist Alan Di Perna later described it, "between Beck's past and possible future." Should he so wish, Beck also had a fine group at his disposal, and one who were champing at the bit to take things to the next level. "I know we all wanted to go straight back on the road after that, or at least into the studio," said Mo Foster. "But Jeff being Jeff, well, he'd again begun to lose interest and wanted to do something new."

Unfortunately, Beck spent most of the eighties trying to find out what that 'something new' was.

Chapter 18

Intermission (The Cars Are Getting Very Shiny)

Following *There And Back*'s respectable run on the charts and successful tour, Jeff Beck again went to ground. "I suppose I could get a group together, go out there and clean up singing about rot and playing 'I Ain't Superstitious'," he said in 1981. "You know, just turn it into nostalgia. But that's nothing new." Having grown used to − and one suspects, rather enjoying the freedoms − of being a 'major cult artist', he was also in no mood to entertain record company whims about turning him into a superstar. "I don't want to 'break'," he growled to *Guitar World*. "When you say 'break', you mean getting to the AM market and becoming a widespread name with household acceptance. No way." A serious plunge into the 'proper' jazz market sounded unlikely too. "If I were to really pursue jazz, I'd have to have a lot more understanding of it under my belt," he said. "It's just too late for me to start delving back into the old, great jazz records... Ornette Coleman, stuff like that. It's beyond my grasp now, so it's natural for me to go back to the way I've always played, which is from the gut... a spur of the moment type thing."

For the time being at least, Beck seemed more content to get his fingers greasy with engine oil than cut up by strings. With his collection of 1932/4 Fords now close to a baker's dozen − including a cherished black roadster, two freshly painted yellow coupes and an ebony 'five door' with red flames licking its sides − the garage rather than the

273

stage seemed the place to be. "Jeff's main obsession was, is, and always will be hot rods," said Mo Foster, who was then a regular visitor to Beck's home. "So if you strike up a conversation about guitars, often he just doesn't want to know. Then you see the cars he's made, these beautiful cars, works of art in fact, and you understand." Part relaxation, part therapy, but mostly pure enjoyment, Jeff's obsession with spraying, modifying, rebuilding, driving or just looking at hot rods was becoming legendary. "His dedication is total," Mo continued. "One night, he got the 'Jeff urge' to go down to the garage during the night. So he goes in with his light torch and starts working. Soon enough, he falls asleep, then a little while later wakes up covered in moths..."

According to Beck himself, there was also a strangely musical element to the business of constructing hotrods. "It keeps the brain going," he said. "I get dizzy building a rod because it's so thrilling. You burn your fingers, there's grinding and welding. Remember Lee Dorsey's 'Working In A Coalmine'? He was supposedly a panel beater. If you listen to the rhythm, there's an anvil as a backbeat. There's rhythm all around a workshop – machines, compressors, music is everywhere." On the rare occasions he could be separated from his car collection, Jeff had taken to playing the drums, bashing away at "an old Premier kit" he purchased some years before. A confirmed 'skins freak' since his teens, Beck had always built his groups around the drummer. Now he seemed determined to master the instrument himself. "It was a good way of working out actually," he said, "but I was never going to be a convincing drummer." Still, he persisted with it for a while, building up a daily routine of drum practice before again returning to his cars. "When the cars are shiny, I'm not playing," he once said. "And when they're gathering dust, the guitars are out of their boxes."

After a near six-month lay-off, Beck dipped a cautious toe in the musical waters when he was approached by Simon Phillips to appear at *The Secret Policeman's Other Ball*, a regular fund-raising event in support of Amnesty International. "I was asked to play and while I was speaking to the producer, I said that I might be able to get Jeff to play," said Phillips. "Then, when I spoke to Jeff he said 'I might be able to get Eric Clapton to come along' and that's how that all happened." As evidenced, during the sixties Beck and Clapton had often been painted by the press as bitter rivals: one cast as the lonesome blues aesthete whose principles forbade him to indulge the fripperies of pop, the other a temperamental, but gifted soloist secretly still resentful that his break into the big time had only come after 'the anointed one' ascended to 'godhead'. God knows, there might have been some truth in it – at least for a little while. But away from the clichés, the facts seemed somewhat less romantic. Eric had actually jammed with Jeff at The Marquee soon after the latter joined The Yardbirds, the two even sharing a hug to mark the occasion. In New York two years later, Clapton, Beck and Jimi Hendrix appeared onstage together, though sadly no one caught it on tape. And while the two had remained distant throughout the seventies, May 1980 again found them sharing the boards, this time at Guildford's Civic Hall where Eric was playing the last night of his UK tour. Seemingly out of nowhere, Jeff bounded on at encore time for a brisk run-through of 'Ramblin' On My Mind', following which he was covered in foam.

Beck and Clapton's subsequent career paths could not have been more divergent since the days of JBG and Cream. On hearing Bob Dylan's backing group The Band in 1968, Eric had all but renounced blues-rock in favour of wider musical horizons, first with Stevie Winwood in Blind Faith, then Delaney & Bonnie and Derek & The Dominoes before heroin addiction threatened to end it all in the early seventies. However, Clapton's subsequent recovery had allowed him to re-establish himself within the marketplace as a "legitimate survivor", his brand now extended to include not only blues, but also folk, bluegrass, reggae and soft-rock styles. In short, 'God' had mellowed a bit. Jeff, on the other hand, had ping-ponged all over the place during the same period, but latterly found some stability within the jazz-rock/fusion community. Given time, tide and a hell of a lot of water under the bridge, surely no one was expecting 'the age of the gunslinger' to return at London's Theatre Royal. "You know, there's something cool and mean about Becky that beats everyone else," said Eric. How right he was.

The Secret Policeman's Other Ball took place on September 9, 1981 with its cast drawn from the worlds of both comedy and music. "It was a fun gig for sure and a lot of laughs with the likes of Billy Connolly and Rowan Atkinson doing these sketches," recalled Phillips. "Though the strange thing was how unfunny and serious John Cleese was offstage!" Scattered among the comic turns were solo spots from the likes of established pop icons Sting, Phil Collins and Donovan with Simon Phillips and Mo Foster among the musicians providing back-up. "Yes, but it was nothing like our own gig," said Simon. "This was a different level." On the night, Clapton and Beck performed three songs together, with Eric taking the lead on a fine version of Robert Johnson's 'Crossroads' before Jeff turned in a typically heart-rending solo on Stevie Wonder's 'Cause We've Ended As Lovers'. The finale, Bobby Bland's 'Further On Up The Road', was supposed to see them trade a few good-natured licks before an inevitable round of applause drowned the hall. Except Jeff didn't read the script. "One couldn't help feeling a bit sorry for Eric," said journalist David Sinclair when reviewing the show. "Having shouldered all the donkey work, only to then have Beck whip in and steal the number right from under his nose." In what can only be termed 'a musical mugging', Jeff didn't so much turn up the heat during his solo pass on 'Further On Up The Road' as incinerate Eric where he stood. To Clapton's enduring credit, his only response was to raise an arm in surrender while smiling at the audacity of the crime. "Eric's a great player, but that gig missed it by a million miles," Jeff later said, while returning his gun to its holster.

Away from the whizzing bullets fired at the Theatre Royal, the next 18 or so months provided precious few sightings for Beck watchers, with the guitarist seemingly ever-more fixated on building cars than playing guitars. "It's difficult to have fun all the time," he said. "The best time to play is when you're having fun, when you're really enjoying it. I just can't see the sense of rushing it. There are certain problems with me, at this time in my life, with the lead guitar. I mean, what do you do with the electric guitar? I have to play to the max or not at all." On the odd occasion that Jeff did venture into the studio, it was always as a guest musician. In this guise he appeared on former JBG2 colleague Cozy Powell's second solo album, 1981's *Tilt*, contributing feisty lead breaks to 'Hot Rock' and 'Cat Moves', two tunes written by Jan Hammer and originally performed by Beck on his 1978 tour with Stanley Clarke.

Though both songs were inessential at best, 'Cat Moves' was of some interest if only for the fact that Jeff used a guitar synthesiser on record for the first time, its stringy tones providing a slight distraction from the workmanlike funk rock going on in the background. Beck didn't stay a fan of the device for long. "What a waste of time. I really didn't think there was much point in a guitar emulating a keyboard, but I gave it a go," he said later. "Then, in a hot climate, the pitch voltage interface wouldn't work, and the [tracking] would go all over the place. You'd play one note and it'd jump an octave. I just thought, 'Put it back in the box and forget about it'. Besides, you're never going to sound like a keyboard player anyway. I just don't believe it works. I don't think the two cross over. Jan Hammer, of course, is the exception. He can make a keyboard sound better than a guitar."*

Catching up with another pair of old friends, Beck also made an uncredited appearance on PHD's second album, *Is It Safe?*. The trio, comprising Tony Hymas, Simon Phillips and singer Jim Diamond, had already scored a Top Three UK hit with the 1982 single 'I Won't Let You Down', and were hoping for even bigger things with their next 45, 'I Didn't Know', which featured a short, but exceedingly sweet solo from Jeff. Oddly, 'I Didn't Know' died a death in the UK, though it did top the Italian charts.

After keeping a positively subterranean profile throughout 1981/82, Jeff Beck finally began a slow, but sure walk back into the spotlight in March 1983 when he appeared on a televised tribute to his boyhood hero, Les Paul. The US TV show – entitled '*Rock 'N' Roll Tonight*' – was filmed at LA's Perkins Palace, featured Billy 'The Stroke' Squier on compere duties, and gave the 68-year-old guitarist another chance to remind everyone why he had been dubbed 'The Wizard of Waukesha'. In the end, neither Les Paul nor Beck disappointed, trading licks, laughs and the odd prank or two during their loose jam on 'Chicken Shack' and another on-the-spot 'blues ramble'. Looking trim and healthy in a white jacket, black waistcoat and jeans, Jeff was content to play up to Les' penchant for

---

* Powell's previous album, *Over The Top*, featured a tune called 'The Loner' which was written by Max Middleton and dedicated to Beck. 'The Loner' was to have featured Jeff on guitar, but as he proved unavailable for the session, the marvellous Gary Moore filled in instead: "Not a bad replacement, eh?" quipped Cozy.

onstage tomfoolery as the old master mock-detuned his new '57 sunburst Strat (reissue) after a particularly tricky piece of tremolo bar manipulation. Beck hit back by trying to pull the lead out of Les' own signature model. "Meeting Les Paul," he said later, "just seeing him play again, was a triumph in every sense of the word." Paul was equally complimentary about Beck, and indeed, the Englishman's intimate knowledge of his own back catalogue. "I just met Jeff and the first thing he says to me is 'You did 'San Antonio Rose' and I've been playing that damned thing for the last 20 years! I still haven't got it yet! Would you play it for me?'" he said soon after the event. "I told him 'To be honest, I don't remember making it... I guess I made it and just forgot it'. So Jeff started to play it for me and I remembered some of the things I'd done. I like Jeff's playing and not because he's taken something from me. We all take from somebody. We all have to learn somewhere."

With the '*Rock 'N' Roll Tonight*' appearance behind him, Jeff continued to amuse himself with more sessions and the odd, impromptu gig – each solo or concert bringing him ever closer to the inevitable task of trading once again under his own name. One thing, however, remained clear. Beck's next release would not be found in the jazz or fusion section of any record stores: "'Fuzak'. Pah. I wish I hadn't done any of them, they're mistakes. I wish I'd stayed with earthy rock'n'roll. I just got sucked [in]. It all reminds me of flared trousers and double-breasted jackets!" That said, Jeff seemed more than content to make an exception for his friend Stanley Clarke. "Beck was in town and I was doing my new LP *Time Exposure*, and we just wanted to play," remembered Clarke. "There was so much musicality to his solos, like little compositions in themselves. It had nothing to do with technique, though he had that too. You see, for us it wasn't about whether you could play 'Giant Steps' or Miles Davis or Stravinsky, it was how heartfelt it was. And Jeff's just a fierce guitar player, with a sense of fun. Upbeat, good sense of humour, a great guy to be around." As ever, Stanley was also impressed by Beck's humility during the recording process: "Jeff's like an 'anti-rock hero'. No prima donna airs and graces. If anyone could get away with that rock-star thing, you'd think it'd be him. But he doesn't. He's generous to other musicians and so, so funny. Get him on a stage though, and he can turn it on." Beck ended up contributing three fine solos to *Time Exposure*, including a soaring pass on the title track itself and a sinewy run on 'Are You Ready (For The Future)'.

Back in London, the seeds were being sown for further collaboration. After a break of 15 years, The Yardbirds had assembled for a reunion gig to mark the 20th anniversary of London's Marquee club on June 22 and 23, 1983. Given that Keith Relf died in 1976 and Paul Samwell-Smith had forsworn the stage since relinquishing his duties as bass player to Jimmy Page 10 years before that, the idea of Beck's old group reforming – even for two nights – seemed unlikely. Yet, events had conspired in recent years to set things in motion. In 1980, for instance, Jeff had worked with Samwell-Smith on West End star Murray Head's disc *How Many Ways*: Paul acting as producer and Jeff cutting three solos on 'Last Days Of An Empire', 'Children Only Play' and 'Affairs Across A Crowded Room' (*How Many Ways* was re-issued as a CD in Austria under the title *Voices* in 1993). Equally, Jim McCarty, Chris Dreja and Samwell-Smith's paths continued to cross in one way or another over the years – more often than not in the pub. "Well, when looking back, we were a sensitive and creative band and there was just no way it could have lasted then," said Jim. "At that time, we earned our money on the road, not from record sales, so we couldn't take a break. We became exhausted, and one by one, handed in our cards. But you know, no regrets really." Yet, old habits die hard, and when Samwell-Smith agreed in principle to "doing something" to mark the Marquee's birthday, the reunion was on. "It was really a case of 'Why the hell not?'" laughed Chris Dreja.

With their line-up augmented by former Medicine Head singer John Fiddler and sturdy guitarist Dzal Martin, The Yardbirds returned to the sweaty West End club that had set them on the way, with a set list drawing from each point of their illustrious career: 'Heart Full Of Soul', 'Happenings Ten Years Time Ago', even the dreaded 'For Your Love' were all dispatched with passion, humour and, thankfully, not a single raspberry blown at the gathered crowd. Enthused by their efforts, the group set about securing a record deal from their former label, Epic, though to gain some distance from the past (and avoid any legal action from Giorgio Gomelsky), they rechristened themselves 'Box Of Frogs'. "It just grew," said McCarty. "We'd done the reunion gigs for the Marquee anniversary, John came along on vocals and then someone had the bright idea of asking Jeff to join in for a record. And so he did." Beck's appearance on Box Of Frogs' self-titled 1984 album remains a little treasure to this day, his typically moody runs and silvery slide work on 'Back Where I Started', 'Another Wasted Day', 'Two Steps Ahead' and 'Poor Boy' a genuine pleasure to listen to: "If I didn't think it was valid, I wouldn't have done it. But they sent me a demo tape and I was pleasantly surprised."*

Momentum still gathering for his comeback, Beck's next move was a charitable one. On September 20 and 21, 1983, he joined an all-star gathering at London's Royal Albert Hall in aid of Action for Research into Multiple Sclerosis (MS) or as it was better known, 'ARMS'. The story behind the concerts was a touching one. Former Small Faces bassist Ronnie Lane had been diagnosed with MS in 1977 while recording the album *Rough Mix* with The Who's Pete Townshend. Though Lane continued to tour regularly, by 1983 his condition had worsened to a point where he spent an increasing amount of time seeking effective treatments. During this period, Ronnie encountered many others suffering from the disease as well as a number of doctors, scientists and specialists. As a result, he helped set up ARMS as a blanket charity committed to researching a cure for MS. Seeking a way of raising further funds, Lane's girlfriend, Boo Oldfield, duly contacted promoter Harvey Goldsmith with a view to organising some kind of event that drew support from the rock community. As Goldsmith was in the midst of arranging Eric Clapton's performance for The Prince's Trust with Glyn Johns at the time, he extended the Royal Albert Hall booking for an extra night, with proceeds raised now benefiting both charities.

The subsequent concerts proved truly glitzy affairs, with "rock royalty meeting actual royalty" in the grand surroundings of the Royal

---

* Though Box of Frogs did reasonably well Stateside, a second release – 1986's *Strange Land* featuring Jimmy Page on the track 'Asylum' – did not fare well commercially and the band subsequently broke up. However, Dreja and McCarty once again resurrected The Yardbirds' name in the nineties, releasing an album *Birdland* in 2003, with Beck appearing on 'My Bind Life'. They continue to gig regularly throughout Europe and the States.

Albert Hall. Both Prince Charles and his wife, Princess Diana, were in attendance, while the musical contingent was represented by Clapton and Beck, with Traffic/Blind Faith's Steve Winwood, Andy Fairweather-Low and The Rolling Stones' rhythm section of Charlie Watts and Bill Wyman also along for the ride. To potentially top it all, Jimmy Page agreed to do a short set, thus ending an absence of nearly three years from the concert stage. However, there were real concerns regarding the guitarist's health. "At rehearsals, we weren't even sure Jimmy was going to make it through," Jeff later said. And for good reason. Since appearing with Beck at Hammersmith Odeon in March 1981, Page had gone into further decline. Now a virtual recluse, the only music that he had involved himself was the soundtrack to director (and neighbour) Michael Winner's 1982 movie, *Death Wish II*. "I lived next door to Jimmy for many years," said Winner. "It was a very bad time for him. John Bonham had died and he was in a very inactive period."

Ultimately, the ARMS gigs went like a dream, even if the second night was marred by a distinctly muted atmosphere, thanks in large part to the presence of a certain visiting Princess. "She put the muckers on the audience by making them very subdued," Beck said. "The whole atmosphere was intense... 'Don't shout, don't swear, don't act like hooligans'." As the resultant TV broadcast (and video) was filmed on the first night, those watching from their armchairs didn't have to worry unduly. Following a strong set from Clapton and an upbeat take of 'Gimme Some Lovin'' by Steve Winwood, Jeff turned in what can only be described as a virtuoso performance to those gathered in the RAH. Backed by Simon Phillips, Tony Hymas and 1976 US tour bassist Fernando Saunders, Beck's renditions of 'Star Cycle', 'Goodbye Pork Pie Hat', 'Led Boots' and a quite wondrous 'The Pump' were arguably the highlights of the night – at least for the musicians in attendance. "For many months after that," said Eric, "I began to think of Jeff as probably the finest guitar player I'd ever seen." Obviously in a cheeky mood, Beck ended his set with an unexpected blast from the past: "You ain't gonna believe this," he laughed, "but I still do it for special occasions..." Assisted by Stevie Winwood and Andy Fairweather-Low on backing vocals, Jeff then proceeded to murder 'Hi Ho Silver Lining', as an ecstatic audience bellowed every line of the song with him.

The man cursed with following Beck was Jimmy Page: "All bets," said Jeff, "were off." As ever, Page managed to pull it out of the bag. Arriving onstage in a plume of cigarette smoke, his trademark Cheshire cat grin disguising "a bucketful of nerves", Page not only managed to get through his set, but also provide some fireworks on the way. Drawing on material from the aforementioned *Death Wish II*, with Stevie Winwood providing lead vocals on 'Who's To Blame' and a suitably rocking 'City Sirens', Jimmy finally rewarded those assembled with what they had really come to hear: a messy, but heartfelt instrumental version of Led Zeppelin's 'Stairway To Heaven', played – of course – on his doubled-necked Gibson 1275.

"Same old Jimmy," said an admiring Beck, "hovering on the brink of disaster, then... magic." As the applause for Page's efforts subsided, those gathered were treated to the sight of Jeff, Eric and Jimmy working their way through 'Tulsa Time' before ripping into Clapton's signature tune, 'Layla'. It was the first time all three had ever performed together in public. "Worked, didn't it?" Eric later said. To end the evening, Ronnie Lane joined the band for an emotive take on the old folk standard 'Goodnight Irene'. "I genuinely didn't think I'd get such a huge response," said Lane at the time. "I mean, that was 'The Best of British' out there tonight."

Suitably inspired by their collective efforts, the ARMS team next headed to the States for nine extra dates, culminating in a fine performance at New York's Madison Square Garden on December 8. "It's fantastic that it's... got this far," Ronnie told *Creem*. "Really, I intended originally for it to get a hyperbaric oxygen chamber for London, and that was it. But the musicians really enjoyed playing with each other, I provided the excuse, and [we] put out the same vibe in America about what ARMS is doing in England. You know, maybe life is worth living."

On the American leg, various changes in line-up were made, with singers Joe Cocker and ex-Free/Bad Company front man Paul Rodgers replacing a now otherwise engaged Steve Winwood. "No stars and no moods, which was a little bit of a surprise, really," Cocker later said. As far as Beck's backing band were concerned, the only addition was Jan Hammer who now took over keyboards from Tony Hymas. "I think it should have gone on for another month,"

And then there were three. A cigar-smoking Jeff Beck alongside new 'BBA' band mates Carmine Appice and Tim Bogert in 1972. (L-R): Carmine, Jeff and Tim. MICHAEL OCHS ARCHIVES/GETTY IMAGES

Jeff lets fly with his 'Oxblood' Gibson Les Paul at Crystal Palace in London, 1972. MICHAEL PUTLAND/GETTY IMAGES

Happier times. Carmine and Jeff ham it up backstage for the cameras, while Beck cracks a rare smile onstage with Tim in June, 1973. It would all be over within a year. CHRIS WALTER. DAVID WARNER ELLIS/REDFERNS

The Strat King. Beck performing at London's Roundhouse in 1976. ANDRE CSILLAG/REX FEATURES

Jeff at home with partner and former fashion model, Celia Hammond. Their relationship would last nearly two decades.
EVENING STANDARD/REX FEATURES

"Hey Grease Monkey, show me what you got…" Jeff arrives at the Hollywood Palladium for the Rock Awards in one of his beloved hot rods. MARK SULLIVAN/CONTOUR BY GETTY IMAGES

Beck in amp heaven. An ecstatic Jeff and his new Jackson guitar surrounded by several walls of Seymour Duncan amplifiers in 1985. ROBERT KNIGHT ARCHIVE /REDFERNS

...an and Jeff are a match made in heaven. When they start licking those lips and firing up the licks, it's game over." Jan Hammer ...d Beck onstage at the A.R.M.S. benefit concert at San Francisco's Cow Palace on December 3, 1983. CLAYTON CALL/REDFERNS

The *Guitar Shop* boys. L-R: Terry Bozzio, Jeff and Tony Hymas. ROBERT KNIGHT ARCHIVE/REDFERNS

A dream line up. (L-R): Andy Fairweather-Low, Jimmy Page, Eric Clapton, Bill Wyman and Jeff performing in aid of A.R.M.S. at the Royal Albert Hall, London, in September, 1983. RICHARD YOUNG/REX FEATURES

The Holy Trinity. Former Yardbirds Jimmy Page, Jeff and Eric Clapton united onstage for A.R.M.S. EBET ROBERTS

"Les was an innovator... he created the most incredible sounds and he was also my friend." Jeff and the legendary Les Paul share a riff or two on the *Rock And Roll Tonite* TV Show in 1983. CHRIS WALTER

The Fire and The Fury. Jeff and Stevie Ray Vaughan toured the States together in the autumn of 1989. Sadly, Vaughan died in a helicopter crash in August, 1990. ROBERT KNIGHT ARCHIVE/REDFERNS

Beck in relaxed mood with his Surf Green Fender Strat, 'Little Richard'. MICHAEL PUTLAND/GETTY IMAGES

Weapons of mass destruction – the many guitars of Jeff Beck. The 'Hot Rod' Prototype, the Signature Strat, the 1959 Gibson Les Paul and 1956 Gretsch Duo Jet. NIGEL OSBOURNE/REDFERNS

Who needs a pick? Beck points his Fender Telecaster at the camera in New York City on August 9, 1985. EBET ROBERTS

said Jeff, "but... initially we didn't know how well it would be received. Because it was Jimmy, Eric and myself for Ronnie Lane, the whole thing seemed to really mean something. It was an amazing experience all over."

Amazing, but still occasionally competitive. As song arrangements changed – with Jeff and Eric now joining Jimmy for a blazing, three-guitar run-out at the end of 'Stairway To Heaven' and Beck nabbing the main riff on 'Layla' – the gunslinging antics of *The Secret Policeman's Other Ball* were always only a whisker away. "Yeah, there was a little element [of competition] there I suppose, with the three of us up there plunking away," Jeff admitted to *Guitar Player*. "But... we weren't up there to have a battle. We traded solos and that's as close as it came. In the end, I just wanted to play as well as I could for Ronnie Lane."

Undoubtedly true, but Eric Clapton still heard the unlocking of holsters once or twice. "Well," he told journalist Dan Forte. "It was very much there between me and Jeff, and I think it was also there between Jeff and Jimmy – but because I'm not familiar with Jimmy's playing, I'd never really worked with him – we had no time to develop a rapport. So, as a 'three-part thing', it couldn't happen. Besides, Jimmy was under pressure as it was, and to have thrown him under more of that would have been unfair. He was very nervous... and very frail." Though undoubtedly the most technically gifted of 'The Holy Trinity', Beck also knew that no amount of onstage shoot-outs were likely to challenge the legacy of Led Zeppelin, Cream or 'God' himself: "My postman will know who Eric Clapton and Jimmy Page are, but he won't know who I am," he later joked. "And he probably plays a Strat..."

In the end, the ARMS tour did no harm to any of those involved. Aside from the obvious benefits for Ronnie Lane's cause, the experience also seemed to positively reinvigorate Eric Clapton, who in all honesty had become increasingly complacent since his glory days with Cream. Within the space of just 18 months, 'EC' was again looking like his old self – but this time in much sharper suits – as hits like 'Forever Man' and 'Behind The Mask' found a new audience in Europe and America. Jimmy Page too, had much to thank ARMS for. Before agreeing to participate, he was in his own words "a bit lost", the death of John Bonham and his band leaving him without clear purpose or definition. However, fate, or more specifically, singer Paul Rodgers had quickly intervened – the two striking up an on-the-road friendship which eventually led to the formation of Jimmy's next million-selling group, The Firm: "I thought if I stop now, I'm just a bloody fool." As for Beck, ARMS represented an opportunity to again test his skills alongside world-class musicians, but without carrying the burden of a group on his own shoulders: "At the time, I was still waiting for a little bell to ring, to know I was ready to go forward..."

It was a while yet before said bell rang. Still trying to figure out exactly what to do next, Jeff continued to procrastinate throughout early 1984, more content to mark time with the odd jam or session than form a long-term band. For a while, it even looked like he might return to jazz-rock, as bassist Mo Foster explained: "Well, Jeff had been planning a new tour and we'd been rehearsing with Tony Williams on drums. I mean, I walk in, and there's Tony Williams. From The Tony Williams Lifetime. And Miles Davis. I really wanted to say 'I've got all your records', but resisted it. You know, play it cool. Anyway, we had two rehearsals and that turned out to be it." Yet again, Beck appeared unsure how to proceed. "Jeff's problem – always has been – is he knows exactly where he wants to go musically, but he doesn't know how to articulate it," said Mo. "He couldn't say why it was wrong. So he'd just blunder through. And if it wasn't going in the right way, he'd just get up and leave." Jeff was all too aware of the dilemma, but also knew this musical wanderlust was intrinsic to his nature. "If you've got a licence to play guitar, there shouldn't be any perimeters and fences," he later explained to *Mojo*. "It'd be like saying you can only have egg and chips for the rest of your life. You're entitled to express yourself in any way you think you should."

One episode that did allow Beck a break from all the soul-searching and provide him with "a bloody good laugh" came in March 1984 with the release of *This Is Spinal Tap*. A 'mockumentary' based on the fictitious career of rock survivors Spinal Tap, the movie struck a chord with just about every musician who saw it: "When I first saw… *Spinal Tap*," said Aerosmith singer Steven Tyler, "I took it real personal." Satirising the overwhelming pretensions and lunatic behaviour of hard rock/heavy metal bands, the film's plotline centred around the two-decade relationship between veteran rockers David St. Hubbins, Derek Smalls and Nigel Tufnel – played to perfection by Michael McKean, Harry Shearer and Christopher Guest respectively – and a revolving cast of mysteriously unreliable drummers. However, for Beck acolytes, it was the character of lead guitarist Tufnel that really caught the eye: moody, rooster-haired, obsessed with guitars, cars and women, and possessed of a distinctly 'Thames Delta' accent, one didn't need a degree in psychology to draw a conclusion about who 'Nigel' might be based on. "There's one scene at an airport and Nigel Tufnel's reading a hot-rod magazine," Beck roared. "I mean, C'mon, the bloody bastard!"

Jeff first saw ...*Spinal Tap* with Mo Foster at a screening held in London's Portobello Road. "The opening night of *Spinal Tap* was at the Electric Cinema and I went with Jeff after rehearsals," Foster recalled. "He was on the floor throughout the film, just laughing his head off at this Nigel Tufnel character. Actually, I've never heard someone laugh that much. He was literally peeing himself." According to Beck, Tufnel's character was so astoundingly rendered, it just couldn't be deemed offensive: "I thought it was the best thing I'd ever seen... the most fantastic piss take. It's [also] cringe-worthy... because we all got kicked up the arse." As to the physical similarities between Jeff and the hapless Nigel, again there were few complaints: "Well, the hair was the wrong colour, but still pretty close. Obviously, they'd studied me, but it was mostly from bands like Black Sabbath, because I've never worn make-up or spandex pants. But..." he concluded, "I was still sobbing with laughter. You know, there were all these people around me, 'shooshing' me!" For Mo Foster, Jeff's reaction was indicative of the guitarist's ability not to take anything – including himself – too seriously: "Ah, Jeff's got a great sense of humour. Very funny man. Of course he wasn't insulted. He bloody loved it!"

As the spring of 1984 rolled on, there were more sessions for Beck to attend to. Fulfilling a personal ambition to work with vocalist Robert Plant, Jeff joined the former Led Zeppelin front man's latest project, The Honeydrippers, in the studio for a notable afternoon's soloing. A loose, sax-driven pick-up band Plant had put together to record some old fifties rock'n'roll and soul tunes, The Honeydrippers also called on the services of his former bandmate Jimmy Page, who cut his leads after Beck's work was done: "Well, I heard Beck's solo on 'Rockin' At Midnight' and thought 'Bloody hell, that's good'. It's absolutely beautiful, his solo..." In addition to providing a fine, mischievous break on 'Rockin' At Midnight', Jeff also let his fingers do the walking on Ray Charles' 'I Got A Woman' and the doo-wop classic 'Sea Of Love', though it was Page's solo that made the final cut on the latter track. Released as an EP in November 1984, *The Honeydrippers: Volume One* spawned a number three US single with 'Sea Of Love', while 'Rockin' At Midnight' also made number 25 in the States.

An even greater success came from Beck's brief, but fruitful association with Tina Turner. In London to record her latest LP, Turner's career had undergone major change since Beck last shared a bill with the Nutbush-born singer at the Royal Albert Hall in September 1966. Having enjoyed a fine run of singles into the mid-seventies, Tina's fortunes had fallen into steady decline until a bold remake of Al Green's timeless 'Let's Stay Together' in 1983 rewarded her with a Top 10 hit in the UK. As the song had also scored a measure of US success, there was now much to play for with what was being referred to as her 'comeback' album. In an effort to find quality material, Turner's label Capitol Records had thrown out a wide net to a variety of songwriters, including Dire Straits singer/guitarist Mark Knopfler. On the suggestion of Knopfler's manager, Ed Bicknell, Turner's attention was drawn to 'Private Dancer' – another of those world-weary ballads the Dire Straits man seemed capable of knocking out in his sleep. Taken by its storyline of a jaded woman forced to dance for cash in a seedy club, Tina immediately called Knopfler into the studio. Unfortunately, he only had time to provide a guide vocal/guitar track before another recording date beckoned in the States. One man's loss, as they say, is another man's gain: "I'd have crawled over broken bottles to play with Tina Turner," said Beck.

Called in by Tina's manager Roger Davies, Jeff contributed an astounding solo to 'Private Dancer', his choice of notes inspired, his tone like glass. With the take completed in just half an hour, Beck had time to provide another startling lead break on Turner's version of Paul Brady's 'Steel Claw' – using his brand new, two-octave, pink

Jackson Soloist, replete with Kahler locking tremolo arm, to scare the living daylights out of dogs everywhere. "The Soloist's a bit heavy metal looking," Jeff told *Guitar World*, "but it's bloody good. It goes up to high C... and it sounds almost like a whistle. That's on 'Steel Claw'. It's almost beyond human hearing."* On completion of recording Jeff asked Tina to sign his guitar. But when a felt-tip pen failed to make an enduring mark on the Jackson's polished finish, more extreme measures were called for. "She said 'Do you want it to stay there for a long time?' I said 'Yeah... go for it'." Turner pulled a knife out of her handbag which she then used to chip away at the Jackson, first very neatly, but after some encouragement from Beck, with ever-increasing intensity: "She just tore into it and then rubbed nail polish (to seal the wound). I was totally speechless, but very proud." To no one's great surprise, the guitar has since become known as 'The Turner'.

'Private Dancer' would change Tina Turner's fortunes forever, the single reaching number seven in the US charts, its parent album of the same name selling over five million copies on its first run when released in May 1984, with an eventual tally of over 20 million units. "I had a fantastic time," said Jeff, "and we got blasted at the end of the session!"

The next icon requiring Beck's particular skills set was Rolling Stone Mick Jagger, who after 20 odd years of avoiding the temptation, had finally begun recording a solo album at Compass Point Studios in the Bahamas during the summer of 1984. "[The producer] Bill Laswell... said it's very important that we use people who have personalities," Jagger recalled to *Musician*'s Mark Hunter. "It's no good getting people who don't as it will come across on the record. Bill then said, 'You've worked with such good guitar players, you should really use someone good, like Jeff. And I thought 'Hmm, yeah, that'd be good'."

Though he didn't know it at the time, Beck was walking into a potential minefield by accepting Jagger's invitation to the dance.

---

* So impressed was Beck with Grover Jackson's three pick-up war machines, he ordered two more, both in 'DayGlo orange' to match the colour of his trainers.

When the Stones had signed a new record deal with CBS in 1983, a clause was opened for members of the group to pursue individual projects and Mick had jumped at the prospect. Keen to lose his associations with the sixties and reposition himself as a 'contemporary artist' in an increasingly youthful market, the Peter Pan-like Jagger was now ready to test the waters with a solo LP. Except of course, the Stones, and in particular his longtime Glimmer Twin, Keith Richards didn't like the idea at all. "The timing's very strange," Richards told anyone willing to listen, "bringing out... an obviously commercial album just before we were due to start on a new Stones record. I mean, if he'd done his favourite Irish folk songs with a lady harpist or have Liberace accompany him on some Frank Sinatra tunes... that would have been fine. [But] to my mind, a Mick Jagger album should be a ginormous event, not just another record. I told him it was dumb timing." Jagger, however, was not listening: "Well, they're not very keen, but they've all done things on their own, so they can't really say anything. Anyway, it's [1984], not 1964 any more."

Exhibiting a previously hidden gift for diplomacy, Beck kept his own counsel over Mick and Keef's growing feud and simply got on with the task at hand. And a very good job of it he did, too. Laying down guitar parts for six songs in all over a three-week period, Jeff's work on Jagger's first solo disc *She's The Boss* proved another small triumph. On 'Lonely At The Top', for instance, he was all wildness and edges, using the tremolo arm of his fifties Strat reissue to spruce up an otherwise traditional blues-rock song. 'Lucky In Love' saw Jeff take matters even further by adding dog barks, octave leaps and low-end growls to Mick's tale of a down-at-heel gambling man. With 'Hard Woman', the emphasis was again on enlivening a fairly ordinary tune as Beck's quicksilver solo turned an ambling, Celtic-themed ballad into something a bit more audacious, at least for a while. 'Just Another Night', on the other hand, saw Jeff tearing the wires from Jagger's Gibson J-200 acoustic and replacing them with electric strings to add a bit of flamenco-like passion to reggae star Sly Dunbar's bouncing electronic drum pattern. Unfortunately, little had changed since the guitarist's last encounter with Mick in early 1975. Solo album or not, everything still ran on 'Stones time', with the singer given to disappearing at short notice while Beck worked into the night on tracks: "Well, I was on his dollar." That said, Beck seemed to enjoy the overall experience, and readily agreed to work with Jagger in the future – an event made almost inevitable when *She's The Boss* sold a million copies in the US on its release in February 1985.

What Jeff did next, however, confounded all expectation. After 15 years of sniping at each other in the press, or simply pretending the other one didn't exist, Jeff Beck and Rod Stewart announced they were to tour in the summer of 1984. Together. "Well, I met him again at the Record Plant in LA and he threw his arms around me," said Beck. "I didn't hate him any more after that." Since parting ways so acrimoniously in 1969, the once dynamic duo had taken extraordinarily divergent paths, with each fulfilling their destiny in very different, albeit distinguished ways. As evidenced, Jeff's musical choices proved maverick, occasionally eccentric, but never less than interesting. Plotting Stewart's progress, on the other hand, could be tied down to one telling phrase: "The boy done good."

Having left behind the strident blues rock of JBG, the vocalist's time with The Faces was the stuff of legend: a five-year long drinking binge held together by an 'all for one, one for all' siege mentality that bestrode every calamity in its path until Stewart's parallel career as a solo artist ended the party once and for all. In fact, for every hit The Faces had, Rod damn near had two of his own, from 1971's 'Maggie May' to 'You Wear It Well', 'Farewell' and beyond. By 1976, Stewart was officially a superstar in his own right, as 'Sailing''s million-selling UK success paved the way for an onslaught on the States, where 'You're In My Heart', 'Hot Legs' and the ridiculous, but entertaining 'Da Ya Think I'm Sexy?' all reached the US Top Five. But each victory had successively chipped away at Rod's original roguish charm, with newsprint tales of Hollywood actresses, knicker-wearing and leopard-print spandex trousers far outweighing stories about 'beers with the boys'. Still, as the saying went, 'blonds have more fun' and Stewart's now peroxide locks were the living proof of it.

The first thawing between Jeff and Rod in 1982 was orchestrated by Carmine Appice, who had taken up the drum stool in Stewart's backing group after co-writing 'Da Ya Think I'm Sexy' with the singer. When Jeff and Rod failed to kill each other on sight at LA's Record Plant, Appice took it as a good sign, and one that might be worked on at a later date. The plot thickened further when Beck agreed to appear on Vanilla Fudge's reunion album, *Mystery*, in 1983, cutting solos for the tracks 'Jealousy' and 'My World Is Empty' under the pseudonym 'J. Toad'. Still working with Stewart at the time, Carmine suggested that Jeff have dinner with Rod and his band the next time he was in LA. When the ARMS tour arrived on the West Coast, the stars finally aligned and Beck took the plunge over a curry. "[Rod said] 'What about this new band of ours?'" said the guitarist. "This was right in front of his guys, but they seemed to think that it was a good idea, so..."

Beck and Stewart actually tested their own resolve in the following days by working on an idea for Jeff's own – long delayed – album, which will be returned to in due course. But the first fruits of their newly repaired friendship emerged with the release of Rod's 13th studio disc, *Camouflage*, in June 1984. A partial return to Stewart's rock roots after the cod-balladry of 'Sailing' and bum-shaking of 'Da Ya...', *Camouflage* also featured Beck's screaming leads on three cuts, including 'Bad To Me' and the single 'Infatuation', which reached number six in the American charts. Given that Jeff was still only at 'demo stage' for his own LP, the idea of he and Rod combining their star-power for a high-visibility (and highly profitable) US tour probably seemed like the best idea since the wheel to their respective managers. Even Jeff sounded vaguely hopeful: "I think they'll find a bit of room on the ticket for my name..."

If reports are to be believed, 'An Evening with Rod and Jeff' was originally structured to highlight both performers, with Beck opening the show for 30 minutes before Stewart took over with his own band. After an interval, the pair would then team up for a joint set featuring tunes from Rod's new album followed by a few vintage cuts from JBG, including the likes of 'Shapes Of Things', 'Plynth' and 'I Ain't Superstitious': "The meaty stuff," Jeff said. After this portion of the show, Beck would again disappear to let Rod get on with "his thing" before returning for the encores. As Stewart was one of America's biggest-selling artists at the time, this seemed an entirely reasonable and exceedingly generous distribution of labour, with both parties benefiting from the arrangement. Suffice to say, it didn't quite work out that way.

Scheduled to run for 70 nights over a four-month period, the Stewart/Beck bill lasted just six dates in all before Jeff called it quits: "I stopped because I didn't like Calgary. I wanted to go home after that. It would have been a musical disaster for me to continue. My career would have been in shreds. I'd have been a millionaire, though it wasn't a very good trade-off." In stark contrast to Beck's original hopes, his contributions onstage appeared limited to a measly run-through of 'The Pump' before Rod joined him for a medley of 'I Ain't Superstitious/Rock My Plimsoul'. From there it was a quick gallop through 'Bad To Me' and 'Infatuation' before Stewart returned to safer waters with his 1981 hit 'Young Turks'. "I actually thought he wanted to get his jeans back on and get out of the velvet," said Jeff, "[but] he wanted to use me as a sort of cabaret: 'Here's the little guitar player'." For Beck, the equation was simple: "He was the star, I was the sideshow." For Rod, it was 1969 all over again, albeit with the polarities reversed: "It was so good to work with Jeff, it really was – until the tour started. And I still love to play with him. [But] he's his own worst enemy as many of us are."

Surprisingly, there was no enmity between Stewart and Beck following the latter's decision to pull the plug so early into the tour. In fact, the singer sounded as if he was expecting it all along. "I don't think Rod thought I'd last more than a week with him," Jeff later recalled. "He said he was actually amazed I turned up on the first night." For some, Beck's choice to call time on the enterprise might have smacked of sour grapes, the trading of roles between 'master' and 'servant' proving simply too much for his ego. For others, the fault may have been with Jeff's distaste of Rod's pop-star theatrics, a view certainly echoed by the guitarist in later years. "[It was] like vaudeville with him shaking his ass. I just couldn't take it seriously."

In the end, the true cause was irrelevant. After four years of various sessions, guest appearances, favours to friends and gallons of used car polish, Beck's withdrawal from "The Rod Stewart Revue" had forced his hand. It was again time to get working on a new album.

Chapter 19

Lost In The Eighties

Since Jeff Beck released *There & Back* in July 1980, the musical landscape had changed beyond all recognition. After punk threatened so much and even delivered some of it, new wave had fleetingly run with the ball before synth-pop came along and threw everything back in the blender. An ephemeral movement, as the best ones so often were, synth-pop (or futurism to give its other name) had made stars of Gary Numan, Duran Duran, Japan, Soft Cell, Depeche Mode and a host of others. Festooned with wedge haircuts, frilly shirts and immaculately crafted make-up, these performers appealed to a generation that had missed glam the first time round and were now looking for something a little more exotic to wear at the school disco. But underneath all the robot moves, retina-detaching stares, J.G Ballard lyrical imagery and faux-existential angst, something potentially wondrous was also happening. Synthesisers and drum machines were gradually taking over the world.

In reality, both the synth and drum machine had both been around for a while, with early Moogs making an appearance on sixties records by The Monkees, The Beatles and even Simon & Garfunkel, while The Bee Gees' Robin Gibb and Sly Stone dabbled with electronic drums at the same time. Ironically, the progressive rockers punk was so keen to dethrone also used such technology, with ELP's Keith Emerson and Yes' Rick Wakeman both early converts to the synthetic cause. Yet, it was the pioneering work of German groups such as Faust, Can and Kraftwerk, and David Bowie's 'Berlin Trilogy' in the late seventies that struck a profound chord with young musicians – turning their heads away from hackneyed blues and metal sounds towards a radically different agenda.

As technology became cheaper, so guitars and snares were exchanged for Roland Jupiter Fours and CR-78s, with their 'pre-sets' and in-built sequencers making them easily programmable – albeit occasionally temperamental things – to use. As a result, unlike Jan Hammer, one did not have to be a virtuoso to gain dominion of a synth or a 'beat box'. Instead, just a modicum of interest, degree of persistence or the ability to understand the technical manual that accompanied such devices could reap rich melodic rewards. In this respect, synth-pop was little different from punk – returning music to people brave or enthused enough to simply press the buttons and see what happened. As a result, songs such as The Human League's 'Don't You Want Me', Visage's 'Fade To Grey' and Gary Numan's immortal 'Cars' became statutory listening as the eighties bloomed, their influence being steadily absorbed by mainstream acts and record producers. With the advent of samplers and Midi, enabling the form to blossom in even bolder directions, that influence only grew stronger.

Across the Atlantic, things were also changing fast. In August 1981, Music Television or 'MTV' was launched, immediately impacting on US culture and soon trickling out to the watching world. With the advent of a TV channel wholly devoted to promotional videos, image and fashion became even more fundamental to the marketing of pop and rock stars – their choice of shoes now as important as their vocal prowess – and in a number of cases, perhaps more so. As a result, a new breed of camera-friendly hyper-star was born, with Michael Jackson, Madonna and Prince birthing lookalikes in every Stateside shopping mall. Even previously gnarly propositions like Bruce Springsteen and ZZ Top were not immune to the need for change, shaving their beards or growing them more in an effort to cultivate their style and sell more records. From 'Kings of the Grand Gesture' such as U2's Bono and re-animated punk Billy Idol to the exploding hairstyles of Cyndi Lauper and Flock Of Seagulls, MTV had changed the game forever.

So far, Jeff Beck had managed to avoid – or more accurately hide from – most of the insanity. But he was aware it was there, ready to snatch him up when his defences were low. "The eighties were bereft of any music I would want to be involved in," he later said. "You had to have a video which was cost prohibitive for me. Everything had to be video for MTV and I didn't like the idea of power rotation and force-feeding people with stuff on TV. Rock'n'roll is a moment, it's an exciting jab in the arm [and] I didn't go along with that force-feeding and power rotation." But try as he might, there was no escape. By 1984, he had already starred in a promo for Rod Stewart's 'Infatuation', hamming it up uncomfortably with his 'Turner' as Rod minced his way around a swimming pool. Unless he remained diligent, further such traps lay ahead.

As time came to show, Jeff could avoid neither the rigours of programming nor the tortures of film-making when recording and promoting his new album, on which he began pre-production at New York's Record Plant at the end of April, 1984. It was tentatively titled 'Get Workin'', and Beck had scored one of America's hottest young producers, Nile Rodgers, to aid his return. A composer, arranger and superb funk guitarist, Rodgers started his career as a session musician before forming disco act Chic with bassist Bernard Edwards and drummer Tony Thompson in 1977. Using singers Norma Jean Wright and Luci Martin to front the band, Chic literally owned the dance floor in the late seventies, with a steady stream of hits including 'Le Freak', 'I Want Your Love' and 'Good Times' providing an immaculate soundtrack for clubbers across the world. By the eighties, Rodgers' production skills were also in high demand, as he racked up international hits for David Bowie ('Let's Dance'), INXS ('Original Sin'), Duran Duran ('The Reflex') and Madonna ('Like A Virgin'). In short, Nile was a good catch for Jeff Beck.

Of course, CBS/Epic Records' installation of Rodgers in the producer's chair was a quite deliberate attempt on their part to reposition Beck as a still relevant and important artist in a bold new era of bold new superstars. "They've been the most wonderful, enduring record company," Jeff told *Guitar World*. "They have respect for me and haven't pushed me about. Any other one would have potted me away by now! But nowadays record companies really want hits." Yet, behind the scenes, Epic's reluctance to have Beck record another all-instrumental album after the reasonable, but not overwhelming success of *There & Back* had proved a stumbling block between their A&R department and the guitarist: "Well, I was told discreetly to forget the idea of another instrumental album," Jeff later confirmed, "so I went and sulked for three years."

In fact, Beck had tried to force the record company's hand over this issue in 1983, when he approached the renowned electronic musician Vangelis in the hope of collaborating on a 'vocal-free' album. Having been suitably enthused by the Greek composer's rousing soundtrack to the 1981 movie *Chariots Of Fire*, Jeff was hoping to fuse his own guitar style to Vangelis' lush keyboard patterns. However, when the latter's house burned down and forced him to return home, the project crumbled before a single note was played. For the first time since 1973's 'Black Cat Moan', Beck would now have to step in front of the microphone. In Nile Rodgers' mind, Jeff's previous lack of singing experience did not create a problem. "He insisted," Beck later told journalist Steven Rosen. "He said there was nothing wrong in that, it was the norm in 1984, people who couldn't even sing were being sampled." The two would wrestle over the matter throughout the making of the LP.

Despite Beck's concerns regarding vocals, sessions for his latest record began well enough, with Rodgers like so many before him simply astounded by Jeff's abilities on guitar. "I've never seen anyone play guitar like Beck, with the exception of Hendrix," he said. "Beck just knocks me out. The guitar is part of his body. He holds it and it's making music. Then he puts it on the ground and it's still making music." Jeff too, seemed genuinely pleased with early progress, remaining hopeful that his vision of bolting a "Chicago blues feel onto modern-day technology" might work well. But Niles' status as New York's top producer made for frequent interruptions in their schedule, with visits from pop and soul icons a regular occurrence. "I was in the studio overdubbing with Niles and Diana Ross arrived," Jeff recalled. "We were introduced and she said 'My God, it's so hot in here. I mean, your music's so hot. Would you like to put some heat on my record one day?'"

As Rodgers had co-produced Ross' multi-platinum 1980 album *Diana*, it was perhaps unsurprising that the former Supreme was keen to commune with him while working on her latest effort – and indeed, steal Beck away while she was there: "We went to Soundworks studio and I was in awe of that golden voice. I did a couple of tracks, but it was a bit of a naff album. I really wanted to play on 'Ain't No Mountain High Enough'."

The results of Jeff's fleeting visit to Soundworks can be heard on 'Forever Young', Ross' cover of the old Bob Dylan tune that subsequently appeared on her 1984 LP *Swept Away*. While Beck might have respected Diana Ross' status as a genuine soul/R&B legend, he seemed to have less time for another of Niles' previous clients, who appeared increasingly impatient to have her producer quickly returned to her virginal arms. "Basically, I was being squeezed in between two Madonna singles," Jeff later told *Musician*. "She kept coming in, saying 'How's it going with Nile? When's he going to be free?' I said 'He ain't going to be free until I'm finished. Piss off!'"

By the time Beck temporarily broke off from the project to begin touring with Rod Stewart in early June, four semi-complete tracks had been recorded with Rodgers, two featuring Jeff on lead vocals. But when the Rod tour collapsed, the opportunity to reconvene came rather more quickly than anyone had anticipated. With Nile now committed to other interim duties, Jeff was left potentially twiddling his thumbs unless a new producer could be found. He turned to Arthur Baker to seal the gap: "It was Arthur Baker's turn then. It was a great move, because... he was going in saying, 'Hey, I'm taking over Nile's job now.' But he was great. He didn't say, 'Oh God, those four Nile tracks have to go.' He loved them."

By 1984, Arthur Baker was almost as much in demand as Nile Rodgers, though for somewhat different reasons. A former DJ from Boston, Baker came to real prominence as a producer for Tommy Boy Records in 1982, when his work on Afrika Bambaataa & The Soul Sonic Force's 'Planet Rock' scored the label its first real success. Turning his attentions to the growing remix market, Arthur then provided Cyndi Lauper and Bruce Springsteen with two monster singles: the perma-bright 'Girls Just Wanna Have Fun' and the slightly more adult 'Dancing In The Dark'. A huge fan of Kraftwerk's synthetic textures, a stern advocate of New York's dazzling new hip-hop scene and an early exponent of interloping, looping and sampling technologies, Baker was representative of a whole new breed of producer – and one potentially capable of providing Beck with a runaway hit.

Ultimately, Baker's arrival seemed to bring new impetus to the project, as he, Jeff and an occasionally available Nile Rodgers all cobbled together a complete recording. They also invited a selection of old friends and new acquaintances in to help. One of these was singer Jimmy Hall. A true Southern gentleman, Hall was then best known for his work with Wet Willie, a soulful R&B-flavoured rock band he had formed with his brother Jack and sister Donna in 1969. Enjoying several hits, the biggest of which was 'Keep On Smilin', Wet Willie kept Jimmy busy throughout the seventies and early eighties. However, but for family ties, things might have been very different. "Wet Willie formed in 1969, and we soon ended up supporting Vanilla Fudge in Arkansas," Hall remembered. "Anyway, Carmine and Timmy said they were talking to Jeff at that point about putting together a four-piece 'super group'. They asked whether I'd consider being the singer. Well, I was a huge fan of Jeff's and told them that I was flattered, but my own band were about to sign a record deal. Still, there were a few phone calls back and forth. Anyway, somewhere around then, Jeff had his auto accident, which kind of made the decision for everybody. I went ahead with Wet Willie and Carmine and Timmy formed Cactus."

Fate lent a helping hand in 1970 when Jeff and Jimmy finally met following Beck's stalled experiment at Motown studios: "Well, Cozy and Jeff came down to check out Macon and its studios after they'd been to Motown. We hung out for a few days, ate some soul food and we showed them the town. Soon, we were playing together. I was singing 'Forty Miles Of Bad Road' and some made-up blues. It was recorded, but Jeff and his manager Ernest kept a tight control on all tapes, so I never got to hear it." As the years progressed, the two kept in touch, with Hall joining Beck occasionally onstage whenever he was in the South. "I was there when BBA played Georgia," Hall said. "Just standing on the side of the stage, soaking it all up. Then I got the call to come on. We'd do 'Going Down' or 'You Shook Me'. I'm not sure BBA were the perfect vehicle for him, but they rocked with lots of power. Then Jeff said to me 'One of these days, we've got to get you into the studio, one of these days we're going to do it'."

In 1984, Beck finally made good on his promise, "The keyboard player Chuck Leavell and Jeff were working on the *She's The Boss* sessions, and my name came up," continued Jimmy. "Now I knew Chuck from working together in Betts, Hall, Leavell and Trucks in 1982, 1983 and Jeff asked him for my number. My wife was just about to give birth to my second son when I actually got the call. Jeff said 'Can you fly to New York, meet me at the Record Plant and sing some tunes?' Of course I wanted to do it, but I needed to talk with my wife first! She was cool:'Go to New York, sing with Jeff and just get an open return.' Jeff was great about it. He said 'Anytime you need to go home, just go.' So I got on the plane and headed East."

Arriving on June 20, Hall spent three days at The Record Plant cutting vocals: "I just wanted to do a good job, prove myself to be something other than a skinny white kid from Alabama. And in the end, I had a ball." By the time he returned home, Jimmy was a father for the second time. "June 24, Sunday morning, I seem to remember, my son was born. Well, we decided to name him 'Alexander Jeffrey' because he was born on Jeff's birthday. Of course, Jeff later met Alex and my other son[s]. He even sent him a card on his 21st birthday." Having suffered at the mike himself for too long, Jimmy Hall was Beck's first choice when he finally persuaded Nile Rodgers and Arthur Baker to 'stop the pain' and get in a real singer on the album. "I'd always wanted to work with Jimmy, but I wasn't living in America to ever put something together," he said. "He was tied to home and I wasn't going anywhere either. But as I was doing the album in the States, Jimmy was only half an hour's flight away."

Another musician brought in to enhance proceedings was Doug Wimbish. A gifted, innovative bassist, Wimbish had already played on some of the finest recordings ever to come out of the New York hip–hop and rap scene. Alongside guitarist Skip McDonald and drummer Keith LeBlanc, Doug's planet-eating bass sound had been responsible for propping up Grandmaster Flash's 'The Message,' Melle Mel's album *White Lines* and Angie Stone's debut single, 'Funk You Up', to name but a few. A Sugar Hill Records regular and longtime comrade of Arthur Baker, Wimbish was over the moon when he got the call. "Arthur had his own studio and was the 'go to' guy at that time for primo remixes," he said. "I mean, everyone wanted to work with him. Bruce, Cyndi Lauper, the Stones, and we just hit it off. Whenever there was a session Arthur would bring me in, and that's how I met Jeff." However, Doug was also fully aware of Nile Rodgers' continuing association with the record: "Nile and his [sometime] co-producer Bernard Edwards were rated at that time and he'd become so popular, as had Arthur. So it was like two different camps on the project."

By the autumn of 1984, Rodgers and Baker had concluded work on the album, leaving Beck to fiddle about with the final mix until he was satisfied with the results. After nearly six months working in the States, one would have thought Jeff was due a rest, but he wasn't quite through with playing guitar just yet. "When we met at Electric Ladyland Studios, Beck and I just hit it off instantly," said Wimbish. "The next thing I know, I'm getting a call from his manager Ernest Chapman who said, 'Hey Doug, I was just talking to Jeff and we were wondering would you like to come over to London for a gathering'..." The 'gathering' was actually Beck's excuse to pull together musicians for a possible tour in support of his new record, with band rehearsals conducted at the Brixton Academy in January 1985. During this period, Jeff and Doug also involved themselves in a brief alliance with The Art Of Noise, an avant-garde synth outfit formed by esteemed producer Trevor Horn, arranger Anne Dudley and music journalist Paul Morley. It was during these sessions that the alternative theme tune to Channel Four's *The Tube* was recorded. As mentioned, this was a scintillating blast of early techno meets hard rock with the addition of some stunning solo flourishes from Beck, and it remains a crime that the theme is still gathering dust in someone's drawer to this day.

After an ongoing promotional campaign by Epic Records throughout the spring of 1985, which drummed up considerable interest in Beck's return as a solo artist, the guitarist's new disc was finally released in June of that year. Its title, *Flash*, though short and sweet, was potentially loaded with meaning and promise – both a knowing nod to Jeff's unique brand of guitar fireworks and a bold statement of intent from the artist himself. Regrettably, while it delivered admirably on the first part of the equation, it sometimes fell well short on the second. Of the four tracks produced by Nile Rodgers, only two could be deemed essential additions to the Beck catalogue. Album opener 'Ambitious' was an excellent attempt to update Jeff for the eighties, its mechanistic dance groove, growling Jimmy Hall vocal and 'chain-gang' drum pattern steadily building to a crescendo before Beck tore the doors off the song with a mind-bending solo. "Jeff just played the shit out of it," said engineer Jason Corsaro. "Every time you thought he'd played the most amazing lick you'd ever heard, he did it again and again and again." With its endless trills, screaming harmonics and a whammy bar abused to breaking point, Beck's head-on collision with his Jackson Soloist on 'Ambitious' was undoubtedly the high point of the album.

'Get Workin'' was also a creditable effort on Rodgers' part to align Jeff with the demands of a new generation, its funky, 'behind the beat' feel mining similar musical territory to David Bowie's 'Let's Dance'. Sung by Beck in a low and surprisingly soulful voice, the tune also featured a novel lead break from the guitarist, with Jeff popping the strings of his '53 Tele against their pick-ups, the treble rolled right back so as to enhance the overall percussive effect: "It's like what funk bass players do when they 'snap'." 'Night After Night' and 'Stop, Look And Listen' again provided ample opportunity to admire Beck's way with six strings as he waltzed his way impeccably through verse and chorus. But neither song was particularly memorable, their presence on the LP little more than an excuse for Niles to endlessly trigger the 'orchestral stab' setting of his Synclavier II keyboard.

Arthur Baker's work was equally hit or miss. On the one hand, 'Gets Us All In The End' was a tremendous tune, roaring in on a psychotic, backwards-sounding solo from Jeff before Jimmy Hall again justified the cost of his air fare: "When they played the song to me, it just seemed so depressing. The lyric ran 'Life's so hard, it gets us all in the end...' It sounded like someone who wanted to hang themselves: no hope, no use in living, life's just too hard. I said, 'Can we put some hope in it? What about 'Love's so hard?' Make it about a relationship, you know, 'Love gets us every time' instead of all the doom and gloom. So they liked that, we took a new road and I think it came out as a much better song." And one with a positively Herculean vocal take: "There was no time for key changes and the key was high on the song, kind of like opera. Arthur and Jeff were saying to me, 'Are you sure you can do this?' So, when I hit the highest note on the chorus, Beck jumped out of his chair, he was applauding so much, I thought I'd hit a home run."* However, the other Baker-produced track, 'Ecstasy', was a profound disappointment – its tempo and construction sounding slow

---

* Jimmy was subsequently nominated for a 'Best Rock Vocal Performance' Grammy for his work on 'Gets Us All In The End'.

and jarring – though Beck's resurrection of his Roland G-707 guitar synth for the solo section did pique the interest temporarily.

Of *Flash*'s remaining notable tracks, two seemed to have an element of appeasing 'old school' fans about them, while the other was surely recorded for the purpose of giving Jeff a long-needed hit single. With Tony Hymas' instrumental 'You Know, We Know', Beck hinted at the sound and style of *There & Back*, his guitar gliding over the melody in the same mad, but magisterial fashion it had on 'The Golden Road' and 'The Pump' some four years before. Jan Hammer's 'Escape' was even more whimsical. Full of odd percussive effects, tears and cuts in the rhythm, and a glistening Fairlight synthesiser guitar sample Hammer had already made his own on the million-selling 'Miami Vice Theme', 'Escape' was "mood music for the mid eighties". Memorable only for Jeff's against-the-grain solo interludes, the Beck/Rodgers-produced 'Escape' still somehow managed to win Best Instrumental Performance at the 1985 Grammys: "Go figure," Jeff might have said.

When Beck cut 'People Get Ready' with Rod Stewart, he must have thought all his Christmases had come at once. A chiming, soulful ballad Jeff first played live with BBA (and almost recorded for the band's debut album), 'People Get Ready' had already been a hit for its writer, Curtis Mayfield, in 1965 and was surely due a remake. However, the song almost didn't get off the ground at all. After their 'kiss and make up' curry in late 1982, Stewart was eager to get working immediately and asked Beck if he had any suitable demos that could be adapted for his voice, but nothing came to mind. Fortunately, a spot of lunch at former Cactus keyboardist Duane Hitchings' home in Venice Beach, California solved the problem: "[Duane] had a guitar lying about and he wanted to show me his desk [console]," Beck told *Guitar Player*'s Steve Rosen. "It was such a rotten guitar that the only chord in intonation was D. And I thought, 'What can I play in D?' He got me a fantastic sound on it and I continued playing. And within seconds, he had dialled in this breathy voice and I came up with 'de de dee dee' [the guitar hook to 'People Get Ready']. We took it up to Rod that night." By next day, with Beck behind the production desk, the track was on tape: "He sings that stuff better than anybody else. I thought it was brilliant, two hours work boiled down to a few magic moments."

Despite its undoubted quality, 'People Get Ready' languished in the vaults for two further years with Epic Records biding their time until the single was ripe for release. By August 1985, that time had come. To enhance its chances of gaining blanket rotation on MTV, a twee, but well-meaning video was shot with a hobo-style Beck hopping trains across America on his way to meet Stewart for a friendly hug in an unnamed Western town. "I was glad about doing [it]," Jeff later said, "because people could see we didn't hate each other. That it was all good, so to speak." Filmed in sepia tone, and featuring a cast of firemen, cowboys, field workers, cute children and Jeff and Rod in toe-curlingly tight trousers, the clip showed that no demographic had been spared by Epic's marketing department in their efforts to make the song a success. However, 'People Get Ready' inexplicably stalled at number 48 in the US charts, with the single actually failing to make the UK charts at all.*

Keen to see a substantial return on its investment, Epic Records again dug into *Flash* for another potential hit, this time turning its attention to 'Ambitious'. Though the song tanked when released in October 1985, its accompanying video was an absolute hoot, with Jeff mock-auditioning a score of would-be vocalists – famous and otherwise – to sing the song. "The promo was a cattle call made through connections at A&M studios," explained Jimmy Hall. "They got a Madonna 'lookalike', and put fake hair under her arms, and had mad characters like Hervé Villechaize [Tattoo from 'Fantasy Island'] and Cheech Marin, from Cheech & Chong. There were other celebrities too, like Parker Stevenson, Marilyn McCoo and Herb Alpert, who was just so cool. They threw everything into that video, including the kitchen sink. Ten in the morning until 10 at night with a cast of thousands."

Aside from Hall, who inevitably won the audition – only fair, as he did sing the original tune – Donny Osmond also made a comedic, but utterly convincing stab at becoming Jeff's new front man. "Donny was such a down to earth nice guy who just wanted to deliver," said Jimmy. "He took me aside and said, 'Show me how the song goes, I want to do this right.' So I coached him on his vocal. It sounded really great." When filming concluded at LA's Chaplin's Studios, Beck had a special

---

* A 1992 UK re-release fared slightly better with the song getting to a semi-respectable number 49.

treat in store for the winner. "After the shoot, Jeff said, 'All right, I'm giving you a lift back to the hotel'," Hall remembered. "Well, we jump in this shiny red hot rod convertible and he's revving this baby up and down Sunset Boulevard. It was a great way to end the day..."

Without a real hit to prop it up or give it legs, *Flash* had to make do with its original meagre chart placing of number 42 on the US charts, while reaching a rather desultory 83 in the UK. For Nile Rodgers, Beck quipped, "It's probably a blot on his career." That said, at least one British music paper gave the album a decent review: "*Flash* is an engaging sortie into the field of funk metal mayhem that also nestles alongside a collection of eighties blues and soul ditties redolent of Johnny 'Guitar' Watson and Elvin Bishop at their best," wrote *Sounds'* Andy Hurt. "All this and more, more, more. Yippee." In spite of Hurt's unerring enthusiasm, *Flash* was – and is – a hard record to love. Though Jeff fought hard to "humanise" its synthetic backbone, bringing in stickmen like Jimmy Bralower, Carmine Appice and Curly Smith to either programme drum machines for a more organic feel or even add live parts of their own, the disc still has a crisp, almost brittle quality more suited to pop than rock. No bad thing if championed by a more temperate artist, but hardly the stuff of a 'classic' Beck release. "It was in the middle of the robot music phase, and I just didn't think that I could attract any of the musicians I wanted to play with using that approach," he later said. "In the end, I was caught up in a New York whirlwind. Nile was producing Madonna and Duran Duran and I just didn't feel that I was given a fair crack of the whip. Still, the two songs I wanted, 'Escape' and 'People Get Ready', which really had little or nothing to do with Niles, ended up getting recognised."

Despite the cool sales accorded *Flash*, there was still plenty of interest from guitar magazines and their readers concerning how exactly Beck had produced the molten-sounding lead breaks featured on the album. The results were surprising. In addition to his use of the Jackson Soloist, '53 and '58 Telecasters, 'Marriot' Strat, 100-watt Seymour Duncan Convertible amp and Pro Co Rat distortion unit, Jeff had also entirely dispensed with guitar picks, now preferring to use the fingers of his right hand to sound, tease and torture notes. "We used to do a lot of booze [when touring] and I'd drop the picks all the time," he explained. "The embarrassment of constantly looking for them onstage during a song... it just wasn't worth it. It was like falling off a bike and trying to continue the race. Somehow, I pulled it off with just fingers so my days as a Chet Atkins fan paid off. Then, I found I liked it, [and] could get more out of five fingers than just one pick."

Having first begun the process of returning to 'finger style' during the *There & Back* tour of 1980/81, Beck soon became so comfortable with the technique that he used it almost exclusively when playing alongside Eric Clapton and Jimmy Page for ARMS in 1983. "Actually, Eric had seen me doing it during the seventies, and said, 'Drop all the country shit,'" Jeff laughed. "Then what did he do? Four soddin' country albums." Enjoying the visceral thrill of "flesh on the string", Beck used the nail of his first finger when negotiating "the fast stuff", while pulling, snapping or picking the strings with the remaining digits for slower passages or country-style rolls. "I listened to Chet Atkins [when I was young] and tried to copy him, but it was a dead end street," he told *Guitar World*. "After all the labour and heartbreak, everyone would go, 'Yeah, great, great copy of Chet Atkins'. I can play country-style within reason, Merle Travis kind of stuff, but that's not quite the way I play now... it's more bluegrass with rock'n'roll in mind." It was a 'hybrid' style, allowing him to produce bell-like tones from even the most distorted amplifier settings, and Beck would only improve with practice, his decision to abandon the pick in favour of a multi-fingered assault reaping extraordinary results in coming years.

If *Flash* has sold in the millions, there would no doubt have been a major tour to promote the album. But when sales proved modest rather than stupendous, all such plans were abandoned. Instead, Beck spent most of the summer and autumn of 1985 either doing interviews, the odd session or guest appearance with other artists. In August, for instance, he was the cover star of *Auto Week*, relishing the opportunity to talk about his ever-growing car collection rather than once again explain the worth of his latest record. "The rods are an escape from rock'n'roll," he said tellingly. "I have to have an even balance [so] one has to offset the other. I'm so fed up with the music thing." Pictured in the magazine surrounded by various '32 and '34 Fords (all in one stage or another of completion) and a sparkling 1984 Corvette positioned in pride of place on the driveway of his mansion home, Jeff seemed lights years away from his day job: "I just love turning the key and watching peoples' faces."When faced with Beck's obvious love for rods, one couldn't help but recall Hollywood star Steve McQueen's answer when asked whether he preferred acting to racing cars: "Well, I'm not sure whether I'm an actor that races or a racer who acts..."

At around this time, Jeff added a lick or two to 'Back It Up', a track from Earth, Wind & Fire singer Phil Bailey's solo LP *Inside Out*, while also joining former Police front man Sting onstage for a bluesy interlude at Los Angeles' Greek Theatre, a benefit gig in aid of cancer research. Beck's contribution to Sting's set can be heard on 'I've Been Down So Long', which was later released on the 1986 charity disc *Live! For Life*.

Perhaps the most interesting dalliance Beck involved himself with was a one-off experiment with former Stray Cats rhythm section Lee Rocker and Slim Jim Phantom. Only four years before, The Stray Cats had been at the forefront of an electrifying rockabilly revival that briefly threatened to up-end synth-pop's domination of the charts. Led by Cliff Gallup-channelling guitarist Brian Setzer, the group's miraculous debut single, 'Runaway Boys', and subsequent follow-ups 'Stray Cat Strut' and 'Rock This Town' gained them a huge following, with their first album selling over a million copies in the US alone. However, interest in their reanimated brand of fifties rock'n'roll proved temporary and the band went their separate ways in 1984. Since then, Lee and Jim had been working with former David Bowie guitarist Earl Slick, but were more than happy to accommodate the rockabilly-mad Beck when he suggested a jam. Ultimately, the results were disappointing – "Jim wanted me to be like 'Jeff Beck', they wanted to be themselves, and the two things didn't work" – though the experience did cause Jeff to dabble with the idea of doing a rock'n'roll album of his own. In typically contrary fashion, the guitarist also expressed interest in pursuing a "classical-type" disc with a full backing orchestra during the same period.

Both dreams would have to wait a while as in the spring of 1986 it was announced that Beck was to hit the road for a limited series of dates in Japan where, sales-wise at least, *Flash* had performed considerably better than elsewhere. His backing band was to be a mixture of old and new friends, with Jan Hammer and Simon Phillips returning to the fold while *Flash* cohorts Jimmy Hall and Doug Wimbish took on vocal and bass duties respectively. Significantly, Carlos Santana would also be part of the proceedings, appearing as a 'special guest' with Beck. In his own way as much a guitar legend as Jeff, Santana's expressive, fluid runs and Latin-tinged rock songs had made him difficult to avoid during the seventies, with multi-platinum albums such as *Abraxas*, *Amigos* and *Moonflower* spanning that decade in some style. Unfortunately, the eighties had been a less fertile period thus far, with only the odd Top 20 single to add to his previous successes. However, Carlos and his group remained a strong live draw both in the US and abroad, where his name on a concert ticket was still capable of drumming up gate receipts. Combined with Beck's enduring Japanese profile, the presence of Santana ensured the tour could be nothing but a profitable affair.

After rehearsals at S.I.R studios and a loose warm-up at the Greek Theatre, the ensemble arrived in Nagano, Japan on June 1 for their first date at Karuizawa Prince Hotel's Open Air theatre, playing before a crowd of several thousand. "That was my first big rock'n'roll gig," remembered Doug Wimbish. "That's the concert that busted it all open for me, and Jeff was the guy behind it. It's still a milestone in my life. That man helped me find my voice."

After a fine set from Santana, Beck took to the stage to the sounds of 'Star Cycle', immediately finding his old partner Jan Hammer a willing foil for another night of "fireworks". "It was just wonderful," said Jan. "Jeff and I hadn't been on stage for three years, so it was great to get back out there and do it." According to Wimbish, it was almost impossible to stop the two when they started playing: "When they meet up, they just want to play all day," he confirmed. "There are certain musicians who you can just feel through the shape of the notes. Jan and Jeff are a match made in heaven, from the frequencies they use, the way they play, to the sheer challenge of it. And when Jan starts licking those lips, it's game over. It's a masterclass watching those two guys play. They just become one string. Just question, answer, question, answer, answer, answer, answer. Astounding."

Playing a funky yellow Strat for much of the gig, Beck and his band drew on over two decades' worth of material for the show, with old favourites such as 'Going Down' and 'Freeway Jam' rubbing shoulders with Jeff's latest single – a combustible version of The Troggs' 1965 hit 'Wild Thing'. Once described as "the best garage rock song ever", 'Wild

Thing"s thrilling amateurism had been behind much of its original appeal. Yet in Beck hands, it more resembled Jimi Hendrix's version of the tune, with his guitar grunting and growling its way through verse and chorus before the squealing harmonics and whammy bar theatrics took over. "When Jeff gets that smile on, you can feel the excitement," said Wimbish. "Some guitar players want to be cool all the time. Not Jeff, fuck that shit. He gets excited and then you get excited."*

At encore time, it really was every man for himself, as Beck, Santana and their respective groups piled onstage for "a huge fucking party". Joining them at this juncture was Toto's Steve Lukather. A recent addition to the pantheon of modern day guitar heroes whose outro solo on 1982's 'Rosanna' featured some of the most complex lead passages ever committed to tape, Lukather was also a planet-sized fan of Beck. "God," he once concluded, "plays guitar with Jeff Beck's hands." The resultant jam also included former Jimi Hendrix drummer/ vocalist Buddy Miles, who was working with Carlos Santana at the time. "A very special moment for me was during soundcheck," said Simon Phillips. "I swing around on my drum stool... and there was Buddy Miles on the back of my riser checking out the kit with this huge smile. He was just a sweetheart."

The subsequent encores, which included a three-guitar pile-up entitled 'Super Boogie' and a sterling rendition of 'People Get Ready', brought out the very best of those present. "So many legends on that tour. Jeff, Carlos Santana, Buddy Miles," said Jimmy Hall. "The crowd went wild, singing along. Steve Lukather, Carlos and Jeff jamming together, it was just a great atmosphere." And one, it has to be said, ably held together by Simon Phillips, who was working overtime as a human metronome while those in front of him went to hell in a hand basket. "For Jeff, the drummer is the key," confirmed Doug Wimbish. "He starts there and it gives him the fuel. It's a primary human instinct for him, the drums. If he's got a drummer behind him that sets fire to his ass, gets him moving, then it's all there for him. That's why he loves Simon – Simon gives him fire." With two songs already behind

---

* Released in July 1986, 'Wild Thing' – replete with a heavily processed, vocoder-assisted vocal from Jeff and a quite mad guitar solo – did not bother the charts.

them, it was time to bring things to a close, but no one was exactly sure how. "Well, backstage for the final encore, everyone was saying we need something big to go out with," said Hall. "Buddy Miles suggested 'Johnny Be Goode', saying 'Everyone knows the song'. Jeff wasn't sure, though. He thought it was a bit of an old stalwart. But by the time everyone had jammed three solos and we'd got the crowd singing, it was utter madness. Buddy got me to jump on his back and the two of us were racing across the stage, trying not to fall off."

Inevitably, the night didn't end onstage, as Beck and his merry pranksters partied on into the wee small hours of the morning in the plush grounds of the Prince's Hotel. "I remember driving electric golf carts around in the dark with our lights off as fast as these things would go," said Phillips. "Jeff was in one cart and I was in another with about five or six people hanging off the side. We were intent on colliding with each other but somehow managed to miss!"

Striking up a friendship that would see them combine their musical talents in Toto and several other projects over the next two decades, Phillips and Steve Lukather also proved to be the best of "beer buddies". "Ha! Those two boys had a good time that evening," said Doug. "If I'm remembering right, they took those golf carts out and had a drunken ride around the fucking hotel." For Simon, Jeff's idea to bring Lukather along to the party was among his very best. "Well, meeting Luke of course was quite an event and [it's been] a lasting relationship ever since, and yes, I think he might have been one of my 'passengers' on my golf cart! Little did we know at the time that we'd be in the same band together for over 18 years."

Concluding with two nights at Tokyo's Budokan Theatre where The Bangles offered able support, the Beck/Santana Japanese dates still brings a smile to all those involved. "The 'Hot Rod Man'," smiled Doug Wimbish. "Jeff represents to me a James Dean kind of thing, kind of a timeless cool. And those fingers have got some real grease underneath them. Great tour."

For Beck, Wimbish and Phillips, things didn't end in Japan. Within months, the trio found themselves hard at work on Mick Jagger's second solo album, *Primitive Cool*, which was recorded at Holland's Wisseloord Studios and reggae star Eddie Grant's Blue Wave complex in Barbados during late 1986/early 1987. "I'd met Mick in late 1985," said Doug. "He and Jeff had done *She's The Boss* and Jagger was thinking of making another record with a view to touring. So Jeff put my name in the hat for the project. Then there was a huge cattle-call audition and a couple of days later I got the phone call saying I'd got the gig. Strangely, all the musicians that made it through were all replaced or moved on, except for me, Simon and, of course, Jeff."

In fact, Jagger was scheduled to start *Primitive Cool* some months earlier, but the sudden death of keyboardist Ian Stewart from a heart attack in December 1985 had stunned The Rolling Stones camp: "Stu was the one guy we tried to please," Mick said. "We wanted his approval when we were writing or rehearsing a song. We'd want him to like it." As a tribute, the band staged a memorial gig in Stewart's honour at London's 100 Club on February 23, 1986. Keen to pay his respects to the man who lent him some of his first blues albums, Jeff joined the Stones and fellow guest Eric Clapton onstage at encore time for 'Mannish Boy'.

In the end, Beck's efforts on *Primitive Cool* were not as immediately compelling as they had been on *She's The Boss*, his guitar considerably less prominent in the mix than before. Worse, Mick's songs also lacked any real bite or distinction, with only the title track, 'Let's Work' and 'Throwaway' of enduring quality. That said, on the latter tune Jeff had left an indelible mark – his guitar providing both 'Throwaway''s central, soaring riff and a slick, angular solo that showed what could be done when a tremolo arm found itself in the right hands.

With the Stones' last album *Dirty Work* an absolute disaster, and Keith Richards now publicly referring to Jagger as 'Brenda' during interviews, the singer was in little hurry to return to base camp. Instead, he concentrated ever more on establishing himself as a solo artist. As a consequence, *Primitive Cool*'s release date was pushed back to September 1987, giving Mick time to assemble a touring band in which Beck would play a critical part. "I like watching people's faces when they see Mick because they're just so into him," Jeff said at the time. "Also, that takes the strain off me. I can just play a more supportive role, concentrate on just guitar."

The first glimpse of 'Old Rubber Lips'' new ensemble came in October 1987, when Jagger, Beck, Doug Wimbish, keyboard player Phil Ashley and an astounding young drummer named Terry Bozzio gathered at the LA Country Club to film a video for 'Throwaway'. During breaks in schedule, Mick and the band amused the extras by performing a variety of tracks, including the Stones' 'Miss You', a stinking cover of Hendrix's 'Foxy Lady' and an explosive take on James Brown's 'Sex Machine':"We beat the shit out of that one."Though Jeff appeared to be enjoying himself whole-heartedly, he also had one ear firmly locked on the drum kit. "I was there went he and Terry Bozzio met up," said Wimbish. "Love at first sight, you might say. It was the frequency Terry had, all the different stuff he brought to the table... the mood, the swing, the whole sonic template. Jeff could instinctively hear how Terry could apply himself to Jeff's own music." That Bozzio was an ex-Frank Zappa graduate who had only recently disbanded his own successful group, Missing Persons, mattered not. In Beck's mind, he had found his next drummer:"[Terry] blew my socks off. I grabbed him by the collar and said 'You're playing with me now, pal."

However, there was still the matter of Jagger's forthcoming tour to attend to before Jeff could hatch any new plot for his own band. Importantly, his loyalties still lay with Mick, Doug and Simon Phillips, who had now returned to active duty with Jagger after a spell playing alongside *Tubular Bells* guitarist Mike Oldfield. At first, rehearsals between the four were riveting. "All I can say is that when we got together to jam in New York in '87 with just Jeff, Mick, Doug and myself it sounded awesome," said Phillips. But much to Beck's dismay, Jagger had no intention of ever touring as a quartet. "It would have needed different music written specifically for [that] line-up," Simon continued. "Mick never had any intention of doing it that way and [always] had other musicians lined up."As the weeks went by, it became apparent to Jeff that Jagger was not only intent on supplementing the line-up with another guitarist and keyboard player, but also using a host of backing vocalists too. "To be honest, Jeff was always more into the idea of it being a four piece, with myself, Mick, Simon and him," said Doug. "That would have been a motherfucker of a group! But then Mick started expanding the band, adding musicians... and that wasn't Jeff's thing. And you've got to remember, [the core] of it was kind of Jeff's band."

When Jagger finally confirmed he would tour the Far East and Australia in the autumn of 1988 with a vastly augmented group playing a set largely drawn from the Stones' back catalogue, Beck bailed on the project: "Jeff called me, and said, 'Doug, I know I got you the gig, but I can't do it like this... I didn't sign up for this shit and I'm not coming back'. I understood that, but the tour was booked. We'd even taken the pictures for the programme," Wimbish remembered. "And Mick, well, he's got to do what he's got to do. The music business is like that. What's said on Monday can be changed by Friday. Remember, we're talking about the real big boys now. So I guess Jeff had to take care of himself, stay true to himself, and I respected that. And truth to tell, Mick was good to me, he's always been good to me, so in the end it all turned out OK."

Simon Phillips came to the same conclusion as Wimbish: "We had a few false starts, but by February 1988, we were up and running with Mick's solo project and that turned out great too." Looking back on his decision to part ways with Jagger, Beck seemed to vacillate between regret and anger – but mostly anger. "Probably the worst backing out of a tour I've ever done," he told *Q* after the event. "To make me happy, Mick allowed me to use Simon Phillips and Doug Wimbish and he obviously thought 'I've got Jeff because I've got his band'. But as each day unfolded, it turned out there were 15 Rolling Stones songs and I didn't want to go to Australia and Japan to play a load of Keith Richards licks. I was not happy." By 1995, he was a tad more philosophical. "We got on great and I wanted to forge a new band, a new career for him. [In a way] I was thinking 'Great, Mick's my new vocalist!' He wasn't. I was his guitarist."

With Simon Phillips and Doug Wimbish now a part of Mick Jagger's ongoing band, Beck must have wondered where it all went wrong. But there were worse fates than agreeing to disagree with a Rolling Stone. In November 1987, while working at home in a six-feet deep inspection pit under the chassis of one of his cars, Jeff enacted every guitarist's worst nightmare. "I don't have a cover for the [pit] other than these oak planks," he told journalist Gene Santoro. "I picked up one of them... pulled it, and the other end went about four feet into the pit and kicked, pinching my finger up against the chassis." The accident left him with a broken thumb and finger on his right hand. "Yeah, I heard it go," he continued. "The pain was excruciating. I wandered round sweating and fainting." Attempting to anaesthetise himself, Beck headed for the drinks cabinet and drank a bottle of whiskey. Waking some three hours later, he flexed the hand and "went through the ceiling". Within an hour, Jeff was in hospital and his digits were in a splint. Thankfully, the breaks were not so severe as to jeopardise his career. In fact, they might have even provided some unexpected fringe benefits. "I practised with the remaining fingers for six months and started up using the thumb even though it was bound up," he said. "I'd get sticky plaster all over the strings."

Bandaged, but defiant, Beck was well enough to travel to New York in January 1988 where he inducted his childhood hero Les Paul into the Rock & Roll Hall Of Fame. "He's given me 33 years of inspiration and good vibes," Jeff said on the night. However, a session date with former Sex Pistols manager Malcolm McLaren had to be commuted to later in the year. "I think Malcolm responded to me nudging him in a club one night and I said, 'What do you think about doing some work together?'" Beck recalled. "To my amazement he said, 'Yeah, I'd love to,' because I thought my style would have been a bit out for him... not useable enough, that kind of deal. But he called up and said, 'Yeah, let's talk about some ideas.' And it was strange because he sent me all these cassettes of [this] wonderful sort of 1890s music hall music, surf music and classics. And he said, 'What do you make of that?' One thing led to another."

Since playing "Fagin" to the Sex Pistols' "artful little dodgers" in the mid-seventies, McLaren had abandoned management and transferred his skills to the UK charts, a fact conclusively proved by 1982's Top 10 hit 'Buffalo Gals'. Inspired by a visit to New York, where he witnessed the city's blossoming hip-hop scene in full flow, Malcolm teamed up with the World's Famous Supreme Team to cut the single, which appropriated almost every rap technique in the book. A subsequent album, 1983's *Duck Rock*, saw him repeat the trick – this time liberating South African, South American and Caribbean rhythms for his own ends. Its immediate success made McLaren an unlikely, but still entertaining pop star. Further experiments with fusing R&B, rap and opera (1984's 'Madame Butterfly') were even more lucrative. "When I first heard 'Buffalo Gals', I got the same charge as when I heard Elvis Presley's 'Hound Dog'," said Beck, "It really got me going. I loved the way he manipulates people and I wanted to see what he'd do with me."

When Jeff's hand was sufficiently healed, he provided two fine solos on 'Call A Wave' and 'House Of The Blue Danube' for Malcolm's 1989 album *Waltz Darling*, the latter track making an unlikely appearance on the soundtrack to the film *Teenage Mutant Ninja Turtles*.

Of course, this was not the first time Beck's guitar had been heard soothing or scaring audiences in the background of a Hollywood movie. Aside from 'The Pump' popping up at a crucial juncture in 1983's *Risky Business*, Jeff had also cut a wonderfully faithful rendition of Santo Farina's 'Sleepwalk' for 1985's gross-out comedy *Porky's Revenge*. 1988 was little different, with the guitarist actually making it to the screen this time for the Arnold Schwarzenegger/Danny DeVito vehicle *Twins*. Assembling a band for the recording – comprising Tony Hymas, comedian/drummer Peter Richardson, rock/soul singer Andrew 'Cuddly Toy' Roachford and 'occasional guest' Terry Bozzio – Beck provided *Twins* with four songs in all. On 'Train Kept A Rollin', it was a case of all-out attack as the group boldly (and violently) updated Johnny Burnette's rockabilly anthem for the late eighties. Conversely, Freddy King's 'The Stumble' and Booker T & The MGs' 'Green Onions' were treated with the upmost care and attention, Jeff's solos on both tunes sticking rigidly to their original – and some might say – unsurpassable templates. The last composition, 'I'd Die For This Dance', featuring singer Nicolette Larson, was even more gentile, with Beck using his gift for lyrical phrasing to maximise the emotional content of an already uplifting country ballad. Stealing a brief cameo as a bandleader in the movie, Jeff can be seen watching agog as a fight breaks out in a bar, his acoustic guitar snatched from its stand by Danny DeVito before being used to batter a gangster over the head. Subtle, *Twins* was not. "Well, I got a free holiday to California," he later quipped.

The winter of 1988 brought more jamming, but no more new music. In a sketch a damn sight funnier than his turn in *Twins*, Beck joined English comedian Lenny Henry onstage at the Hackney Empire, providing some fiery background licks for Henry's latest creation, an ageing blues singer named 'Low Down Finger Lickin' Dirty Hound Dog Smith': "Bent down to pick up a rabbit's foot, got knocked down by a truck... I got the 'I'm in deep shit blues'." Jeff also appeared onstage for another comedy gig at The Marquee in December 1988 with Peter Richardson's cod heavy metal band Bad News. The stars of a recent

Channel 4 spoof that owed a great debt to ... *Spinal Tap*, Bad News might have been a tad derivative, but in its own very British way, was just as amusing. Accompanying Beck on the night for this charity concert was Queen's Brian May, who some 24 years earlier had been in the audience for one of Jeff's first shows with The Yardbirds at the same venue. Now a guitar hero in his own right, May was still full of admiration for his teenage hero. "Jeff produces... so much beauty," he said. "[He] is the greatest living guitarist."

Probably the highest-profile charity event Beck threw his weight behind at this time was in aid of the Celia Hammond Animal Trust. Joining other distinguished guests Eric Clapton, Jimi Hendrix's old rhythm section of Mitch Mitchell and Noel Redding, and The Yardbirds' Jim McCarty, Jeff performed several blues numbers at the Hard Rock Cafe, an intimate venue in the heart of London's Covent Garden, on November 28, 1988. While they remained close, Beck and Hammond's relationship had actually ended two years before, with Celia now focusing all her energies on providing rescue and homing shelters for unwanted or abused cats, dogs and other pets.*

Though Jeff Beck had kept himself reasonably busy throughout the eighties, there was also the distinct feeling that for the best part of the decade, he had simply been treading water. With just one album to his name since 1981, the sessions might have been prolific, the guest appearances numerous and the associations notable, but it was still just pocket change when compared with his workload throughout the seventies: "For most of the eighties, the business went to a place I just didn't want to go," he later said. "The clothes were more important than the music at one point, I think. The video prerequisite is something I wasn't interested in, and the domination of synthesisers made me very depressed...to think that they could overshadow real playing. And they did for a while. But then, lo and behold, real playing came back." And when it did, Beck was armed and ready.

---

* By 2010, Hammond had opened three such centres in London and its surrounding areas, dealing with over 110,000 neglected animals. In 2004, she was also presented with the RSPCA's most prestigious honour – The Richard Martin Award – for her lifelong dedication to animal welfare.

Chapter 20

Old Dog, New Tricks

Since Jeff Beck crash-landed on the international charts with 'Heart Full Of Soul' in 1965, each day, month, year and decade had brought with it another potential candidate to claim the title 'Ultimate Guitar Hero'. Of course, before Jeff, there had been dozens, hundreds, thousands of immaculate stylists – from Segovia, Barrios, Robert Johnson, Django and Charlie Christian to Les Paul, BB King, Jimmy Bryant and Chet Atkins, to name but a few. But the advent of rock'n'roll and all that came with it had upped the ante and turned the spotlight on guitarists as never before: Scotty, Cliff and Chuck begat Hank, George and Keith, only to have the 'Holy Trinity' of Clapton, Beck and Page again shock the world before Hendrix shocked them. The warm shivers of Bloomfield and Green. The deceptive simplicity of Townshend and T-Bone Walker. So many talented players. Forget just one and you risk offending many.

Yet as the seventies proved, there was to be no let-up in the guitar hero stakes. Deep Purple's Ritchie Blackmore introduced a welcome classical influence to hard rock, while Black Sabbath's Tony Iommi downtuned his strings and invented heavy metal. Progressive artists such as Yes' Steve Howe and King Crimson's Robert Fripp also removed boundaries as they went, using everything from bluegrass, folk and ragtime influences to tape looping to inform their sound and startle their audiences. Aside from John McLaughlin, jazz fusion had been a fertile breeding ground for virtuosos, as the saxophone-like breaks of Larry Carlton and extended blues vocabulary of Robben

315

Ford underlined. And as the decade progressed, so did the number of notable guitarists: Al Di Meola's whiplash-flamenco runs, Steve Morse's stunning dexterity, Gary Moore's express train picking and Michael Schenker's elegant, almost mathematical solo excursions. Again, there were far too many to name, but they knew who they were.

Then in February 1978, a one minute, 42 second solo called 'Eruption' changed the course of guitar history in much the same way that Jimi Hendrix had a decade before. The solo was the work of Eddie Van Halen, a Dutch-born, American-raised 23-year-old guitarist whose band (of the same name) had just released their debut LP. A frightening thing to behold, 'Eruption' showcased Eddie's extraordinary command of two-handed tapping, a technique executed by using the fingers of the 'pick' hand to tap the strings against the fingerboard, thus producing a stream of cascading, arpeggiated notes. Though tapping wasn't strictly new – Zep's Jimmy Page, Queen's Brian May, ZZ Top's Billy Gibbons and several others had all dabbled with it in previous years – the breakneck speed, breathless delivery and shocking control exercised by Van Halen during 'Eruption' made his solo simply revolutionary. When one factored in that tapping was just one of many tricks in the guitarist's magic hat, and that he was as gifted a songwriter and rhythm player as he was a soloist, the revolution wasn't going to stay a local one for long.

Hence by the mid-eighties, a slew of Van Halen-influenced guitarists were fighting the good fight against synthesiser and beat-box domination. Mostly found in metal bands – though not exclusively so – these players expanded considerably on Eddie's original template, incorporating sweep picking and extended legato techniques to further develop and define the form. The advent of the Floyd Rose 'locking tremolo' system only helped their cause, allowing strings to literally fall from the neck but return perfectly in tune after a particularly vigorous spot of whammy bar abuse. The arrival of Randy Rhoads and Yngwie Malmsteen on the hard-rock scene in 1980 and 1982 respectively brought other, even more bold possibilities, with both displaying a strong neo-classical bent in their choice of notes and riffs. Not content with the 'blues box' pentatonics used by the guitar heroes of the sixties, these latter-day Paganinis utilised augmented, diminished, Phrygian and diatonic scales to inform their solos, their speed and definition stupendous to ear and eye. George Lynch. Greg Howe. Shawn Lane.

Marty Friedman. Paul Gilbert. Jason Becker. From 'Mr. Scary' to 'Racer X'. These boys were good and Jeff Beck knew it: "Yngwie's great, Van Halen's great. What can you say, young kids. Blond, good looking, they play great. Where does that leave me? Playing a bloody banjo?"

Not quite. Though this new breed boasted both youth and often classically-trained chops, they actually had several things in common with Beck. Their love of heavily modified or customised guitars, for instance, mirrored Jeff's teenage (and many subsequent) attempts at building the perfect beast – even if his earliest efforts were driven by lack of money rather than the pursuit of ultimate tone. In fact, Eddie Van Halen had started the trend for such personalised instruments among Shredders when he originally constructed his own 'Frankenstrat' circa 1975/6. Desperate to combine the sound of a Gibson Les Paul with the physicality of a Fender Stratocaster, Van Halen inserted a PAF humbucker into a Strat-styled body, purchased for a paltry $50 from LA-based luthier Wayne Charvel. When said body was attached to a maple neck (again bought from Charvel, this time for $80) and a '58 tremolo arm bolted on to complete the package, Edward wrapped it in red and white stripes, dispensed with a tone control in favour of a single volume knob and the 'Frankenstrat' was born. After the initial blast of 'Eruption' and Van Halen's subsequent success, a plethora of guitar manufacturers began producing their very own brand of 'Super Strats', with Kramer, Ibanez and, indeed, (Wayne) Charvel all profiting from the trend. Even Beck himself had benefited from this revolution, his Jackson 'Tina Turner' Soloist one of the first models to incorporate 'Super Strat' features.

Another area of commonality for Jeff was the dedication these guitarists showed to their cause, which sometimes beggared belief. When learning the instrument, Randy Rhoads and Eddie Van Halen had often locked themselves away for weekends at a time, forgoing normal adolescent pleasures in favour of endless hours at the strings. This devotion even followed Rhoads into adulthood. Before he tragically died in an aircraft accident in 1982 while on tour with Ozzy Osbourne, Randy was still taking classical guitar lessons whenever he could, seeking out a teacher in each town his band visited. Yngwie Malmsteen was equally obsessed. As a child in Sweden, he covered his bleeding fingers with plasters in an effort to keep practising. Given that

317

Beck had attempted a similar exercise after breaking his thumb and finger in 1987, he must have understood such compulsion – even if hot rods sometimes got in the way. "You know, these guys are fantastic," he said at the time. "There's no way you can get near them. Theirs is a dedicated talent, which I envy. If I had that application, I'd be a lot better. [In America], there are no half measures. It's always all or nothing. Unfortunately, I don't have that kind of discipline. I wander off and do something else."

If Beck expressed admiration for this next generation of six-stringers, albeit peppered with the occasional, good-natured insult ("They symbolise youth, vigour, energy, power... and they deserve to have their fingers broken!"), they too were keen to return the favour. "Jeff Beck's the tastiest guitar player ever," said Dokken's George Lynch. Solo artist and tapper extraordinaire Tony MacAlpine was also quick to shout Jeff's praises from the rooftops: "Singing tone, great vibrato, unmistakable sound." But it was Jake E. Lee, who replaced Randy Rhoads in Ozzy Osbourne's group in 1983, who perhaps paid Beck his highest compliment at the time: "Jeff's the epitome of tasteful playing. Start to finish, he just did everything right. Top of my list."

Kind words all and extremely well spoken. But another and perhaps even more crucial element in aiding Jeff's future cause had arrived with this new movement: a reactivation of interest in instrumental guitar albums. Mike Varney had been first to spot the potential trend in 1980, when at the tender age of 22 he set up Shrapnel Records, a label dedicated to finding new six-string talent and bringing them to public attention. As a result, Yngwie Malmsteen, Marty Friedman, Jason Becker, Paul Gilbert, Tony MacAlpine, Vinnie Moore, Greg Howe and the marvellous Richie Kotzen all released their debut discs via Shrapnel. Soon, other artists and record companies were in the race. Former Frank Zappa protégé and "king of impossible guitar parts" Steve Vai self-funded his first LP, *Flexible*, in 1983 – the $5,000 cost of making the LP recouped at least a hundred times over within a year of it landing in stores. Not to be outdone, Vai's original guitar teacher Joe Satriani followed suit, first with *Not Of This Earth* and then 1987's ground-breaking *Surfing With The Alien*. Issued by Interscope Records, *Surfing...* sold a million copies in the US alone, the first vocal-free guitar album to do so since Jeff Beck's *Wired* 21 years before. Even a fool could see a pattern emerging here, and as previously stated, Jeff was no fool.

In truth, *Flash's* middling chart performance had taught Beck a valuable lesson. Against his better judgement and on the advice of CBS/Epic, he had allowed himself to be talked into making an 'eighties' record: not a crime if said disc was Prince's almost perfect *Purple Rain* or Peter Gabriel's uplifting *So*, but *Flash* was neither. Coming across as a silken compromise, bereft of the classic belligerence or bold vision that made *Truth* and *Blow By Blow* such fine statements of intent, *Flash* often sounded like a Nile Rodgers solo album with Jeff's solos grafted on as an afterthought. "It was a very sad sort of time for me," he later told *Guitar Player*. "I didn't have a grip on what I should be doing or what was expected of me. It was in the hands of the gods of New York. At that time it just seemed the right thing to do, to try and get a sneaky hit album with Niles. [And] I'm not making any bones about it. We were after a hit album." However, with instrumental guitar albums again in the ascendant and his record company no doubt mindful of the fact, Beck could now return to a genre he helped invent: "I wanted a band and a record with some nifty guitar on it, and that's what I was going to get."

To turn that idea into reality, Beck enlisted the help of the ever-dependable Tony Hymas and his latest drumming discovery, Terry Bozzio. "I was flattered," said Bozzio, "[but also] adamant about it being an instrumental album. Having heard *Flash,* which I wasn't too pleased with, I said to Jeff 'Look, why do mediocre songs...with [the listener] wading through bullshit waiting for a brilliant guitar solo?' You're Jeff Beck, it's your album!'" From his point of view, Beck was just happy to have two such distinguished musicians on board for the project. "Terry's my dream drummer, but he's a dangerous machine to have around if you haven't got finished songs – he'll plug into a groove within the first five seconds and make a simple jam sound great!" As ever, Hymas also made Jeff's 'honours' list. "I'm so flattered Tony's playing with us," he told *Guitarist*. "He's so musical, classically trained, nothing whatsoever to do with rock'n'roll, that I sometimes feel inferior. He's a very deep person, but as long as he puts up with my cocking about, as long as he can bear that, we'll have something good."

Work began on Beck's new record in mid-1988 with a series of casual jams at Tony Hymas' house. At first, Jeff was reportedly keen to explore an amalgamation of rockabilly-type sounds with high-tech production values, or as one critic put it: "Duane Eddy meets The Art Of Noise", but no one was particularly thrilled with the results. Instead, the trio took a different road as Hymas began stitching together phrases and riffs emanating from Beck's Strat until they became something of real substance: "[Tony] took the mad bits, little scratches really, scratches in the sand... and started playing with them. He somehow makes my minimal writing capacity blossom into something."

Having worked with Jeff on and off for nigh on a decade, Hymas was also aware of the guitarist's belief that he could always top an already perfect idea or solo – a persistent foible that had led to much pain in previous endeavours. "I've never seen any wobblers from Jeff," said Tony. "[But] the only danger with him is he'll record a blinding solo and then want to go over it. There have been some tragedies in the past." Strong measures would be taken to ensure no such tragedies occurred when they got to the studio.

After a month of jamming and more formal rehearsals, it became apparent to all that they didn't have a bassist. Yet, as Hymas was doing such a fine job of covering the gap with his keyboards, the decision was made to press on as a trio. "The chemistry between us was so good, we decided not to rock the boat," said Beck. Despite the additional workload, Tony was of an equal mind. "If we added a standard bass player," he said, "I think everything would have been done in a more traditional fashion and the music would have suffered." By dispensing with the services of a traditional bass player, it also allowed Hymas the luxury of controlling all orchestral aspects of the group's sound, giving Beck a clear run at doing what he did best. "My job," concluded Jeff, "was to light the fireworks."

Preliminary recording began at Oxfordshire's Chipping Norton Studios in the autumn of 1988, where Gerry Rafferty had cut his monstrous 1978 hit, 'Baker Street'. But Beck, Hymas and Bozzio were again on the move by January 1989 as Jimmy Page's Sol Studios became unexpectedly vacant. "[Until then], the studio was unavailable," said Jeff. "It had downtime for about three to six months at really reduced rates so we jumped in there. We conceived, wrote, arranged, demoed, and produced it all in one big bang." Once owned by legendary sixties producer Gus Dudgeon before Page snapped it up at a bargain price, Sol Studios was an idyllic location in which to work, situated near the River Thames close to the leafy village of Cookham, Berkshire. In fact, so perfect were the surroundings, Beck had trouble concentrating on the business of making music. "When you're a resident, you flop out in bed, it's all too easy and time flies by. I should have been in a crappy studio that was falling to bits and I had to drive to every day." He was also mindful who was profiting from his stay. "It hurt, though... knowing Jimmy made all that bread," Jeff later joked to *Musician*. "I even left my bicycle behind in his shed, so he got that too."

With Sol Studios came its attendant manager, Leif Mases. An engineer of distinction, the Swedish-born Mases began his career working with Abba and ELO at Stockholm's Polar Studios before becoming part of Led Zeppelin's team during the making of their final LP, 1979's *In Through The Out Door*. When Zeppelin broke up in 1980, Leif also engineered their subsequent out-takes album, 1982's *Coda*. Mases reunited with Jimmy Page in 1988 for the guitarist's first solo record, *Outrider*, again in an engineering capacity. A calm, affable presence, Mases earned a co-production credit alongside Beck, Hymas and Bozzio for his efforts at Sol as well as becoming a regular fixture during Jeff's studio recordings of the nineties. "We were all convinced we were onto something [at Sol]," said Jeff, "so none of us really wanted to rush it."

The guitarist's hunch was proved correct with the release of *Jeff Beck's Guitar Shop With Terry Bozzio and Tony Hymas* in September 1989. A special record that rightly gave 'featured billing' to Jeff's collaborators, *Guitar Shop...* was undoubtedly his best effort since *Blow By Blow* 14 years before, and some might say his most complete and satisfying album ever: "[*Guitar Shop...*] was me, digging deep, deep down into my boots." From the cover onwards, *Guitar* Shop... was keen to make its mark: a clever illustration of Beck working in his garage under a car-sized guitar (obviously a pun on the title and his love of hot rods); one immediately knew some real thought and no little humour had been put into the disc.

This fact was confirmed by the opening track, 'Guitar Shop' itself.

Opening with the Bonham-esque roar of Terry Bozzio's drum kit, 'Guitar Shop' mimicked the sounds emanating from any guitar store in any country on any given weekend – with Jeff's multi-tracked riffs, solos and sonic interjections invoking all the chaos and mad beauty of such places. "It was just the way I hear the sound coming out of the guitar shops like Manny's on a Saturday morning," Beck told *Guitar Player*. "All these would-be guitar heroes in there, struggling away. There's always a dozen of them in there, and that's where I got the idea, trying to capture that energy." To accompany Jeff's howls and squeals, Bozzio had laid down a clever (and very funny) mock-sales pitch, his Zappa-approved voice dryly extolling the virtues of "killer cabs", "dangerous distortion, serious sustain", and 'Balls Deluxe", with each phrase echoing various over the top advertisements from guitar magazines. "Jeff was a rock star with a great sense of humor, a cut-up," he said, "and there were certain aspects of his personality that I really fitted with."

After 'Savoy's canny melding of hard-rock textures with post-WWII rockabilly swing – on which Beck dug out his Oxblood Les Paul to provide some rich harmonics and a Gretsch Duo-Jet for some authentic 'Cliff Gallup' twang – came the delightful 'Behind The Veil'. Conceived at Chipping Norton, 'Behind The Veil' allowed Beck the rare opportunity to hang out with a reggae tune, his guitar gently slip-sliding in and out of the melody before turning up the overdrive at the end.

This mixture of gentility and steel was also present on 'Two Rivers', a song recorded in five minutes flat, with "six months of messing around" after the fact to perfect its appeal. Originally titled 'Two Trains' ("We all closed our eyes and it sounded more like a landscape with rivers meandering through it"), 'Two Rivers' came to life as a short note cluster Jeff was casually chewing over during a break in recording. Overheard and subsequently developed by Tony Hymas with Beck, it became one of the highlights of the album. A masterclass in how to play ascending harmonics, 'Two Rivers' also featured a flawless slide-guitar break from Jeff, which found him leaving behind the limits of the fret board and venturing over the pick-ups towards the bridge itself: "It's almost unbearable, there's something about the polished metal going up on the string that high." Testing the limit of human hearing, Jeff's slide work on 'Two Rivers' remains a constant of his live set.

322

'Big Block', on the other hand, was all about wielding the wilder moments of Jimi Hendrix onto the bangs and crashes of big band leader/drummer Buddy Rich. Once called 'Big Block Chevy' in honour of Beck's hot-rod fetish, the track was recorded with a Strat and Marshall 100-watt amp at full pelt, giving Jeff's guitar a hugely aggressive and overloaded tone of which he took complete advantage. "It helps to be angry, but not destructively aggressive," Beck said. "You've got to choose the pinnacle of the moment, the peak of creativity."

Over a stunning backbeat from Terry Bozzio and a rumbling bass line courtesy of Tony Hymas, Jeff's solo on 'Big Block was full of deceptively careful abandon, with trills, scuffs, whammy dive bombs and even the occasional bit of 'tapping' all fighting for supremacy at various times. Ironically, all this menace had come out of a loose jam with former *The Young Ones/ Bad News* comedians Nigel Planer, Ade Edmondson and Rik Mayall, who along with Beck's close friend Peter Richardson visited the guitarist during the making of the album. While Jeff, Bozzio, Hymas and these amateur, but no doubt enthusiastic musicians were "sodding about", Jeff hit upon the riff for 'Big Block', causing an immediate clearance of all non-essential personnel: "Well, there's a time for comedy, but that wasn't it."

Thankfully, the attendant humour on *Guitar Shop* didn't disappear with the expulsion of the comedians, a fact evidenced by 'A Day In The House'. Parodying a typical afternoon's debate in the House of Lords, 'A Day In The House' again made clever use of spoken-word interludes as Jeff and Terry aped the sound of peers and politicians debating the environment. "Much is being said, me Lords," intoned a billiard-ball-gobbling Bozzio, "but nothing is being done." On the Speaker's command "I suggest the issue be passed to Mr. Beck," Jeff provided one of his finer solos on the album, handing in an abstract, chord-wrenching blast of politically incorrect guitar. In comparison, 'Stand On It' (another hot-rod term) was positively muted, its mixing and matching of major and minor chords pleasant enough, but hardly essential. 'Slingshot', however, was a much more thrilling ride, as Bozzio and Hymas gave chase to Beck's almost thrash-metal riff, while towing a forest of sheet music behind them.

Given the sheer quality of *Guitar Shop…*'s wares, it was perhaps greedy to ask for the stars when one had already been handed the moon and several small planets. But as 'Where Were You' showed, Jeff Beck was in a very generous mood. Perhaps the finest guitar instrumental of the last 30 years, 'Where Were You''s enduring beauty not only brought a tear to the eye, but also an unhinging of the jaw as guitarists the world over tried to figure out exactly how Beck had pulled it off. The tune (for want of a better word) was inspired by *Le Mystere Des Voix Bulgares*, a collection of Bulgarian folk songs sung by a female folk choir. Dispensing with the traditional Western harmonic system, these singers created an eerily beautiful atonality, where one drone-like voice held the root note while the others gathered sang in 'seconds' – capturing major, minor, quarter or even eighth tones – and sometimes with a tremolo effect. When Jeff first borrowed *Le Mystere...* from Tony Hymas, he was profoundly affected by what he heard: "I heard this strange, wonderful folk music with these incredible voices on it. They just had a way of breaking the voice and cascading the notes without a break." Beck being Beck decided to re-create the unique sound of this choir of Bulgarian women with just his Stratocaster. "I thought 'I can do that on guitar...'"

In the end, 'Where Were You' did require some additional help from Hymas and Bozzio before Jeff was satisfied. As Beck developed the central melody, Tony added "these strange, supporting chords" while Terry suggested the odd change of note, here and there. When the trio were certain "it played right", it was time for recording. Using a '59 Strat equipped with Alnico pick-ups and a '62 or '63 neck for the take, Beck plugged his guitar into a brand new Fender Twin Reverb and eight-year-old Fender Princeton amp (set up in combination), while also adding a Pro Co Rat distortion pedal for a little 'grain'. The signal was then processed with a long, repeating echo to provide a "bit more majesty", at which point he was ready to go. By all accounts, the resulting takes were among the hardest of Jeff's long and illustrious career.

Aside from its principal melody, 'Where Were You' was to be played using a series of false harmonics, with Beck raising or lowering the tremolo arm to control the pitch of notes. When executed correctly, the end result would be a seamless progression of unfretted "grace notes", fluttering voice-like across Tony Hymas' supporting keyboard chords. However, man and machine were at war several times during recording. First, due to the sheer complexity of his task, Beck had to remember exactly when to raise or lower the tremolo arm in advance of striking each harmonic. More, he also had to mute strings and create volume swells, often at the same time. To add insult to injury, Jeff's original, unaccompanied opening to the tune was scrapped due to too much amplifier static and a slight, though jarring effect when it linked to the incoming melody. "It was heartbreaking," he remembered. "The soul was there, the performance was there, the hesitancy was there, but we couldn't use it."

Worse still, because of problems with the '59 Strat's metal nut killing the sustained harmonic at the end of the solo, Beck was forced to use his brand new Surf Green 'Jeff Beck' prototype signature Strat with Wilkinson-equipped tremolo to finish the take – a fine guitar for sure, but one that represented an unwanted break in continuity and tone. Witnessing all these trials and tribulations was Mo Foster, who had come to visit Jeff at precisely the moment his friend was busy testing the limits of sound. "Yep, I was there when he was recording it. Just staring in fucking amazement at this... thing. I mean, the technique was astonishing. But there were problems with the echo repeat picking up the sound of the tremolo bar – a little glitch every now and then that was creating this 'err, err, err' sound in the background. Flawed mechanics, but incredibly frustrating. So after a while, Jeff picked up the echo unit, flung it down hard and shouted 'No! This has got to sound like the voice of God!'"

At risk of blasphemy, the end result probably did. A stupendous achievement with Beck's thumb and fingers turning false harmonics into "little drops of heaven" while simultaneously guiding the whammy bar to determine whether those drops lived, died or simply re-ascended to the firmament, 'Where Were You' was/is/always will be Jeff's greatest recorded moment on guitar. "I wanted to do something that moved the listener almost to tears," he said, "[and] it's probably the best thing I ever wrote, a milestone in my playing." Mo Foster whole-heartedly agreed, seeing the composition as a breakthrough moment not only for Beck, but for a whole generation of guitar players: "Of course, Jeff really changed the sound of the guitar with 'Where Were You'. Nobody else, before or since, has done anything like that. It was just frontier stuff and we're still all in awe of it. You know, so few people actually redefine the sound of an instrument. Jeff, Jaco Pastorius on bass, Miles Davis, maybe. And that's the mark of an artist, not a chancer."

As the guitar-playing community reeled in wonder at 'Where Were You', the critics were equally busy reeling out the superlatives for its parent album. "*Guitar Shop...*," said *Mojo*'s Colin Harper "confirms Beck's place as the guitarist's guitarist... [with] humour, power, virtuosity [alongside] a winning amalgam of studio trickery, organic brinksmanship and an utterly distinctive touch." *Q*'s Charles Shaar Murray was also quite taken with the disc: "[It's] a full tilt guitar orgy... that runs the gamut from tear-at-your-heartstrings ballads to tear-your-ears-off hard rock. If stunt guitar is your cup of meat, it doesn't get much better than this." For a guitarist once accused of "incoherent blazing" by the music papers, this was high praise indeed.

For an album full of colour, texture, complexity and humour, one would have hoped that *Guitar Shop* followed Joe Satriani's *Surfing With The Alien* in attaining platinum status, but it had to make do with number 49 in the US charts – one place lower than the considerably inferior *Flash* had managed. As ever, the UK proved a fickle mistress. Starved of a tour from Jeff since 1981 and then in thrall to Manchester's 'baggy' movement', British punters completely ignored *Guitar Shop* with the record failing to even dent the charts. As evidenced, this snubbing of a Beck release was not uncommon at home, where musical fashions changed more frequently than Jeff replaced his strings, but the record's disappointing showing in America was somewhat harder to fathom. Perhaps unlike other 'shred'-related product, Beck's decision to follow a tune rather than cram each bar with a thousand notes had proved uninteresting or even unexciting to a new generation of guitar fans. Or as likely, his position as 'elder statesman' in a market always devoted to the 'shock of the new' had failed to engage their ears. Whatever the case or cause, *Guitar Shop* deserved better, and a few clever souls within the record industry knew it. In just reward of their services, Beck, Bozzio and Hymas were awarded a Grammy for 'Best Rock Instrumental Performance of 1989'.

Despite *Guitar Shop*'s middling sales performance, Jeff appeared philosophical with his lot when meeting the press, even appearing happy to champion the guitar's enduring appeal as a primary instrument in the rock and metal market: "There was one point where I thought, 'This is it, we're all finished. Me, Eric, you name it... all on the bus to nowhere'. Then, wouldn't you know it, the heavy metal kids came along. It was just one of those things the kids wouldn't let die. The guitar just keeps floating on." However, his memories of the mid-eighties remained vivid and depressing: "I was in despair at what had happened to the music industry... with this endless, powerful corporate cock up moving along at 100 miles an hour and of which I was no part of whatsoever," he told *Musician*'s Scott Isler. "There was nobody rooting for me in any powerful position. As my record company's based in New York and I live in the depths of the country in England, I just didn't feel I was even in the business."

That said, one always got the distinct impression that success remained a double-edged sword for Beck: "Success? Are you talking in terms of high pay, high profile, getting pissed, falling over and being put in the headlines? That's not success. That's total disaster. I could have been a lot richer, but a lot of extra money wouldn't satisfy me. I look at Eric and I don't envy him one bit." As Clapton's latest album *Journeyman* had just entered the US charts at number 16 and would go on to sell over two million copies, this was quite a statement.

One country that always stayed faithful to Jeff Beck was Japan, where he had retained near superstar status for close to two decades. This fact was reconfirmed when *Guitar Shop* reached number one in the Japanese charts. Given such enduring kindness, it made perfect sense for Beck to begin his first world tour in eight years there in August 1989. "I was once talking to Mr. Udo, Japan's biggest promoter," Simon Napier-Bell remembered, "and I asked him who his favourite performer was. Now, given the fact he runs The Budokan, he's seen a lot of acts. Anyway, without hesitation, he smiles and says 'Jeff Beck. Perfect gentleman, very humble and his bands are always gracious'. High praise indeed." Backed by Bozzio and Hymas, Jeff did not disappoint on this occasion either, playing six dates in all at various venues throughout the country. "I've always enjoyed going to Japan," Beck said. "The audience really listens to what you're trying to get across."

Jeff's next step was a 28-date tour of the US which began at Minneapolis' Northrop Memorial Auditorium on October 25. Sharing the bill with him for these dates was Texan legend Stevie Ray Vaughan and his group, Double Trouble. A breed apart from the neo-classicists, shredders and technocrats that had flooded the market in recent years, Vaughan was something of a throwback to simpler times, though his brand of hot-wired guitar blues still had the power to strip paint. Heavily influenced by the likes of Muddy Waters, BB King, Lonnie Mack and Jimi Hendrix, Stevie first came to light on David Bowie's album *Let's Dance*. Using the publicity generated from his stint with Bowie as a springboard, Vaughan and Double Trouble enjoyed great success with their debut album, 1983's *Texas Flood*, and its follow-up, *Couldn't Stand The Weather*. Though problems with cocaine subsequently threatened to derail the guitarist's career, his drug-free 'comeback' LP, 1989's *In Step*, had once again re-established his profile as an exciting torch-bearer for electric blues.

Beck and Vaughan had first met in March 1984 at a convention held by CBS records in Honolulu, Hawaii. "When I met Stevie," Jeff remembered, "he was eating fried chicken through the bottom of the bucket. Just putting his hand through the bottom. It was really funny." Vaughan's recollections were no less amusing: "Jeff was smoking cigars and talking hot rods. Then he was up onstage, his hand punching the air. Man, he played in the most beautiful way." Forming an immediate mutual admiration society, the two jammed together at the convention, playing Lonnie Mack's 'Wham' and Don Nix's 'Going Down' and several other tunes.* For Stevie, the opportunity to talk with Jeff – let alone share the same stage on tour – was a genuine privilege. "I started listening [to Beck] when I was about eight or nine, and it's an honour to be out here with [him]," he told *Guitar Player* in 1989. "He takes the roots of the blues and is able to make it go way out there. And I'm not a parrot talking shit. It's the real deal."

Advertised as *The Fire Meets The Fury*, Beck and Vaughan's US jaunt featured no 'headliner' per se. Exactly as he had done with John McLaughlin in 1975, Jeff simply alternated top billing with Stevie each night: "Saved on the egos." A 'must have' ticket, the two acts often found themselves playing for visiting rock dignitaries, with Eddie Van Halen, Steve Vai and Guns N' Roses' Slash – then the latest addition to

---

* Though these songs were never officially released, video footage of the event can easily be found in the usual places.

the pantheon of guitar gods – all dropping in at one point or another to see the show. "Compared to Jeff Beck I'm just a peon, man," said Slash somewhat harshly, but accurately. Though each solo set had its undoubted share of highlights, Beck and Vaughan were usually at their best during encore time, where both made good on their promise of 'Fire and Fury' by taking to the stage for a shared version of 'Going Down'. A feast for Strat lovers (Jeff using his 'Surf Green', Vaughan his beloved 'Number One'), the two dug so deep into their heavy-gauge strings that the pick-less Beck was left with severely torn fingernails by the end of the tour at Denver Sports Arena on November 29, 1989. Tragically, it was also the last time they played together as Vaughan died in a helicopter accident while on tour with Eric Clapton in August 1990. "Stevie Ray was just great," Jeff later said. "He had a large chunk of Hendrix in him and Hendrix carried a large chunk of Buddy Guy."

Mercifully for his fans at home, Beck took no slight from *Guitar Shop*'s no-show on the UK charts and booked a five-date British tour during the late spring of 1990. However, following a particularly lively concert at Manchester Apollo, the guitarist injured several ligaments in his back and a two-night stop-off at London's Hammersmith Odeon scheduled for May 12 and 13 had to be postponed until the end of July. For those lucky to be able to rework their calendars accordingly, the 'Hammy' gigs proved among the best of Jeff's career. Showcasing material from *Guitar Shop*, *Blow By Blow*, *Wired*, *There & Back* (though wisely not *Flash*), Beck and his band were given a heroes' welcome, with Bozzio and Hymas both displaying a musicality and vigour on par with their fearless leader.

Predictably, the moment those gathered in the hall had been waiting for came with 'Where Were You'. Already a topic of wild debate among guitarists, there were many who believed Jeff simply couldn't channel 'the voice of God' in a live environment. Even Beck himself had his doubts: "Yeah, I know. I've made a rod for my own back." Three wonderful minutes later, the doubting Thomases were sent back whence they came as the former Yardbird delivered a near pitch-perfect rendition of the tune: "Fucking unbelievable," being *Melody Maker*'s sage assessment of his performance. Though he would occasionally struggle replicating each note to his own exacting standards in years to come, 'Where Were You' has retained its place in Jeff's concert set since 1989/90, a sure highlight of nearly every show. In fact, the guitarist has been known "to jump about a bit" during its execution so "they know it's me playing it rather than the keyboards!"

On completing his first full tour in nearly nine years, Beck was full of enthusiasm for the future, making quick plans for another album while also pointing out the virtues of his current band: "Tony's the powerhouse, the power station. The strings, the bass line, he was in charge of all that. He should have got more recognition." Jeff was also keen for Terry Bozzio's contribution to be recognised: "Terry's like Miles Davis... a bullet through the brain, right between the eyes." But it wasn't to be. When the trio reconvened for rehearsals in the summer of 1990, a heatwave of sweltering proportions descended on the UK, sending Beck in search of the coastline and Hymas home to his newborn baby. Hoping for the best Bozzio held out a little longer. Yet when Jeff seemed in no great hurry to return, he formed The Lonely Bears with Tony Hymas, a temporary project that ran a year or so before Terry moved on to former Frank Zappa alumnus Steve Vai's group in 1993.

In the meantime, and repeating a pattern one could set a clock by, Jeff again returned to the business of cars. "I get out there and I get in my garage, and I can saw up things. I can cut plate. I can modify something. I can get a project going," he later said. "I mean, I've built cars and driven them and sold some. And now I've got a cross section of cars that's enough for me, so I don't think I'll be doing any more. Probably. I don't know." In addition to his love for old Fords, Beck had also taken to the streamlined joys of the Chevrolet Corvette: "I'm into early Corvettes at the moment. I've got enough early Fords. The '63 Corvette is what I'm into at the moment, with the late-model suspension. So I can have the look of the '63, which is a great-looking car, and have all the ride characteristics of a later car, and economy as well. So it'll be a super car, I hope." For Jeff, it was always going be a choice between Fenders and fenders.

Chapter 21

Apocalypse Twang

Though he didn't greatly care for the decade, Jeff Beck had finished the eighties on a high, releasing a superb album to strong critical acclaim and then touring it proudly into the summer of 1990. And if circumstances meant that another potentially great band had gone their separate ways, so be it. As before, he'd simply form another. For the time being at least, Jeff appeared content to step away from the studios and concert halls and recharge his batteries under the bonnet of a Corvette. After all, it kept him sane. "I would have loved to have been two people, but I was determined not to devote my entire life just to my 'career'," he said. "In the last 22 or 24 years, I've stolen at least half of that for myself. And the only reason I'm sitting here now is because I've done that. Had I not done that, I wouldn't be fresh and wanting to go again."

Such a philosophy had obviously served him well. At 46, he looked at least 10 years younger, his face and frame showing little real change from the man who had toured *There & Back*. Perhaps there was a portrait locked in the attic of his mansion home. Or it might just have been good genes, a vegetarian diet and the physical benefits gleaned from working long hours in a chassis pit. Hard to know, and Beck wasn't really telling: "It's just change, variety, that keeps the thing from kicking over."

In his personal life too, there was reason to be cheerful. Following the end of his relationship with Celia Hammond, Jeff dated several women, but the early nineties saw him settle down with former glamour model Sandra Cash. A head-turning, blue-eyed blonde, Cash was considerably younger than Beck, but shared both his sense of humour and his love of fine art – being an accomplished amateur painter herself. As the years went by, she even managed to smooth away his previous reluctance to attend music industry events and 'gong shows', with the guitarist slowly but surely accepting that such soirees were not the work of the devil, but more a chance to catch up with old friends. In fact, the sight of Cash smiling stoically for the cameras while Beck ducked out of shot in the background became an oddly touching, if still comical sight. There was also the beginning of some change on the business front as Ralph Baker began to take on a more important role in the management of Beck's affairs. However, "Chief Cook and Bottle Washer" Ernest Chapman remained strongly at the heart of the guitarist's career, aside from the occasional break to enjoy some quality golf.

Under no great obligation to do much of anything for the time being, Beck continued to work on his rods and Corvettes, though as ever before he peppered such activity with the odd session. Repaying a favour to Tony Hymas for all his hard work on *Guitar Shop*, Jeff had already contributed two fine solos to the keyboardist's first solo album, *Oyaté*, in early 1990. A France-only release, *Oyaté* was full of spoken-word passages, swirling synths and shifting rhythms, its overall concept honouring Hymas' interest in Native American culture and 1800s war chiefs in particular. Around the same period, Beck also flew to Los Angeles for several days' work on the soundtrack to *Young Guns II,* a movie with a decidedly different take on the old west. Leading on the project was hair-metal icon Jon Bon Jovi, who was providing several songs for the film. The bastard son of Bruce Springsteen and Aerosmith's Steven Tyler, Bon Jovi's career had been built on a combination of pop-metal hooks and lyrics that either extolled the virtues of the working class or celebrated his own band as modern-day cowboys – his 1986 mega-hit 'Wanted Dead Or Alive' an anthem to the "steel horse" and "loaded six string". Given such preoccupations, Jon really was the perfect choice to write the musical backdrop for a movie in which Hollywood played fast and loose with the legend of 'Billy The Kid' while also looking to ramp up the profit margin with a million-selling tie-in album.

As one might expect, the resulting soundtrack to *Young Guns II* was bumper entertainment, with Bon Jovi providing 10 songs full of tumbleweed imagery, brave, but doomed outlaws and men generally doing what they had to do while riding a horse. Taking the place of Jon's regular guitarist Richie Sambora (who like the rest of Bon Jovi's band was pursuing other interests at the time), Beck made great sport of it, appearing on seven cuts in all. Saving his best work for the single 'Blaze Of Glory', where he provided a typically hypersonic lead break, and 'Miracle', which found him sailing sweetly over a female choir, Jeff thoroughly enjoyed his experience, even if the constant presence of a cameraman during recording did grate: "I didn't like having a video camera in the corner all the time. He was filming me learning and playing, and making mistakes, which I didn't get off on."

Meeting Little Richard more than made up for the inconvenience, however. Introduced to Beck by Bon Jovi in an LA nightclub, Jeff's teenage hero did not let him down, the still-pompadoured singer regaling the guitarist with countless, untold stories about the birth of rock'n'roll. Like Tina Turner before him, Little Richard carved his signature into the body of a Jeff Beck guitar, though this time it was the Surf Green Strat that was marked for posterity. "'Lucille' was the only record that shocked me as much as Gene Vincent... but in a porno way," Jeff later recalled. "You had to play it when your parents were out..."

Beck wasn't finished with the film industry just yet, though it almost finished him. His next session appearance was on the soundtrack to Tom Cruise's *Days Of Thunder*, a racing drama that promised much, but delivered little. Working alongside Oscar-winning composer Hans 'The Lion King' Zimmer, Beck recorded at least four guitar parts for the film, but only one can be heard distinctly in the final cut. Worse still, the plane he was travelling on was almost struck by lightning on the way to the studio session in Fort Lauderdale, Florida. Jeff was certainly safer when working in television as his 1990 cameo in *The Comic Strip Presents: South Atlantic Raiders* proved. It was almost a decade since the Comic Strip cast had first lampooned, spoofed and torn into cultural and literary stereotypes, their debut show, *Five Go Mad In Dorset*, first airing on UK's Channel Four in 1982. Made up of a revolving cast of comedians that included Nigel Planer, Ade Edmondson and Rik Mayall as well as Kathy Burke, Dawn French and Jennifer Saunders, their best work included *The Bullshitters* (a riff on bad macho cop shows), the Golden Rose Of Montreux-winning *The Strike* and the heavy metal satire *Bad News*. Little assassinations all, the mainstay behind their toxic brilliance was Peter Richardson, who had written many of the best episodes and, as already evidenced, happened to be one of Beck's closest friends.

Jeff's cameo in the half-hour TV special was brief, but very funny. Seated on a plane ordering food alongside girlfriend Sandra Cash, his one line "I'll have the same, with garlic. And can I have some mushrooms too?" was one part Oliver Twist and one part Nigel Tufnel, even down to trying to hide his cigarette from the camera. Watched by over a million viewers, the episode also featured several musical snippets from *Guitar Shop*, including 'Stand On It', 'Two Rivers' and an early demo of 'Where Were You', which incorporated a passage from Ravel's 'Bolero'. Obviously a natural at this acting lark (though being mates with executive producer Peter Richardson surely didn't hurt), Jeff became a semi-regular in subsequent Comic Strip episodes, popping up as a guitar-wielding politician in *The Red Nose Of Courage* and a hot-rod driving serial killer in *Gregory – Diary Of A Nutcase*. He was also there as both musician and actor when Richardson directed his first movie, 1991's slight, if entertaining *The Pope Must Die,* featuring rotund comedian Robbie Coltrane in the title role. Contributing heavily to the soundtrack alongside The Art Of Noise's Anne Dudley – but without fear of being struck by lightning, this time – Beck also turned up on screen as a bicycle-riding postman. Retitled *The Pope Must Diet* for the American market (Coltrane must have been beside himself with laughter over the religiously driven change), the movie was only a moderate success.

Away from the cameos and comedy, Beck continued to involve himself with the occasional session. A collaboration with The Pretenders' Chrissie Hynde and the group Moodswings proved an interesting diversion, with Beck lending his guitar to 'Skinthieves', a song recorded for supposed inclusion on Tame Yourself – a charity album in support of People for the Ethical Treatment of Animals (PETA). Unfortunately, 'Skinthieves' was not included on the final track listing and languished in the vaults until 1992, when a heavily remixed version found its way on to Moodswing's own disc, *Moodfood*. Against Jeff's original wishes (he only agreed to the session if all profits went to PETA), 'Skinthieves' was then released as a US promo single, causing Hynde to intercede on his behalf and have it hastily withdrawn. A less complicated – and one suspects, far more gratifying – appearance occurred in January 1991, when Beck was asked to guest on Buddy Guy's first album in over a decade, *Damn Right I Got The Blues*. An all-star confection, it had additional contributions from Dire Straits' Mark Knopfler and Eric Clapton; Jeff turned up on the old R&B standard 'Mustang Sally', whooping and hollering away in the background as Guy ripped out a world-class vocal on top. As expected, Beck couldn't believe his luck: "I couldn't even see why Buddy wanted me on it, considering his skill." Guy was more than happy to explain: "When Jeff plays, I don't care if I'm asleep. Please wake me up so I don't miss a thing." Cast as an irascible baseball cap-wearing grease monkey who ends up playing guitar with his hero outside 'Mustang Ranch' in the resulting promotional video, Beck had seldom looked happier.

After a best forgotten studio date in July 1991, which found Jeff writing and recording an advertising jingle for clothing giant C&A (it subsequently turned up on German TV), he then turned his hand to a far more substantial project. Having been pursued with some vigour by Roger Waters for the best part of six months, Beck finally agreed to join forces with the former Pink Floyd front man on his third solo disc, *Amused To Death*. A concept album based in part on Neil Postman's 1985 book *Amusing Ourselves To Death* – which analysed and critiqued television's effect on culture – Waters' latest effort was to be a typically 'Floydian' affair: musically ambitious, intellectually challenging and obsessed with the decline and disillusionment of post-war Western society and values. In truth, Jeff had his doubts. Eric Clapton had been the 'featured' guitarist on Roger's first solo LP, 1984's *The Pros And Cons Of Hitch-Hiking*, and having done it once already, Beck wasn't keen to follow in his footsteps. Equally, the subject matter was dense, intricate and, in Jeff's mind, somewhat disheartening. Yet, when he heard the tracks Waters was working on, he couldn't fail to be anything other than impressed. "When you get through the brushwood and see what the subject is, it's deeply depressing, but I liked the music. Roger writes good stuff."

Cut in five distinct sessions during the summer of 1991, Jeff Beck's guitar work on *Amused To Death* was devastating to behold. Geed on by Roger, who had loved 'Where Were You' and keenly encouraged Jeff to adapt a similar approach to his own songs, Beck stole the album from under his boss' feet. Melancholy but menacing on opening track 'The Ballad Of Bill Hubbard', angry but amusing on 'What God Wants, Part I' and lazy but lethal on 'Three Wishes', Jeff's six-song contribution to *Amused To Death* made one wonder how mighty a prospect Pink Floyd might have been if he joined them in 1968. Still a relatively hidden gem in the Beck 'sessions' catalogue – though if truth be told a difficult listen when he's not actually playing guitar – *Amused To Death* reached number 21 in the UK charts when released in September 1992.

As Jeff continued to whittle away his time on soundtracks, sessions, cameos and rods, Epic Records stepped in on behalf of devotees awaiting new product from the man himself and issued *Beckology* in November 1991. The brainchild of Epic's Head of A&R, Greg Geller, *Beckology* followed the same rough business model as Eric Clapton's 1988 collection *Crossroads* and Led Zeppelin's 1990 release *Re-masters* by capturing a mixture of classic, rare and unreleased material in one lavishly packaged three-CD box set. In Beck's case, this translated to 55 tracks spanning a 26-year period, from an early 1963 Tridents session ('Trouble In Mind') to 1989's masterpiece 'Where Were You'. At first, Jeff was suspicious of such a release, seeing it less as a tribute to a fine career and more an 'ego trip'. There was also the notion of "bad apples" to consider. Always keen to find fault with his own work, Beck was not filled with joy at the prospect of previous mistakes or embarrassments making their way onto the final track listing. But Geller's combination of patience and persistence finally paid off as he worked with the guitarist to whittle down a rather rangy 80 songs to a more manageable 55.

Inevitably, there was always going to be jostling among fans and critics as to what should and should not be included. For some,

Beckology represented a perfect opportunity to unearth Jeff's long-lost Motown sessions or live cuts from his 1978 tour with Stanley Clarke. Others – who could not afford to purchase every session Beck had involved himself with over the years – wanted to hear his contribution to the work of Dorian Passante, Badger or The Holy Smoke. In the end, Jeff, Greg Geller and Epic made a fair stab at keeping both sides reasonably happy. BBA followers, for instance, were rewarded with the unreleased (if already heavily bootlegged) 'Jizz Whizz' and a corking in-concert medley of 'Blues Deluxe/ BBA Boogie'. Yardbirds enthusiasts, on the other hand, received a whopping 19 tracks, including three tunes ('Mr You're A Better Man Than I', 'Love Me Like I Love You' and 'Too Much Monkey Business') recorded live at the BBC in 1965. And for Beck's session hunters came the beautiful 'Sleepwalk' from *Porky's Revenge* and '... Train Kept A Rollin'' and 'The Stumble' from *Twins*.

There was, as was often the case with such collections, the odd, peculiar omission or equally baffling addition. 'Star Cycle', surely one of Jeff and Jan Hammer's finest instrumentals, was nowhere to be found. Yet, four tracks from Flash had somehow found their way through quality control. On the upside, 'Plynth...' was present and correct, but 'Spanish Boots' had surrendered its place in the pecking order to 'I've Been Drinking'. 'Tallyman', yes. 'El Becko', no. However, with all songs remastered, an informative 64-page booklet containing rare photos, a strongly written, authoritative essay from journalist Gene Santoro, and its packaging daintily made to look like a tweed guitar case, *Beckology* still represented a fine addition to any Beck freak's collection: "*Beckology* chronicles Jeff Beck's stylish development and innumerable contributions to the electric guitar," said *Guitar World*, "paint[ing] a clear picture of the experimental passion that has always defined his approach." (A single, 17-track CD collection, *The Best Of Beckology*, was also released in November 1991).

At approximately the same time that Epic was asking Jeff's fans to dig deep into their pockets for *Beckology*, Fender was launching its second wave of 'Jeff Beck Signature Stratocasters'. A long-gestating project, the idea had originally presented to Jeff as far back as 1986 when he requested two custom Strat reissues from the company. Seizing the possibility of working with the guitarist on his own custom model, Fender presented him with two workable 'prototypes' – one in a bold 'hot rod' yellow that strongly recalled the famous Deuce Coupe in George Lucas' 1973 movie, *American Graffiti*. With Beck still reticent to officially endorse a guitar, Fender simply reworked its idea, adding Lace Sensor pick-ups – as used in Eric Clapton's 'Signature Strat' – and a Wilkinson tremolo arm, and called it the 'Strat Plus'. These finally got Jeff's attention. Replacing the original maple neck with a rosewood one, Fender sent Beck three new models which included the Surf Green Strat he used to finish 'Where Were You' (and which subsequently became 'Little Richard'), and the 'Midnight Purple' Jeff clutched so fondly in the video for Buddy Guy's 'Mustang Sally'.

But before Beck was completely happy, major modifications were needed for the neck. Never a lover of "the new thin ones", Jeff asked for the fattest possible option – akin to an early fifties Strat design or even similar to his Oxblood Les Paul. "Dan Smith at Fender kept asking 'How big do you want it?'" he said. "I said 'Just picture the biggest lump of wood you can grab hold of with your fingers coming around the front. That's how big I want it.'" And that's what he got. In fact, the earliest official 'Beck prototypes' (for want of a better term) had necks that more resembled baseball bats than anything else. Urgent measures were called for. Hence, 'Prototype Two' shaved things down a bit, but the result remained an acquired taste. A third stab at the problem seemed to bring some resolution, though the guitar was still not for all. "People usually pick up my guitar and say 'Jesus, you can keep that! Take that thing out of here!'" he laughed. "But that's the way I like it, and if people want to buy a 'Jeff Beck' guitar, that's the way I have it." Finally settling on a four pick-up Strat, with two Lace Sensors tied together in the treble position and a floating bridge to provide maximum range for tremolo work, the Beck 'Signature' was a curious, but strangely alluring thing – rewarding those who put in the hours with some rich, throaty sounds.*

---

* Following Fender's first wave of manufacture in 1990, 1992's 'JB' Strats were subsequently modified to include an LSR nut. The original colour schemes on offer were also expanded in due course.

Though already honoured with exclusive box sets and personalised guitars, Jeff Beck had to share his next prize, which came on January 19, 1992 when The Yardbirds were inducted into the Rock & Roll Hall Of Fame. An award bestowed for the group's original efforts, their lasting influence on the rock scene and the fact they managed to house not one but three of the world's great guitarists in their ranks at one time or another, such recognition was a long time coming but still thoroughly deserved. After a word or two onstage from various band members including Jimmy Page, Jeff finally got his chance to talk. The results were hilarious. "I have done other music after The Yardbirds you know," he began. "Anyway, somebody told me I could be proud tonight, but I'm not. Because they kicked me out. No, they did. Fuck 'em." After which, he strolled off laughing. Behind the scenes, he was more serious when encapsulating the band's worth: "We paved the way for barbarism," he said. "We set fire to things."

A much more worrying incident occurred at Paris' Hippodrome de Vincennes on June 6, 1992, where Beck had agreed to join Guns N' Roses onstage for an encore of 'Train Kept A Rollin''. Then officially 'The World's Most Dangerous Band', GNR's ascent to stardom had remained unchecked since the release of their 1987 debut album, *Appetite For Destruction*. True 'Sons of Aerosmith' (who were also appearing as guests at the Paris show), with an added chunk of punk credibility, the group featured a fine, surprisingly soulful guitarist in Slash, who had loved Jeff's work with a passion since his teens. In fact, the two had recently worked together when they provided brief solos alongside Joe Satriani and Steve Lukather on the title track of Spinal Tap's 1992 comedy album, *Break Like The Wind*. "When I finally got to meet Nigel Tufnel face to face," said Beck, "it was just too, too good."* Therefore, when Slash invited Jeff to join Guns for a spot of riffing at their pay-per-view Paris gig, it was an offer he couldn't refuse. But during final rehearsals, Beck found himself in agony: "We'd rehearsed in the dressing room and then went out to do a soundcheck. Matt [Sorum, Guns' drummer] hit one bass drum and it was like 40 million watts going through me. I just had to walk away."

---

* Sadly, no one thought to capture this pivotal moment on video.

As Jeff knew already, the pain he experienced was a result of tinnitus. "I remember my mum warning me about tinnitus," he later told *Clashmusic*. "She told me clearly what was going to happen. And that was when amplifiers were [only] five watts. She'd read about someone who had a continuous ringing in his ears. At the time, I equated loud noise with being good. [But] in about 1990, which was when I got it, my drummer was using these giant cymbals, which crashed into each other. I think they're the worst thing ever. I won't have them onstage with me ever again." Best defined as a persistent buzzing, ringing or whistling in one or both ears, tinnitus was often caused by a specific condition such as infection, the side effect of certain drugs, a blocked auditory tube or even head injury. But in musicians it was usually more attributable to the results of playing at high volumes over a protracted period of time, with subsequent (and often irreversible) damage caused to the inner eardrum.

Aside from Beck, other high-profile tinnitus sufferers included Neil Young, singer Barbra Streisand and, most notably, Pete Towshend, whose hearing had suffered terribly due to endless nights onstage with the 'high-decibel' Who. That said, Jeff could take little consolation from the fact he was not alone in having to deal with it. "You just wouldn't believe how depressed you get," he told journalist Richard Johnston. "When you get the slightest bit under the weather, like lack of sleep or depressed, it moves in like a bailiff to kick you out of your head."

In Beck's case, tinnitus manifested itself as a recurrent "hissing sound" and he investigated several possible cures for the problem – from cochlear implants (only for the deaf) to various drugs and herbal remedies. Yet, while it proved immensely irritating in crowded rooms, where hearing individual voices became maddeningly difficult, the greatest threat was to his livelihood. Without a solution, the potential damage caused by playing an amplified electric guitar at any real volume for even the shortest period of time was too horrible to contemplate. Pursuing a course of trial and error, Jeff was able to finally isolate what worked for him. By rolling all the bass off his amp and carefully adjusting the mid and presence controls, he was able to minimise much of his discomfort, while the use of in-ear monitors for stage work also provided great relief. In the coming years, additional experimentation and further medical treatment would help alleviate much of his distress.

Surprisingly, though Beck was audibly crippled by his experience with Guns N' Roses in Paris, it did not stop him contributing to two songs – 'Fucked Up Beyond Belief' and 'Swamp Song' – on former GNR drummer Duff McKagan's first solo album, *Believe In Me*. "'Fucked Up...' was a song Matt Sorum and I would screw around with at GNR soundchecks," said Duff, "And the two of us went to the studio and recorded in one take. Months later in Paris, Jeff Beck was staying in the hotel room across from me and heard it. He asked if he could 'Have a go'. My hands shaking, I called our manager, and studio time was booked in London the following day." Beck's work on 'Fucked Up...' and 'Swamp Song' was to his usual exacting standards – his Strat literally surfing a wave of artificial harmonics on the former while playfully toying with a flattened fifth before finally deciding to kill it stone dead on the latter.

If the onset of tinnitus had shaken Jeff, it did not dent his need to work, a fact evidenced by the release of *Frankie's House* in February 1993. Written as an accompanying soundtrack to an Australian TV mini-series of the same name, the project teamed Beck with New York-born composer Jed Leiber and was his first effort at scoring for film. In fact, Jed was akin to rock nobility, being the son of Jerry Leiber who alongside Mike Stoller had penned several of Elvis Presley's early classics, including 'Hound Dog', 'King Creole' and the surely perfect 'Jailhouse Rock'.

When in 1981 while touring *There & Back* Beck approached Leiber Snr. about the possibility of re-creating some of that magic for him, Jerry explained his days as an angry young rock'n'roller were long gone. However, he did recommend his keyboard-playing son Jed to Beck, calling him "a holy terror", full of the requisite "piss and vinegar" Beck was after. For the guitarist, this was almost a sign from God: "It was like a blessing from the father of rock'n'roll, or something." When Jed subsequently attended Jeff's show in Manhattan, the two went for a beer afterwards to discuss the prospect of working together. "He's a street kid, he knows what's going on," Beck later told *Guitar Player's* Chris Gill, "and we have the same thread running through his father [into] my childhood." After 10 years of trying to find precisely the right endeavour, *Frankie's House* finally fell into their laps in early 1992.

A drama focusing on the precarious life of a photojournalist documenting the Vietnam War, *Frankie's House* was directed by Peter Fisk and not easy viewing – its plot covering the brutal violence and often appalling excesses that accompanied the conflict. Because of this subject matter, Beck was initially reticent to become involved. "I have to say right up front that I never wanted to get involved with the Vietnam War," he said. "I hated it. The Vietnam vets hated it. I thought, 'This is fucked. This is horrible'. It was such a senseless thing. [And] I'm really a bit annoyed that my first chance at scoring was something like that. Just senseless, like all war." But having read the plot and seen Fisk's rushes, he was soon won over: "I was so touched by the photographer's story that I agreed to do it. A four-part, low-budget, but fantastic series with a great Australian director."

Forming a writing/recording team with Leiber, Beck immersed himself in music from the region, focusing in particular on the koto, a traditional Japanese 13-stringed instrument with a haunting, reedy tone: "It's very deep, very soulful, [with] these painful notes coming up." Working with Jed at first in a home studio, the duo produced some 20 minutes of ideas for the director, including two compositions entitled 'The Jungle' and 'Sniper Patrol'. In 'The Jungle''s case, the emphasis was on combining Beck's newfound ability to emulate koto-like lines on his 'Little Richard' over Leiber's funky, yet obviously Vietnamese-influenced chord voicings. 'Sniper Patrol' was a much more menacing proposition, as Jeff's feedback-skirting solo flight slowly wound its way around Jed's droning synths. Fisk loved the results so much he immediately picked 'The Jungle' as the series' theme tune.

Knowing they had "cracked the nut", Beck and Leiber now moved into a professional studio environment to begin work properly. Dispensing with established practice, Jeff chose not to use an amp to record his parts, but instead ran his Strat straight into the console via a Digitech GSP 21 Legend. An unusual step, it nevertheless provided Beck with the crystal-clear tones required for the 'koto' interludes while also allowing him to reproduce some searing rock tones through the Legend processor. Crucially, it saved his stricken ears a daily battering as well.

In the end, the results were striking. 'Vihn's Funeral' had the same keening aspect to its nature as 'Where Were You', with Beck bending a series of natural and false harmonics with the bar of his 'Little Richard' until they almost cried. Conversely, 'Cat House' was all about 'The Rock', as Jeff cheekily referenced the main riff from his own 'Rice Pudding' in its tight, three-chord progression. 'In The Dark' again saw Beck's returning to his recent koto studies, with an unaccompanied solo pinging soulfully along for a minute or so before ending with a slow tremolo dive, while 'In The Dark' re-created the effect against a backdrop of moody keyboards. There were also some moments of light relief. 'Innocent Victim' began life with some upbeat King Sunny Ade-approved Nigerian Juju music before turning to the dark side as Beck scratched out a trail of dissonant note clusters. But in the case of 'Hi Heel Sneakers', it truly was all sweetness and light, with Jeff even pulling out a Fender Twin reissue, Gretsch Duo-Jet and Tele-Gib for a four-to-the-floor boogie hoedown. Quoting the melody line to 'Mustang Sally' before trading solos with Leiber on his barrel-house piano, 'Hi Heel Sneakers' was the only cover version on *Frankie's House* – its inclusion on the soundtrack coming at the request of Peter Fisk, who learned that Tommy Tucker's 1964 original was a big favourite among US helicopter pilots during the Vietnam conflict.

This devotion to old standards was also present when Beck and Leiber took a break in recording during March 1992 to provide a faithful, if frenetic instrumental version of 'Hound Dog' for the Nicolas Cage/Sarah Jessica Parker comedy *Honeymoon In Vegas*. A huge Presley fan (he even married 'The King''s daughter, Lisa Marie), Cage had been drawn to the movie as one of its pivotal scenes involved a group of Elvis impersonators skydiving from a plane. Furthering the conceit, the film's soundtrack also featured a mixture of Presley originals and newly recorded covers by well-known artists, with Bruce Springsteen, Billy Joel and Willie Nelson belting out the likes of 'Viva Las Vegas', 'Heartbreak Hotel' and 'Blue Hawaii'. Covering all instruments between them, Jeff and Jed cut their contribution to *Honeymoon...* in just half an hour, with Beck pulling double duty on his trusty Duo Jet and the now omnipresent 'Little Richard'. Keen to capture an authentic Jordanaires-like feel to the track, the duo tried singing some 'doo wop' backing vocals behind Jeff's solo, but the experiment didn't work. Clutching at straws, they then asked 'Lance the drum roadie' to try his proverbial hand at the mike. "He went 'Wah...' and [it was]pitch perfect," said Beck. "So we set him down, put the headphones on him, but he didn't know when to stop. So he sang... until he was blue in the face and was collapsing on the floor. I said, 'No, don't stop now, Lance...'" Though the now-collapsed roadie could sing only one note in tune, a little studio trickery enabled his torturers to vary its pitch, thus magically transforming Lance into a ready-made quartet. Recorded in Jerry Leiber's honour – and quite right too, he had co-written the tune – the duo's take on 'Hound Dog' was obviously as irreverent as it was well-intentioned.

With the release of *Frankie's House* and *Honeymoon In Vegas* came a surprising, but thoroughly deserved number of accolades. Both 'Hi Heel Sneakers' and 'Hound Dog' found themselves nominated for 1993's 'Best Rock Instrumental Performance' Grammy while Beck and Leiber's work on *Frankie's House* won a British Academy of Film and Television Arts (BAFTA) award for 'Best Original Television Music'. "I [only] went along [to the presentation] for the ride really," said Beck, "and initially, to tell you the truth, I wasn't really into it. I just sat there criticising it [until] there's me going up there!" Beck's admission was typically self-deprecating, but also hid some real pride. A wet, humid, dank and claustrophobic soundtrack, with the occasional, uplifting blast of rock'n'roll and African music to change mood and motivation, *Frankie's House* was a well-deserved winner, and Beck knew it.

Astoundingly, though *Frankie's House* was released in February 1993, Beck devotees only had to bide their time for three months before his next album hit the stores. For ardent fans, this was the musical equivalent of waiting patiently for a bus only to have two arrive at once...

Entitled *Crazy Legs*, Jeff's latest disc, some 35 years in the making, was a lovingly rendered homage to the music of Gene Vincent & The Bluecaps, and guitarist Cliff Gallup in particular, who had sadly died on October 9, 1988. Beck and his new accomplices The Big Town Playboys had recorded 18 cover versions of classic Vincent material, from beloved singles such as 'Race With The Devil' to lesser-known gems such as 'Catman' and 'You Better Believe'. Almost fractal in his devotion to re-creating the snap, crackle and pop of Vincent's originals, one felt at times that Jeff and the Playboys were less a group and more apostles for a cause. Beck certainly agreed. "I see myself as a sort of evangelist," he said, "[saying] 'listen to the gospel of Cliff Gallup...'"

As evidenced, the idea of cutting a rockabilly-themed album had long possessed Jeff. In the mid-eighties he spoke at length with Rockpile guitarist/singer and fellow rock'n'roll enthusiast Dave Edmunds about getting such a project off the ground, but the idea floundered when Beck heard the work of Telecaster genius Albert Lee: "Albert [already] had that stuff covered. He can just make your toes curl, but in a good way." Another experiment with former Stray Cats Lee Rocker and Slim Jim Phantom died before it had time to settle in the Petri dish, with Rocker and Phantom expecting 'Jeff Beck' to turn up when all he wanted to do was play Cliff Gallup licks. Even Beck's early jams with noise-terrorists The Art Of Noise were driven by a wish to chain the deep growl of Duane Eddy's Gretsch '57 6120 to some "real sonic thuggery". But each new effort only ended in frustration and eventual abandonment – at least until The Big Town Playboys turned up.

Formed in 1984, the Playboys soon established a reputation as a fine live act, their ability to channel the sound of post-WWII swing and West Coast R&B/jump blues marking them out as a spirited alternative to the "robot music" then currently in vogue. Citing influences such as Little Willie Littlefield, Willie Egans and the wonderful Amos Milburn, the band obviously had little truck with synthesisers or drum machines, preferring a combination of piano, upright bass and tenor/baritone saxophones to inform their sound. A 'cult group drawing a cult audience' of greasers, swing kids and other like-minded souls, the Playboys also started to pick up quite the celebrity following, as Robert Plant, Jimmy Page, Dave Edmunds and Eric Clapton became early converts to their cause. By the early nineties, this had ballooned into something of a sect in itself, with the rich and famous chasing the band to perform at events, parties and shindigs in the UK and abroad.

Beck had first heard of the Playboys from his friend Peter Richardson, when they played at his sister's wedding. Unfortunately, Jeff was on tour at the time and missed the show, but he eventually caught up with them at a small London club in 1991. "When I saw them, they had an energy about them that wasn't reliant on high volume," he said. "And even though they weren't playing Gene Vincent stuff, there was that kind of aura... I just loved it." At first, he had concerns about approaching the group – "I couldn't see the sense of pushing myself on them" – but a subsequent jam calmed nerves on both sides: "I got to thinking about how I could work with them, and the Vincent thing just seemed right."

After a period of intense rehearsals which found them covering 31 Bluecaps songs in all, Beck and the Playboys entered west London's Townhouse Studios to begin recording. With engineer Leif Mases returning to the engineer's chair, the project was helmed by Stuart Colman, a producer who had already overseen several eighties hits by rock'n'roll revivalist Shakin' Stevens, including 'This Ole House' and the infectious 'Green Door'. A rockabilly fanatic of long standing who also had his own radio show devoted to playing obscure gems from the fifties, Colman knew his proverbial eggs from his onions. "The Playboys are the coolest form of slime I've ever seen," he said at the time. "They ooze greatness. It's always a joy to capture hot guitar solos on tape and for me, Jeff has taken that joy to a new level."

From the off, Beck was homicidally intent on capturing each click, trill and subtle nuance of Cliff Gallup's style, while also seeking out exactly the right equipment with which to do the job. To this end, in addition to using Gallup's preferred choice of a 1956 Gretsch 6128 Duo Jet with fixed-arm Bigsby tremolo arm as his main instrument, Jeff found a Fender Tremolux combo and Twin/ Bassman amps to further nail down the tone. Even his choice of strings was painfully authentic as he equipped the Duo Jet with a set of Flatwounds, including a hard-to-bend 'G' string. Seeking ultimate closure, Beck also learned to replicate Cliff's picking technique with a thumbpick/fingerpick combination. However, it later came to light that while Gallup had employed fingerpicks on his middle and ring fingers, he did not use one on his thumb – preferring to hold a huge triangular flatpick between first finger and thumb instead. Beck learned this from *Guitar Player's* Chris Gill, who kindly gifted Jeff a set of Gallup's very own picks. "Are you kidding me?" he said after receiving the present, "I'm having a religious moment!"

In a further attempt to clone the unique Gene Vincent sound, Beck and the Playboys reduced the volume of their instruments to the same levels used by The Bluecaps. "The thing that hit me like a ton of bricks was that you didn't play loud," Jeff said later. "I couldn't equate that because I always thought [Vincent's] records sounded loud. But the quieter we played, the better it sounded. Our drummer Clive Deamer hit the nail on the head when he said, 'The whole approach must be controlled... a quiet, but intense input.'" For Beck, this meant volume settings seldom strayed above 'two' on his amp, providing a beautifully clean, but resolutely unforgiving tone. "It's... very honest... almost a dangerous thing. It was 'How good can I really play?' No distortion, no power chords, minimal overdubs, just stripped right back to you with a perfect, clean, pure tone. When you make a fluff, everybody looks around!" To add to his pain, Jeff was also receiving no favours from producer Stuart Colman: "Colman was a bastard – he wouldn't let me off anything! I thought I'd played great, and he'd say 'Almost, no cigar yet.' I thought... maybe he wants to sit in the producer's chair a bit longer. But sure enough, I'd take the tape home and 99% of the time, he'd be right." Though Beck didn't know it, Colman often recorded him without his knowledge, intent on capturing the guitarist at his "spontaneous best".

Cut wherever possible live with all the musicians playing together in the same room, *Crazy Legs* turned out to be one of those curious records that could start an argument at a pub table in a matter of seconds. For some, it was a near-flawless approximation of what made Gene Vincent & The Bluecaps great, with Beck and The Big Town Playboys almost imprisoning the spirit of 'The Virginia Devil' and his band on tape. For others however, it was a static, even sterile exercise in musical reconstruction, with Jeff and his cohorts needlessly tampering with perfection when none was required. Whichever side of the argument one took, there could be little doubt that *Crazy Legs* represented a sincere attempt on Beck's part to shine a light and even reactivate interest in a group and guitarist that had set fire to his head almost three decades before: "[Cliff Gallup's] an incredible smudge on me. The greatest unsung hero of all time. He didn't know I existed. The awe I would have been in… and he would have been sitting there, wishing he was fishing. I would just like to have heard [him say] one syllable. That would have been good enough for me."

Gallup would probably have been in shock at Jeff's attempt to do him justice. On tracks such as 'Cruisin'', 'B-I-Bickey-Bi-Bo-Bo-Go', 'Catman' and 'Who Slapped John', Beck chased and caught every slur, pull-off, dissonant clang and chromatic ascent Cliff had ever called his own – the tone frighteningly correct, the execution flawless. He also made great efforts to reproduce the sense of fun and abandon present in Gallup's playing, with 'Pink Thunderbird', 'Race With The Devil' and 'Blues Stay Away From Me' fizzing away like a well-shaken coke bottle. Not every line or solo was an exact replication of Gallup, however, with Jeff content to introduce his own ideas when required. "I didn't sweat for hours learning every little thing," he said. "Obviously, on the ones that were note perfect and a showcase for his style, I did. [Other times], I'd find myself in trouble halfway through a solo and have to modify it. But [overall], the feeling is pretty close." Equally, it wasn't all about Cliff. Doffing his blue cap to Gallup's replacement, Beck had chosen three Johnny Meeks-era tunes for inclusion on *Crazy Legs*, pulling out a white '62 Strat to fine effect on 'Say Mama', 'Lotta Lovin'' and 'Baby Blue'. "Playing with Gene was the greatest period of my life," Meeks once said. "I was 19, 20 years old, travelling the country… girls every night, a new guitar neck every week if I wanted it. Everything was so beautiful during that era." To Jeff, this must have read like a list of instructions during his time with The Yardbirds.

The Big Town Playboys were certainly worthy of their share of the praise too. Founding member/bassist Ian Jennings and drummer Clive Deamer made for a propulsive rhythm section, while rhythm guitarist Adrian Utley's fluid, meticulous lines were like bedrock for Jeff's more acrobatic fretboard assaults: "Adrian's less a berserker than me!" Saxophonists Nick Lunt and Leo Green's low stabs and high screams also helped prop up the material at play, turning 'Say Mama' into a little party all its own. But if there was a Playboy who walked from the enterprise deserving a medal, it was surely singer/pianist Mike Sanchez. Given the unenviable task of playing Gene Vincent to Beck's Gallup/Meeks, Sanchez was a revelation, his vocals on 'Woman Love', 'Catman' and 'Hold Me, Hug Me, Rock Me" sometimes as earthy and animalistic as the great man himself.

Ultimately, the one track that would define or destroy Beck and the Playboys' dalliance with Gene and his Bluecaps was their rendition of 'Be Bop A Lula'. In a stroke of near genius on Jeff's part, he ducked it. "I deliberately left it out because everyone would expect it," Beck told Chris Gill. "We did play it, and it sounded great and felt great. But it was the post-'Be Bop...' period we were interested in. If we put [it] on the record, it would be the one most likely to be played. If we don't put it on, then they can't play it. Anyway," Jeff concluded, "I'm an awkward son of a bitch when it comes to doing the expected." Never a truer word spoken.

Released in June 1993, *Crazy Legs* was never going to be an easy sell, even to the most passionate Beck aficionado. Neither rock, blues, fusion, techno-boogie or funk, the disc was an obvious love letter from the guitarist to his youth, and bore little or no relation to his own previous releases – even if Gallup's influence was writ large across them all. Therefore, it came as no great surprise that *Crazy Legs* only managed to graze the US charts with a number 171 placing while failing to even register in the UK. Still, Jeff's regrets were less focused on the album's commercial performance and more to do with how Mike Sanchez's vocals were recorded. "The only thing I regret about that record is we didn't distort the vocals," he said. "The original rockabilly records in the fifties had that, and with Gene Vincent, his vocals had a progressive distortion. The more he shouted, the more distorted it became and that's what gave it its power. Take that away, and it loses some of the dynamics. Still..."

Originally, there were plans to take *Crazy Legs* to the US for a nine-date tour. But aside from a one-off gig at Paris' La Cigalle theatre in front of 1,400 crazed fans on April 23, 1993 (if anyone understood the appeal of Gene Vincent, it was surely the French), Beck and the Playboys were content to end it there. "I'm not pretending that we did a better job than the original," said the guitarist. "In fact, I hope people actually go back and check the original. The original still has an incredible aura about it and maybe we've missed that, but we've been able to improve on the quality of the sound – not that that makes it necessarily better, but you know, we've got the right atmosphere and the grooves are right. We really tried to re-create the warmth of those early records."

Following his adventures with the ghosts of Gene Vincent and Cliff Gallup, Jeff again found himself back in the CD racks on a number of titles, though this time all of them featured him in his other guise as special guest rather than star performer. First out of the traps in the summer of 1993 was former Free/Bad Company singer Paul Rodgers' *Muddy Water Blues...*, a high-profile tribute album to the seminal Louisiana bluesman. In a clever marketing move, Rodgers had enlisted the help of 11 of the world's more gifted/notable guitarists to help him cover some of Muddy's best-known tunes, including 'I Can't Be Satisfied', 'I'm A Hoochie Coochie Man' and 'I'm Ready'. Among those lending their talents were Buddy Guy, Pink Floyd's David Gilmour, Queen's Brian May, Journey's Neal Schon, former Stray Cat Brian Setzer, Guns N' Roses' Slash and the always emotive Gary Moore. Unlike the rest, who were usually allotted only one track, Beck was given three songs by Rodgers on which to shine. And shine he did, almost taking the roof off 'Rollin' Stone', slip-sliding around 'Good Morning Little Schoolgirl (Part One)', and providing his meanest performance in years on 'I Just Want To Make Love To You'. When asked why Jeff was so prominently featured throughout the disc, Paul gave a blunt, but probably very honest answer: "Well, there's Jeff Beck and then there are other guitar players."*

The next two sessions Jeff turned his attention to were with female singer/songwriters, albeit both operating at resolutely different ends of the musical spectrum. In Beverley Craven's case, this amounted to piano-led pop melodies sung in a breathy, melancholic style – not a territory one normally associated with Beck. "I think she was wondering why the hell I was there, and to be perfectly honest, so was I," he said. "I suppose I'd become fascinated by her demeanour

---

* Beck and Rodgers were to collaborate again soon, recording a surprisingly sensitive version of 'On Broadway' for the 1994 movie *The Cowboy Way*.

when she was playing the piano. Anyway, I found out [Paul Samwell-Smith] was producing the record, so I went along. She just sat there, staring at the floor while I was playing. And I thought, 'This is the most miserable time I've ever had.' But then she said, 'That was amazing'. Then I just went home." Jeff's confusion was there for all to hear on Craven's twee cover of Abba's 'The Winner Takes It All', his barking mad first solo clearly the work of a man who would rather be somewhere – anywhere – else. That said, his second pass was much more conciliatory, its 'wounded trombone' tone sounding like an apology for losing his temper in the first place.

In comparison with Beverley Craven, Beck's choice to work with Kate Bush made far more sense. A national treasure in the UK, Kate's musical career was almost as difficult to chart as Jeff's own. Beginning her assault on the senses with 1978's 'Wuthering Heights', Bush's subsequent experiments had come to define an eccentric, yet quite brilliant form of art-pop uniquely her own, the likes of 'Running Up That Hill', 'Army Dreamers' and 'Cloudbusting' all treats for the ear. However, Kate was somewhat surprised by Beck's choice of guitar for the session, recoiling in horror at the sight of his Surf Green Strat. "She said it was the ugliest guitar she'd ever seen," he laughed. "She nearly vomited at the sight of it."

Once equilibrium was restored, Jeff was given the opportunity to illustrate what his 'Little Richard' could do, the guitarist providing a serene, tremolo-heavy break on 'You're The One', a wistful track on Bush's album of November 1993, *The Red Shoes*.

In the same month, Beck's contribution to *Stone Free: A Tribute To Jimi Hendrix*, was also released. Again joining a starry cast that included Eric Clapton, Buddy Guy, Slash, Paul Rodgers and punk violinist Nigel Kennedy, Jeff teamed up with R&B singer Seal and old friend and former Upp drummer Jimmy Copley for a brisk run through of Jimi's 'Manic Depression'. A perfect alliance of soulful vocals and ferocious guitar, Beck and Seal enjoyed working together so much they did it again on 'Bring It On', a tune recorded for the vocalist's second, self-titled album, released seven months later. "I need somebody around that I can believe in," Jeff confessed when recalling Hendrix's impact and influence on him. "I don't believe in anyone else."

1994 brought further small treats, with Beck putting in a comedic turn whèn asked to speak at Rod Stewart's induction into the Rock & Roll Hall of Fame on January 19. "Rod loves me," he said from the podium, "and I hate him." From there, it really was a case of 'good friends and a bottle of wine' for the rest of the year. Returning a previous kindness for his work on 'The Train Kept A Rollin'' from 1988's *Twins* soundtrack, Jeff's brief, but telling appearance on 'Emergency' – a fine tune from singer Andrew Roachford's much underrated disc, *Permanent Shade Of Blue* – was finally released in the spring of 1994. Jan Hammer was next to benefit, as Beck popped up as a guest for two instrumentals on his former musical partner's album *Drive,* providing a languid, jazzy solo on the title track and a slow-burning break on 'Underground'.

Obviously keen to catch up with as many old comrades as possible, Jeff also threw his lot in with Stanley Clarke's soundtrack for 1994's teen baseball movie, *Little Big League.* It was a mixture of incidental music and sixties surf covers, and Beck was credited for his laboratory-like restorations of The Ventures' 'Walk, Don't Run' and The Surfaris' self-defining 'Wipeout', though he also contributed to Clarke's overall score. "You know, it was a lot of fun seeing Jeff making music for a movie," recalled Clarke. "He was a natural. I'd love to see Jeff do a movie score. I don't know what movie it'd be... maybe a car movie. You know, he could have done the music for the *Fast And Furious* movies, he'd have been perfect for that!"

A second film Beck was briefly associated with during this period was *Blue Chips*, yet another baseball drama this time top-lined by *Rich Man, Poor Man*'s Nick Nolte. The draw for Jeff here was the chance to reunite with Jed Leiber, but after a disagreement with a producer over what tone the soundtrack should take, the two cited 'musical differences' and quickly left the project. At a momentary loss for something to do, Beck took up John McLaughlin's kind offer to duet with him on his new album, *The Promise.* As with *Muddy Water Blues...* and *Stone Free...*, *The Promise* was awash with celebrity musicians, as guitarists Al Di Meola and Paco De Lucia, saxophonists Michael Brecker and David Sanborn, and even Sting joined McLaughlin for a walk on the jazz high-wire. Jeff and John's subsequent work on 'Django' was an absolute delight, with both men paying tribute to the pioneering Manouche Gypsy virtuoso in their own unique ways, Beck floating over the melody with his tremolo arm – volume swells here and there adding emotional impetus to certain notes and flourishes – while McLaughlin attacked the tune like a drunken sax player, high-speed scales and trills shooting this way and that. "No one's born with John's talent," Jeff later said. "You just have to sit and study. I'd just like to know what he did study... the guy's something else." An exceptional disc, *The Promise* was eventually released in February 1996.

From lightning sessions with bassist Will Lee to a slight, but endearing solo on Italian rock/R&B singer Zucchero's 'No More Regrets', Beck had lent his guitar to no less than a dozen albums, singles or soundtracks since 1993's *Crazy Legs*. But as 1995 beckoned, there was still no announcement as to when he might again release something under his own steam. Behind the scenes, however, Jeff had been far from idle. In fact, he spent much time during 1994 working with Tony Hymas and former Police drummer Stewart Copeland on several tracks of his own, even pulling in Paul Rodgers and Canadian rocker Bryan Adams to add the occasional vocal. Yet, these sessions had proved unsatisfactory, Beck's initial idea of experimenting with world-music beats and lush synth patterns eventually coming to nothing.

The installation of a new home studio in the attic of his East Sussex fortress, replete with separate control room and eight-track recording machine brought several other guests to the party. Sade percussionist Martin Ditcham was one such visitor, as was drummer Richard Bailey, with whom Jeff had last engaged on 1976's *Wired*. Obviously in hot pursuit of a rhythmically-driven sound, Beck later described these experiments as "really strong, really tribal", an attempt on his part to combine the spirit of Hendrix with African beats. Nonetheless, this too went the way of the dodo. "There's not many days I don't pick up the guitar, much to my girlfriend's annoyance," he said at the time. "She'll be watching *Coronation Street* and I'll be giving it a Cliff Gallup accompaniment. I do a rocking version of the *Coronation Street* theme." For anyone familiar with *Coronation Street's* dreary, brass band-driven theme tune, one can only hope Beck was joking.

By the summer of 1995, the guitarist had grown sufficiently bored of trying out various ideas only to fail, or holding out for potentially lucrative, but maddeningly ephemeral soundtracks, and accepted an offer from Carlos Santana to share the bill on a North American tour. Though Beck had already toured with Carlos in 1986, it still always seemed a strange pairing on paper: Jeff, the maverick who had walked away from Woodstock ("I was never more pleased that I wasn't involved in that shit") and Carlos, the perpetual San Francisco hippie who became a star after playing at the event. But despite such differences in outlook, the two admired each other greatly. "It's always an honour and a privilege to play with Jeff, and it's great to see people respond to our playing, especially when we play together," said Santana. "Once it all happens, it's like seeing there's no division between his consciousness and my consciousness. We both love the blues." Beck's assessment was shorter, but just as sweet: "Santana is one of the guys. Like a big oak tree, he's always there."

Sagely, Jeff gathered the best possible group he could for the shows, once again bringing back Tony Hymas and Terry Bozzio to cover keyboards and drums while also adding an impressive new recruit in bassist Pino Palladino. First turning heads in 1983 as a member of English R&B singer Paul Young's backing band, Palladino's ever-blossoming session diary had brought him into Beck's circle of friends nine years later, when they worked together on the jingle for clothing giants C&A. Since that intriguing moment in time, Pino had only consolidated his worth, backing Jeff on 'Manic Depression' and 'Django'. An exceptionally tall, exceptionally talented fretless bass player, Palladino's slippery, progressive jazz style suited Beck well: "He's got guts, melody, and is also one of the best bass players in the country. He's also pro-basketball tall, so we'll have to sink him into the stage."

Though there were some concerns about Jeff's tinnitus causing havoc due to the high volume required at 5–10,000 seater venues, they proved unfounded – his 'Future Sonics' in-ears system keeping him well protected from the excesses of the Pro Co Rat, Marshall Super Lead Plexi and Fender Bassman he used for the tour. Opening with a two-night stopover at Vancouver's Wolftrap theatre on July 31, Beck's set mixed well-trodden classics such as 'Star Cycle' and 'The Pump' with a blast or two of new material, including 'Hurricane', which had come out of the guitarist's sessions with Jed Lieber some time before. Full of those 'jungle drums and droning synths', Beck wasn't kidding about the Hendrix angle either, his Strat tormenting 'Hurricane''s odd atonalities with the same type of bends, squeals, tears and rips present on 'Voodoo Child (Slight Return)'. Crossing into the US in early August, the Jeff/Carlos double-header ran 44 dates in all, coming to an end at New York's Paramount Theater on October 9, 1985. "I don't want to be touring like this when I'm 80," Jeff said archly, "Well, maybe I do, but I'm [also] quite happy staying at home." Presumably, so was his 'Little Richard Strat', which took a repeated onstage pounding during the tour, with Beck even throwing into it into the overhead lights on one occasion. Suffice to say, he missed his catch on the way down, and the instrument was lucky not to have been broken in two.

With no new product to promote for these dates, Epic Records had strung together another Jeff compilation to tempt fans with, its title the accurate, but rather dry *Best Of Beck*. A 14-track disc, which ran the gamut from The Yardbirds' 'Shapes Of Things' to 1989's 'Where Were You' (no room for Gene Vincent tunes here), it actually proved a serviceable, even thoughtful collection. In addition to the tunes, inestimable Living Colour guitarist Vernon Reid had also provided liner notes and a brief essay for the album. "God, Vernon loves Jeff's stuff," said Doug Wimbish, who had joined Living Colour on bass in 1992. "Brothers in sonics. They both sound as mad as each other!"

Of equal interest was *Jeffology*, a tribute album to Beck released in November 1995 on Shrapnel/Triage records. The first of many such honorifics to come, *Jeffology* once again proved how much the eighties wave of shredders held him in esteem. From Def Leppard guitarists Vivian Campbell and Phil Collen's semi-faithful treatments of 'Led Boots' and 'Cause We've Ended As Lovers' to Jake E. Lee's radicalised version of 'Rice Pudding', all appeared eager to show their respect by blowing valves and snapping whammy bars. If one had to pick a proverbial 'King of the Hill', then it was probably Warren DeMartini's bold, but still reverential take on 'New Ways Train Train', which pulled Jeff's early seventies classic kicking and screaming into the new age.*

---

* For those seeking the 'ultimate' Beck cover, however, Paul Gilbert's two-handed battering of 'El Becko' remains hard to beat.

1995 ended on a bittersweet note for Jeff. Having completed a successful tour with Carlos Santana, he was presented with *Guitar Player*'s 'Lifetime Achievement Award', joining a 'Gallery of Greats' that included the likes of Les Paul, Bo Diddley, José Feliciano, Eric Clapton and Steve Howe. Distinguished company, indeed. Sadly, this good news was tempered by the death of Beck's former manager Peter Grant from a heart attack on November 21. He was among the mourners when Grant was buried at Hellingly Cemetery in East Sussex on December 4. A giant of the industry both figuratively and physically, Peter had done little of real note since the demise of Led Zeppelin in 1980. But his influence on how record companies, promoters and merchandising outlets treated bands still resonated throughout the business. "We owe so much to that man," said The Yardbirds' Chris Dreja. "He changed the balance for musicians. His vision was amazing. His dedication was with Led Zeppelin and between them they had a very powerful tool." Beck echoed Dreja's thoughts: "People talk about Peter in a strange way, sometimes. I only saw the professional side of him, the good. No funny business."

After four years of wavering levels of activity, all was then radio silence as Jeff once more went to ground, the guitarist content to scurry home and lock the door behind him until the next wave of inspiration came knocking. "If people like what I've done up to now, I'll just carry on that way... bend the rules," he said. "I don't like the thought of being booted out of the music business, [but] sometimes I'm just amazed I've still got a job." At 51 years old, he really had nothing left to prove: pioneer, inspiration, now in the 'Gallery of the Greats'. If he so wished, Jeff could simply walk away, his status sealed, his legend assured.

Not a hope in Hell.

Chapter 22

Starting Fires With Guitars

1 996 brought little news of Jeff Beck, with only the occasional 'bleep' on the radar to assure fans he was still twanging away: a quick, personal appearance in Los Angeles to have his hands captured in cement on Hollywood's 'Rock Walk of Fame'; a strong nod of approval on hearing that his hero Cliff Gallup had been recently honoured by *Guitar Player* with the very same 'Lifetime Achievement Award' he received in 1995; an uncredited solo on 'Reaching Out', a track on *Rock Therapy* – an album in aid of the charity Nordoff-Robbins, whose music centres helped disadvantaged children and adults; and the addition of 'Where Were You' to *Fender's 50th Anniversary Guitar Legends* disc, where it joined the legendary likes of Ritchie Blackmore's 'Smoke On The Water', Mark Knopfler's 'Sultans Of Swing' and Buddy Holly's 'That'll Be The Day'. All in all, these were quiet times.

That said, Jeff did end 1996 with a bang, when he flew to Ireland to join Ronnie Wood and original Elvis Presley guitarist Scotty Moore and drummer DJ Fontana for the recording of 'Unsung Heroes', a track to be featured on *All The King's Men*. A tribute album to mark the 20th anniversary of Presley's death, *All The King's Men* found Moore and Fontana remembering their boss alongside the likes of Keith Richards, The Band, Cheap Trick and The Jordanaires. "Jimmy and I used to dribble over Scotty and DJ's playing when we were kids," Beck said later. With Big Town Playboy Ian Jennings filling in for the sadly deceased (and third 'King's Man') Bill Black on bass,

'Unsung Heroes' proved a real treat, with Beck and Wood trading licks over a spongy, rockabilly rhythm.

In comparison with 1996, 1997 was yet more tranquil, with Jeff committing to only two recordings throughout the year. Finding the lure of another teenage hero impossible to resist, the guitarist duetted with BB King on the old standard 'Three O'Clock Blues', a tune scheduled to appear on King's next disc, *Deuces Wild*. But contractual problems saw the song removed from the track listing at the 12th hour, its eventual resting place on a rare CD promo or in bootleg heaven. However, Beck's contribution to the Steve Vai-compiled *Merry Axemas* did make the cut. It was a clever idea from an astounding musician – Vai had approached 11 of the world's finest players and asked them to record a Christmas-related carol/tune of their choice. "The challenge was to invite special guests [for a] Yuletide extravaganza," he said in the disc's liner notes, "players who could coax, caress or just slam a unique voice from [their] instrument and unite the spirit of Christmas with the beautiful tones of silver strings."

He wasn't kidding. With Aerosmith's Joe Perry bashing the living daylights out of 'Blue Christmas', Rush's Alex Lifeson gently picking his way through 'The Little Drummer Boy' and Vai himself coming across as a 'Shred Sinatra' on 'Christmas Time Is Here', *Merry Axemas* was nothing if not great fun. For Jeff, there was always only one choice for the project: 'Amazing Grace'. Backed by the angelic voices of the London Choral Society – with Tony Hymas stepping in to conduct for the occasion – Beck's elegiac reading of the 18th-century hymn was almost as touching as his work on 'Where Were You'. "Well, I turned up looking like a rocker," he laughed, "and [the choir] wondered what the hell I was doing creeping around the studio. There were a few accidents because I wasn't used to not having drums, and I was [recording] in a room on my own, because if I messed up it would have gotten on the vocal track. But it was real fun – I just wanted to get out there among them all. Bit of a wrestle, but it didn't turn out too bad."

After an extremely low-key two years, 1998 finally saw some real bustling in the hedgerow. On January 19, Jeff flew into New York to perform 'Be Bop A Lula' alongside blues young gun Jonny Lang for the induction of Gene Vincent into the Rock & Roll Hall of Fame. Having been a group recipient of the award with The Yardbirds in 1992, and a comic speaker at Rod Stewart's moment in the sun during 1994, this was his third visit to the ceremony in six years. One suspected it was probably the most satisfying: "Gene Vincent floored me."

However, there were several musicians on whom Beck had performed a similar trick. Following the death of Freddie Mercury in 1991, Queen guitarist Brian May had cautiously rebuilt a career on his own terms, with 1992's *Back To The Light* marking his debut as a solo artist. On completing work on a Queen posthumous release, 1995's *Made In Heaven*, he returned to his home studio to begin penning songs for a proposed movie and second solo album. When the film fell through, May found himself in possession of a throaty, hard-rock tune but no soundtrack on which to put it. Thinking on his feet, he turned the song into a Jeff Beck tribute called 'The Guv'nor' and asked Beck to play on it, which he did. "Jeff is the 'Guv'nor,'" Brian later said. "He's the best pop-type oriented guitar player there is, really. Everybody loves to play his licks."

The result was one of the standout tracks on May's 1998 disc *Another World*, with Jeff providing ample evidence that when it came down to it, he really was in a league of his own. Unfortunately, the making of *Another World* was marred by tragedy. In a curious twist of fate, Beck's old friend Cozy Powell had been providing drums for the album, but was killed in a car accident halfway through recording. In his honour, Brian decided to take samples of Cozy's unused work to complete the project. One of rock's great journeyman drummers, who had enlivened the work of Black Sabbath, Rainbow, Whitesnake as well as JBG2, Powell was going to be missed: "Simply one of a kind," said Jeff.

There was no such sadness to *In My Life*, a compilation of Beatles cover tunes complied and produced by Sir George Martin to mark his retirement from the music industry at the grand old age of 72. With half the known entertainment world trying to prise their way onto the album, space was tight, but Beck was not to be denied – least of all by the producer of *Blow By Blow*. "I was so thrilled that George chose me to be one of the guests," said Jeff. "And then, when

I found out that Goldie Hawn was on it with Jim Carrey, I went, "Wait a minute…" With actors Hawn and Carrey tackling 'A Hard Day's Night' and 'I Am The Walrus' respectively, and Sean 'James Bond' Connery whispering his way through 'In My Life' itself, this was to be no ordinary enterprise. But Beck's choice of Beatles cover proved inspired. "I chose 'A Day In The Life'," he said. "I pulled that song out of the air in the studio on the day. And I'd just wondered what the hell I'd done. [But] it couldn't have been a better choice, really. And George said that he would do the strings…"

One of Lennon and McCartney's most evocative compositions, which took part of its lyrical inspiration from the death of their close friend (and Guinness heir) Tara Browne, 'A Day In The Life' still held fond memories for Sir George. "I first heard it with John just playing his guitar in front of me," he said. Rising gently from Lennon's spare acoustic chord progression, 'A Day…' was turned by The Beatles and Martin into one "big orchestral orgasm", as a bank of 40 strings drove the principal melody skyward, seemingly never to return. "What I did was to write the lowest possible note for each of the instruments in the orchestra," the producer confirmed. "At the end of the 24 bars, I wrote the highest note… near a chord of E major. Then I put a squiggly line right through the 24 bars, with reference points to tell them roughly what note they should have reached during each bar. Of course, they all looked at me as though I were completely mad." Nonetheless, it worked. Wondrously, Beck managed to encapsulate this delirious turn of musical events with just his Stratocaster and a Marshall amp. Following Lennon's vocal closely to begin, the guitarist soon added his own character to the melody, with Martin's strings holding up each twist, trill and tremolo-assisted bend. Rightly nominated for 'Best Pop Instrumental Performance' at the 2000 Grammys, 'A Day In The Life' subsequently became a signature tune for Jeff himself, joining 'Where Were You' and 'Star Cycle' as one of the 'must play' tunes in his concert set.

Before *In My Life* was released in October 1998, Jeff had struck out on the road for his first tour in nearly three years, with three new musicians in tow. Taking over duties on bass was Randy Hope-Taylor, a fine, soulful player who had cut his teeth with British acid-jazz pioneers Incognito, before expanding his portfolio in the world of sessions. Every bit his equal on drums was Steve Alexander, who first found fame as part of English eighties boy band Brother Beyond. Like Hope-Taylor, Alexander subsequently found work as a studio musician, though by 1998 he had followed Terry Bozzio's path and taken up the drummer's stool with pop icons Duran Duran. "The first time [I played with them was] in front of 20,000 people in Chicago. And stuff like 'Rio' and 'The Reflex' are great fun to play," he said. "I enjoyed making it sound like the records, because the drums were always a major, major part of the Duran sound." Through serendipity and several industry contacts, Steve found himself jamming with Jeff and several other musicians at the guitarist's country home: "They said to me, 'We're only looking at you. Don't think of it as an audition, let's just see how we get along.'" Obviously, it went well. A powerhouse in the truest sense of the word, but one also imbued with a strong funk sensibility, Alexander was the latest in a long and distinguished line of drummers there to light a fire under Beck's skinny posterior.

The final recruit joining Jeff's cause was a delightful surprise named Jennifer Batten. "A demon with six-foot hair," she had first met Beck in 1992 when she was lead guitarist on Michael Jackson's *Dangerous* world tour. Having sold close to 200 million albums and then the reigning 'King of Pop', Jackson was a difficult man to upstage, but Jennifer had almost done it – her wondrous abilities picking up a fanbase not only among Michael's own supporters, but also Jeff himself: "She could piss rings around most everybody." The two soon became friends, with Batten staying at Beck's home during breaks in touring. Inevitably, talk turned to the possibility of future collaboration, but various commitments on both sides halted progress until 1998 when Jennifer was free to join Jeff on tour.

The responsibility she was taking on her shoulders was considerable. In addition to backing up Beck's solo excursions, Batten would also be responsible for covering all keyboard parts via a midi-guitar interface – her six strings responsible for summoning up the sound of Hammond organs, banjos, synth lines and a plethora of other settings (some 60 in all). When questioned as to why he was joining forces with another guitarist for the first time since Ronnie Wood's brief tenure in 1967, Jeff was emphatic: "Jen's no ordinary guitar player. She's a warrior woman... a vital ingredient, the driving force in the band." For her sins, Batten just sounded relieved to be standing next to Beck rather than staring down at him in the audience: "Everybody looks up to Jeff... because he has that magic thing. [But] I'm a lot more comfortable onstage with him than I'd be if he was in the audience watching me!"

Initially scheduled to last 21 dates and visit several European countries including Germany, Switzerland and Italy, Beck's summer tour of 1998 was extended from July to October as the group ventured to South America for more concerts in Mexico, Uruguay, Argentina and Chile. In fact, by the time Jeff got to Brazil, he was breaking box-office records, his show at Rio's Free Jazz Festival topping previous ticket sales set by old friend Stevie Wonder the year before. As he had never played Brazil before – let alone any part of South America – this was an impressive feat. Broadcast on national TV, the Free Jazz Festival found the new band in excellent form: Randy Hope-Taylor and Steve Alexander a two-headed rhythm machine, Beck and Batten a remarkable pairing. This was best illustrated on 'Star Cycle', as Jennifer ably covered all Jan Hammer's Moog parts with her guitar and a small army of foot-triggered effects, while Jeff soloed himself like a whirling dervish over the top. This contrast of the professorial and auto-didactic worked a treat, though when Batten stepped from behind her bank of switches and cut loose with the occasional lead break on tracks such as 'Savoy', she gave Beck a run for his money: "Jen's a monstrous talent."

Batten, Alexander and Hope-Taylor would all feature prominently on Jeff's next album, *Who Else!*, which was released in March 1999. Truthfully, the uphill struggle to get a disc into shops at all had already weighed heavily on the guitarist's shoulders for over two years. At first, Beck's latest enterprise appeared in safe hands when Toto's Steve Lukather took up the role of producer in 1997, the two working on ideas both at Jeff's home and at Steve's LA studio, The Steakhouse. Here, demos of 'Hurricane' and several other "heavily rhythmic" tunes were developed. "We've cut 18 songs already and six or seven are still in the running," Lukather told *Guitar World* in early 1998. "We've re-recorded some songs three or four times. Jeff demands the best from himself, and it's my job to keep him from erasing things. You wouldn't believe the amazing performances we've chucked..."

But as the sessions continued, Beck became increasingly wary of the results: "[Steve's] enthusiasm started to overtake the quality of the writing. I'd play some stupid, single-note riff and he'd freak out and say it was great." Whether Lukather's inability to put side his own longtime admiration of Jeff's skills and focus on the job in hand was the stumbling block remains uncertain. But producer and guitarist parted company – though still on the best of terms – before the summer tour of 1988: "Good players can make anything sound good. You need a captain telling you where it's going, or you'll hit an iceberg, and we hit a few icebergs on the way."

There were other hurdles to negotiate along the way. According to Beck, 'The Steakhouse Sessions' (as they have come to be known) had also coincided with an ongoing struggle to create something genuinely new with the guitar – a simple creative block that led to an altogether more distressing problem. "My guitar had just become a symbol of misery," he said later. "I was thinking 'What the hell did I waste my time on this for?'" Forward momentum came from an unexpected source. While visiting a cranial osteopath treating him for persistent head and backaches caused by his car crash in 1969, Jeff talked of his current woes. Evidently as good a therapist as she was a physician, the osteopath managed to persuade the guitarist he was experiencing nothing more than a temporary aberration and should continue working with the instrument. The advice stuck and Beck found a new sense of purpose. Though now mentally back on track, he was still without a producer, or indeed, strong enough material from which to craft an album. The matter was resolved by the arrival of Tony Hymas, who stepped into the breach and began writing as quickly as his fingers would allow. By Christmas Eve, 1998, Jeff's new record was complete.

Quite the surprise, goodly portions of *Who Else!* found Jeff Beck in thrall to the sound of techno and big beat, two genres of electronic dance music that had their origins in the clubs of Detroit in the mid-eighties, but soon barged their way into pop, rock and even heavy metal. At first, techno appeared little more than a bolting of electronic pioneers such as Kraftwerk and Yellow Magic Orchestra onto African-influenced rhythms. Yet, by the early nineties it had become a foundation stone for the UK's big-beat scene, with acts such as The Propeller Heads and The Chemical Brothers beefing up their sound with heavy break-beats, synthesizer-loops and other high-energy sampling patterns.

In 1996, The Prodigy took the movement worldwide, pulling the sound out of DJs' hands at parties and raves, and adding a little punk-friendly attitude and rock-like bombast to the mix. As a result, their parent-baiting single 'Firestarter' and album *Fat Of The Land* sold in the millions and gave big beat its first US number one. Though Beck first engaged with electronic music in the sixties while listening to avant-garde composer Tom Dissevelt with Jimmy Page – "It was like other-world music, white noise and heavy bass lines... it screwed my head up for good" – this new, propulsive jungle noise terrorism was just what the doctor ordered. "I was aiming for rave music, Ibiza, house. I didn't care too much about playing live," said Jeff. "I just wanted something that might take off in the clubs, maybe. I'd always loved that music, the wildness, the outrageous volume you can get in those clubs, and I'd never really heard any guitar playing on that sort of stuff, just drum and bass, or vocal samples."

For a man who had treated the advent of eighties synth-pop with such suspicion, this might have sounded like a volte-face. But as evidenced, Beck never really had anything against synthesizers, a fact borne out by his longtime associations with keyboard kings Jan Hammer and Tony Hymas. Instead, his objection related to the 'robotic' aspects of those early pop records, their glacial splendour and maddeningly precise rhythms an anathema to the earthy rock'n'roll he originally connected with. However, over time, technology had been bested to the point where programmable beats and drum patterns were now capable of surpassing anything generated by two beefy forearms and a strong right foot. "The energy levels and levels of intricacy that can be obtained with techno [drum programming] are far greater than those that can be achieved by using real drums," Jeff said at the time. "But I didn't actually want [that] to overshadow anything else. The samples and beats [we used] were really there for stylistic effect." Ultimately, Beck was aiming for a new kind of fusion, one where he and the likes of drummer Steve Alexander could harness such advances to their own ends: "The computer is like a Zimmer frame. You play one note and you can make a whole album out of it. It's convenient but it's not real. It's just graphics. Where's the music?"

Despite such ambitions, the music of *Who Else!* was only partially successful in bringing Jeff's grand scheme to life, sounding more like a man circling the challenges of a new age rather than really mastering them. That said, there was much to admire about the record, its sheer sense of musical gall often overcoming at least some of those nagging doubts about Beck's latest musical endeavour. This was nowhere more apparent than on the opening track, 'What Mama Said'. With its central, galloping riff written by Jennifer Batten and combination of programmed break-beats, real drums and bass, the tune was a real techno/hard rock stew, with Jeff pouring his own brand of sonic gravy on top. "Mel Wesson did the programming on that," he later confirmed. "A real young guy, great attitude, [like] 'Chop it up!'" 'What Mama Said' also contained several samples of dialogue from one of the guitarist's favourite films, 1963's *It's A Mad, Mad, Mad, Mad World*. "Oh yeah," remembered The Yardbirds' Jim McCarty. "Beck used to love that movie, he watched it loads of times. He much preferred it to *Blow Up* anyway!"

The passion for techno, ambient, trance and other electronic textures continued throughout *Who Else!*. 'THX 138' – its title taken from the licence plate of the yellow rod featured in George Lucas' *American Graffiti* – was also indebted to the big beat, as Beck hammered his way across a bank of complex rhythms. 'Psycho Sam' fell into a similar area. Originally called 'Arab Hoot' and salvaged from Steve Lukather's 'Steakhouse Sessions', the tune was akin to a jittery 'sabre dance', as synth stabs and triggered snares fought a running battle with Jeff's heavily compressed guitar bursts. Dubious name aside, 'Hip-Notica' was also beholden to electronica, though this time the emphasis was chilling rather than rocking out. Essentially a long jam, with Beck using his slide to invoke Indian sitar moods, 'Hip-Notica' was a musical flip side to 'Blast From The East' – a rowdy Asian-themed instrumental cut in 7/4 time that featured Jeff bizarrely emulating the vocals of forties vocal act The Andrews Sisters.

On both tracks, Beck's approach was heavily influenced by the work of renowned Indian bottleneck slide guitarist Vishwa Mohan Bhatt: "His [playing's] almost too exquisite for words. Like Ravi Shankar, but on guitar..." Bhatt's inspiration was also a telling factor on 'Space For The Papa', a languid piece that again found Jeff quoting from Indian scales and 'Arabic Madams' to inform his melodic choices. In addition to its trance-like quality, the track featured a breathy (uncredited) vocal sample from The Pretenders' Chrissie Hynde, a friend of Beck's for close to a decade. He returned Hynde's favour by adding a burst of whammy bar and the odd pinched harmonic to 'Legalise Me', a winning rocker on The Pretenders' 1999 disc, *Viva El Amour!*.

For those left reeling from Jeff's new obsession with Pro-Tools technology and rampant techno beats, the remaining tracks on *Who Else!* must have seemed like a soothing balm. 'Angel (Footsteps)' was another of those lush Tony Hymas compositions that allowed Beck to soar into the heavens: thematically similar to 'Two Rivers' and 'Behind The Veil', Jeff again took listeners to the edge of heaven as his steel slide crept way beyond the limits of the fretboard towards the very bridge of his '52 reissue Telecaster. 'Even Odds', on the other hand, saw Jan Hammer returning to the fold with a tune that gave Beck a chance to turn up the volume and follow a very jazz-rock course, the two trading licks as if the eighties never happened. 'Declan', however, offered a real change of pace. A misty-eyed tribute to bouzouki/guitar player Donal Lunny, whose efforts with Planxty and The Bothy Band had fundamentally changed the sound of Irish folk music in the seventies, 'Declan' was written by Lunny himself. "I'd heard Declan's work in the past," said Jeff, "and it stole my heart." Backed by a group of traditional folk musicians using ethnic flutes and violins, Beck's take on 'Declan' was another showcase in tremolo arm control and lyrical, voice-like phrasing: "You know, if I had a singer for all these years, I probably wouldn't have developed into the player I am," he later laughed. Reportedly, Jeff was so overcome with emotion when listening to his fellow musicians' efforts he fluffed his take, eventually deciding to leave the offending note as a mark of respect for a job well done.

But if there was a 'classic' to be had on *Who Else!,* it was probably the album's most traditional tune, 'Brush With The Blues'. Recorded live in a 2,500 seater hall in Munich during his 1998 European tour, 'Brush...' was Jeff's first real 'slow blues' since *Truth's* 'Blue Deluxe' and it was a pleasure to hear him return to first principles, even if by the middle of the track he was tearing the most profoundly lunatic sounds from his Strat this side of Hendrix. "[My friend] Peter Richardson, told me after hearing the new stuff that he thought it was what Hendrix would be doing, if he were alive today," Beck later said. "I took that as the ultimate compliment." A mind-altering replacement for 'Goodbye Pork Pie Hat' in Jeff's live set, 'Brush With The Blues' became another of those instrumentals crowds demanded from the guitarist before he went home for the night.

Ending with the short and sweet-sounding 'Another Place', which used a combination of polyphonic scales and arpeggios to make its point, *Who Else!* was probably Jeff's most schizophrenic release since 1971's *Rough And Ready*. Occasionally brilliant, sometimes wilfully obtuse, its mixture of electronic styles and more familiar Beck trademarks could often confuse, with one almost cancelling out the other. Given such issues to negotiate, it was perhaps unsurprising the album divided critics right down the middle. "The last time Jeffery had a proper album out," said *Mojo*, "things still came in vinyl and he was the only 'Beck' in the record racks. Nobody can accuse Jeff Beck of saturating his market, but his market was in danger of forgetting he was [still] out there. It's like the guy waits for the odds to mount up against him, then delivers an album's worth of killer punches. No frills, no contest. He's still the Guv'nor." *Q's* Paul Elliot, however, felt there was considerably less to champion: "The loud stuff is mostly horrible... forming a boffin rock onslaught of bad Van Halen and Herbie Hancock's 'Rockit'-period robo funk. In short, a guitarist's album for guitarists only." With benefit of hindsight, *Jamming's* Tony Fletcher was probably closest to the money: "*Who Else!* was heavy-going," he said, "as if [Beck] was finding his feet again after so long away."

Co-produced by Jeff and Tony Hymas, *Who Else!* was also notable for the fact that it actually performed better at home than in the US charts, reaching number 74 in the UK while only scratching the *Billboard* Top 100 at a paltry 99. Despite receiving a now inevitable Grammy nomination for 'Best Rock Instrumental Performance', this lack of attention from Beck's long-established American fanbase was mildly distressing. "A bit of a nightmare. An album that, I suppose, was meant to put me back in there," he later confirmed. "But there was a lack of focus on how the whole project was handled. So we brought Tony Hymas in to save the day. And even he wasn't sure about the music we'd recorded, or the techno direction I'd taken, but he warmed up when he saw where we trying to go. Really, we wasted a lot of money on the first attempt. It was only when we got a friend in who could programme things that the music was saved from going in the bin." Ever honest, Beck understood his position better than most: "The truth is we didn't have enough material when we started, [but] if I had one small hit single, well, I'd be away."

If Beck was disappointed by *Who Else!* failing to set new sales records, he didn't show it. Instead he once again hit the road with Jennifer Batten, Steve Alexander and Randy Hope-Taylor, touring the album across America, Japan and Europe until the late autumn of 1999. Aside from the welcome return of a blast of 'Rice Pudding' to open the show, the new highlight of these concerts was surely Beck's rendition of The Beatles' 'A Day In The Life'. Without an orchestra to rely on for crucial string parts in the middle and end sections, it was once again up to Batten to save the day. Her solution was to suggest turning both passages into a heavy metal-like bombardment, replacing Sir George Martin's violins and cellos with a crescendo of whammy bar screams, power chords and Midi-guitar interfaces. As a result, the song lost not a jot of power in its transfer from studio to stage. "She said 'Why don't we just put a heavy metal riff in it?'" Beck later recalled, "'Or a heavier riff to enable me to play a solo a bit longer?' So she had a lot to do with that arrangement."

Evidently, Jeff hadn't lost his sense of humour either, as a guest spot on ZZ Top's disc *XXX* ably demonstrated. An enormous fan of the Texan trio, he had credited Top's guitarist Billy Gibbons' solo on 1983's 'Rough Boy' as one of the finest he had ever heard. More, their disc *Eliminator* had also given him hope that sequencers and drum machines did not necessarily mean the death of music, as the band's fusion of such technology with their own brand of molten blues rock resulted in hit after sweaty hit. "Just one of the best groups out there," Beck rightly said.

Sharing Billy's love of hot rods (the 'Eliminator' of the album title was actually a real red customised 1933 Ford coupe Gibbons had been working on since 1976) and "mad love" of guitars, one would have thought Jeff's contribution to *XXX* would be one full of swollen pick-ups and feisty solos. Instead, despite having pitched his skills against some of the finest players in Christendom, Beck chose to mark his appearance alongside America's pre-eminent boogie king by singing rather than gunslinging. In a marvellously sardonic turn, the only billing Jeff received on ZZ Top's 'Hey Mr. Millionaire' was a backing vocal credit, letting Billy get on with the sharp-shooting on both their behalfs. The two would turn this missed opportunity around several times and in several spectacular ways in years to come.

As the next millennium dawned, so Beck disappeared. This time, however, it was not so much to tinker with cars, but more to pull a new album together. Content to mark the year 2000 with just one guest session – a 'blink or you'll miss it' appearance on Seal's fey 'This Could Be Heaven' from the soundtrack to the Nic Cage-starring *The Family Man* – Jeff worked on behind the scenes. Retaining the services of Jennifer Batten, Steve Alexander and Randy Hope-Taylor, the guitarist was also committed to securing new blood in the form of Aidan Love and Andy Wright. In Love's case, Beck was impressed with the young programmer's innate ability to mesh and meld complex time signatures with Gypsy, Balkan and Asian musical stylings, this gift opening new doors of melodic and rhythmic opportunity.

As far as Wright was concerned, the producer's track record spoke for itself. Beginning his career as a driver for a recording equipment firm, Andy had used his downtime to learn the in and outs of drum machines and synths, eventually leading to an impromptu programming session with Goth kings The Cure. Following a period of near bankruptcy trying to properly break into the music scene, his luck turned as a run of credits with the likes of The KLF, Tom Jones and Simply Red established his name as both a keyboardist and promising engineer/producer. However, linking up with one of the world's great guitarists had him initially flummoxed. "At first I couldn't imagine how collaboration between us would work, but Jeff's got a great sense of humour and we got on famously," said Wright. "I thought he'd been somewhat marginalised in the fusion world, so we went for a bit of a Chemical Brothers vibe with some of the grooves."

Spurred on by these new recruits to his cause, Beck and the band worked fast, though several eggs had to be broken to make a proverbial omelette. "As usual, I didn't have much to bring to the table," he confessed to *Guitar*. "We had some scrappy ideas of mine and some full-blown compositions from Jennifer, which were really great. But when we weighed it up, Jennifer's stuff stylistically clashed with the stuff I was writing. And as I began to get the air beneath my wings with this new way of writing I felt I'd rather carry on in that direction than have a sudden left turn when you [heard] one of Jennifer's pieces. So we had to weed through [some] of the contributions from the rest of the band, must to their disgust. I'm still having to explain myself to them."

As Beck's new album proved, such conversations might have been difficult, but in the end were of merit. Released on February 6 2001, *You Had It Coming* at last found Jeff in full control of all this electronic business, with the resultant disc his finest since *Guitar Shop* 12 years before. In the tradition of all previous records, *You Had It Coming* opened with a bang, as 'Earthquake' rattled the speakers and loosened the teeth. A relentless, chromatically ascending riff 'Pro-Tooled' within an inch of its life by Aiden Love and Andy Wright, 'Earthquake''s aggressive slant and heavy vocal sampling landed Beck squarely in the noughties – the guitarist sounding not only 'current', but positively youthful. "I've tried to take the thrust from house and dance music which gets young kids jumping up and down like I did when I first heard rockabilly in the fifties," he said. Nonetheless, there was also a distinct nod to the past on 'Earthquake'. Just as he had on 1966's 'The Nazz Are Blue', Jeff cut away mid-track from a blazing solo to let a single note of feedback reign for seven long seconds, this high-pitched scream chilling the listener in the same manner it did some 35 years before.

Like 'Earthquake' (which, ironically, was written by Jennifer Batten), 'Loose Cannon' was also given to the odd bout of belligerence, being somewhat slower in pace, but no less destructive in its impulses. It wasn't all blood and gore, of course. 'Suspension' was a much more contemplative proposition with Beck's Strat shimmering over a spare, East European-sounding melody, while 'Blackbird' found him almost communing with nature – his guitar playing a game of 'call and response' with the blackbirds of the title. "I rented the BBC's sound library of birdsong, went to 'Blackbird', and chose about 10 of [the] best 'riffs'," said Andy Wright on his website. "We had to tune the bird's song down two octaves and then Jeff was able to play [along with] it on guitar. The comedian Vic Reeves asked me how we did it, and when I explained he said, 'Oh, I'm really disappointed. I thought a blackbird landed on Jeff's shoulder and they just started jamming together...'" A strange but compelling ditty, 'Blackbird''s heavily reverbed stratospheric-sounding parts were played by Beck using a kitchen fork.

Away from the odd disappointment such as 'Rosebud' and 'Left Hook', which both sounded like a series of samples in search of a tune, the rest of *You Had It Coming* was of resolutely superior class. Written in honour of his friend legendary San Francisco hot-rod builder Roy Brizio, 'Roy's Toy' showcased Beck's playful side, a tune full of revving '32 Ford engine noises, growling ring modulators and "dollops of sonic grease". "Many's the time I've thought I might just go and work at 'Brizio's Street Rods'," he later laughed. Conversely, 'Nadia' illustrated that Jeff had continued to mine the potentially rich soil in which he first struck gold with 'Where Were You'. Composed by the British-Indian jazz-electronic musician Nitin Sawhney for his 1999 disc *Beyond Skin*, 'Nadia' was originally an exquisite, break-beat-driven love song sung delightfully by Swati Natekar. But like 'Cause We've Ended As Lovers' before it, Beck had liberated the tune for his own purposes, following Natekar's swooping vocal lines with a steel slide and the tremolo arm of his guitar, creating a feast of micro/quarter-tones and rich, harmonic textures. "Nitin's an Asian guy," he said. "Absolutely amazing. He lets people feature on his records. He's kind of like the catalyst. A keyboard player [and] guitarist. And he has Trilok Gurtu on tabla drums. They're into crossover music. They're coming toward a Western rock groove. It's much simpler than traditional Indian stuff, and I'm going more that way, so [Nadia's] kind of a happy medium there."

Though Beck's guitar work was increasingly indebted to the sounds of the Indian subcontinent – a natural lineage that started with 'Heart Full Of Soul' and continued with 'Nadia' – *You Had It Coming*'s final tunes bowed in remembrance of Jimi Hendrix and Muddy Waters. With 'Dirty Mind', Jeff was again caught communing with the spirit of Hendrix, his Strat burning the same brand of midnight oil as Jimi had on 'Manic Depression', 'Foxy Lady' and 'Crosstown Traffic'. 'Dirty Mind' also featured a distinctly salty vocal sample or two from singer-songwriter Imogen Heap, her breathy voice blaspheming its way all over Beck's slash-chording. "I met Imogen at a writing festival in Bordeaux, France," he told *Guitar*'s Vic Garbarini. "Andy Wright knew her... we made the call to see if she was interested in singing...and she was in the studio within 15 minutes. [The] sampled voice on 'Dirty Mind' is pretty erotic. To tell the truth, we actually tricked her into doing it, the breathing and all. She was a really good sport about it. Maybe she was just running up the stairs," he concluded, "and [maybe] you have a dirty mind too." A brazen little strumpet of a song, 'Dirty Mind' won a well-deserved Grammy for 'Best Rock Instrumental Performance' in 2002.

Obviously blessed with a good sense of humour, Imogen Heap was also a major factor in Beck's totemic cover of Muddy Waters' 'Rollin' And Tumblin'', though this time she was singing from her heart rather than just breathing suggestively. An old blues standard Waters had made his own before Cream covered it on their 1966 debut album, 'Rollin' And Tumblin'' was a perfect choice for Jeff to meddle with: "I loved the original Baby Face Leroy version from 1928. [His] version had this guy playing a single bass drum beat with his foot [while also] playing the guitar and hollering the words." Given this skeletal structure, 'Rollin'...' could potentially be manipulated into beat-breaking paradise. Obsessed with finding just the right rhythm, Beck programmed a snare/bass drum pattern at his home studio and then used a Mackintosh computer to "fit it with the perfect time". After adding Heap's battle-cries and some fluid chords, roaring slide and whammy bar theatrics of his own, Jeff and Andy Wright had *You Had It Coming*'s best track saved forever on disc. "I could take this amazing old blues," he said, "preserve what's great about it and yet give it a brand new veneer."

From its self-referencing cover sleeve – with Beck's hands close to camera covered in engine oil – to the strength of material on show,

You Had It Coming deserved its fair share of attention, a view strongly borne out by critics reviewing it at the time. "Techno is still very much on his mind," said *Entertainment Weekly*, "but this forward-thinking veteran now sounds comfortable melding his adventurous fret work with studio wizardry." *Mojo* went even further: "The most visceral... instrumental album Jeff Beck has ever made... this is peerless playing ability made over into pools of bodily fluids." *Q* was even thinking about hit singles: "You could fantasise an improbable hit single out of 'Rollin' And Tumblin', all tangled bedsheet moan from guest singer Imogen Heap and consensual guitar thrusts from Beck and Jennifer Batten. Visceral, spunky-stinky, *You Had It Coming* is a coat-trailing challenge to the likes of Eminem and Limp Bizkit." Sadly, record buyers were fantasising about something else entirely. Despite its undoubted worth, Jeff's latest record hardly clipped the charts at all, having to make do with number 110 and number 132 chart placings in the US and UK respectively. A disc he proudly referred to as "really like my first album... a pure Beck album, all me doing just what I want to do", *You Had Me Coming*'s poor sales performance (now something of a recurring theme) must have stung.

In spite of it all Beck persisted, taking the songs on tour to replenish his finances and once again meet up with "the ever faithful" who continued to purchase every album for the promise of every note he played. Opening his account in Seattle on February 15, 2001 Jeff and his group worked their way across America for the next two months. From set opener 'Earthquake' through 'Brush With The Blues', 'Psycho Sam' and 'Nadia' to encores 'Where Were You', 'Goodbye Pork Pie Hat' (with a smudge of 'Rosebud' thrown in) and the clattering finale of 'What Mama Said', it remained a fine show. Even the lighting was impressive, with swirls of violet and aquamarine blue circles floating above Beck's head as he got down to business. Now retired after over 10 years of road abuse, the 'Little Richard' had been ably replaced by an Olympic White reissue Strat: its rosewood fingerboard and locking Sperzels familiar to the eye, even if the standard pick-ups with custom tone controls specifically built to roll off all treble from bridge and middle positions were wholly new. Once again seeking the benefits of an old friend, Jeff retained his Marshall 100 watt amp (a JCM 2000 model), but his

Snarling Dog wah-wah pedal was not as 'worn in' – being a recent, but valuable addition to the Maestro ring modulator, Boss chorus pedal and (occasional) Pro Co Rat he relied on to vary tone, attack and general weirdness. "But you know," he later said, "my set-up for *You Had It Coming* was basically my Strat, a Marshall, a mike and my fingers." As they say, 'You can't beat simplicity'.

With America behind him, Beck next turned his attentions to Europe, with a fairly short, but still strong showing in the UK during the early summer of 2001, where he supported Sting in front of an audience of at least 25,000 at London's Hyde Park. From there, it was on to Italy, France and even Corsica, where Jeff played an 80-minute set at the 'Nuits de la Guitare', a long-established shindig in the village of Patrimonio, which had previously played host to the likes of John McLaughlin and Al Di Meola. Though he ceased touring later in the year after several concerts in Japan, there was one more chunk of Beck-related ephemera to contend with before the end of 2001. Joining a veritable legion of rock legends that included Jimmy Page and Robert Plant, Eric Clapton, Bob Dylan and Elton John, the guitarist contributed a riotous interpretation of Elvis' 'Mystery Train' for *Good Rockin' Tonight: The Legacy Of Sun Records*. Another of those increasingly popular tribute discs Jeff apportioned some of his time to in the last decade, *Good Rockin' Tonight...* was actually a fine collection, made all the better for his involvement. With Chrissie Hynde covering vocals on 'Mystery Train', Beck sounded in his element – memories of his own experiences scowling at Sam Phillips while Keith Relf grew ever drunker behind the drum kit at Sun Studios surely coming to mind.

Enlivened by his new-found interest in all things electronica, Jeff waxed lyrical about releasing an album a year in 1999, and so far, had almost made good on the promise. But a combination of disappointing sales figures and a need to produce "something spectacular" next time around slowed Beck's ratio of product per annum, meaning that 2002 was something of a dry spell for the guitarist. As ever, there was the odd session, beginning with a sedate appearance on 'Hobo Blues' – a track featured on *From Clarksdale to Heaven: Remembering John Lee Hooker* that not only reunited him with drummer Richard Bailey but also honoured the passing of one of the true giants of the Mississippi Delta. Jeff was in equally good form on 'Drown In My Tears', an old Ray Charles cover that former Squeeze pianist and BBC music presenter Jools Holland had recorded for his latest disc, ... *More Friends*. "Sadly, Ray Charles is gone," Beck said. "I'd have loved to have worked with him."

Though the album featured the likes of U2's Bono, jazz supremo George Benson and Roxy Music's Bryan Ferry, Beck's rendition of 'Drown In My Tears' was a genuine standout, his interpretation of Charles' soulful ballad again underlining exactly why so many musicians called on his skills. Jeff subsequently performed the tune with the Big Band Rhythm & Blues Orchestra on Holland's show, *Later...*, in a 'New Year's Eve' special – with Robert Plant, Solomon Burke and Tom Jones emerging from the wings to accompany him for an impromptu version of 'Shake, Rattle & Roll'. And on the live front, Beck turned up at New York's Carnegie Hall on April 13, 2002 to make his contribution to the 'Rainforest Foundation Benefit Concert'. Organised by Sting's wife Trudi Styler with old friend Narada Michael Walden acting as musical director, the event found the former Police front man, Elton John and James Taylor all onstage for a song or two. Keen to join in, Jeff was nonetheless in awe at fellow guest and soul legend Patti Labelle's singing voice. "Patti Labelle sang and I couldn't play," he said. "There are not many singers that make you incapable of playing because they're giving it out so loud and so clear and so powerfully."

As his actions suggested, Beck had spent much time and effort honouring old souls, good causes and those sadly passed away. But his next course of action actually found him paying tribute to himself, even if he put up a hell of a fight to stop it from happening. In early 2002, Jeff was approached by one of the Directors of London's Royal Festival Hall and asked to consider performing a career retrospective at the venue. At first – and wholly in character – the guitarist baulked at the idea, offering various excuses about "always wanting to go forward rather than look back". Yet, the RFA man was persistent in his cause: "He practically wrote the set list!" Finding such enthusiasm infectious, Beck finally relented and gave in to the idea.

Taking place over three nights from September 12–14, 2002, 'From The Yardbirds To The Future' was an event and a half as Jeff turned on the musical taps and went for broke. Treating the retrospective as less of a formal occasion and more of a party, Beck invited along a number of distinguished guests, including old ARMS comrade Andy Fairweather-Low and the *Guitar Shop* team of Terry Bozzio and Tony Hymas. Though Steve Alexander had now moved on to pastures new, Jennifer Batten returned, bringing with her Roger Waters for the first two concerts. Truthfully, Waters' rendition of 'What God Wants…' was a slightly shambolic affair, with the singer forced to read his own lyrics from a piece of paper on opening night. Looking more like a teacher giving an end of term speech to a gathered assembly than the man responsible for Pink Floyd's *The Wall*, he corrected the oversight next time around. Flown in from the States to handle vocals on vintage material such as 'I Ain't Superstitious', 'I'm A Man' and 'Morning Dew' was another longtime Beck cohort, Jimmy Hall. "You know, it really was a massive undertaking," he said, "a complete overview of Jeff's career. But for me, it was wonderful, getting to sing the old Yardbirds stuff, and of course, some songs off *Beck-Ola*."

On the final night, Jeff went decidedly off-piste. Opening the show with a rendition of the much-missed 'Beck's Bolero', followed by the likes of 'Blue Wind', 'Angel (Footsteps)', 'Big Block' and 'Freeway Jam', all appeared relatively normal: just another night of superlative guitar playing, accompanied by some of the finest musicians to walk the earth. However, with a minimum of fuss, Jeff then ceased trading under his own name and introduced Detroit's The White Stripes to the stage. Now, this was novel. After all, when the grunge movement of the early nineties reared its tousled head, Beck had largely ignored it – more content to dig into the wonders of Kotos and Gene Vincent covers than engage with down-tuned riffs, psychologically dislocated lyricism and plaid shirts. Offering too much rock, but not enough roll, groups such as Nirvana, Alice In Chains, Pearl Jam and Soundgarden appeared lost on him. Yet, the minimalism and garage grunts of The White Stripes obviously touched a nerve. A two-piece pressure cooker of a band, comprised of singer/guitarist Jack White and Meg White on drums, The White Stripes' strident respect for the blues, coupled with a distinctly 'can do' punk spirit obviously met with Jeff's approval. "Look what The White Stripes did in their last album," he said. "They went into a studio in England and cut an album the old way. The idea is to make the album sound fresh and as raw as possible." Backstage, however, there were rumblings from those in attendance: "Some of the musicians involved had concerns about The White Stripes' minimalism," said Jimmy Hall. "But Jeff really defended them. He said, 'Trust me, Jack and Meg sound like The Yardbirds when we first started. They're like a garage band, playing raw blues as it should be'. And you know, they were amazing."

Arriving on the well-trodden boards of the Royal Festival Hall, The White Stripes were the surprise of the evening, though there were clues from the off the duo had come to show their respects rather than abuse their host's goodwill. Painted proudly by Jack White on the skin of his musical partner's bass drum in red and white were the words 'The Yardbirds', a kind and knowing gesture to both Beck's past achievements and a band never forgotten by America. Kicking off with 'Train Kept A Rollin'', Jeff and his new backing group (assisted by Jack Lawrence on bass) had a whale of a time re-creating some of the Thames Delta's finest moments, from 'Heart Full Of Soul' and 'Mister, You're A Better Man Than I' to corrosive renditions of 'I Ain't Done Wrong' and final number 'I Ain't Got You'. An admirable addition to the roster of talent already on show and full of a vim and vigour one could only marvel at, it was almost a shame when The White Stripes left the stage.

Having provided a causal link between his Yardbirds' past and a musical future he now deemed in reasonable hands, the rest of Beck's celebrations centred on doing justice to his own back catalogue. As a result, old friends and new were invited to join him, with Imogen Heap adding sex and sass to 'Rollin' And Tumblin'' and tabla player Aref Durvesh providing a perfect accompaniment for Jeff's slide/tremolo high-wire act 'Nadia'. John McLaughlin made a welcome appearance, popping up for a duet with Beck on his own 'Django' before skipping around the strings on the always popular 'Scatterbrain'. From there, it was 'vocalist heaven' as Paul Rodgers arrived to deliver a rousing version of 'Going Down' before Jimmy Hall returned from the wings to sing 'People Get Ready'. "Those three nights, the way they were presented, the light shining on Jeff on his home turf, playing those old songs, well, it was just magic," said Hall. "And you know, on one of the nights, Jeff introduced me to the stage by saying, 'Ladies and gentlemen, here's my favourite singer in the whole world.' For someone who's worked with some of the best in the world, he really didn't have to say that, though it just about made my whole career."

After the now familiar one-two punch of 'A Day In The Life' and 'Where Were You', Beck then led his guests into a final run-through of his age-old nemesis 'Hi Ho Silver Lining'. Sadly, for one critic, the guitarist's behaviour throughout the song was a little too much on an empty stomach. "As Beck signed off with a spine-tingling interpretation of Lennon and McCartney's 'A Day In The Life', the man's awesome musicianship was not in doubt," said *The Times*. "But his... reluctant encore of 'Hi Ho Silver Lining' – complete with puking gestures to indicate his disdain for the song – was insulting and embarrassing." And funny.

An odd but endearing enterprise then, 'From The Yardbirds To The Future' might have been a departure from Beck's normal way of doing business, but it did have its supporters. "Whatever your take on rock guitar heroics, Jeff Beck's three-night South Bank residency was certainly the most miscellaneous gig of the year," said *The Guardian's* John L. Walters. "It was also a logistical triumph, as more than a dozen performers moved on and off the stage without a hitch, a howl or a bruised ego. [In fact], any suspicion of rock-star idiocy is blown away the second he plays. Beck is an intelligent guitarist, with technique, range and fire – His sound... particularly effective when paired with a belting rock singer, such as Jimmy Hall or Jack White of The White Stripes."

Undoubtedly true. But there was one nagging doubt about the Royal Festival Hall "career retrospective" gigs. Despite the presence of fusion giants such as John McLaughlin, "gauche, but talented youngsters" like The White Stripes and a 'House Full' sign outside the venue for all three nights, it all seemed a bit... small. For a man who had stood toe to toe with Hendrix, arguably bested Jimmy Page and Eric Clapton on six strings, and pioneered a way of life for many a guitar player, a three-night stopover at the RFH was small beer for such an influential life in music. Surely, Beck deserved better. Sadly, he would have to wait a while longer before the world did anything about it.

Beck in action at Hammersmith Apollo, 1990. This was his first British tour in nine years. DAVID REDFERN/GETTY IMAGES

Jeff hams it up backstage with The Yardbirds following the group's induction into the Rock 'N' Roll Hall Of Fame in January, 1992. His onstage speech concerning how he 'left' the band in 1966 remains a thing of beauty. ROBIN PLATZER/TWIN IMAGES/TIME LIFE PICTURES/GETTY IMAGES

Country life, Beck Style. Jeff pictured at his manor with two of his favourite rods. STEVE LYNE/REX FEATURES

'Strat city. Jeff backstage at The 12th Annual Rainforest Foundation Concert, held at Carnegie Hall in New York on April 13, 2002. The white Fender Strat at the front of picture was christened 'Anoushka' after famed sitar player Anoushka Shankar signed the instrument for him. K. MAZUR/WIREIMAGE

"Do you play an instrument too?" Queen Elizabeth II meets Jeff, Eric Clapton, Jimmy Page and Brian May at the "Music Day At The Palace" event at Buckingham Palace on March 1, 2005 in London. FIONA HANSON/TIM GRAHAM PICTURE LIBRARY/GETTY IMAGES

"The kid is amazing." Beck and Tal Wilkenfeld perform at Eric Clapton's Crossroads Guitar Festival in 2007.
BARRY BRECHEISEN/GETTY IMAGES

Jeff and Les Paul sharing a beer and a hug. Beck would pay homage to Paul with his 2011 CD/DVD, *Rock 'N' Roll Party*.
TIME & LIFE PICTURES/GETTY IMAGES

Blue Cap and his Missus. Jeff shares a backstage kiss with wife Sandra Cash. LARRY BUSACCA/GETTY IMAGES

eff and Jimmy Page pose for the cameras following Beck's nduction into the Rock 'N' Roll Hall of Fame at Cleveland's ublic Hall on April 4, 2009. STEPHEN LOVEKIN/GETTY IMAGES

Brothers in blues. B.B. King and Beck attend the 25th Anniversary Rock & Roll Hall of Fame Concert at Madison Square Garden on October 29, 2009. DIMITRIOS KAMBOURIS/WIREIMAGE

Z Top guitarist and fellow hot rod enthusiast 'Reverend' Billy Gibbons performed a superb version of Jimi Hendrix's 'Foxy ady' with Jeff at the 25th Anniversary Rock & Roll Hall of Fame Concert. THEO WARGO/WIREIMAGE

Jimmy Page, Jeff, Ron Wood and Metallica's Kirk Hammett on stage at the finale at Beck's induction into the Rock 'N' Roll Hall Of Fame. THEO WARGO/WIREIMAGE

The Rockabilly Queen. Jeff joins Imelda May and her band at London's Indigo2 Arena on September 21, 2009.
CHRISTIE GOODWIN/REDFERNS

pinstriped Beck picks up his 'Outstanding Contribution'
ong at the Classic Rock Awards in 2008. MARK ALLAN/WIREIMAGE

God Save The Queen, Hendrix style. Jeff plays the national
anthem at Wembley Stadium on 31 October, 2010.
MICHAEL ZAGARIS/SAN FRANCISCO 49ERS/GETTY IMAGES

e won't be playing 'For Your Love'…" Eric Clapton and Jeff together in concert at New York's Madison Square Garden on
bruary 18, 2010. STARTRAKS PHOTO/REX FEATURES

"If you dream of something you really like to do, then I suggest you follow it..." Jeff drops a few wise words when receiving an honorary degree from the University of Sussex for an 'Outstanding musical career' in July, 2011. MATT KENT/WIREIMAGE

Chapter 23

The Good Soldier

Rumours followed Jeff Beck into 2003. Though Jimmy Page had played no part in his recent concerts at the Royal Festival Hall, it was reported that he and the former Led Zeppelin guitarist might pool their talents for a joint album. On paper, this was a mouth-watering prospect, and one that made some sense. Since Zeppelin's demise in 1980, Page had worked only sporadically: the *Death Wish II* soundtrack, ARMS tour and fruitful, if short-lived collaboration with Paul Rodgers in The Firm during the mid-eighties. There was a solo album of varying quality towards the end of that decade, and an ill-advised, though moderately entertaining disc with Whitesnake singer David Coverdale followed by an infuriating, on-again-off-again reunion with Robert Plant under the 'Unledded' banner in the nineties. Finally, a one-off, 'blink or you'll miss it' project with The Black Crowes marked the new millennium. All these projects had passed his time well enough, but none held a candle to Jimmy's work with the mighty Zep. Surely collaboration with his decades-spanning friend might help stoke those creative juices and produce something of lasting worth.

Ultimately, even if Beck seemed willing, it all came to nothing. Elsewhere, flags continued to be raised in the hope that Jeff and eighties funk-rock icon Prince could see their way to crossing paths and guitars, a delicious prospect for even the most cynical mind. Again, while Jeff remained a gargantuan fan of the diminutive wonder, talk proved cheap. Beck stayed in England, Prince in Minneapolis, and the amps remained on stand-by.

However, by August 2003, Beck was back with a new record of his own. Entitled *Jeff* (no highfallutin titles here), the disc again found him working alongside Andy Wright, with several new names in the frame. House/electronica producer/bassist Dean Garcia had been drafted in to help write two songs, while Liverpudlian dance/rock trio Apollo 440 also made a contribution here and there. "They were in the same studio as us," said Beck. "They walked by and heard what Andy and I were doing, and said, 'Wow, what's going on?' We asked them if they could do a serious remix of one of our tunes. They said, 'We'll do one better, we'll write some stuff'. They wrote me six [drum loops], and we chose two or three."

Aside from writer/programmer Ron Aslan, whom Jeff cut initial demos with, and Dave Bloor on recording/engineering duties, the final piece of the puzzle came with former Everyman Band/David Sylvian guitarist David Torn, who now traded under the name Splattercell: "I got this CD from a friend in New York who collects weird music," Beck told *Guitar Player*, "I said to myself, 'What is this Spattercell?' And boom, within a minute, I was sitting there riveted. I thought 'This guy's twisted and I want twisted.'" An avant-garde treasure, who shared Beck's frontier spirit when it came to the possibilities of sound manipulation, Torn's arrival on the project proved both telling and profitable.

Recorded in large part at Metropolis Studios in West London, *Jeff* concluded Beck's 'techno' trilogy with some aplomb, though as the guitarist was the first to admit, there was an element of "pinning tails on donkeys" about the whole enterprise. The album began well enough with 'So What', a rip-snorting instrumental that came to life while Jeff was searching "for the right riff to attach to the right drum groove". With some real fire in its belly, 'So What' bore absolutely no relation to Miles Davis' cool jazz classic of the same name, more resembling an irritated tribal stomp with Beck's guitar the principal cause of anger.

'Seasons' was also a groove in search of a bad mood, as British comedian Ronni Ancona's heavily sampled voice advised listeners to 'Play me in the winter, play me in the summer, play me in the autumn, any order' over a thumping back beat. Yet, as one's ear grew used to all the bangs and crashes, the tune suddenly deviated from purpose with Jeff abandoning its stabbing riff for a contemplative solo played over lush strings provided by the London Session Orchestra. 'JB's Blues' only enhanced this atmosphere, the instrumental drifting along like a vintage Tony Hymas piece, that again allowed Beck to indulge his gentler inclinations.

In fact, Hymas' influence was writ large elsewhere: his own composition, 'Why Lord Oh Why?', provided Jeff the opportunity to soothe and slash with his choice of notes, its slow pace, rising strings and ominous tone providing a perfect bedrock for Beck's flittering Strat. And even though 'Bulgaria' was a traditional Bulgarian air again played over a luscious accompaniment from the London Session Orchestra, one couldn't help but recall Jeff and Tony's most enduring tune 'Where Were You'. "I wanted it to sound like a voice and not too much like a guitar," Beck said. "To save me embarrassment, we cut the orchestra first so that I didn't have to follow the conductor." Played on a new, fat-stringed Strat called 'Anoushka' – like the 'Tina' and 'Little Richard' before it, Jeff had asked Ravi Shankar's sitarist daughter Anoushka to sign the instrument – 'Bulgaria' was Beck's latest heartbreaker and another fitting tribute to *Le Mystere Des Voix Bulgares.*

Away from these melancholic airs, Jeff was still capable of locating his inner hooligan. Obvious homages to the joy of rods, both 'Grease Monkey' and 'Hot Rod Honeymoon' were full of meat and gristle, the former bouncing along on a Bonhamesque drum loop (courtesy of Apollo 440), the latter soldering Buddy Merrill-like steel guitar runs and Beach Boys melodies to a rousing drum loop: "It ended up like The Prodigy meets The Beach Boys." On both tracks, comedian Vic Reeves' wife Nancy Sorrell provided some genuinely funny vocal samples, her mock American tones demanding that the titular mechanic "make it dirty" while showing her "what you've got". Sorrell was also a welcome addition to the James Brown-worshipping 'My Thing', which found Beck's main riff wobbling like a drunken sailor as a mad woman shouted in the background. "[Nancy] is something else," he confirmed to *Guitar Player.* "We were having a party at my house, and as we were playing, she grabbed the mic and started ranting to her then-to-be husband, 'Don't mess with me'. I had the recorder going and thought this is the coolest thing!" The joke sample, and indeed a writing credit for Nancy, both made it to the record intact.

With 'Trouble Man', the stress was again on Jeff harnessing some of the hoodlum spirit that had played such a central role in all his endeavours. This time, however, he really exceeded himself. In essence "a barbaric jam" with Beck seemingly content to lose the plot over what sounded like a runaway train, 'Trouble Man' was a magnificent example of free-jazz like lunacy. "It's like a Jackson Pollock painting," he later said. "We wanted to have fun with no boundaries, with a drum loop and a real drummer. We just let rip for about 10 minutes [but] it was too long... so we edited it. Maybe someday I'll release the full version. It's really crazy, a bit wild... like Mothers Of Invention wild." To achieve the insane tone that permeated 'Trouble Man', Jeff plugged his Strat into the old, but still capable Maestro Ring Modulator that had been part of his set up since 1976's *Wired*: "It's great for moments of madness, stirring things up and just adding some general weirdness. At the end, the men in white coats were waiting to take me away."

Still looking for that elusive hit, or at least a stab at some radio play, Beck and composer Eric Martin had come up with 'Pay Me No Mind', featuring a soulful vocal from the curiously credited 'Me One'. Best described as 'techno meets The Neville Brothers', 'Pay Me No Mind' really sounded like a Prince outtake – a good thing if Jeff was ever to set up that elusive collaboration – but in reality, an unlikely candidate for a future number one. While 'Pork-U-Pine' was never in fear of being released as a single, it was actually a far more satisfying ride, the instrumental's sombre mood, use of Arabic scales and Snarling Dogs Whine-O-Wah growls giving it a sense of real danger.

For *Jeff*'s remaining tunes, the proverbial tapes were handed over to David Torn to "reproduce, mix and manipulate" to his heart's content. On 'Line Dancing With Monkeys', this translated into literally throwing most of the original backing track away and "rebuilding the scaffolding" around Beck's guitar lines: "David's... even more 'Jackson Pollock' than I am. He chopped up the stuff and saved it from the bin." Though only Jeff and Andy Wright had a clue as to what 'Line Dancing...' sounded like before Torn got his hands on it, the final version resembled the soundtrack to a spy film; all twisting keyboard sounds, sharp edits and 'dark corridors', with Jeff's Strat cautiously poking its head in out of the mix, this was radical stuff.

'Plan B' was even more atmospheric. Reportedly akin to "ZZ Top on speed" before winging its way to New York and the Splattercell man, 'Plan B' came back in little, but exquisitely cut pieces. "It's almost unrecognisable from what I gave him," said Beck, "He 'Splatterized' it." Again taking electronic scissors to the original version, Torn had kept the body of Jeff's guitar work, but added a new dimension of his own, reorganising chords and lead lines to create a brand new melody. However, despite such tinkering, he also remained fulsome in his praise for one of the few, original sonic architects committed to pushing back the boundaries of sound. "Jeff's 59 years old and still kicking like a beast," David said. "He's one of the only electric guitar players who has the sound of the whole electric guitar in his hands." Joining the likes of 'Escape' before it, 'Plan B' was to eventually win a Grammy for 'Best Rock Instrumental Performance'.

With its cover sleeve featuring a photograph of a wooden 'Caveman guitar' – the name 'Jeff' written on the headstock and bearing the warning "If you find this gitar you give it back else yo get yo ass bit" – Beck's latest album was by no means perfect. At times, it meandered too much for its own good, the tunes harder to find or less compact than *You Had It Coming*. Worse, like 1971's *Rough And Ready* before it, Jeff seemed bored by the contents before it was even released: "I wound up hating the sound of my own guitar," he told *Guitar World*. "This is probably the last album I do with a mouse!" Yet, pound for pound, the disc was another creditable stab at blending Beck's passion for rampant six-string abuse with the brazen cuts and beats of electronica.

Even the critics agreed: "A whole generation of axe-maulers have used Beck's flashy template as an excuse to disappear up their own flange pedals (we're talking Steve Vai, Joe Satriani etc. here)," said BBC Music's Chris Jones. "But most forget that Beck himself, even in his most self-indulgent fusion moments, always strove for something different. A true 'Psychedelicist' until the last, his youthful joy in making an unholy racket is only matched by his unimpeachable expertise. There's plenty of life in this old dog." Jones was not alone in his opinions: "Wild-fire instrumental affairs set in fat, dirty jungles of looped percussion and synth licks," said *Rolling Stone*, while *Mojo* described *Jeff* as "13 tracks that are beat-driven, heavy and unrepentant".

These were strong reviews to a man, full of support for the record and praise for the artist. Reading them might even want to make people want to buy the album. But *Jeff* again performed dismally in the US and UK charts, with only ever-faithful Japan rewarding the disc with a Top 20 placing. For Beck, being simultaneously ignored on both sides of the Atlantic was an undistinguished first. Of course, there were reasons, and ones that had been mounting for decades. Ever since 1975 and *Blow By Blow*, his decision to abandon the strictures of a traditional rock band, pursue 'fusion' and release purely instrumental music had proved a ticking time bomb. Though the original idea paid off in spades, it also marginalised his mainstream appeal over time, with 1985's *Flash* doing little to stem the tide. By putting the guitar front and centre, with no flaxen-haired, barrel-chested vocalist to distract the ear or eye, Beck's position had become increasingly isolated – his face regularly appearing on the cover of guitar magazines but never the broad-band music papers that drove sales and confirmed fashion.

Of equal importance was his age. Nearing 60, Jeff's latest dalliance with 'techno' might have appeared vulgar or grasping to a younger audience, a man of middle years trying to hold on to youth via a genre they saw belonging to them and not him. That Beck was pioneering such aural chaos with just a Telecaster, Vox AC30 and fuzz box decades before laptops began cutting sounds into bite-size pieces and spitting them out any which way you wanted mattered not. Techno and all its variations was largely a young man's game, and as ever, its followers had little respect for bandwagon jumpers, no matter how well meaning. Further, unlike Jimmy Page or Eric Clapton, Jeff could not rely on 'brand recognition' or sell himself as a 'heritage product', his penchant for changing musical hats at will making him increasingly difficult to market, impossible to predict. When mainstream journalists did write about him, the standfirsts and banners read 'Maverick', 'Shapeshifter', 'Non-Conformist' or simply 'Rebel'. Apt descriptions one and all, but more often than not ones that implied 'Cult Artist' or worse 'Buy, but only if you fancy something a bit different'. While Led Zeppelin remained 'Giants who walked the earth' 30 odd years after their passing and Eric was still a 'deity in human form', Beck stayed Beck: loved by his peers, respected by his contemporaries. Probably the most gifted British guitarist of his generation – any generation, actually. "Jeff's better than any of them, always was, always will be," said one of his former bandmates, "He's a fucking cannonball." But he was still hell to sell.

Someone who could offer Jeff a pointer or two about the ups and downs of a life in music was B.B. King. A true blues superstar, Riley 'Blues Boy' King escaped life as a tractor driver in Greenwood, Mississippi through ownership of an astounding voice and some of the most emotional guitar playing of the 20th century. Armed with his beloved Gibson ES355 'Lucille', King scored hit after hit in the fifties on the R&B charts, before 1965's high-selling *Live At The Regal* defined his sound and appeal in 35 blissful minutes. Nonetheless, the guitarist – like most blues musicians – had often ebbed and flowed in terms of commercial appeal. Despite one of the most punishing touring schedules known to man (King performed 342 concerts in 1956 alone), his successes were peppered with years out of the spotlight, before associations and albums with U2 and Eric Clapton again established his status as 'King of the Blues' for a new generation of followers.

Raising an odd eyebrow, Beck took the 'Guest Spot' on King's 2003 American tour, billed as the '12th Annual BB King Blues Festival'. Though the two had known each other since 1985 when they both appeared at the 50th anniversary of Harlem's legendary Apollo Theater, and as mentioned, collaborated for B.B's 1997 disc, *Deuces Wild*, it was the first time they would tour together. It was something of an odd pairing. "I was a bit worried that maybe we were too different, but you know, it's all rooted in the blues," Beck said. "No matter what techno-nonsense I come up with, it's always overlaid with recognisable blues anyway, and I don't have to look too far to find that." For King, there were no such worries: "I'd say that [Jeff's] the number one rock'n'roll guitarist in my opinion, and he plays blues better than most of us!" At 78 years old, he was also more than happy to play 'elder statesman' to Jeff's 59-year old 'pup': "You know what I was doing when you were born?" he asked Beck in an interview at the time, "I ain't gonna tell you! I got you by 17 years, young man..."

Jeff's group for the tour was another pleasant surprise. With Steve Alexander, his temporary replacement Andy Gangadeen, Randy Hope-Taylor and Jennifer Batten now all pursuing other projects,

Beck had seized the opportunity to recapture a pair of former bandmates in the form of Terry Bozzio and Tony Hymas: "[As a trio], we'll be kind of like The Jimi Hendrix Experience, but a 2003 version of that." It turned out to be an accurate statement, as 'BBH' provided a refreshing (and extremely spirited) alternative to B.B. King's brass-driven brand of blues across the US in the autumn of 2003. Drawing from a set list that included old favourites ('Goodbye Pork Pie Hat', 'Scatterbrain'), and new upstarts ('Seasons', 'My Thing'), the trio sounded as fresh and powerful as they had on the *Guitar Shop* tour some 13 years before.

This fact was confirmed with the release of *Live At B.B. King Blues Club*, a Japan-only CD recorded on October 9, 2003 at Mr. King's very own New York venue. A warts and all document of their concert set, what *Live At BB's...* might have lacked in polish, it more than made up for with vim, vigour and some startling musicianship. As always, Jeff was in singular form, coaxing a bamboozling array of screams, sighs, howls and hoots from his 'Anoushka' and reissue Strats, the latter's pick-ups rescued from 'Little Richard', and now put back into action. Of the 16 tracks presented on the album, it was a pleasure to hear the return of 'You Never Know' from 1980's *There And Back* to live duty, though emotional renditions of 'A Day In The Life' and 'People Get Ready' really stole the show on the night.

While Beck's US tour concluded in the winter of 2003, his presence continued to be felt on the airwaves and on TV screens as several unlikely sessions/appearances recorded earlier in the year emerged. In the case of Luciano Pavarotti, this was entirely uncharted territory as Jeff joined the Italian opera singer for the Andy Wright-produced 'Caruso'. Appearing on the disc *Ti Adoro*, the combination of world famous tenor and guitarist appeared unlikely on paper but actually worked a treat, Pavarotti's melancholic vocal being shadowed throughout by Jeff's hesitant, sighing guitar lines. Dependable country star Wynonna Judd was also a recipient of the Beck Strat, his short, but sharp lead break on 'What The World Needs Now' stirring up an otherwise formulaic Nashville tune.

As evidenced, Jeff also turned his attentions to a reactivated Yardbirds during this period, putting a little sass and slide behind *Birdland*'s 'My Blind Life': "I heard the tapes and was knocked over by the fact they still had the enthusiasm for it."That said, a full-blown reunion with his former band was unlikely:"Not a bloody chance." Finally, there was a tidy contribution to director Mike Figgis' 'Red Hot & Blues', one instalment of Martin Scorsese's *The Blues,* a seven-part series chronicling the history and impact of blues from its roots in Africa to the modern day. Figgis' film concentrated on the role the music had played in post-war Britain, tracking its movement from minor cult to major influence on the UK blues boom of the sixties. Though Jeff was little seen in the documentary itself, his presence in the DVD extras proved notable, with the guitarist playing an informal version of 'Nadia' while also providing a solid, sentimental backbone for Tom Jones' emotive take on Elvis Presley's 'Love Letters'.

After the burst of activity that accompanied the release of *Jeff,* quietness reigned until June 2004, when Beck returned once again, though this time his attentions were focused on the UK. Undertaking his first British tour in several years, the guitarist again changed the line-up of his backing group, bringing in brothers Michael and Mark Mondesir on bass guitar and drums respectively. Both were proper 'jazz heads': Michael had cut his teeth with the likes of Billy Cobham and saxophonist Courtney Pine, while Mark also shared Pine as a former employer alongside John McLaughlin and pianist Julian Joseph. As one had come to expect, both musicians were of outstanding quality, which was just as well because Jan Hammer was also returning to Jeff's camp on keyboards. "A long time coming!" he said of his first live appearances with Jeff since 1983. With two near sold-out nights at Manchester Apollo and two more at London's prestigious Royal Albert Hall, Beck might have had recent trouble shifting albums, but there were evidently still thousands of fans willing to part with their cash to see him live – even if 90% of them were now probably guitarists. Ultimately, it turned out to be a fine brace of shows with Jeff's appearance at the RAH on June 24 marking the occasion of his 60th birthday, an event he celebrated onstage with several friends. Aside from Hammer, who brought The Mahavishnu Orchestra's 'Resolution' and his own 'Nothing But Love' to the set (which featured some rare acoustic work from Jeff), Beck was also joined by Ronnie Wood for a rollicking version of 'Rice Pudding' and a funky run-through of The Meters' 'Cissy

Strut'. "Happy birthday Jeff Beck!" shouted an affable-sounding Wood, before departing for the wings, lest he be sacked again.

Nancy Sorrell was next to emerge from stage left, lending her vocals to a surprisingly effective rendition of Julie London's 'Cry Me A River'. Unlike 'My Thing', there were no comedy turns to be had here, as the duo played it straight all down the line, with Sorrell hitting the high notes and Beck plucking at the heartstrings. Singer Imogen Heap was also there to mark Jeff's accession to 'The Sixties Club', performing the captivating 'Blanket'. A torch song written by Imogen herself, its slow, assured pace and open, ringing chords were a perfect canvas for Jeff to once again open up, providing a flighty solo that strongly recalled his work on Stevie Wonder's 'Cause We've Ended As Lovers'.* Back at the Royal Albert Hall in 2004, however, Heap was leading the charge at encore time, taking the vocal on 'People Get Ready' with a now returning Ron Wood and Nancy Sorrell providing spirited accompaniment. Also smiling ear to ear in the audience as Jeff received a bouquet of flowers at the finale – though a set of spanners and a monkey wrench would probably have been more appropriate – were Jennifer Batten and Jimmy Page.

Arguably a far more poignant occasion than the Royal Festival Hall concerts of 2002, one couldn't help but notice how well Beck looked for his age at the RAH. Casually dressed in black jeans, vest and waistcoat, rooster-hair still thick and suspiciously free from any strand of grey, the wiry, bovver-booted guitarist might easily have shaved a decade off his 60 years without hint of suspicion. "I don't go to parties, I don't get drunk all the time," he said. "I live in the country where I go to my auto shop every day, about 10 times. And then there are animals on the land that need to be tended to. So I do about four miles a day, walking and running, plus physical lifting of things. It keeps me in good shape." Another factor that surely kept

---

* Thanks to canny internet marketing, Heap's second album, 2005's *Speak For Yourself*, would soon establish her as a major artist in her own right. In return for the favours the singer had bestowed on *You Had It Coming*, Beck would make a brief appearance on 'Goodnight And Go', a track from *Speak For Yourself* that reached number 56 in the UK when released as a single in May 2006.

Jeff on the move and in the rudest of health was his dedication to session work and guest appearances throughout 2004 and 2005. In addition to accompanying Robert Plant on 'Look Out Mabel', a track from The Big Town Playboys' disc, *Roll The Dice*, he also found time for a soulful turn on esteemed singer Joe Cocker's cover of the sixties heartbreaker 'I (Who Have Nothing)'. Originally an Italian tune penned by Carlo Donida with lyrics by Giulio 'Mogol' Rapetti, Jerry Leiber and Mike Stoller had translated 'I...' for the American market in 1963, gifting R&B vocalist Ben E. King with a Top 30 hit. When Tom Jones took up the song in 1970, he made it even more melodramatic and orchestral, stealing a number 14 spot in the US singles chart for his trouble. That said, Cocker's version was altogether more gritty, his gruff voice squeezing out every note as if in pain while Beck purred gently along behind him. A quick solo on the Zucchero/Macy Gray duet 'Like The Sun', a feisty slapping of the whammy bar on Steve Alexander's 'Flashman' project and a reteaming with Jed Leiber for 'Above The Clouds' – a track featured on Cyndi Lauper's 2005 CD *The Body Acoustic* – also allowed Beck to meet his engine oil bills during the same period.

One side of Jeff's playing that had always called for more exploration was his simpatico with reggae and other Afro-Caribbean musical forms. Since his calypso-themed cover of The Beatles' 'She's A Woman' in 1975, he had dabbled little with such genres, despite showing undoubted proficiency and genuine flair for their sound and style. Thankfully, British soul singer (and possibly the nicest person in the music industry) Beverley Knight managed to steer Beck back into reggae territory with a tribute to Bob Marley at the UK Music Hall of Fame awards in the late autumn of 2004. Performing a marvellous cover of Marley's 'Is This Love', the pairing of Knight's rangy, emotive voice and Jeff's clipped, clear Strat tones (he even used a pick for the occasion) caused a delightful chill. Though he and Knight's association sadly ended there, Jeff had already lent a hand to another reggae act some six months before, providing a fierce solo on Toots & The Maytals' '54–46 Was My Number', a hit originally recorded by the band in 1968 and brought back into commission for their all-star comeback disc, *True Love*.

Despite the thrills of hearing Beck re-engage with a form of music that had brought out the best in him on tunes such as 'Behind The

Veil', marking his progress during this period was still no easy task. But with Jeff, the very act of attaching rhyme or reason, strategy or plan to his actions had always been a fool's game. In his own words, he was always ready for "Career change No. 47", being content to drop a project to the ground while simultaneously picking up another one as he ran. As ever, these changes in mood, peppered with regular withdrawals from view were as much a part of his charm as the way he bent a string. In short, you never really knew which way the note was headed. However, after the failure of *Jeff* in 2003, the guitarist appeared at sixes and sevens – the lure of electronica now seemingly behind him, but with no new inspiration to replace it. Returning to a well-established pattern of 'bob and weave', Beck continued to alternate sessions with tours, and tours with hot rods, waiting for that "little bell" to ring inside his well-thatched head.

2005 confirmed this theory as Jeff once again played a game of hide and seek with his audience, popping up here and there, and sometimes in the most unexpected places. Early in the year, he was to be found on *Zugzwang,* the debut release from Tony Hymas' latest group Ursus Minor. As one might expect from anything bearing Hymas' name, the album was quick to reveal its quality, with the French-based act successfully brewing a potent mix of rap, funk, rock and jazz. Billed as 'The Traveller', Beck lent a hand to four tracks in all, his battles with Ursus Minor's guitar player Jef Lee Johnson alternating between tasteful and frenzied within a matter of seconds. "As guitarists," Johnson later said, "we're all trying to carry the torch for Jimi Hendrix, though sometimes it starts raining very heavily!" Despite such self-deprecation, his and Jeff's work on the likes of 'Lists' and 'She Can't Explain' were obviously captured during extremely clement weather.

In wilful contrast, Beck's next appearance came on *Les Paul And Friends: American Made, World Played*, this time backing the ghost of Sam Cooke. Joining Keith Richards, Joe Perry and Journey's always interesting Neal Schon on a starry project organised by Les himself, Jeff added a few well-executed licks to the original master tape of Cooke's vocal on 'Ain't That Good News', cut by the R&B giant shortly before his death in 1964. Nonetheless, while Paul and Beck's dual interjections were brisk enough, the disc itself was thematically hard to fathom, with songs picked for no apparent reason and having little or nothing in common with Les himself.

If Beck's presence alongside old friends such as Tony Hymas and Les Paul was understandable, his meeting with Queen Elizabeth II in March 2005 had an element of the truly surreal about it. Visiting Buckingham Palace for a reception to celebrate the British music industry, Jeff found himself lining up with Eric Clapton, Jimmy Page and Brian May waiting for the royal handshake. If reports are correct, the monarch's knowledge of the quartet's achievements was hazy at best. In fact, when May pointed out he had been honoured to play the national anthem atop a palace turret in 2002 as part of the rock concert marking her Golden Jubilee, the Queen replied, "Oh, was that you?" Similarly, the sight of Clapton brought no great recognition. After Her Royal Highness asked, "Have you been playing long?" he was left to ponder for a moment, before saying "God, it must be 45 years now." Sensing their host was unlikely to pull out a copy of *Blow By Blow* from her handbag and request an autograph, Beck simply introduced himself with "I'm Jeff" before scoping the nearest exit.

After his brush with sovereignty, Beck again returned to plain sight in July for a guest spot at the 2005 Meltdown festival, hosted by punk troubadour Patti Smith and held in London's auspicious Royal Festival Hall. Causing no great surprise among long-standing fans, the guitarist had once again changed the line-up of his group for the show, now recalling singer Jimmy Hall and bassist Pino Palladino to active service while adding Vinnie Colaiuta and Jason Rebello on drums and keyboards respectively. One could find no fault in either musicians' pedigree, and in Colaiuta's case, it was probably easier to list the artists and groups he hadn't played with rather than the ones he had. Beginning his career behind the kit with Frank Zappa, Vinnie's session history included spells with Barbra Streisand, Joni Mitchell, The Beach Boys and Chaka Khan, before he took a more permanent spot with Sting's touring band. A terrifying technician with a wry sense of humour, Colaiuta would last longer with Jeff than many a drummer before him. Jason Rebello was also no slouch. Arriving on the scene as a promising solo artist in 1990 with the Wayne Shorter-produced *A Clearer View*, Rebello had topped the jazz charts for five solid months. His reputation established, further stints alongside Branford Marsalis, Jean Toussaint, Des'ree and Mica Paris came and went before Jason became a sizable weapon in Sting's musical armoury, replacing keyboardist Kenny Kirkland following his untimely death in 1998. Like Colaiuta, Rebello had a draw full of plaudits from his fellow musicians and a profound sense of the absurd, two crucial qualities required when serving time with Beck.

Jeff's set at the RFH was an unusual one, its dedicated theme to honour the music of Jimi Hendrix. Frankly, there were few guitarists brave, foolish or capable enough to attempt such a conceit, the risk of failure always only a chord or solo away. But as Beck proved with his cover of 'Manic Depression' in 1993, he was more than equipped for the task and carried this one out admirably. Introduced by Patti Smith as "the jewel in our crown", Jeff handed in an assured, ballsy set full of shock and stun guitar. Whether tackling 'Hey Joe' or 'All Along The Watchtower', he appeared in control of the complexities of the material and challenges it brought, his solos vexatious, strident and in the case of 'Red House', happily revisiting the well of blues influences that informed part of his early style. Following a deserved encore of 'Castles Made Of Sand', where Beck was joined onstage by Smith, he packed up his gig bag and flew with his new band to Japan, the Hendrix portion of his RFH appearance becoming a part of his set while on tour.

Jeff marked his return to England in the best possible way. In a ceremony held in Tunbridge Wells, with guests Jimmy Page, Paul McCartney, Terry Bozzio, Jennifer Batten, Peter Richardson and Robbie Coltrane all in attendance, the guitarist married his long-term girlfriend Sandra Cash. By all accounts it was a well-lubricated, but tasteful event that ended with Beck, Page and McCartney jamming together onstage; English tabloid *The Sun* risked the newlyweds' ire when they mistakenly reported it was the groom's sixth trip up the aisle. One hasty retraction later, and all was well. "I remember Jeff saying he wanted Billy Gibbons from ZZ Top to officiate at his wedding," laughed Jimmy Hall. "He was yelling 'Yeah, I want Reverend Gibbons to marry us!' Man, he loves Billy." Though the Good Reverend certainly had the credentials, a more traditional overseer was eventually sought. With much to celebrate, Beck was also cheered by the news he had won 'Best Re-issue of

The Year' for *Truth* at *Classic Rock*'s annual awards show in 2005. A lavish repackaging of his seminal album, containing alternative takes of 'You Shook Me' and 'Blues Deluxe', *Truth* was soon followed by *Beck-Ola* in the reissue stakes, as BB King's 'Sweet Black Angel' and 'Throw Down A Line' were rescued from the archives for everyone's listening pleasure.

Those pining for a new release from Jeff would have to wait a while longer as 2006 brought more touring, but no real product. Presumably keen to reimburse his bank balance after the cost of a wedding and reception, Beck hit the road in a sustained manner for much of the year. Beginning his run with several dates on the US West Coast in the spring, which included a headlining slot at Fender's '60th Anniversary' show in Tempe, Arizona, the guitarist then soldiered on to Europe. Looking for somewhere "a little less ordinary" to play in England, Jeff teamed up with Buddy Guy for an outdoor 'double header' at the Tower of London on July 10. Once a location where monarchs imprisoned their more unruly subjects (and a couple of their own princes, if rumours are to be believed), the Tower gig made for a fine night's entertainment, its location next to the River Thames and a distinctly uncharacteristic spell of fine weather combining to send fans home with suntans rather than sniffles.

From there, the 'Mustang Sally' boys headed to Japan and the Udo Music Festival, where they joined fellow performer Paul Rodgers for a gig that was later made available on DVD. By now, Beck had brought a new addition to his set in the form of '(Somewhere) Over The Rainbow'. Written in 1939 for the movie *The Wizard Of Oz* by Harold Arlen and Yip Harburg, '... Rainbow' had subsequently become actress/singer Judy Garland's signature tune, its ever-hopeful lyric taking on added impetus as she fell victim to several bad marriages and increasing levels of drug abuse. However, Garland could not claim exclusivity to the song, as it continued to be recorded by new artists each year and decade, not least by Eva Cassidy, who enjoyed a posthumous hit with the song after BBC Radio 2 DJ Terry Wogan played it regularly on his morning show in 2000. Les Paul provided the definitive, instrumental version at his weekly 'Fat Tuesdays' shows in New York during the late eighties – definitive that is, until Jeff got his hands on it. Like 'Where Were You' and

'Nadia' before it, Beck stole '... Rainbow' for his own – his tremolo arm negotiating every change of pitch, his volume swells squeezing out every drop of emotion it could offer. Another masterclass in a long line of masterclasses, Beck's cover of '... Rainbow' soon earned its place in the running order at most future concerts.

By September 2006, Jeff was back on tour in the States, and again adding a surprise or two for his audience. This time, she came in the form of Beth Hart, a respected rock, blues and gospel singer who had come to Beck's attention after providing a spicy vocal on 'I Wanna Know', one of the few essential tracks on Les Paul's *American Made, World Played*. Taking up the role of 'Rod Stewart' in the band (which had now substituted Randy Hope-Taylor for an otherwise engaged Pino Palladino), Hart's nightly renditions of 'You Shook Me', 'I Ain't Superstitious' and 'Morning Dew' were both respectful and immaculately rendered. However, they again brought to mind how effective a weapon Jeff was when teamed with a vocalist, and that things might have been very different if the JBG had stomached the hippies and turned up at Woodstock after all.

Unfortunately, none of Beth Hart's contributions made it to *Official Bootleg USA '06*, a disc recorded in April during Beck's spring tour of America and later sold at merchandising stands when he returned for a second leg in the autumn of 2006. But as demand from fans unable to attend concerts increased – buoyed, no doubt, by those seeking a memento of a night already well spent with Jeff – the album was finally made available via his official website in February 2007.

Realistically, as with *Live At BB King's....*, *Official Bootleg USA '06* was hardly a vital addition to the Beck canon, even if its sound quality was arguably superior to any previous concert releases. Yet, for those willing to make the purchase, *Bootleg...* did serve up some tasty morsels from the Captain's table. Back in action was 'Beck's Bolero', as beguiling as ever, and with a middle-section even more ferocious than the 1966 version, the track worked well as a natural segue into Billy Cobham's 'Stratus'. Always loved by Jeff and now a part of his own set, 'Stratus' in turn allowed Rebello, Palladino and Colaiuta the opportunity to show off their chops until 'The Guv'nor' stepped in with a well-placed sonic boot of his own. While 'Angel (Footsteps)' and a bold new arrangement of 'Scatterbrain' also marked their place strongly, it was surely 'Cause We've

Ended As Lovers' that deserved the lion's share of the plaudits. Seeking the comfort of an old flame, Jeff's solo pass on the tune was a pleasure to behold and might well have bested the original.

The end of 2006 also saw the return – or rather, the reconstruction – of another old lover, as Fender guitars introduced the 'Relic Esquire', "a historically accurate recreation of the Blonde '54 Esquire Beck used so famously throughout his career with The Yardbirds". The latest in a long line of 'custom shop' tributes that included from-the-ground-up reworkings of Eric Clapton's hybrid 'Blackie' Strat and Stevie Ray Vaughan's tireless workhorse 'No.1', Fender had spared no detail in capturing every dent and ding of Jeff's beloved blonde: "Prematurely aged to match the wear and tear of the original, even down to the chipped and dinged pickguard." The company also re-created the '57 one-piece maple neck in a soft 'V' shape, while augmenting the design with a '51 'Nocaster' single bridge pick-up. The only drawback for those seeking to own a painstakingly rendered piece of Beck's illustrious history was its price: one such example was recently sold at auction for $13,000. At such a high mark, it was probably only the very rich or Jeff himself who could afford to buy it. Or not: "People think I'm a multi-millionaire," he grimaced, "but that's not the case. There are people who came up at the same time as me who are in a far better financial position."

Though Beck named no names, it was easy to do the maths. For every hit record he had produced, there was at least the same number of commercial disappointments trailing in its wake. Unlike Clapton, Jeff's back catalogue contained no 'Wonderful Tonight' or 'Layla'. And unlike Jimmy Page, there were no monster albums selling by the truckload every week some 40 years after their release or a £50 box set that sold over a million copies. Of course, the guitarist had often fought against such success – setting his own perimeters of comfort around the fame game and where he sat within it. But the truth was he remained a working musician, dependant on tours and sessions rather than daily radio play to supplement his royalty payments. Financially comfortable, without doubt. Rich by everyman's standards, very probably. However, it was a fleet of rods that sat in Beck's backyard, not a fleet of aircraft: "Yeah, to get a hit, that'd be good," he said in 2001. In the end, he got two.

Chapter 24

With A Little Help From My Friends

The year 2007 brought the first signs of a change in the air around Jeff Beck, an electrostatic charge imperceptible to the naked eye that nonetheless seemed to permeate his aura and play with the molecules above his rooster-thatched head. Given that Jeff began to wear sunglasses on stage at this time, perhaps he noticed it first. More likely, he would have brushed off any such idea as hippie nonsense. He was probably right. Whatever the case, the crackles and sparks were there all the same.

The first manifestations of this electrical activity occurred on April 24, when Beck guested alongside singer Kelly Clarkson on *American Idol Gives Back*. A charity-themed spin-off from the hugely successful *American Idol* TV series that had launched the careers of several US singers, ... *Gives Back's* purpose was raising money for underprivileged children. With stars the magnitude of Tom Cruise and Matt Damon either manning phones or performing sketches, and acts such as Green Day and The Black Eyed Peas' Fergie contributing the odd tune, ... *Gives Back* was never destined to fail. But it was Kelly and Jeff that actually stole the 'Telethon' from under everyone's suspiciously perfect noses.

In Clarkson's case, she had proved the deserved winner of *American Idol's* inaugural season in 2002, rising above the crassness of the series' reality TV roots by actually being very good indeed. A stage-natural singer with a humungous voice and some real down-to-earth charm, Kelly established herself quickly on the charts, a succession of Stateside hits coming fast before the sad/sweet 'Since You've Been Gone' broke worldwide in 2005. Back to honour the programme that pushed her into the spotlight while simultaneously donating her time for a good cause, Clarkson was there to perform country vocalist/songwriter Patty Griffin's soulful 'Up To The Mountain' with Jeff. Aside from sharing the same record company, Sony, the two could hardly be said to have much in common: one a manufactured, albeit talented pop star, the other a quixotic lead guitarist whose last notable US chart success was an instrumental album dating back to 1976. Yet, as the cliché went, together they were dynamite. In a performance that activated the tear ducts, pulled on the heartstrings and left viewers wanting more, Kelly and Jeff's rendition of 'Up To The Mountain' not only got the phones ringing, but also put them in the charts, with a live recording of the song later making number 56 on the *Billboard* Top 100.

While 'Up To The Mountain''s success was fully deserved, Clarkson later cast a dubious light on the internecine politics behind such events, and the fact she and Beck might not have performed it at all: "My record label wanted me to sing 'Never Again,'" she told *Elle*, referring to the first single from her 2007 album, *My December*. "And I was like, 'To promote yourself on a charity event is beyond crass.' People are starving and dying and I'm up there singing some bitter pop song? And believe me, everyone wanted me to sing it. Because they are jaded and they have no soul. Imagine sitting in a room full of people totally against you. Can't they hear themselves speaking? Capitalise on AIDS? Are you kidding? Insulting an entire nation of people? I just refused."

If Beck shared Kelly's views on the subject, he chose not to share them with the press. Never one to court controversy on such matters, he was also no doubt aware that Sony (or 'Epic', as it was before being absorbed by the media/entertainment giant in 2004) had put up with his own foibles for close to 40 years, keeping faith when some might well have floundered. Instead of chucking in his tuppence worth, Jeff kept it clean and focused his remarks purely on Kelly's singing abilities: "It was the depth of her voice that struck me," he said. "She's got this maturity, you know, this fully developed soul voice that I wasn't expecting. It just knocked me out. It was quite riveting to listen to. At one point, the audience started to stand up. They were so moved by her. She's got that quality that demands attention, which is rare." Evidently, the hand that had fed Beck for so long was spared any sign of his teeth.

In spite of such potential controversies, 'Up To The Mountain' generated some real heat around Jeff, putting him back in the US public eye after a long period where his only real followers appeared to be fellow guitarists or those still waiting for *Blow By Blow: The Sequel*. Yet, while the crackles in the air continued to pop, it was to be more a slow, but steady climb back to the top than a furious sprint. His first steps on that path were taken in the summer of 2007 when he began a short European tour that included a headline appearance at the Montreux Jazz Festival, followed by a return visit to Patrimonio's 'Les Nuits De La Guitare' on the island of Corsica: "I love it," he said.

From there, Beck made his way back to America in late July for an appointment at the Crossroads, or more specifically, Eric Clapton's 'Crossroads Festival'. Making its debut in 2004, the Crossroads festival was a benefit concert devised and overseen by Clapton in aid of his own 'Crossroads Centre' – a drug treatment facility, again founded by Eric and located in Antigua. Since first recovering from drug and then alcohol addiction in the late eighties, Clapton had committed an increasing amount of time to this cause, and remained keen to raise funds when he could. By staging such an event for the public, where the emphasis was firmly placed on spotlighting guitar talent from across the world, he could not only fill the coffers of his charity, but also provide a showcase for a variety of players chosen by his own slow hand.

This was not Beck's first time at the Crossroads cavalcade. He had been there in 2004, when it was held in Dallas and attracted such guitar luminaries as Buddy Guy, Steve Vai, Pat Metheny, B.B. King, Sonny Landreth and Jeff's personal favourites, the "bottleneck wonder" Vishwa Mohan Bhatt and the peerless ZZ Top. 2007's line-up was not less distinguished, as country picker Vince Gill and bluesmen Robert Cray and Hubert Sumlin were joined by talented young guns like Derek Trucks, Doyle Bramhall II and Strat killer/ serial pantsman John Mayer at Toyota Park in Bridgeview, Illinois. Though Jeff was firmly behind Eric's hopes for the event and the aim it supported, he was initially sceptical about taking part: "They said 'You've got 40 minutes'. And I went 'Oh no, you're not putting me out there in front of those blues fanatics.' Truck drivers with 'CAT' written across their forehead, scowling in 100 degree heat. But I came off and they were all still standing up, which was amazing." Stirred by his initial experiences, he was back to give it another try.

Walking onstage in his now customary shades, Sioux necklace and black pants, Beck gave his usual virtuoso performance, alternating between old and new material with consummate ease and even the odd smile. But it was the new member of his group that was raising an equal number of eyebrows among the crowd. Though both Vinnie Colaiuta and Jason Rebello had retained their place in the line-up, Jeff's previous bassist Pino Palladino was unavailable for the concert. Instead, taking his place stage left appeared to be a tousled-haired, teenage girl. "Well, Pino couldn't do the gig," said Beck, "because he'd committed to a year's worth of work with The Who, so Vinnie recommended this girl. And, to be honest, I thought 'Ah, Vinnie's fallen in love'. But he was adamant she was fantastic. Anyway, he brings her over, I open the door, and he's right up here [gesturing to Colaiuta's height] and alongside him is this... child!"

Aged 21, Tal Wilkenfeld could hardly be described as a 'child', though admittedly the Australian bassist was nowhere near as tall as Palladino (that would take several chairs and a gift for balancing). Emigrating from Sydney to Los Angeles in 2002, Wilkenfeld had initially studied guitar before moving to four strings. The reduction of two wires from the neck seemed to bring her some good fortune, however. On graduating from LA's Academy of Music in 2004, she was on the move again, this time for New York and its vibrant jazz scene. Picking up several gigs and the patronage of The Allman Brothers Band, Tal cut her first disc, *Transformation*, in 2006. Showing guile as well as ambition, she promptly sent a copy of the album to pianist Chick Corea, who employed her services for an American tour.

From there, her route to Jeff Beck proved straight and swift. "She just sort of pushed past me, and said 'I'm hungry, I want some food'. So she went straight to the bread bin," he said of their original introduction courtesy of Vinnie Colaiuta. "Within an hour, the band is upstairs and she's right in the middle of it. I'd play a line and Tal would play it straight back to me. The kid [was] amazing." The group's subsequent visit to a night club went less well. "I remember they threw us out," said Beck. "The guy walked up to Tal and said 'You can't be here. You're 14.' I thought, 'Well, that's pretty specific.' She was 21 at the time."

If Tal Wilkenfeld still looked like a teenager, she actually played like a wizened old sage – or would, had their hands magically avoided the advances of age or been cloned from the cells of the sadly deceased bass giant Jaco Pastorius. "She has the smallest hands, but plays like Jaco," Jeff laughed. Like Beck, Wilkenfeld's command of melody and phrasing was also head-turning, her own solo excursions at the Crossroads Festival on 'Cause We've Ended As Lovers' drawing nearly as many cheers from those in attendance as the ones reserved for the maestro himself. That said, Tal appeared a team player with some genuine respect for her boss. "I was always a fan of instrumental music, jazz and fusion, things like that," she said. "But Jeff's stuff is extra special. It maintains dynamics, great composition, melody and sheer musicality all the time. Sometimes, jazz can ignore some of that 'song sensibility'. For me, this is almost the perfect situation, with Jeff's music having all those elements." Respectful, talented and possessed of the "biggest shit-eating grin this side of Jimmy Page", Wilkenfeld would also bring more than a little luck with her to Beck's cause.

That run of luck – or as likely serendipity coupled with astute marketing – began in the autumn of 2007 when Jeff was asked to consider playing five back-to-back shows at Ronnie Scott's. As well known a jazz venue to Londoners as the Blue Note was to New Yorkers, Ronnie Scott's had been a Mecca for bebop heads, fusion freaks, free, trad and cool jazzers since it was first opened its doors on October 30, 1959. Run by Ronnie himself – who in addition to being a fine tenor saxophonist, also acted as a withering 'Master of Ceremonies' until his death in 1996 – the club's status and reputation only grew with time as every visiting or home-grown jazz dignitary worth his or her salt dropped in to play a set or soak up the cigarette-stained atmosphere. Housing just 250 punters, the club was tiny, with the audience literally onstage beside the performer rather than behind a photographers' pit. Brimful of history and also a tad imposing, the idea of playing Ronnie's seemed to put the fear of God into Beck. "When we were preparing for the gigs, I was so nervous," he said later. "I didn't eat a single piece of solid food for four days... only water. Actually, only one meal when we started rehearsals. I couldn't face food and nearly fainted."

From an outsider's perspective, this might have looked an overreaction on Jeff's part. After all, he surely could not have conceived the attention these appearances would later bring him, nor their lasting importance on his career. Being nervous, nauseous even, was perfectly understandable for a guitarist facing such an intimate venue when more used to halls, theatres and the occasional field. And as evidenced, the club's reputation might have been a tad intimidating: no wall of amps turned up to 10 to compensate for the odd, fluffed note or scuff, no displays of onstage theatrics to save the day. The spectators were far too close for such tomfoolery. But, in the end, it really was just a set of gigs. Small, high pressure, even high profile, but gigs, nonetheless. Yet, on some level Beck seemed to understand that this might be his moment in the sun, and he better get it right. "Oh, it really was a bit of a gulp moment. Looking down from the stage, seeing friends, it was just... astounding." Suffice to say, he went for it.

Bolstered by the formidable trio of Colaiuta, Rebello and Wilkenfeld, Beck's blitzkrieg of London's 'Home of Jazz' from November 27 to December 1 turned out to be a bumper affair, with an array of famous faces either joining him onstage or nodding appreciatively from the audience. The guitarist's set was well chosen too, reflecting over 40 years of dizzying career choices and musical volte faces, his probing, listless nature and downright refusal to do what might be expected of him reflected by the material on show. From vintage gems such as '...Bolero' and 'Scatterbrain' right through to latter-day pearls like 'Nadia' and 'Brush With The Blues', Beck scattered four decades' worth of precious stones before the crowd. With the inclusion of Billy Cobham's 'Stratus' and John McLaughlin's 'Eternity's Breath', he also seemed intent on honouring the men who had presented him with bold new directions to follow when he hit a creative block in the seventies. "I played 'Stratus' and 'Eternity's Breath' because I want[ed] people to realise that music was around, plus it's still fun to play," Jeff told *Guitar World*. "I'm just a messenger for John on those songs, because I want people to listen to him. If people enjoy my version of it, then my job is done. John is so far ahead of his time, he really is. He's not half as well known as I'd like him to be. So, those songs are played with the most heartfelt respect."

As stated, aside from his own group – "If I didn't have the band, I probably couldn't have done it. They were such a leaning post for me" – Beck peppered the residency with a host of guest appearances. Imogen Heap was back to add fire and ice on 'Rollin' And Tumblin'' and 'Blanket', while a relatively new acquaintance, British soul ingénue Joss Stone, sang 'People Get Ready'. For those of a more old-school persuasion, Eric Clapton also visited Jeff at Ronnie's, the two having grown friendly again after losing touch in the late nineties. Always musically chalk and cheese – with Clapton's stoic blues classicism an anathema to Beck's sonic fireworks – one might have yelled 'mismatch' and left it there. But the former Yardbirds gelled surprisingly well on Muddy Waters' 'Little Brown Bird' and Willie Dixon's 'You Need Love', their respective styles as complimentary as their manners were deferential. "I might as well fuck off home now," said Jeff when introducing a humble-looking Eric to the stage.

While Beck may have understating his own talent in the presence of 'God', Ronnie Scott's really did belong to him during the duration of his stay at the club. Armed with a Marshall JTM45 (the smaller amp choice reflecting the size of the venue), his trusty combination of Snarling Dogs wah, ring modulator, flanger and a new Klon Centaur that provided a little "clean gain", Jeff also gave audiences a close-up of his most trusted of guitars. Unofficially known as 'The Hybrid' or 'Strat One' – though 'Mongrel' might be a more apt description – Beck's main white Strat featured the neck from 'Little Richard' bolted to a basswood body and fitted with John Suhr/Bill Turner pick-ups. "It's got a number of dings," said his guitar tech Andy Prior, "and like all his guitars, he plays it to destruction." And the edge of heaven. Whether communing with angels on 'Where Were You' or teasing out grace note after grace note during 'A Day In The Life', Jeff had the critics drowning him in superlatives: "An absolutely jaw-dropping display of the most exciting, imaginative and inspirational jazz-rock guitar witnessed in years," said *Jazzwise*. *Classic Rock* wasn't far behind: "The guitarist's guitarist reaches jazz-rock nirvana."

Watched with both delight and wonder by Jimmy Page and Robert Plant – who were gearing up for their own 'once and very much once only' Led Zeppelin reunion at London's O2 Arena on December 10 – Beck's stand at Ronnie Scott's also brought out Queen's Brian May and Jon Bon Jovi to witness the spectacle. Indeed, a couple of Jeff's old bandmates made the trip to Soho too. "I was just in awe of him," said a visiting Mo Foster, "and I was also knocked out by Tal Wilkenfeld. I was watching her play 'Space Boogie' so beautifully. Afterwards I said 'God, you weren't even born when I was playing that on tour!'" For her part, Tal enjoyed the shows, even if she was onstage: "It was great for me... every night in the same club, I adjusted really well." Deemed "a triumph in every sense of the word", just 1,000 people saw Beck at Ronnie's at the time. Thanks to the presence of a discreet camera crew and a bold stroke of managerial genius, that number would change exponentially in due course.

Following the excellent reviews accorded his latest endeavour, and a stop-off at the O2 Arena to see Jimmy Page play to an audience of over 20,000 (it probably could have been six million if there were enough seats), Jeff again reverted to type and headed back to his rods in East Sussex. Sightings throughout the spring and summer of 2008 were restricted to the odd session and a surprise turn at London's Royal Albert Hall on July 19 where he became the first rock guitarist to play The Proms in its 113-year history. An annual event predominantly held at the RAH, the Proms offered classical music lovers the opportunity to revel in various symphonies and sonatas over an eight-week period, before they all got to sing a finale of 'Land Of Hope And Glory' and head for the pub.

Though Beck was bestowed a considerable honour by the organisers in being asked to appear, there had been the odd, non-orchestral usurper at the Proms before. In 1970, avant-garde jazz rockers Soft Machine were guests at the celebrations, while more recent years saw the likes of Ravi Shankar and West End musical star Michael Ball also stepping upon the stage of the RAH. But make no mistake, Jeff's presence was real news, both to him and the press. "It's absolutely monumental to be playing at the Proms," he said. Joining jazz/punk/classical violinist Nigel Kennedy's quintet for a rendition of 'Hills Of Saturn' – one of Nigel's own compositions – Beck did his best to stir up a hornet's nest, as a blast of false harmonics, whammy bar drops and howling overbends emanated from 'Strat

One': "Kill! Kill! Kill!" shouted the mohawked Kennedy by way of encouragement. From the wry smile on the guitarist's face at the end of his solo, he really didn't need the support. In Jeff's mind, it was the 1966 San Remo Festival all over again. "The Proms," said *The Times'* Richard Brooks, "but not as we know it..." Quite right too.

Having scared the horses at the RAH, Beck seemed content to avoid the boards for the rest of 2008, preferring to mull over how he might consolidate the sense of forward momentum gained from ... *Idol Gives Back* and Ronnie Scott's. However, there were one or two guest spots for his fans to chew on in the meantime. A posthumous release of sixties session drummer Carlo Little's first (and sadly) only solo record, *Never Stop Rockin'*, featured Jeff combining "postmodern splatter guitar" with more traditional rockabilly licks on a cover of Elvis' 'Mystery Train'. The album, originally cut in the early noughties, also found Ron Wood and Long John Baldry contributing to a track or two. Elsewhere, he joined former Smiths front man Morrissey for 'Black Cloud', a tune recorded for the arch-miserablist's ninth disc, *Years Of Refusal*. "I met Morrissey in a hotel in Los Angeles and he put a note under my door saying, 'Would you like to play on my album?' That's how things are with me most of the time," said Beck. "I knew his work with The Smiths and knew he was iconic. I was also aware he was particular about how he liked to do certain things. That suited me because I'm a bit like that myself." Sharing a mutual friendship with The Pretenders' Chrissie Hynde, the two ended up bonding over a glass of bourbon: "I've always found him fascinating, I like the guy, he's a close friend of my mate Chrissie, and when the opportunity presented itself to play on the record after a few Jack Daniel's, then why not?"

A far more important, and indeed, far-reaching meeting for Jeff Beck occurred on November 3, 2008 at the 'Classic Rock Awards'. Another industry-themed event run by *Classic Rock* magazine, the CRAs usually bestowed their honours on bands, performers and managers who had been around the block once or twice – with gongs going to key influencers rather than those simply influenced. Hence, Jimmy Page, Whitesnake's David Coverdale, Guns N' Roses' Slash, Black Sabbath's Ozzy Osbourne and Irish bluesman Gary Moore were all there to see Jeff Beck receive his award for 'Outstanding Contribution', presented to the guitarist by an ever-smiling Ronnie Wood. Also at London's Park Lane Hotel to pick up his own 'VIP Award' for exceptional services to the music business was promoter Harvey Goldsmith. A "proper legend" in a world where the term was often hideously overused to denote minor contributions rather than genuine achievements, the North London-born Goldsmith began promoting concerts while still a pharmacy student in Brighton during the sixties – putting on live acts at his own 'Club 66' for fellow scholars. Finding himself to be very good at it, he abandoned compounds and tinctures for the rigours of staging gigs and tours. By 1978, Harvey was organising 'Concerts for Kampuchea' at Hammersmith Odeon, the first major global music TV shows of their kind, and supported by artists such as Paul McCartney, The Who and Queen.

But if there were an event that forever defined him in the public eye it had to be *Live Aid*. Working alongside Bob Geldof, Goldsmith masterminded 1985's 'Global Juke Box', which saw two concerts running simultaneously at London's Wembley Stadium and Philadelphia's JFK Stadium in aid of the Ethiopian famine. With over 150 countries showing the 17-hour event live on television, 172,000 people at Wembley and JFK and an estimated 1.9 billion also watching from their armchairs, a dream line-up of stars and superstars performed before the cameras: from David Bowie, Queen and U2 to Tina Turner, Mick Jagger and Bob Dylan, all turned up on time to the ticking of Harvey's watch. Given that £150 million was eventually raised for the cause, one might have forgiven him if he returned to a simpler, less frenetic life. Yet, the next two decades found Goldsmith back at Wembley promoting or producing shows by Pavarotti and Bruce Springsteen, 1992's Freddie Mercury Tribute Concert to raise AIDs awareness and even venturing to Berlin to oversee Pink Floyd's live performance of 'The Wall'. Indeed, when Led Zeppelin reformed in 2007 for their historic O2 appearance, it was Goldsmith they asked to run the show. Trusted advisor, influential businessman and armed with a contacts book the size of the King James Bible, Harvey Goldsmith's mettle had not only been tested over time but also suffused with large shards of tungsten steel.

Beck had known Goldsmith for over 30 years before their meeting again at Park Lane. As younger men, Harvey promoted BBA's British tours, and was heavily involved in The Prince's Trust with which Jeff became temporarily affiliated via Ronnie Lane's ARMS concert in 1983. Long before that, Goldsmith had also introduced Narada Michael Walden to Beck, their subsequent friendship leading to the drummer's strong contribution on *Wired*. Old friends and well-connected then, the two were happy enough to chew the cud about the respective projects and accolades at the CRAs: Kelly Clarkson, Ronnie Scott's and the Proms for Jeff; 'Live 8', 'The Merchants Of Bollywood' and a recent CBE from the Queen for Harvey. However, talk soon turned to the subject of Jeff's current career trajectory and the matter of his managerial status. With Ernest Chapman happily retired to a golf course of his own choosing and Ralph Baker now committed to several pressing projects, Beck felt somewhat in limbo. On one hand, he could sense the tide might be turning in his direction. On the other, he desperately needed someone to help him push the boat out before the last waves were lost. Probably to his own surprise as much as anyone else's, Jeff asked Goldsmith a question: "Do you fancy managing me?" To his surprise, Harvey said yes.

From that moment, things moved very quickly indeed.

Goldsmith's opening gambits as Jeff Beck's new manager were clear, concise and, with benefit of hindsight, extremely profitable for his client. Though a DVD of the Ronnie Scott's gigs was due an imminent release for the Christmas market, Goldsmith stalled it until the New Year, allowing more work to be done on its sound quality while also ensuring Jeff's best concert run in years was not lost in a seasonal crush. "I didn't want the Ronnie's thing to just vanish," he said. "If it was held over to the spring of 2009, it'd get a clear run of its own and the word of mouth could build." As Beck set off on his first Australian tour for over 30 years in January 2009 (with former Bruce Springsteen/Peter Gabriel keyboardist David Sancious temporarily replacing Jason Rebello), word also began circulating that the guitarist might well be inducted into the Rock & Roll Hall Of Fame in his own right. "I'm not sure how the voting is, but you have to be put forward to a panel and they decide," said Jeff. "It's a big one though and in rock'n'roll terms, it doesn't get much bigger. I'm very flattered."

Flattered and, indeed, inducted. Having already received the honour as a Yardbird, and spoken with wit and wisdom on behalf of several previous recipients, Beck found himself at Cleveland's Public Hall on April 4, 2009 in front of a crowd specifically cheering his own name. "I'd listen to Jeff along the way," said Jimmy Page as he introduced his friend to the stage, "and I'd think, 'He's getting really, really good'. Then you'd hear him a few years later, and he just kept getting better and better and better. And he's still getting better now. He leaves us mere mortals wondering... [with] sounds and techniques totally unheard of before. An amazing feat and I'm just honoured to be here to induct him."

Accepting the honour dressed all in white (bovver boots included), Beck's acceptance speech was a typical mixture of humility and humour. "I've been naughty all my life and I really don't deserve this at all," he began, "but I'll continue to be naughty, I think." After namechecking both Ernest Chapman and Harvey Goldsmith for services rendered, he then turned his attention to those who helped and those who hindered: "There are so many people who've helped me, and I'd like to extend a huge thanks to them. Oh, and a huge thanks to those that didn't." As the last remark reverberated around the auditorium, the cameras caught Beck rubbing the middle finger of his left hand up and down his nose in animated fashion.

With the honorifics now out of the way, it was time to hear the music that had earned Jeff his accolade. But even then, he remained in a mischievous mood. After Beck had toyed with 'Beck's Bolero' for a minute or so, Jimmy Page promptly emerged from the wings to join the guitarist and his group for a manic blast of Led Zeppelin's 'Immigrant Song' before the tune again returned to its original template. "I change plans all the time," Jeff said. "When I was playing... we were going to have Jimmy Page come on and play 'Bolero'. But I didn't think it would be right for him to be playing rhythm guitar all the way through that one number. Then the phone rang and it was Tal. She was on the way down in the elevator and told me we should play 'Immigrant Song'. We were going on in 10 minutes and had no time to rehearse. She said, 'Oh, when you stop at the middle of 'Bolero', when the rhythm changes, we'll kick in to 'Immigrant Song'. That's what I like, right on the hoof. Nobody knew, the lighting and sound guys didn't know, the organisers didn't know. I just grabbed the microphone and shouted, 'Jimmy Page!'

and went straight into the song. I loved that. That's what you call dangerous, that's living on your reflexes."

After another unexpected turn with the 'Peter Gunn Theme', the stage became crowded with guitarists and bassists as Page, Ronnie Wood, Aerosmith's Joe Perry, fellow Hall Of Fame inductees Metallica and The Red Hot Chili Peppers' Flea paid tribute to their hero by grinding 'Train Kept 'A Rollin'' to a meaty pulp. "There were all these guitar guys, Jimmy, Ronnie, Kirk Hammett from Metallica and me," said Perry, "and we all just naturally kind of formed a semi circle around Jeff, just waiting to see what he'd do. There was no plan to it, we just wanted to watch what he was doing." But like many before them, watching Beck at close quarters didn't always guarantee enlightenment. "Well yeah, you can watch," laughed Joe, "but that doesn't mean you can figure it out..."

Following Jeff's induction into the Rock & Roll Hall Of Fame, interest in the guitarist inevitably began to build, a fact proved by the healthy ticket uptake for his spring/summer tour of 2009 and the sales figures accorded ... *Live At Ronnie Scott's*. As Harvey Goldsmith predicted, interest in the concert film grew throughout the year as guitarists and fans both old and new purchased the one chance they had to bring Beck out of the club and into their living rooms. By roughly the time he won yet another Grammy for his performance of 'A Day In The Life' at Ronnie's, the DVD had attained platinum status, with over one million units sold. For a straightforward film of its type, with no airs, graces, dry ice or exploding cannons to enhance the spectacle, this was no mean feat. "I was around at a friend's house for a dinner party when BBC Four first showed [highlights of] it on TV," remembered Max Middleton, "and I said 'I'm really sorry as I never normally do this, but I have to watch Jeff.' Well, it was just astounding. So, I called him up the next day to tell him how good it was. And he was still grumbling about the sound quality. That's typical Jeff. Performs a miracle and then spends his time worrying it wasn't good enough!"

As ... *Live At Ronnie Scott's* continued to do brisk business in stores and on the internet, so demand increased for Beck's live appearances. After a sell-out tour of the Far East and the Antipodes at the beginning of 2009, the guitarist's stroll across America in the spring was also well received and well attended – with John

Mayer turning up to trade a lick or two with Jeff on Hendrix's 'Manic Depression' at LA's El Rey Theatre on April 22. June and July found Beck back in Canada and then Europe, this leg marked with a two-night stop-over at the Royal Albert Hall where he was joined onstage by Dave Gilmour for an emotional take on the hymn 'Jerusalem'. "Oh, Jeff's the best there is," said Pink Floyd's front man. Though many might agree with Gilmour's sentiments, his own soaring lead lines on William Blake's homage to England's "green and pleasant land" were also worthy of serious comment, providing a tasteful contrast to Beck's swallow-like dips above and below Sir Hubert Parry's haunting melody. It wasn't all gentile sophistication, however. Having dispensed with the serious part of the evening, the duo led the crowd through a comedic rendition of 'Hi Ho Silver Lining' – a tune Dave begged Jeff to let him sing. "I thought it would be a great tongue in cheek twist," Beck said of the tune he had now occasionally grown to love, but mostly still hated.

New ground for Jeff was broken on September 21 when he threw his weight behind the British Music Experience, a permanent exhibition housed in the grounds of Greenwich's cavernous O2 entertainment arena. Taking up more than 20,000 square feet, the 'BME' offered a retrospective look at the British music industry since 1944 and featured a wide variety of exhibits, interactive media displays, artefacts and donations; from David Bowie's 'Ziggy Stardust' costume and Roger Daltrey's 'Woodstock' outfit to Noel Gallagher's 'Union Jack' guitar and some of Elton John's more outrageous spectacles. A charitable trust spearheaded by Harvey Goldsmith, the BME's latest project was a range of 'masterclasses' held by famous musicians for the general public, with Beck (accompanied by Jason Rebello) cast as head teacher for the day. "Jeff fits right in the middle of the BME ethos," said Harvey at the time, "and [he's] taking the first of these masterclasses, where he'll talk about [his] history, play a little bit and explain his approach [to music]. What we're trying to do here at the BME is have a whole series of 'Firsts', where we honour the heritage of our music and celebrate the artistry of our icons [like Jeff]."

At the end of a class that saw Beck communing with fans, explaining his guitar techniques and even playing a few tunes ('Superstition', 'Where Were You' and 'Cause We've Ended As

Lovers') came a gig at the IndigO2. This, however, was not a standard set as Jeff was backed by The Imelda May Band onstage. Another of those prestigiously talented individuals Beck seemed to collect like hot rods, May was for all intents and purposes a postmodern composite of Gene Vincent and Mary Ford, but with cleaner nails and funkier hair. Discovering the wonders of rockabilly and blues while still a child, the singer made a small splash in her native Dublin before moving to England in 1998 where she provided backing vocals for former Big Town Playboy Mike Sanchez.

By 2007, Imelda was working full tilt under her own steam, with her second solo album, *Love Tattoo*, reaching number one in the Irish charts and her UK club appearances coming to the attention of Jools Holland, who gave her a spot on his own BBC TV show, *Later...* From there, it was only a matter of months before she was headlining the Royal Albert Hall in her own right. "When I was on the way out to the soundcheck," she said, "Al Gare, our double bass player, said, 'Take a deep breath', so I took it all in, got myself prepared, and then we were on. The audience was just brilliant." A vampish rock'n'roller blessed with what one critic described as "a burn down the houses voice", May was also married to the lug-handsome Darrel Higham, once The Big Town Playboys' rhythm guitarist and latterly another of Beck's guests at Ronnie Scott's in November 2007. Of course, these were all qualities that drew Jeff to the singer like a proverbial moth to the flame. "Ah, he's a lovely man," she laughed. "Me, Darrel, Jeff and his wife, Sandra, really get on. We even go to pub quizzes together!"

While the Indig02 gig was advertised as a fairly low-key affair, it was to have lasting ramifications for both Beck and May's career plans. Performing before an audience that included Jimmy Page and the ever-present Ronnie Wood (Jeff laughingly accused them both of being "too chicken" to join him onstage), the set was awash with old rockabilly, R&B and forties classics. 'Green Onions', 'The Girl Can't Help It' and 'Rock Around The Clock' were all given the Beck treatment, while May dispatched stupendous versions of 'Lilac Wine' and '(Remember) Walking In The Sand', her lilting vocals melting into Beck's fluid guitar lines. "All respect to Imelda and her band," Jeff said, "they really live this music. They look like they have just stepped out from a fifties catalogue. I really want people to hear more of the stuff from the fifties, not just Elvis but things from before him, and I'd love to take the show to the West End. If *Mamma Mia* can be a success then I don't see why a show like this wouldn't be as well." In time, he would make good on his promise.

A little over a month later Beck was in action again at New York's Madison Square Garden, taking up the baton at 'The 25th Anniversary Rock & Roll Hall Of Fame' concert on October 30/31 for an indisposed Eric Clapton. Jeff hit an immediate high note on the first night when he teamed up with Stevie Wonder for a furious rendition of 'Superstition', the keyboardist howling "Do your thing son!" as Beck tore the face off his white Strat with another one of those whiplash solos. Obviously in the mood to mingle, Jeff and his group were also joined onstage during night two by Buddy Guy, Sting and ZZ Top's Billy Gibbons – the latter contributing some gut-bucket riffs to a cover of Jimi Hendrix's 'Foxy Lady' while also giving his own 'Rough Boys' a proper shaking off. "Billy just does things I would never think of," said Beck, "and nobody has that tone."

Thus far, 2009 had proved an extraordinary year for the guitarist, bestowing him with accolades and awards, platinum discs and sell-out tours. Some six years before, such progress would have been frankly inconceivable. Beck's career – by his own admission – was then at something of a nadir, his third techno-themed disc failing to chart, and leaving him vulnerable to accusations of bandwagon jumping while also confusing his core audience. But dogged persistence, an unfailing work ethic and the acquisition of a superb manager had re-established him in the marketplace, shifting Jeff from 'Cult Artist' to 'Mainstream Success' in just 14 months. He was in no doubt as to who to thank the most for this upturn in his fortunes: "Harvey's a livewire. He gets things done." Yet, for the war to be truly won, there had to be a further consolidation and repositioning of 'Brand Beck'. To this end, Goldsmith now played another excellent card by teaming his charge with Eric Clapton for an ocean-spanning series of shows.

Creating the proverbial 'Dream Ticket', it was announced that Jeff would hit the road as a 'Special Guest' to Eric at various airport-sized venues in London, New York, Toronto and Montreal during early 2010. A marvellously simple idea (first tested in Japan in early 2009), both guitarists were committed to playing separate sets with their own groups before taking to the stage to perform together at the finale. The benefits of such an arrangement were potentially enormous for Beck. Not only would he be given a wide-ranging platform to display his wares, but also seek to make converts from Clapton's own fanbase. If the strategy worked, it could provide the perfect springboard from which to launch his new studio album, scheduled for release in the spring of 2010.

Suffice to say, the plan went perfectly as Jeff found himself taken to heart by Eric's fans while also profiting from a surge of media interest in the pairing of two former Yardbirds on the same stage. "We did 45 minutes to establish who I was within Eric's audience," he said soon after two sold-out shows at London's O2 Arena in February 2010. "So I [was] playing largely to Eric's people. [But] it worked fine for me. I was full of gratitude for that, to get my music across to his people. Then there was a turnaround, and he came back on to do his 45 minutes. Then we did 35 or 40 minutes together. So it was a triple show really, [and] very good fun."

Sticking close to a near approximation of his Ronnie's set before Clapton performed a 'Greatest Hits' package that included 'Layla', 'Motherless Child' and the double whammy of 'Crossroads' and 'Cocaine', when Beck returned for the concluding part of the show, there was a genuine air of anticipation as the two gunslingers readied themselves for battle. But for both Jeff and Eric, those days were long gone. "No, because Eric shines playing the blues," said Beck. "To me, you don't go there. I do one blues, which is full-on. It starts off moody and it builds into hysteria. So that's my version of his kind of music. But I don't mess with Eric and he doesn't get in my way with my style. We've both developed very, very distinguished styles. So whoever wants to put us in a boxing ring together is slightly misguided. Why not just enjoy both?"

Ultimately, the Clapton/Beck finale provided no blood and gore, but instead concentrated on playing to the strengths of both parties: a little bit of The Yardbirds with 'Outside Woman Blues', a nod to Ronnie Scott's with a reprise of Muddy Waters' 'Little Brown Bird' and an occasional, rip-snorting run through of Sly Stone's '... Take You Higher'. If there was a winner to be had during the set, it actually came with a supremely well-judged cover of Johnny Mercer and Henry Mancini's Academy Award-winning 'Moon River'. The theme tune of the 1961 movie *Breakfast At Tiffany's* (when it was sung by actress Audrey Hepburn) and later a hit for crooner Andy Williams, 'Moon River''s quaint melodic structure and whispering chords proved fertile territory for Eric and Jeff's contrasting styles: Clapton content to seek out the blue notes with both his voice and Strat, Beck taking the opportunity to once again sail into the sunset using his tremolo arm as a paddle: "Beautiful tune, that."

Billed as 'Together And Apart', the short, but extremely well-attended shows also put some old differences to bed between two of the 20th century's finer musicians. When asked by *Rolling Stone*'s David Fricke why it had taken so long for him and Jeff to strike out together on tour, Eric was cripplingly frank with his response: "Because we were enemies, basically. To be absolutely honest, I wanted to be as critical of him as I could. It hurt me because I could see what [The Yardbirds] were getting with Jeff. [It was] something beyond what I was capable of. His thing was so unique and advanced." More, any post-Yardbirds enmity had now melted into pure, unadulterated respect: "Jeff is the most unique guitar player, and also probably the most devoted. He's either fixing his cars or playing guitar. There's just no 'in between' for him." Beck was equally kind in his assessment of Clapton's abilities. "I just love playing with him," he said. "I like to play these big band chords while he's soloing, you know, give him a proper backup!" How things change.

Bolstered by his recent successes and a mini-tour with Eric Clapton that put him back on the front covers of the mainstream press, Jeff was now ready to unveil his first studio album in seven years. Released in April 2010, *Emotion & Commotion* presented an older, wiser and very much more chart-friendly Beck, its 10 well-honed tunes immaculately produced and covering a broad gamut of styles, from R&B and rock to old standards and classical music. In marketing terms, the disc was akin to a box of quality chocolates – the contents offering something for every palette, though some might also come away disappointed at the lack of 'nutty' treats Jeff usually had on offer. That said, *Emotion & Commotion*'s quite deliberate, broadband appeal and occasionally safe flavours did not detract from the magnificent displays of guitar that were at the heart of the record.

413

As one might expect, there had been several shifts of emphasis and planning before Beck settled on the material chosen for *Emotion & Commotion*. For some while, he pondered making a purely 'classical' CD, and even went as far as to start the process with the New York Philharmonic Orchestra. "I had to do an album, that was a given, kind of like being forced into a corner," said Jeff. "So I listened to some jams I'd recorded with various musicians, but didn't care for most of them. [But] I'd always wanted to record with an orchestra, something very melodic. Originally, I was going to record a full-on classical album, interpretations of Mahler's 5th Symphony and the like. And I did some stuff with the New York Philharmonic where I morphed the guitar into the orchestra. The record company loved it, loved the idea." Stirred by his collaboration with Pavarotti, Beck also considered working up Puccini's 'O Mio Babbino Caro' from the opera *Gianni Schicchi*. The French composer Maurice Ravel was explored as another possible source of inspiration, but prohibitive costs and unfeasible logistics brought such ideas to a quick halt: "It wasn't really feasible, travelling around the world with a hundred-piece orchestra to tour the thing."

Instead, Jeff began to concentrate his mind on what might be achieved on time and within budget: "I wanted to explore the idea of simple melodies that could reach people. Not techno, funk, esoteric or grunge, just simpler tunes that people could connect with. Me being a bit more accessible, if you like." He was also adamant that his new album not be purely instrumental, but also feature contributions from a number of female vocalists: "I just got into women singers, the way they approached things. There was no macho, bare-chested testosterone element there... just singing. [And] that [also provided] a sense of restraint. When a vocalist is doing their thing, they should be given space, not just trampled over by guitar."

Having honed his ideas to this point, and remaining 100% sure that the backbone of his album should retain an orchestral slant, Beck became concerned that his own group might not have a place in the new regime. But they would not be denied: "It didn't make too much sense to fly Tal and Vinnie over from the States for three or four tracks, but they ended up contributing to one or two things anyway!"

Clear on his approach and encouraged in his choices by Harvey Goldsmith, Jeff sought out two fine producers to oversee the project.

Taking a hands-on role was Steve Lipson, who in addition to production duties was responsible for engineering and mixing the album. A gifted guitarist who began his studio career with The Rolling Stones before extending his CV to include Cher, Paul McCartney and The Pet Shop Boys, Lipson had also co-written Grace Jones' 'Slave To The Rhythm', one of the eighties' finer dance tracks. "Sitting six feet away from Jeff while he casually plays something no one else could get close to [was] an extraordinary experience," he said. "He makes the instrument sing like a voice... with total apparent ease." In the role of executive producer on *Emotion & Commotion* was Trevor Horn. Perhaps the finest sound manipulator of his generation, Horn's work with The Buggles, Yes, ABC, Frankie Goes To Hollywood, Seal and his own Art Of Noise had brought him awards and platinum albums by the truckload (with an incoming CBE from the Queen to be added to his treasure trove by the end of 2010). A friend of Beck's since they collaborated together on the unused *Tube* theme in 1985, and one never given to lending his name to something unless it stood an excellent chance of selling in droves, Trevor's presence on *Emotion & Commotion* almost guaranteed a hit.

And a hit it proved to be. Though Jeff's original conceit of recording a full-on classical disc was stymied by cost and practicality, much of *Emotion & Commotion* retained an air of lush strings and orchestral settings, a point driven home by its opening track, 'Corpus Christi Carol'. Discovered by an apprentice grocer in a tome written around 1504, 'Corpus Christi...' was a seven-stanza example of the classic Middle English hymn, its religious overtones possibly pertaining to the quest for the Holy Grail. While the original author's name remains sadly unknown, English classical composer Benjamin Britten resurrected its melody for his own purposes on 'A Boy Is Born' (Opus 3) in 1933. From there, the hymn gained a new following, with jazz pianist Nina Simone highjacking it for her own purposes in the late fifties. But it was singer/guitarist Jeff Buckley's interpretation on his 1994 album *Grace* that caught Beck's ear: "Well, it was just one listen to the Jeff Buckley album... so beautiful, so effective, [this] delicate voice and so I just wanted to give it a shot. Originally, I was going to do [Jeff's version of] 'Hallelujah', but a girl group [Alexandra Burke] ruined it, though it did go to number one, and I just thought 'No, don't go there'." With keyboards and orchestra arranged by Richard Murray, Jeff's treatment of 'Corpus Christi...' set the tone for much to follow: mellow, soulful, keening and crisp, his singing lines and gentle phrasing more evocative than ever. Sandra Beck was reportedly moved to tears when she first heard it: "My wife begged me to put 'Corpus Christi...' on the album," said the guitarist.

This brush with the classics continued with 'Elegy For Dunkirk', a mournful piece written by Dario Marianelli for the 2007 film *Atonement*, based on the novel by Ian McEwan. Heard during a lengthy, heart-stopping, panoramic travelling shot across the violence and chaos of angry soldiers stranded on the beaches at Dunkirk in 1940, the music adds immeasurably to McEwan's anti-war subtext, winning 'Film Music Composition of the Year' at the Golden Globes. "Steve Lipson suggested [it]," Beck said in *Emotion's* sleeve notes. I picked out the main melody from the cellos and when I played it on the guitar, it made a lot of sense." Later described by Jeff as "probably the deepest thing I've ever done", 'Elegy For Dunkirk' featured a drifting vocal interlude from English opera singer Olivia Safe, who also lent her voice to 'Serene', a track written by Beck and Jason Rebello that recalled some of his more reflective work with Tony Hymas.

After three years causing sharp intakes of breath in concert halls worldwide, Jeff finally committed his version of '(Somewhere) Over The Rainbow' to disc on *Emotion & Commotion*. Nevertheless, he did not use the studio setting to overcook the melody, preferring to keep things straight and simple: "I've heard so many people try and strangle that song," said Beck. "If you got the sound, why add the gymnastics? I was just after a melodic approach, without excessive embellishment."

This approach was also prevalent on 'Nessun Dorma', an aria liberated from the final act of Giacomo Puccini's opera *Turandot* by Luciano Pavarotti, who by degrees turned it into his own signature tune before the tenor died in 2007. "Pavarotti never ceased to amaze me," recalled Jeff. "The *bellowing,* the big, deep, proper opera singing is something I love and I was keen to try 'Nessun Dorma', which he sang so magnificently." Tailor-made for Beck, 'Nessun Dorma''s bold, open nature and frequent switches between major and minor chords allowed the guitarist to once again soar off into the skies –

his final, ever-spiralling note at its rousing conclusion causing much quivering of the upper lip and reaching for the hankies.

Away from Jason Rebello's well-intentioned, if somewhat slight 'Never Alone' and one other tune to be returned to in due course, the rest of *Emotion & Commotion* "belonged to the girls". Reprising her role as one of Jeff's favourite singers of the moment was Imelda May on the fifties torch ballad 'Lilac Wine'. Again drawn to the song after hearing Jeff Buckley's subtle treatment on *Grace*, Beck and May's version was probably as good as anything on the album: Imelda's voice close miked and silky, Jeff's Strat quietly tracing the notes she left behind. "I just loved the song and wished I'd seen Jeff before he tragically [died] in 1997," he said of Buckley. "It was just made for guitar. I could take the melody, the power from his voice and do something with it. But then, I thought, why don't I add a great singer who isn't that well known, and should be. That was Imelda. She's great on the track, and takes it away from just being an endless solo."

Another vocalist making a strong mark on *Emotion & Commotion* was Dover-born, Devon-raised soul queen Joss Stone. Since entering the public's consciousness with her UK number one album *Mind, Body And Soul* in 2004, Stone's combination of gravelly screams and soothing sighs had also won over America where her first three discs had sold over 2.5 million copies by 2008. She had been a Beck devotee since she sang 'People Get Ready' at Ronnie Scott's, and the guitarist returned the favour by appearing on Joss' 'Parallel Lines', one of the saltier tracks featured on her 2009 disc *Colour Me Free*. Now she was back again, adding her voice to 'There's No Other Me' and 'I Put A Spell On You'. Composed by Rebello and Stone herself, 'There's No Other Me' was in Beck's own words "a bit of a mix and match thing", originally using 'call and response' themes to inform much of its content. But as Beck's guitar excursions threatened to overlap Joss' voice, some hasty rewriting was called for: "Joss sat there quietly writing lyrics for an hour or so, got the feeling of the song, did three or four takes and there you are. It turned out really well."

'I Put A Spell On You', on the other hand, required no extensive root canal work to get to the bottom of the problem. A bone-shivering blues, written in 1956 by the one and only Screamin' Jay

Hawkins, Stone's performance had Jeff literally reaching for the ice cubes: "Joss was wearing a backless dress, and I'm telling you, that was the most erotic, beautiful thing I've ever seen. The muscles she was using and everything about her breath... just an amazing sight. I wish I'd filmed it."

When Beck had sufficiently recovered from his experience, he was able to give a more objective opinion of Joss' vocal take and the choice of song: "We wanted something that really suited her," he said. "And she's a wild one. So we wanted something with a screaming quality... and she just nailed it." Stone and Beck subsequently performed 'I Put A Spell On You' on US TV's *...Idol Gives Back* on April 21, 2010. The guitarist got through the tune more or less intact.

Thus far, Beck's latest disc had been heavy on the 'Emotion', but less given to delivering on the 'Commotion' side of things. Thankfully, 'Hammerhead' remedied the oversight. A powerful instrumental, propelled by a bank of cellos and violins, and featuring one of Jeff's most waspish riffs in years, 'Hammerhead' was born backstage at the Royal Albert Hall on July 4, 2004: "Before the show, [David Gilmour] asked if I was going to sing 'Hi Ho Silver Lining'. I said 'Absolutely not'. So he asked if I would mind him singing it. I thought it would be a great... twist. Jason Rebello suggested we write a different riff to play underneath it, instead of [that] stomping rhythm. [So] he wrote an amazing riff with Jan Hammer in mind... that later evolved into 'Hammerhead'."

Inspired by the Czech master and cooked to perfection by Jeff and Jason, 'Hammerhead''s fusion of orchestral clout and sizzling fret work was a wonderfully vivid antidote to an album that sometimes sacrificed firepower for mood and atmosphere. "I didn't come up with the title *Emotion & Commotion* first. But towards the end of recording, it was obvious that there was a lot of emotion on the album," Beck later conceded. "Then we were cutting 'Hammerhead', which was pure 'blow the house down' stuff, where the full orchestra comes in. And that's where the 'Commotion' came in... at least in my small little brain, anyway!" Despite the huge tones present on 'Hammerhead', Jeff had actually used small amps for the majority of recording, with two fifties Fender Champs – one set clean, one slightly distorted – and a Marshall Plexi reissue there to cover all remaining bases: "Pure tones to reflect the size of the orchestra." Additionally, while he also experimented with Gretsch and Guild guitars, his Strat nearly always won out. This penchant for smaller-sized amps was set to continue, as Jeff took to using a 15-watt Fender Pro Junior for live shows.

A mature record deliberately conceived to present Beck as an elder statesman of the six-string, master of most genres and mentor to new talent, even *Emotion & Commotion*'s cover sleeve seemed specifically designed to court favour with his biggest potential audience; featuring a white-headed eagle descending from a big, broad sky, wings spread wide with a white Fender Strat held tight in its talons, there was little doubt that Jeff and Harvey Goldsmith were hoping to fly the CD straight into the arms of America. And it worked. Giving Beck his highest chart position in 34 years, *Emotion & Commotion* swooped into the US charts at number 11, selling over 26,000 copies in its first week of release. The album was not just embraced in the States. It debuted at number one in the Japanese charts and at 21 in the UK, providing Jeff with his most successful British album ever. For the guitarist, this was vindication of the highest order: "Right now, everyone's trying to write the heaviest rock riffs ever, wear the most outrageous clothes, create the biggest stage shows, the best dancing, the best gymnastics. We were just trying to make some music. Remember that old chestnut?"

Sticking to long established rules of rock'n'roll marketing, Jeff set out on the road in the spring of 2010 to promote *Emotion & Commotion* in as many territories as would have him. Opening in the Far East and Australia before plane-hopping into his primary market of the USA in mid-April, this latest round of dates also introduced two new group members to his camp. With Vinnie Colaiuta and Tal Wilkenfeld having moved on to other projects and solo album deals respectively, Jeff once again beguiled Narada Michael Walden back to the fold and behind the drum kit. According to Walden, he had never really been away: "Whenever I was in London, I'd always pop over to Jeff's house, hang out, and hear what he was up to."

The last recruit to join 'Camp Beck' was the wonderful Rhonda Smith. Canadian by birth, Smith's background read like a 'Who's

Who' of jazz, funk and soul, with the bassist having worked with Chaka Khan, Beyoncé, Erykah Badu, Patti Labelle, Lee Ritenour, Little Richard and George Clinton in her time. Yet, it was Rhonda's 10-year stint with Prince that most defined her style and sass: "I couldn't help but learn a lot from him. He's still the greatest performer, musician and business mind in the game today," she said. "When he speaks, you should listen and respect the music." Having made her debut with Beck alongside Narada Michael Walden and the long-serving Jason Rebello on the 'Together And Apart' dates in early 2010, Smith was now part of another royal household: "Narada recommended me for [the gig]. He thought we would be good together. It's a wonderful experience. I've always been a fan of Jeff, but he's absolutely amazing! His sound, his technique. [And] it doesn't hurt that he's the nicest guy in the world, along with Narada, Jason and the rest of the touring family."

Drawing on a set of old and established favourites that included 'Led Boots', 'People Get Ready', 'Big Block', 'Blast From The East' and 'A Day In The Life', Beck also incorporated a reasonable amount of *Emotion & Commotion* into his shows. 'Corpus Christi Carol' and 'Hammerhead' made for a playful, back-to-back experience while '(Somewhere) Over The Rainbow' gained a friend or two for those visiting Jeff's music for the first time. As one might expect, the presence of Rhonda Smith also brought a far funkier element to proceedings, with the bass player even contributing the odd vocal or two. A strong singer who had trained her lungs well while with Prince, Smith covered Imogen Heap's previously smoky renderings on 'Rollin' And Tumblin'' with considerable aplomb while also providing an able Sly Stone impersonation on 'I Want To Take You Higher'.

After a prestigious spot at the New Orleans Jazz Festival on May 1, and a trail blazed up and down America's East Coast, Jeff made time to play a novel version of the US national anthem at a Detroit Tigers baseball game before again returning for a spot at Eric Clapton's Crossroads Guitar Festival on June 26. This time the event was held at Chicago's imposing Toyota Park, but as ever it brought out a plethora of guitarists to show their support, with James Burton, Johnny Winter, Albert Lee and Earl Klugh keenly representing country, blues, rockabilly and jazz styles. Another performer on the Crossroads bill was Joe Bonamassa. An excellent singer/guitarist who had slowly but surely built up a sizeable following both as a solo artist and one part of the rock supergroup Black Country Communion, Bonamassa was a major fan of Beck. In fact, he had not only named his 2003 album *Blues Deluxe*, but also covered the tune. Unhappy to leave it there, Joe's latest disc, 2010's well-received *Black Rock*, also found him dabbling purposefully with 'Spanish Boots'. "Jeff was always a major, major influence on me," he said. "Jeff Beck, Jimmy Page, those guys were my guys." Beck evidently felt a degree of affection for Bonamassa too, as he asked the New Yorker to be his opening act for a number of European festival appearances throughout July.

By the late summer of 2010, Jeff had pushed his frequent flyer points to a whole new level as France, Belgium, Switzerland, Spain, Ireland and even debut visits to Russia and Israel were all crossed off the itinerary. It must have come as some relief then for the guitarist to find himself back on British soil for the UK leg of the *Emotion & Commotion* tour. Opening his account with a gig at Bournemouth's BIC on October 15, Beck travelled along the coast to Brighton before veering north for further dates in Birmingham, Manchester and Glasgow. Having ensured many of England and Scotland's major conurbations were properly attended to, he returned to his 'home from home' for two sold-out shows at London's Royal Albert Hall on October 26 and 27.

Memorable occasions for all concerned, Beck and his group were joined onstage by Olivia Safe for a wistful version of 'Elegy For Dunkirk' on the first night, while Imelda May turned up twice to barnstorm her way through The Shangri-Las' 1964 classic 'Remember (Walking In The Sand)'. Another surprise guest at the RAH was Sharon Corr, one part of the multi-million selling Irish folk/pop quartet The Corrs. An elegant soul and accomplished violinist, Sharon's first solo album (2010's *Dream Of You*) had featured Jeff emoting beautifully on the traditional air 'Mná Na h'Éireann' and she was there to repay the debt. "I played on Sharon's album," Beck confirmed. "How did that happen? Simply because she came to the show when we played Ireland. And, as you do, you get talking about different things and I love Davy Spillane, the uilleann pipe player. [So] she said, 'Well that's amazing, he's on my record and I'd love you to play a track on it.'" A misty affair, allowing both musicians to play safe and sure with its slow-moving melody, 'Mná Na h'Éireann' drew strong applause from an already receptive crowd.

Away from the guest spots and Celtic tear-jerkers, the undoubted highlight of Beck's two-night stand at the RAH was the presence of the Royal Harmonic Orchestra – albeit in reduced numbers – to back the guitarist on several tunes. With over a dozen violinists and cellists, a similar number of French horn players and trombonists and a conductor to boot, Jeff finally managed to bring an idea that had been kicking around his head for 40 odd years to the concert stage. It didn't disappoint either. Whether adding ballast and sweep to 'Hammerhead', majesty and grandeur to 'A Day In The Life' or simply supporting Beck's fearless tremolo work on 'Corpus Christi Carol', the RHO earned their fee and then some. However, it was 'Nessun Dorma' that proved the perfect marriage of orchestra and guitar. Introduced by Jeff as "a little bit of Italian rock'n'roll", the execution of Puccini's aria was simply flawless: "Good lord," said a shaken-looking Beck after the performance.

During the same week that Jeff was knocking them over in the aisles at the Royal Albert Hall, another disc emerged from the shadows and onto the CD racks. Bearing the title *Live And Exclusive From The Grammy Museum*, the album was actually a faithful rendition of a webcast performance given by Beck and his group in front of an audience of just 200 at LA's titular Grammy Museum on April 22, 2010. Given that Jeff had won five Grammys himself, both the choice of venue and nodding of his head towards the concept made some sense. But the issuing of new product so soon after the success of *Emotion & Commotion* was somewhat harder to fathom, especially when four of the eight live tracks presented were drawn from the guitarist's latest studio album. Nonetheless, as a memento of the Beck/Rebello/Walden/Smith line-up, *Live And Exclusive...* more than served its purpose, with 'A Day In The Life' and '(Somewhere) Over The Rainbow' both especially pleasing to the ear. Like the *Live At Ronnie Scott's* CD before it – which only reached 143 in the US charts as opposed to the million plus selling DVD – ...*Grammy Museum's* sales figures proved predictably low, though the downloadable version fared slightly better.

For the rest of 2010, Beck pared down his activities, as the reclamation of his status, the rebalancing of his finances and the rebranding of his image in the marketplace were achieved. An excellent year to be the guitarist, even he had trouble believing the course of events that had transpired since teaming up with Harvey Goldsmith. "It's great at this time of my life just to be listened to," he said. "Of course, I still worry about putting on a great gig, but the fact that people still want to listen, well, that makes the effort worth it. To be honest, I just try not to be boring, and if I make a mistake, let's hope it's a great mistake." Yet, he harboured no great regrets as to the roads he had taken on the way: "To be honest, laziness has helped. I've used it to great effect. It's enabled me to duck out of some hard work, and at the same time watch the parade go by while thinking 'Fuck me, thank God I didn't do that.'"

That rebel spirit was still in full bloom on October 31, 2010 when Beck trotted out at Wembley Stadium to perform the British national anthem before a televised game between The San Francisco 49ers and the Denver Broncos. Part of a new initiative to bring American football to a world stage, 83,000 fans were gathered for the spectacle and the guitarist appeared justly nervous as he took to the platform. Indeed, when he first broke into 'God Save The Queen', the notes seemed hesitant, the approach perhaps overtly respectful. But at the climax of the tune, he just couldn't help himself: turning up the volume knob, and depressing the tremolo arm as low as it would allow, Beck walloped the hell out the last chords before ending the piece with a quote from Hendrix's immortal 'The Wind Cries Mary'. Evidently, despite re-establishing himself as one of the world's finer guitarists in the public mind, Geoffrey Arnold Beck wasn't quite ready for a knighthood just yet.

Chapter 25

The More Things Change

Those expecting Jeff Beck to pull his usual trick of retreating into the world of hot rods and country life following the heady events of 2010 were to be disappointed. Bucking old trends, the guitarist was back in action only 13 days into 2011, appearing at London's Hammersmith Apollo for a benefit gig in aid of Killing Cancer. The charity, whose work funded research into a new, photodynamic treatment to help fight the disease, brought out a glut of stars in support of its cause: Apart from Jeff, The Who, Bryan Adams, Blondie and former Verve frontman Richard Ashcroft had all pledged their services. Following his own short set, Beck was back onstage with Debbie Harry for several Blondie hits including 'Call Me' and 'Heart Of Glass', before again disappearing until the show's finale – which included a well-meaning, if shambolic version of The Who's 'Join Together': "At the end," observed the *Evening Standard*'s David Smyth, "Beck and Pete Townshend edged towards each other like wary rhinos." Perhaps they had been debating who invented feedback in the bar beforehand.

Beck's next stop-off was on February 13 at Los Angeles' Staples Center, where he attended the 53rd Grammy Awards. A regular winner at the ceremony for over three decades, he excelled himself on this occasion by being nominated in four categories for *Emotion & Commotion*: 'Best Rock Album', 'Best Rock Performance By A Duo Or Group With Vocals' for 'I Put A Spell On You' with Joss Stone, 'Best Pop Instrumental Performance' for 'Nessun Dorma' and 'Best Rock Instrumental Performance' for 'Hammerhead'. In an associated category, Steve Lipson was also honoured, taking a nod for 'Best Engineered Album, Non Classical'. Ultimately, Beck had to make do with just two wins for 'Nessun Dorma' and 'Hammerhead', though his brief solo on Herbie Hancock's rendition of 'Imagine' (featuring old friend Seal and pop/rock singer Pink) also made off with 'Best Pop Collaboration With Vocals'. That brought his overall Grammy tally to eight. As ever, the guitarist was self-effacing about the importance of such gong shows, even if he seemed happy to take his victories where he found them. "Yeah, well, there's always a lot of categories," he once joked. "'Best Use Of A Comb', 'Best Paper Clip'. You're bound to win something if you've been around as long as me..."

Though Beck tried to make light of his achievements, he remained aware that the Grammys had been an important part of maintaining his US profile during leaner years, their dedication to his cause reciprocated by his last live disc and an exclusive concert at their museum. "The ceremony is a very long day, but you can't help but have a good time," he said. "You never expect to win any Grammys, so it's always a surprise to hear your name called. The most nerve-racking part is the acceptance speech, because I'm always going to miss out thanking someone. So three more Grammys to add to my collection, thank you very much!" In fact, his latest DVD/CD also owed something in part to the organisation's previous kindnesses, though one had to backtrack a year or so to put it all in perspective.

On February 5, 2010 Jeff and Imelda May had performed 'How High The Moon' at the 52nd Grammy Awards, the song a fitting tribute to Les Paul, who passed away some six months before at the grand old age of 94. "When you're doing that type of tribute," said May, "you just want to get it right, right, right. The stuff Les did by himself and with Mary Ford was so fantastic, so ahead of its time... well, we just wanted to do it as best we could." Having already paid a partial debt to Paul by airing a couple of his tunes at the post-BME Masterclass show with Imelda in September 2009, Beck had seen the possibilities of taking his teenage hero's music to a wider audience. Therefore, when their rendition of 'How High...' turned heads at the Grammys ceremony, he felt justified in pursuing the project with a newfound vigour.

By June 7 and 9, 2010, Jeff's idea had become reality as the guitarist, Imelda May and several others hijacked New York's

Iridium Club for two nights to honour the memory and music of Les Paul at the venue he continued to play weekly until his death. Breaking from his own touring schedule for *Emotion & Commotion*, Beck's appearance was perfectly timed to mark what would have been Les' 95th birthday (June 9). "Les was an innovator," he said. "He created the most incredible sounds and was also my friend. I felt that I wanted to put on a tribute show to him, which I knew he would have appreciated and enjoyed." A lovingly crafted affair, Jeff, Imelda and her band (including husband Darrel Higham on guitar/vocals) turned what might have been an austere occasion into "one bloody big party", as they delved into Paul's illustrious history before an audience that included David Bowie, Metallica's Kirk Hammett, Meat Loaf and Government Mule's Warren Haynes.

Pre-recording her backing vocals to emulate Mary Ford's lush multi-tracked harmonies in a live environment, May proved herself equal to the complex material at play. Whether negotiating her way through the verbal minefield that was 'Tiger Rag', hitting the high notes on 'I'm Sitting On Top Of The World' or coming over all winsome on 'Vaya Con Dios', the Irish singer did Ford's memory a lasting service.

Beck wasn't resting on his laurels either. Frequently changing guitars to capture the appropriate tones of the era he was paying homage to, Jeff's signature white Strat saw only limited action at the Iridium, being often replaced by a cast of Gibson ES-175s, Telecasters, Duo Jets and inevitably a Gibson 'Les Paul'. "I couldn't not play a Les Paul!" he laughed. "Les always used to point to my Strat and say, 'Why do you have that piece of crap around your neck?' I'd say, 'Yours are too heavy, I've had to drill holes in it!'"

As he had done when honouring Cliff Gallup on *Crazy Legs* 17 years before, Beck was not looking to exclusively replicate each note and subtle nuance of Les Paul's style, but also capture the humour and mischievous spirit behind it. "Les had an impish personality as a musician," he told *Guitar World's* Chris Gill. "Mary Ford was more the straight person in their act, and Les was the comedian." But when the situation demanded it – as on 'The World Is Waiting For The Sunrise' – his chops and memory were more than up to the task: "That solo is amazing. I had that record on vinyl and remember lifting up the needle and listening to the solo again and again trying to figure out what it was all about. I was 15 years old when I finally had that solo down. Your mind is going at a million miles an hour at that age, and things are so vivid. First-time experiences stick with you forever."*

Jeff's Iridium Club gigs did not wholly concentrate on the music of Les Paul, however. Taking the view that "it would be very time-consuming to do a full set of [just] Les' songs," Beck threw his net a little wider to include a few tunes from a similar era, give or take the odd few years. As a result, The Shadows' 'Apache' was given its first real outing since Jeff played the instrumental with The Deltones in the early sixties, the guitarist duplicating Hank Marvin's trebly shivers and echoing lead lines to an eerie degree. Santo And Johnny's 'Sleepwalk' was also dusted off and returned to active service from the soundtrack to *Porky's Revenge,* Jeff now largely dispensing with the steel slide he used when first cutting the track in favour of the whammy bar of his Strat. And given that he was dressed head to toe in various shades of blue – with a matching 'Blue Cap' to set off the whole ensemble – it was perhaps unsurprising that some rockabilly songs sneaked their way into the set. Hence Gene Vincent's 'Cruisin'' and Johnny Burnette's 'Train Kept A Rollin'' were performed at breakneck speed, with Darrel Higham deftly handling the vocals while David Bowie grinned from ear to ear: "David was just blown away," said Beck. "He noticed [my blue cap] was signed by one of the members of Gene's band and said, 'Where did you get that?' It revealed that he was as nutty about the whole thing [as I was]."

Unfortunately, Bowie did not join Jeff at encore time, which might have been a blessing as there probably wasn't room onstage. Aside from a horn section which included special guests Trombone Shorty (more of him later) and Leo Green blowing away like madmen during the 'Peter Gunn Theme', Gary US Bonds was also there to add some soul and grit to 'New Orleans', his voice riding over a wave of saxophones, rumbling basses and thunderstruck snares. Brian Setzer was next to try and make himself heard above the racket, hauling his Gretsch G612O across his shoulders for a duet with Jeff on Eddie

---

* As with Fender's 'Yardbirds Esquire replica, Gibson issued an exact reproduction of Jeff's famous 'Oxblood' Les Paul in 2009. Heavy as a horse, it nonetheless plays beautifully.

Cochran's '20 Flight Rock'. A master of that curious hillbilly/jazz/ country/rock'n'roll alchemy called rockabilly, Setzer's lightning runs were so reminiscent of Cliff Gallup's style that Beck mock-bowed to him during his solo: "Brian's a fantastic player," he said. "He just digs into that guitar."

Homage, tribute, labour of love and a fine's night's entertainment, Jeff's stand at the Iridium Club was finally issued under the title *Rock 'N Roll Party (Honouring Les Paul)* on DVD, CD and download in late February 2011. "It was a crazy few days and I couldn't believe the atmosphere in the Iridium and also the people who turned up," he said. "We didn't get too much time to rehearse and that was worrying me the most, especially having the guests join me onstage. [But] the audience seemed to love it and honestly, I don't think we could have got a better reaction. I just wish Les had been alive to see it." Gleaning extremely positive reviews – "Beck's immaculate rockabilly finger picking instantly transports you back to an era of giant quiffs and jukebox jives," said *The Mirror* – Jeff had no hesitation in getting behind the release, cajoling Imelda May and her band into an 11-date US tour which started on March 24. "It'll be a party every night," he said in advance of the shows. "Rock'n'roll music is just feel-good and puts a smile on everyone's face." Striking out in Washington before crossing the States through Texas and Chicago, the 'Rock 'N' Roll Party' came to an end at Jeff's old stomping ground, The Fillmore in San Franscisco on April 9. He seemed unwilling to rule out future collaborations with May, or indeed, another such 'themed' release. "Who knows what the future holds," he said.

In the guitarist's case, the answer seemed be ceaseless touring. Having just downed tools with Imelda May, Jeff was back on the road by mid-April with his own group, reuniting Jason Rebello, Rhonda Smith and Narada Michael Walden for another comprehensive haul across the States and Europe. "The music for *Emotion & Commotion* seems to fit in anywhere," he told Gibson.com, "and nothing beats a live performance. The audience create the atmosphere and push us to give the best show we can."

Determined to play every nook and cranny of the Big Sky Country, Beck and his band gamely sauntered from coast to coast throughout late spring, making pit-stops in Utah, Kansas, Ontario,

Buffalo and a goodly portion of Florida while they were at it. "Well," laughed Jeff, "Once you're on a roll..." With North America and Canada temporarily behind them, the group then pushed on to Norway, Germany, Poland and the Czech Republic, hitting the European summer festival circuit with a vengeance. Typically, the notoriously unstable British weather hit right back when they appeared at the Isle of Wight festival on June 12, 2011, drenching revellers with rain at the foot of the stage while Beck tortured his Strat above their heads. "Well, I was actually trying to get wet to join in with the fans," he said, "but the rain just didn't come in that far."

Despite the atrocious conditions – in addition to slashing rain, fans were summarily battered by strong winds throughout the set – both band and leader put in a proper day's work, with Jeff providing a touching surprise for those brave enough to face the elements. "I saw Jimi play here," he said, referring to Hendrix's set at the IOW festival just days before his death in September 1970, "and I'd like to play a little tribute to him." Without further ado, Beck launched into a soulful rendition of Hendrix's sweetest tune, 'Little Wing', his creamy chords and flittering lead lines ably supplemented by a strong vocal from Narada Michael Walden. "I was amazed at the response we got," Jeff later confirmed, "I'd seen big festivals before and seen the way huge bands go over. But I honestly thought I'd never (get) that. Yet, there we were and all I could see were smiling faces." Wet smiling faces at that.

As Beck's never-ending global shindig in support of *Emotion & Commotion* continued throughout the autumn of 2011, he as ever found time to lend his skills to several new recordings while also making the odd guest live appearance. First out of the traps was a short, but bone-rattling blast of guitar on 'Do To Me', a prime cut from Trombone Shorty's latest album, *For True*. Born in the Tremé district of New Orleans, Shorty (or Troy Andrews as he was better known to his family) had spent his earliest years avidly studying trombone and trumpet – studies so successful that he was asked to join rock/soul king Lenny Kravitz's touring band while still a teenager. "Lenny was a really good friend to me," he confirmed. "I joined his brass section and went on tour with him for two years straight out of high school."

Sessions with the likes of U2 and Green Day soon followed, nestling comfortably alongside an ever-growing profile as both a solo artist and group contributor to the American jazz, r&b and hip hop scenes. In fact, by 2007 Shorty was named *Offbeat* magazine's 'Performer of the Year' – his Latin-flavoured honks with post-Hurricane Katrina charity band The New Orleans Social Club and scene-stealing musical cameo on the US TV comedy *Studio 60 On The Sunset Strip* – only consolidating his appeal.

Jeff Beck needed no persuasion regarding Shorty's gifts. Indeed, he was more than willing to forsake a good night's sleep to see the trombone man play an 'after-after-hours set' in his own backyard. "Well, Jeff came to one of my late-night shows in New Orleans (in early 2010)," Shorty told *The Aquarian*. "Damn show didn't even start until like 3:00 a.m., but he hung out and afterwards came backstage, and invited me to play with him in New York at his Les Paul tribute. Next thing you know, he invites me to open up for him in England. I've been a big fan of his for a long, long time." As good as his word, in addition to getting Shorty up onstage at New York's Iridium Club and booking him as opening act on his 2010 British tour, Jeff also called on his services when appearing at New Orleans jazz festival a year later. Come encore time, a grinning Beck pulled the local boy from the wings to join him and his band for an incendiary take on Sly Stone's 'I Want To Take You Higher'. Suffice to say, the two soloists soon entered instrumental hyperspace, each chasing some truly twisted blues scales along the way. "Now that," said Jeff after the event, "was bloody good fun."

While Beck was surely wild about Trombone Shorty, he was equally smitten with several other artists throughout 2011. Returning a gentle favour from some months before, he proved himself a welcome guest at London's O2 Academy on August 24, where violinist/singer Sharon Corr was performing in support of her latest solo album, *Dream Of You*. Again adding some sprinkles of magic to the ballad 'Mná na hÉireann' (which the two first played onstage in October 2010 at the RAH), Jeff was persuaded to stick around for the show-closer: a ramshackle, if well-intentioned hop through Fleetwood Mac's 'Go Your Own Way'.

Beck's next stop-off on the all-star trail saw him back in the USA during September, where he joined his old pal Seal for a valiant attempt at redefining the ageless anthem 'Like A Rolling Stone'. Specially recorded for *Chimes Of Freedom*, a charity compilation album that celebrated the 50th birthday of Amnesty International by having various artists rework the songs of the legendary Bob Dylan, Jeff and Seal's latest effort found itself nestling among some distinguished company. In addition to established names such as Mark Knopfler, Carly Simon and a posthumous contribution from the late, great Johnny Cash, acts as diverse as My Chemical Romance, Patti Smith, the Kronos Quartet and even Miley Cyrus had also thrown in their lot covering old Dylan classics.

Truthfully, Beck/Seal's new take on the sacred '... Stone' wasn't quite up to par with their last collaboration, where the duo fought a marvellous battle with 'Manic Depression' for 1993's Hendrix tribute CD, *Stone Free*. On that occasion, drummer Jimmy Copley's genius level idea of radically slowing down the established tempo mid-tune allowed Beck's guitar to literally breathe fire. This time around, however, 'Like A Rolling Stone' was treated with far more respect as Jeff and Seal stuck rigidly to the original's pace and feel, their version more deferential than revolutionary. Still, both the project's cause and inspiration were never in doubt. "Oh, the cause was great, Dylan's the greatest ever lyricist and I got to sing with Jeff Beck," said Seal. "I mean, how could you pass that up?"

In the same way that Jeff had recently honoured Les Paul, Jimi Hendrix and Bob Dylan in his thoughts and deeds, so others now enthusiastically honoured him. First out of the traps was the University of Arts London, who bestowed a fellowship on Beck for his "Outstanding contribution to the field of Music" on July 18, 2011. Looking dapper (if surreal) in a grey suit, purple gown and mortarboard, Jeff's acceptance speech at the Royal Festival Hall to graduating students from his former 'alma mater', Wimbledon College, was a marvellous thing to behold: Part humble mumble, part bad comedy routine, it was also extremely truthful and genuinely touching in its central message.

"I was never much of a success at school," he said quietly. "Honestly, my main memory of Wimbledon (Art School) was the amazing pineapple crumble they served in the canteen. But seriously, my advice to you is that if you dream of something you'd really like to do, I suggest you follow it. It's not always about the money, and in my case, it certainly wasn't... but in difficult times, stick with the dream, and go with your passion. A talent to do something you love is far more satisfying for the soul. I wish you only luck in your future endeavours and don't be put off by any setbacks," Beck sagely concluded. "After all, it will only make you stronger." And he would surely know.

Only three days later, the academics were besieging him again, as Jeff was presented with an honorary doctorate from the University of Sussex. This time, the title was conferred for his "Outstanding musical career and celebrat(ing) the relationship between the University and the Brighton Institute of Modern Music (BIMM)." Swopping a purple cloak for a yellow one, Jeff stuck more or less to the same speech made at the RFH, though he did go worryingly off-pisté while receiving his scroll from Sussex University's resident chancellor, the TV actor, writer and comedian Sanjeev '*Kumars at No. 42*' Bhaskar. Squaring up to his prey like a prize fighter, Beck threw a mock punch at Bhaskar before warmly embracing him only a moment later. "I really didn't know who you were talking about when you gave that introduction," he later joked with his friend.

If Jeff sometimes appeared out of his comfort zone when accepting scrolls or balancing mortarboards on that famous thatched head of his, the next honorific bestowed on him was at least granted in a more familiar setting. Seven days after completing the final leg of his North American tour, Beck arrived in London on November 9 to collect a very special prize: *Classic Rock* magazine's 'Living Legend' award.

Previously given to shock-rock king Alice Cooper, prog-rock monarchs Rush and the elastic-limbed Godfather of Punk Iggy Pop, the trophy was three-pronged in its relevancy. For one, it was able proof of a stunning career rehabilitation that began with a five night stand at Ronnie Scott's in 2007 and had lately taken Beck to within spitting distance of the US Top Ten. Of equal impact, the gong also represented his full absorption into a new type of rock hierarchy – one where long-standing artists and bands were rewarded as much for their endurance as their original impact. But perhaps most importantly, in an age where back catalogues now often outsold any new product, treasures like Jeff Beck – who was still finding fresh audiences well into his sixties – had to be acknowledged, encouraged and even protected.

After all, the evidence for such a viewpoint was compelling. For years, nay decades, he had exemplified the 'cult artist', forever cast as a classic outsider looking over the fence while his contemporaries made merry inside. Loved by guitarists, revered by the critics, his abilities were often spoken of in hushed tones, with one phrase gently resonating over and over again: "How the hell does he do that?" Yet recent years had seen a huge reassessment of his place in the scheme of things. Beck was now openly acknowledged as one of the primary architects behind a new, bold style of sixties blues rock that Jimmy Page later sharpened into a monster called Led Zeppelin.

His later dalliances with jazz, funk and even techno styles had also immeasurably pushed back the boundaries of what was expected from supposed "old rockers", with Jeff's inability to stand stylistically still opening doors to new places where odd time signatures, spiralling riffs and queasy break beats clanged loudly from every corner. Crucially, Beck's recent success with *Emotion & Commotion* and elsewhere was again as striking as it was unexpected. While his Yardbird contemporaries Page and Eric Clapton were now often accused of trading on past glories (ah, but what glories they were), Jeff was still busy throwing shapes with "cool rockabilly chicks," willowy violinists and melismatic trombone players. In short, the stars had aligned, the clouds had departed and Jeffrey Arnold Beck was finally having his time in the sun. "Yeah," he said before the ceremony began, "but I'm actually shaking in my boots, you know... hoping to keep it together..."

The nail chewing wasn't required. As Jeff climbed on the stage at Camden Town's Roundhouse to accept his 'Living Legend' award from Queen's Roger Taylor, the room fair shook with applause. "I'm thrilled to bits," he told an assembled throng of rock stars including The Who's Pete Townshend and Roger Daltrey, various Manic Street Preachers, and in Beck's own words "a whole load of metal dudes". Acknowledging his fans, manager Harvey Goldsmith and the plethora of musicians he had worked with in previous years, Jeff then cut to the chase regarding his recent career renaissance and the strategy behind it. "My career seems to have just snowballed again during the last couple of years," he said. "Don't get me wrong, I have been working very hard (and) I've made myself known in places that I've never been before. But it's definitely been worth it."

In return for proclaiming him a 'Living Legend', Beck graced the *Classic Rock* awards with a short live set, which also happened to mark the British debut of his latest drummer. Filling in for a now absent Narada Michael Walden was New Yorker Veronica Bellino. A tip-top percussionist whose past credits included stints with rapper LL Cool J and Carmine Appice's multi-drum project SLAMM, Jeff knew nothing of Bellino's work – or indeed, her connection to his former BBA bandmate – when he happened upon her while browsing *You Tube*. "Yes!" she laughed to *Tom Tom*, "I got an e-mail one morning from Jeff's management saying that he saw some video of me on *You Tube*... and was interested in working on a new project. I didn't believe it was real at first, so I asked them if Jeff would call me later that day. And sure enough, he did."

One 20-minute conversation later, Veronica was not only convinced it was actually Beck she was talking to, but was also the proud possessor of a lunch invitation for the next time he visited New York. "We met for lunch at his hotel in the afternoon and he gave me VIP passes to the (*Rock & Roll Hall of Fame*) show that night." By the summer of 2011, Bellino was demoing new tracks with the guitarist. "And you know," she later said, "I was actually thinking of taking down that post from *You Tube*. But, if that video was good enough for Jeff Beck, I must be doing something right."

As with most every drummer who had taken a seat behind the guitarist, Veronica Bellino found herself thrown in at the deep end almost immediately, with Jeff's 15 minute *Classic Rock* set proving no exception. Eager to give those gathered something a little different to accompany their post-dinner revels, Beck opened proceedings with a blindsiding (and extremely loud) cover of Lady Gaga's recent hit 'Bad Romance' before walloping them over the head with a bruising rendition of his own 'Big Block'. Frankly, those industry types closest to the stage looked stunned. Beck, on the other hand, looked like a six-year old with a new bike. Thankfully, he chose to play fair with his last two numbers, gathering up Joss Stone from stage right for a none-more-blue 'I Put A Spell On You' before The Pretenders' Chrissie Hynde strolled on to close the show with a rousing take on her own 'I'll Stand By You'.

For some, receiving the title 'Living Legend' might cause them to assess whether the hard work was done, and it was time instead to seek out the rock star equivalent of a pipe, slippers and daily dose of *Countdown* or *Jeopardy*. Not so Jeff Beck. Though now 65 years young, Beck's onstage mutilation of Lady Gaga's 'Bad Romance' illustrated in no uncertain terms he was still very much engaged with the present rather than the past. This fact was underlined just a day or so after his appearance at the *Classic Rock* awards, when he returned to the studio with Veronica Bellino and bassist Rhonda Smith to continue work on his latest project: an update on the classic power trio. "I want to do something that has that immediacy, that kick," he said by way of explanation, "… but with a whole modern spin. It's time for me to stand up and do something really special." Working with Bellino and Smith on melody lines and riffs – and with Veronica also acting as occasional vocalist – several ideas were subsequently caught on tape. But it was another project with Jeff's name attached to it that was really making media waves. "Yeah," said the guitarist, "Rod and I are thinking about doing an album…"

Since news broke that Beck and Rod Stewart were once again to record together, men of a certain age and musical taste had been weeping tears of grateful joy. A reunion of sorts was first muted between the two over lunch at the end of 2010. Yet, instead of said idea being left at the table with the cheque, a few weeks later Rod and Jeff were holed up at the latter's LA-based studio. Astoundingly, the duo – neither of whom was particularly prolific or fast-paced when it came to the songwriting process – managed to produce 11 workable tunes within in a matter of days. "I put in a lot of effort over the week we were together in the studio," Beck told *Classic Rock* at the time, "(and) we've co-written 11 tracks… (that) might be a good starting point. Hopefully, we can come to an exciting agreement as to what to do with all this stuff."

Of course, there were several challenges to attend to before any real work could begin. Both artists had pressing commitments outside the project: Jeff's ever-rolling tour schedule for *Emotion & Commotion* was pulling him one way while the birth of Stewart's latest child, Aiden Patrick, with wife Penny Lancaster in February 2011 was pulling Rod another. But Beck was still hopeful that the voice and guitar behind the likes of *Truth* and *Beckola* could pull together at least one more time. "I really want to see that Rod is genuinely into the idea and that it's not just a weekend's fancy," he said. "(But) I don't think it is because his manager – Arnold Stiefel – is well into it." Such was Jeff's enthusiasm, he was even talking up possible gigs. "It makes no sense not to tour it, (we) have to! We can do… a couple of Hollywood Bowls here and some Madison Square Garden there. Then there's England. I'd… do three or four nights at the old Hammersmith Odeon. I'd want it to be right in your face, and the sound has to be just right. The sound is my number one priority." Given previous engagements between them, one might have said booking some solid studio time was a more realistic priority.

While the doubting Thomases were busy placing their bets against Beck and Stewart's latest team-up, there was genuine reason to hope against hope. Despite the disasters of their shared 1984 US tour where 'special guest' Jeff had bailed after just six performances, there had been no real fall-out between the two because of it. Rod was philosophical regarding his former boss's reasons for leaving the tour (let's be honest, he was probably expecting it), while Beck seemed equally sanguine about walking away so soon. Further, both parties had at least got something out of their brief re-association: a near-miss hit single for Jeff with 'People Get Ready' and a salty, Beck-assisted 45 in the shape of 'Infatuation' for Rod. Indeed, as the decades rolled by, the terrible twosome seemed to inch ever closer together. Jeff had almost joined Stewart onstage in 2004 for a concert at the Royal Albert Hall with fellow JBG veteran Ronnie Wood. On that occasion, they even got as far as rehearsing 'I Ain't Superstitious' and 'Rock My Plimsoul' before the guitarist's toes grew cold. But it was at a Beck one-nighter at Los Angeles' El Rey theatre in April 2009 where things finally turned a corner. Gliding unexpectedly onstage in an immaculate white jacket, black tie and shirt loosened 'just so' at the top button, Rod Stewart's impromptu, note-perfect renditions of 'People…' and '… Superstitious' not only brought the house down but also pointed clearly to the fact that this combustible pairing might not be done with each other just yet.

And for a while at least, that seemed the case. In conjunction with his power trio aspirations, Jeff continued to work up various ideas and send them to Stewart for comment during 2011/12. Harboring no illusions that they were likely to make a techno album – "Rod loves the sixties, the blues, the old stuff and that's just fine" – he concentrated on either writing or finding appropriately themed material for the singer. Sadly, the first in a series of alarms bell went off when Stewart complained that none of the songs he had received were in the right key for his voice. Another shot at re-entering the studio also fell at the last hurdle, with Rod reportedly unable to make the proposed dates.

After a year or so of trying to advance the project without success, Beck's patience began to wear thin. When asked by the *Wall Street Journal* what exactly was halting progress, he was as blunt as an overused bread knife. "Him. His Football, his family, him and his manager. Get rid of them and we'd have an album out." Even when he softened slightly, the familiar ring of crushed hope was never far away. "It really depends on his voice and if Rod even wants to sing that sort of stuff anymore. He just needs the right material, but can he concentrate long enough to find it? I'm the one that's doing all the looking... combing *Spotify*, you know, just trying to find that one 'right' song." As yet, that song remains missing in action, its fate unknown.

If Beck could not manage to tie down the mercurial Stewart to an album, tour or even tune, then he could at least be encouraged by the slew of other vocalists queuing up to work with him. On 24 September 2011, Jeff teamed up with Steven Tyler and Sting to perform a loose-limbed version of Aerosmith's evergreen 'Sweet Emotion' at the i-HeartRadio music festival in Las Vegas. A good-natured jam, where the former Police frontman seemed content to just play bass while Tyler spun among his scarves and howled at the moon, Beck even pulled out an old voice bag for the song – his teeth no doubt rattling as he mimicked Joe Perry's original guitar moves on '... Emotion''s woozy intro.*

Having now performed alongside the lead singer of "America's greatest rock 'n' roll band", there was only one way to up the ante: try the same trick with the lead singer of "the greatest rock 'n' roll band in the world". And so it was that Beck joined Mick Jagger at the White House on February 21, 2012 for a landmark TV special

---

* Beck enjoyed himself so much during rehearsals for the iHeartRadio festival that he ended up contributing to the Aerosmith singer's entire set, including Steven's duet with Pussycat Doll Nicole Scherzinger on '(It) Feels So Good' and a ultra-funky version of Sly Stone's 'Thank You'.

celebrating the blues in the company of US President Barack Obama. Billed as 'Red, White and Blues', the event brought together BB King, Buddy Guy, Booker T. Jones, Susan Tedeschi, Derek Trucks and the ever-present Trombone Shorty among others to help America's 44th President champion a music which in Obama's own words "had humble beginnings, (its) roots in slavery and segregation...(and that) bore witness to... hard times... and like so many of the men and women who sang (it), refused to be limited by the circumstances of (its) birth."

A night of several wonders – including a quite astounding pre-concert take on 'Rollin' And Tumblin'' by the husband/wife team of Tedeschi and Trucks – Beck was here, there and everywhere during the broadcast. Whether bashing out 'Let Me Love You Baby' in the company of Buddy Guy, hamming it up with BB King on 'Let The Good Times Roll' or producing a rasping version of his own 'Brush With The Blues'*, the guitarist was seldom off camera. But it was his efforts with Mick Jagger that perhaps yielded the best results. Joining the rubber-lipped icon on 'Commit A Crime' and 'Five Long Years', Jeff's ability to stir, shake or simply set fire to Mick's voice once again raised serious doubts as to whether turning down the Stones in Rotterdam all those years ago might have been a serious mistake.

Those wanting to know what he could have brought to that particular party didn't have to wait long. After Beck again jammed with Jagger in mid-May for the season finale of US TV skit show *Saturday Night Live* (the result, 'President's Blues', really wasn't either's finest moment), he finally ended decades of speculation by actually joining The Rolling Stones – albeit for just one night. Keen to honour the band's 50th anniversary celebrations at London's 02 Arena on November 25, 2012, the guitarist clambered onstage with Mick, Keith Richards, Charlie Watts and Ronnie Wood for a six-minute run at Don Nix's old blues chestnut 'Going Down'.

Wholly familiar to both parties, with Beck having already covered it on his own 1972 LP, '...Down' was in many ways the perfect track to

---

* While Beck performed a marvellous version of 'Brush...' with Veronica Bellino and Rhonda Smith on the night, due to tight running times, the track was actually dropped from the final broadcast. However, the power trio's performance can be accessed easily enough on *You Tube*.

emphasise the gaping chasm that had always existed between Jeff and The Stones. While as ever, his unique Strat stylings – all rude bursts of energy and sharp harmonic twists – sat well with Mick's wayward vocal swaggers and elongated vowels, Beck's approach was still much at odds with the another key element of The Stones' signature sound: AKA Mr. Richards. As Keith sat in the proverbial pocket throughout 'Going Down', massaging both melody and groove into a simple, but mesmeric whole, Jeff flew fighter-pilot style above his head, dropping bombs and firing missiles at unseen targets in the distance. From the audience's perspective, it was akin to watching Iron Man stray into shot during *The Godfather*: fascinating stuff all right, but for all the wrong reasons. In short, when Beck opted for *Blow By Blow* over *Black And Blue*, he really was doing both himself and The Rolling Stones a favour.

Away from the various superstar blues jams and creative cul-de-sacs involving Rod Stewart, Beck continued to formulate plans regarding his own future, though finding a stable musical line-up to help execute them was proving difficult. Following in Narada Michael Walden's footsteps, longtime keyboardist Jason Rebello finally left Jeff's employ for pastures new, while bassist Tal Wilkenfeld temporarily returned to the fold for several gigs. A fan favourite from Ronnie Scott's days, Tal's reappearance for sections of Steven Tyler's set at the iHeartMusic festival was roundly welcomed, as was her backing of Jeff and Mick Jagger during their spot on *Saturday Night Live*. But Wilkenfeld was still busy pursuing her own solo interests, making her permanent involvement in whatever line-up Beck finally chose to pursue aspirational rather than actual. Similarly, the much-lauded power trio idea with Rhonda Smith and Veronica Bellino also seemed to have run aground for the moment, with the guitarist growing increasingly silent about his need to re-create a female-backed BBA for the 21st century. As ever with Jeff, it really was a case of 'the more things change, the more they stay the same'.

If history proved anything, there was no doubt Beck could deal with any number of possible line-ups. In fact, he seemed to positively thrive on it. But the same might not be said of managers. For decades, he had worked closely and unswervingly with Ernest Chapman and later Ralph Baker, the connection steadfast and remarkably faithful on both sides. But in late 2008, Jeff had sought change and found it in the form of Harvey Goldsmith, leading to a new association that marked a rapid upturn in both his critical and commercial fortunes. Further, Goldsmith's seemingly endless contacts within the musical community and elsewhere can surely have not hurt Beck's increasing public profile, with all the honorary degrees, awards and fellowships recently accorded him better enhancing his reputation – now and for the ages. It came as something of a surprise then, to learn that at the end of 2012 that Goldsmith and Beck had chosen to end their association.

For a time, David Gilmour's manager Paul Loasby seemed to be in the frame as a replacement for Harvey. But as the smoke cleared, it became apparent that Jeff was following a growing number of digital age performers who now chose to represent their own affairs. By securing the services of a good publicist (in Beck's case, Melissa Dragich-Cordero at *Mad Ink PR*), restructuring his website and showing an enthusiasm for Twitter and Facebook that was finally being embraced among his contemporaries, Jeff could connect with his fans, negotiate with tour promoters and even oversee the future release of any recorded material. In this respect, not only keeping up with new music, but also new technology and marketing strategies would serve him – at least in the short term – very well indeed.

By early 2013, there was also some clear signs of artistic stability too, as a new band line-up slowly but surely began to coalesce around their leader – give or take the odd bass player. Following in the footsteps of many before him, Miami-born Jonathan Joseph was the latest incumbent to set up his drum kit behind Jeff. A Grammy-winning percussionist whose previous credits included time spent with David Sanborn, Pat Metheny, Randy Brecker and the omnipresent Joss Stone (he was actually her step father), Joseph's high command of jazz, rock, blues and funk boded well for a sustained run with a man who had spent 50-odd years chewing them all into new shapes. "Jeff's music has had a profound effect on my career," said Jonathan, "and having an opportunity to follow in the footsteps of Vinnie Colaiuta and Narada Michael Walden is both humbling and exciting." And given the turnover in previous drummers, possibly quite scary too.

A more-left field addition to Beck's latest band was violinist Lizzie Ball, who in a short, but already sharp career, had carved out a formidable reputation as a multi-functioning classical, Latin and rock player – her 'Concertmaster''s position with Nigel Kennedy's Orchestra of Life and creation of 'Classical Kicks' night at Ronnie Scott's just two notable achievements thus far. "I've always wanted to push boundaries," she said. "Growing up near Sheffield I played in bands (while at) the same time... I performed in classical concerts. So, there were these two sides to me which have now fused into a career path."

For some, Jeff's choice to include "a fiddler" as part of his new set-up was greeted with raised eyebrows, but there were precedents here: as far back as 1977, he had worked alongside violinist Steve Kindler when touring the US with Jan Hammer, while more recently, Sharon Corr's winsome melody lines on 'Mná na hÉireann' had again reminded him of an instrument he loved listening to (if hating playing) as a child. "Lizzie's utterly spectacular," he gushed of his newest recruit, though on this occasion, he was probably understating rather than overstating her skills with a bow. Having received a MA from St. Johns College at Cambridge University (with further diplomas gained at the from Royal College of Music & the Guildhall), Ball was viewed by those in the know as a world-class prospect, her former boss (and Beck collaborator) Nigel Kennedy even quipping, "Your appointment as leader of my Orchestra of Life has been so amazing that I am even proud of myself for asking you!"

With Tal Wilkenfeld temporarily filling up the one remaining instrumental space, Beck decided to put his band to the test with a high-profile, if brief set at Eric Clapton's annual Crossroads guitar festival, this time held in New York's Madison Square Garden on 12-13 April. Joining a bill that also featured Steve Vai, The Eagles' Joe Walsh, jazzer Larry Carlton and (one of Jeff's favourite players) Vishwa Mohan Bhatt, the new line-up meshed well from the off. Using Lizzie Ball to lull the assembled hordes with a plaintive stroll through show opener 'Mná na hÉireann', Beck's quartet kept things on a reasonably even keel by then covering John McLaughlin's lush 'You Know, You Know'. Having soothed those gathered before them into a relaxed heap, it was now time to fire things up with the introduction of Beth Hart. Always a fine onstage foil for Jeff*, the LA-born singer had no trouble in acclimatising to his latest set up or geeing up the crowd, her voice as throaty and raw as Beck's wah-wah growls and pinched harmonics on show closers 'I Ain't Superstitious' and 'Going Down'.

Tested to his satisfaction in NYC, Jeff temporarily parked up his new group and headed off for yet another kind of new and potentially very profitable experience, this time on the west coast of America. For years, fans and amateur musicians had dreamed of playing alongside their idols in an intimate setting, watching every bend of the string or crash of the cymbal from mere inches away. Rock'n'Roll Fantasy Camp (RNRFC) offered that opportunity – and indeed, much more – albeit for a price. Founded by producer/ sports agent David Fishoff in 1997, RNRFC sold itself as an interactive and unique experience, where those attending could not only play, write songs and record them in state-of-the-art facilities, but also work in close proximity with the very stars that originally inspired them – gaining advice, instrumental and vocal training from their heroes, and even getting to perform with them onstage. And what heroes they were. Thus far, The Who's Roger Daltrey, former Rolling Stone Bill Wyman, Aerosmith's Steven Tyler, Kiss' Gene Simmons, Meat Loaf, Alice Cooper, members of Def Leppard and Motley Crue, as well as guitar stars Slash, Ace Frehley and Zakk Wylde had all signed up to provide tuition, advice and a twinkling of stardust at various RNRFC events. Now it was Jeff's turn.

By all accounts, Beck turned out to be quite the teacher, his laconic but encouraging manner going over well with students. Arriving at RNRFC's new permanent site in Las Vegas on April 18, he was soon stuck in with a core group of admirers all keen to learn how the guitarist pulled off his particular magic. Taking questions on technique, scales, inspirations and how in hell he managed to

---

* For ample proof of how well Beck and Hart complement each other, one should seek out their cover of 'I'd Rather Go Blind' on Beth's 2013 CD, *Bang Bang Boom Boom*. A fine tune, '...Blind' was first played live by the duo at the Kennedy Center during a show honouring veteran bluesman Buddy Guy in December, 2012.

stay in tune when "abusing the whammy bar so much", Jeff also led the class through several practical examples of what his job entailed, showing those present the rudiments of tracks like Santo & Johnny's 'Sleepwalk'. Matters then concluded with 'Professor Beck' leading his charges through some old Presley tunes, before taking yet another pass at 'Going Down'.

It is easy to be cynical about … *Fantasy Camp*. Some less charitable souls, for instance, might see the idea as a novel way for musicians to supplement their pension funds in the face of increased downloading and falling CD sales. Others might feel the very idea of such a camp was elitist in the extreme, giving only those who could afford it a chance to play with the great and the good. However, for those lucky or rich enough to be able to buy their entry into rock paradise, the rewards were simply immeasurable. "Everyone, and I mean everyone in that class," said one attendee, "got to solo with Jeff fuckin' Beck!"

One delightful if not wholly unexpected aspect of Jeff's involvement with RNRFC was where it led him next. While sharing his knowledge with those who wished to learn in Las Vegas, a good friend of the guitarist was doing exactly the same thing in a different part of the … *Fantasy Camp* complex. Just two years older than Beck, Brian Wilson was also one of the few performers alive who could convincingly be referred to as a 'Living Legend'. Co-founder, chief songwriter and principal visionary behind California's Beach Boys, Wilson was responsible for some of the 20th century's finest tunes, his talent perhaps only eclipsed by John Lennon and Paul McCartney – and even then, the jury was out in some quarters. A multi-instrumentalist, arranger and producer as well as tunesmith, Brian had taken surf music and turned into an art form. 'Surfin'', 'Surfin' USA', 'Surfin' Safari', 'In My Room', 'I Get Around' and 'California Girls' – all were written or co-written by Wilson by the time he was 22. And then he grew even more ambitious.

Following a nervous collapse in 1964, Brian had completely withdrawn from live performance with The Beach Boys. But this withdrawal had its own benefits, as it allowed him more time to focus on recording technology, production techniques and song-writing. The results were startling. By treating the studio as yet another instrument at his disposal, Wilson fashioned 1966's *Pet*

Sounds — an album held by many as the pinnacle of his career with The Beach Boys — and perhaps one of the finest LPs ever recorded. Unfortunately, ... *Sounds* and the unforgettable single 'Good Vibrations' seemed to mark a break point for its creator, his behaviour growing ever more erratic and his use of LSD and other drugs escalating to worrying levels. After *Pet Sounds'* follow-up, *Smile,* was cancelled due to Brian's mental fatigue (among other issues), his "creative directorship" of The Beach Boys began to slip in earnest, leaving fellow band member and co-writer Mike Love to pick up the reins of the group. Matters for Wilson deteriorated further as subsequent years went by, with tales of reclusive or odd behaviour becoming far more newsworthy than his current — or even previous — musical endeavours. Unfortunately, it appeared that Brian Wilson might be lost to history.

Or, as it turns out, not. Though much of the seventies and eighties were blighted by health scares, continuing psychic frailties and several other debilitating artistic/legal issues, Wilson somehow found the strength to rally. By the mid-nineties, he was not only regularly recording again, but also working alongside The Beach Boys, albeit in a more relaxed capacity this time around. Brian even returned to his past to re-inform his present, bringing the songs he had abandoned in 1967 back to life as *Brian Wilson Presents Smile*, a hugely successful album and world tour that ran across 2004/5. Healthy and in his own words "hugely happy", Wilson's presence as tutor/guru at RNRFC was yet another sign of an artistic and rehabilitation many thought impossible. Jeff Beck, for one, was thankful Brian was back from the brink.

"Oh God," he said, "*Pet Sounds. Smiley Smile. 20/20.* All these great albums containing songs that weren't just 'surf' songs, but other types too. And those were the songs that appealed to me. It's hard to describe what that music did to me. The melodies were so strong, the sheer musicality of it all. It transcended surf into a form of wild psychedelic pop. And that inspired me to make some wild sounds of my own."

Given Beck's ceaseless appetite for collaboration, it was almost inevitable that he and Wilson would team up sooner or later. The pair had first met back in 2005 when Jeff performed 'Surfin' USA' and 'Surf's Up' at the Hollywood Palladium for a *Musiccare* event honouring Brian as their 'Person of the Year'. But their dual attendance at RNRFC was just the catalyst required to set the wheels in motion anew. By early June 2013, announcements signalled not only Beck's "serious involvement" with Wilson's forthcoming album, but also their plans to tour together in the autumn. "Jeff really blew my mind, so we thought we'd have him join us on (my) album," Brian said. "He plays the most goddamn greatest guitar you've ever heard. He really brings quality notes, more notes per bar than you can ever imagine."

Subsequent sessions for Wilson's new project took place at Hollywood's Ocean Way Recording studios with Beck very much in attendance – the guitarist contributing chords, solos and even some 12-string acoustic (a Jeff first) to several tracks. In fact, such was the optimism generated by these sessions, that rumours began to circulate Brian was to release a three-CD set, with one disc mainly comprised of instrumentals featuring Beck. But before work on the project was anywhere near completion, there was the not insubstantial matter of a US tour to consider and prepare for. For Jeff, however, hitting the road without anything new or tangible to promote might have be a case of putting the cart before the horse. "I'm not sure," he later told *Rolling Stone*. "As far as I know, they made a mistake by... opening up the floodgates for a tour prematurely instead of finishing the tracks. And so we left the studio with half-finished tracks, three, four tracks I was supposed to be on and they're still unfinished. To me, it was a bit stupid because they should have done the album, had a *killer* album, and then gone out on the road. But I think they wanted to grab me while I was still available. (That said)," he concluded, "It'll be a complete honour to be on stage with Brian."

In the end, Wilson and Beck's 21-date trawl across the USA during September/October of 2013 turned out to be both an artistic and commercial success, even if there was no new album for punters to take home at the end of the evening. Taking the form of a three-tier event, each night saw Brian and his 10-piece band open proceedings, the likes of 'California Girls', 'Surfer Girl' and the golden nugget 'Heroes And Villains' providing ample entertainment for his own ever-faithful clan. To gee up things up some more, Wilson had also brought Beach Boys Al Jardine, David Marks (and occasionally Blondie Chaplin) with him on the road, giving vintage material such as 'Forever' and 'Little Bird' even greater authenticity. After a spirited charge through the immortal 'I Get Around' and 'Good Vibrations', Brian then left the stage to Beck.

Following a national treasure responsible for re-defining the borders of American pop was never going to be easy, more especially in his own back yard. The additional fact that Jeff's peculiar amalgam of rock, jazz, blues and God only knows what else could at times challenge the ear (even of his own audience) was another potential stumbling block. But his faith in that guitar, his band and what they could do was unshakeable. "Yes, Brian's got a truckload of hits to play," he said. "But we'll build on that and interact. Brian will kick things off, but I'll also be given enough time to establish what I'm about. In the end, we'll mix and match."

To Beck's credit, it worked, and worked well. Not shirking his reputation as a maverick for one second, he performed a highly eclectic set full of musical left turns, but one never in danger of losing those in attendance because Brian Wilson's name was on the ticket. Opening their account with the tried and tested 'Eternity's Breath/ Stratus', the band dabbled in cool fusion ('The Pump'), invoked old gods (Hendrix's 'Little Wing') and even visited Beck's personal Mount Everest ('Where Were You') before playing a masterstroke by bringing on Wilson and his own group for some mix-and-match surprises.

With more than a football team's worth of musicians onstage, Jeff, Brian and friends cut the proverbial rug on the likes of 'Our Prayer', 'How High The Moon', 'Surf's Up' and 'A Day In The Life', tossing each other's signature tunes this way and that to the obvious delight of both themselves and those watching. Come encore time, more rabbits were pulled from the hat as 'Do You Wanna Dance', 'Surfin' USA' and 'Fun, Fun, Fun' had everyone dancing out the door. "Seeing Beck's aggressive rock fusion five-piece after a 20-song Beach Boys hits set was like bingeing on the sweetest birthday cake ever and then sitting down for a steak dinner," said the *Houston Chronicle* of Jeff's latest gambit, "But to the credit of all involved, it wasn't jarring. In fact, grown men in the audience were staring mouths agape for the man."

As the *Houston Chronicle*'s review hinted, Beck's tour with Wilson had again seen him dabble with the group's line-up, as a fifth member was now being added to his team. Arriving alongside Rhonda Smith (who returned to the fold after Tal Wilkenfeld again moved on) was guitarist Nicolas Meier, the first six-stringer to take up arms with Jeff since Jennifer Batten over a decade before. Like relative newcomer Lizzie Ball, Meier was also a virtuoso on his chosen instrument, his teenage studies having taken him from his native Switzerland to the USA, when he gained a scholarship to Berklee's hallowed halls of music. Following that adventure, Nicolas moved to London where he soon became a regular face on the Capital's classical, jazz and fusion circuits.

"(At that time) I also deeply studied South American sounds," he confirmed, "and this opened a world of Flamenco and Latin forms for me." Concentrating his efforts on nylon acoustic guitar (though somewhat improbably, he is also a huge fan of heavy metal), Meier soon added Turkish, Tango and Arabic influences to the pot, making him a veritable encyclopaedia of world guitar styles. With at least 17 albums worth of material connected to his name and a plum role teaching students their way around a neck at Goldsmiths University, Nicolas was another one of those classic finds Beck could be depended upon making when the mood took him. "You didn't think I did other guitar players, did you?" he joked, "Well, I do now!"

From opening night at Hollywood's Hard Rock Cafe & Casino on September 21 to their last truck stop at Milwaukee's Riverdale Theatre on October 30, 2013, the "Brian/Jeff revue" appeared to be one of the most enjoyable tours either had involved themselves in. "I felt having Jeff Beck co-headline with me (was) a cool and exciting addition," said Wilson. Beck was no less succinct in his appraisal of events. "No dramas, just good music." Away from the shared bonhomie, the dates also allowed Jeff to more strenuously road test his band and their capabilities, with each show played taking him one step nearer to realising the sound he wanted for that new, but still maddeningly elusive album of his. "It's now two years behind schedule!" he said. "I (know) I could easily do a rock album, but so could a million other people. It's not recording it (that causes the delay). It's the gathering, and the writing, and the arranging. That's what takes the time. Once you've done that, open up the studio and let's go! It shouldn't take that long, but I've got to get on with it..."

For those seeking a fix before he did, at least 2013 ended with some tasty Beck-related morsels to chew on. First up was typically fiery intrusion on 'Gasoline And Matches', a duet featuring country chanteuse Leann Rimes and Matchbox 20 singer Rob Thomas. "I was worried at first, when (Leann) asked me," Jeff confirmed. "Would this work? Was this me? Should I be working alongside a country singer? But she's really good, and you soon find a place where that guitar will fit." Essentially a middle-of-the-road country rocker riding on the strength of Rimes and Thomas' vocals, Beck still managed to make his appearance on 'Gasoline...' count. Barging into the middle of the tune like an angry bear, he flailed around for 20 or so seconds before leaving again in a flurry of quite mad descending scales.

If Jeff's contribution to 'Gasoline And Matches' indulged his devilish side, then the grace notes he summoned for Roger Taylor's gentle 'Say It's Not True' put him right back on the side of the angels. Originally written by the Queen drummer for Nelson Mandela's Aids Foundation '46664', '... Not True' was first released on December 1, 2007 to mark World Aids Day. Always fond of the tune, Taylor was keen to have another stab at it and duly resurrected the ballad – most recently at a cancer benefit concert on May 25, 2013 (with Jeff on guitar) – and then for inclusion on his latest solo album *Fun On Earth*. Described by renowned Beck expert Dick Wyzanski as one of the guitarist's finest ever solos, Jeff fair sailed over 'Say It's Not True', his sympathetic accompaniment of Roger's voice and exquisite passing melodies throughout the track soothing both heart and ear.

Rod Stewart. Steven Tyler. Mick Jagger. Brian Wilson. Now Roger Taylor. All had benefitted from Beck's gift with "six strings and one hell of an attitude". Yet, as 2013 passed, 'God's Guitarist' appeared little closer to releasing his own follow up to *Emotion & Commotion*. For Jeff, that follow-up had to be just perfect, or all might fail. "I think I've drawn attention," he confessed to *Rolling Stone* in early 2014. "I've worked, worked, worked for the last three years (and) now is the time really. I thought it was time for a really, really good studio album I had control over and time to do properly." Ever the perfectionist, he was once again fighting with himself to deliver something truly astounding. "As long as it sounds unique and fresh... so be it."

By April 2014, the engine started rumbling again.

Epilogue:

The Wire And The Wood

4 April, 2014
NHK Hall, Toyko

The crowd's clapping remains polite, but insistent. It also serves a purpose. Since someone dimmed the house lights 30 seconds before, those gathered at Tokyo's NHK Hall know they are only moments away from show time. By slamming their hands together in ever-louder peals, they are letting the man in the wings know they are ready for their night's entertainment. They don't have to wait long. As Stevie Wonder's wondrous 'Sir Duke' fades (rather abruptly, it has to be said) from the speakers, eight white spotlights burst into life and start sweeping the still dark stage as if looking for a stray bomber plane. At precisely the same moment that one of Japan's premier arenas is being turned into a scene from the Blitz, an ungodly drone also begins to creep forward, first rattling the chests of those in the front rows before finally singeing the ears of those at the back. Then, among all this immaculately staged lunacy, a black-clad, rooster-haired figure of indeterminate age emerges from stage left, taking cacophonous chunks out of a gleaming white... Telecaster. It's all immensely confusing of course, but as we've come to learn, Jeff Beck seldom does predictable.

The first night of a continent-jumping world tour due to run until early August 2014, Beck's appearance at the NHK Hall threw down the gauntlet for what might be another year of surprises from the guitarist. And that portentous opening number was as good a place as any with which to start. A grim, one chord rumble, overlaid with all manner of spiky, bad-tempered solo outbursts, 'Loaded' not only kicked off proceedings in Tokyo, but was also the first of three brand new tracks on his latest EP, *Yosogai*, or 'Unexpectedly'. Released to coincide with the Japanese leg of the tour, *Yosogai* covered most all recent bases in the Beck canon, with 'Loaded''s grumbling techno leanings soon deferring to 'Why Give It Away', a much funkier proposition featuring up and coming French pop/soul singer Sophie Delila. Born out of a recording session with London hip-hop production team SMV that Jeff involved himself in 2010 while scouting tunes for his next album, 'Why Give It Away' had sat untended if not unloved until it was sent to Delila – an occasional SMV collaborator. When Beck heard the sample phrases Sophie sung on top of 'Why…''s central melody, he loved the results so much she was invited to the studio to help complete the song. Slinky, sultry, and revolving around a twitching drum loop, the tune's combination of Delila's smooth/rough vocals and Jeff's clipped guitar made it a natural successor to the "greasy sex funk" he had first experimented with on 2001's 'Rollin' And Tumblin'' and 'Dirty Mind'.

Far more chaste was *Yosogai*'s last tune, a quite magnificent reading of the ageless ballad 'Danny Boy' recorded live in Austin, Texas with Imelda May back on the *Rock 'n' Roll Party* dates of early 2011. Approaching the tune with the same combination of reverence and dominance he summoned for the likes of 'Amazing Grace', 'A Day In The Life' and 'Nessun Dorma', Beck's guitar brushed quietly against May's voice for much of 'Danny Boy' before providing the crowd with a solo so heartbreakingly lovely he really should have provided complimentary hankies with each entrance ticket. "That's Jeff," said Upp drummer and old friend Jimmy Copley*, "he can make the melody sing like no other guitarist. It doesn't matter what equipment he's using or even what guitar. He just picks it

---

* In addition to working alongside Jeff on various Upp releases and the Seal-sung 'Manic Depression', Jimmy Copley also captured the guitarist at full throttle for his own solo CD, 2008's *Slap My Hand*. A fine release, Beck's contributions to the tracks 'Everyday I Have The Blues' and 'J Blues' are well worth seeking out.

up, plugs it in and he's off, flying away into the distance." As with several standards Beck made his own over the years, 'Danny Boy' has become a major part of his repertoire, the song even being used to close the shows he did with Brian Wilson in the autumn of 2013.

If 'Danny Boy' caused the heart to flutter and the eyes to well up, there was also the odd tear shed by fans over the fact that an EP rather than full-blown album was being released in conjunction with Jeff's Japanese shows. With four years gone since 2010's *Emotion & Commotion* – and the tantalising prospect of a collaborative disc with Brian Wilson still yet to materialize – fans were perhaps expecting more than three tunes (albeit good ones) for their continued patience. But as this book goes to press in April 2014, news has emerged that Beck might finally pull the proverbial rabbit from the hat soon enough, with his latest CD/download landing before the end of the year. Suffice to say, the contents sound typically intriguing.

In addition to stories of his working with choir and orchestral samples to stoke the creative fires, Jeff's new association with Nicholas Meier has also been a source of real inspiration for him. "I've never had a rhythm guitarist on stage with me, but (Nicholas) is more than that," he told *Billboard*. "He has a Turkish style, a Middle Eastern flavour, and we've been writing stuff with that... trying to probe the depths of some Turkish scales just to do something different. I'm trying to absorb some of the more interesting movements that are available... in Middle Eastern music (and) Ireland is another place with powerful, emotional melodies."

A sure hint of what might be coming is 'Yemin', a trance-like composition of deep, swirling sands and scales that Meier brought with him to Jeff's band, and which they have been performing live since late 2013. "(It) enables me to play my style wedged into those scales, so in one song you've got two fairly strong elements there," said Beck. "I can do gymnastics with a Stratocaster. That's part of the reason Nicolas wrote (the tune). It's a chance of a lifetime, really, to have someone like him and Lizzie Ball on violin, because the violin also adds a very unique sound to rock 'n' roll."*

---

* It is worth noting that Lizzie Ball moved on from Jeff's band in mid-2014, though she may still appear on his new album.

Of course, as mouth-watering as it all sounds – the Arabic Madams twirling off into infinity, Jeff's lonesome Stratocaster turning pirouettes over a sad-sounding violin – he might just change his mind again next month and strike out instead with a French marching band. After all, with Beck, one is never quite sure.

And that really encapsulates the appeal of the man.

After five decades ducking in and out of the spotlight, leaving a trail of wonder and awe, carnage and near calamity behind him, it seems pathologically insane to even try predicting Jeff Beck's next move. A human pinball, whose choices have regularly veered between delight and delirium, he remains one of music's most intriguing and mercurial propositions. Give him five career options and he'll start six others, only to put them all down again in favour of a new spin at the wheel. This has always been the case. It probably always will be.

Yet, one persists with Beck. While he can be infuriating in his frequent changes of heart and cavilier in his choices, he can also be startling in his self-effacement. Often called "the greatest living guitarist of his generation", he genuinely seems to baulk at the description, preferring to shrug his shoulders and peck irritably at his own efforts. But this stance might be less false modesty and more hard won wisdom. "I don't think about accolades," he says. "My mum (once) said to me, 'Whatever you do, don't listen to that shit. Don't get delusions of grandeur.' And I was like, 'Why not?' But she was absolutely right. When she died, I knew that the one thing I had to listen to was that advice. I've seen people look really stupid by being too confident. You get these bands now that weren't anything a year ago and (are) giving it large and acting out more (of a) fantasy than they ever deserved to. I spent too long struggling to even know what to do if I became really famous. I don't think anybody can rest on their laurels. There's always a very, very cold wind blowing up my back."

If Jeff refuses to wallow in or even conscience his own gifts, there remains a queue of musicians willing to do it for him. "Like many of us, Jeff's got a lot of insecurities," his friend Terry Bozzio said. "He's a sensitive person. But if he has a problem, it's simply that he doesn't know how good he is."

Bozzio is not alone in that opinion. "The problem for Jeff is he always has to think in terms of what he's going to do next," said Jim

McCarty. "He has to live up to his name. I still think he's the greatest rock guitarist there is... but he's a complex character, isn't he? He plays from his heart all the time and it takes a lot out of him. But he's always come back."

Indeed he does. Over the years, Beck has often skirted disaster. When he finished with The Yardbirds in 1966, for instance, it was difficult to see how he might prosper on his own, He was a guitar player – not a singer or songwriter – and his options appeared limited, his chances few. Yet, within months, he was again back in the spotlight, spearheading his own group and slugging it out with Hendrix, Clapton and Page in the race to create new sounds, shapes and styles.

Fast forward over 40 years and he seemed in trouble again. Having parted from Epic/Sony after a series of critically well-received, but poor-selling albums, one might have thought he would retire to hot rod heaven. Then came Ronnie Scott's, a new deal with Atco/ Rhino Entertainment, the Rock 'n' Roll Hall Of Fame and the success of *Emotion & Commotion*. Whether he was being thrown from a sports car, sacked from a band or simply breaking up another one of his own, Beck has never truly seemed out of the game, the next corner turned bringing either luck, opportunity or the prospect of an intriguing new start.

Of course, things might have very been different without his guitar. Found in childhood, nurtured in adolescence and used as a weapon for 50 odd years to keep away a world where "designing cornflake packets" might have been his only option, Beck's guitar – or more specifically his terrifying command of it – has proved invaluable for both him and us. "If you've got a licence to play guitar, there shouldn't be any perimeters and fences," he once said. "It'd be like saying you can only have egg and chips for the rest of your life. You're entitled to express yourself in any way you think you should." No matter the make or model (though the Fender Strat seems to have won), Beck's dedication to six strings remains total: "The guitar's like a slippery Eel. You're always trying to catch it. Next to the wheel, it's the best invention ever."

A self-confessed "awkward son of bitch" Beck also remains the rarest of things within his own community: a guitarist's guitarist. Whether imitating ouds and sitars, chasing grace notes or mimicking collapsing stars, he has maintained the respect of his fellow musicians while also proving inspirational to those beginning their own exploration the instrument. "You have to understand Jeff's a stylist," said Stanley Clarke. "He stepped away from the pack and became his own man. Of course, he honours those who came before him like Les, but it's the way he approaches the guitar, that distinct character that sets him apart. There are so few guitar players who really know how to approach a melody, but he really does. There are so many good players, some many fine technicians, but nobody – and I mean nobody – can play a melody like Jeff. If you listen to the totality of his work, you'll hear that. Most guitar players are waiting for their chance to scream and forget the tune. Not Jeff. He's a man apart."

Even the man who inducted him into the Rock 'N' Roll Hall Of Fame agrees. "Jeff has been instrumental in creating a blueprint totally unique to him that's been so inspirational, that everyone can learn from," said Jimmy Page. "No one's ever equalled what's he's done. He's shifted the whole sound and face of electric guitar music."

One of the few musicians to genuinely improve with age, and one pathologically adverse to the re-hashing of old ideas, Jeff Beck continues to beguile, bewilder and "blow minds" – his independence to be championed, his stubbornness to be commended. "I've no regrets," he said. "Let's face it, I'm centre stage, the ticket's got my name on it, I go out and play and there's no singing. Who wants to swap that for being part of someone else's band? It's change and variety – that's what keeps the thing from kicking over."

That variety, or in his own words "dabbling", is still at the very heart of Beck's approach. A guitarist for nearly 60 years – and despite his protestations, one of the best there ever was or probably ever will be – his devotion to the wire and the wood remains unswerving. And it's unlikely to stop any time soon. "It's a form of insanity, like Tourettes or something. A bit of everything, really. Rockabilly licks, Jimi Hendrix, Ravi Shankar, all the people I've loved to listen to over the years. Cliff, Les, Eastern and Arabic music, it's all in there.

"And I have a guitar in every room, on every sofa and on every chair – just to remind me to get on with it. Not one in the car, though..."

Just as well, really.

Acknowledgements

There are so many people to thank...

In the course of researching this book, I consulted the following television/radio networks, magazines, newspapers, websites and weeklies (some of which have now ceased publication). In some cases, I extracted previously published/broadcast material. For this, I remain truly grateful to: *96 Rock, ABC Dig Music, Allmusic, Audio Magazine, Auto Week, BAM, BBC, California Chronicle, Car Crazy, Clashmusic.com, Classic Rock, Creem, Disc, Drummer, Drummerworld, Electric Guitar Review, Elle, Elsewhere.com, Evening Standard, Fender News, For Bass Players Only, Gibson.com, Guitar, Guitarist, Guitar Center, Guitar Classics, Guitar For The Performing Musician, The Guitar Greats, Guitar Heroes, Guitar International, The Guitar Magazine, Guitar One, Guitar Player, Guitar Shop, Guitar World, The Independent, Inside Musicast, International Musician And Recording World, Ireland.com, Jeff Beck.com, KMET, Let It Rock, Living Legends Music, Making Music, Melody Maker, Modern Drummer, Modern Guitars, The Montreal Gazette, Mojo, Musician, Music Radar.com, The New York Times, NME, Nuva News, The Observer, Palestra.net., Q, Record, Record Collector, Repertoire Records, Rhino Entertainment, Rolling Stone, RTE, Sounds, Sound International, Synthtopia, The Tommy Bolin Archives, Truth In Shredding, Ultimate Guitar.com, Uncut, Vanilla Fudge Journal, Vintagerock.com, Wharf.co.uk, Yahoo* and the miracle of *YouTube* (including the thousands who have posted rare Yardbirds/Jeff Beck clips online).

For providing additional source material, I'd like to offer kind thanks and much appreciation to the following individuals/ journalists: Billy Altman, Billy Amendola, Robin Bextor, Eddie Cabello, Annette Carson, Lowell Cauffiel, Alan Clayson, Barry Cleveland, Alice Cooper, Jamie Crompton, Liz Derringer, Alan Di Perna, Robert Duncan, Bruce Eder, Paul Elliott, Dan Forte, Cynthia Foxx, David Fricke, Dave Fudger, Vic Garbarini, Steve Gett, Chris Gill, Joe Giorgianni, Scoop Goldman, Joe Gore, Stuart Grundy, Bob Gulla, Colin Harper, Simon Hayes, Martin Hayman, Tom Hibbert, Danny Holloway, Mark Hunter, Andy Hurt, Chris Jones, Josh Jones, Tim Jones, Richard Johnston, Nick Kent, Joe Lalaina, John Liebman, Tom Lisanti, John Lewis, Mac, Rob Mackie, Peter Makowski, Neil McCormick, Jerry McCulley, Neville Martin, Peter Mengaziol, Mark Michaels, Charles Shaar Murray, Howard Mylett, Dan Neer, H.P. Newquist, Kris Nicholson, Douglas Noble, Jas Obrecht, Rob Patterson, Joe Perry, Pierre Perrone, Shawn Perry, B. Pinnell, John Platt, Paul Quinn, Graham Reid, Matt Resnicoff, Tim Rice, Steven Rosen, Dave Rubin, Greg Russo, Gene Santoro, Jesse Shrock, Alana Sculley, David Sinclair, David Smyth, John Stix, Rich Such, Phil Sutcliffe, Ray Telford, Art Thompson, John Tobler, Brad Tolinski, Kieron Tyler, Steve Vai, Paolo Vittes, Chris Welch, David Wells, Edward Wessex, Valerie Wilmer and Alan Yentob.

I must also sing the praises of the excellent 'Jeff Beck' website (http://www.ainian.com), which alerted me to several magazine articles and various facts of which I had no prior knowledge. Genuine thanks then to Dick Wyzanski, Bill Armstrong, David Terralavoro, Eric Engler, Eric Mirell, JP Lamon and Louie Cruz.

Many thanks also to Colleen Curtis, Vic Firth, Gary Graff, Shawn Hammond, *Billboard*, *Modern Drummer*, *Premier Guitar.com*, Rolling Stone, *Tom Tom* and *Wall Street Journal*, and again, and a huge thank you goes to the one and only Dick W and his fellow Beck enthusiast Sid Johnson for all the help. The coffee, as they say, is on me…

Another large debt of gratitude to Jeff's "backroom boys", who over the years have kept the guitars strung and in shape, the amps humming and loud, and their boss ever sure that if it all goes to hell onstage, they'll be someone behind the scenes trying to fix it. All thanks then to guitar techs Mike Peters, Steve Prior, Dan Dearnley,

Al Roberts and the inimitable Al Dutton. I'm just sorry that I couldn't get all your stories into this book.

Last but not least, a huge thank you to the people who kindly gave up their time and thoughts for this project: John Arrias, Stanley Clarke, Tyron Dawson, Chris Dreja, Michael Fennelly, Mo Foster, Diane Hadley, Jimmy Hall, Jo Hill, Mike Jopp, Nigel Kerr, Jim McCarty, Roger Mayer, Max Middleton, Simon Napier-Bell, Simon Phillips, Tony Smith and Doug Wimbish. And for those who wished their contributions to remain 'behind the scenes', I also remain extremely grateful.

Several honourable mentions: first (as always), a king big thanks to Chris Charlesworth, who has guided me through the trip wires of rock and pop writing for over 16 years. For continuing to find the right photo to fit every page, I thank Jacqui Black. And for publicising my endeavours so diligently, I am indebted to Charlie Harris.

Some personal doffing of the cap: to John Constantine. Just a quick one: Duma wants the key back, but won't say why. As ever, to David Kelly, Stephen Joseph and Andrew Robinson – gentlemen, thanks for listening. Also a special mention to Colin Stewart: a superb guitarist, Mr. Stewart's sage views on Jeff Beck have helped immeasurably in the writing of this book. Maestro, if you die first, the Suhr is mine. A final round of thanks: to Anthony and Elisabeth, yours remains the kindest home in South London. To Samson, Solomon and Rebel: bring me back some socks. And last, but certainly not least, to Trish: thanks for saying "Yes".

Of course, there remains one huge debt of gratitude: God bless you, Mr. Beck. Long may you reign.

Discography

Given that Jeff Beck has been making records for over five decades and has appeared on hundreds (if not thousands) of singles, albums and videos/DVDs during that time, it would be impossible to catalogue each and every release here. What follows then, is a selective discography of the guitarist's recorded output from the early sixties to 2011, mixing 'classic' releases, sessions and guest appearances with other items of interest.

(All UK releases unless otherwise stated, bootlegs not considered. MP3 downloads will also be available for many of the major titles listed below.)

Early Appearances
Jeff Beck contributed guitar to the following recordings before joining The Yardbirds in March, 1965. As studio/record company information is sketchy or simply no longer available as to exactly when these sessions took place, singles/LPs have been placed in order of their market release date.

Singles

Phil Ryan & The Crescents
Mary, Don't You Weep/Yes I Will
Columbia DB 7406 7" 1964

Johnny Howard Band
Rinky Dink/Java
Decca F 11925 7″ June 1964

Screaming Lord Sutch
Dracula's Daughter/Come Back Baby
Oriole CB 1962 7″ October 1964

Fitz & Startz
I'm Not Running Away/So Sweet
Parlophone R 5216 7″ December 1964

The Nightshift
Stormy Monday/That's My Story
Piccadilly 7N 35264 7″ 1965

Paul Young
You Girl/Baby You Blow My Mind (Beck appears on B-side)
Phillips (Sweden) PF 350 316 7″ 1966

LPs

Blues Anytime
Someday Baby/Steelin'/L.A. Breakdown/Chuckles/Down In the
Boots/Piano Shuffle/Miles Road/Porcupine Juice/Albert/Rubber
Monkey/Howlin' for My Darling

N.B. Jeff Beck appears on two tracks from this anthology LP
recorded circa 1965: 'Steelin'' and 'Chuckles'. Both Jimmy Page and
Eric Clapton also appear on the LP.
Immediate IMLP 019 LP 1968
(Reissued on CD as *The Great Jeff Beck And Friends... Featuring
Jimmy Page And Eric Clapton*: GREAT O20 CD 1994)

With The Yardbirds

Singles/EPs

Heart Full Of Soul/Steeled Blues
Columbia DB 7594 7″ June 1965
Epic (US) BN 9823 7″ July 1965

Five Yardbirds: My Girl Sloopy/I'm Not Talking/I Ain't Done
Wrong
Columbia SEG 8421 7″ EP Aug 1965

Evil Hearted You/Still I'm Sad
Columbia DB7706 7″ October 1965

I'm A Man/Still I'm Sad
Epic (US) BN 9857 7″ November 1965

Shapes Of Things/Mr. You're A Better Man Than I
Columbia DB 7848 7″ February 1966

Shapes Of Things/I'm Not Talking
Epic (US) BN 9891 7″ March 1966 (Single withdrawn)

Shapes Of Things/New York City Blues
Epic (US) BN 10006 7″ March 1966

Over Under Sideways Down/Jeff's Boogie
Columbia DB 7928 7″ May 1966

Over Under Sideways Down/Jeff's Boogie
Epic (US) BN 10035 7″ June 1966

Happenings Ten Years Time Ago/Psycho Daisies
Columbia DB 8024 7″ October 1966

Happenings Ten Years Time Ago/The Nazz Are Blue
Epic (US) BN 10094 7″ November 1966

Over Under Sideways Down: Title Track/I Can't Make Your Way/
He's Always There/What Do You Want
Columbia SEG 8521 7″ EP January 1967

LPs

For Your Love

For Your Love/I'm Not Talking/Putty In Your Hands/I Ain't
Got You/Got To Hurry/I Ain't Done Wrong/I Wish You
Would/A Certain Girl/Sweet Music/Good Morning Little
Schoolgirl/My Girl Sloopy

N.B. While Eric Clapton plays guitar on seven of the 10 tracks
included on this 1965 US compilation album, Jeff Beck does appear
on three songs: 'I'm Not Talking', 'I Ain't Done Wrong' and 'My
Girl Sloopy'.

Epic (US) BN 26167 (LN 24167) LP July 1965

(An expanded German 24 track CD reissue of the album –
Repertoire Records 4757 CD – includes Jeff's 'Steeled Blues', a
sitar-driven 'Heart Full Of Soul' and Beck's reluctant contributions
to the B-side of The Yardbirds' 1966 Italian single 'Questa Volta/
Paff...Bum'.)

Having A Rave Up With The Yardbirds

Mr. You're A Better Man Than I/Evil Hearted You/I'm A Man/Still
I'm Sad/Heart Full Of Soul/The Train Kept A Rollin'/Smokestack
Lightning/Respectable/I'm A Man/Here 'Tis

N.B. Beck appears on the first six tracks. The rest are taken directly
from February 1965's 'Five Live Yardbirds' and again feature Eric
Clapton on guitar.

Epic (US) BN 26167 (LN 24177) LP November 1965

Columbia SCXC 28 LP January 1966

Having A Rave Up With The Yardbirds (Expanded Version)

Mr. You're A Better Man Than I/Evil Hearted You/I'm A Man/Still
I'm Sad/Heart Full Of Soul/The Train Kept A Rollin'/Smokestack
Lightning/Respectable/I'm A Man/Here 'Tis

Bonus Tracks: Shapes Of Things/New York City Blues/Jeff's Blues
(Take 1)/Someone To Love (Part 1)/Like Jimmy Reed Again/
Chris' Number/What Do You Want/Here 'Tis/Here 'Tis (Version
For RSG)/Stroll On

Repertoire REP 4758 WY (German CD Reissue) 1999

461

The Yardbirds

Lost Woman/Over Under Sideways Down/The Nazz Are
Blue/I Can't Make Your Way/Rack My Mind/ Farewell/Hot
House Of Omagarashid/Jeff's Boogie/He's Always There/Turn
Into Earth/What Do You Want/Ever Since The World Began
Columbia SCX 6063 LP July 1966 (Stereo)

The Yardbirds (US Title: Over Under Sideways Down)

Lost Woman/Over Under Sideways Down/ I Can't Make Your
Way/ Farewell/Hot House Of Omagarashid/Jeff's Boogie/
He's Always There/Turn Into Earth/What Do You Want/Ever Since
The World Began
Epic (US) BN 26210 LP August 1966 (Mono)

Roger The Engineer

The UK stereo release of 'The Yardbirds' was subsequently
renamed/reissued as 'Roger The Engineer' on CD and LP in 1983.
This reissue also contains the single: 'Happenings Ten Years Time
Ago'/'Psycho Daisies'.
Edsel ED CD 116 1983
Epic (US) FE 38455 1983

Roger The Engineer (Mono/Stereo)

A further reissue of 'Roger The Engineer' collects the Mono and
Stereo versions of 'The Yardbirds' on one CD. It also includes The
Yardbirds single 'Happenings Ten Years Time Ago/Psycho Daisies'
and Keith Relf's solo singles/B-sides: 'Mr. Zero', 'Knowing', 'Shapes
In My Mind' (Versions 1 & 2) and 'Blue Sands (Excerpt).
Airline Records (US) GA 211 CD 2000

The Yardbirds

I'm Not Talking/Crying Out For Love/The Nazz Are Blue/For
Your Love/Please Don't Tell Me 'Bout The News/Train Kept
A Rollin'/Mr. Saboteur/Shapes Of Things/My Blind Life/Over
Under Sideways Down/Mr. You're A Better Man Than I/Mystery
Of Being/Dream Within A Dream/Happenings Ten Years Time
Ago/An Original Man (A Song For Keith)
N.B. Beck joined a newly reformed Yardbirds (albeit with only Jim
McCarty and Chris Dreja remaining from the original line-up) to

provide guitar on 'My Blind Life'.
Favored Nations FN2280 2 CD April 2003

Compilations/Collections:

A vast number of 'Greatest Hits', compilations and other assorted
collections have been gathered together since The Yardbirds 'Mark
V' split on 7 July 1968. To include them all here would take several
pages. Therefore, please find below two comprehensive releases that
– while they include material from both the Clapton and Page era
(surely no bad thing) – also capture much of Jeff Beck's best and
rarest work with the band:

The Yardbirds Story by Giorgio Gomelsky (4 CD Box Set)
Disc One: Smokestack Lightning/You Can't Judge A Book By
Looking At The Cover/Let It Rock/I Wish You Would/Who Do You
Love/Honey In Your Hips/Bye, Bye, Bird/Mister Downchild/The
River Rhine/23 Hours Too Long/A Lost Care/Pontiac Blues/Take It
Easy, Baby/Out On The Water Coast/Western Arizona/Take It Easy,
Baby/Do The Weston/Baby, What's Wrong
Disc Two: Boom, Boom/Honey In Your Hips/Talkin' 'Bout
You/I Wish You Would (Demo Version)/A Certain Girl (Demo
Version)/Slow Walk/Highway 69/My Little Cabin/Too Much
Monkey Business/Got Love If You Want It/Smokestack Lightning/
Good Morning, Little Schoolgirl/Respectable/Five Long Years/
Pretty Girl/Louise/I'm A Man/Here 'Tis/I Wish You Would/A
Certain Girl/Good Morning, Little Schoolgirl (Backing Track)/Good
Morning, Little Schoolgirl (Backing Track Plus Harmonica)/Good
Morning, Little Schoolgirl (Master)/I Ain't Got You
Disc Three: For Your Love/Got To Hurry (Take 2, False Start)/
Got To Hurry (Take 3, Master)/Got To Hurry (Take 4)/Putty (In
Your Hands)/Sweet Music (Take 3)/Sweet Music (Take 4)/I'm Not
Talking/I Ain't Done Wrong/My Girl Sloopy/Heart Full Of Soul
(Version with Sitar)/Heart Full Of Soul/Steeled Blues/Evil Hearted
You/Still I'm Sad/Shapes Of Things/Shapes Of Things (Alternative
Mix)/Mr. You're A Better Man Than I/I'm A Man/New York City
Blues/Train Kept A-Rollin'/Paff...Bum/Questa Volta/Mr Zero

(Keith Relf)/Knowing (Keith Relf)
Disc Four: New York City Blues (Stereo Remix)/Jeff's Blues
(Take 1)/Jeff's Blues (Take 2)/Someone To Love, Part One (Take 2,
Instr.)/Someone To Love, Part One (Take 4, Instr.)/Someone To Love,
Part One (Take 14, Instr.)/Someone To Love, Part One (Take 15,
Vocal)/Someone To Love (Part Two)/Like Jimmy Reed Again/Chris'
Number (Take 1)/Pounds And Stomps (XYZ)/Pounds And Stomps/
What Do You Want (Take 1)/What Do You Want (Take 2)/What Do
You Want (Take 3)/What Do You Want (Take 4)/Here 'Tis (Stereo
Instrumental Version)/Here 'Tis (Version For R.S.G.)/Crimson
Curtain (Edit Of Take One And Insert)/Stroll On/I'm A Man (Live
In Germany, 1967)/Shapes Of Things (Live In Germany, 1967)
Charly SNAJ 736 CD 4 CD Box Set 2007

The Yardbirds: The BBC Sessions (1965–1968)
I Ain't Got You/ Keith Relf Talks About The Band's Background/
For Your Love/I'm Not Talking/I Wish You Would/ Keith Relf
Talks About USA Tour/Heart Full Of Soul/I Ain't Done Wrong/
Too Much Monkey Business/Love Me Like I Love You/I'm A
Man/Evil Hearted You/Interview About The 'Still I'm Sad' Single/
Still I'm Sad/Hang On Sloopy/ Smokestack Lightning/Yardbirds
Give Their New Year's Resolutions/Mr. You're A Better Man Than
I/Train Kept A-Rollin'/Shapes Of Things/Dust My Broom/Baby
Scratch My Back/ Keith Relf Talks About His Solo Single/Over
Under Sideways Down/ Shapes Of Things (Version 2)/Most Likely
You Go Your Way (And I'll Go Mine)/Little Games/Drinking
Muddy Water/Think About It/Interview With Jimmy Page/
Goodnight Sweet Josephine/ My Baby
Repertoire RR 4777 CD 1999

Jeff Beck Group

Singles
Hi Ho Silver Lining/Beck's Bolero
Columbia DB 8151 7″ March 1967
Epic 10157 7″ April 1967

Tallyman/Rock My Plimsoul
Columbia DB 8227 7″ July 1967
Epic 10218 7″ July 1967

Love Is Blue/I've Been Drinking
Columbia DB 8359 7″ February 1968

Plynth (Water Down The Drain)/Jailhouse Rock
Epic (US) 5 10484 7″ June 1969
Columbia DB 8590 7″ (Single withdrawn) September 1969

Got The Feeling/Situation
Epic (US) 10814 7″ December 1971
Epic (UK) EPC 7720 7″ January 1972

Definitely Maybe/HI Ho Silver Lining
Epic 10938 7″August 1972

Hi Ho Silver Lining/Beck's Bolero/Rock My Plimsoul
RAK Replay RR3 Maxi Single 7″ October 1972

I've Been Drinking/Morning Dew/Greensleeves (featuring Rod Stewart)
RAK RR4 Maxi Single 7″ April 1973

Hi Ho Silver Lining/Beck's Bolero/Rock My Plimsoul
RAK Replay RR3 Maxi Single (Reissue) 7″ September 1982

Albums
Truth

Shapes Of Things/Let Me Love You/Morning Dew/You Shook
Me/Ol' Man River/Greensleeves/Rock My Plimsoul/Beck's
Bolero/Blues De Luxe/I Ain't Superstitious
Epic (US) PE 264 13 LP July 1968
Columbia SCX 6293 LP October 1968
(Reissued in July 1985 on LP: ATAK/TC ATAK 42, and again in
June 1986 as part of 'Fame series': FA/TC FA 3155).

Truth (Bonus Tracks/Re-mastered Edition)

Shapes Of Things/Let Me Love You/Morning Dew/You Shook
Me/Ol' Man River/Greensleeves/Rock My Plimsoul/Beck's

Bolero/Blues De Luxe/I Ain't Superstitious
Bonus Tracks: I've Been Drinking (Stereo mix)/You Shook Me
(Take 1)/Rock My Plimsoul (Stereo Mix)/Beck's Bolero (Mono
Mix)/Blues De Luxe (Take 1)/Tallyman/Love is Blue/High Ho
Silver Lining (Stereo Mix)
EMI 873 7492 CD 2005

Beck-Ola

All Shook Up/Spanish Boots/Girl From Mill Valley/Jailhouse
Rock/Plynth (Water Down The Drain)/The Hangman's Knee/
Rice Pudding
Epic (US) RN 26478 LP June 1969
Columbia SCX 6351 LP September 1969
(Reissued in July 1985 on LP: Capitol ED 260600 1 4).

Beck-Ola (Bonus Tracks/Re-mastered Edition)

All Shook Up/Spanish Boots/Girl From Mill Valley/Jailhouse
Rock/Plynth (Water Down The Drain)/The Hangman's Knee/
Rice Pudding/Sweet Little Angel/Throw Down A Line/All Shook
Up (Early Demo)/Jailhouse Rock (Early Demo)
EMI 578750 CD 2004

Rough And Ready

Got The Feeling/Situation/Short Business/Max's Tune/I've Been
Used/New Ways Train Train
Epic (US) PK 309 73 LP
Epic EPC 4710 47 2 LP January 1972
Epic 4710 472 CD (Reissue) 1990

Jeff Beck Group

Ice Cream Cakes/Glad All Over/Tonight I'll Be Staying Here With
You/Sugar Cane/I Can't Give Back The Love I Feel For You/
Going Down/I Got To Have A Song/Highways/Definitely Maybe
Epic (US) PE 31331 LP May 1972
Epic EPC 40 64899 LP June 1972
Epic 4710 462 CD (Reissue) 1990

Beck Bogert Appice

Singles
Black Cat Moan/Livin' Alone
Epic 1251 7″ February 1973

Lady/Oh To Love You
Epic (US) 11027 7″ April 1973

I'm So Proud/Oh To Love You
Epic (US) 10998 7″ July 1973

Albums
Beck Bogert Appice
Black Cat Moan/Lady/Oh To Love You/Superstition/Sweet Sweet
Surrender/Why Should I Care/Lose Myself With You/Livin'
Alone/I'm So Proud
Epic (US) EK 32140 LP March 1973
Epic 40 65455 LP April 1973
Epic ESS 011 CD (Reissue) November 1989

BBA Live In Japan
Superstition/Lose Myself With You/Jeff's Boogie/Going Down/
Boogie/Morning Dew/Sweet Sweet Surrender/Livin' Alone/I'm
So Proud/Lady/Black Cat Moan/Why Should I Care/Plynth
(Water Down The Drain) – Shotgun (Medley)
EPCJ 5 6 (Japanese Import) LP September 1973
Abraxas Records B000ZYL9GU (Import) CD Reissue 2007

Jeff Beck

Singles/EPs
She's A Woman/It Doesn't Really Matter
Epic EPC 3334 7″ May 1975

You Know What I Mean/Constipated Duck
Epic (US) 50112 7″ June 1975

Come Dancing/Head For Backstage Pass
Epic (US) 50276 7″ August 1976

The Final Peace/Space Boogie
Epic 8806 7″ July 1980

The Final Peace/Too Much To Lose
Epic (US) 50914 7″ August 1980

The Final Peace/Scatterbrain/Too Much To Lose/Led Boots
Epic EPCA 1009 7″ EP February 1981

People Get Ready/Back On The Street
Epic EPCA 6387 7″ June 1985

People Get Ready/Back On The Street/You Know, We Know
Epic TA 6387 12″ June 1985

Stop, Look And Listen/You Know We Know
Epic EPCA 6587 7″ September 1985

Stop, Look And Listen/ Stop, Look And Listen (Remix)/
You Know, We Know
Epic TX 6581 12″ September 1985

Gets Us All In The End/You Know, We Know
Epic (US) 05595 7″ September 1985

Ambitious/You Know, We Know
Epic (US) 34 5595 7″ October 1985

Ambitious/Escape/Nighthawks
Epic EPCA TA 6981 12″ March 1986

Wild Thing/Gets Us All in The End/Nighthawks
Epic EPCA 7271 March 1986

Guitar Shop (Version)/People Get Ready/Behind The Veil (with
Terry Bozzio And Tony Hymas)
Epic BECK 1 7″ October 1989

Guitar Shop/Cause We've Ended As Lovers/Blue Wind (with Terry Bozzio And Tony Hymas)
Epic BECK 1 CD October 1989

Day In The House/People Get Ready (with Terry Bozzio And Tony Hymas)
Epic BECK 1 7" October 1989

Day In The House/Guitar Shop (Guitar Mix)/Cause We've Ended As Lovers (with Terry Bozzio And Tony Hymas)
Epic BECK 1 T 12" October 1989

Day In The House/People Get Ready/Cause We've Ended As Lovers/Blue Wind (with Terry Bozzio And Tony Hymas)
Epic BECK 1 CD October 1989

People Get Ready/The Train Kept A Rollin' (Twins Soundtrack) (A-side with Rod Stewart)
Epic 657756 7 7" February 1992

People Get Ready/Cause We've Ended As Lovers/Where Were You
Epic 6577 56 2 CD February 1992

Crazy Legs (EP) (Track Listing Unavailable)
Epic CD 1993

Up To The Mountain (with Kelly Clarkson)
MP3 Download Only (US) May 2007

I Put A Spell On You (featuring Joss Stone)
Rhino/Atco (US) (MP3 Download) April 2010

Lilac Wine (featuring Imelda May)
Rhino (MP3 Download) September 2010

Yosogai
Loaded/Why Give It Away (featuring Sophie Delila)/Danny Boy (featuring Imelda May – Live At Moody Theater, Austin, TX. *Warner Music Japan* WPCR-15682 CD (and download) April 2014

Albums

Blow By Blow

You Know What I Mean/She's A Woman/Constipated Duck/AIR
Blower/Scatterbrain/Cause We've Ended As Lovers/Theolonius/
Freeway Jam/Diamond Dust
Epic EPC 40 691 17 LP April 1975
Epic (US) EK 33409 LP March 1975
Epic 469012 2 CD (Reissue) 1994

Wired

Led Boots/Come Dancing/Goodbye Pork Pie Hat/Head For
Backstage Pass/Blue Wind/Sophie/Play With Me/Love Is Green
Epic EPC 40 860 12 LP July 1976
Epic (US) EK 33849 LP July 1976
Epic 860 12 CD (Reissue) 1988

Jeff Beck With The Jan Hammer Group Live

Freeway Jam/Earth (Still Our Only Home)/She's A Woman/Full
Moon Boogie/Darkness-Earth In Search Of A Sun/Scatterbrain/
Blue Wind
Epic EPC 40 860 25 LP March 1977
Epic (US) PE 33433 LP March 1977
Epic 471055 2 CD (Reissue) 1989

There & Back

Star Cycle/Too Much To Lose/You Never Know/The Pump/El
Becko/The Golden Road/Space Boogie/The Final Peace
Epic EPC 40 832 88 LP July 1980
Epic (US) EK 35684 LP July 1980
Epic EPC CD 83288 CD 1989

Flash

Ambitious/Gets Us All In The End/Escape/People Get Ready
(With Rod Stewart)/Stop, Look And Listen/Get Workin'/Ecstacy/
Night After Night/You Know, We Know
Epic EPC 30 261 12 LP June 1985
Epic (US) FE 39483 LP June 1985

Flash

Ambitious/Gets Us All In The End/Escape/People Get Ready
(With Rod Stewart)/Stop, Look And Listen/Get Workin'/Ecstasy/
Night After Night/You Know, We Know/Nighthawks/Back On
The Streets
Epic EPC CD 261 12 CD July 1985

Jeff Beck's Guitar Shop With Terry Bozzio And Tony Hymas

Guitar Shop/Savoy/Behind The Veil/Big Block/Where Were You/
Stand On It/Day In The House/Two Rivers/Sling Shot
Epic 4634 472 1 LP October 1989
Epic (US) EK 443 13 LP October 1989
Epic 4634 472 2 CD October 1989

*Frankie's House (Music From The Original Soundtrack) Music By Jeff Beck
& Jed Leiber*

The Jungle/Requiem For The Bao-Chi/Hi-Heel Sneakers/
Thailand/Love And Death/Cathouse/In The Dark/Sniper Patrol/
Peace Island/White Mice/Tunnel Rat/Vihn's Funeral/Apocalypse/
Innocent Victim/Jungle Reprise
Epic 472 494 1 LP February 1992
Epic (US) EK 53194 LP June 1993
Epic 472 494 2 CD February 1992

Crazy Legs: Jeff Beck & The Big Town Playboys

Race With The Devil/Cruisin'/Crazy Legs/Double Talkin' Baby/
Woman Love/Lotta Lovin'/Catman/Pink Thunderbird/Baby Blue/
You Better Believe/Who Slapped John?/Say Mama/Red Blue
Jeans And A Pony Tail/Five Feet Of Lovin'/B-I-Bickey-Bi-Bo-Bo-
Go/Blues Stay Away From Me/Pretty Pretty Baby/Hold Me, Hug
Me, Rock Me
Epic 473 597 1 LP June 1993
Epic (US) EK 535 62 LP June 1993
Epic 473 597 2 CD June 1993

Who Else!

What Mama Said/Psycho Sam/Brush With The Blues/Blast From
The East/Space For The Papa/Angel (Footsteps)/THX138/Hip-

Notica/Even Odds/Declan/Another Place
Epic 493 041 2 CD March 1999
Epic (US) EK 679 87 CD March 1999

You Had It Coming
Earthquake/Roy's Toy/Dirty Mind/Rollin' And Tumblin'/Nadia/
Loose Cannon/Rosebud/Left Hook/Blackbird/Suspension
Epic 5010 18 2 CD February 2001
Epic (US) EK 616 25 CD February 2001

Jeff
So What/Plan B/Pork-U-Pine/Seasons/Trouble Man/Grease
Monkey/Hot Rod Honeymoon/Line Dancing With Monkeys/JB's
Blues/Pay Me No Mind (Jeff Beck Remix)/My Thing/Bulgaria/
Why Lord Oh Why?
Epic 510 820 2 CD August 2003
Epic (US) EK 761 215 2 CD August 2003

Jeff Beck Live At BB King Blues Club
Roy's Toy/Psycho Sam/Big Block/Freeway Jam/Brush With The
Blues/Scatterbrain/Goodbye Pork Pie Hat/Nadia/Savoy/Angel
(Footsteps)/Seasons/Where Were You/You Never Know/A Day In
The Life/People Get Ready/My Thing
Sony Music Online Download (Japan) 2004
Sony Music (Japanese Import) MHCP 784 CD 2006

Jeff Beck Official Bootleg USA '06
Bolero/Stratus/You Never Know/Cause We've Ended As Lovers/
Behind The Veil/Two Rivers/Star Cycle/Big Block/Nadia/Angels/
Scatterbrain/Led Boots/Goodbye Pork Pie Hat – Brush With The
Blues/Blue Wind/Rainbow
Sony Music Online Download (Japan) 2007
Sony Music (Japanese Import) MHCP 1362 CD February 2007

Jeff Beck: Performing This Week...Live At Ronnie Scott's
Beck's Bolero/Eternity's Breath/Stratus/Cause We've Ended As
Lovers/Behind The Veil/ You Never Know/Nadia/Blast From The

East/Led Boots/ Angel (Footsteps)/Scatterbrain/Goodbye Pork
Pie Hat – Brush With The Blues/Space Boogie/Big Block/A Day
In The Life/ Where Were You
Eagle Vision EAG CD396 CD November 2008

Emotion And Commotion
Corpus Christi Carol/Hammerhead/Never Alone/Over The
Rainbow/I Put A Spell On You (featuring Joss Stone)/Serene
(featuring Olivia Safe)/Lilac Wine (featuring Imelda May)/Nessun
Dorma/There's No Other Me (featuring Joss Stone)/Elegy For
Dunkirk (featuring Olivia Safe)
Rhino/Atco 8122 798 10 5 CD April 2010
Rhino/Atco (US) 52 369 5 CD April 2010
(A vinyl LP version of *Emotion And Commotion* is also available).

Emotion And Commotion (Deluxe edition)
Corpus Christi Carol/Hammerhead/Never Alone/Over The
Rainbow/I Put A Spell On You (featuring Joss Stone)/Serene
(featuring Olivia Safe)/Lilac Wine (featuring Imelda May)/Nessun
Dorma/There's No Other Me (featuring Joss Stone)/Elegy For
Dunkirk (featuring Olivia Safe)
Bonus DVD – Live From The Crossroads Guitar Festival 2007:
Stratus/Behind The Veil/Nadia/Big Block/Brush With The
Blues/A Day In The Life
Atco 8122 798 10 5 CD DVD April 2010

Emotion And Commotion (Japanese Edition: Bonus Tracks)
Corpus Christi Carol/Hammerhead/Never Alone/Over The
Rainbow/I Put A Spell On You (featuring Joss Stone)/Serene
(featuring Olivia Safe)/Lilac Wine (featuring Imelda May)/Nessun
Dorma/There's No Other Me (featuring Joss Stone)/Elegy For
Dunkirk (featuring Olivia Safe)/Poor Boy (featuring Imelda May)/
Cry Me A River
Sony Music (Japanese Import) 991 499 657 CD April 2010

Jeff Beck: Live And Exclusive From The Grammy Museum
Corpus Christi Carol/Hammerhead/Over The Rainbow/Brush
With The Blues/A Day In The Life/Nessun Dorma/How High

The Moon/People Get Ready
Atco (US) 52 6419 CD November 2010

Rock'n'Roll Party – Honouring Les Paul from Jeff Beck
Double Talking Baby/Cruisin'/The Train Kept A Rollin'/Cry
Me A River/ How High The Moon/ I'm Sitting On Top Of The
World/Bye Bye Blues/ The World Is Waiting For The Sunrise/
Vaya Con Dios/ Mockin' Bird Hill/I'm A Fool To Care/Tiger
Rag/Peter Gunn/ Rockin' Is Our Bizness/Apache/Sleep Walk/
New Orleans/(Remember) Walking In The Sand/Please Mr. Jailer/
Twenty Flight Rock
Atco (US) 52 662 9 CD February 2011

Collections/Compilations

As with The Yardbirds, there is a plethora of Jeff Beck-themed
product on the market, including a vast array of 'Best Of' packages.
However, there are two compilations which had considerable input
from Beck himself. The first, *Beckology*, is a definitive 3-CD box set
collection that gathers the cream of Beck's recordings – including
previously unreleased, rare and live material – from his days with
The Tridents (1963) right through to 1989's *Guitar Shop*. The
second, *The Best Of Beckology*, is a single CD featuring selected
highlights from the larger collection. Track listings below.

Beckology
Disc One: Trouble in Mind/Nursery Rhyme (live)/Wandering
Man Blues/Steeled Blues/Heart Full of Soul/I'm Not
Talking/I Ain't Done Wrong/The Train Kept a Rollin'/I'm A
Man/Shapes of Things/Over Under Sideways Down/Happenings
Ten Years Time Ago/Hot House of Omagarashid/Lost Woman/
Rack My Mind/The Nazz Are Blue/Psycho Daisies/Jeff's Boogie/
Too Much Monkey Business (live)/The Sun Is Shining (live)/Mr.
You're A Better Man Than I (live)/Love Me Like I Love You (live)/
Hi Ho Silver Lining/Tally Man/Beck's Bolero.
Disc Two: Shapes of Things/I Ain't Superstitious/Rock My
Plimsoul/Jailhouse Rock/Plynth (Water Down The Drain)/I've

Been Drinking/Definitely Maybe/New Ways Train Train/Going Down/I Can't Give Back The Love I Feel For You/Superstition/ Black Cat Moan (live)/Blues De Luxe-BBA Boogie (live)/Jizz Whizz
Disc Three: Cause We've Ended as Lovers/Goodbye Pork Pie Hat/ Love Is Green/Diamond Dust/Freeway Jam (live)/The Pump/ People Get Ready/Escape/Gets Us All In The End/Back On The Street/Wild Thing/The Train Kept A Rollin'/Sleep Walk/The Stumble/Big Block/Where Were You
Epic/Legacy (US) E3K 48661 3 CD Box Set November 1991
Epic/Legacy EPC 4692 262 2 3 CD Box Set February 1992
N.B. *Beckology* also includes a 64 page booklet, with a written appreciation of Jeff Beck by Gene Santoro and many rare photographs.

The Best Of Beckology

Heart Full Of Soul/Shapes Of Things/Over Under Sideways Down/Hi Ho Silver Lining/Tally Man/Jailhouse Rock/I've Been Drinking/I Ain't Superstitious/Superstition/Cause We've Ended As Lovers/The Pump/Star Cycle/People Get Ready/Wild Thing/ Where Were You/Trouble In Mind
Epic 471 348 2 CD March 1992
N.B. An American CD edition is also available.

Sessions/Guest Appearances

Jeff Beck has been much in demand as a session player or 'Special Guest' over the years, appearing on scores of singles, albums and CDs. What follows is a chronological listing of his more notable appearances. Again, UK releases unless stated otherwise.

John's Children

Just What You Want, Just What You'll Get/But She's Mine (Beck
appears on B-side)
Columbia EMI DB 8124 7″ February 1967

Johnny Walker

I See Love In You/If I Promise (Beck appears on the A-side)
Phillips BF 1612 7″ October 1967

Paul Jones

And The Sun Will Shine/The Dog Presides (Beck appears on the
B-side)
Columbia DB 8379 7″ March 1968

Donovan And The Jeff Beck Group

Goo Goo Barabajagal (Love Is Hot)/Trudi
Pye 17778 7″ June 1969

GTOs: Girls Together Outrageously

Permanent Damage
Beck appears on 'The Captain's Fat Theresa Shoes', 'The Eureka
Springs Garbage Lady' and 'The Ghost Chained To The Past,
Present And Future (Shock Treatment)'
Straight (US) STS 1059 LP December 1969
Enigma (US) 7 73397 2 CD Reissue July 1989

Screaming Lord Sutch

Lord Sutch And Heavy Friends
Beck appears on 'Gutty Guitar'
Atlantic 2400 008 LP February 1970
Wounded Bird 6848363 CD Reissue August 2006

The Holy Smoke

If You've Got A Little Love To Give/It's All In The Camera (Beck
appears on A-side)
Capitol CL 156 77 7″ 1971

Stevie Wonder
Talking Book
> Beck appears on 'Lookin' For Another Pure Love'
> Motown (US) T7 319 R1 LP October 1972
> Motown STMA 8002 LP January 1973
> Motown AFZ 076 (Gold Edition CD) 2010

Eddie Harris
E.H. In The U.K.
> Beck appears on 'He's Island Man' and 'I've Tried Everything'.
> Atlantic K 50029 LP Feb 1974
> Collectables CD Reissue 1999

Badger
White Lady
> Beck appears on the title track
> Epic 800 09 LP June 1974
> Epic (Japan) 7077 CD Reissue 2002

Michael Fennelly
Lane Changer
> Beck appears on the title track and 'Watch Yerself'
> Epic 802 30 LP June 1974
> PID Records (US) CD Reissue 2010

ZZebra
Panic
> Beck appears on 'Put A Light On Me'
> Polydor 2383 326 LP July Feb (?) 1975
> Disconforme (Spain) DISC 1955 CD Reissue 1999

Upp
Upp
> Beck produces this LP and appears on five tracks: 'Bad Stuff',
> 'Friendly Street', 'Get Down In The Dirt', 'Give It To You' and 'Jeff's One'
> Epic 806 25 LP April 1975
> Epic 4809 642 CD Reissue August 1995 (Beck appears on two
> bonus tracks: 'Count To Ten' and 'It's A Mystery')

Stanley Clarke

Journey To Love
> Beck appears on 'Hello Jeff' and 'Journey To Love'
> Epic 468 221 2 LP September 1975
> Nemperor (US) 433 LP September 1975
> Epic 468 221 2 CD Reissue 1994

Upp

This Way
> Beck appears on 'Dance Your Troubles Away' and 'I Don't Want
> Nothing To Change'
> Epic 813 22 LP May 1976
> Epic/Sony (Japan) ESCA 7542 CD Reissue July 1994

Billy Preston

Billy Preston
> Beck appears on 'Bad Case Of Ego'
> A&M AMLH 645 87 LP November 1976
> Polydor (Japan) POCM 2039 CD Reissue October 1995

Narada Michael Walden

Garden Of Love Light
> Beck appears on 'Saint And The Rascal'
> Atlantic K 503 29 1976
> Wounded Bird CD Reissue 2006

Dorian Passante

Dorian
> Beck appears on 'Inside Looking Out' and 'Destination Nowhere'
> Amerama (US) A 1001 LP 1977

Stanley Clarke

Modern Man
> Beck appears on 'Rock'N'Roll Jelly'
> Epic EPC 82674 LP July 1978
> Nemperor (US) 353 03 LP July 1978
> Epic 506 106 CD Reissue 2008
> (Beck also appears on Clarke's next LP, *I Wanna Play For You*, on the
> track 'Jamaican Boy': CD Reissue Epic 22133)

Murray Head

How Many Ways

Beck appears on 'Last Days Of An Empire', 'Children Only Play' and 'Across A Crowded Room'

Music Lovers MLP 101 GB LP April 1981

(Beck's appearance with Murray Head was reissued on CD under the title *Voices* in 1993: GAH 102 CD)

Cozy Powell

Tilt

Beck appears on 'Cat Moves' and 'Hot Rock'

Polydor POLD 239 1513 LP September 1981

(Jeff's contributions to *Tilt*, plus 'The Loner' – a track dedicated to Beck by Powell – were reissued on CD as part of *The Best Of Cozy Powell*: Polydor 537 724 2 CD 1992)

PHD

Is It Safe?

Beck appears on 'I Didn't Know' (also released as a single in Italy)

Warner Bros WEA U 0050 LP July 1982

Warner Bros WEA 25 0052 1 CD 1983

Stanley Clarke

Time Exposure

Beck appears on the title track, 'I Know Just How You Feel' and 'Are You Ready (For The Future)?'

Epic EPC 254 86 LP April 1984

Nemperor (US) FE 386 88 LP April 1984

Sony Music (Japan) 5236 CD Reissue 1990

Vanilla Fudge

Mystery

Billed as 'J. Toad', Beck appears on 'My World Is Empty' and 'Jealousy'

ATCO (US) 901 49 1 LP May 1984

WEA (US) 51901 CD Reissue 2004

Rod Stewart
Camouflage
> Beck appears on the single 'Infatuation', 'Bad For You' and 'Can We Still Be Friends?'
> Warner Bros 7599 25095 2 CD May 1984
> Warner Bros (US) 250 95 1 CD May 1984

Box Of Frogs
Box Of Frogs
> Beck appears on 'Back Where I Started', 'Another Wasted Day', 'Two Steps Ahead' and 'Poor Boy'
> Epic EPC 259 96 LP June 1984
> Epic (US) BFE 39327 LP June 1984
> (Beck's contributions to the LP were reissued as part of a double pack CD – *Box Of Frogs/Strangelands* in 2008 – RMED 106 CD)

Tina Turner
Private Dancer
> Beck appears on the title track and 'Steel Claw'
> EMI CDP 7460 41 2 CD June 1984
> Capitol (US) ST 123 30 CD June 1984

The Honeydrippers
The Honeydrippers Volume I
> Beck appears on 'Rockin' At Midnight' and 'I Got A Woman'
> Es Paranza 7902 220 1 EP September 1984
> Rhino CD Reissue 2007

Diana Ross
Swept Away
> Beck appears on 'Forever Young'.
> EMI CDP 746 053 2 CD September 1984

Mick Jagger
She's The Boss
> Beck appears on the title track, 'Lonely At The Top', 'Running Out Of Luck', 'Hard Luck Woman', 'Just Another Night' and 'Lucky In Love'
> CBS Columbia CDC CBS 86310 CD February 1985

Atlantic (US) 825 53 2 CD February 1985
(Beck also contributes guitar to Mick Jagger's second solo disc,
Primitive Cool, most notably on 'Throwaway' and 'Let's Work':
Atlantic 7657 82524 2 CD September 1987)

Philip Bailey
Inside Out
Beck appears on 'Back It Up'
CBS Columbia CDCBS 26903 CD May 1986

Malcolm McLaren & The Bootzilla Orchestra
Waltz Darling
Beck appears on 'House Of The Blue Danube' and 'Call A Wave'
Epic EPC 4607 736 2 CD July 1989
(Beck's contributions to McLaren's project also surface on the
single 'House Of The Blue Danube (Dub Mix) and (Shorthouse
Mix): Epic WALTZ C 44 CD November 1989)

Tony Hymas
Oyate
Beck appears on 'Tashunka Witko' and 'Crazy Horse'
NATO (French import) 530 10 2 CD 1990

Jon Bon Jovi
*Blaze Of Glory: Songs Written And Performed By Jon Bon Jovi For The
Film Young Guns II*
Beck appears on the title track, 'Billy Get Your Guns', 'Miracle'
'Justice In The Barrel', 'Bang A Drum' 'Never Say Die', and 'Dyin'
Ain't Much Of A Living'
Vertigo 8464 73 2 CD August 1990
Mercury (US) 846 473 CD August 1990

Buddy Guy
Damn Right I Got The Blues
Beck appears on 'Mustang Sally', which was also released as a single
Silvertone (US) ORE CD 516 CD August 1991

Spinal Tap
Break Like The Wind
  Beck appears on the title track
  MCA D 105 14 CD March 1992

Moodswings
Moodfood
  Beck appears on 'Skinthieves'
  Arista 74321 111 702 CD August 1992

Roger Waters
Amused To Death
  Beck appears on the title track, 'What God Wants (Parts One &
  Three)', 'The Ballard Of Bill Hubbard', 'Watching TV', 'It's A
  Miracle' and 'Three Wishes'
  Columbia 468 761 2 CD September 1992
  Columbia (US) CK 471 27 CD September 1992

Paul Rodgers
Muddy Water Blues
  Beck appears on 'Rollin' Stone', 'Good Morning Little School Girl
  (Part One), and 'I Just Want To Make Love To You'
  Victory (US) 828 424 2 CD April 1993

Duff McKagan
Believe In Me
  Beck appears on 'Fucked Up Beyond Belief' and 'Swamp Song'

  Geffen GED 246 05 CD September 1993

Kate Bush
The Red Shoes
  Beck appears on 'You're The One'
  EMI CD EMD 1047 CD November 1993

Various artists
Stone Free: A Tribute To Jimi Hendrix
  Beck appears alongside Seal to cover 'Manic Depression'
  Warner Bros CD 1779 CD December 1993

Roachford

Permanent Shade Of Blue
  Beck appears on 'Emergency'
  Columbia 4758 42 2 CD April 1994

Seal

Seal
  Beck appears on 'Bring It On'
  Warner Bros 4509 962 56 2 CD June 1994

Will Lee

Oh
  Beck appears on 'Driftin''
  Polystar (Japanese Import) PSCS 5015 November 1994

Jan Hammer

Drive
  Beck appears on the title track and 'Underground'
  Miramar (US) 2501 December 1994

Zucchero

Spirito DiVino
  Beck appears on 'Papà Perchè'
  London 527 785 2 CD October 1995

John McLaughlin

The Promise
  Beck appears on 'Django'
  Polydor/Verve 529 828 2 CD February 1996

Scotty Moore And DJ Fontana

All The King's Men
  Beck appears on the title track and 'Unsung Heroes'
  Polydor (US) 5390 066 2 CD November 1997

Various artists

Merry Axemas: A Guitar Christmas
  Beck appears on the instrumental 'Amazing Grace'
  Epic (US) EK 677 75 CD November 1997

George Martin

In My Life
> Beck appears on 'A Day In The Life'
> Echo/MCA MCAD 118 41 CD May 1998

Brian May

Another World
> Beck appears on 'The Guv'nor'
> EMI Parlophone 4949 73 2 CD June 1998

The Pretenders

Viva El Amor
> Beck appears on 'Legalise Me'
> WEA 3984 2715 52 2 CD May 1999

ZZ Top

XXX
> Beck provides backing vocals on 'Mr. Millionaire'
> RCA (US) 74321 69372 2 CD September 1999

Stevie Ray Vaughan

Stevie Ray Vaughan And Double Trouble
> Beck appears on 'Going Down', a live duet with Vaughan recorded
> on their 1989 US tour
> Epic/Legacy EPC 5009 302 3 CD Box Set December 2000

Various artists

Good Rockin' Tonight: The Legacy Of Sun Records
> Beck appears alongside The Pretenders' Chrissie Hynde on
> 'Mystery Train'
> London/Sire (US) 31165 2 CD October 2001

Various artists

From Clarksdale To Heaven: Remembering John Lee Hooker
> Beck appears on 'Hobo Blues' and 'Will The Circle Be Unbroken'
> with The Kingdom Choir
> Eagle (US) WK23629 CD September 2002

Jools Holland & His Big Band Rhythm & Blues Orchestra
Small World, Big Band Volume Two: More Friends
> Beck appears on 'Drown In My Own Tears'
> Rhino/WSM R2 73884 December 2002

Wynonna Judd
What The World Needs Now Is Love:
> Beck appears on 'I Want To Know What Love Is'
> Curb (US) D2 78811 CD August 2003

Luciano Pavarotti
Ti Adoro
> Beck appears on 'Caruso'
> Decca 470 635 2 CD October 2003

Toots And The Maytals
True Love
> Beck appears on '54–46 Was My Number'
> Virgin V2 63681 27186 2 April 2004

Zucchero
Zu & Co
> Beck appears on Zucchero and Macy Gray's duet 'Like The Sun
> (From Out Of Nowhere)'
> Polydor (Italy) 9810953 CD May 2004

The Big Town Playboys
Roll The Dice
> Beck appears alongside Robert Plant on 'Look Out Mabel'
> Mi5 MUK 007 CD November 2004

Joe Cocker
Heart And Soul
> Beck appears on 'I Who Have Nothing'
> EMI (UK) CD September 2004/New Door (US) January 2005

Imogen Heap
Speak For Yourself
    Beck appears on 'Goodnight And Go'
    Megaphonic Mega 001 CD July 2005
    ('Goodnight And Go' was made available online via Imogen Heap's
    official website in December 2004)

Ursus Minor
Zugzwang
    Beck (under the pseudonym 'The Traveller') appears on 'Won't
    Stop Raining', 'Square Dance Rap', 'She Can't Explain' and 'Lists'
    Hope Street/Nocturne (France) HS 10046 NT096 CD Summer
    2005

Les Paul & Friends
American Made, World Played
    Beck appears on '(Ain't That) Good News)' playing guitar along to
    Sam Cooke's original master vocal track
    Capital (US) 09463 6934370 1 CD September 2005

Cyndi Lauper
The Body Acoustic
    Beck appears on 'Above The Clouds'
    Epic/Daylight 82796 94569 2 CD November 2005

Carlo Little All Stars
Never Stop Rockin'
    Beck appears on 'Mystery Train'
    Angel Air 1JILSB2 CD January 2009

Morrissey
Years Of Refusal
    Beck appears on 'Black Cloud'
    Polydor B001NPUGX2 CD February 2009
    Lost Highway/Attack (US) B0012578-01 CD February 2009

Joss Stone
Colour Me Free
    Beck appears alongside Sheila E on 'Parallel Lines'
    Virgin (US) 509 994 58018 22 CD October 2009

Sharon Corr
I Dream Of You
> Beck appears on 'Mná Na h'Éireann'
> Rhino/Warner Bros 2564 6788 39 CD September 2010

Jimmy Copley (and Friends)
Slap My Hand
> Jeff appears alongside Jimmy, Go West's Peter Cox and Pino
> Palladino on 'Everyday I Have The Blues' and 'J Blues'
> Nina Records EWSR008 CD 2008

Beth Hart
Bang Bang Boom Boom
> Jeff appears on 'I'd Rather Go Blind'
> Provogue Records B00B9LND2Q (Import) CD April 2013

Leann Rimes
Spitfire
> Jeff appears alongside Matchbox 20's Rob Thomas on 'Gasoline
> And Matches'
> Rhino B00B9KP3C0 CD April 2013

Roger Taylor
Fun On Earth
> Jeff appears on 'Say It's Not True'
> Virgin EMI B00FAZ01I6 CD November 2013

Videos/DVDs

The Yardbirds – The Story Of The Yardbirds
> Available in one format or another for several years, this 52 minute
> DVD still remains a brisk but entertaining account of The Yardbirds'
> memorable assault on the sixties blues, pop and rock scene. Beck,
> Clapton and Page are all on hand to air their views (and on
> occasion, vent their spleen), while vintage footage from the band's
> heyday makes one nostalgic for simpler times.
> Zeit Media B001DGFGRC DVD 2008

The ARMS Concert: The Ronnie Lane Appeal For ARMS, Royal Albert Hall, London 1983

Includes Jeff Beck performing 'Star Cycle', 'The Pump', 'Goodbye Pork Pie Hat', 'Led Boots' and 'Hi Ho Silver Lining'. Also features Beck on encores 'Layla' and 'Goodnight Irene'.

A reasonable transfer from VHS to DVD helps makes this all-star 1983 concert an appealing prospect. That it remains the only documentary evidence of The Yardbirds' 'Holy Triumvirate' appearing under one roof and on one stage together only heightens that appeal. Solo performances from a blue-suited, professorial-looking Clapton and a jittery, whip-thin Page are interesting (and in Jimmy's case, even touching to behold), though Beck again steals the show by pulling 'Hi Ho Silver Lining' out of mothballs for a rare live outing. The three-pronged guitar attack on 'Layla''s monolithic riff at the show's climax is also likely to raise a smile.

VIP Productions B001EQVP3U Region 3 DVD 2008

The Nagano Session: Jeff Beck with Carlos Santana & Steve Lukather

Includes Jeff Beck performing 'Cause We've Ended As Lovers', 'Wild Thing', 'Freeway Jam' 'Going Down' and encores 'Super Boogie', 'People Get Ready' and 'Johnny B Good'.

Recorded within the luxurious grounds of Karuizawa Prince Hotel, at the foot of Mt. Iwate in Nagano, Japan on June 1, 1986, this in-concert DVD certainly doesn't lack for beautiful scenery. Featuring accomplished solo sets from Santana and Beck (including a frankly lunatic rendition of 'Wild Thing'), things climax with an entertaining, if sometimes shambolic three-guitar jam session with special guest Steve Lukather. Jan Hammer, Jimmy Hall, Buddy Miles and Chester Thompson also add to the musicianship on show.

Woodstock Tapes 7934 C DVD 1986/2005

Jeff Beck: Performing This Week… Live At Ronnie Scott's

Beck's Bolero/Eternity's Breath/Stratus/Cause We've Ended As Lovers/Behind The Veil/You Never Know/Nadia/Blast From The East/Led Boots/Angel (Footsteps)/People Get Ready (with Joss Stone)/Scatterbrain/Goodbye Pork Pie Hat/Brush With The Blues/Space Boogie/Blanket (with Imogen Heap)/Big Block/A Day In The Life/Little Brown Bird (with Eric Clapton)/You Need

Love (with Eric Clapton)/Rollin' And Tumblin' (with Imogen Heap)/Where Were You

Bonus Features: Interviews With Jeff Beck and band.

For decades, any close quarters footage of Jeff Beck at work was only to be found on grainy VHS bootlegs, or uninspired concert films where cameramen dwelled lovingly on the drummer while Jeff played exquisitely – albeit completely out of shot. *...Live At Ronnie Scott's* forever remedies such oversights, capturing Beck and his best band in years within the intimate surrounds of a small London jazz club. Guest stars abound, Jimmy Page grins from the audience and "God's Guitarist" is on fire from start to finish. With over one million copies sold, and a Grammy won for Beck's emotive rendering of The Beatles' 'A Day In The Life', *...Live At Ronnie Scott's* is the pick of the Jeff Beck visual litter.

Eagle Vision EREDV 723 DVD 2008 (2009 Blu Ray edition also available)

Rock'n'Roll Party – Honouring Les Paul from Jeff Beck

Double Talking Baby/Cruisin'/The Train Kept A Rollin'/Cry Me A River/ How High The Moon/ I'm Sitting On Top Of The World/Bye Bye Blues/ The World Is Waiting For The Sunrise/ Vaya Con Dios/ Mockin' Bird Hill/I'm A Fool To Care/Tiger Rag/Peter Gunn/ Rockin' Is Our Business/Apache/Sleep Walk/ New Orleans/(Remember) Walking In The Sand/Please Mr. Jailer/ Twenty Flight Rock

Filmed on June 9, 2010 at New York's cosy Iridium Jazz Club on what would have been Les Paul's 95th birthday, this homage from Jeff Beck to his childhood hero is sentimental and scintillating in equal measure. With the delightful Imelda May playing Mary Ford to Jeff's spot-on Les impersonation, songs such as 'How High The Moon', 'Walking In The Sand' and 'Bye Bye Blues' were never destined to fail. Moreover, Beck's backing band led by May's husband, Darrel Higham, and a raft of special guests including ex-Stray Cat Brian Setzer, Gary US Bonds and Trombone Shorty only add to the overall party atmosphere.

Eagle Vision EREDV 824 DVD February 2011
Eagle Vision ERBRD 5075 Blu Ray February 2011